DOCUMENTS SUPPLEMENT TO
CASES AND MATERIALS ON
LEGISLATION
STATUTES AND THE CREATION
OF PUBLIC POLICY
Fourth Edition

■ ■ ■

By

William N. Eskridge, Jr.

John A. Garver Professor of Jurisprudence
Yale University

James J. Brudney

Professor of Law
Fordham University School of Law

with

Brian Richardson and
Jayme Herschkopf
Yale Law School, Class of 2011

AMERICAN CASEBOOK SERIES®

WEST®
A Thomson Reuters business

Mat #40889405

© 2011 Thomson Reuters
    610 Opperman Drive
    St. Paul, MN 55123
    1–800–313–9378
Printed in the United States of America

ISBN: 978–0–314–20816–3

Contents

CONTENTS

CONTENTS

INTRODUCTION AND ROADMAP

This Supplement contains statutory, congressional, and regulatory materials that are not often found in law school casebooks—including most Legislation or Regulatory State casebooks. We hope the Supplement complements (and not just supplements) the Casebook itself, which has more theoretical and background materials than most other classroom books and presents appellate decisions with less editing than is typical in casebooks.

Like the Casebook, the Supplement reflects our interest in creating a learning experience with respect to both practical and separation-of-powers aspects of statutory meaning that is richer than can be obtained through exposure to severely edited judicial decisions.

The decisions included in most of the Casebook (chapters 2 through 5 notably excepted) were chosen not to illustrate a particular legal doctrine, but rather as vehicles to consider questions about the meaning, interpretation, and implementation of statutes. Accordingly, the reproduced excerpts from these decisions often focus in some detail on competing approaches to judicial reasoning and the use of various interpretive assets. Subject matter doctrine is relevant in these decisions primarily for illustrative purposes. We do not intend that students mastering the course will or should become sophisticated about civil rights law, tax law, criminal law, antitrust law, or any other substantive aspect of federal regulation.

In addition, and importantly, the Casebook selection of decisions often includes judicial discussion of a statute's legislative background. Typically, this discussion features presentation of how the House and Senate debated, negotiated, and reached agreement on a law's enactment. It also may include description of what administrative agencies then did in an effort to fulfill responsibilities and duties conferred upon them by the enacted law. The process of ascertaining what a statute means and how it applies is distinctive in our legal system. Courts are the exclusive arbiters of what the common law means, and—although this is more often debated—they are the predominant arbiters of what the Constitution means. For statutes, however, the interpretive dialogue is more complex: it ordinarily reflects an evolving and at times dynamic conversation among all three branches of government.

This Supplement further develops the legislative process orientation of the Casebook. It consists primarily of excerpts from the legislative record during the process of statutory enactment. Excerpts come from initial or earlier versions of a bill, congressional hearings, committee reports, and floor debates. These are the so-called raw materials of statutory interpretation, in addition to the statutory text itself. In order to understand how the lawmaking enterprise functions, why a statute is different from a private law instrument such as a sales contract or a property lease, and how statutes come to have certain meanings over time, students must get "up close and personal" with these raw materials.

The Supplement also includes some excerpts from the executive branch record when implementing and enforcing the text Congress has enacted. These include formally promulgated documents such as executive orders, regulations, guidelines, and policy directives, plus certain less public or formal documents such as internal agency memoranda.

The first part of the Supplement addresses legislative and regulatory materials related to Title VII of the Civil Rights Act of 1964. The story of Title VII, covered in chapter one of the Casebook, provides an in-depth introduction to statutory lawmaking. We include legislative materials leading up to enactment of the 1964 law, regulatory materials implementing the law between 1964 and 1991, and some additional legislative materials from 1972 and 1991. At several points, we insert Explanatory Notes and also suggested Questions to help guide group discussion or individual inquiry. By relying on these chapter-one-related materials, professors and students can deepen their understanding of Title VII as a paradigm for public lawmaking and use this deeper appreciation to inform their approaches to subsequent chapters.

The balance of the Supplement consists mainly of legislative materials discussed, relied upon, or criticized in relation to judicial decisions that are found in chapters six through eight of the Casebook. Specifically, we include materials useful for an enriched understanding of the Baseball Antitrust Exemption Case in chapter six; the Holy Trinity and Expert Witness Fee Cases in Chapter 7; and the Spotted Owl, Carrying a Gun, Catholic Bishop, Contingent Attorney's Fee, Family Farm, and Native American Job Preference Cases in Chapter 8. These briefer excerpts are accompanied in each instance by Questions that aim to generate probing analysis into the reliability and legitimacy of how judges use legislative history.

The Supplement concludes with an extended Case Study involving the Age Discrimination in Employment Act. This study, including statutory text, legislative history, and two Supreme Court decisions, reflects a 25-year dialogue between Congress and the Supreme Court on the meaning of a certain statutory phrase. The dialogue, which involves two congressional overrides, raises interesting and potentially troubling separation of powers issues that professors and students may wish to explore.

THE CIVIL RIGHTS ACT OF 1964

Employment discrimination because of race, ethnicity, or national origin is nothing new in the United States, but such discrimination did not become an object of national political concern until the mid-twentieth century. In 1941, A. Philip Randolph, President of the Brotherhood of Sleeping Car Porters, pressed the federal government to address discrimination against African Americans in federal, state, and private workplaces. When President Franklin D. Roosevelt was slow to respond, Randolph publicly called for a March on Washington by people of color and their allies to protest continuing discrimination by the federal government and defense contractors. Faced with a messy protest by an estimated fifty thousand people, Roosevelt issued Executive Order 8802 in June 1941, prohibiting job discrimination not only by the federal government, but also by any defense contractors and establishing the Fair Employment Practices Committee (FEPC) to investigate charges of racial discrimination. In return, Randolph cancelled the March on Washington. By 1945, nearly two million workers of color were employed in defense work.

After the war, however, the FEPC lapsed and discrimination returned with a vengeance. Although the federal segregation of soldiers within the armed forces ended in 1948-54, segregated workforces remained the norm in the United States, to the great detriment of black workers, who were relegated to lower-paying jobs. The civil rights movement of the 1950s primarily targeted state-sponsored segregation of schools and public accommodations, but also objected to workplace discrimination and low wages. Following the model of civil rights laws in states like New York, proposed civil rights bills in the 1950s would have prohibited job discrimination by private employers—but procedural roadblocks in Congress thwarted such efforts.

The new decade—the 1960s—offered a great window of opportunity for civil rights hopes. In the 1960 presidential election, both John F. Kennedy and Richard M. Nixon called for sweeping civil rights legislation. Kennedy won both the black vote and the election, and his Department of Justice worked with Democrats and Republicans in Congress to develop strong civil rights legislation. But grass-roots leaders thought they needed a popular push to motivate the Washington, DC insiders.

In this spirit, Randolph and his longtime associate, Bayard Rustin, called for a new March on Washington, specifically, for Jobs and Freedom. The revered Randolph united bickering civil rights organizations to support the idea. Rustin's brilliant organizing helped attract 200,000 persons to assemble in Washington, DC and to march for the cause of civil rights legislation. Speaking less than a mile from the U.S. Capitol, Dr. Martin Luther King Jr. delivered his "I Have a Dream" Speech on August 22, 1963 and galvanized a nation for civil rights legislation.

I. Civil Rights Bills are Introduced by Republican and Democrat Members and Referred to Committee (January and June 1963)

By the time Dr. King spoke to the marchers and to the nation, legislation was already pending before Congress. The first step in the federal legislative process is the introduction of the proposed law as a "bill" in either the House of Representatives or the Senate (or both).

The House Republicans were the first to introduce civil rights legislation, on January 31, 1963. H.R. 3139 was introduced by Rep. Lindsay and supported by eight Republican cosponsors, led by the ranking minority member of the House Judiciary Committee Bill McCulloch (see Casebook, p.7).

1

a. Republican-sponsored Civil Rights Bill of 1963

* * * *

REPUBLICAN-SPONSORED CIVIL RIGHTS BILL OF 1963

Mr. McCULLOCH. Mr. Speaker, I ask unanimous consent to address the House for 1 minute and to revise and extend my remarks.

The SPEAKER. Is there objection to the request of the gentleman from Ohio?

There was no objection.

Mr. McCULLOCH. Mr. Speaker, earlier today I introduced a civil rights bill which is comprehensive in scope and moderate in application. Congressmen LINDSAY, MOORE, CAHILL, MacGREGOR, MATHIAS, BROMWELL, SHRIVER, and MARTIN of California joined with me in introducing identical bills.

In this bill, the Civil Rights Commission is made permanent and is given additional authority to investigate vote frauds, including the denial of the right to have one's vote counted.

Secondly, there is established a seven-man Commission for Equality of Opportunity in Employment. This Commission shall have the power to investigate discrimination in employment in any business concern which holds a Federal Government contract or any labor union which works on such contract. I stress, this authority is limited to Federal Government contracts. In addition, employment agencies which are wholly or partially financed by Federal funds shall be subject to the Commission's jurisdiction, while equality of job opportunity in Federal employment is placed under the Commission's inspection.

If the Commission finds a clear pattern of discrimination, it is given the authority to cut off Government contracts, halt the flow of funds to employment agencies, and order labor organizations to cease discriminating, at the risk of running afoul of nondiscrimination amendments to the National Labor Re-lations Act. In granting such authority to the Commission, however, we have sought to impose strict safeguards for the rights of all individuals. The right to judicial review is concisely spelled out, while the party affected is given the opportunity to end discriminatory practices prior to the issuance of a formal order by the Commission.

This civil rights bill also authorizes the Attorney General to institute a civil action on behalf of a citizen who claims that he is being denied the opportunity to enroll in a nonsegregated public school. In so granting this right, however, a Federal court is restrained from enjoining a State or local official in such civil action, if there has been instituted a plan to desegregate with all deliberate speed, and unless the complainant has exhausted all State legal remedies.

In the same vein, this civil rights bill authorizes Federal appropriations to aid state or local school boards in desegregating, if a request is made by them for such assistance. The financial aid so authorized, however, is limited to administrative and special, nonteaching professional services, developmental programs and technical assistance. The payment of teachers' salaries, or the financing of construction costs are in no way involved.

Finally, this civil rights bill provides that anyone, otherwise qualified to vote in a Federal election, is presumed to have sufficient literacy and intelligence to vote if he has completed six grades of an accredited elementary school. This provision, of course, does not eliminate the right of a State to use literacy or other intelligence tests as a means of qualifying voters. Even if an individual has a sixth-grade education, the State may show that he is, in fact, illiterate. But the bill does provide a presumption of literacy which will materially assist a court in determining whether literacy tests—and tests of a similar nature—are being used in a manner which unfairly discriminate against certain classes of citizens.

Here, then, is a comprehensive bill which seeks to advance the cause of civil rights in the United States. At the same time, however, it is a bill keyed to moderation. And the reason for moderation is obvious. We members of the Republican Party are honestly desirous of proposing legislation which stands a chance of enactment. Anyone, of course, can introduce grandiose legislative schemes. But, reaching for the sky, rather than aiming for the possible is a form of showmanship we do not wish to engage in. Reality is what we live by and accomplishment is what we seek.

Of equal importance is the fact that we are a Nation of many people and many views. In such a nation, the prime purpose of a legislator, from wherever he may come, is to accommodate the interests, desires, wants and needs of all our citizens. To alienate some in order to satisfy others is not only a disservice to those we alienate, but a violation of the principles of our Republic. For, only in compromise, moderation, and understanding are we able to fashion our so-ciety into a cohesive and durable structure.

I sincerely hope that all Members of Congress, of the executive department and the public will carefully study this proposed legislation and reach out to support it in the spirit in which it is introduced. The sincerity of its purpose, the moderation of its scope, and the reality of intended accomplishment should, we hope, attract wide support.

* * *

In other words, the bill creates a presumption in favor of the citizen, a presumption which could be rebutted and taken to the court, if necessary. But here the court comes into play again, that wonderful lubricant in this area, the Federal court structure. But nevertheless the citizen is given the benefit of the doubt if he has had a sixth grade education.

In conclusion I urge and hope that all Members of Congress will join together to give us a civil rights bill. And I would like once again to extend my eternal gratitude to the Republican members of the House Judiciary Committee who are here on the floor today, particularly the ranking minority member, the gentleman from Ohio [Mr. McCulloch]; and to the gentleman from New Jersey [Mr. Cahill]; the gentleman from Minnesota [Mr. MacGregor]; the gentleman from Maryland [Mr. Mathais]; the gentleman from Iowa [Mr. Bromwell]; the gentleman from California [Mr. Martin]; the gentleman from Kansas [Mr. Shriver] and the gentleman from West Virginia [Mr. Moore].

With the backing of the Republican leadership, which we have with the blessing of the Republican National Chairman Bill Miller—and he has given it—we on this side offer this measure today. We ask the majority side of the aisle that dominates this Congress to join with us in enacting meaningful and comprehensive civil rights legislation to protect the rights of all Americans and to fulfill the promise of the American Constitution.

Mr. Speaker, I ask unanimous consent to revise and extend my remarks; and that all Members may extend their remarks in the body of the Record at the conclusion of today's proceedings.

At this point in the Record I wish to include the text of the bill which we are introducing and an analysis of its provisions.

The SPEAKER pro tempore (Mr. Libonati). Is there objection to the request of the gentleman from New York?

There was no objection.

H.R. 3139

A bill to amend the Civil Rights Act of 1957, and for other purposes

Be it enacted by the Senate and House of Representatives of the United States of America in Congress assembled, That this Act may be cited as the "Civil Rights Act of 1963".

* * * *

* * * *

TITLE II—EQUAL EMPLOYMENT OPPORTUNITY

Part A. Establishment of Commission

The Commission on Equality of Opportunity in Employment

Sec. 201. (a) There is hereby created a Commission to be known as the Commission on Equality of Opportunity in Employment, which shall be composed of seven members who shall be appointed by the President by and with the advice and consent of the Senate. Not more than four of such members may be of the same political party. One of the original members shall be appointed for a term of one year, one for a term of two years, one for a term of three years, one for a term of four years, one for a term of five years, one for a term of six years, and one for a term of seven years, but their successors shall be appointed for terms of seven years each, except that any individual chosen to fill a vacancy shall be appointed only for the unexpired term of the member whom he shall succeed. The President shall designate one member to serve as Chairman of the Commission. Any member of the Commission may be removed by the President upon notice and hearing for neglect of duty or malfeasance in office, but for no other cause.

(b) A vacancy in the Commission shall not impair the right of the remaining members to exercise all the powers of the Commission and four members thereof shall constitute a quorum.

(c) The Commission shall have an official seal which shall be judicially noted.

(d) The Commission shall at the close of each fiscal year report to the Congress and to the President concerning the cases it has heard; the decisions it has rendered; the names, salaries, and duties of all individuals in its employ and the moneys it has disbursed; and shall make such further reports on the cause of and means of eliminating discrimination and such recommendations for further legislation as may appear desirable.

(e) Each member of the Commission shall receive compensation at the rate of $20,000 a year.

(f) The office of the Commission shall be in the District of Columbia, but it may meet or exercise any or all of its powers at any other place. The Commission may, by one or more of its members or by such agents as it may designate, conduct any investigation, proceeding, or hearing necessary to its functions in any part of the United States. Any such agent, other than a member of the Commission, designated to conduct a proceeding or a hearing shall be a resident of the judicial circuit, as defined in section 41 of title 28, United States Code, within which the alleged unlawful employment practice occurred.

(g) The Commission shall consider and adopt rules and regulations consistent with this title to govern its proceedings.

(h) The Commission shall consider reports as to progress under this title.

Rules of Procedure of the Commission ←

Sec. 202. (a) The Chairman or one member of the Commission designated by him to act as Chairman at a hearing of the Commission shall announce in an opening statement the subject of the hearing.

(b) A copy of the Commission's rules shall be made available to the witness before the Commission.

(c) Witnesses at the hearings may be accompanied by their own counsel.

(d) The Chairman or Acting Chairman may punish breaches of order and decorum and unprofessional ethics on the part of counsel, by censure and exclusion from the hearings.

(e) If the Commission determines that evidence or testimony at any hearing may tend to defame, degrade, or incriminate any person, it shall (1) receive such evidence or testimony in executive session; (2) afford such person an opportunity voluntarily to appear as a witness; and (3) receive and dispose of requests from such person to subpena additional witnesses.

(f) The Chairman shall receive and the Commission shall dispose of requests to subpena additional witnesses.

(g) No evidence or testimony taken in executive session may be released or used in public sessions without the consent of the Commission. Whoever releases or uses in public without the consent of the Commission evidence or testimony taken in executive session shall be fined not more than $1,000, or imprisoned for not more than one year.

(h) In the discretion of the Commission, witnesses may submit brief and pertinent sworn statements in writing for inclusion in the record. The Commission is the sole judge of the pertinency of testimony and evidence adduced at its hearings.

(i) Upon payment of the cost thereof, a witness may obtain a transcript copy of his testimony given at a public session or, if given at an executive session, when authorized by the Commission.

(j) A witness attending any session of the Commission shall receive $4 for each day's attendance and for the time necessarily occupied in going to and returning from the same, and 8 cents per mile for going from and returning to his place of residence. Witnesses who attend at point so far removed from their respective residences as to prohibit return thereto from day to day shall be entitled to an additional allowance of $12 per day for expenses of subsistence, including the time necessarily occupied in going to and returning from the place of attendance. Mileage payments shall be tendered to the witness upon service of a subpena issued on behalf of the Commission or any subcommittee thereof.

(k) The Commission shall not issue any subpena for the attendance and testimony of witnesses or for the production of written or other matter which would require the presence of the party subpenaed at a hearing to be held outside of the State wherein the witness is found or resides or transacts business.

Powers of the Commission

SEC. 203. (a) The Commission shall have power—

(1) to appoint, in accordance with the Civil Service Act, rules, and regulations, such officers, agents, and employees, as it deems necessary to assist it in the performance of its functions, and to fix their compensation in accordance with the Classification Act of 1949, as amended; attorneys appointed under this section may, at the direction of the Commission, appear for and represent the Commission in any case in court;

(2) to furnish to persons subject to this title such technical assistance as they may request to further their compliance with this title or any order issued thereunder;

(3) to make such technical studies as are appropriate to effectuate the purposes and policies of this title and to make the results of such studies available to interested governmental and nongovernmental agencies.

(b) All departments, agencies, and independent establishments in the Executive branch of the Government shall cooperate with the Commission and shall carry out the orders of the Commission relating to the termination of contracts and subcontracts, the refusal to enter into or permit the entering into of such contracts and subcontracts, and the withholding of Federal funds from employment agencies.

Investigatory Powers

SEC. 204. (a) For the purpose of all investigations, proceedings, or hearings which the Commission deems necessary, the Commission, or any member thereof, shall have power to issue subpenas requiring the attendance and testimony of witnesses and the production of any evidence relating to any investigation, proceeding, or hearing before the Commission, its member, or agent conducting such investigation, proceeding, or hearing.

(b) In case of contumacy or refusal to obey a subpena issued to any person under this title, any district court within the jurisdiction of which the investigation, proceeding, or hearing is carried on or within the jurisdiction of which said person guilty of contumacy or refusal to obey is found or resides or transacts business, upon application by the Commission shall have jurisdiction to issue to such person an order requiring him to appear before the Commission, its member, or agent, there to produce evidence if so ordered, or there to give testimony relating to the investigation, proceeding, or hearing.

(c) Complaints, orders, and other process and papers of the Commission, its member, agent, or agency, may be served either personally or by registered mail or by leaving a copy thereof at the principal office or place of business of the person required to be served. The verified return by the individual so serving the same setting forth the manner of such service shall be proof of the same, and the return postoffice receipt therefor when registered and mailed as aforesaid shall be proof of service of the same.

Part B. Provisions relating to Government contractors

Provisions To Be Included in Contracts

SEC. 210. (a) There shall be included in every contract entered into by any department, agency, or independent establishment in the executive branch of the Government a provision in such form and containing such terms as the Commission may prescribe (including compliance reports), designed to insure that in the employment practices (including but not limited to upgrading, demotion, transfer, recruitment or advertising therefor, layoff or termination, rates of pay or other forms of compensation, and selection for training, including apprenticeship) of the contractor, and of each person with whom the contractor enters into a subcontract of such contract, such contractor or subcontractor, as the case may be, will not discriminate against any person because of his race, creed, color, or national origin.

(b) The discriminatory practices covered by subsection (a) shall include, but not be limited to, any practice whereby an employer shall—

(1) discharge, lay off, or fail or refuse to hire, any individual, or otherwise shall discriminate against any individual with respect to his compensation, terms, conditions, or privileges of employment, because of such individual's race, color, or national origin; or

(2) limit, segregate, or classify his employees in any way which would deprive or tend to deprive any individual of employment opportunities or otherwise adversely affect his status as an employee, because of such individual's race, creed, color, or national origin.

(c) The Commission may exempt any contract or class of contracts from the operation of this title.

Enforcement of Contract Provisions

SEC. 211. (a) Whenever a charge has been filed by or on behalf of any person claiming to be aggrieved by reason of a discriminatory employment practice covered by section 210(a) of this title the Commission shall investigate such charge and if it shall determine after such preliminary investigation that probable cause exists for crediting such charge, it shall issue and cause to be served upon the contractor or subcontractor involved, as the case may be (hereinafter called the "respondent"), a complaint stating the charges in that respect together with a notice of hearing before the Commission, or a member thereof, or before a designated agent, at a place therein fixed, not less than ten days after the service of such complaint. No complaint shall issue based upon any practice occurring more than six months prior to the filing of the charge with the Commission and the service of a copy thereof upon the respondent.

(b) The respondent shall have the right to file a verified answer to such complaint and to appear at such hearing in person or otherwise, with or without counsel, to present evidence and to examine and cross-examine witnesses.

(c) The Commission or the member or designated agent conducting such hearing shall have the power reasonably and fairly to amend any complaint, and the respondent shall have like power to amend its answer.

(d) All testimony shall be taken under oath.

(e) At the conclusion of a hearing before a member or designated agent of the Commission, such member or agent shall transfer the entire record thereof to the Commission, together with his recommended decision and copies thereof shall be served upon the parties. The Commission shall afford the parties an opportunity to be heard on such record at a time and place to be specified upon reasonable notice. In its discretion, the Commission upon notice may take further testimony.

(f) With the approval of the member or designated agent conducting the hearing, a case may be ended at any time prior to the transfer of the record thereof to the Commission by agreement between the parties for the elimination of the practice complained of on mutually satisfactory terms.

(g) If, upon the preponderance of the evidence, including all the testimony taken, the Commission shall find that the respondent has violated the provision included in the contract pursuant to section 210 of this title, the Commission shall state its findings of fact and shall notify the contractor or subcontractor involved that it intends to issue an order to the contracting agency requiring that such agency terminate the contract or, where a subcontractor is involved, make appropriate arrangements for the termination of the subcontract involved. Unless within thirty days, or such additional period as the Commission may determine, the Commission is furnished satisfactory assurances that the respondent will cease to violate such provision, and has established and will carry out personnel and employment policies as specified in such provision, the Commission shall issue such order.

(h) Where the Commission has issued an order under subsection (g) of this section, the Commission shall take appropriate steps to insure that no department, agency, or independent establishment in the Executive branch of the Government shall thereafter enter into a contract with the respondent, and that no subcontract of such a contract shall be entered into with the respondent, until the Commission has determined that the respondent has established and will carry out personnel and employment policies as specified in the provision included in the contract pursuant to section 210.

(i) Proceedings held pursuant to this section shall be conducted in conformity with the Administrative Procedure Act.

Hearings

SEC. 212. (a) The Commission may hold such hearings as the Commission may deem advisable for compliance, enforcement, or educational purposes under this part. Such hearings shall be public unless all parties thereto agree that they be private.

(b) No order for debarment of any contractor from further Government contracts or subcontracts shall be made without opportunity for a hearing.

Educational Program

SEC. 213. The Commission shall encourage the furtherance of an educational program by employer and labor groups in order to eliminate or reduce the basic causes of discrimination in employment on the ground of race, creed, color, or national origin.

Part C. Discriminatory practices by employment agencies and labor organizations

Employment Agencies and Local Labor Organizations

SEC. 220. (a) It shall be a discriminatory employment practice for an employment agency supported in whole or in part by Federal funds to fail or refuse to properly classify or refer for employment, or otherwise to discriminate against any individual because of his race, color, religion, national origin, or ancestry.

(b) Where any employer has a contract with the United States, or a subcontract of such a contract, it shall be a discriminatory employment practice for any local labor organization which represents employees of such employer for the purposes of collective bargaining—

(1) to exclude or to expel from its membership, or otherwise to discriminate against, any individual because of his race, religion, color, national origin, or ancestry;

(2) to limit, segregate, or classify its membership in any way which would deprive or tend to deprive any individual of employment opportunities, or would limit such employment opportunities or otherwise adversely affect his status as an employee or as an applicant for employment, because of such individual's race, religion, color, national origin, or ancestry; or

(3) to cause or attempt to cause an employer to discriminate against an individual because of such individual's race, religion, color, national origin, or ancestry.

(c) It shall be a discriminatory employment practice for any employer having a contract with the United States, or a subcontract of such a contract, or for any labor organization, or joint labor-management committee of such employer and organization controlling apprenticeship or other training programs to discriminate against any individual because of his race, religion, color, national origin, or ancestry in admission to, or employment in, any program established to provide apprenticeship or other training. With respect to employers, the discriminatory employment practices covered by this subsection shall be included in the practices forbidden pursuant to section 210(a).

(d) It shall be a discriminatory employment practice for any such employment agency or local labor organization to discharge, expel, or otherwise discriminate against any person, because he has opposed any unlawful employment practice or has filed a charge, testified, participated, or assisted in any proceeding under this title.

(e) For the purposes of this title, the term "local labor organization" means, with respect to the employees of any employer, an organization—

(1) which is the certified representative of such employees under the provisions of the National Labor Relations Act, as amended, or the Railway Labor Act, as amended; or

(2) which, although not so certified, is a national or international labor organization or a local labor organization recognized or acting as the representative of such employees.

Proceedings Before the Commission

SEC. 221. (a) Whenever a written charge has been filed by or on behalf of any person claiming to be aggrieved that any employment agency or local labor organization is engaged in any discriminatory employment practice described in section 220 of this title, the Commission shall investigate such charge and if it shall determine after such preliminary investigation that probable cause exists for crediting such written charge it shall issue and serve upon such employment agency or local labor organization, as the case may be, a complaint stating the charges in that respect, together with a notice of hearing before the Commission, or a member thereof, or before a designated agent, at a place therein fixed, not less than 10 days after the service of such complaint. No complaint shall issue based upon any discriminatory employment practice occurring more than six months prior to the filing of the charge with the Commission and the service of a copy hereof upon the agency or organization complained against.

(b) (1) If, upon the preponderance of the evidence, including all the testimony taken, the Commission shall find that any employment agency supported in whole or in part with Federal funds has engaged in any discriminatory employment practice prohibited by section 220, the Commission shall state its findings of fact, and shall notify such agency that the Commission intends to order the Federal agency or agencies providing such Federal funds that such funds be withheld from such employment agency. Unless within thirty days or such additional period as the Commission may determine, the Commission is furnished satisfactory assurances that such employment agency will cease to engage in such discriminatory employment practices, the Commission shall issue such order, and thereafter no Federal funds shall be made available for such employment agency until the Commission shall otherwise determine.

(2) If, upon the preponderance of the evidence, including all the testimony taken, the Commission shall find that any local labor organization has engaged in any discriminatory employment practice prohibited by section 220, the Commission shall state its findings of fact and shall notify such local labor organization that the Commission intends to issue an order to such local labor organization under this paragraph. Unless within thirty days or such additional period as the Commission may determine, the Commission is furnished satisfactory assurances that such local labor organization will cease to engage in such discriminatory employment practice, the Commission shall issue and cause to be served on such local labor organization an order requiring such local labor organization to cease and desist from such discriminatory employment practice and to take such affirmative action as will effectuate the policies of this title. Such order may further require the local labor organization to make reports from time to time showing the extent to which it has complied with the order. Such order shall be effective during all periods thereafter in which employees who are members of such local labor organization are employed on any work being done under a contract with the United States, or any subcontract of such a contract.

(3) If the Commission shall find that any employment agency or local labor organization has not engaged in any discriminatory employment practice, or has ceased to engage in such a practice before the issuance of an order under paragraph (1) or (2), the Commission shall state its findings of fact and shall issue and cause to be served on such agency or representative and other parties an order dismissing the complaint.

(c) Proceedings held pursuant to this section shall be conducted in conformity with the Administrative Procedure Act.

Enforcement of Orders Covering Employee Local Labor Organizations

SEC. 222. (a) The Commission shall have power to petition any United States Court of Appeals or, if the court of appeals to which application might be made is in vacation, any district court within any circuit or district, respectively, wherein any discriminatory employment practice by a local labor organization occurred, for the enforcement of such order and for appropriate temporary relief or restraining order, and shall certify and file in the court to which petition is made a transcript of the entire record in the proceeding, including the pleadings and testimony upon which such order was entered and the findings and the order of the Commission. Upon such filing, the court shall conduct further proceedings in conformity with the standards, procedures, and limitations established by section 10 of the Administrative Procedure Act.

(b) Upon such filing the court shall cause notice thereof to be served upon the local labor organization and thereupon shall have jurisdiction of the proceeding and of the question determined therein and shall have power to grant such temporary relief or restraining order as it deems just and proper and to make and enter upon the pleadings, testimony, and proceedings set forth in such transcript a decree enforcing, modifying, and enforcing as so modified, or setting aside in whole or in part the order of the Commission.

(c) No objection that has not been urged before the Commission, its member, or agent shall be considered by the court, unless the failure or neglect to urge such objection shall be excused because of extraordinary circumstances.

(d) The findings of the Commission with respect to questions of fact if supported by substantial evidence on the record considered as a whole shall be conclusive.

(e) If either party shall apply to the court for leave to adduce additional evidence and shall show to the satisfaction of the court that such additional evidence is material and that there were reasonable grounds for the failure to adduce such evidence in the hearing before the Commission, its member, or agent, the court may order such additional evidence to be taken before the Commission, its member, or agent and to be made a part of the transcript.

(f) The Commission may modify its findings as to the facts, or make new findings, by reason of additional evidence so taken and filed, and it shall file such modified or new findings, which findings with respect to questions of fact if supported by substantial evidence on the record considered as a whole shall be conclusive, and its recommendations, if any, for the modification or setting aside of its original order.

(g) The jurisdiction of the court shall be exclusive and its judgment and decree shall be final, except that the same shall be subject to review by the appropriate United States court of appeals, if application was made to the district court or other United States court as hereinabove provided, and by the Supreme Court of the United States as provided in title 28, United States Code, section 1254.

Judicial Review

SEC. 223. (a) Any contractor, subcontractor, employment agency, local labor organization, or other person who is aggrieved by a final order of the Commission under this title may obtain a review of such order in any United States court of appeals of the judicial circuit wherein the discriminatory employment practice in question was alleged to have been engaged in or wherein such person resides or transacts business or the Court of Appeals for the District of Columbia, by filing in such court within the sixty-day period which begins on the date of the issuance of such order a written petition praying that the order of the Commission be modified or set aside. A copy of such petition shall be forthwith served upon the Commission and thereupon the aggrieved party shall file in the court a transcript of the entire record in the proceeding certified by the Commission, including the pleadings and testimony upon which the order complained of was entered and the findings and order of the Commission. Upon such filing, the court shall proceed in the same manner as in the case of an application by the Commission under section 222, and shall have the same exclusive jurisdiction to grant such temporary relief or restraining order as it deems just and proper, and to make and enter a decree enforcing, modifying, and enforcing as so modified, or setting aside in whole or in part the order of the Commission.

(b) Upon such filing by a person aggrieved the reviewing court shall conduct further proceedings in conformity with the standards, procedures, and limitations established by section 10 of the Administration Procedure Act.

(c) The commencement of proceedings under this section shall not, unless specifically ordered by the court, operate as a stay of the Commission's order.

(d) When granting appropriate temporary relief or a restraining order, or making and entering a decree enforcing, modifying, and enforcing as so modified, or setting aside in whole or in part an order of the Commission, as provided in this section, the jurisdiction of courts sitting in equity shall not be limited by the Act entitled "An Act to amend the Judicial Code and to define and limit the jurisdiction of courts sitting in equity, and for other purposes", approved March 23, 1932 (29 U.S.C., title 29, secs. 101–115).

(e) Petitions filed under this title shall be heard expeditiously.

Part D. Nondiscrimination in Government Employment

SEC. 230. (a) The Commission shall continually scrutinize and study employment practices of the Government of the United States, and consider and recommend such affirmative steps as should be taken by executive departments and agencies to realize fully the national policy of nondiscrimination within the executive branch of the Government.

(b) All executive departments and agencies shall continually conduct studies of Government employment practices within their responsibility. The studies shall be in such form as the Commission may prescribe and shall include statistics on current employment patterns, a review of current procedures, and the recommendation of positive measures for the elimination of any discrimination, direct or indirect. Reports and recommendations shall be submitted to the Commission at regular intervals as prescribed by the Commission. The Commission, after considering such reports and recommendations, shall report to the President from time to time and recommend such positive measures as may be necessary to accomplish the objectives of this part.

Enforcement of Orders Directed to Government Agencies

SEC. 231. (a) The President is authorized to take such action as may be necessary to conform employment practices within the Federal Government with the policies of this title and the recommendations of the Commission.

Part E. General provisions

Notices To Be Posted

SEC. 240. (a) Every person having a contract with the United States or a subcontract of such a contract, every local labor organization representing employees of such a contractor or subcontractor, and every employment agency supported in whole or in part by Federal funds, as the case may be, shall post and keep posted in conspicuous places upon its premises where notices to employees, applicants for employment, and members are customarily posted a notice to be prepared or approved by the Commission setting forth excerpts of this title and such other relevant information which the Commission deems appropriate to effectuate the purposes of this title.

(b) A willful violation of this section by a contractor, subcontractor, or labor organization shall be punishable by a fine of not less than $100 or more than $500 for each separate offense.

(c) Where an employment agency willfully violates this section, the Federal agency or agencies providing Federal funds for such agency shall withhold such funds until the employment agency complies with subsection (a) and furnishes satisfactory assurances that it will continue to comply with that subsection.

Veterans' Preference

SEC. 241. Nothing contained in this title shall be construed to repeal or modify any Federal, State, or local law creating special rights or preference for veterans.

Forcibly Resisting the Commission or its Representatives

SEC. 242. The provisions of section III of title 18, United States Code, shall apply to officers, agents, and employees of the Commission in the performance of their official duties.

Cooperative Arrangements

SEC. 243. The Commission is authorized to establish and maintain cooperative relationships with agencies of State and local governments, as well as with nongovernmental bodies, to assist in achieving the purposes of this title.

Separability Clause

SEC. 244. If any provision of this title or the application of such provision to any person or circumstance shall be held invalid, the remainder of this title or the application of such provision to persons or circumstances other than those to which it is held invalid shall not be affected thereby.

Amendments

SEC. 245. (a) Section 8(b) of the National Labor Relations Act (29 U.S.C. 158(b)), is amended (1) by striking out "and" at the end of paragraph (6) thereof, (2) by striking out the period at the end of paragraph (7) and inserting in lieu thereof ": and", and (3) by adding at the end thereof the following new paragraph:

"(8) to discriminate among the members of such labor organization on the basis of race, color, creed, or national origin in violation of an order of the Commission on Equality of Opportunity in Employment issued under section 221 of the Civil Rights Act of 1963."

(b) Section 9(c)(1) of such Act (29 U.S.C. 159(c)(1)) is amended by adding immediately before the period at the end thereof the following: "; except that the Board shall refuse to certify the results of any election which would result in a labor organization becoming the representative of employees for the purposes of collective bargaining, if such labor organization in any of its activities discriminates among its members on the basis of race, color, creed, or national origin in violation of an order of the Commission on Equality of Opportunity in Employment issued under section 221 of the Civil Rights Act of 1963".

Repeal

SEC. 246. Executive Order 10925 (except section 203 thereof) is repealed. All references in contracts and other documents to such order and to the Committee established thereby, shall hereafter be held and considered to refer to this title and to the Commission, respectively. All records and property of or in the custody of the said Committee are hereby transferred to the Commission, which shall wind up the outstanding affairs of the Committee.

Effective Date

SEC. 247. This title shall become effective sixty days after enactment.

* * * *

On June 23, 1963, Rep. Celler introduced the Administration bill, HR 7152, in the House; Senator Mansfield introduced the same bill, S.1731, in the Senate. The House bill was referred to the Judiciary Committee, while the Senate bill was held at the desk.

b. Colloquy Between Senate Leadership (Sens. Mansfield and Dirksen) and Sen. Johnston from South Carolina

---

1963   **CONGRESSIONAL RECORD — SENATE**   **11075**

* * * *

CIVIL RIGHTS LEGISLATION

Mr. MANSFIELD, Mr. CURTIS, and Mr. JOHNSTON addressed the Chair.

Mr. MANSFIELD. Mr. President, I was seeking recognition.

The VICE PRESIDENT. The Chair did not hear the Senator from Montana.

The Senator from Montana is recognized.

Mr. MANSFIELD. Mr. President, I introduce, and send to the desk, a bill which has been proposed by the President of the United States, dealing with one of the most compelling questions now facing the United States. This is the question of whether all our citizens, regardless of the color they may have been born with, shall have an equal chance to participate in the responsibilities and opportunities of our Nation.

Mr. President, on behalf of the distinguished Senator from Washington [Mr. MAGNUSON], I introduce, for appropriate reference, a bill designed to eliminate discrimination in places of public accommodation. This is one aspect of the total legislative problem with which the President's message deals. The bill covers a particularly difficult problem in an area much in need of adjustment.

It is my hope that the bill will be referred to the committee of which the distinguished Senator from Washington is chairman. I am confident it will there receive the careful examination and consideration which this new and complex area requires.

It is my intention later this afternoon, together with the distinguished minority leader, to submit to the Senate an additional bill which will cover a great many of the legislative questions involved in the present issue, and on which we are in accord.

Our Nation was built on the ideal that each individual, if given the opportunity to develop those gifts that God has given him to the fullest extent possible, would make the greatest contribution in return to both himself and his society as well. Upon this principle we have developed the greatest nation the world has ever seen. But we have not in all cases kept true to this ideal; and the time has come when those to whom we have denied it ask to be included. This is all they seek—elemental things, like a chance to go to school and vote, which the rest of us have enjoyed without a moment's thought. What they wish is only that which other Americans have always had.

In the last weeks, many people throughout the country have willingly begun what is always a painful process of change. They have recognized their obligation to resolve this question in those ways of which they are capable. Shortly, it will be our time here. We do not fool ourselves that it will be easy; but with the honest support of all those Members in this great body who truly believe that men are born free and that freedom was meant for all our people, we will pass a law which will advance this end.

Let me say that those men who agree on this end will have to bring their disagreement on means to a common point of view. Democrats, Republicans, liberal, moderate or conservative, we must respect the right of others to honestly defend their opinion. But if we are to bring this matter to a successful finish, we must be willing to exercise the most demanding qualities of the legislative process.

We will work and wrestle with each suggestion for improvement, in committee and on the floor. But if those who agree that something must be done do not, at the final moment, agree on something that can be done, there will be no bill. Those who then say the bill did not go far enough or went too far will do their cause and the Nation they serve and this institution in which they serve a great disservice.

It is in the attempt to approach this agreement on means that Senator DIRKSEN and I have worked together, in consultation with the President of the United States, on this bill.

We are not in accord on every point, such as the provisions dealing with public accommodations; but we are still constantly working toward agreement. Some approach—and we are greatly indebted to Senator AIKEN for his concise statement of the problem—will, I predict, eventually be reached.

These bills will now be referred to the appropriate committees. It is my hope—and I now appeal to the chairmen concerned and all Senators—to give these measures their immediate and closest attention, so that we may begin debate on the floor at the earliest possible time.

In the days ahead, two great questions will be decided. The first I have already mentioned: it is simply whether American freedom and ideals are meant to be for all our people. The second question will be whether our free and balanced Government is capable of bringing to conclusion this issue which so divides us. I am hopeful that the answer of the Senate to both of them will be "Yes."

Mr. President, I ask that the two bills now introduced and the one to be introduced later this afternoon be held at the desk until the conclusion of business on Monday next, for the purpose of giving an opportunity to all Senators who may desire to do so to join in sponsoring them.

Mr. JOHNSTON. Mr. President, on the same subject——

The VICE PRESIDENT. The Chair does not understand the request of the Senator from Montana. Will he rephrase his request, so the Chair can understand to which bill he refers?

Mr. MANSFIELD. Yes, Mr. President, the bill having to do with title II only—the public accommodations bill—and the administration's bill, both of which are at the desk. I ask that they and the bill which the distinguished minority leader, Mr. DIRKSEN, and I will introduce later this afternoon be held at the desk until the conclusion of business on Monday next, for the purpose of allowing other Senators who may desire to do so to join in sponsoring them.

The VICE PRESIDENT. Is there objection?

Mr. JOHNSTON. Mr. President, I believe that the majority leader, at the beginning of his statement, asked that a bill be referred to a particular committee.

Mr. MANSFIELD. No; I asked that it be referred to the appropriate committee.

Mr. JOHNSTON. I thought the Senator made the statement that one of the bills should be referred to the committee headed by the Senator from Washington [Mr. MAGNUSON].

Mr. MANSFIELD. I expressed the hope that it would be so referred.

Mr. JOHNSTON. The question I raise refers to that statement. There is a statute which provides what committees shall handle certain proposed legislation.

Mr. MANSFIELD. The Senator is correct.

Mr. JOHNSTON. I am only asking that the law be carried out, and that no special or preferential treatment be started in the Senate in regard to the referral of bills. If it is, we shall have trouble in the future in regard to other subjects. I ask that the rules be strictly carried out in regard to the introduction of any bills.

Mr. MANSFIELD. Mr. President, I am in wholehearted accord with what the distinguished senior Senator from South Carolina has said. For the edification of the Senate, I repeat the particular paragraph of my statement to which the Senator has referred:

It is my hope that it will be referred to the committee of which the distinguished Senator from Washington is chairman.

I did not ask that the bill be referred to that particular committee; I am hopeful that it will be so referred.

The VICE PRESIDENT. Is there objection to the request of the Senator from Montana? The Chair hears none, and it is so ordered.

Mr. DIRKSEN. Mr. President——

The VICE PRESIDENT. Does the Senator from Illinois wish the Senator from Montana to yield?

Mr. DIRKSEN. No; I seek recognition in my own right.

The VICE PRESIDENT. Has the Senator from Montana concluded?

Mr. MANSFIELD. I have.

The VICE PRESIDENT. The Senator from Illinois is recognized.

Mr. DIRKSEN. Mr. President, first I should like to express my appreciation for the restraint which the majority leader has exercised over a considerable period of time with respect to the highly emotional subject of civil rights. Numerous conferences have been held at the White House. There have been party conferences on both sides of the aisle. We are aware of the sharp diversity of opinion with respect to the whole subject matter. The approach now taken will give every Senator an opportunity to manifest not only his interest, but what he proposes to do about its disposition.

Mr. JOHNSTON. Mr. President——

Mr. DIRKSEN. I would appreciate it if the Senator would permit me to conclude my statement.

We refer to the administration bill as "the package bill." It contains eight titles.

The first title of the bill deals with voting. It includes a presumption of literacy on the basis of a sixth grade certificate.

The second title is the highly controversial title dealing with accommodations and public services. It has been modified somewhat from the original draft, which is the one that I could not accept—first, because I do not believe it would be enforcible; second, I think it would contravene the Constitution and would be an invasion of a private right.

The third title deals with desegregation of schools. It provides for loans and grants as well as special training.

The fourth title deals with the setup of a community relations service in the Office of the President.

The fifth title would extend the Civil Rights Commission until December 1967 and would spell out some of its procedure in the statute.

The sixth title is a negative approach with respect to facilities and projects in which Federal funds would be used. Of course, it deals with segregation, discrimination and the interpretation which is to be placed upon them.

The seventh title is the so-called equality-of-job-opportunity title, presently covered by the President's Commission, of which the distinguished Vice President is now the Chairman. It has no statutory authority. It was created by Executive order and, of course, it must get its funds by assessing the appropriate agencies and departments of Government.

The eighth title deals with appropriations.

What is now before the Senate and will be before the committees in due course is the entire package containing eight titles. There will be another bill which will be introduced this afternoon, from which the highly controversial title II has been deleted.

Finally, there will be a separate bill which will deal entirely with title II and nothing more.

I believe everyone appreciates that the problem is a national one. As a party leader, I try to remember that I have some obligation to fulfill the pledges that my party made to the country in its platform of 1960. I have an obligation to my party members, and I try to see it as objectively as possible.

The bills will be at the desk until the end of business on Monday, and Senators who care to join in cosponsorship can do so. I do not believe a more extended statement is necessary at this time. Certainly there will be hearings, and those hearings will be thorough on every part of the program before it finally comes to the Senate for action.

Mr. CASE. Mr. President, will the Senator yield?

The VICE PRESIDENT. Does the Senator from Illinois yield, and if so, to whom?

Mr. DIRKSEN. I yield to the Senator from New Jersey.

Mr. CASE. As a matter of information, will the Senator advise whether the so-called package of bills contains what is commonly called proposed FEPC legislation?

Mr. DIRKSEN. No.

Mr. MANSFIELD. Mr. President, will the Senator yield?

Mr. DIRKSEN. I yield.

Mr. MANSFIELD. I believe that if the Senator will read the President's message with reference to such proposed legislation which has already been introduced, he will see that the President expressed his hope that it will be given serious consideration.

Mr. CASE. I have read the President's message. As the Senator said, the President indicates that he favors pending proposed legislation which a number of us have introduced, but it is not included in the package which he has presented.

Mr. JOHNSTON. Mr. President, I wonder if it would be in order at this time to ask that the bill lie on the desk and that Senators be notified, say, 1 day before the bill is referred to the committee to which it is to be referred. The reason I make that suggestion is that heretofore such measures have been referred to the Judiciary Committee.

The VICE PRESIDENT. Did the Senator from Montana ask unanimous consent that the bills remain at the desk and not be referred until next Monday?

Mr. MANSFIELD. No; I did not. I asked that the bills be referred to the appropriate committees.

At this time I ask unanimous consent that the bills be printed, and that they also be printed at this point in the RECORD.

Mr. JOHNSTON. I have no objection.

The VICE PRESIDENT. The bills will be received and appropriately referred; and, without objection, the bills will be printed in the RECORD, and will be held at the desk, as requested by the Senator from Montana.

The bill (S. 1731) to enforce the constitutional right of vote, to confer jurisdiction upon the district courts of the United States to provide injunctive relief against discrimination in public accommodations, to authorize the Attorney General to institute suits to protect constitutional rights in education, to establish a Community Relations Service, to extend for 4 years the Commission on Civil Rights, to prevent discrimination in federally assisted programs, to establish a Commission on Equal Employment Opportunity, and for other purposes, introduced by Mr. MANSFIELD, was referred to the Committee on the Judiciary and ordered to be printed in the RECORD, as follows:

Be it enacted by the Senate and House of Representatives of the United States of America in Congress assembled, That this Act may be cited as the "Civil Rights Act of 1963."

SEC. 2. (a) Discrimination by reason of race, color, religion, or national origin is incompatible with the concepts of liberty and equality to which the Government of the United States is dedicated. In recent years substantial steps have been taken toward eliminating such discrimination throughout the Nation. Nevertheless, many citizens of the United States, solely because of their race, color, or national origin, are denied rights and privileges accorded to other citizens and thereby subjected to inconveniences, humiliations, and hardships. Such discrimination impairs the general welfare of the United States by preventing the fullest development of the capabilities of the whole citizenry and by limiting participation in the economic, political, and cultural life of the Nation.

(b) It is hereby declared to be the policy of this Act to promote the general welfare by eliminating discrimination based on race, color, religion, or national origin in voting, education, and public accommodations through the exercise by Congress of the powers conferred upon it to regulate the manner of holding Federal elections, to enforce the provisions of the fourteenth and fifteenth amendments, to regulate commerce among the several States, and to make laws necessary and proper to execute the powers conferred upon it by the Constitution.

(c) It is also desirable that disputes or disagreements arising in any community from the discriminatory treatment of individuals for reasons of race, color, or national origin shall be resolved on a voluntary basis, without hostility or litigation. Accordingly, it is the further purpose of this Act to promote this end by providing machinery for the voluntary settlement of such disputes and disagreements.

* * * *

* * * *

109 Cong. Rec. 11081:

TITLE VII—COMMISSION ON EQUAL EMPLOYMENT OPPORTUNITY

SEC. 701. The President is authorized to establish a Commission to be known as the "Commission on Equal Employment Opportunity," hereinafter referred to as the Commission. It shall be the function of the Commission to prevent discrimination against employees or applicants for employment because of race, color, religion, or national origin by Government contractors and subcontractors, and by contractors and subcontractors participating in programs or activities in which direct or indirect financial assistance by the United States Government is provided by way of grant, contract, loan, conferred upon it by the President. The Commission shall have such powers to effectuate the purposes of this title as may be conferred upon it by the President. The President may also confer upon the Commission such powers as he deems appropriate to prevent discrimination on the ground of race, color, religion, or national origin in Government employment.

SEC. 702. The Commission shall consist of the Vice President, who shall serve as Chairman, the Secretary of Labor, who shall serve as Vice Chairman, and not more than fifteen other members appointed by and serving at the pleasure of the President. Members of the Commission, while attending meetings or conferences of the Commission or otherwise serving at the request of the Commission, shall be entitled to receive compensation at a rate to be fixed by it but not exceeding $75 per diem, including travel time, and while away from their homes or regular places of business they may be allowed travel expenses, including per diem in lieu of subsistence, as authorized by section 73b–2 of title 5 of the United States

Code for persons in the Government service employed intermittently.

SEC. 703. (a) There shall be an Executive Vice Chairman of the Commission who shall be appointed by the President and who shall be ex officio a member of the Commission. The Executive Vice Chairman shall assist the Chairman, the Vice Chairman, and the members of the Commission and shall be responsible for carrying out the orders and recommendations of the Commission and for performing such other functions as the Commission may direct.

(b) Section 106(a) of the Federal Executive Pay Act of 1956, as amended (5 U.S.C. 2205(a)), is further amended by adding the following clause thereto:

"(52) Executive Vice-Chairman, Commission on Equal Employment Opportunity."

(c) The Commission is authorized to appoint, subject to the civil service laws and regulations, such other personnel as may be necessary to enable it to carry out its functions and duties, and to fix their compensation in accordance with the Classification Act of 1949, and is authorized to procure services as authorized by section 14 of the Act of August 2, 1946 (60 Stat. 810; 5 U.S.C. 55a), but at rates for individuals not in excess of $50 a day.

c. Questions on The Early Legislative History of Title VII

1. The first two excerpts from the House and Senate floor debate set forth the initial approach to combatting employment discrimination offered by the House Republicans in January 1963, and the approach proposed by the Kennedy Administration in June 1963. Which approach is a more serious effort, in terms of the status of the Commission? How do the two bills compare in terms of their enforcement and remedial powers?

2. What exactly is going on in the floor exchange between Senators Mansfield and Johnston? What procedural protection is Senator Johnston seeking, and why?

d. Hearings Before Subcommittee No. 5 of the H. Comm. on the Judiciary, 88th Cong. (1963) (statement of Robert F. Kennedy, Att'y Gen. of the United States)

CIVIL RIGHTS

2014—

HEARINGS

BEFORE

SUBCOMMITTEE NO. 5

OF THE

COMMITTEE ON THE JUDICIARY
HOUSE OF REPRESENTATIVES

EIGHTY-EIGHTH CONGRESS

FIRST SESSION

ON

MISCELLANEOUS PROPOSALS REGARDING THE CIVIL RIGHTS
OF PERSONS WITHIN THE JURISDICTION OF THE
UNITED STATES

MAY 8, 9, 15, 16, 23, 24, 28; JUNE 13, 26, 27; JULY 10, 11, 12, 17,
18, 19, 24, 25, 26, 31; AUGUST 1, 2, 1963

Serial No. 4

PART II

Printed for the use of the Committee on the Judiciary

U.S. GOVERNMENT PRINTING OFFICE
23–340   WASHINGTON : 1963

1372   CIVIL RIGHTS

(material omitted)

STATEMENT OF ATTORNEY GENERAL ROBERT F. KENNEDY, ACCOMPANIED BY ASSISTANT ATTORNEY GENERAL BURKE MARSHALL, CIVIL RIGHTS DIVISION, DEPARTMENT OF JUSTICE

Attorney General KENNEDY. Just Mr. Marshall, Mr. Chairman.

The CHAIRMAN. Mr. Burke Marshall.

Attorney General KENNEDY. He is head of the Civil Rights Division.

The CHAIRMAN. You may proceed, Mr. Attorney General.

Attorney General KENNEDY. Thank you, Mr. Chairman, and members of the committee.

I am here today to testify in support of a bill that will go a long way toward redeeming the pledges upon which this Republic was founded—pledges that all are created equal, that they are endowed equally with unalienable rights and are entitled to equal opportunity in the pursuit of their daily lives.

In this generation, we have seen an extraordinary change in America—a new surge of idealism in our life—a new and profound insistence on reality in our democratic order. Much has been done. But quite obviously much more must be done—both because the American people are clearly demanding it and because, by any moral standard it is right.

The 10½ percent of Americans whose skin is not white are required to meet all the duties of citizenship. They must obey the same laws as white citizens, they must pay the same taxes, they must fight side by side in the same wars.

Nothing is more contrary to the spirit of the Constitution—and even to the spirit of commonsense—than to deny the full rights and privileges of citizenship to people who are so obligated. And the Constitution provides the means for redressing this inequity. If we do not use those means, we compound the wrong.

On June 11, the President called for action by all Americans to assure Negroes the full rights of citizenship. He asked for the same action at all levels of government. And he asked in particular that

Congress "make a commitment it has not fully made in this century to the proposition that race has no place in American life or law".

The bill before you today embodies that commitment.

Technically speaking, it is an omnibus bill, H.R. 7152, to carry out recommendations contained in the President's civil rights message of February 28, 1963, and his more recent message of June 19.

The bill contains seven titles dealing with problems of racial discrimination in our country. Two of the titles are virtually identical to bills already introduced by the chairman of this committee and which have the support of the administration. Title I, with minor exceptions, is the same as H.R. 5455, concerning voting rights, and title V is the same as H.R. 5456, which would extend the life of the Commission on Civil Rights.

However, titles relating to discrimination in public accommodations, education, and federally assisted programs are new, as are titles providing a statutory basis for a Community Relations Service and a Commission on Equal Employment Opportunity.

In his message to Congress of February 28 the President pointed out that more progress has been made to secure civil rights for all Americans in the last 2 years than in any comparable period in our history. But he emphasized that harmful and wrongful racial discrimination still occurs in virtually every part of the country and in virtually every aspect of our national life—in public accommodations, in employment, in education and in voting.

The events that have occurred since the President's first message—in Birmingham, in Jackson, in nearby Cambridge, in Philadelphia and in many other cities—make it clear that the attack upon these problems must be accelerated.

The demonstrations show not only that an ever-increasing number of our Negro citizens will no longer accept an inferior status, they have drawn sharp attention to the handicaps which so many Negro citizens experience simply because they are not white—or because years of unjust deprivation have left them in poverty and without the means or hope of improving their condition.

Two titles of the bill—those relating to the Commission on Equal Employment Opportunity and to nondiscrimination in federally assisted programs—bear on the problem of poverty. However, much more will have to be accomplished in this regard, and the June 19 message details the President's proposals to stimulate economic growth, to provide employment opportunities and to equip individuals with the ability to take advantage of enlarged opportunities.

PUBLIC ACCOMMODATIONS

(material omitted)

(material omitted)

(material omitted)

EQUAL EMPLOYMENT

At the beginning of my statement I touched briefly upon the economic handicaps to which our Negro citizens are subjected and pointed out that measures to deal with this problem are contained in bills not before this committee. However, two titles of H.R. 7152 have an important bearing upon this problem.

By Executive order issued shortly after the President took office, he established the Committee on Equal Employment Opportunity which has opened large areas of employment to Negroes by preventing racial discrimination by Government contractors and subcontractors.

Although it contains some public members, the Committee is financed as an interdepartmental group, and therefore must rely for its operating funds upon contributions by various departments and agencies.

Under the leadership of the Vice President, the Committee has made outstanding progress toward the elimination of discriminatory employment practices in business and industry. It has won the confidence and obtained the cooperation of the leading firms and labor organizations of the country.

Title VII of H.R. 7152 would provide the Committee with a statutory base and would establish its as a permanent body. No change in its composition or manner of operations is intended, and it would remain under the direction of the Vice President.

In short, the new organization will have the same leadership and use the same personnel as the Committee now has and will have the same powers and functions as the President has conferred upon it to date. But it will have, in addition, the prestige of congressional authorization and direct access to appropriated funds to meet its needs.

(material omitted)

(material omitted)

The CHAIRMAN. As I say, we will terminate these hearings at 5 o'clock and there are still some more subjects open for discussion, namely: the Commission on Civil Rights, Equal Employment Opportunities, use of Federal funds, community relation services. My suggestion is, Mr. Attorney General, we hold you here to 5 o'clock and then at some subsequent meeting, we should like to have Mr. Burke Marshall here to discuss a lot of these technical questions. We could have Mr. Marshall back in executive sessions when the subcommittee goes into details concerning the bill.

Attorney General KENNEDY. That will be fine, Mr. Chairman.

Mr. CRAMER. Mr. Chairman, is there any reason why such a session should be in executive session. This would involve basic policy questions in which testimony from the Attorney General's office is vital. Why should it be held secretly and in executive session, rather than to proceed in a public session?

The CHAIRMAN. If you make it public, I don't mind that.

Mr. MILLER. Mr. Chairman, I have one question. Mr. Attorney General, I am looking for information. I am not trying to politic in this question. The President's message of June 19, 1963, states, "I renew my support of pending Federal fair employment practices, legislation applicable to both employers and unions." What legislation is referred to?

Attorney General KENNEDY. I think there are a number of bills that are before the Congress at the present time.

The CHAIRMAN. We do not have that bill before us. That is before Education and Labor.

Mr. MILLER. When did the President previously indicate his support of such legislation?

Attorney General KENNEDY. Arthur Goldberg testified before that committee a year ago or 2 years ago.

Mr. MILLER. As a matter of fact, the Assistant Labor Secretary and Director of Labor's Bureau on Apprenticeship testified in open session to H.R. 10144 providing for an Equal Employment Opportunity Commission and power to eliminate discrimination in employment practices. Mr. Goshen said the bill would "not be helpful to any group and we do not support it." I have never seen a statement where the President does support this. Could you supply this committee with some quote from the President or some statement by him?

Attorney General KENNEDY. Arthur Goldberg appeared before the committee on behalf of it. I can't tell you specifically about that particular bill. But he appeared on FEPC legislation and said although the administration was not tied to any particular bill, that it supported FEPC in principle. I don't know what the date was. But he spoke on behalf of the administration.

Mr. McCULLOCH. Mr. Chairman, I have a question. Mr. Attorney General, Are labor unions covered under title VII of the administration bill entitled, "Commission on Equal Employment Opportunities"?

Attorney General KENNEDY. Yes; they are.

Mr. McCULLOCH. Will you tell me? I read it and I could not find where labor unions were covered.

Attorney General KENNEDY. It is just Government contracts or subcontractors and labor organization that have dealings with them.

1442 CIVIL RIGHTS

I don't think our authority goes beyond that. What we have attempted to do is to bring in——

Mr. McCulloch. Can you point it out to me because I read it two or three times and have not been able to find it, or if that is an improper question today, point it out for the record tomorrow.

Attorney General Kennedy. Very Well.

Mr. Cramer. It is not in there.

Mr. Miller. Mr. Marshall, could you point out where the labor unions are covered in title VI?

Attorney General Kennedy. I expect it is probably in the Executive order.

Mr. McCulloch. The reason I ask that was because the legislation which was introduced by me late in January has a title which unequivocally and unmistakably covers labor unions. I should like to say this: I think this is one of the most effective approaches to equal employment opportunity in America.

Attorney General Kennedy. I would agree with you.

Mr. McCulloch. Because if apprentices are not accepted by labor unions at an age when they will begin their job training there is going to be discrimination against them as long as they live.

Attorney General Kennedy. I agree.

Mr. McCulloch. I hope the Attorney General, if the administration bill does not have that specific provision, will support this title in our bill because it is very carefully drawn.

Mr. Miller. It does not have it, does it, Mr. Marshall?

Attorney General Kennedy. Congressman, I think it is fundamental. It is included in the Executive order. I have been on the committee that has dealt with these problems. We have done a great deal of work with labor organizations. A number of them, a large number, a high percentage have signed these agreements. But I think what you say is fundamental to this whole operation.

Mr. McCulloch. I am very happy to hear you say that and would be glad to have you join in this title of our bill.

Attorney General Kennedy. Fine. I think if it is not clear in the bill that it should cover labor organizations, I am sure we can clear that up.

The Chairman. The counsel wishes to call attention to the Executive order which contains this provision.

Attorney General Kennedy. If you want it in the bill, it would be fine because I think it is essential.

Mr. McCulloch. The reason we want it in the bill is to give it legislative status and dignity. We can work on that with your representatives.

Mr. Foley. I am referring to part III, superpart (a) under section 302(c). It reads as follows:

Whenever the contractor or subcontractor has a collective bargaining agreement or other contractor understanding with a labor union, or other representative of workers, the compliance report shall include such information as to the labor unions or other representatives' practices and policies affecting the compliance as the committee may prescribe. *Provided,* That to the extent that such information is within the exclusive possession of a labor union or other workers' representative and the labor union or representative shall refuse to furnish such information to the contractor, the contractor shall so certify to the contracting agency as part of its compliance report and set forth what efforts he has made to obtain such information.

Mr. McCulloch. I would like to again ask if there are any sanctions if it be violated by labor unions?

Mr. Foley. Only to the enforcement of the contract itself.

Mr. McCulloch. And that is against the contractor and not against the union?

Mr. Foley. That is correct.

Mr. McCulloch. That is one of the points we were trying to make and which we think is so important.

Mr. Cramer. That refers also not only to title VII, but also to title VI. Nondiscrimination in federally assisted programs relates only to the contractor or subcontractor and has no relationship whatsoever to unions either.

Mr. McCulloch. Yes, if I might interrupt again. There was lengthy testimony in this committee within the last 2 or 3 weeks that on the interstate highway program in several Southern States there was continued discrimination by reason of color. Is my memory correct?

Mr. Miller. That is correct.

Attorney General Kennedy. May I point out title VII and perhaps, Congressman, it should be clearer, but it does say the President is authorized to establish a Commission on Equal Employment Opportunity hereinafter referred to as the Commission, and just a second sentence therein that it shall be the function of the Commission to prevent discrimination against employees or applicants for employment because of race, color, or religion. Although it doesn't spell out labor unions, it spells out people who are employees which should obviously cover labor unions. If there is any question about it, we will be glad to put it in.

Mr. McCulloch. We are very glad to hear that. We carefully studied this title in this bill.

Mr. Cramer. Assuming if it were in title VII, or title VI, or both, what form of sanctions against labor unions could be employed? You are talking about withdrawing contracts with relation to the employer. What sanctions against the labor unions?

Attorney General Kennedy. I think then the employer would have a suit against the labor organization if through their discrimination the contract had to be withdrawn.

Mr. Cramer. Then the responsibility is on the employer to bring the suit.

Attorney General Kennedy. It is also possible that we would have some authority.

Mr. Cramer. I would like to suggest that proper language proposing sanctions relating to both contractors and labor unions and proper amendments to bring both title VI and title VII in line consistent with what the Attorney General has stated, should be submitted by the Attorney General's Office for consideration.

Attorney General Kennedy. Would you be in favor of both VI and VII?

Mr. Cramer. If you are going to put management in, you should put labor in; yes, I certainly would.

Attorney General Kennedy. Would the gentleman vote for the bill if we put that in?

Mr. Cramer. I reserve my right to see what kind of bill we get out.

23-340—63—pt. 2——35

1444   CIVIL RIGHTS

Mr. McCulloch. I will be glad to answer the chairman, with the perfecting amendments, I will join with him as I joined in 1957 and 1959 in this field.

Mr. Lindsay. In section 7, do you think the bill would be strengthened if there were a subpena power provision inserted?

Attorney General Kennedy. Could I study that and submit it?

Mr. Meader. Mr. Chairman, before the deadline, may I ask one question about the community relations service.

The Chairman. Certainly.

Mr. Meader. I notice on page 26 you appoint a Director at $20,000 a year but do not require confirmation by the Senate. Is there a reason for that?

Attorney General Kennedy. No. I never really got into much of a discussion about it, Congressman. I just do not know whether we would suggest that or not.

Mr. Meader. Is there any objection to requiring Senate confirmation of a position of that importance?

Attorney General Kennedy. No. I would like to reserve my answer on that. I think there are more advantages in having the individual operate out of the personal household of the President and possibly there might be some disadvantage in having ratification by the Senate. Let me think about that.

The Chairman. Could you get confirmation under these circumstances?

Attorney General Kennedy. I think that is something that would have to be considered.

Mr. McCulloch. Would the gentleman yield at that point?

Mr. Meader. Yes.

Mr. McCulloch. The Equal Employment Opportunities Commission provided in H.R. 3139 would require the Commissioner to be nominated by the President and confirmed by the Senate. Would the Attorney General have the same tentative objection to that proposal as he would to the way in which the members of the community service organizations are to be selected?

Attorney General Kennedy. That is the Civil Rights Commission you are talking about?

Mr. McCulloch. No. I am talking about the **Equal Job Opportunity Commission.** The Commission on Equality of Opportunity in Employment. We proposed that the members of this Commission have staggered terms and that they be nominated by the President and confirmed by the Senate. That it be a bipartisan Commission. Would there be objection to that?

Attorney General Kennedy. I think it should be bipartisan. I would like to think a little bit more about whether it should be confirmed by the Senate. I would like to give it a little more thought. Maybe that is the answer. Maybe it should be. I don't know.

Mr. McCulloch. The last sentence of section 401 on page 26 reads:

The Director is authorized to appoint such additional officers and employees as he deems necessary to carry out the purpose of this title.

There is no reference to the civil service or classification laws. Is it intended that the Director shall have power to appoint assistants without regard to the classification and civil service laws?

Attorney General Kennedy. No. It would be covered by the classification and civil service regulations.

Mr. McCulloch. I notice this office is not created in any existing department or even in the office of the President; it seems to be a completely autonomous agency that is being created here. I wonder if that is the intent here in light of the statement you made recently that it ought to be close to the White House. Should this be an office created in the office of the President?

Attorney General Kennedy. That is the intention—that it should operate out of the White House or out of the Executive Office Building.

Mr. McCulloch. Is there any estimate of the number of personnel and the cost that this agency will involve?

Attorney General Kennedy. No, we have none. I would expect that it would be quite small and as much as possible perhaps you could utilize people on a voluntary basis who would come down and devote their services.

Mr. McCulloch. From the discussion in the President's message, it would appear that there is a desire that this not be an office in the Department of Justice.

Attorney General Kennedy. That is correct.

Mr. McCulloch. Althought such mediation as has occurred has occurred under your Civil Rights Division.

Attorney General Kennedy. Yes. But our responsibility really is the enforcement of the law and to see that the statutes are enforced. We have gotten into this because there has not been any other group to do it. I think it would be better if that responsibility was taken from us and put over into another department. I think the best way that can be done, as I said.

Mr. McCulloch. As you know, Mr. Attorney General, I served on the Government Operations Committee on which you served as counsel in the Senate for many years, and there is a reluctance on the part of Congress to create new independent agencies without being responsible to anyone in the established executive branch of the Government. I am just wondering if there is any reason why this mediation service could not be performed under the Civil Rights Commission rather than to have a new autonomous agency in orbit without control by anybody.

Attorney General Kennedy. I think it has a different function than the Civil Rights Commission, Congressman. It is to examine, and offer its good services in particular problem areas. The Civil Rights Commission has a broader responsibility. I think it can have a very valuable function if it has the right kind of people running it, in bringing white persons and Negroes together in discussing the facts and trying to work out some of these matters at a local level rather than having the Federal Government involved. I don't think it is going to require a large number of personnel. I don't envision that it will be more than a half-dozen people altogether, which would include the staff. I don't look upon it as a major operation. I think they can call on people to volunteer their services as well. So I think it would be better if it operated out of the White House and the Executive Offices rather than the Civil Rights Commission or Department of Justice.

Mr. McCulloch. I understand you do intend to provide the committee with some kind of estimate of how many people and how much this new agency would cost.

Attorney General Kennedy. I would be happy to. I might say we gave a good deal of thought whether it should be in the Department

1446   CIVIL RIGHTS

of Justice or in the Executive Offices, and we decided we thought it could function better in the White House.

Mr. McCULLOCH. The message indicated that the President intended to establish such a service by Executive order. That message was dated June 19. I presume he has not yet done so.

Attorney General KENNEDY. He has not. We are giving some thought to some people that might head it up. We make our report to the President when he returns from Europe. I hope it would be done quickly. I say, Congressman, right at this very time we have probably a half-dozen people from the Department of Justice in areas across the South trying to perform this function. I have my administrative assistant away. Mr. Marshall has a number of people who would otherwise be meeting other responsibilities. I think this is extremely valuable and helpful at this time and perhaps can head off a good deal of difficulty in some of these areas.

The CHAIRMAN. I think we have reached a little after 5 o'clock. I want to say, Mr. Attorney General, you have been patient and helpful and forthright and cooperative, and we are very grateful to you as we are to Mr. Marshall. At this point I wish to insert the presidential message of June 19, 1963.

(The message follows:)

(material omitted)

e. H. Comm. on the Judiciary, Civil Rights Act of 1963, H.R. Rep. No. 88-914 (Nov. 20, 1963)

88TH CONGRESS 1st Session	HOUSE OF REPRESENTATIVES	REPORT No. 914

CIVIL RIGHTS ACT OF 1963

NOVEMBER 20, 1963.—Committed to the Committee of the Whole House on the State of the Union and ordered to be printed

---

Mr. RODINO, from the Committee on the Judiciary, submitted the following

REPORT

[To accompany H.R. 7152]

The Committee on the Judiciary, to whom was referred the bill (H.R. 7152) to enforce the constitutional right to vote, to confer jurisdiction upon the district courts of the United States to provide injunctive relief against discrimination in public accommodations, to authorize the Attorney General to institute suits to protect constitutional rights in education, to establish a Community Relations Service, to extend for 4 years the Commission on Civil Rights, to prevent discrimination in federally assisted programs, to establish a Commission on Equal Employment Opportunity, and for other purposes, having considered the same, report favorably thereon with amendments and recommend that the bill do pass.

The amendments are as follows:

Amendment No. 1: Strike all after the enacting clause and insert in lieu thereof the following:

That this Act may be cited as "The Civil Rights Act of 1963."

TITLE I—VOTING RIGHTS

SEC. 101. Section 2004 of the Revised Statutes (42 U.S.C. 1971), as amended by section 131 of the Civil Rights Act of 1957 (71 Stat. 637), and as further amended by section 601 of the Civil Rights Act of 1960 (74 Stat. 90), is further amended as follows:

(a) Insert "1" after "(a)" in subsection (a) and add at the end of subsection (a) the following new paragraphs:

"(2) No person acting under color of law shall—

"(A) in determining whether any individual is qualified under State law or laws to vote in any Federal election, apply any standard, practice, or procedure different from the standards, practices, or procedures applied under such law or laws to other individuals within the same county, parish, or similar political subdivision who have been found by State officials to be qualified to vote;

25-610—63——1

(material omitted)

TITLE VII—EQUAL EMPLOYMENT OPPORTUNITY

FINDINGS AND DECLARATION OF POLICY

SEC. 701. (a) The Congress hereby declares that the opportunity for employment without discrimination of the types described in sections 704 and 705 is a right of all persons within the jurisdiction of the United States, and that it is the national policy to protect the right of the individual to be free from such discrimination.

(b) The Congress further declares that the succeeding provisions of this title are necessary for the following purposes:

(1) To remove obstructions to the free flow of commerce among the States and with foreign nations.

(2) To insure the complete and full enjoyment by all persons of the rights, privileges, and immunities secured and protected by the Constitution of the United States.

DEFINITIONS

SEC. 702. For the purposes of this title—

(a) the term "person" includes one or more individuals, labor union, partnerships, associations, corporations, legal representatives, mutual companies, joint-stock companies, trusts, unincorporated organizations, trustees, trustees in bankruptcy, or receivers.

(b) The term "employer" means a person engaged in an industry affecting commerce who has twenty-five or more employees, and any agent of such a person, but such term does not include (1) the United States, a corporation wholly owned by the Government of the United States, or a State or political subdivision thereof, (2) a bona fide private membership club (other than a labor organization) which is exempt from taxation under section 501(c) of the Internal Revenue Code of 1954: Provided, That during the first year after the effective date prescribed in subsection (a) of section 719, persons having fewer than one hundred employees (and their agents) shall not be considered employers, and, during the second year after such date, persons having fewer than fifty employees (and their agents) shall not be considered employers.

(c) The term "employment agency" means any person regularly undertaking with or without compensation to procure employees for an employer or to procure for employees opportunities to work for an employer and includes an agent of such a person; but shall not include an agency of the United States, or an agency of a State or political subdivision of a State, except that such term shall include the United States Employment Service and the system of State and local employment services receiving Federal assistance.

(d) The term "labor organization" means a labor organization engaged in an industry affecting commerce, and any agent of such an organization, and includes any organization of any kind, any agency, or employee representation committee, group, association, or plan so engaged in which employees participate and which exists for the purpose, in whole or in part, of dealing with employers concerning grievances, labor disputes, wages, rates of pay, hours, or other terms or conditions of employment, and any conference, general committee, joint or system board, or joint council so engaged which is subordinate to a national or international labor organization.

(e) A labor organization shall be deemed to be engaged in an industry affecting commerce if the number of its members (or, where it is a labor organization composed of other labor organizations or their representatives, if the aggregate number of the members of such other labor organization) is (A) one hundred or more during the first year after the effective date prescribed in subsection (a) of section 719, (B) fifty or more during the second year after such date, or (C) twenty-five or more thereafter, and such labor organization—

(1) is the certified representative of employees under the provisions of the National Labor Relations Act, as amended, or the Railway Labor Act, as amended;

(2) although not certified, is a national or international labor organization or a local labor organization recognized or acting as the representative of employees of an employer or employers engaged in an industry affecting commerce; or

(3) has chartered a local labor organization or subsidiary body which is representing or actively seeking to represent employees of employers within the meaning of paragraph (1) or (2); or

(4) has been chartered by a labor organization representing or actively seeking to represent employees within the meaning of paragraph (1) or (2)

10   CIVIL RIGHTS ACT OF 1963

as the local or subordinate body through which such employees may enjoy membership or become affiliated with such labor organization; or

(5) is a conference, general committee, joint or system board, or joint council, subordinate to a national or international labor organization, which includes a labor organization engaged in an industry affecting commerce within the meaning of any of the preceding paragraphs of this subsection.

(f) The term "employee" means an individual employed by an employer.

(g) The term "commerce" means trade, traffic, commerce, transportation, transmission, or communication among the several States; or between a State and any place outside thereof; or within the District of Columbia, or a possession of the United States; or between points in the same State but through a point outside thereof.

(h) The term "industry affecting commerce" means any activity, business, or industry in commerce or in which a labor dispute would hinder or obstruct commerce or the free flow of commerce and includes any activity or industry "affecting commerce" within the meaning of the Labor-Management Reporting and Disclosure Act of 1959.

(i) The term "State" includes a State of the United States, the District of Columbia, Puerto Rico, the Virgin Islands, American Samoa, Guam, Wake Island, the Canal Zone, and Outer Continental Shelf lands defined in the Outer Continental Shelf Lands Act.

EXEMPTION

SEC. 703. This title shall not apply to an employer with respect to the employment of aliens outside any State, or to a religious corporation, association, or society.

DISCRIMINATION BECAUSE OF RACE, COLOR, RELIGION, OR NATIONAL ORIGIN

SEC. 704. (a) It shall be an unlawful employment practice for an employer—

(1) to fail or refuse to hire or to discharge any individual, or otherwise to discriminate against any individual with respect to his compensation, terms, conditions, or privileges of employment, because of such individual's race, color, religion or national origin; or

(2) to limit, segregate, or classify his employees in any way which would deprive or tend to deprive any individual of employment opportunities or otherwise adversely affect his status as an employee, because of such individual's race, color, religion, or national origin.

(b) It shall be an unlawful employment practice for an employment agency to fail or refuse to refer for employment, or otherwise to discriminate against, any individual because of his race, color, religion, or national origin, or to classify or refer for employment any individual on the basis of his race, color, religion, or national origin.

(c) It shall be an unlawful employment practice for a labor organization—

(1) to exclude or to expel from its membership, or otherwise to discriminate against, any individual because of his race, color, religion, or national origin;

(2) to limit, segregate, or classify its membership in any way which would deprive or tend to deprive any individual of employment opportunities, or would limit such employment opportunities or otherwise adversely affect his status as an employee or as an applicant for employment, because of such individual's race, color, religion, or national origin; or

(3) to cause or attempt to cause an employer to discriminate against an individual in violation of this section.

(d) It shall be an unlawful employment practice for any employer, labor organization, or joint labor-management committee controlling apprenticeship or other training programs to discriminate against any individual because of his race, color, religion, or national origin in admission to, or employment in, any program established to provide apprenticeship or other training.

(e) Notwithstanding any other provision of this title, it shall not be an unlawful employment practice for an employer to hire and employ employees of a particular religion or national origin in those certain instances where religion or national origin is a bona fide occupational qualification reasonably necessary to the normal operation of that particular business or enterprise.

OTHER UNLAWFUL EMPLOYMENT PRACTICES

SEC. 705. (a) It shall be an unlawful employment practice for an employer to discriminate against any of his employees or applicants for employment, for an employment agency to discriminate against any individual, or for a labor organization to discriminate against any member thereof or applicant for membership, because he has opposed any practice made an unlawful employment practice by this title, or because he has made a charge, testified, assisted, or participated in any manner in an investigation, proceeding, or hearing under this title.

(b) It shall be an unlawful employment practice for an employer, labor organization, or employment agency to print or publish or cause to be printed or published any notice or advertisement relating to employment by such an employer or membership in such a labor organization, or relating to any classification or referral for employment by such an employment agency, indicating any preference, limitation, specification, or discrimination, based on race, color, religion, or national origin, except that such a notice or advertisement may indicate a preference, limitation, specification, or discrimination based on religion when religion is a bona fide occupational qualification for employment.

EQUAL EMPLOYMENT OPPORTUNITY COMMISSION

SEC. 706. (a) There is hereby created a Commission to be known as the Equal Employment Opportunity Commission, which shall be composed of five members, not more than three of whom shall be members of the same political party, who shall be appointed by the President by and with the advice and consent of the Senate. One of the original members shall be appointed for a term of one year, one for a term of two years, one for a term of three years, one for a term of four years, and one for a term of five years, beginning from the date of enactment of this title, but their successors shall be appointed for terms of five years each, except that any individual chosen to fill a vacancy shall be appointed only for the unexpired term of the member whom he shall succeed. The President shall designate one member to serve as Chairman of the Commission, and one member to serve as Vice Chairman. The Chairman shall be responsible on behalf of the Commission for the administrative operations of the Commission, and shall appoint, in accordance with the civil service laws, such officers, agents, attorneys, and employees as it deems necessary to assist it in the performance of its functions and to fix their compensation in accordance with the Classification Act of 1949, as amended. The Vice Chairman shall act as Chairman in the absence or disability of the Chairman or in the event of a vacancy in that office.

(b) A vacancy in the Commission shall not impair the right of the remaining members to exercise all the powers of the Commission and three members thereof shall constitute a quorum.

(c) The Commission shall have an official seal which shall be judicially noticed.

(d) The Commission shall at the close of each fiscal year report to the Congress and to the President concerning the action it has taken; the names, salaries, and duties of all individuals in its employ and the moneys it has disbursed; and shall make such further reports on the cause of and means of eliminating discrimination and such recommendations for further legislation as may appear desirable.

(e) Each member of the Commission shall receive a salary of $20,000 a year, except that the Chairman shall receive a salary of $20,500.

(f) The principal office of the Commission shall be in the District of Columbia, but it may meet or exercise any or all of its powers at any other place. The Commission may establish such regional offices as it deems necessary, and shall establish at least one such office in each of the major geographical areas of the United States, including its territories and possessions.

(g) The Commission shall have power—

(1) to cooperate with and utilize regional, State, local, and other agencies, both public and private, and individuals;

(2) to pay to witnesses whose depositions are taken or who are summoned before the Commission or any of its agents the same witness and mileage fees as are paid to witnesses in the courts of the United States;

(3) to furnish to persons subject to this title such technical assistance as they may request to further their compliance with this title or an order issued thereunder;

(4) upon the request of any employer, whose employees or some of them refuse or threaten to refuse to cooperate in effectuating the provisions of this title, to assist in such effectuation by conciliation or other remedial action;

(5) to make such technical studies as are appropriate to effectuate the purposes and policies of this title and to make the results of such studies available to interested governmental and nongovernmental agencies.

(h) Attorneys appointed under this section may, at the direction of the Commission, appear for and represent the Commission in any case in court.

12   CIVIL RIGHTS ACT OF 1963

(i) The Commission shall, in any of its educational or promotional activities, cooperate with other departments and agencies in the performance of such educational and promotional activities.

PREVENTION OF UNLAWFUL EMPLOYMENT PRACTICES

Sec. 707. (a) Whenever it is charged in writing under oath by or on behalf of a person claiming to be aggrieved, or a written charge has been filed by a member of the Commission (and such charge sets forth the facts upon which it is based) that an employer, employment agency, or labor organization has engaged in an unlawful employment practice, the Commission shall furnish such employer, employment agency, or labor organization (hereinafter referred to as the "respondent") with a copy of such charge and shall make an investigation of such charge. If two or more members of the Commission shall determine, after such investigation, that reasonable cause exists for crediting the charge, the Commission shall endeavor to eliminate any such unlawful employment practice by informal methods of conference, conciliation, and persuasion and, if appropriate, to obtain from the respondent a written agreement describing particular practices which the respondent agrees to refrain from committing. Nothing said or done during and as a part of such endeavors may be used as evidence in a subsequent proceeding.

(b) If the Commission has failed to effect the elimination of an unlawful employment practice and to obtain voluntary compliance with this title, or in advance thereof if circumstances warrant, the Commission, if it determines there is reasonable cause to believe the respondent has engaged in, or is engaging in, an unlawful employment practice, shall, within ninety days, bring a civil action to prevent the respondent from engaging in such unlawful employment practice, except that the Commission shall be relieved of any obligation to bring a civil action in any case in which the Commission has, by affirmative vote, determined that the bringing of a civil action would not serve the public interest.

(c) If the Commission has failed or declined to bring a civil action within the time required under subsection (b), the person claiming to be aggrieved may, if one member of the Commission gives permission in writing, bring a civil action to obtain relief as provided in subsection (e).

(d) Each United States district court and each United States court of a place subject to the jurisdiction of the United States shall have jurisdiction of actions brought under this title. Such actions may be brought either in the judicial district in which the unlawful employment practice is alleged to have been committed or in the judicial district in which the respondent has his principal office. No such civil action shall be based on an unlawful employment practice occurring more than six months prior to the filing of the charge with the Commission and the giving of notice thereof to the respondent, unless the person aggrieved thereby was prevented from filing such charge by reason of service in the Armed Forces, in which event a period of military service shall not be included in computing the six-month period.

(e) If the court finds that the respondent has engaged in or is engaging in an unlawful employment practice charged in the complaint the court may enjoin the respondent from engaging in such unlawful employment practice, and shall order the respondent to take such affirmative action, including reinstatement or hiring of employees, with or without back pay (payable by the employer, employment agency, or labor organization, as the case may be, responsible for the unlawful employment practice), as may be appropriate. Interim earnings or amounts earnable with reasonable diligence by the person or persons discriminated against shall operate to reduce the back pay otherwise allowable. No order of the court shall require the admission or reinstatement of an individual as a member of a union or the hiring, reinstatement, or promotion of an individual as an employee, or the payment to him of any back pay, if such individual was refused admission, suspended, or expelled or was refused employment or advancement or was suspended or discharged for cause.

(f) In any case in which the pleadings present issues of fact, the court may appoint a master and the order of reference may require the master to submit with his report a recommended order. The master shall be compensated by the United States at a rate to be fixed by the court, and shall be reimbursed by the United States for necessary expenses incurred in performing his duties under this section. Any court before which a proceeding is brought under this section shall advance such proceeding on the docket and expedite its disposition.

(g) The provisions of the Act entitled "An Act to amend the Judicial Code and to define and limit the jurisdiction of courts sitting in equity, and for other

---

CIVIL RIGHTS ACT OF 1963   **13**

purposes," approved March 23, 1932 (29 U.S.C. 101–115), shall not apply with respect to civil actions brought under this section.

(h) In any action or proceeding under this title the Commission shall be liable for costs the same as a private person.

(material omitted)

---

16   CIVIL RIGHTS ACT OF 1963

(material omitted)

Purpose and Content of the Legislation

The bill, as amended, is designed primarily to protect and provide more effective means to enforce the civil rights of persons within the jurisdiction of the United States. In furtherance of these objectives the bill: (1) provides for the appointment of a three-judge district court in voting suits and for the expeditious determination of such suits, and also provides against the discriminatory use of literacy tests in Federal elections; (2) prohibits discrimination in enumerated public establishments; (3) authorizes the Attorney General to initiate suits to desegregate public facilities, other than public schools, and to intervene in suits charging deprivation of equal protection of the laws; (4) authorizes the Attorney General to initiate suits to desegregate public schools; (5) makes the Civil Rights Commission a permanent agency; (6) prohibits discrimination in any Federal financial assistance program; (7) establishes a Federal Equal Employment Commission designed to eliminate discriminatory employment practices by business, labor unions, or employment agencies; (8) provides for the compilation of registration and voting statistics by race, color, and national origin; (9) makes a remand of a civil rights case from a Federal court back to a State court reviewable on appeal.

History of the Legislation

Early in the 88th Congress a substantial number of broad civil rights bills were introduced by members of both political parties.

On February 28, 1963, the President of the United States transmitted to the Congress a message of recommendations pertaining to civil rights (H. Doc. 75, 88th Cong., 1st sess.). Subsequently, on June 19, 1963, the President of the United States transmitted to the Congress a second message containing recommendations pertaining to civil rights (H. Doc. 124, 88th Cong., 1st sess.).

A judiciary subcommittee conducted hearings on 172 bills which had been referred to it. These proposals related to almost every aspect and facet of civil rights including such topics as voting; public accommodations; school desegregation; prohibition of discrimination in Federal financial assistance programs; equal protection of laws; antilynching; fair employment practices; the Civil Rights Commission; establishment of a Community Relations Service; voting and registration statistics according to race, color, and national origin; and authorization for the Attorney General to institute civil actions to protect and enforce civil rights.

Hearings were held on May 8, 9, 15, 16, 23, 24, 28; June 13, 26, 27; July 10, 11, 12, 17, 18, 19, 24, 25, 26, 31; and August 1, 2, 1963 (civil rights hearings before Subcommittee No. 5 of the Committee on the Judiciary, House of Representatives, 88th Cong., 1st sess., serial No. 4).

During the course of these hearings, the testimony related to all the subjects of the legislative proposals. The witnesses included the congressional authors of the proposals; other Members of both Houses of Congress; the Attorney General; the Secretaries of Labor and of Health, Education, and Welfare; representatives of the Civil Rights Commission; and of the President's Committee on Equal Employment Opportunity, State and local officials, private citizens, as well as representatives of various organizations specifically concerned with this legislation. The subcommittee afforded to all who were interested a reasonable opportunity to present their views on the proposals. Those who did not appear personally were given an opportunity to submit any relevant matter for the record.

Upon conclusion of the hearings, the subcommittee met in executive session a total of 17 days to consider the legislation. Thereafter the subcommittee struck out of H.R. 7152, as amended, all after the enacting clause and inserted in lieu thereof an amendment in the nature of a substitute. The amended version was recommended to the full Judiciary Committee.

The substitute version of the legislation before the full Judiciary Committee contained 11 titles. Briefly, these were:

(I) Voting rights;

(II) Injunctive relief against discrimination in public accommodations;

(III) Authorization to the Attorney General to institute civil proceedings to protect against the deprivation of rights;

(IV) Desegregation of public education and other public facilities;

(V) Establishment of a Community Relations Service;

(VI) Permanent extension of the Civil Rights Commission;

(VII) Nondiscrimination in federally assisted programs;

(VIII) Creation of a Federal Equal Employment Opportunity Commission;

(IX) Provision for the compilation of registration and voting statistics according to race, color, and national origin;

(X) Provision for review of an order remanding a civil rights case from a Federal court back to a State court; and

(XI) A general separability provision and a general appropriations authorization.

The full Judiciary Committee in its deliberation and consideration of the bill, H.R. 7152, adopted an amendment in the nature of a substitute. This substitute retained amended titles on voting rights; public accommodations; authorization to the Attorney General to intervene in or initiate certain civil rights suits; desegregation of public education; permanent extension of the Civil Rights Commission; nondiscrimination in federally assisted programs; creation of a Federal Equal Employment Opportunity Commission; compilation of registration and voting statistics according to race, color, and national origin; a separability provision; and general appropriation authorization. The substitute deleted the title establishing a Community

18 CIVIL RIGHTS ACT OF 1963

Relations Service and retained intact the title providing for review of an order remanding a civil rights case from a Federal court back to a State court.

GENERAL STATEMENT

In various regions of the country there is discrimination against some minority groups. Most glaring, however, is the discrimination against Negroes which exists throughout our Nation. Today, more than 100 years after their formal emancipation, Negroes, who make up over 10 percent of our population, are by virtue of one or another type of discrimination not accorded the rights, privileges, and opportunities which are considered to be, and must be, the birthright of all citizens.

Considerable progress has been made in eliminating discrimination in many areas because of local initiative either in the form of State laws and local ordinances or as the result of voluntary action. Nevertheless, in the last decade it has become increasingly clear that progress has been too slow and that national legislation is required to meet a national need which becomes ever more obvious. That need is evidenced, on the one hand, by a growing impatience by the victims of discrimination with its continuance and, on the other hand, by a growing recognition on the part of all of our people of the incompatibility of such discrimination with our ideals and the principles to which this country is dedicated. A number of provisions of the Constitution of the United States clearly supply the means "to secure these rights," and H.R. 7152, as amended, resting upon this authority, is designed as a step toward eradicating significant areas of discrimination on a nationwide basis. It is general in application and national in scope.

No bill can or should lay claim to eliminating all of the causes and consequences of racial and other types of discrimination against minorities. There is reason to believe, however, that national leadership provided by the enactment of Federal legislation dealing with the most troublesome problems will create an atmosphere conducive to voluntary or local resolution of other forms of discrimination.

It is, however, possible and necessary for the Congress to enact legislation which prohibits and provides the means of terminating the most serious types of discrimination. This H.R. 7152, as amended, would achieve in a number of related areas. It would reduce discriminatory obstacles to the exercise of the right to vote and provide means of expediting the vindication of that right. It would make it possible to remove the daily affront and humiliation involved in discriminatory denials of access to facilities ostensibly open to the general public. It would guarantee that there will be no discrimination among recipients of Federal financial assistance. It would prohibit discrimination in employment, and provide means to expedite termination of discrimination in public education. It would open additional avenues to deal with redress of denials of equal protection of the laws on account of race, color, religion, or national origin by State or local authorities.

H.R. 7152, as amended, is a constitutional and desirable means of dealing with the injustices and humiliations of racial and other discrimination. It is a reasonable and responsible bill whose provisions are designed effectively to meet an urgent and most serious national problem.

(material omitted)

(material omitted)

TITLE VII—EQUAL EMPLOYMENT OPPORTUNITY BACKGROUND AND PURPOSE

General

The purpose of this title is to eliminate, through the utilization of formal and informal remedial procedures, discrimination in employment based on race, color, religion, or national origin. The title authorizes the establishment of a Federal Equal Employment Opportunity Commission and delegates to it the primary responsibility for preventing and eliminating unlawful employment practices as defined in the title.

Section 701(a) sets forth a congressional declaration that all persons within the jurisdiction of the United States have a right to the opportunity for employment without discrimination on account of race, color, religion, or national origin. It is also declared to be the national policy to protect the right of persons to be free from such discrimination.

Section 701(b) states that the title is necessary to remove obstructions to the free flow of interstate and foreign commerce and to insure the complete and full enjoyment by all persons of the rights, privileges, and immunities secured and protected by the Constitution.

Section 702 contains definitions of a number of the terms used in the title.

"Employer" is defined to mean a person engaged in an industry affecting commerce who has 25 or more employees, except that during the first year after the date the enforcement provisions of the title become operative employers having fewer than 100 employees will not be covered, and during the second year after such date, employers with fewer than 50 will not be covered. The definition excludes from the term "employer" all Federal, State, and local government agencies, and bona fide membership clubs (other than labor organizations) which are tax exempt under the Internal Revenue Code (sec. 702(b)).

"Employment agency" is defined to mean any person who regularly undertakes to procure employees for an employer or to procure, for employees, opportunities to work. The U.S. Employment Service and the system of State and local employment services receiving Federal assistance are specifically included. Other governmental agencies are not included (sec. 702(c)).

"Labor organization" is defined in substantially the same way that the term is defined in the Labor-Management Reporting and Disclosure Act of 1959, except that State and local central bodies will be treated as are other labor organizations (sec. 702(d)).

Labor organizations will be covered only if they are engaged in an industry affecting commerce within the meaning of the title, and subsection (e) of section 702 describes the labor organizations which are so engaged. This provision is the same as the comparable provision in the Labor-Management Reporting and Disclosure Act of

1959, except that it excludes any labor organization having fewer than 25 members. Also, during the first year after the date on which the enforcement provisions of the title become operative, a labor organization having fewer than 100 members will be excluded from coverage, and during the second year after such date, those having fewer than 50 members will be so excluded (sec. 702(e)).

The terms "person," "employee," "commerce," "industry affecting commerce," and "State" are defined for the purposes of the title in the manner common for Federal statutes (secs. 702 (a), (f), (g), (h), and (i)).

Section 703 provides that the requirements of the title will not apply with respect to the employment of aliens outside a State, or to religious corporations, associations, or societies.

Section 704(a) describes a number of activities which, if engaged in by employers, will constitute unlawful employment practices. It will be an unlawful employment practice for an employer to fail or refuse to hire or to discharge any individual, or otherwise discriminate against any individual with respect to compensation, terms, conditions, or privileges of employment, because of race, color, religion, or national origin. It will also be an unlawful employment practice for an employer to limit, segregate, or classify his employees in any way which would deprive or tend to deprive any person of employment opportunities or otherwise adversely affect his status as an employee because of his race, color, religion, or national origin.

Section 704(b) provides that it will be an unlawful employment practice for an employment agency to fail or refuse to refer an individual for employment or otherwise to discriminate against him because of race, color, religion, or national origin, or for such an agency to classify or refer any person for employment on the basis of race, color, religion, or national origin.

Section 704(c) describes a number of unlawful employment practices of labor organizations. Under this subsection it will be an unlawful employment practice for a labor organization to exclude or expel or otherwise discriminate against any person from membership because of race, color, religion, or national origin. It will be an unlawful employment practice for a labor organization to limit, segregate, or classify its membership so as to deprive or tend to deprive any person of employment opportunities or to limit such opportunities, or otherwise adversely affect his status as an employee or as a job applicant because of his race, color, religion, or national origin. It will also be an unlawful employment practice for a labor organization to cause or attempt to cause an employer to discriminate against an individual in violation of this section.

Section 704(d) makes it an unlawful employment practice for persons controlling apprenticeship or other training programs to discriminate because of race, color, religion, or national origin in admission to, or employment in, such a program.

Section 704(e) provides for a very limited exception to the provisions of the title. Notwithstanding any other provisions, it shall not be an unlawful employment practice for an employer to employ persons of a particular religion or national origin in those rare situations where religion or national origin is a bona fide occupational qualification.

Section 705(a) makes it an unlawful employment practice for an employer to discriminate against any of his employees or applicants for employment, for an employment agency to discriminate against any individual, or for a labor organization to discriminate against any member or applicant for membership, because he has made a charge, testified, assisted, or participated in any manner in the enforcement of the title.

Section 705(b) makes it an unlawful employment practice for an employer, labor organization, or employment agency to be responsible for the publishing of any notice or advertisement indicating a preference, limitation, specification, or discrimination based on race, color, religion, or national origin, except where such preference, limitation, specification, or discrimination is based on religion when religion is a bona fide qualification for employment. The prohibitions of this section do not require newspapers and other publications to exercise any control or supervision over, or to do any screening of, the advertisements and notices published by them.

Section 706 creates an Equal Employment Opportunity Commission of five members appointed by the President subject to Senate confirmation. The Commission will be bipartisan in character. Members of the Commission will receive the usual salaries of members of independent regulatory agencies. The members of the Commission will have staggered terms of 5 years each, and will have the usual powers and duties with respect to employment of personnel, quorum, right to act while vacancies exist, use of official seal, reports to Congress and the President.

The Commission will have power to cooperate with and utilize regional, State, and other agencies, both public and private, and individuals. It will also be authorized to furnish technical assistance to persons subject to this title who request it to further their compliance therewith or with an order issued thereunder. If the employees of an employer refuse or threaten to refuse to cooperate in effectuating the provisions of the title, the employer may request assistance from the Commission in effectuating such provisions by conciliation or other remedial action. The Commission may make such technical studies as may be appropriate to effectuate the purposes of the title and may make the results of its studies available to interested agencies. It is also empowered to pay witness fees in the usual amounts (sec. 706(g)).

Attorneys appointed under this section will be permitted, at the direction of the Commission, to appear for and represent the Commission in any case in court (sec. 706(h)). The Commission is directed to cooperate with other departments and agencies in the performance of its educational and promotional activities (sec. 706(i)).

Section 707 contains the provisions relating to enforcement of the title. The first stage in the enforcement process is the filing of a charge in writing under oath by or on behalf of a person claiming to be aggrieved or the filing of a written charge by a member of the Commission, alleging that an employer, employment agency, or labor organization has engaged in an unlawful employment practice. When the Commission receives such a charge, it will furnish the employer, employment agency, or labor organization against whom the charge is made a copy of the charge and shall make an investigation of that charge. If two or more members of the Commission believe after such investigation that reasonable cause exists for crediting the charge, the Commission must endeavor to eliminate any such unlawful employment practice by informal methods of conference, conciliation, and persuasion and, if appropriate, to obtain from the charged party a written agreement describing particular practices which he agrees to refrain from committing. Nothing said or done during and as a part of these endeavors may be used as evidence in a subsequent proceeding (sec. 707(a)).

Section 707(b) provides that if, through these informal methods, the Commission has failed to effect the elimination of an unlawful employment practice (or in advance thereof if circumstances warrant), it shall, if it determines there is reasonable cause to believe that the charged party has engaged in or is engaging in an unlawful employment practice, bring a civil action within 90 days to prevent the charged party from engaging in such unlawful employment practice, except that the Commission is to be relieved of any obligation to bring a civil action in any case in which it has by affirmative vote determined that the bringing of such action would not serve the public interest.

Section 707(c) provides that if the Commission has failed or declined to bring a civil action within the time required, the person claiming to be aggrieved may, if one member of the Commission gives his permission in writing, bring a civil action himself to obtain relief.

Section 707(d) provides that the district courts of the United States (including each U.S. court of places subject to the jurisiction of the United States) are given jurisdiction of actions brought under this title. These actions will be brought either in the judicial district where the unlawful employment practice is alleged to have been committed or in the judicial district in which the charged party has his principal office. No civil action may be based on an unlawful employment practice occurring more than 6 months prior to the filing of a charge with the Commission, except in cases in which the party aggrieved was prevented from filing the charge within the prescribed time by reason of service in the Armed Forces.

Section 707(e) provides that if the court finds that the charged party has engaged or is engaging in an unlawful employment practice as charged in the complaint, it may enjoin him from engaging in such practice and shall order him to take such affirmative action as may be appropriate. This affirmative action may include the reinstatement or the hiring of employees with or without back pay (payable by the employer, employment agency, or labor organization, as the case may be, responsible for the unlawful employment practice). In a case in which the payment of back pay is ordered interim earnings or amounts earnable with reasonable diligence by the person or persons discriminated against will reduce the back pay otherwise allowable. No order of the court may require the admission or reinstatement of an individual as a member of the union or the hiring, reinstatement, or promotion of an individual as an employee or payment of any back pay if the individual was refused admission, suspended, or separated, or was refused employment or advancement, or was suspended or discharged for cause.

Section 707(f) permits the court to appoint masters to hear the evidence in these cases. The court may require the master to submit a recommended order together with his findings of fact. The court must also expedite these cases.

Section 707(g) provides that the provisions of the Norris-LaGuardia Act are waived in the case of these civil actions.

Section 707(h) makes the Commission liable for costs in any action brought under the title.

(material omitted)

ADDITIONAL VIEWS OF HON. ARCH A. MOORE, JR.

The right to be free from all forms of racial intolerance is so fundamentally the privilege of each and every citizen of the United States that it cannot be made the plaything of politics. The shame of our times, however, is that the subject of civil rights has from the early days of the 88th Congress been made the butt of political opportunism. It was only after public pressure began to mount, however, did the administration stir itself to fashioning a civil rights package. This game of lonemanship by the administration was further spotlighted when the subcommittee of the House Judiciary Committee reported a bill which the committee chairman was forced to label the bill "drastic" irrespective of the fact that it was his bill. The fog of indecision and the quagmire of inaction became so great when the Judiciary Committee began to debate the subcommittee's bill, that the prospects for civil rights legislation faded to all but the vanishing point. Amendments were offered and withdrawn. Signals were called and then missed. Coalitions formed and then dissolved. Pleas of assistance were made and rejected. To rescue this hopeless mess, then, a motion was made to report the subcommittee bill to the House in an effort to salvage civil rights and to permit the Congress to work its will on this most needed subject. But, although majority support existed for this course of action, a "compromise" bill was sprung upon the committee from out of the night. Where it came from or who were its benefactors remains to this day a deep, dark secret. The bill reported was conceived in segregation, born in intolerance, and nurtured in discrimination.

As I have stated earlier, civil rights is the foremost issue of our times. But, to attempt to enact civil rights legislation in the heavyhanded and politically motivated manner that is presently being attempted is a disservice to the democratic process and a disservice to all citizens who want and expect effective legislation in this Congress.

ARCH A. MOORE, JR.,
Member of Congress.

MINORITY REPORT UPON PROPOSED CIVIL RIGHTS ACT OF 1963, COMMITTEE ON JUDICIARY SUBSTITUTE FOR H.R. 7152

HISTORY OF THE LEGISLATION

This legislation is being reported to the House without the benefit of any consideration, debate, or study of the bill by any subcommittee or committee of the House and without any member of any committee or subcommittee being granted an opportunity to offer amendments to the bill. This legislation is the most radical proposal in the field of civil rights ever recommended by any committee of the House or Senate. It was drawn in secret meetings held between certain members of this committee, the Attorney General and members of his

62

staff and certain select persons, to the exclusion of other committee members.

Sometime prior to October 22, 1963, Subcommittee No. 5 of the Judiciary Committee of the House of Representatives had prepared a substitute bill for H.R. 7152. Title I of the substitute was read and discussed by the full Judiciary Committee prior to October 22, and at a meeting held on that date a motion was made by the gentleman from West Virginia to report the subcommittee substitute to the House of Representatives. Before final action could be had on this motion, a point of order was made that the House of Representatives was then in session. The chairman of the committee called a meeting for the following morning, the 23d, and then on the 23d, within an hour of the time of the meeting it was postponed to the 24th, and then on the 24th, a short while before the meeting was scheduled, it was postponed again, and later postponed to Tuesday, October 29. These various postponements were made by the chairman without any prior consultation with any of the signers of this report.

On October 29, the full committee met at 10:30 a.m. The motion of the gentleman from West Virginia was promptly voted down, after which Chairman Celler offered a 56-page mimeographed substitute which he described as an amendment and moved that the committee approve the bill. The chairman announced that he would recognize a member of the committee to move the previous question and in it were ordered that no amendments could be offered to his proposal; no debate had; and no questions asked or answered.

The bill was, upon order of the chairman, read hastily by the clerk, without pause or opportunity for amendment. Several members of the committee repeatedly requested to be permitted to ask questions, have an explanation of the bill, discuss it, consider its provisions, and offer amendments. The Chair refused to grant such requests or to recognize these members of the committee for any purpose. After the reading of the bill in the fashion hereinabove described, the chairman announced that he would allow himself 1 minute to discuss the bill, after which he would recognize for 1 minute the ranking minority member, the gentleman from Ohio. This was an ostensible attempt to comply, technically, with the rules of the House but did not amount to debate, as debate is generally understood. Neither of these gentlemen discussed the bill for more than 1 minute; both of them refused to yield to any other member of the committee; and neither of them debated the bill nor discussed it in any fashion other than to say that they favored it. They made no effort in the 2 minutes consumed by both together to even so much as explain the provisions of the bill. In short, there was no actual debate or even any opportunity for debate.

Immediately upon the conclusion of the remarks from the gentleman from Ohio, the ranking minority member, the chairman recognized a member of the committee friendly to the chairman's proposal who moved for the previous question. The clerk of the committee immediately called the roll upon the motion to approve the bill and before the tally could be completed or the vote announced, the House was in session. The committee met later in the afternoon and, the tally of vote upon the motion to approve the bill having been completed and announced at the morning meeting after the House session had commenced, a motion was made and adopted that H.R. 7152 be re-

64   CIVIL RIGHTS ACT OF 1963

ported to the House.   The chairman treated the vote taken upon the bill at the morning session as being valid.

The signers of this minority report in reciting these facts relating to the procedures employed in the full committee do not do so in any captious spirit, but relate these facts to inform the Congress of the tactics employed to bring this bill before the House.

GENERAL NATURE OF THE LEGISLATION

As stated above, the full-committee substitute for H.R. 7152 was railroaded through the Committee on the Judiciary without an opportunity by members of that committee to discuss, debate or amend the 56-page mimeographed document.   While this document was being forced through the committee wholly without study, it was hailed as "moderate" legislation and as a "compromise" when in truth and in fact it was no less extreme and vicious than the subcommittee proposal.   In coordination with these statements, the reported bill was denounced, publicly, by civil rights political pressure groups for the apparent purpose of creating the impression the substitute measure was, in fact, a "watered down" version of the unacceptable subcommittee proposal.

Now that we, as members of the committee, have had some opportunity to compare the reported bill with the subcommittee proposal, we find that the bill, as reported, is no compromise at all.   It actually broadens and strengthens many powers conferred upon the Attorney General in the subcommittee proposal and grants new sweeping and unlimited authority to the President, while retaining all of the most viscious and harsh provisions of the subcommittee proposal.

Throughout this entire report the construction we have placed upon the provisions of the reported bill are based upon that which we believe will be advanced by the administration, evidenced by numerous Executive orders, other administrative actions and statements of officials in the executive branch of the Federal Government.   We do not mean to say that such construction is necessarily correct or that the powers granted are constitutional.   Broad, obscure, and undefined wording is repeatedly used in the bill.

The reported bill is not a "moderate" bill and it has not been "watered down."   It constitutes the greatest grasp for executive power conceived in the 20th century.

We hereinafter analyze in detail each title of the reported bill and compare it to the subcommittee proposal.

(material omitted)

[page 65:]

In brief, the proposed bill now reported to the House by the committee does the following:

1. Amends every Federal statute setting up or appropriating money for any program or activity involving Federal financing by a mandatory requirement that every Federal department and agency "shall take action to effectuate" the purposes of the act (secs. 601-602). Persons with less than 25 employees are not excepted from this title of the bill.   This makes available to the President and his chief law enforcement officer, the Attorney General, enormous and unlimited funds for sociological manipulation in the field of civil rights.

25-610—63——5

66   CIVIL RIGHTS ACT OF 1963

2. The various definitions contained in the bill, particularly titles II and VII, would extend "interstate commerce" so as to encompass substantially all intrastate commerce and thus bring under Federal control all phases of commerce, whether interstate or intrastate. Actions of any persons under color of local custom or usage, or which are encouraged, fostered, or required by any State or political subdivision thereof are classified as "State action" and subject to Federal control. This authority, if granted, would extend Federal control into the business and the home of almost every individual in the United States (secs. 201 and 202).

3. The reported bill creates an Equal Employment Opportunity Commission to police and control the hiring, discharge, and terms of compensation, conditions and privileges of employment of all persons employed by any business or industry "affecting commerce" and which has 25 or more employees (title VII). The administration's original bill was much more limited, in that it applied only to employers involved in programs and activities financially assisted by the Federal Government. The Commission is to be supported by $2,500,000 for the first year and $10 million per year thereafter. The power granted by this title, if invoked, would destroy seniority in unions, corporate employment and apparently in civil service. Precedents destroying seniority have already been set in limited fields by Executive orders and administrative regulations. The exception of employers who have less than 25 employees (the exception is fixed at 100 employees for the first year and 50 employees for the second year) does not apply to those participating in any program or activity receiving Federal financial assistance by way of grant, contract, or loan under title VI coupled with section 711(b).

(material omitted)

[page 68:]

It will be noted that the word "discrimination" is nowhere defined in the bill.

The destruction of individual liberty and freedom of choice resulting from the almost limitless extension of Federal Government control over individuals and business, rather than being in support of the Bill of Rights, is directly contrary to the spirit and intent thereof.

Judge Learned Hand, in 1958, said in his "Oliver Wendell Holmes Lectures":

> * * * the Bill of Rights is concerned only with the protection of the individual against the impact of Federal and State law.

Dean Roscoe Pound, dean emeritus of Harvard University School of Law, said in 1957 in his "The Development of Constitutional Guarantees of Liberty":

> Analytically the bills of rights are bills of liberties. They define circumstances and situations and occasions in which politically organized society will keep its hands off and permit free, spontaneous, individual activity; they guarantee that the agents and agencies of politically organized society will not do certain things and will not do certain other things otherwise than in certain ways.

In determining whether this bill should be adopted, it must be remembered that when legislation is enacted designed to benefit one segment or class of a society, the usual result is the destruction of coexisting rights of the remainder of that society. One freedom is destroyed by governmental action to enforce another freedom. The governmental restraint of one individual at the behest of another implies necessarily the restriction of the civil liberties and the destruction of civil rights of the one for the benefit of the other. This legislation, then, brings to mind the wise statement of George Washington:

> Government is not reason, it is not eloquence—it is force.
> Like fire, it is a dangerous servant and a fearful master.

CIVIL RIGHTS ACT OF 1963   69

EFFECT OF THE LEGISLATION

The depth, the revolutionary meaning of this act, is almost beyond description. It cannot be circumscribed, it cannot be said that it goes this far and no farther. The language written into the bill is not of that sort. It has open-end provisions that give it whatever depth and intensity one desires to read into it. In the language of the bill, "The President is authorized to take such action as may be appropriate to prevent * * *" (sec. 711(b)), and "Each Federal department and agency * * * shall take action to effectuate * * *" (sec. 602). This vests, of course, almost unlimited authority by the President and his appointees to do whatever they desire.

It is, in the most literal sense, revolutionary, destructive of the very essence of life as it has been lived in this country since the adoption of our Constitution. Because this is true, the undersigned members of this committee believe it wise to demonstrate, by example, the effects of this legislation on people; to demonstrate, by example, the meaning of lost liberty; to demonstrate, by example, the power in this bill to completely dominate the lives of even the least of us.

To this end, there follow nine examples of the effect of the bill upon persons covered by it. There might be offered innumerable examples, because this bill encompasses directly or indirectly nearly every American.

(material omitted)

Labor unions and members

To millions of working men and women, union membership is the most valuable asset they own. It is designed to insure job security and a rate of pay higher than they otherwise would receive. As none knows better than the union member, himself, these two benefits are dependent upon the system of seniority the unions have followed since their inception. Seniority is the base upon which unionism is founded. Without its system of seniority, a union would lose one of its greatest values to its members.

The provisions of this act grant the power to destroy union seniority. The action of the Secretary of Labor already mentioned is merely the beginning, if this legislation is adopted. With the full statutory powers granted by this bill, *the extent of actions which would be taken to destroy the seniority system is unknown and unknowable.*

To disturb this traditional practice is to destroy a vital part of unionism. Under the power granted in this bill, if a carpenters' hiring hall, say, had 20 men awaiting call, the first 10 in seniority being white carpenters, the union could be forced to pass them over in favor of carpenters beneath them in seniority, but of the stipulated race. And if the union roster did not contain the names of the carpenters of the race needed to "racially balance" the job, the union agent must, then, go into the street and recruit members of the stipulated race in sufficient number to comply with Federal orders, else his local could be held in violation of Federal law.

Neither competence nor experience is the key for employment under this bill. Race is the principal, first, criterion.

Specific penalties are provided for violation of this bill (title VII). However, in addition, the President "is authorized to take such action as may be appropriate to prevent the committing or continuing of an unlawful employment practice" in connection with title VI of the bill (sec. 711(b)). This, of course, amounts to practically unlimited authority. Unions held in violation of this bill may lose their rights

72 CIVIL RIGHTS ACT OF 1963

and benefits under such labor statutes as the National Labor Relations Act, the Railway Labor Act, the Davis-Bacon Act, the Walsh-Healey Act, and other legislation beneficial to labor. Representation rights and exclusive bargaining privileges could be canceled. Unions could be denied access to NLRB or National Mediation Board procedures.

Moreover, this bill affects unions from the other end, that of the employer, since the law applies to the employer, as well. It extends to railroads, motor carriers, airlines and steamship companies handling mail or other Government shipments, enterprises receiving loans from the Small Business Administration, construction contractors financed through FHA or GI home loan insurance, the rural electrification program and practically all others (secs. 601, 602).

Consequently, however meticulous a local union may be as pertains to *its* racial practices, if a contractor, for example, has been adjudged guilty of discrimination and must, therefore, hire 100 or 1,000 workers of a given race—in preference to all others—before his job becomes "racially balanced," it means the local which supplies his labor can send him only union members of that particular race—and the members of other races will sit until that number has been employed. If the union does not have among its membership the number required, it must recruit membership of that race to supply the contractor's needs. This is a specific instance of the Federal Government interfering in the contract rights of unions and employers.

By threat of contract cancellation and blacklisting, contractors could be forced to actively recruit employees of a specified race and upgrade them into skilled classifications, although this would displace union members in the skilled trades. Where skilled tradesmen of the specified race were not available from union sources, the agency could direct that they be recruited from nonunion sources, notwithstanding existing union shop or exclusive referral agreements.

Individuals at work

Union members are not the only working people affected by this bill. All employees of private industry and apparently those under Federal civil service will be affected. Assume that a nonunion individual is employed by a corporation which has more than 25 people on its payroll (title VII), or is employed by a smaller corporation which has an SBA, FHA, or other federally supported loan or contract (title VI, sec. 711(b)). Assume that his firm, in his job classification, historically has employed people only of his particular race, whatever that race may be. Assume that a demand is made that his firm abide by a Federal regulation requiring racial balance in his department. To comply—unless unneeded employees are to be hired—somebody has to go. Who?

Assume two women of separate races apply to that firm for the position of stenographer; further assume that the employer, for some indefinable reason, prefers one above the other, whether because of personality, superior alertness, intelligence, work history, or general neatness. Assume the employer has learned good things about the character of one and derogatory things about the character of the other which are not subject to proof. If his firm is not "racially balanced," under such regulation he has no choice, he must employ the person of that race which, by ratio, is next up, even though he is

> **CIVIL RIGHTS ACT OF 1963**   **73**
>
> certain in his own mind that the woman he is not allowed to employ
> would be a superior employee.
>   That such mandatory provisions of law approach the ludicrous
> should be apparent. That this is, in fact, a not too subtle system of
> racism-in-reverse cannot be successfully denied.

f. Additional Questions About the Early Legislative History of the Civil Rights Act

1. The House Judiciary Committee report describes the version of Title VII that emerged from committee deliberations in November 1963. In what ways is this bill stronger (more protective) than either the House Republicans' bill or the Administration bill, reproduced at pp. 2-9 above?

2. Why would House Democrats draft a bill that goes beyond what their President has requested?

g. Note: What Happens After the Committee Report

After the Judiciary Committee reported the civil rights bill to the House, the bill was assigned to one of the House Calendars. But if the sponsors wanted the House to deliberate and vote on the bill, it needed to be expedited on the Calendar—and that expedition required a Rule, at the recommendation of the Rules Committee.

The House Rules Committee was chaired by Representative Howard Smith (D-VA), an opponent of civil rights legislation. Chairman Smith put off hearings on the proposed bill for months, until the Republicans and the liberal Democrats on the Committee threatened a mutiny. At the hearings, Representative Celler, the Chairman of the Judiciary Committee, explained the bill and changes that his Committee had made to accommodate changes the Senate had made to a previous civil rights bill.

The Rules Committee recommended an expediting Rule, which was taken up by the House of Representatives on January 31, 1964. Because Chairman Smith was opposed to the Rule, Representative Madden (D-IN), the senior Democrat in favor of the Rule, spoke for the Committee to present the Rule. The debate that followed was largely a debate about the merits of the proposed Civil Rights Act of 1964.

II. Debate in the House

a. The Bill is Considered by The Committee of the Whole (January 31, 1964)

| 1964 | CONGRESSIONAL RECORD — HOUSE | 1511 |

(material omitted)

CIVIL RIGHTS ACT OF 1963

Mr. MADDEN. Mr. Speaker, by direction of the Committee on Rules, I call up House Resolution 616 and ask for its immediate consideration.

The Clerk read the resolution, as follows:

Resolved, That upon the adoption of this resolution it shall be in order to move that the House resolve itself into the Committee of the Whole House on the State of the Union for the consideration of the bill (H.R. 7152) to enforce the constitutional right to vote, to confer jurisdiction upon the district courts of the United States to provide injunctive relief against discrimination in public accommodations, to authorize the Attorney General to institute suits to protect constitutional rights in education, to establish a Community Relations Service, to extend for four years the Commission on Civil Rights, to prevent discrimination in federally assisted programs, to establish a Commission on Equal Employment Opportunity, and for other purposes, and all points of order against said bill are hereby waived. After general debate, which shall be confined to the bill, and shall continue not to exceed ten hours, to be equally divided and controlled by the chairman and ranking minority member of the Committee on the Judiciary, the bill shall be read for amendment under the five-minute rule. It shall be in order to consider without the intervention of any points of order the substitute amendment recommended by the Committee on the Judiciary now printed in the bill, and such substitute for the purpose of amendment shall be considered under the five-minute rule as an original bill, and shall be read by titles instead of by sections. It shall also be in order to consider, without the intervention of any point of order, the text of the bill H.R. 980, 88th Congress, as an amendment to the said committee substitute amendment. At the conclusion of such consideration the Committee shall rise and report the bill to the House with such amendments as may have been adopted, and any Member may demand a separate vote in the House on any of the amendments adopted in the Committee of the Whole to the bill or committee substitute. The previous question shall be considered as ordered on the bill and amendments thereto to final passage without intervening motion except one motion to recommit, with or without instructions.

The SPEAKER. The gentleman from Indiana [Mr. MADDEN] is recognized for 1 hour.

Mr. MADDEN. Mr. Speaker, this Resolution No. 616 calls up for consideration H.R. 7152, the first really comprehensive civil rights legislation in our history.

This bill is composed of eight titles dealing with the major problems concerning constitutional rights of American citizens. The Judiciary Committee of the House has held hearings and has deliberated weeks and months on provisions set out in these major titles dealing with Title I: Voting; Title II: Public Accommodations; Title III: Public Facilities and Authority of the Attorney General To Intervene in Equal Protection Cases; Title IV: Education; Title V: Civil Rights Commission; Title VI: Nondiscrimination in Federally Assisted Programs; Title VII: Equal Employment Opportunities; and Title VIII: Registration and Voting Restrictions.

Yesterday, the Rules Committee completed hearings which started on January 9. This resolution calls for an open rule with 10 hours debate and waiving all points of orders. Amendments to be offered to this legislation will be to each separate title.

The Rules Committee heard the testimony of 40 Members of Congress, consisting of proponents and opponents. No doubt, we will hear during this debate numerous charges that this legislation is saturated with unconstitutional provisions, and if enacted, will build up a monumental bureaucracy. I do hope all Members will remain on the floor during these extended discussions and learn firsthand complete facts regarding the contents of this legislation so they can vote with intelligence and knowledge on various amendments, which, I presume, will be offered. I have great faith in the good judgment of the House Members that if any provisions of this bill are unconstitutional, they will be deleted or amended.

JUDICIARY COMMITTEE

The Judiciary Committee which reported this civil rights legislation is composed of 35 experienced and high-grade lawyers. These members are schooled in parliamentary and legislative procedure. I cannot imagine a majority of the Judiciary Committee, trained in the law, voting for legislation so filled with unconstitutional boobytraps as charged by some of the bill's opponents. I think the members of the Judiciary Committee should be commended for the outstanding work and sacrifice they have made in devoting weeks and months to this complicated legislation. This debate gives a great opportunity for the Members of the House to learn from these experienced lawyers regarding the contents of this bill as to constitutionality and effectiveness in extending protection to the constitutional rights of all our people.

Congressmen CELLER, McCULLOCH, and ROGERS, Minority Leader HALLECK, Congressman BROWN, and other leaders on both sides, have worked in a highly unpartisan manner to succeed in bringing this legislation on the floor of the House. In my long service in Congress, this is the first major legislation on a controversial issue in my memory, wherein the provisions set out therein are almost identical with the platforms of the two major parties in the immediately preceding presidential election. This morning, I hold here in my hand copies of the 1960 platforms adopted at the Republican and Democratic National Conventions, and in a few minutes, I want to read some of the excerpts from both the Republican and Democratic planks on civil rights—the issues which both major parties used in their presidential and congressional campaigns of 1960.

For that reason, both major political parties are to be commended for supporting a major bill of this importance in carrying out their national party platforms.

VOTING

This legislation set up protections for all citizens to avail themselves of their basic right to vote in a free American election. This gives the disenfranchised citizens preferential and immediate remedies in courts so they can exercise their franchise, the greatest basic privilege possessed by all Americans.

SCHOOL DESEGREGATION

The bill provides constitutional remedies and financial assistance to aid school districts in the process of desegregation in compliance with the Constitution.

PUBLIC ACCOMMODATIONS

This legislation gives the Attorney General and the aggrieved citizen authority to institute a civil action in Federal court against any person who denies an individual, because of race, color, religion, or national origin, access to public transportation, interstate travel, public eating houses, hotels, admission to places of exhibition and public entertainment, and other establishments supported by public taxation. These provisions are limited in minor restrictions and exemptions considering the magnitude of the public operation as to size and scope of the business.

CIVIL RIGHTS COMMISSION

The Civil Rights Commission is to be made permanent and is authorized to serve as a national clearinghouse for information in respect to equal protection of the laws.

NONDISCRIMINATION IN FEDERALLY ASSISTED PROGRAMS

Each Federal department or agency, empowered to extend financial assistance by way of grant, contract, or loan, is authorized to terminate or withhold financial assistance to any recipient who, on account of race, color, or national origin, excludes citizens from participation or benefits thereof.

EQUAL EMPLOYMENT OPPORTUNITY

This legislation provides that there shall be no discriminatory practice by employers having 25 or more employees in the hiring, promotion, compensation, or other employment practices of an employee or an individual seeking employment.

REGISTRATION AND VOTING STATISTICS

Under this title, the Secretary of Commerce, through the Bureau of the Census, is to conduct a survey and make a compilation of voting statistics for the purpose of counting persons of voting age by race, color, and national origin, and for the determination of the extent to which such persons are registered to vote and individuals voting in any Federal election since January 1, 1960. This compilation shall be made in the geographical areas recommended by the Civil Rights Commission.

Some 30 States and numerous cities covering some two-thirds of this Nation's population have already enacted laws against discrimination in places of public accommodations—many in response to the recommendation of President Truman's Committee on Civil Rights in 1947. The failure of more States to take effective action makes it clear that this Federal legislation is necessary. The voluntary approach has been tried but has been found unable to eliminate widespread discrimination. Clearly, the Federal Government has both the power and the obligation to eliminate these discriminatory practices. Congress has been specifically empowered under the 14th amendment to enact legislation to make it a certainty that no State laws will sanction or give unequal protection or treatment to any of its citizens.

CONSTITUTIONALITY

The enactment of this legislation is clearly consistent with the Constitution and our concepts of both human rights and property rights. The courts have consistently rejected the theory that it is unconstitutional to interfere with the rights of citizens as they pertain to restrictions on voting laws, minimum wages, collective bargaining, air pollution, smoke control, pure food laws, and countless other measures designed to make certain that the use of private property must be utilized in conformity with the public interest.

Next week, a great number of our Members have set up a program to extoll President Abraham Lincoln on the anniversary of his birth. History reveals that in issuing his Emancipation Proclamation 100 years ago, he was accused by many of violating the property rights of slave owners. It is farfetched to believe that a man engaged in soliciting business from the American public for profit has an inherent right to exclude part of that public on the grounds of his race or color. Both human rights and property rights are basic foundations of our society, and the combination of both is highly essential to our economy.

CITIZENS IN WAR AND PEACE—WORLD WARS I AND II

Our Nation has fought to preserve liberty and freedom in a number of wars. The heroes who fought and died in World Wars I and II, as well as in the Korean war, saw no signs erected marked "White" or "Colored" in the trenches, foxholes, battleships, or in Flanders Field.

It is a deplorable situation that 100 years after the emancipation, it should be necessary for an American citizen to demonstrate in the streets for the opportunity to stop at a hotel or to eat at a lunch counter in the very department store where he is shopping, or to enter a motion picture house, recreation area, or other public places of accommodation on the same terms as any other customer.

The great struggle for civil liberties is a moral struggle demanding the effort of every American citizen who believes in democracy and freedom for themselves. They also should realize that freedom for minorities is indivisible with freedom for the majority and that unless everyone enjoys freedom, no one's freedom is secure. That is probably why all the major churches in the land, Protestant, Catholic, Jewish, and others, have endorsed the legislation which we are about to consider in Congress today.

CIVIL RIGHTS BILL OF 1960

In 1960, civil rights legislation was paralyzed and emasculated by a bitter and carefully calculated debate and filibuster.

It was severely weakened by amendments and its failure to provide sufficient power to enforce its provisions and to enact certain safeguards for other minority groups, and proved to be a weak watered-down bill in final form. It failed to make effective provisions for employment to improve the unemployment situation as it pertained to Negroes. In 1947 to 1951, the rate of unemployment for Negro men and women was 50 percent more than it was for whites.

This measure provides effective consideration for proper educational facilities for millions of the Negro children in America.

Both Presidents Kennedy, and Johnson, Eisenhower and Truman have urged the Congress for effective action on civil rights legislation. The time for citizenship equality for all Americans is here.

What greater event could come about in 1964 to 15 percent of our population than to realize that final victory is at hand. To be attained, not by demonstrations, sitdowns, and riots but by peaceful legislative processes under our Constitution. Both major political parties adopted strong, almost identical civil rights planks in their national platforms at their 1960 national conventions. To refresh the minds of our Members, I hereby read excerpts and pledges from the 1960 Republican and Democratic presidential election platform.

(material omitted)

(material omitted)

(material omitted)

previous inclinations, and listen to the debate both on the bill and proposed amendments. Hear both sides of the issue, and consider what is proposed, in this revolutionary manner, to be done to all of the freedom-loving people of this country.

The other would be that whatever temptation there might be to wave the flag of sectionalism would be taboo.

For while it may be that some people have in mind that this is a loaded pistol aimed at a particular section of this country, from which I have the honor to come, I point out to you and I challenge you to deny—after you have considered this bill, if it is not also a scatter-gun that reaches every section of this country from north to south and from east to west.

So let us approach this consideration—let us approach this bill with all of its ramifications, not as southerners, not as so-called northerners or westerners or easterners. But I beseech you in the name of the Supreme Being, please let us consider this bill upon its merits, upon its constitutionality and upon the effect that it is going to have upon the future generations of this country who will follow you and me.

Oh, yes, I know, I am realistic too—I know of the political implications. I have had private conversations—and, of course, I would not call names—with many of you. I know how you feel about this legislation, those of you in high and those of you in low places in this House. I know of the popular political and sectional vote appeal of this legislation. But all I am asking you to do is to consider it upon its merits—to listen to the great constitutional lawyers on this committee—yes, on both sides—and weigh and consider the matter for yourself.

You know, you and I—and some of us have been here a long time and some of us have been here a short time—you and I prize these seats in this Congress of the United States. But our stay here is but transitory.

We sit here today—tomorrow we are gone. Someone else comes in to take our place. In other words, we are like the little bird which flies into the door of our living room on a summer's day. He flits about the room for a few seconds and then flies out an open window.

I ask you, as I have asked myself on many occasions, is the cherished privilege of sitting in this body worth the price that we are often asked to pay?

Every one of us—some of us 15 times, some of us more and some of us less—have stood in this House and held our hand to high heaven and obligated ourselves, in most solemn covenant with God to uphold the Constitution of the United States. Now I say to you, this bill, if not in whole, at least in part is unconstitutional, and I challenge you again to listen to the debate and determine that for yourselves.

I do not impugn the motives of anyone. I do not intend to reflect upon anyone. All I ask is for your honest and sincere consideration.

I have lived with this bill for some time myself during the past several weeks. I wish I had time to point out

some of the unconstitutional proposals which have been made. I wish I had the time to point out the assaults being made upon the Constitution of the United States and our way of life. When I talk about "our way of life" I am talking about the American way of life as guaranteed to us in the Constitution by the Founding Fathers.

I do not have sufficient time to do so here. They will be pointed out by members of the Judiciary Committee.

My friends, consider the public accommodations title of the bill. There are those who say that the Supreme Court's ruling is the law of the land. I challenge the constitutional lawyers on the other side—on whichever side of the aisle they sit—to deny that the law of the land today is that an innkeeper cannot be required to take in somebody he does not want to take in, regardless of the color of his skin.

The Congress, in the hysteria which followed the fratricidal War Between the States, attempted to write such a provision. Congress wrote a statute in very much the same language we have in this bill. That was in 1875.

Eight years later, when some of the hysteria had passed, the Supreme Court of the United States jerked the Congress back on its feet and said that law was unconstitutional. I do not have the time to develop that case, either.

Let me remind Members of another thing. What is proposed to be done? It is proposed to grant the most extraordinary powers to the executive department.

I appeal to you conservatives. I point particularly to some of my Republican brethren, who regard themselves as conservative. I wish you would consider what we are asked to do here by way of granting power to the executive department. Is there anyone who has studied the bill who can deny that under the terms of the bill—as pointed out by the gentleman from Virginia [Mr. Poff] and the gentleman from Florida [Mr. Cramer] in the report; and as shown on page 104 of the report—power would be given not only to the President and to the Attorney General but, more than that, given to every bureaucrat in the executive department to cut off all Federal aid from your hometown, from your county, and from your State.

Of course, the advocates of this legislation are in favor of helping the Negro. So am I; but the fact that those people would be cut off apparently makes no difference to them.

Yes, we are asked to delegate to some man in a department, wherever he may be in all of the agencies of the Government, the power to cut off the school lunch program, the Federal aid to education program, aid to the farmers, to the bankers, to every citizen who is the beneficiary in any way of Federal assistance from this Government.

The Civil Rights Commission in its 1963 report had recommended that the President have the powers conferred in this title VI. At his April 17 press conference, the late President Kennedy was asked to comment on that recommendation. In response the President said:

I don't have the power to cut off aid in a general way as was proposed by the Civil

Mr. McCULLOCH. The rule meets our approval. It makes in order a good bill, the passage of which is necessary without further unnecessary delay. I hope the rule is adopted unanimously.

Mr. BROWN of Ohio. I do hope that the rule will be adopted without any intervening difficulty.

Mr. MADDEN. Mr. Speaker, I yield the remainder of the time to the gentleman from Mississippi [Mr. COLMER].

Mr. COLMER. Mr. Speaker, I possibly will not have another opportunity to speak to you on this most important and far-reaching bill, a bill to which I have given considered, thorough, and meticulous consideration. Now, if I may have your attention, realizing as I do, and as you must, that no man in this House far superior though he may be in intellect to an ordinary Member like me, could intelligently discuss this highly technical bill in 15 minutes. Therefore, I can only hope to touch upon some of the highlights and to call your exploring minds to the consideration of some of these provisions that I regard as most vicious assaults upon the Constitution of the United States and our great heritage, its institutions.

Let me at the outset, if I may, say that I wish I had the power to set the ground rules for the consideration of this debate. If I could, I would have at least two fundamental rules.

One of them would be that we stay on the floor of this House, every Member, regardless of party alinements and

Rights Commission, and I would think it would probably be unwise to give the President of the United States that kind of power.

Yet "that kind of power" is given the President of the United States in title VI of this bill.

Mr. Speaker, in this connection may I point out that if this legislation was bad in the Kennedy administration, it is bad in the Johnson administration.

What do you do here? You put $100 billion, the annual budget, in the hands of the bureaucrats of this Government to say when the water will be cut off from your hometown or your district or your State. If you want to do that, go ahead with it. However, I finish where I started. I know some of the facts of life, too. I know—I hate to say this, but I am going to say it because some things ought to be said—I know when this bill is starting to be considered here, up to this time, there has not been 10 percent of the Members of this House who have read it. I know that when it is over many of you will not have read it.

Really, you are asked to legislate by labels. You are told that this is a moderate or watered down bill. I can assure you that it is neither moderate nor watered down. It is in reality as stringent as the original committee bill. In some instances, it is even stronger.

I hate to say what I am going to say now, but I think it ought to be said. I wish it were possible to have a secret ballot on this bill to see just what the real status of it is. I doubt that it would receive 20 percent of the votes.

Mr. Speaker, finally I ask, what is all this furor about?

What is the rush?

Why was this bill now under consideration rammed through the Judiciary Committee in a star chamber proceeding without debate, without an opportunity to offer amendments and with only a 2-minute discusson, 1 minute for Chairman CELLER and 1 minute for his counterpart, Congressman McCULLOCH?

Why was all the pressure placed on the Rules Committee to clear the bill to the floor of the House with a minimum of hearings?

Why did the chairman of the Judiciary Committee file a petition to discharge the Rules Committee from consideration of the bill so prematurely, while at the same time fail to have hearings on the bill before his committee that would override the Supreme Court's decision permitting prayer in the schools of the land?

I ask, Mr. Speaker, is all of this done out of fear? Is the Congress of the United States to yield to threats of further demonstrations by minority group leaders—blackmail, if you please?

I ask you in all candor, to what end will this bring us? Is the Congress to comply by legislation with the demands and even riots of every organized minority group in the country?

We are confronted today with demonstrations and riots in the Canal Zone. Are the President and the Congress to surrender to unreasonable demands in that area?

If we are prepared to follow that course of appeasement, then it would appear that the end of this glorious young Republic is near.

The SPEAKER. The time of the gentleman from Mississippi has expired.

(material omitted; sections repaginated)

Mr. CELLER. Mr. Chairman, I yield myself 40 minutes.

Mr. Chairman, this is an opportunity for which we have been anxiously awaiting. You know, the Lord's best gifts to us are not things, but opportunities, and we now have bestowed upon us a golden opportunity to do a great thing.

Furthermore, it was John Milton who said "Peace hath her victories no less renowned than war."

I fervently believe that in the passage of this civil rights bill we are participating in a historic event in peacetime, an event that will shine in our history. It will be a triumph as great as many a marshal's victory. It will bring happiness to 20 million of our people and will impart to a great many of the rest of us the comfort of having done our duty.

(material omitted)

UNFAIR REFLECTIONS ON THE BILL

Much unfair and unreasonable criticism has been leveled at the civil rights bill of 1964.

This criticism falls into three main categories and we heard some of that criticism just a few moments ago from the very distinguished and eminent Member of the House, the gentleman from Mississippi.

Opponents cry with alarm about what they claim are infringements of the rights of nonminority American citizens.

They invoke the baleful specter of Federal inspectors wielding unlimited power over innocent victims of governmental tyranny.

Finally, they attack the constitutional validity of the proposed legislation.

No one can object to legitimate criticism of any bill, no matter how worthy its objectives. What is objectionable about much of the criticism directed against the civil rights bill is that it seriously misrepresents what the bill would do and grossly distorts its effects.

The bill seeks simply to protect the right of American citizens to be free from racial and religious discrimination and to guarantee to them the full enjoyment of the rights of citizenship. It is a constitutionally and morally justified exercise of the obligations and authority of the Federal Government.

Let me cite some specifics.

EMPLOYERS, EMPLOYEES, AND LABOR UNIONS

It has been claimed that the bill would deprive employers, workers, and union members of their right to be free to control their business affairs and their membership. Specifically, the charge has been made that the Equal Employment Opportunity Commission to be established by title VII of the bill would have the power to prevent a business from employing and promoting the people it wished, and that a "Federal inspector" could then order the hiring and promotion only of employees of certain races or religious groups. This description of the bill is entirely wrong. The Equal Employment Opportunity Commission would be empowered merely to investigate specific charges of discrimination and to attempt to mediate or conciliate the dispute. It would have no authority to issue any orders to anyone.

In the event that wholly voluntary settlement proves to be impossible, the Commission could seek redress in the Federal courts, but it would be required to prove in the court that the particular employer involved had in fact, discriminated against one or more of his employees because of race, religion, or national origin. The employer would have ample opportunity to disprove any of the charges involved and would have the benefit of the protection of all the usual judicial procedures.

No order could be entered against an employer except by a court, and after a full and fair hearing, and any such order would be subject to appeal as is true in all court cases.

Even then, the court could not order that any preference be given to any particular race, religion or other group, but would be limited to ordering an end to discrimination. The statement that a Federal inspector could order the employment and promotion only of members of a specific racial or religious group is therefore patently erroneous.

Nor, as charged, would the fair employment provisions reach all employers and all businesses of any size or importance. Only businesses which affect interstate commerce would be covered, and, initially, even these businesses would be subject to the act only if they have more than 100 employees. In the later years, the act would apply to employers of 25 or more persons.

Finally, in order to provide an opportunity for adjustment and transition, the specific prohibitions on job discrimination would not become effective until 1 year after passage.

It has been asserted also that the bill would destroy worker seniority systems and employee rights vis-a-vis the union and the employer. This again is wrong. The bill would do no more than prevent a union, as it would prevent employers, from discriminating against or in favor of workers because of their race, religion, or national origin.

It is likewise not true that the Equal Employment Opportunity Commission would have power to rectify existing "racial or religious imbalance" in employment by requiring the hiring of certain people without regard to their qualifications simply because they are of a given race or religion. Only actual discrimination could be stopped. And there is, of course, no provision whatever for depriving unions of the rights and benefits under existing law.

The assertion that this is so is simply a total invention. Section 711 of the fair employment portion of the bill covers employment in the Federal Government and employment in firms having contracts with the Government. The President is authorized to take necessary action to insure equal employment opportunities in these areas. Contrary to the innuendos of certain critics of the bill, the President's authority is not unlimited. It is clearly confined to Government and Government contract employment. It is only just and reasonable that the Federal Government, representing and supported by all of its citizens, of whatever race or religion, insist upon fair and impartial employment procedures which allow equal opportunity to all qualified workers.

* * * *

(material repaginated)

(material omitted)

THE CONSTITUTIONALITY OF THE PUBLIC ACCOMMODATIONS PROVISIONS OF TITLE II

Title II of H.R. 7152 provides a remedy by suit for injunction against discrimination at certain places of public accommodation. These provisions are applicable to certain designated establishments—places of lodging, eating places, gasoline stations, and places of exhibition or entertainment—if (1) their operations affect commerce or (2) discrimination or segregation by them is supported by State action (sec. 201). These tests are in the alternative, and an establishment is covered by title II if either one of them is met. Thus, as to the establishments designated in section 201, title II is an exercise of the power of Congress to regulate commerce among the several States under article I, section 8, clause 3, of the Constitution, and also of the power of Congress to enact appropriate legislation to enforce the 14th amendment.

In addition, title II is applicable to any establishment or place at which segregation or discrimination is or purports to be required by State or local law (sec. 202). As to the places or establishments covered by section 202, title II is an exercise of the power of Congress to enact appropriate legislation to enforce the 14th amendment. The provisions of title II may also derive support from the power of Congress to enact appropriate legislation to enforce the 13th amendment.

There is no objection to invoking several sources of constitutional authority to achieve a legislatively desired result. Federal statutes often rest on more than one source of congressional power.[1] In many cases, a particular establishment will clearly be subject to congressional power under both the commerce clause and the 14th amendment; in other cases, however, proof of effect on interstate commerce may be easier, factually or legally, than proof that discrimination is supported by State action, or vice versa. By relying on both sources of power, section 201 will facilitate proof and avoid doubts or gaps as to coverage which might result if exclusive reliance were placed on a single source. In title II Congress would state the result

---

[1] For example, the TVA Act was sustained as an exercise of the war and commerce powers. *Ashwander* v. *Tennessee Valley Authority,* 297 U.S. 288, 326–330.

it seeks to achieve, and would marshal all available sources of congressional power in support of that result.

The danger of tying the public accommodations provisions to a single source of congressional authority is illustrated by the original *Civil Rights* cases, 109 U.S. 3 (1883). In view of the Supreme Court, sections 1 and 2 of the Civil Rights Act of 1875 had been tied by Congress exclusively to section 5 of the 14th amendment. The Court held the statute unconstitutional as based upon that amendment, and refused to consider whether it would be constitutional in some of its applications under the power to regulate interstate commerce (id. at 19). See also *Butts* v. *Merchants and Miners Transportation Co.,* 230 U.S. 126. Section 201 of the present bill avoids this danger.

I. The commerce clause

Insofar as title II rests on the power of the Congress to regulate commerce, its provisions are amply supported by well-established constitutional principles.

The power of Congress over interstate commerce and activities affecting interstate commerce is broad and plenary. "The congressional authority to protect interstate commerce from burdens and obstructions," Chief Justice Hughes said in *Labor Board* v. *Jones and Laughlin Steel Corp.,* 301 U.S. 1, 36–37, "is not limited to transactions deemed to be an essential part of a 'flow' of interstate or foreign commerce. * * * The fundamental principle is that the power to regulate commerce is the power to enact 'all appropriate legislation' for 'its protection and advancement' * * * to adopt measures 'to promote its growth and insure its safety' * * * 'to foster, protect, control and restrain.'"

Congress may exercise this power notwithstanding that the particular activity is local, that it is quantitatively unimportant, that it involves the retail trade, or that standing by itself it may not be regarded as interstate commerce "[W]hatever its nature, [it] may be reached by Congress if it exerts a substantial economic effect on interstate commerce, and this irrespective of whether such effect is what might at some earlier time have been defined as 'direct' or 'indirect'." *Wickard* v. *Filburn,* 317 U.S. 111, 125.

Thus, in *Wickard* v. *Filburn,* the Agricultural Adjustment Act was applied to a farmer who sowed only 23 acres of wheat and whose individual effect on interstate commerce amounted only to the pressure of 239 bushels of wheat upon the total national market. In *Mabee* v. *White Plains Publishing Co.,* 327 U.S. 178, the Fair Labor Standards Act was applied under the commerce clause to a newspaper whose circulation was about 9,000 copies and which mailed only 45 copies—about one-half of 1 percent of its business—out of State.[1] And in *United States* v. *Sullivan,* 332 U.S. 689, the Supreme Court held, without dissent on this point, that Congress has power to forbid a small retail druggist from selling drugs without the form of label required by the Federal Food, Drug, and Cosmetic Act (21 U.S.C. 301 et seq.), even though the drugs were imported in properly labeled bottles from which they were not removed until they reached the local drugstore and even though the drugs in question had reached the State 9 months before being resold.[2]

Of course, there are limits on congressional power under the commerce clause. It may be conceded that Congress does not have the power to regulate all of a man's conduct solely because he has some relationship with interstate commerce. What is required is that there be a relationship between interstate commerce and the evil to be regulated. Over the course of the years, various tests have been established for determining whether this relationship exists. The proposed legislation clearly meets these tests.

1. Restrictions on interstate travel

Congress has long exercised authority under the commerce clause to remove impediments to interstate travel and interstate travelers. As long ago as 1887, legislation was enacted (49 U.S.C. 3(1)) forbidding a railroad in interstate commerce "to subject any particular person * * * to any undue or unreasonable prejudice or disadvantage in any respect whatsoever." Similar statutory authority is provided with respect to motor carriers (49 U.S.C. 316(d)) and air carriers (49 U.S.C. 1374(b)).

These provisions have been authoritatively construed to proscribe racial segregation of passengers on railroads (*Mitchell* v. *United States,* 313 U.S. 80; *Henderson* v. *United States,* 339 U.S. 816; *NAACP* v. *St. Louis-San Francisco Ry. Co.,* 297 I.C.C. 335), on motor carriers (*Boynton* v. *Virginia,* 364 U.S. 454; *Keys* v. *Carolina Coach Co.,* 64 M.C.C. 769), and on air carriers (*Fitzgerald* v. *Pan American World Airways,* 229 F. 2d 499 (C.A. 2)). The decisions in these cases are, of course, direct authority for the proposition that Congress may enact legislation appropriate to secure equality of treatment for Negroes using the facilities of interstate commerce.

The constitutional authority of Congress under the commerce clause, moreover, extends beyond the regulation of the interstate carriers themselves; it covers all businesses affecting interstate travel (i.e., interstate commerce). Thus the wages of employees engaged in preparing meals for interstate airlines, sandwiches for sale in a railroad terminal, and ice for cooling trains have all been held subject to Federal regulation under the commerce clause. *Walling* v. *Armstrong,* 68 F. Supp. 870, affirmed, 161 F. 2d 515; *Sherry Corine Corp.* v. *Mitchell,* 264 F. 2d 831, cert. denied, 360 U.S. 934; *Mitchell* v. *Royal Baking Co.,* 219 F. 2d 532; *Chapman* v. *Home Ice Co.,* 136 F. 2d 353, cert. denied, 320 U.S. 761.

Similarly, Congress' authority under the commerce clause extends to restaurants at a terminal used by an interstate carrier. In *Boynton* v. *Virginia,* 364 U.S. 454, 463, the Supreme Court declared:

"Interstate passengers have to eat. * * * Such passengers in transit on a paid interstate * * * journey had a right to expect that this essential transportation food service voluntarily provided for them under such circumstances would be rendered without discrimination prohibited by the Interstate Commerce Act."

While in *Boynton* the Court held as a matter of statutory construction that the Interstate Commerce Act reached only restaurants connected with the carrier itself, its reason-

ing with respect to effect on commerce is no less applicable to service stations, hotels, motels, and other establishments serving interstate travelers. Such establishments affect travelers, and therefore, interstate commerce, in the same manner as restaurants. Just as travelers need food, they must have gasoline and places to sleep. Clearly, discrimination by such establishments severely burdens and restricts interstate travel and may therefore be regulated by the Congress.

In removing impediments to interstate travel, Congress is not limited to forbidding discrimination against interstate travelers alone; it may forbid discrimination against local customers as well. Congress may "choose the means reasonably adapted to the attainment of the permitted end, even though they involve control of intrastate activities." *United States* v. *Darby,* 312 U.S. 100, 121. Interstate commerce is burdened if interstate travelers are required to carry with them proof that they are in the course of a trip through more than one State. See *Baldwin* v. *Morgan,* 287 F. 2d 750 (C.A. 5). And interstate travel is discouraged if the interstate traveler is aware that those of his race who are not involved in interstate travel are refused service or accommodations in facilities needed by interstate travelers. Congress may eliminate these incidental impediments to interstate travel along with the more direct burdens discussed above. *United States* v. *Darby,* 312 U.S. 100; *Currin* v. *Wallace,* 306 U.S. 1; *Thornton* v. *United States,* 271 U.S. 414; *Shreveport Rate Cases,* 234 U.S. 342.

Under the foregoing authorities there can be no doubt that Congress has power to legislate so as to prohibit discrimination in eating places and gasoline stations which serve or offer to serve interstate travelers (sec. 201(c)(2)); and in establishments which provide lodging to transient guests and hence by their very nature serve or offer to serve interstate travelers (sec. 201(c)(1)). Obtaining lodging, food, gasoline and related services and conveniences is an essential part of interstate travel, and discriminatory practices which restrict the availability of such goods, services and conveniences, or expose interstate travelers to inconvenience or embarrassment in obtaining them, constitute burdens on interstate commerce which Congress has clear authority to remove.

2. Artificial restrictions upon the market for goods

Supreme Court decisions have many times sustained the power of Congress to enact legislation which would remove artificial restrictions upon the markets for products from other States. The removal of such restrictions, as the Supreme Court recognized in *Stafford* v. *Wallace,* 258 U.S. 495, promotes interstate traffic and therefore constitutes an appropriate object for the exercise of congressional authority. On that basis, restraints involving the local exhibition of motion pictures have been the subject of Federal regulation under the Sherman Act (*Interstate Circuit* v. *United States,* 306 U.S. 208; *White Bear Theatre* v. *State Theatre Corp.,* 129 F. 2d 600; *Youngclaus* v. *Omaha Film Board of Trade,* 60 F. 2d 538; *IPC Distributors* v. *Chicago Moving Picture Machine Operators Union,* 132 F. Supp. 294), and so have restraints involving stage attractions (*United States* v. *Shubert,* 348 U.S. 222), professional boxing matches (*United States* v. *International Boxing Club,* 348 U.S. 236), and professional football games (*Radovich* v. *National Football League,* 352 U.S. 445).

Like unlawful monopolies, racial discrimination and segregation in the establishments covered by the proposed legislation constitute artificial restrictions upon the movement of goods in interstate commerce, and they may be dealt with by the Congress for

---

[1] See also, *Labor Board* v. *Fainblatt,* 306 U.S. 601, 607; *United States* v. *Darby,* 312 U.S. 100, 123.

[2] Laws enacted pursuant to the commerce power have been applied to businesses furnishing accommodations to interstate travelers (*Hotel Employees Local 255* v. *Leedom,* 358 U.S. 99), to retail auto dealers (*Howell Chevrolet Co.* v. *National Labor Relations Board,* 346 U.S. 482) to drugstores (*United*

States v. *Sullivan,* 332 U.S. 689), to department stores (*J. L. Brandeis* v. *National Labor Relations Board,* 142 F. 2d 977 (C.A. 8), certiorari denied, 323 U.S. 751; *May Department Stores, Co.* v. *National Labor Relations Board,* 326 U.S. 376), to theaters (*League of New York Theaters, Inc.,* 129 N.L.R.B. 1429; *National Labor Relations Board* v. *Combined Century Theaters,* 278 F. 2d 306 (C.A. 2)), and other retail enterprises (see e.g., *Meat Cutters* v. *Fairlawn Meats,* 353 U.S. 20; *San Diego Building Trades Council* v. *Garmon,* 353 U.S. 26; *National Labor Relations Board* v. *Reliance Fuel Corp.,* 371 U.S. 224; *National Labor Relations Board* v. *Gene Compton's Corporation,* 262 F. 2d 653 (C.A. 9).

that reason. The restrictive impact of discriminatory practices is perhaps best illustrated by reference to the motion picture industry.

Motion picture theaters which refuse to admit Negroes will obviously draw patrons from a narrower segment of the market than if they were open to patrons of all races. The difference will often not be made up by separate theaters for Negroes because there are localities which can support one theater but not two (or two but not three, etc.) and because the inferior economic position in which racial discrimination has held Negroes often makes their custom alone financially inadequate to support a theater. Thus, the demand for films from out of State, and the royalties on such films, will be less. What is true of exclusion is true, although perhaps in less degree, of segregation. During any particular performance, a segregated theater may well lack sufficient seating space in the "white" section while offering ample seating in the "Negro" section, or vice versa. Moreover, the very fact of segregation in seating discourages attendance by Negroes.

These principles are applicable not merely to motion picture theaters but to other establishments which receive supplies, equipment or goods through the channels of interstate commerce. If these establishments narrow their potential markets by artificially restricting their patrons to non-Negroes, the volume of sales and therefore the volume of interstate purchases will be less. Although the demand may be partly filled by other establishments that do not discriminate, the effect will be substantial in those areas where segregation is practiced on a large scale. The economic impact is felt in interstate commerce. The commerce clause vests power in the Congress to remedy this condition.

On the foregoing authorities it is clear that Congress has power to prohibit discrimination at places of exhibition and entertainment which customarily present films, performances, athletic teams, exhibitions, or other sources of entertainment which move in interstate commerce (sec. 201(c)(3)), and at eating places and gasoline stations which sell goods, a substantial portion of which has moved in such commerce (sec. 201(c)(2)).

3. *Elimination of adverse effects on the allocation of resources and flow of interstate commerce*

The commerce clause also vests Congress with the authority to deal with conditions which adversely affect the allocation of resources and the flow of interstate commerce.

The Federal Government has, of course, a legitimate interest in the interstate movement of capital and goods, and Congress has frequently acted in furtherance of that interest. Thus, in the Agricultural Adjustment Act of 1938 (52 Stat. 31, 46, et seq.), Congress provided for restrictions on production of certain agricultural products "in order to promote, foster and maintain an orderly flow of [supply of such products] in interstate and foreign commerce." Similarly, the Fair Labor Standards Act (29 U.S.C. 201, et seq.) speaks of the effect of "labor conditions detrimental to the * * * minimum standard of living necessary for health, efficiency and general well-being of workers" upon "the orderly and fair marketing of goods in commerce." See also the declaration of policy in section 1 of the National Labor Relations Act (29 U.S.C. 151 et seq.).

Experience shows that discrimination and segregation, when widely practiced throughout sections of the country, have a markedly adverse effect upon the interstate flow of both capital and goods. Capital is reluctant to invest in the region. Skilled or educated men who will be the victims of discrimination are reluctant to settle in the area even when opportunities are available. The inferior economic position to which general discrimination and segregation relegate a large segment of the population in some regions reduces their purchasing power, thus reducing the flow of goods and the incentive to bring capital into the area. It is perfectly apparent that Congress may legislate with respect to such conditions.

4. *Elimination of causes of disruption in the flow of interstate commerce*

There is a parallel congressional power to eliminate the causes of disputes that may curtail the flow of interstate commerce—power which was recognized and sustained in a number of decisions under the National Labor Relations Act. These decisions show that Congress may, by legislation, deal with labor disputes which halt production or the resale of manufactured goods because, based on the Federal interest in the elimination of obstructions to the free flow of commerce, there is a corresponding power to remove the causes of the disputes which are responsible for these obstructions. See *NLRB v. Jones & Laughlin Steel Corp.*, 301 U.S. 1; *NLRB v. Suburban Lumber Co.*, 121 F. 2d 829, cert. denied, 314 U.S. 693; *J. L. Brandeis v. NLRB* 142 F. 2d 977, cert. denied, 323 U.S. 751; *NLRB v. Reliance Fuel Corp.*, 371 U.S. 224.

Disputes involving racially discriminatory practices of places of public accommodation frequently give rise to picketing and other demonstrations which interfere with interstate travel and with the sale of goods and thus affect interstate commerce in precisely the same manner as would labor disputes involving such establishments.

*   *   *   *   *

Thus, insofar as the coverage of section 201 is based on an effect on commerce, the provisions of that section are clearly supported by a long line of decisions interpreting the power of Congress over interstate commerce. Nothing in the *Civil Rights* cases, 109 U.S. 3, creates any question as to congressional power under the commerce clause. In its decision holding the public accommodations provisions of the Civil Rights Act of 1875 beyond the power of Congress under the 14th amendment, the Court did not pass upon the power of Congress to enact similar legislation under the commerce clause. It had been argued to the Court that the act was effective at least as to public conveyances, since they were plainly in interstate commerce, but the Court felt that "as the sections in question are not conceived in any such view," the statute could not even be considered under the commerce clause and had to stand or fall on the power of Congress under the 14th amendment (109 U.S. at 19).

The fact that the proposed civil rights bill rests ultimately on a concept of justice and morality presents no reason for Congress not to avail itself of its powers over interstate and foreign commerce. Congress may exercise its commerce power to prevent injuries to "the public health, morals or welfare." *United States v. Darby*, 312 U.S. 100, 114. See also *Lottery Cases*, 188 U.S. 321; *Hipolite Egg Co. v. United States*, 220 U.S. 45; *Caminetti v. United States*, 242 U.S. 470. "The authority of the Federal Government over interstate commerce does not differ in extent or character from that retained by the States over intrastate commerce." *United States v. Rock Royal Cooperative*, 307 U.S. 533, 569–570. Congress power over interstate commerce "is complete in itself, may be exercised to its utmost extent, and acknowledges no limitations, other than are prescribed in the Constitution." *Gibbons v. Ogden*, 9 Wheat, 1, 196. Congress has frequently exercised its powers over interstate commerce to protect the public health, safety and morals, to protect various groups in society from exploitation or unjust treatment, and to prohibit or regulate practices deemed injurious to the public welfare.[4]

II. THE 14TH AMENDMENT

Section 1 of the 14th amendment provides that—

"No State shall * * * deny to any person * * * the equal protection of the laws."

Section 5 provides that "Congress shall have power to enforce by appropriate legislation, the provisions of this article."

On its face the amendment is aimed at discrimination by a State, and laws enforcing the amendment must therefore be aimed at State action. As the Supreme Court recently stated in *Burton v. Wilmington Parking Authority*, 365 U.S. 715, 722:

"It is clear, as it always has been since the *Civil Rights Cases*, [109 U.S. 3] that 'Individual invasion of individual rights is not the subject matter of the amendment,' at page 11, and that private conduct abridging individual rights does no violence to the equal protection clause unless to some significant extent the State in any of its manifestations has been found to have become involved in it."

To the same effect see *Shelley v. Kraemer*, 334 U.S. 1, 13; *Peterson v. Greenville*, 373 U.S. 244, 247.

In the *Civil Rights* cases, 109 U.S. 3, the Court held invalid sections 1 and 2 of the Civil Rights Act of 1875. Section 1 declared the right of all persons to the full and equal enjoyment of "the accommodations, advantages, facilities and privileges of inns, public conveyances on land or water, theaters and other places of public amusement." Section 2 made it a crime for "any person" to deny such rights to any other person. Because the statute "makes no reference whatever to any supposed or apprehended violation of the 14th amendment on the part of the States" (109 U.S. at 14), it was held to be beyond the power of Congress. The 14th amendment, and Congress' power to enforce it, were limited, in the Court's view, to cases in which "some State law has been passed, or some State action through its officers or agents has been taken, adverse to the rights of citizens sought to be protected by the 14th amendment." 109 U.S. at 13.

The provisions of title II, insofar as they rely on the 14th amendment, are limited to situations in which the requisite "State action * * * has been taken." Title II is therefore clearly distinguishable from the provisions of the Civil Rights Act of 1875 which were held unconstitutional in the civil rights cases. The constitutional validity of title II, insofar as it rests on the 14th amendment, is fully supported by the civil rights

[4] For a few out of the many examples, see the Federal Food, Drug, and Cosmetic Act, 21 U.S.C. 301 et seq.; the Meat Inspection Act, 21 U.S.C. 71 et seq.; the Poultry Products Inspection Act, 21 U.S.C. 451 et seq.; the Plant Quarantine Act and related legislation, 7 U.S.C. 150–167; legislation regulating intrastate and interstate traffic in biological products, 42 U.S.C. 262; legislation prohibiting interstate traffic in lottery tickets, in liquor contrary to State law and in women for immoral purposes, 18 U.S.C. 1301 et seq., 1261 et seq., 2421 et seq.; prohibitions against interstate transmission of gambling devices and of switch blade knives, 15 U.S.C. 1171 et seq., 1241 et seq.; the Fair Labor Standards Act, 29 U.S.C. 201 et seq.; the Welfare and Pension Plans Disclosure Act, 29 U.S.C. 301 et seq.; the Labor-Management Relations Act, 20 U.S.C. 141 et seq.; the Federal Trade Commission Act, 15 U.S.C. 41 et seq.; the Securities Exchange Act, 15 U.S.C. 78a.

cases, as well as by later decisions applying the concept of State action.[5]

It is settled that judicial relief can be obtained against private individuals and organizations who engage in discrimination with which the State is sufficiently involved to warrant invocation of the 14th amendment. *E. G. Turner v. City of Memphis,* 369 U.S. 350 (action against city and a private restaurant); *Burton v. Wilmington Parking Authority, supra* (same); *Evers v. Dwyer,* 358 U.S. 202 (action against city and private transit company); *Browder v. Gayle,* 142 F. Supp. 707 (M.D. Ala.) aff'd, 352 U.S. 903 (same); *Flemming v. So. Carolina Electric and Gas Co.,* 224 F. 2d 752 (C.A. 4) (action against private transit company); *Baldwin v. Morgan,* 251 F. 2d 780, 287 F. 2d 750 (C.A. 5) (action against city officials and private terminal company); *Kerr v. Enoch Pratt Free Library,* 149 F. 2d 212 (C.A. 4) (action against privately endowed library); *Simkins v. Moses Cone Memorial Hospital* (C.A. 4, Nov. 1, 1963) (action against nonprofit hospitals).

A long line of decisions has made it clear that "State action," for purposes of the 14th amendment, is a broad concept which may be satisfied by any of a number of circumstances. Sufficient State involvement may result from "State participation through any arrangement, management, funds or property." *Cooper v. Aaron,* 358 U.S. 1, 4. Any significant "degree of State participation and involvement in discriminatory action" may bring it within the prohibitions of the 14th amendment. *Burton v. Wilmington Parking Authority,* 365 U.S. 715, 724; *Peterson v. Greenville,* 373 U.S. 244, 248. As will be shown below, sections 201 and 202, the provisions of title II which rely on the 14th amendment are based upon a concept of State action or involvement well supported by judicial precedent.

Section 202 would preclude discrimination at any establishment or place "if such discrimination or segregation is or purports to be required by any law, statute, ordinance, regulation, rule or order, of a State or any agency or political subdivision thereof." The section would reach only cases in which there is actually "on the books" a State or local law requiring discrimination.

Not only is it beyond dispute that any such law is patently unconstitutional, but it seems clear that racial segregation or discrimination which is or purports to be required by State law is prohibited by the 14th amendment. *Peterson v. Greenville,* 373 U.S.

---

[5] Of course, arguments could be made for reconsidering and distinguishing or overruling the civil rights cases. Thus it could be urged that historically, public segregation is the product of and has been supported by State action; that Congress' power to enact "appropriate legislation" confers power to take in whatever additional area is necessary to make effective its prohibition of the use of State action causing and supporting racial discrimination and to undo the consequences of such action, compare *Everard's Breweries v. Day,* 265, U.S. 545; and that if Congress finds that the most effective way of eliminating unconstitutional State support for nongovernmental discrimination is to forbid all discrimination, the courts should sustain that determination as a rational one in light of the facts. However, to draft title II so as to make its constitutional validity depend on such theories would raise serious constitutional questions and would delay its practical effectiveness until a definitive constitutional adjudication could be had. These difficulties are avoided by H.R. 7152, which is clearly consistent with and supported by well-settled precedents.

244; *Lombard v. Louisiana,* 373 U.S. 267; *Gober v. City of Birmingham,* 373 U.S. 374. "When the State has commanded a particular result, it has saved to itself the power to determine that result and thereby 'to a significant extent' has 'become involved' in it, and, in fact, has removed that decision from the sphere of private choice." *Peterson v. Greenville, supra,* at 248.

Such a command has been found in a State statute, *Evers v. Dwyer,* 248 U.S. 202; a municipal ordinance, *Peterson v. Greenville, supra;* a regulation of a State agency, *Baldwin v. Morgan,* 251 F. 2d 780, 287 F. 2d 750 (C.A. 5); a practice of segregated seating in a courtroom, *Johnson v. Virginia,* 373 U.S. 61; and public statements of city officials, *Lombard v. Louisiana,* 373 U.S. 267. It is sufficient that the segregation or discrimination is "commanded * * * by the voice of the State," *Lombard v. Louisiana, supra,* at 274.

The cases draw no distinction based on the type of place or establishment involved. Segregation or discrimination commanded by the State has been held invalid in publicly owned facilities of every kind, *Watson v. Memphis,* 373 U.S. 526; in transportation facilities, *Bailey v. Patterson,* 369 U.S. 31; in restaurants, *Burton v. Wilmington Parking Authority,* 365 U.S. 715; *Turner v. City of Memphis,* 369 U.S. 350; in retail stores, *Peterson v. Greenville, supra;* in hospitals, *Simkins v. Moses Cone Memorial Hospital* (C.A. 4, Nov. 1, 1963). And see, as to private employment. *Colorado Commissioner v. Continental,* 372 U.S. 714, 721.

These precedents amply support the constitutionality of section 202.

The constitutional propriety of that portion of section 201 based on the 14th amendment is no less clear. Section 201(b) would preclude discrimination or segregation at any of the establishments specifically enumerated in that section (e.g., hotels, motels, restaurants, and other eating facilities, gasoline stations, places of public entertainment) if such discrimination or segregation is "supported by State action." This provision thus is applicable only to situations in which the constitutional requirement of State action is met.

Section 201(d) provides that discrimination or segregation is supported by State action if it is "carried on under color of any law, statute, ordinance, regulation, custom, or usage." The quoted phrase is taken from section 1 of the Civil Rights Act of 1871, 42 U.S.C. 1983. The constitutionality of that provision, as an implementation of the 14th amendment, is clear. *Monroe v. Pape,* 365 U.S. 167, 171–187.

Section 201(d) also provides that discrimination or segregation is supported by State action if it is "required, fostered, or encouraged by action of a State or a political subdivision thereof." It has already been shown that action "required" by a State is State action under the 14th amendment. It is also clear that State action falling short of a requirement may constitute a sufficient degree of State "participation and involvement" to warrant a holding of State action in violation of the 14th amendment. "It is settled that governmental sanction need not reach the level of compulsion to clothe what is otherwise private discrimination with 'State action'." *Simkins v. Moses Cone Memorial Hospital* (C.A. 4, Nov. 1, 1963) (typewritten opinion, p. 17). See also *McCabe v. Atchison, T. & S.F. Ry. Co.,* 235 U.S. 151; *Baldwin v. Morgan,* 287 F. 2d 750, 754 (C.A. 5). "Overt State approval" may in some cases be sufficient. *Simkins v. Moses Cone Memorial Hospital, supra,* 17, 18. Indeed, in some circumstances, the failure of the State to prevent discrimination in facilities in whose operation it is involved may

constitute State action to which the 14th amendment applies.

Depending on the circumstances, any of a number of factors, singly or in combination, may establish State action.

Thus, the fact that a private establishment is allowed to use publicly owned property and facilities, or receives substantial financial or other benefits from the State, may tend to establish State action. *Burton v. Wilmington Parking Authority,* 365 U.S. 715, *Turner v. City of Memphis,* 369 U.S. 350, *Simkins v. Moses Cone Memorial Hospital* (C.A. 4, Nov. 1, 1963). State action may be found in "State participation" in the functioning of an establishment or institution, "through any arrangement, management, funds, or property." *Cooper v. Aaron,* 358 U.S. 1, 4.

State action may be found in the grant by a State of special franchises or privileges or in the delegating to a private organization of quasi-governmental powers. In *Steele v. L.& N. R. Co.,* 323 U.S. 192, 198, the Court indicated that Congress could not confer exclusive bargaining rights on a labor union, without placing it under a duty to refrain from discriminating against Negro workers. See also *Brotherhood of Railroad Trainmen v. Howard,* 343 U.S. 768. Compare cases holding that the prohibition in the 15th amendment of denial of voting rights by a State on grounds of race, color, or previous condition of servitude "is not to be nullified by a State through casting its electoral process in a form which permits a private organization to practice racial discrimination in the election." *Smith v. Allwright,* 321 U.S. 649; *Terry v. Adams,* 345 U.S. 461, 466. Like principles appear to preclude segregation or discrimination by public utilities which are executing public functions. *Baldwin v. Morgan,* 287 F. 2d 750, 755 (C.A. 5); *Boman v. Birmingham Transit Co.,* 280 F. 2d 531 (C.A. 5); cf. *Pollak v. Public Utilities Commission,* 191 F. 2d 450 (C.A.D.C.), reversed on other grounds, 343 U.S. 451. Mr. Justice Douglas has expressed the view that State licensing and supervision of places of public accommodation constitute sufficient State involvement to make applicable the prohibitions of the 14th amendment. *Lombard v. Louisiana,* 373 U.S. at 281–3 (concurring opinion).

State action may under some circumstances be involved where the State lends its aid to the enforcement of discriminatory practices carried on by private persons. Thus in *Shelley v. Kraemer,* 334 U.S. 1, the Court held that judicial enforcement of private restrictive covenants constituted State action in violation of the 14th amendment. The Court characterized the case as one in which the States "have made available" to individuals desiring to impose racial discrimination, "the full coercive power of government." 334 U.S. at 19. See also *Barrows v. Jackson,* 346 U.S. 249; *Boman v. Birmingham Transit Co.,* 280 F. 2d 531 (C.A. 5); *Lombard v. Louisiana,* 373 U.S. at 278–81 (concurring opinion). Coercion applied by public officials, whether or not authorized by State law, may constitute State action. *Lombard v. Louisiana,* 373 U.S. 267, 273.

The foregoing illustrations are neither comprehensive nor exhaustive. While the concept of State action cannot be circumscribed by "readily applicable formulas," and while the existence of State action "can be determined only in the framework of the peculiar facts or circumstances present," *Burton v. Wilmington Parking Authority,* 365 U.S. 715, 725, 726, the language of sections 201 (b) and (d) clearly would not extend to any case where, as a matter of constitutional law, State action is not present; hence there can be no doubt of its constitutionality as an implementation of the 14th amendment. Moreover, it should be noted that section 201 does not extend to all establishments in which discrimination may be "supported" by the State; section 201 covers, even with regard to State action, only those establishments within the specific categories defined in the section; i.e., hotels, motels, eating places, gasoline stations, places of amusement, etc. This limitation on its coverage, coupled with the fact that enforcement of the section is dependent upon a prior judicial determination that an establishment is covered, gives the section a more than adequate specificity of application.

III. THE 13TH AMENDMENT

It has also been suggested that additional support for the constitutionality of title II may be found in the 13th amendment, which outlaws slavery and involuntary servitude and authorizes Congress to enact appropriate legislation enforcing that prohibition. Unlike the 14th amendment, the 13th amendment contains no requirement of State action. It "denounces a status or condition, irrespective of the manner or authority by which it is created." "Congress may enforce the 13th amendment by direct legislation" which "operates directly on every citizen of the Republic." *Clyatt* v. *United States*, 197 U.S. 207, 216, 218. See 18 U.S.C. 1581; *United States* v. *Gaskin*, 320 U.S. 527. Thus the 13th amendment, if applicable, would support those provisions of title II which are applicable to purely private action as well as those provisions of title II which are applicable to purely private action as well as those provisions which are premised on some form of State involvement.

The first Mr. Justice Harlan, in his dissent in the Civil Rights cases, argued that the 13th amendment permits Congress to prohibit not only the legal institution of slavery itself, but also the collateral burdens and incidents—the civil disabilities and inequalities—which either accompanied or followed it. He said, "the power of Congress under the 13th amendment is not necessarily restricted to legislation against slavery as an institution upheld by positive law, but may be exerted to the extent, at least, of protecting the liberated race against discrimination, in respect of legal rights belonging to freemen, where such discrimination is based upon race," 109 U.S. at 37.

While the most salient characteristic of the institution of slavery was the ownership of one person by another, this was by no means the only one. The slave system also encompassed the imposition on the slaves of many degradations, inferiorities, and disabilities designed to make impossible any relationship of equality between the slaves and their masters. Ownership of one human being by another was itself ended by the 13th amendment, but racial segregation, promoted by State law and other State action, replaced it as a device for perpetuating the inferior position of the Negroes. Outlawing of this substitute for slavery, it is argued, is also within the reach of congressional power and under the 13th amendment, which was intended, along with the 14th and 15th amendments, to raise the Negro to a position of first-class citizenship with full civil rights.

The majority of the Supreme Court did not adopt the first Mr. Justice Harlan's views, perhaps because at the time the Civil Rights cases were decided State-imposed racial segregation was not yet a widespread fact. It was only in the latter part of the 19th century that Jim Crow laws, requiring segregation in establishments dealing with the public, spread throughout the South. These were the laws which reimposed on the Negro the badge of inferiority from which the 13th amendment, as read by Justice Harlan, sought to relieve him, and it is these laws, and their aftermath, with which we must deal today.

Thus, the arguments advanced by Justice Harlan lend support to the constitutionality of Federal public accommodations legislation under the 13th amendment. It must be recognized, however, that there is no decisional law to support such an approach and that the scope of the power of Congress under the 13th amendment is unclear. Hence, the 13th amendment may be available, not as a primary source of constitutional power for title II, but as possible additional authority for legislation which is believed to be fully authorized by the commerce clause and the 14th amendment.

IV. TITLE II DOES NOT VIOLATE EITHER THE 5TH OR THE 10TH AMENDMENTS

It has been suggested that for Congress to require places of public accommodation not to discriminate would be a taking of private property without due process of law in violation of the 5th amendment and would interfere with powers reserved to the States under the 10th amendment. Both arguments are clearly without merit.

A. *The fifth amendment*

So far as the fifth amendment is concerned, any Federal regulatory legislation is, to a certain extent, a limitation on the use of private property. "It is of the essence of regulation that it lays a restraining hand on the self-interest of the regulated and that advantages from the regulation commonly fall to others." *Wickard* v. *Filburn*, 317 U.S. 111, 129. See also *German Alliance Insurance Co.* v. *Kansas*, 233 U.S. 389.

The type of regulation proposed in title II is hardly novel. Some 30 States presently have public accommodations laws forbidding racial or religious discrimination. Many of these laws date back to the period immediately after the Civil War.

The power of the Federal Government to pass such laws is also clear. See *Boynton* v. *Virginia*, 364 U.S. 454. "The authority of the Federal Government over interstate commerce does not differ in extent or character from that retained by the States over interstate commerce." *United States* v. *Rock Royal Cooperative*, 307 U.S. 533, 569–570.

B. *The 10th amendment*

The 10th amendment provides that "The powers not delegated to the United States by the Constitution, nor prohibited by it to the States, are reserved to the States respectively, or to the people." In the annotation of the Constitution, Senate Document No. 170, 82d Congress, 2d session, page 915, it is pointed out:

"That this provision [the 10th amendment] was not conceived to be a yardstick for measuring the powers granted to the Federal Government or reserved to the States was clearly indicated by its sponsor, James Madison, in the course of the debate which took place while the amendment was pending concerning Hamilton's proposal to establish a national bank. He declared that: 'Interference with the power of the States was no constitutional criterion of the power of Congress. If the power was not given, Congress could not exercise it; if given, they might exercise it, although it should interfere with the laws, or even the constitutions of the States.'"

Prior decisions invalidating Federal legislation on the ground of conflict with the 10th amendment were overruled, expressly or impliedly, in *United States* v. *Darby*, 312 U.S. 100, 123–124. It is clear that legislation enacted by Congress pursuant to a power delegated to the Federal Government by the Constitution cannot be validly attacked upon the ground that it infringes upon rights reserved to the States by the 10th amendment. See *Everard's Breweries* v. *Day*, 265 U.S. 545, 558, in which the Supreme Court held that:

"If the act is within the power confided to Congress, the 10th amendment, by its very terms, has no application, since it only re-

serves to the States 'powers not delegated to the United States by the Constitution.'"

Similarly, speaking of legislation enacted by Congress pursuant to the enforcement clause of the 14th amendment, the Supreme Court has said that State sovereignty cannot, by definition, be invaded by the enactment of a law "which the people of the States have, by the Constitution of the United States, empowered Congress to act." *Ex parte Virginia*, 100 U.S. 339, 346.

(material omitted)

(material omitted)

THE LEGALITY OF THE PROVISIONS OF TITLE VII

Section 701(b) of the bill declares that the provisions of title VII are necessary "to remove obstructions to the free flow of commerce among the States and with foreign nations" and "to insure the complete and full enjoyment by all persons of the rights, privileges, and immunities secured and protected by the Constitution of the United States." Title VII is amply supported by Congress' power to regulate commerce among the States and with foreign nations (article I, section 8, clause 3).[1]

Title VII covers employers engaged in industries affecting commerce, that is to say, interstate and foreign commerce and commerce within the District of Columbia and the possessions. The title also applies to employment agencies procuring employees for such employers and labor organizations engaged in such industries. In order to protect the free flow of commerce, Congress has previously legislated with respect to the practices of employees and labor unions in industries affecting such commerce, National Labor Relations Act, 29 U.S.C. 151, 160; Labor-Management Reporting and Disclosure Act, 29 U.S.C. 401, 402. The power of Congress to legislate in this area is no longer subject to question, *National Labor Relations Board v. Jones and Laughlin Steel Corp.*, 301 U.S. 1 (1937); *Lawson v. United States*, 300 F. 2d 252, 254 (C.A. 10–1962), and the amount of commerce affected in any particular case is not a material consideration in determining Congress' constitutional power, *National Labor Relations Board v. Fainblatt*, 306 U.S. 601, 606 (1939). (See also *Mabee v. White Plains Publishing Co.*, 327 U.S. 178 (1946), holding the Fair Labor Standards Act, 29 U.S.C. 201 et seq., applicable to the business of publishing a daily newspaper, only about one-half of 1 percent of whose circulation is outside the State of publication.)

---

[1] Insofar as the title applies to commerce within the District of Columbia and the possessions of the United States, it is based on Congress' legislative authority over the District, article I, section 8, clause 17, and over the territories and possessions, article IV, section 3.

The term "affecting commerce" has a long history of judicial application under the National Labor Relations Act, *National Labor Relations Board v. Fainblatt, supra* at 606; *National Labor Relations Board v. Reliance Fuel Corp.*, 371 U.S. 224, 226 (1963), and thus there should be little difficulty as to its meaning. As the Court said in the *Polish National Alliance, etc. v. National Labor Relations Board*, 322 U.S. 643, 648 (1944):

"Whether or not practices may be deemed by Congress to affect interstate commerce is not to be determined by confining judgment to the quantitative effect of the activities immediately before the Board. Appropriate for judgment is the fact that the immediate situation is representative of many others throughout the country, the total incidence of which if left unchecked may well become far-reaching in its harm to commerce."

* * * *

[page 1529:]

Mr. McCULLOCH. Mr. Chairman, I yield myself such time as I may consume. I rise to support the civil rights bill, H.R. 7152, as amended.

The bill now before the committee has been ably and accurately discussed title by title by the chairman of the Committee on the Judiciary. It is, therefore, not necessary for me to cover the same ground. I should, however, say that the bill is comprehensive in scope, yet moderate in application.

There are no primary criminal sanctions provided in the legislation. A sincere effort has been made to eliminate from the bill all provisions which improperly invade personal liberty and the rights of States and other political subdivisions. Diligent and effective effort has been made to surround each title with judicial safeguards and administrative limitations in order that fundamental rights and liberties be protected. The bill before you is basically a good bill and a bill that faces a pressing need for enactment.

There is considerable pressure for civil rights legislation from certain quarters on the ground that unless legislation is enacted there will be rioting in the streets, heightened racial unrest, and the further shedding of blood. This kind of activity, in my mind, is highly improper and could do much to retard the enactment of effective civil rights legislation.

No people can gain lasting liberty and equality by riot and demonstration. Legislation under such threat is basically not legislation at all. In the long run, behavior of this type will lead to a total undermining of society where equality and civil rights will mean nothing.

Behavior of this type also creates the false sense of hope that once legislation is enacted, all burdens of life will dissolve. No statutory law can completely end discrimination, under attack by this legislation. Intelligent work and vigilance by members of all races will be required, for many years, before discrimination completely disappears. To create hope of immediate and complete success can only promote conflict and result in brooding despair.

Not force or fear, then, but belief in the inherent equality of man induces me to support this legislation.

I believe in the right of each individual to have his constitutional rights guaranteed. On the other hand, he must always be prepared to shoulder the obligations and to assume the burdens of citizenship.

I believe in the right and duty of State and local authority to be primarily responsible for the conduct of all but limited areas of governmental activity, which it cannot do alone. But, I also believe in the obligation of State and local governments to ever work for the common good.

I believe in the effective separation of powers and in a workable Federal system, whereby State authority is not needlessly usurped by a centralized government. But, I also believe that an obligation rests with the National Government

to see that the citizens of every State are treated equally, without regard to their race or color or religion or national origin.

Where, then, individuals, or governmental authorities, fail to shoulder their obligations, and only stress their rights, it is the duty of the Congress, under constitutional authority, to correct that wrong. To do less would be to shirk our responsibility as national legislators, and as human beings, who honor the principles of liberty and justice.

No one would suggest that the Negro receives equality of treatment and equality of opportunity in many fields of activity, today. Well-informed persons, everywhere, admit that in all sections of the country—North, South, East, and West—the Negro continues to face the barriers of racial intolerance and discrimination. Hundreds of thousands of citizens are denied the basic right to vote. Thousands of school districts remain segregated. Decent hotel and eating accommodations frequently lie hundreds of miles apart for the Negro traveler. Parks, playgrounds, and golf courses continue to be off limits to Negroes whose tax moneys go to support them. Many programs continue to be operated in a discriminatory manner. These, and many more such conditions, point the way toward the need for additional legislation.

In voting, the foundations of our Republic are enhanced by a free elective franchise. In public accommodations, the economy of our country and the enjoyment of its people are bolstered. In equal protection of our laws, the principle of justice is secured. In education, the superiority of our citizens and of our Nation is assured. In employment and Federal assistance, the opportunity and well-being of each individual is advanced and the taproot of the country's economy is strengthened. In every one of these categories, we will be doing ourselves, as well as our Nation, a lasting service by enacting H.R. 7152, as amended.

The constitutionality of certain titles of this bill has been questioned. Whether or not we all concur in the evolution of the law as it has developed at every step, I am of the opinion that the Constitution, as presently interpreted by the courts, supports each title. Congress has already acted in the field of voting. The Supreme Court has stricken down segregation in public education and publicly operated facilities. The Sherman, Taft-Hartley, Food-Drug-Cosmetic, and Fair Labor Standards Acts, and court interpretations thereof, have provided the legal support for the public accommodations and equal job opportunity titles under the interstate commerce clause of the Constitution. And, the Federal Government, through Congress, certainly has the authority, pursuant to the 14th amendment, to withhold Federal financial assistance where such assistance is extended in a discriminatory manner. The fact, moreover, that some 32 States have enacted public accommodations laws, frequently broader in scope than title I of H.R. 7152, as amended, 25 States have enacted fair employment legislation, and many States have enacted other sweeping civil rights provisions clearly demonstrates that Congress will not be invading privacy, overturning the sanctity of private property, destroying personal liberties, or in other ways acting in an illegal manner.

Certain provisions in certain bills, as introduced or as reported by the House Judiciary Subcommittee, very likely exceeded constitutional authority, or were otherwise objectionable and unacceptable; for example, the provisions concerning the elimination of racial imbalance in education and the control over private institutions, such as banks and mortgage companies merely because they were insured by the Federal Government. Such provisions are not a part of H.R. 7152, as amended.

I wish to reiterate that this bill is comprehensive in scope, yet moderate in application. It is hedged about by effective administrative and legal safeguards, which seek to advance the cause of civil rights in the United States. The reason for moderation and necessary safeguards is obvious. Those of us supporting H.R. 7152, as amended, are desirous of presenting legislation which stands a good chance of enactment. Reality is what we live by and solid accomplishment is what we seek.

Of equal importance is the fact that we are a nation of many people and many views. In such a nation, the prime purpose of a legislator, from wherever he may come, is to accommodate the proper interests, desires, wants, and needs of all our citizens. To alienate some in order to satisfy others is not only a disservice to those we alienate, but a violation of the principles of our Republic. For only in compromise, moderation, understanding, and good will are we able to fashion our society into a cohesive and durable whole. I recommend H.R. 7152, as amended, to all my colleagues from wheresoever they may come.

Mr. WILLIS. Mr. Chairman, I yield myself 45 minutes.

Mr. Chairman, I will have something to say about many parts of the bill before you, but I have been assigned the task of discussing titles I and II in particular. Other members of the Committee on the Judiciary, opposed to this legislation, will in turn undertake to discuss titles III to X in greater detail.

If that is your wish, I will be glad to answer questions as we go along but I think it would be better to give my views first. In that way I think we could save time because I suspect I might anticipate many of your questions in my general statement.

Before proceeding, however, I would like to say this: We live in an age of polls, labels, and slogans. In these polls, however, you and I are always the ratees and we are never given an opportunity to rate our raters. I assure you, however, that I do not mind this at all because I regard it as a small price to pay for the rewards that come with public service.

Every year we must be rated by various and sundry groups and organizations such as ADA, ACA, AFL-CIO, NAM, AMA, PTA, NEA, Farm Bureau, and so on and on. And the strange thing is that on identical bills one group might rate us as conservatives, while another might rate us as liberals, each according to their peculiar and rigid notions of the meaning of these relative terms.

I take the ratings as they come and can only draw some consolation from Robert Burns lament, "Oh, would some power the giftee give us, to see ourselves as others see us."

And the same is true with reference to legislation. Bills are almost invariably given "quickie" labels to either pass or defeat them. For example, foreign aid is called the Mutual Security Act. An act to quiet the longstanding title of a State is called tidelands oil. The public works bill is called a pork barrel—and so ad nauseam.

But that is not all, sometimes one can choose between two labels. He can be for medical care for the aged or against socialized medicine. And if he has not read the bill, he can say that he is for medical care for the aged and against socialized medicine at the same time. But for us there is always a day of reckoning. Ultimately we must vote on merits and not on labels and take the consequences—and that, too, is a small price to pay for responsible representation.

Now, some call this legislation civil rights legislation while others call it civil wrongs legislation. But a rose is a rose by whatever name it is called. Therefore, let us consider the proposal not either as conservatives or liberals, or whatever, but as responsible Members and let us study it on the basis of content and not labels.

(material omitted)

(material omitted)

Mr. RODINO. Mr. Chairman, before making a general statement on the need for this bill, I should like to refer to some of the statements made by some of the previous speakers—only very briefly, however—to clarify some of the points which were raised.

With reference to the statement made by the gentleman who preceded me on the question of title VI, I should like to point out to the gentleman that the answers which the gentleman read, which are purported to have been prepared by the Justice Department, are indeed not only reasonable answers to the questions which were raised but also expressly justify the action which would be taken in each particular case under title VI.

Title VI is designed not to cut off Federal financial assistance in any program, but is designed to prevent discrimination. It is true, as the gentleman from Louisiana remarked earlier, that there is a mandatory requirement on the particular agency to set up rules and regulations and requirements to effectuate the provision in section 601, which is intended to end discrimination; but, nonetheless, every opportunity is to be given under that section for the recipient of that assistance to comply. When he complies and there is no longer any discrimination, then there will be no need to cut off financial assistance.

I wish to also point out the fact that the question was raised as to title VII. How did title VII come into the bill? Title VII which deals with Federal employment practices, was a subject which was treated before our committee at great length. Many of the bills introduced and many of the bills spoken on before the Judiciary Committee covered the need to remove, to eradicate, or to eliminate discrimination in employment. As a matter of fact, the original administration bill related itself to the question of an Equal Employment Opportunity Commission, the President's Commission on Equal Employment Opportunity. So it comes with no surprise that title VII is in the bill.

Mr. Chairman, this is a historic week for the House of Representatives and for the Nation. The 88th Congress has had and will have no more important legislation before it than the civil rights bill which we are debating today.

Perhaps, Mr. Chairman, it might also be said that we shall debate no bill more controversial than this. From the time President Kennedy's message on civil rights was first transmitted to the Congress, in June of last year, it has been surrounded by an increasing tempo of debate, emotion, and, I fear, misunderstandings and misstatements of fact.

It is unfortunate that this should be so, for if any bill deserves a dispassionate weighing of needs and facts, this is it. This bill deals with the fundamental American dream that all men are created equal, and that equal opportunity for a better life should be within the reach of all. This bill deals with human beings, with their rights, their well-being, and their dignity.

The debate today has been without rancor and without bitterness.

I hope that, for the duration of this debate, the House will adopt the admonition of Isaiah:

Come now, and let us reason together.

Mr. Chairman, this bill is founded upon those same principles which have formed the cornerstone of our democratic government from the very beginning. Even before our Constitution was adopted, the leaders of the American Revolution created a ringing statement of belief, a declaration of conscience which told the world how Americans felt about people and their governments.

As we debate this bill, I hope all of us will keep in mind these stirring words from the Declaration of Independence:

We hold these truths to be self-evident, that all men are created equal, that they are endowed by their Creator with certain unalienable rights, that among these are life, liberty, and the pursuit of happiness.

It is up to us, 188 years later, to assure to all Americans these unalienable rights.

It is tragic that this should be so, for what we seek to do today should have been done long ago.

For too long Negroes in America have been denied that most fundamental democratic right, the right to vote.

For too long Negroes in America have been shamed by being turned away from a restaurant, a theater, or a hotel simply because of the color of their skin.

For too long Negroes in America have been deprived of equal access to schools and other public facilities, for which they help to pay with their own tax dollars.

For too long Negroes in America have been segregated in the hospitals and schools and other programs paid for in part with Federal funds.

And for too long Negroes in America have been denied the equal opportunity to jobs.

There are too many items on this list, Mr. Chairman. These wrongs cry out for redress.

I am proud to say that it is not only Negroes themselves who are today demanding redress of grievances. Religious and labor groups have been most active in focusing public attention on the problems of civil rights.

National bodies of Catholics, Protestants, and Jews have all taken strong stands in support of civil rights action by the Congress. A large number of priests, ministers, and rabbis in my own congressional district have communicated to me their keen interest in the passage of H.R. 7152. And it appears to me that the laity is in very substantial accord with the bill, for I have received a large number of comments not only in support of the bill, but in support of prompt passage of the bill.

Among the most enthusiastic supporters of civil rights legislation generally, and of H.R. 7152 in particular, is the labor movement. The AFL–CIO and many of its affiliated unions have urged the Congress to pass H.R. 7152, and I have received letters from a number of union members urging passage. Labor is especially interested in the adoption of the fair employment practices section of the bill.

Mr. Chairman, there are those who say that this bill is dangerous to the country, that it will destroy our social fabric and somehow shake the very foundations of our Government.

I may say that our experience in New Jersey is to the contrary. In my State, we have strong statutes assuring fair employment practices, guaranteeing equal access to public accommodations, prohibiting segregation in both public and private schools, and providing against discrimination in private housing.

Our first antidiscrimination law was adopted in 1945, and other laws have continually strengthened the State's antidiscrimination policy in subsequent years.

In all the time these laws have been in effect they have not destroyed the fundamental virtues of the people and government of the State of New Jersey, they have enhanced them. I believe we are stronger economically, politically, and socially in New Jersey than we were before these laws were passed.

The passage and enforcement of these laws have lifted from our consciences a part of the terrible burden which discrimination imposes on both Negro and white, and left us with greater freedom of both mind and spirit; greater freedom to march forward on the road to brotherhood and greater freedom to overcome all the other obstacles to a better life.

As it has been in New Jersey and in the other States which have recognized their responsibilities in the field of race relations and have moved to accept them, so it will be in the Nation as a whole when the Congress follows their example.

Let no man here today forget that this civil rights bill is not just for Negroes; it is for all of us.

Mr. Chairman, the Nation has made some progress in guaranteeing civil rights in recent years. Compared with the progress made in the 80 years following the Civil War, the progress achieved in the last 20 years has been substantial, perhaps even dramatic.

This progress, however, has not been at the hands of the legislative branch of the Government.

Through individual action, much progress has been made in desegregating public facilities and public accommodations. Some of this progress has been made by voluntary action of businessmen and public officials. Some of it has been made by private individuals through appeals to their fellow citizens through public demonstrations. Much of it has been made by quiet efforts at mediation and conciliation.

Through action of the executive branch of the Federal Government, segregation in the Armed Forces has been largely eliminated. Discrimination in employment by Government contractors, a group which includes most of the country's largest employers, is being steadily diminished. The Federal Government itself, the Nation's largest employer, has by order of the President increased its efforts to assure nondiscrimination in Federal employment. And an Executive order of the President has begun the long process of eliminating segregation in publicly assisted housing.

Through action of the Supreme Court, the segregation of public schools and other public facilities has been held unconstitutional, and the courts have begun to deprive the States of their use of police power to enforce segregation in privately owned public accommodations.

Through the Congress of the United States, no substantial progress has been made at all.

Up to this moment the Congress of the United States has yet to recognize in any official act the historic decision of the Supreme Court of the United States which rendered public school segregation unconstitutional.

It has failed to prevent the use of Federal funds to finance segregated schools.

It has failed to prevent the use of Federal funds to build segregated hospitals.

It has failed to provide an effective means for guaranteeing the right to vote.

It has failed to act against discrimination in employment, and in privately owned restaurants, hotels, theaters, and other public accommodations.

Let us end this record of failure with a record of achievement. Let us pass this civil rights bill.

The bill itself merits passage. It is not too moderate, as some have said. It is not extreme, as others have charged. It is a strong bill, designed to meet specific problems and meet them effectively.

The bill is a product of lengthy public hearings and exhaustive discussion and analysis in executive session. Those who say that there are provisions in this bill which were not considered in committee are wrong, because the hearings on civil rights conducted by the subcommittee covered everything in this bill, and far more.

I shall vote for this bill proudly. Although no bill can cure all the ills which our Nation tolerates, although this bill could be drafted to cure more ills than it does, yet this bill will achieve more to advance the cause of civil rights than all the governmental actions of the last 100 years put together.

H.R. 7152 will dramatically improve the opportunities of Negroes to vote. It will hasten the desegregation of public schools and public facilities, a process which has been intolerably delayed. In many areas of the Nation, it will give Negroes confidence to sit at a lunch counter—how modest an advance that is—or take an overnight drive or buy a ticket at a motion picture theater without fear. It will reassure them that the country which they love, the country which they fought for, and for which their fathers and husbands and sons died, the country which they serve as responsible citizens, that that country will honor its promise of respect and brotherhood.

Mr. Chairman, passage of this bill will be a monument to the Nation. It will show the world that we are what we say we are, a democratic society, based on the principle of equality for all men.

It will also be a monument to the great men of this and past generations whose ideas have pointed the way for us. To Thomas Jefferson, whose words in the Declaration of Independence I have already quoted. To Abraham Lincoln, the author of the Emancipation Proclamation. To President Kennedy, who first presented this bill to the Congress, and to President Johnson, who so strongly urges its passage.

For them, but mostly, for our fellow citizens of the United States who need it so badly, let us pass this bill.

Mr. BECKER. Mr. Chairman, will the gentleman yield for a question, please?

Mr. RODINO. I yield to the gentleman from New York.

Mr. BECKER. I think the gentleman is making a very fine speech, but what is bothering me is, if we are going to listen to 5 hours of speeches this afternoon, I wonder about this, because the gentleman said that we should debate this bill. I am wondering when we are going to get an opportunity to do some work on this bill. If we are going to have 10 hours of speeches on this thing, which is the way it looks now, I do not think we will ever get a chance to debate the bill. I wonder if the gentleman agrees with me that we should get a chance to debate this bill section by section, and under the 5-minute rule we will have not enough time.

Mr. RODINO. I am sure the gentleman will have substantial opportunity. There are many sections to this bill, and I understand both sides have agreed that no Member will be precluded from talking on this bill.

Mr. BECKER. As for talking on it, I will agree with the gentleman, but I do not know that that is going to serve any purpose. We would like to talk about what is in each section of the bill so we can get an understanding of it.

Mr. RODINO. I believe the gentleman will have that opportunity when we come to the 5-minute rule and debate each section of the bill.

Mr. BECKER. I disagree.

The CHAIRMAN. The time of the gentleman from New Jersey has expired.

Mr. CELLER. Mr. Chairman, I yield such time as he may desire to the gentleman from Florida [Mr. BENNETT].

Mr. BENNETT of Florida. Mr. Chairman, the bill now before us is unconstitutional for a substantial number of reasons and should therefore be defeated. There are things in race relationships which undoubtedly need remedying, but tyrannical and undemocratic procedures of unconstitutional legislation cannot be excused.

We must not yield to the pressure of mobs, threats, physical obstructions, disregard of public laws and private rights, and bow to the political expediences of the times to flaunt the Constitution. To do so would be a dangerous precedent and an unnecessary weakening of the stability of our Government, not only now, but in the future.

I have drafted a constitutional amendment, House Joint Resolution 728, known as the freedom of association amendment now pending before the House Judiciary Committee, in an effort to properly submit the issues to the country. I asked the Rules Committee to make it possible for this to be offered as a substitute amendment to the bill before us now, but they rejected this request and the House Parliamentarian has advised me it would therefore be out of order to offer this in the present debate.

In an effort to take a positive and helpful approach to the problems of housing, motels, hotels, restaurants, and so forth, for Negroes, I have introduced H.R. 8881, the Voluntary Accommodations Act now pending before the House Banking and Currency Committee. I have asked the appropriate committees to request departmental reports and I have also asked for early hearings to be heard on this legislation, which I hope can be accomplished.

In addition to the constitutional objections that I have to this bill before us now, I have many objections to specific provisions as creating in the executive branch, tyrannical powers both unjustified and improper.

I sincerely hope this bill be defeated.

(material omitted)

(material omitted)

(material omitted)

Mr. WATSON. Mr. Chairman, I am sure all of us are thrilled at the terrific speech which has just been made by my very esteemed colleague from Georgia [Mr. FORRESTER]. It certainly would be a presumption on my part to imagine for a moment I could even attract your attention, let alone measure up to the job he has done. I am grateful to the gentleman from Ohio for yielding me 10 minutes. I did not expect this to come until tomorrow, but I am delighted to have the opportunity and welcome the privilege of saying a word or two concerning this matter which I feel so very strongly about.

Let me say that notwithstanding the accusations which have been made in other places that we of the Southland have put these people of the Negro race under subjugation, that we have treated them wrongly, that we are hatemongers, may I just remind you, Mr. Chairman, for a few minutes that over the past 100 years we have been the true friends of the Negro race.

Notwithstanding our defeat, and being in ashes 100 years ago, when we southerners ate, everybody ate. When we had clothes, everybody had clothes. To be sure, we had varying standards of living down there, just as you have them from one end of the States to the other, but we were continually helping the Negro although our means were very limited. I wonder where were all of these bleeding hearts back over the past 100 years when we of the South were trying to give an education to these people who were unable to pay for it themselves, and most of them were unable to pay any taxes whatsoever. Where were all of these bleeding hearts who want to come out today and say, "Let me be a Moses, let me lead you to the promised land?" Let there be no mistake about it, we in the Southland believe in opportunities for all. We have not had the wealth that many of you in other sections of the Nation have had and therefore we have not been able to make the progress we would have made in lifting the standard of living for all of our people; but at the same time, notwithstanding the heavier burden that we had, we did the best we could.

I think it is just short of treason now that we have so many from other sections of the country that are running down South and stirring up trouble and dividing people who have lived together so well in harmony. Do not think for a moment that it is not easy to create animosity and dissension in every section of the United States, to run over and try to pit this race against another race, and it will work everywhere.

Do you think there is any particular problem in running out there and saying, "Look on the other side of the street, John. Are you not as good as he?" Do

you have that home; do you have that nice car?" But again let me ask you, Where were all of these bleeding hearts for these folks who were supposedly suffering so much? Where have they been over the past 100 years when we of the Southland were trying to give better educational and economic opportunities for all of our people?

Another thing, let me point out to you, the passage of a law is ineffective in dealing with this very delicate problem. The chairman of the committee, the gentleman from New York [Mr. CELLER], said we have 30 States with statutes on their books forbidding discrimination, and 25 forbidding discrimination in employment. Yet at the same time some of those States have been plagued with riots, demonstrations, and disorders not even known to our Southland. I refer to the State of Ohio, in Cleveland. They had demonstrations last year and some 40 were injured. They are having serious racial trouble now. Perhaps you saw on television last night, the Cleveland disorders, demonstrations we have never seen in the Southland notwithstanding the agitation by outsiders who want to run down there and use our people and divide them for the sake of getting some money or some publicity. But do you realize the fact that the State of Ohio has had a law against discrimination I believe since 1955, yet is it effective in putting down or preventing these demonstrations and riots?

I am not trying to oversimplify this thing, but I think you must conclude one of two things. You look at Ohio, you look at Pennsylvania, you look at Colorado. I am not just singling out these States because most of our States have suffered these same problems. If you pass this bill all of the States will suffer this problem. You are agitating, you are asking for trouble, you are deluding, you are perpetrating a fraud on the people you purport to help, because you purport to open the doors of opportunity throughout the United States and you are not taking care of the basic need; that is, better education and economic opportunity for all of our people. That is what we are doing today in the Southland. That will solve the racial problems more than the passage of an unconstitutional and unworkable law.

If we look at these Northern States or other areas that are having trouble, most of which have laws forbidding discrimination on their books, we can either say that the law is ineffective in dealing with this very delicate personal problem of associations or else you must say that these States are not enforcing their civil rights laws. Do not say for a moment that I got up here and said that Ohio, Pennsylvania, Colorado or any of the other States or New Jersey are not enforcing their laws so far as civil rights are concerned. They are doing the very best they can. But it shows you that even a law on a State level is ineffective to deal with this very delicate personal problem.

Let us quit trying to deceive all of the people into believing that you can solve this problem with the wave of a magic legislative wand. All you are doing is

asking for more trouble. History will show you—even recent history will show you—we have had more disorders and demonstrations and racial unrest since the advent of the Civil Rights Commission than we ever had before.

I am privileged to serve on the Manpower Utilization Subcommittee of the House Committee on the Post Office and Civil Service. There was presented to us last year in testimony by the director of the so-called division of equal employment opportunities of the Post Office Department that they have had more complaints in the past 2 years since they introduced or set up this division than they had in the 6 years immediately preceding its establishment.

All you are doing is asking for trouble by the passage of this bill. It has been pointed out so effectively and clearly by Judge Willis and others that the bill is clearly unconstitutional. Certainly, you are going to have to face up to the fact that we need something in America upon which we have to cling and must preserve and respect as one of the most sacred documents that has ever been written—the Constitution. There is a way to amend the Constitution. To be sure, the framers of the Constitution made it difficult to amend—that is one of the things that has made our Constitution survive when other constitutions have crumbled—the fact that it is difficult of amendment. But, yet, the amendment process is easy enough, and if the amendment is necessary, then it will be passed. I would plead with the gentleman from the Committee on the Judiciary and, indeed, with all of you—if this is needed so much and if the people are so much for it, then why do you not follow the orderly process of amending the Constitution by the provisions set forth in the Constitution rather than trying to amend it here by the passage of a bill such as this on the floor of the Congress?

Let me say again, and I believe I speak for everyone down South—when you say this is an emotional issue—we do feel very strongly about it because we yield to no one in our patriotism and our love of country and our love of the Constitution. This is a very emotional problem. We want to preserve our Constitution. We want to give all of our citizens equal rights and equal opportunities. We do not want to deceive any of our citizens into believing that the passage of this law will give them better jobs or will open the doors to all of these areas to them. You are going to find this bill will drive further the wedge of racial dissension and animosity not only in the Southland but throughout the country. Let us be fair with all of the people. I believe in respecting the rights of the minorities as much as any man or woman in this body. But at the same time, I believe in respecting the rights of the majority. You cannot give one excessive rights without in turn trampling upon the rights of others.

This is a serious matter. In fact, it is the most important piece of legislation that we have considered not only in the brief span that I have been privileged to serve here, but I dare say it will be the most important matter that we shall have to consider in this or any other Congress. I do not want to be a fatalist, but if this measure is passed, I predict it will live to curse this Congress.

The CHAIRMAN. The time of the gentleman has expired.

Mr. McCULLOCH. Mr. Chairman, I wish to say to my distinguished colleague from South Carolina that the riots and demonstrations in Cleveland, Ohio, which we so much regret, were not the result of discrimination by reason of race, religion, or national origin, which is prevented by the Constitution. That fact is unmistakably clear.

Mr. WATSON. Mr. Chairman, will the gentleman yield for a minute?

Mr. McCULLOCH. I yield.

Mr. WATSON. I do not know what has precipitated the immediate disorders and dissension there. I understand from the press reports that it is a matter of the forced mixing in the school, perhaps trying to bring in the racial balance system which is foreign to education. Perhaps I am incorrect, but as I recall, the problem there last year arose from discrimination in employment at a hotdog stand at the Cleveland airport. If I am incorrect I apologize to the gentleman. I did not wish to single out Ohio.

Mr. McCULLOCH. I understand that, Mr. Chairman. Again I wish to make it unmistakably clear that the legislation now before the Committee has no effect and can have no effect on racial imbalance. as that term is known.

(material omitted)

———

[From the Washington Daily News, Oct. 18, 1963]

BLACKSTONE ON CIVIL RIGHTS

We are indebted to Representative WILLIAM S. MOORHEAD, of Pittsburgh, for further reminder that the public accommodations section of the civil rights bill is based on ancient Anglo-Saxon tradition.

A requirement that proprietors of public houses serve all comers existed in English law as early as 1450, Mr. MOORHEAD reports, citing a decision in the reign of King Henry VII.

He also calls attention to a section in Blackstone's Commentaries setting forth that "if an innkeeper or other victualler hangs out a sign and opens his house for travelers, it is an implied engagement to entertain all persons who travel that way * * * and an action will lie against him for damages if he, without good reason, refuses to admit a traveler."

Most American States adopted this as common law which still is in at least technical effect in some of the Southern States, though others have repealed it.

Reaffirmation, which is what the civil rights section on accommodations proposes, thus would recognize a traditional courtesy. This, in our opinion, is a key section of the bill. It should be passed.

Mr. TOLL. Mr. Chairman, the House Judiciary Committee, on which I serve, finally last November 20 reported out the compromise civil rights bill, which had been worked on for over 7 months.

This bill is not limited to one group of people. It has provisions which are very beneficial to all the people of our country.

One provision requires an educational survey on lack of opportunity due to race, color, religion, or national origin. The Attorney General is authorized to institute or intervene in cases involving denial of rights to full use of any facility owned, operated, or managed by public authority, where parties are unable to pursue legal remedy.

In connection with Federal aid, the administration bill contained a declaration that no law providing Federal assistance by grant, contract, loan, insurance, guaranty, or otherwise, shall require such assistance to be furnished in circumstances in which persons are discriminated against because of race, color, religion, or national origin. The compromise bill contains a declaration that all persons shall have the right to participate free from discrimination in all programs and activities receiving Federal financial aid.

The bill contains a section providing for the establishment of an Equal Employment Opportunity Commission which is authorized to initiate or receive charges, conduct investigations, seek voluntary solutions in cases where there is

discrimination because of race, color, religion, or national origin. In the event of failure to secure voluntary solution, the Commission is authorized to file a civil action for enforcement in a Federal district court.

The coverage is limited to employment under Federal contract and Federal employment. It applies to most employers of 25 or more employees—100 for the first year, 50 for the second year—and most unions of 25 or more members—100 for the first year, 50 for the second year—and by employment agencies—including State employment agencies assisted by USES—supplying employers covered under this bill.

This is really a fair employment practice section and 23 States, including Pennsylvania, already have FEPC laws. Now an advancement has been made in this bill with the proposal to establish a Federal Fair Employment Practices Commission.

The bill also contains important sections on voting rights in Federal elections; public accommodations—Pennsylvania already has a law on this subject; Civil Rights Commission; and the civil rights protection in which the Attorney General is authorized to intervene in private action to prevent denial of equal protection of law on account of race, color, religion, or national origin.

I very much hope that the Congress will act favorably on this measure.

Mr. CELLER. Mr. Chairman, I move that the Committee do now rise.

The motion was agreed to.

Accordingly, the Committee rose; and the Speaker having resumed the chair, Mr. KEOGH, Chairman of the Committee of the Whole House on the State of the Union, reported that that Committee, having had under consideration the bill (H.R. 7152) to enforce the constitutional right to vote, to confer jurisdiction upon the district courts of the United States to provide injunctive relief against discrimination in public accommodations, to authorize the Attorney General to institute suits to protect constitutional rights in education, to establish a Community Relations Service, to extend for 4 years the Commission on Civil Rights, to prevent discrimination in federally assisted programs, to establish a Commission on Equal Employment Opportunity, and for other purposes had come to no resolution thereon.

———

(material omitted)

b. Floor Amendment Excerpt: Rep. Smith's "Sex" Amendment (February 8, 1964)

The House came to no resolution on the civil rights bill on January 31, and the next day of debate was February 8, 1964. The dramatic moment of the debate came when Representative Smith (D-VA) offered an amendment to add "sex" to the categories of discrimination prohibited in the employment discrimination title of the bill. (Thus, the Smith Amendment would not apply to the public accommodations title, for example.)

In the debate that followed, note that the "conservative" Representative Smith makes arguments in favor of anti-discrimination protections—while "liberal" Representative Celler makes arguments against extending anti-discrimination precepts to sex and gender in the workplace. Why the switch in roles?

Read the arguments of the various sides carefully. Notice that many of the female Representatives rose to speak on this issue, and consider the arguments that they made. After this short debate, the Smith Amendment was agreed-to by a 168-133 majority. Consider the questions about the Smith Amendment that appear on the page following the House Debate. On February 10, the House voted in favor of the civil rights bill, as amended.

(material omitted)

AMENDMENT OFFERED BY MR. SMITH OF VIRGINIA

Mr. SMITH of Virginia. Mr. Chairman, I offer an amendment.

The Clerk read as follows:

Amendment offered by Mr. SMITH of Virginia: On page 68, line 23, after the word "religion," insert the word "sex."

On page 69, line 10, after the word "religion," insert the word "sex."

On page 69, line 17, after the word "religion," insert the word "sex."

On page 70, line 1, after the word "religion," insert the word "sex."

On page 71, line 5, after the word "religion," insert the word "sex."

Mr. SMITH of Virginia. Mr. Chairman, this amendment is offered to the fair employment practices title of this bill to include within our desire to prevent discrimination against another minority group, the women, but a very essential minority group, in the absence of which the majority group would not be here today.

Now, I am very serious about this amendment. It has been offered several times before, but it was offered at inappropriate places in the bill. Now, this is the appropriate place for this amendment to come in. I do not think it can do any harm to this legislation; maybe it can do some good. I think it will do some good for the minority sex.

I think we all recognize and it is indisputable fact that all throughout industry women are discriminated against in that just generally speaking they do not get as high compensation for their work as do the majority sex. Now, if that is true, I hope that the committee chairman will accept this amendment.

That is about all I have to say about it except, to get off of this subject for just a moment but to show you how some of the ladies feel about discrimination against them, I want to read you an extract from a letter that I received the other day. This lady has a real grievance on behalf of the minority sex. She said that she had seen that I was going to present an amendment to protect the most important sex, and she says:

I suggest that you might also favor an amendment or a bill to correct the present "imbalance" which exists between males and females in the United States.

Then she goes on to say—and she has her statistics, which is the reason why I am reading it to you, because this is serious—

The census of 1960 shows that we had 88,331,000 males living in this country, and 90,992,000 females, which leaves the country with an "imbalance" of 2,661,000 females.

Now another paragraph:

Just why the Creator would set up such an imbalance of spinsters, shutting off the "right" of every female to have a husband of her own, is, of course, known only to nature.

But I am sure you will agree that this is a grave injustice—

And I do agree, and I am reading you the letter because I want all the rest of you to agree, you of the majority—

But I am sure you will agree that this is a grave injustice to womankind and something the Congress and President Johnson should take immediate steps to correct—

And you interrupted me just now before I could finish reading the sentence, which continues on:

immediate steps to correct, especially in this election year.

Now, I just want to remind you here that in this election year it is pretty nearly half of the voters in this country that are affected, so you had better sit up and take notice.

She also says this, and this is a very cogent argument, too:

Up until now, instead of assisting these poor unfortunate females in obtaining their "right" to happiness, the Government has on several occasions engaged in wars which killed off a large number of eligible males, creating an "imbalance" in our male and female population that was even worse than before.

Would you have any suggestions as to what course our Government might pursue to protect our spinster friends in their "right" to a nice husband and family?

I read that letter just to illustrate that women have some real grievances and some real rights to be protected. I am serious about this thing. I just hope that the committee will accept it. Now, what harm can you do this bill that was so perfect yesterday and is so imperfect today—what harm will this do to the condition of the bill?

The CHAIRMAN. The time of the gentleman from Virginia has expired.

Mr. CELLER. Mr. Chairman, I rise in opposition to the amendment.

Mr. SMITH of Virginia. Oh, no.

Mr. CELLER. Mr. Chairman, I heard with a great deal of interest the statement of the gentleman from Virginia that women are in the minority. Not in my house. I can say as a result of 49 years of experience—and I celebrate my 50th wedding anniversary next year—that women, indeed, are not in the minority in my house. As a matter of fact, the reason I would suggest that we have been living in such harmony, such delightful accord for almost half a century is that I usually have the last two words, and those words are, "Yes, dear." Of course, we all remember the famous play by George Bernard Shaw, "Man and Superman"; and man was not the superman, the other sex was.

I received a letter this morning from the U.S. Department of Labor which reads as follows:

U.S. DEPARTMENT OF LABOR,
OFFICE OF THE SECRETARY,
Washington, February 7, 1964.

This is in response to your inquiry about the reaction of the Women's Bureau to suggestions that the civil rights bill be amended to prohibit job discrimination on the basis of sex as well as race, creed, color, or national origin.

Assistant Secretary of Labor Esther Peterson who is in charge of the Women's Bureau has replied to requests for support of such an amendment in the following way:

"This question of broadening civil rights legislation to prohibit discriminations based on sex has arisen previously. The President's Commission on the Status of Women gave this matter careful consideration in its discussion of Executive Order 10925 which now prohibits discrimination based on race, creed, color, or national origin in employment under Federal contracts. Its conclusion is stated on page 30 of its report, "American Women," as follows:

"'We are aware that this order could be expanded to forbid discrimination based on sex. But discrimination based on sex, the Commission believes, involves problems sufficiently different from discrimination based on the other factors listed to make separate treatment preferable.'

"In view of this policy conclusion reached by representatives from a variety of women's organizations and private and public agencies to attack discriminations based on sex separately, we are of the opinion that to attempt to so amend H.R. 7152 would not be to the best advantage of women at this time."

So we have an expression of opinion from the Department of Labor to the effect that it will be ill advised to append to this bill the word "sex" and provide for discrimination on the basis of race, color, creed, national origin, and sex as well. Of course, there has been before us for a considerable length of time, before the Judiciary Committee, an equal rights amendment. At first blush it seems fair, just, and equitable to grant these equal rights. But when you examine carefully what the import and repercussions are concerning equal rights throughout American life, and all facets of American life you run into a considerable amount of difficulty.

You will find that there are in the equality of sex that some people glibly assert, and without reason serious problems. I have been reluctant as chairman of the Committee on the Judiciary to give favorable consideration to that constitutional amendment.

The CHAIRMAN. The time of the gentleman from New York has expired.

Mr. CELLER. Mr. Chairman, I ask unanimous consent to proceed for 5 additional minutes.

The CHAIRMAN. Is there objection to the request of the gentleman from New York?

There was no objection.

Mr. CELLER. You know, the French have a phrase for it when they speak of women and men. When they speak of the difference, they say "vive la difference."

I think the French are right.

Imagine the upheaval that would result from adoption of blanket language requiring total equality. Would male citizens be justified in insisting that women share with them the burdens of compulsory military service? What would become of traditional family relationships? What about alimony? Who would have the obligation of supporting whom? Would fathers rank equally with mothers in the right of custody to children? What would become of the crimes of rape and statutory rape? Would the Mann Act be invalidated? Would the many State and local provisions regulating working conditions and hours of employment for women be struck down?

You know the biological differences between the sexes. In many States we have laws favorable to women. Are you going to strike those laws down? This is the entering wedge, an amendment of this sort. The list of foreseeable consequences, I will say to the committee, is unlimited.

What is more, even conceding that some degree of discrimination against women obtains in the area of employment, it is contrary to the situation with respect to civil rights for Negroes. Real and genuine progress is being made in discrimination against women. The Equal Pay Act of 1963, for example, which became law last June, amends the Fair Labor Standards Act of 1938 by prohibiting discrimination between employees on the basis of sex, with respect to wages for equal work on jobs requiring equal skill, effort, and responsibility.

It is a little surprising to find the gentleman from Virginia offering the language he does offer as an amendment to the pending measure. The House knows that this is the language of a proposed constitutional amendment introduced in the House.

Mr. SMITH of Virginia. Mr. Chairman, will the gentleman yield?

Mr. CELLER. It is rather anomalous that two men of our age should be on the opposite sides of this question.

Mr. SMITH of Virginia. I am sure we are not. But I know the gentleman is under obligation not to submit any amendments other than those that are agreed upon between the coalition of the Republicans and Democrats that is controlling the movement of the committee. I wanted to ask the gentleman to clarify what he said. I did not exactly get what he stated about Negroes. He said he was surprised.

Mr. CELLER. I was a little surprised at your offering the amendment.

Mr. SMITH of Virginia. About what?

Mr. CELLER. Because I think the amendment seems illogical, ill timed, ill placed, and improper. I was of that opinion, the amendment coming from the astute and very wise gentleman from Virginia.

Mr. SMITH of Virginia. Your surprise at my offering the amendment does not nearly approach my surprise, amazement, and sorrow at your opposition to it.

Mr. CELLER. As long as there is a little levity here, let me repeat what I heard some years ago, which runs as follows:

Lives there a man with hide so tough
Who says, "Two sexes are not enough."

In any event, I refer again to the President's Commission. They came to the conclusion in these words:

The Commission strongly urges in the carrying out of this recommendation special attention be given to difficulties that are wholly or largely the products of this kind of discrimination.

The Commission says, wait until mature studies have been made. I say, wait, indeed, until more returns are in before we attempt to do anything like this on this bill. In any event, it should not be done piecemeal, it should be done generally and universally.

Mr. DOWDY. Mr. Chairman, I move to strike out the last word.

Mr. Chairman, as I have offered this same amendment to some of the prior titles to which it was applicable, including one concerning education, in which I placed in the RECORD a number of instances where women are discriminated against in getting an education, if the chairman of the committee will permit me to ask a question, this letter he read from the Women's Bureau, was it signed by a man or a woman?

Mr. CELLER. It was signed by a man.

Mr. DOWDY. I had an idea that would be true—the letter from the Women's Bureau of the Department of Labor opposing this equal rights for women amendment was signed by a man. I think there is no need for me to say more. Even the Department set up by the U.S. Government for the benefit of women is opposed to equal rights in employment for women. I urge the adoption of this amendment, I would have offered it myself, but yielded the honor to my beloved colleague from Virginia [Mr. SMITH].

Mrs. FRANCES P. BOLTON. Mr. Chairman, I rise in support of the amendment.

Mr. Chairman, it is always perfectly delightful when some enchanting gentleman, from the South particularly, calls us the minority group. We used to be but we are not any more. I have just had the figures sent me. You males, as you seem to like to call yourselves, are 88,331,494. We females, as you like to call us, are 90,991,681. So I regret to state that we can no longer be the minority; indeed, we have not been for some time.

Also, I would like to suggest that to read the sports news about the winter games in Innsbruck, I think it was a woman who rather saved the United States situation?

I think that perhaps this particular motion of the gentleman from Virginia may be displaced. I do not know enough about parliamentary methods to be certain, and I have not studied it. But I do propose to submit an amendment in the 10th title, which I am told is germane there, and I shall present it at the appropriate time.

Mr. BASS. Mr. Chairman, will the gentlewoman yield?

Mrs. FRANCES P. BOLTON. I yield to the gentleman from Tennessee.

Mr. BASS. With relation to her remarks and her amendment, I just got off an airplane.

Mrs. FRANCES P. BOLTON. You did?

Mr. BASS. Yes, now what I was leading up to is this. A young lady works for an airline company, and she is worried about discrimination against married women because she is about to get married. Then she will lose her job. So she wants something done to prevent discrimination against married women.

Mrs. FRANCES P. BOLTON. May I suggest to the gentleman that married women get along very well because they usually, after they have had their children and brought them to a certain age, go back into business to really protect the family against too little money.

Mr. BASS. I am for all women, I want the record to show that I am for both the unmarried and the married women.

Mr. SMITH of Virginia. Mr. Chairman, will the gentlewoman yield?

Mrs. FRANCES P. BOLTON. I yield to the gentleman.

Mr. SMITH of Virginia. If I understood the gentlewoman correctly, she said, I believe, that she would support this pending amendment that I have offered, but that you expect to offer an amendment to title X?

Mrs. FRANCES P. BOLTON. Yes; that is title X, the miscellaneous title.

Mr. SMITH of Virginia. I do not like the idea here of it going in under "miscellaneous." I think women are entitled to more dignity than that.

Mrs. FRANCES P. BOLTON. My colleague, may I suggest to you, that we are so used to being just "miscellaneous."

Mr. SMITH of Virginia. What I wanted to say is entirely in a cooperative spirit, but I suggest that the gentlewoman examine title X because I do not think there is any place there where it would be suitable and maybe it is not germane.

Mrs. FRANCES P. BOLTON. We can take that up when I offer the amendment. I am so happy to have the gentleman's opinion in the matter.

Mr. SMITH of Virginia. I was just hoping that the good gentlewoman was going to give her full support to my amendment, and then we will talk about her amendment.

Mrs. FRANCES P. BOLTON. I would also like to add at this moment when we have been victorious over there at Innsbruck, this statement: Even your bones harden long before our bones do—we live longer, we have more endurance.

Mrs. GRIFFITHS. Mr. Chairman, I move to strike out the last word and rise in support of the amendment.

Mr. Chairman, I presume that if there had been any necessity to have pointed out that women were a second-class sex, the laughter would have proved it.

Mr. Chairman, I rise in support of the amendment primarily because I feel as a white woman when this bill has passed this House and the Senate and has been signed by the President that white women will be last at the hiring gate.

In his great book "The American Dilemma," the Swedish sociologist pointed out 20 years ago that white women and Negroes occupied relatively the same position in American society.

Before I begin my argument, however, I would like to ask the chairman of the Committee on the Judiciary, the gentleman from New York, a question.

Mr. Chairman, is it your judgment that this bill will protect colored men and colored women at the hiring gate equally?

Mr. CELLER. This bill is all-embracing and will cover everybody in the United States.

Mrs. GRIFFITHS. It will cover every colored man and every colored woman?

Mr. CELLER. Yes, it will cover white men and white women and all Americans.

Mrs. GRIFFITHS. We will find out in just a few minutes how differently it is going to cover them.

Now I would like to ask you, if in your judgment this bill says at any point that a Negro woman will only be protected if she is applying for a job historically held by a white woman?

Could she then invoke the act?

Mr. CELLER. It would apply to a Negro woman if she were proscribed or discriminated against on the basis of race.

Mrs. GRIFFITHS. If she applied for a job which had been historically held by a white man?

Mr. CELLER. I do not know about the "historically." The point is, if there is evidence that she has been proscribed or discriminated against in hiring, firing, promotion, or in matters of seniority, and if there were an element of discrimination which could be proved and demonstrated, then there would be a violation of the act involved.

Mrs. GRIFFITHS. Then may we consider an example. Suppose a Negro woman had been washing dishes in a "greasy spoon," a very poor restaurant, and farther up the street there was a very good restaurant which employed only white people, and all the dishwashers were white men. Suppose they put a sign in the window, "dishwasher wanted." The Negro woman with experience, qualified, let us suppose, applied for the job and was turned away.

In the chairman's judgment, could she invoke the provisions of the act?

Mr. CELLER. If the Negress who applied for the job was disqualified because of the pigmentation of her skin, because she was colored, the act would apply.

Mrs. GRIFFTTHS. Suppose the employer said to her, "No, we will not employ you as a dishwasher. We have only men dishwashers." And suppose she replied, "Sir, you have only white people in this restaurant. I am qualified."

Mr. CELLER. It all involves a question as to whether or not there has been discrimination based upon color. That is a question of fact which has to be determined, finally.

Mrs. GRIFFITHS. In your judgment—and you are a good lawyer—that woman would have made a prima facie case, would she not?

Mr. CELLER. Not necessarily. We would want to get more facts. We would have to inquire.

Mrs. GRIFFITHS. That is the easy case. Let us make it tougher.

Suppose there were three men dishwashers and two women dishwashers and one man dishwasher quit, and they wished to fill one job. Suppose the Negro woman applied, and was qualified.

Would she not have made a prima facie case?

Mr. CELLER. If it can be said that she is qualified and that the employer deliberately refused to accept her because of the color of her skin, then there would be the discrimination covered by this act.

Mrs. GRIFFITHS. Right.

The CHAIRMAN. The time of the gentlewoman from Michigan has expired.

(By unanimous consent, Mrs. GRIFFITHS was given permission to proceed for 5 additional minutes.)

Mr. CELLER. May I add, of course the gentlewoman did not take into consideration the numerical requirements; that in the first year of the operation of the act the place would have 100 employees, in the second year 50 employees, and in the third year 25.

Mrs. GRIFFITHS. We will be glad to make it the first year after the act, and 100 employees. That is no problem at all.

Let us try the next case.

I come from a city in which there is a university. It is my understanding that there has never been a woman political scientist employed at that university to teach political science. Suppose a colored woman political scientist applied for a job. Could she or could she not invoke the act?

Mr. CELLER. Of course, we are addressing ourselves to business activity. It is conceivable that colleges might be covered. There again, if there were discrimination then there would be a violation.

Mrs. GRIFFITHS. Could a white woman turned away from the college or from the restaurant where all the employees were white invoke the act? Would a white woman have any recourse under the act?

Mr. CELLER. I think we covered that in colloquies we had in the earlier part of the afternoon. There could be discrimination against white people and there could be against colored people.

Mrs. GRIFFITHS. Mr. Chairman, you know well and good if every employee of that restaurant were white, that that woman cannot go to the FEPC or to a district attorney and say, "I was turned away from there because I was white," because every employee is white there.

Mr. CELLER. That is speculation. Of course, that may be due to the derelictions of the particular Government agency; and if there are such cases, there is discrimination, and I think we, as Members of Congress, should all complain if it happens. You have, for example, in your own State, I am just informed, an FEPC, and if that occurred in your State, I think they ought to be notified and you ought to ask some questions of that FEPC.

Mrs. GRIFFITHS. Mr. Chairman, I had a white woman come to my office who had been turned away from the FEPC. They refused even to consider her case. She had gone directly to the Michigan Unemployment Compensation Commission. They had not only considered her case, but they gave her compensation on the basis that no person has to work in fear of their life. The Fair Employment Practices Commission of Michigan refused to acknowledge they ever considered the case and that she ever made the complaint.

Mr. CELLER. Knowing the true and dedicated spirit in which you do your work, if that lady came to you, I am sure you would get redress for her.

Mrs. GRIFFITHS. Thank you very much, Mr. Chairman.

Now, Mr. Chairman, I would like to proceed to some of the arguments I have heard on this floor against adding the word "sex." In some of the arguments, I have heard the comment that the chairman is making, which is, that this makes it an equal rights bill. Of course it does not even approach making it an equal rights bill. This is equal employment rights. In one field only—employment. And if you do not add sex to this bill, I really do not believe there is a reasonable person sitting here who does not by now understand perfectly that you are going to have white men in one bracket, you are going to try to take colored men and colored women and give them equal employment rights, and down at the bottom of the list is going to be a white woman with no rights at all.

Let me repeat the example that I have just given you in the case of the restaurant. In that particular case, or in the case of the university, the chairman knows and I know that a white woman, when she asks for that job and is turned away, has no recourse, and nobody on earth has to explain for it. Furthermore, they have been turned away so many times in so many cases, without writing but with laughter, that it will be impossible for any employee to prove that an employer has systematically discriminated against women on account of sex. So, when the colored woman shows up and she is qualified, she is going to have an open entree into any particular field.

Now, when I brought this up with various lawyers on the floor, one of them suggested to me that I was really trying to give a 100-pound woman the right to drive a haulaway truck. So I got to thinking about it. That is not really what I am trying to do, but let us take a case. Supposing a little 100-pound colored woman arrives at the management's door and asks for the job of driving a haulaway truck, and he says, "Well, you are not qualified," and she says, "Oh, yes, I am. During the war I was the motorman on a streetcar in Detroit. For the last 15 years I have driven the schoolbus."

Surely, Mr. Chairman, we are hiring the best drivers to drive the most precious cargo. Of course, that woman is qualified. But he has only white men drivers. Do you not know that that woman is not going to have a right under this law? Merely to ask the question is to answer it.

The CHAIRMAN. The time of the gentlewoman from Michigan [Mrs. GRIFFITHS] has expired.

Mrs. GRIFFITHS. Mr. Chairman, I ask unanimous consent to proceed for 5 additional minutes.

The CHAIRMAN. Is there objection to the request of the gentlewoman from Michigan?

There was no objection.

Mrs. GRIFFITHS. Now, it has been suggested to me by one Member on the floor that if a job were repeatedly filled by colored women, that a white woman would be able to invoke the Federal Employment Practices Act. In my judgment, as long as a majority of the drivers in a haulaway concern were white drivers, as long as the majority of employees in the restaurant, in the university, were white people, no white woman could invoke the act. She will continue to work in the greasy spoon, drive the schoolbus, and do the other under-paid jobs.

Some people have suggested to me that labor opposes "no discrimination on account of sex" because they feel that through the years protective legislation has been built up to safeguard the health of women. Some protective legislation was to safeguard the health of women, but it should have safeguarded the health of men, also. Most of the so-called protective legislation has really been to protect men's rights in better paying jobs.

As late as 1948 such an argument came from the State of Michigan before the Supreme Court of the United States in the case of Goesart et al. against Cleary et al. In the most vulgar and insulting of decisions handed down in this century by the Supreme Court, notable for its lack of legal learning as well as for its arrogant prejudice, the majority of the Supreme Court decided that it was well within the police powers of the State of Michigan for the legislature to draw the most arbitrary and capricious of lines as to who could tend bar in Michigan.

I am happy to say that in the dissenting minority were Justices Rutledge and Frank Murphy of the State of Michigan who said:

> While the equal protection clause does not require a legislature to achieve "abstract symmetry" or to classify with "mathematical nicety" that clause does require lawmakers to refrain from invidious distinctions of the sort drawn by the statute challenged in this case.

In the majority opinion, however, there was a most interesting statement made which, I think when this bill is passed, may be tested. The majority said:

> The Constitution does not require a legislature to reflect sociological insight or shifting social standards any more than it requires them to keep abreast of the latest scientific standards.

Now, of course, that runs directly contrary to the statement made long ago that the decisions of the Supreme Court follow the election returns.

In my opinion, when this bill is passed, some of these arbitrary classifications passed in State statutes will be tested again by colored women, and I have yet to find a lawyer on this floor who cares to state unequivocally that the State law will continue to prevail.

In other words, if labor is seeking to maintain the old distinction, they wil do far better to support this amendment and ask for a savings clause in this law, and we will all start even in the morning.

It would be incredible to me that white men would be willing to place white women at such a disadvantage except that white men have done this before. When the 14th amendment had become the law of the land, a brave woman named Virginia Minor, native-born, free, white citizen of the United States and the State of Missouri, read the amendment, and on the 15th of October 1872, appeared to register to vote. The registrar replied that the State of Missouri had a statute which said that only males could register to vote. Her reply, of course, was, "Why, the 14th amendment says 'No State shall make or enforce any law which shall abridge the privileges or immunities of citizens of the United States.'"

In October 1874 in 13 pages of tortured legal reasoning, the Supreme Court of the United States explained how the Missouri law prevailed, and finally said:

> The amendment did not add to the privileges and immunities of a citizen. It simply furnished an additional guaranty for the protection of such as he already had.

So, Mr. Chairman, your greatgrandfathers were willing as prisoners of their own prejudice to permit ex-slaves to vote, but not their own white wives.

The CHAIRMAN. The time of the gentlewoman has expired.

Mrs. GRIFFITHS. Mr. Chairman, I ask unanimous consent to address the House for 5 additional minutes.

The CHAIRMAN. Is there objection to the request of the gentlewoman from Michigan?

There was no objection.

Mrs. GRIFFITHS. Mr. Chairman, more than 40 years passed before the 19th amendment gave women the right to vote. But white women alone did not secure that right. White men voted for that right; but white people alone did not secure that right. Colored men voted for that right, and colored women were among the suffragettes. Sojourner Truth, a Detroit woman, was the greatest of all of these.

Mr. Chairman, a vote against this amendment today by a white man is a vote against his wife, or his widow, or his daughter, or his sister.

If we are trying to establish equality in jobs, I am for it, but I am for making white women equal, also.

Mrs. ST. GEORGE. Mr. Chairman, I move to strike out the requisite number of words.

Mr. Chairman, I was somewhat amazed when I came on the floor this afternoon to hear the very distinguished chairman of the Committee on the Judiciary make the remark that he considered the amendment at this point illogical. I can think of nothing more logical than this amendment at this point.

This bill, which I support, so that you will know that I am not just talking off the top of my head, this bill if it is to become law will be a law that exists in a stronger form in 32 States of our Union. It will then be imposed on the other 18 States.

In support of this I would like to read a colloquy which was held not in executive session, certainly, but in open session of the Rules Committee, in which I asked the ranking member of the Committee on the Judiciary, the gentleman from Ohio [Mr. McCULLOCH], about this very thing. If you will bear with me a minute, I will read it:

Mrs. ST. GEORGE. Mr. Chairman, there is one question I would like to ask the gentleman from Ohio. Is it a fact that the law as now constituted in your State of Ohio and in my State of New York is, if anything, stronger than the law as it will be if this legislation passes?

Mr. McCULLOCH. The law of the State of New York and the law of the State of Ohio is much stronger in the affected fields than is this legislation.

Mrs. ST. GEORGE. Another question. There are 32 States, as I understand it, that already have civil rights legislation. Are those States also in most cases stronger in their civil rights legislation than they would be under this law?

Mr. McCULLOCH. Without having read every State statute, I would say the States with the large populations without exception have legislation in this field that is stronger than that which we propose.

Mrs. ST. GEORGE. Going on from there, in other words, there are 18 States that do not have such legislation, is that correct?

Mr. McCULLOCH. That is correct.

Mrs. ST. GEORGE. So, this is really being written for those 18 States, to all intents and purposes, because we already have this, so this will not make any very great difference to us, except if it supersedes the law of the State. Is it going to do that?

Mr. McCULLOCH. It is not intended to supersede the laws of the States, except when it is in conflict and grants or insures lesser rights than are provided for in this legislation.

Mrs. ST. GEORGE. Otherwise, as in my State of New York, we will continue to function under the law as it is now written in the State of New York, and in your State of Ohio it will be the same thing?

Mr. McCULLOCH. That is true.

Mrs. ST. GEORGE. So, when we come right back to brass tacks, this is legislation written for 18 States which do not have civil rights legislation at the present time.

Mr. McCULLOCH. I think that is an accurate statement, yes.

The reason I bring that up is that a great many gentlemen, the predominating membership of this House, have a facetious way of saying to any woman on the question of equality, equal rights under the law, and so forth, "But you have all that already."

Mr. Chairman, I am willing to admit that in a great many States we have got it already.

The CHAIRMAN. The time of the gentlewoman from New York has expired.

(By unanimous consent, Mrs. ST. GEORGE was allowed to proceed for 5 additional minutes.)

Mrs. ST. GEORGE. But there are still many States where this equality does not exist.

There are still many States where women cannot serve on juries. There are still many States where women do not have equal educational opportunities. In most States and, in fact, I figure it would be safe to say, in all States—women do not get equal pay for equal work. That is a very well known fact.

Protective legislation prevents, as my colleague from the State of Michigan just pointed out—prevents women from going into the higher salary brackets. Yes, it certainly does.

Women are protected—they cannot run an elevator late at night and that is when the pay is higher.

They cannot serve in restaurants and cabarets late at night—when the tips are higher—and the load, if you please, is lighter.

So it is not exactly helping them—oh, no, you have taken beautiful care of the women.

But what about the offices, gentlemen, that are cleaned every morning about 2 or 3 o'clock in the city of New York and the offices that are cleaned quite early here in Washington, D.C.? Does anybody worry about those women? I have never heard of anybody worrying about the women who do that work.

So you see the thing is completely unfair.

And to say that this is illogical. What is illogical about it? All you are doing is simply correcting something that goes back, frankly to the Dark Ages. Because what you are doing is to go back to the days of the revolution when women were chattels. Of course, women were not mentioned in the Constitution. They belonged, first of all, to their fathers; then to their husbands or to their nearest male relative. They had no command over their own property. They were not supposed to be equal in any way, and certainly they were never expected to be or believed to be equal intellectually.

Well, I will admit from what I have seen very frequently here, I think the majority sex in the House of Representatives may not consider us mentally quite equal, but I think on the whole considering what a small minority we are here that we have not done altogether too badly.

I think for that reason, if for no other, we would like to be given more opportunities.

I can assure you we can take them.

I can assure you that we have fought our way a long way since those days of the Revolution. We have fought our way a long way even since the beginning of this century. Why should women be denied equality of opportunity? Why should women be denied equal pay for equal work? That is all we are asking.

We do not want special privileges. We do not need special privilege. We outlast you—we outlive you—we nag you to death. So why should we want special privileges?

I believe that we can hold our own. We are entitled to this little crumb of equality.

The addition of that little, terrifying word "s-e-x" will not hurt this legislation in any way. In fact, it will improve it. It will make it comprehensive. It will make it logical. It will make it right.

Mrs. GREEN of Oregon. Mr. Chairman, I move to strike the requisite number of words.

Mr. Chairman, I suppose that this may go down in history as "women's afternoon," but the women of the House, I feel sure, recognize that you men will be the ones who finally make the decision.

I wish to say first to the gentleman who offered this amendment and to others who by their applause I am sure are giving strong support to it that I, for one, welcome the conversion, because I remember when we were working on the equal pay bill that, if I correctly understand the mood of the House, those gentlemen of the House who are most strong in their support of women's rights this afternoon, probably gave us the most opposition when we considered the bill which would grant equal pay for equal work just a very few months ago. I say I welcome the conversion and hope it is of long duration.

I do not know whether I am in the minority or whether I am in the majority earlier referred to by the gentleman from Virginia and I do not know whether, after I leave the floor today, I shall be called an "uncle Tom"—or perhaps an "aunt Jane." However, as the author of the equal pay bill and as a member of the President's Commission on the Status of Women, I believe I have demonstrated my concern and my determination to advance women's opportunities in every reasonable way possible. But—I do not believe this is the time or place for this amendment.

Let me say first that I agree with many of the statements my women colleagues have made about the great amount of discrimination against women. Any woman who wants to have a career, who wants to go into the professions, who wants to go to work, I feel cannot possibly reach maturity without being very keenly and very painfully made aware of all the discrimination placed against her because of her sex.

This is true when I am invited to a club in Washington as a guest to attend a conference, and when I arrive at the front door to attend that conference, solely because I am a woman, I have to go to the side door to gain admittance.

I do not know whether you gentlemen realize it, but not long ago—in fact, in September—a group of Latin American editors were invited to the Press Club here in Washington, D.C. When that group of 12 Latin American editors arrived there was one woman among them, and the group was barred admission to the Press Club and held up for 20 minutes because one woman was in the group. After 20 minutes the group, including the woman editor, was finally escorted up the fire steps at the back of the building. That is a matter of record.

I do not feel that anyone can really, honestly deny various discriminations in many ways.

Mr. Chairman, discrimination is also rampant in politics. You gentlemen want the women to work in your campaigns, but I hear more jokes about women in politics than about women in any other field.

If I may digress, I have tremendous admiration for MARGARET CHASE SMITH—for her ability, for her integrity, for her political courage. I do not know—but deep down in her heart I do not believe she feels honestly she could possibly win this year—but what wonderful courage! And perhaps she is making that sacrifice hit which will allow some woman at some time in the future to get to third base or possibly to score.

After I have said all of this Mr. Chairman, I honestly cannot support the amendment. For every discrimination that has been made against a woman in this country there has been 10 times as much discrimination against the Negro of this country. There has been 10 times maybe 100 times as much humiliation for the Negro woman, for the Negro man and for the Negro child. Yes; and for the Negro baby who is born into a world of discrimination.

From the first day of life that baby is the object of discrimination—sometimes subtle, sometimes cruel, and he or she will feel it far more keenly all of his life than I possibly could. Yes—the Negro will suffer far more from discrimination than any discrimination that has been placed against me as a woman or against any other woman just because of her sex. Whether we want to admit it or not, the main purpose of this legislation today is to try to help end the discrimination that has been practiced against Negroes. This becomes almost a way of life. May I submit to my women colleagues, while I join with you in objecting to the discrimination against women, may I say that in all fairness the discrimination against the female of the species is not really a "way of life" and, I repeat, it is a way of life against Negroes in many parts of the country and has been for far too many years. And I must admit to my male colleagues that sometimes, in some ways, maybe women do get some advantages. However, this bill is primarily for the purpose of ending discrimination against Negroes in voting and in public accommodations and in education and, yes, in employment, under this FEPC law. As much as I hope the day will come when discrimination will be ended against women, I really and sincerely hope that this amendment will not be added to this bill. It will clutter up the bill and it may later—very well—be used to help destroy this section of the bill by some of the very people who today support it. And I hope that no other amendment will be added to this bill on sex or age or anything else, that would jeopardize our primary purpose in any way.

The CHAIRMAN. The time of the gentlewoman has expired.

Mr. THOMPSON of New Jersey. Mr. Chairman, I ask unanimous consent that the gentlewoman from Oregon [Mrs. GREEN] may proceed for 5 additional minutes.

The CHAIRMAN. Is there objection to the request of the gentleman from New Jersey?

There was no objection.

Mrs. GREEN of Oregon. Mr. Chairman, in the spirit of American freedom and liberty, cruel discriminations cry out to be corrected in this Nation. Today, I repeat, let us not add any amendment that would place in jeopardy in any way our primary objective of ending that discrimination that is most serious, most urgent, most tragic, and most widespread against the Negroes of our country.

May I also say I am not in complete agreement with everything that has been said by my women colleagues. I think that I, as a white woman, have been discriminated against, yes—but for every discrimination that I have suffered, I firmly believe that the Negro woman has suffered 10 times that amount of discrimination. She has a double discrimination. She was born as a woman and she was born as a Negro. She has suffered 10 times as much discrimination as I have. If I have to wait for a few years to end this discrimination against me, and my women friends—then as far as I am concerned I am willing to do that if the rank discrimination against Negroes will be finally ended under the so-called protection of the law.

May I say, Mr. Chairman, to the best of my knowledge, there was not one word of testimony in regard to this amendment given before the Committee on the Judiciary of the House or before the Committee on Education and Labor of the House, where this bill was considered. I repeat—there was not one single bit of testimony given in regard to this amendment. There was not one single organization in the entire United States that petitioned either one of these committees to add this amendment to the bill. There was not one single Member of the House who came to the Committee on Education and Labor or who came to the Committee on the Judiciary and offered such an amendment.

Finally, Mr. Chairman, may I read a letter which was sent to me yesterday which reads as follows. It is from the American Association of University Women:

Hon. EDITH GREEN,
House of Representatives,
Washington, D.C.

DEAR MRS. GREEN: It has been brought to the attention of the Legislative Program Committee of the American Association of University Women, which is meeting today, that it is probable that an amendment providing for the addition of the word "sex" to section 704 in title 7 of the civil rights bill on discrimination because of race, color, religion or national origin would be offered on the floor this afternoon. In our opinion the inclusion of the word "sex" in this title on discrimination is redundant and could actually work to the disadvantage of this very important legislation. We urge you to speak against this and other amendments which could weaken or impede the passage of this very vital legislation which you, as an AAUW member, know we in the association support.

Sincerely,

MARJORIE C. HAHN
Mrs. George C. Hahn,
Chairman, Legislative Program Committee.

Mr. ROOSEVELT. Mr. Chairman, will the gentlewoman yield?

Mrs. GREEN. I yield to the gentleman from California.

Mr. ROOSEVELT. Mr. Chairman, I want to pay tribute to the courage and to the objectiveness of the very distinguished lady from Oregon. I want to corroborate what she has said. I want to say simply that before the Committee on Education and Labor there was an agreement that the committee of which my mother had the privilege to be chairman, when it was appointed, it was with the understanding that it would finish its work and after it finished its work and a report came from the administration, then a bill would be considered in the proper course of events. I would certainly say to the gentlelady, and I think she will agree, that when that time comes and the recommendation is made we will try to find a way to eliminate the discriminations which have been spoken of without doing the injuries

which we all know also might exist if we legislated in an unwise fashion.

Mrs. GREEN. I thank the gentleman.

Mr. THOMPSON of New Jersey. Mr. Chairman, will the gentlewoman yield?

Mrs. GREEN. I yield to the gentleman from New Jersey.

Mr. THOMPSON of New Jersey. I have the good fortune to be the chairman of the subcommittee of the Committee on Education and Labor which handled the bill of the gentlewoman from Oregon providing, after years and years of effort on her behalf, equal pay for equal work for women. I know perfectly well that although this legislation is great and good, there are still things to be done. But I think the experience which the Congress had with respect to equal pay legislation might well be thought of carefully here.

In the first instance it was not considered carefully enough, moved too fast and was defeated in this body. There is much to be done, that is true. If one were to consider carefully all of the suggestions, there is much to be done. This is a difficult area in which to legislate. I think, however, that we do not want to go so fast and so far that the old rule of abandoning ship will be changed and the woman will have to take her place in line rather than to go first.

I do not think the gentlewoman from Oregon need yield to anyone, with all due respect to her colleagues, in the interests of legislating in behalf of women because she has proven it in the form of legislation. If one were to analyze all of the cases, the hypothetical cases set forth by our distinguished colleague from Michigan [Mrs. GRIFFITHS], it would appear that only color need be substituted for sex in those instances, and the result of every one of them would be changed.

So I thank the courageous gentlewoman from Oregon for her contribution, and I might say that I agree quite clearly with her.

Mrs. MAY. Mr. Chairman, I rise in support of the pending amendment.

Mr. Chairman, this indeed seems to be, as my distinguished colleage from Oregon stated, ladies' afternoon. You have heard eloquent, articulate, logical, and consistent arguments in support of this amendment from my distinguished fellow female colleagues from both sides of the aisle.

Certainly, the gentlewoman from Michigan [Mrs. GRIFFITHS] has outlined in effective legalistic terms what we are asking here today in the way of equal consideration for all women. The gentlewoman from New York [Mrs. ST. GEORGE] and the gentlewoman from Ohio [Mrs. BOLTON] and others have presented additional cogent arguments. I believe the case is fully presented, and I do not wish to prolong the debate.

However, in recognizing my colleague from Oregon [Mrs. GREEN], for her courageous stand, I would say that I do not think we can ever really assume what is in the mind of any one of the 435 Members of the House when he offers an amendment or prejudge any Member on how he intends to vote on a

measure. I would not assume that responsibility. I know the gentlewoman is sincere in her convictions, as I am sincere, because we have worked together in this field of trying to get an equal rights amendment to the Constitution. But may I point out to her that I just cannot assume, as she has, that the addition of this important amendment, no matter who offers it, will jeopardize this bill. We have been trying since 1923 to get enacted in the Congress an equal rights for women amendment to the Constitution.

Since 1923 more and more Members have offered this amendment, but we have never gotten the bill out of the Committee on the Judiciary. The League of Women Voters, some Federated Women's Clubs, the National Federation of Business and Professional Women have joined the National Woman's Party in consistently asking that wherever laws or Executive orders exist which forbid discrimination on account of race, color, religion, or national origin that these same laws and orders should also forbid discrimination on account of sex.

Recently in our congressional mail we received a letter from Emma Guffey Miller, national chairman of the National Woman's Party, which expresses alarm over the complete absence in this bill of any reference to civil rights for women. She says:

We are alarmed over the interpretation that may be given to the words "discrimination on the account of race, color, religion, and national origin" used in the bill, if the meaning of these words is not made clear in the bill itself. We are informed that in the past some government officials have interpreted "race, color, religion, and national origin" in a way that has discriminated against the white, native-born American woman of Christian religion.

I share the views of my colleague from Oregon in her desire to eliminate the proven discrimination which colored women have suffered, but at the same time I feel it is only just and fair to give all women protection against discrimination.

Mr. Chairman, this is to me the crux of the question before us. As I say, I am supporting the amendment on that basis and on behalf of the various women's organizations in this country that have for many years been asking for action from the Congress in this field, and who see this as the one possibility we may have of getting effective action.

I urge your support of this amendment.

Mrs. KELLY. Mr. Chairman, I move to strike the requisite number of words.

Mr. Chairman, I rise in support of this amendment. I feel I would be remiss in my duty if I did not so state. There is little I can add to the arguments of my colleagues who supported this amendment, the gentlewoman from Michigan who presented most legal arguments. My colleague from New York [Mrs. ST. GEORGE] who stated that "fringe benefits" and the protective laws of the several States would not be destroyed by our favorable action on this amendment. I also compliment my colleague from Oregon who is opposed to the amendment, for her arguments, even though I disagree with her position. If this section VII, equal employment opportunity section cannot be perfected to include women, then, it has no place in the bill. Why restore civil rights to all and fail to give equal opportunity to all. My support and sponsorship of this amendment and of this bill is an endeavor to have all persons, men and women, possess the same rights and same opportunities. In this amendment we seek equal opportunity in employment for women. No more—no less.

I do not want any person to secure more rights than any other, all I want is same opportunities and right—on and in all levels of government, or entities.

I do not want anyone to be denied that which is his or her inherent rights as an individual.

Let us recognize that there are many minorities in this country in all groups and organizations. There are minorities within groups as was mentioned this morning by previous speakers. For their opportunity, we seek to secure these rights under this bill—whether group is civic, social, or racial or an economic group.

It is unfortunate that there is not equal opportunity on account of economic status. It is reaching a point in this country when a person cannot seek public office because one lacks the economic status. This must, too, be corrected by proper legislation. Sure, all Americans do not want this. Furthermore, we do not want opportunities obtained on account of race, color, or creed, social status, or economic status—but on account of merit.

I admit there are many places of employment I would prefer not to have women employed but I never want to deny them the right if they wish to seek that employment.

I regret to state that the Department of Labor was against the equal pay bill for many, many years. I had introduced the bill back in 1951 and was delighted to have my colleague, the gentlewoman from Oregon [Mrs. GREEN], achieve its passage last year. Mrs. Peterson whose letter was read in opposition to the present amendment does not speak for all the women of the United States nor do the university women.

Again I state I am not for the equal pay amendment. I introduced the original equal pay bill as the answer to that amendment. I believe in equality for women, and am sure the acceptance of the amendment will not repeal the protective laws of the several States. I therefore urge all to support this amendment and hope it will prevail.

Mr. TUTEN. Mr. Chairman, I move to strike out the last word.

Mr. Chairman, I rise to compliment the performance of the brilliant female Members of this great body.

It has been brought out in the debate here today that I am definitely a member of a minority group. In view of the reference to Innsbruck and the brilliant performance here on the floor today, I accept my place, ladies, as a second-class citizen. Although I am second class and a member of a minority group, I rise

to inform the House that I always take my stand for the majority.

I have been vigorously opposed to this bill—not as a racist—but in the interest of the rights of all of the citizens of this country. Since I am a man, which places me in the minority and makes me a second-class citizen—and the fact that I am white and from the South—I look forward to claiming my rights under the terms of this legislation.

But, Mr. Chairman, the main purpose of my rising is this: Some men in some areas of the country might support legislation which would discriminate against women, but never let it be said that a southern gentleman would vote for such legislation.

Therefore, Mr. Chairman, I rise in support of this amendment.

Mr. POOL. Mr. Chairman, I move to strike out the last word and rise in support of the amendment.

Mr. Chairman, I arise in support of the amendment and point out that the interests and welfare of all American citizens, without distinction as to sex, shall prevail. This principle of equality of rights under the law for all citizens without distinction as to sex would thereby safeguard American women from such inequities with regard to their civil rights as are now threatened in the pending civil rights bill.

Mr. ANDREWS of Alabama. Mr. Chairman, I move to strike out the last word and rise in support of the amendment.

Mr. Chairman, I rise in support of this amendment offered by the gentleman from Virginia [Mr. SMITH]. Unless this amendment is adopted, the white women of this country would be drastically discriminated against in favor of a Negro woman.

If a white woman and a Negro woman applied for the same job, and each woman had the identical qualifications, the chances are about 99 to 1 that the Negro woman would be given the job because if the employer did not give the job to the Negro woman he could be prosecuted under this bill. Failure to employ the white woman would not subject the employer to such action.

Commonsense tells us that the employer would hire the Negro woman to avoid prosecution. The white woman will be at a great disadvantage in the business world unless this amendment is adopted.

Mr. RIVERS of South Carolina. I rise in support of the amendment offered by the gentleman from Virginia [Mr. SMITH] making it possible for the white Christian woman to receive the same consideration for employment as the colored woman. It is incredible to me that the authors of this monstrosity—whomever they are—would deprive the white woman of mostly Anglo-Saxon or Christian heritage equal opportunity before the employer. I know this Congress will not be a party to such an evil.

Mr. SMITH of Virginia. Mr. Chairman, I move to strike out the last word.

Mr. Chairman, I shall not take the 5 minutes but I want to call attention to the fact that the gentlewoman from Oregon read a letter from the Organization of University Women.

I did not mention it, but I assume all of you have received the same letter I received from the American Women's Party urging the adoption of this amendment. I hope you will take that into account in determining how to vote on this amendment.

There is one thing that I want to say that I think is extremely serious about this bill so far as white women are concerned.

If the bill is passed there is a provision in subparagraph (c) on page 79 which would require that every employer in the United States, from General Motors on down to anyone who employs as many as 25 people, keep an accurate record of all hiring and firing activities. That record would have to contain all of the details required by this Commission. The organization woud have to keep records as to why one was not employed and why another was employed.

I put a question to you in behalf of the white women of the United States. Let us assume that two women apply for the same job and both of them are equally eligible, one a white woman and one a Negro woman. The first thing that that employer will look at will be the provision with regard to the records he must keep. If he does not employ that colored woman and has to make that record, that employer will say, "Well, now, if I hire the colored woman I will not be in any trouble, but if I do not hire the colored woman and hire the white woman, then the Commission is going to be looking down my throat and will want to know why I did not. I may be in a lawsuit."

That will happen as surely as we are here this afternoon. You all know it.

I have not heard anybody give any valid reason why the amendment should not be adopted.

Mr. GARY. Mr. Chairman, will my distinguished colleague yield?

Mr. SMITH of Virginia. I yield to my colleague.

Mr. GARY. I wish to associate myself with my colleague in support of his amendment. I believe it is a good amendment and I trust the House will adopt it.

Mr. HUDDLESTON. Mr. Chairman, will the gentleman yield?

Mr. SMITH of Virginia. I yield to the gentleman from Alabama.

Mr. HUDDLESTON. I thank the gentleman for yielding. I shall take only a minute.

I do not wish to delay the further consideration of the bill any longer than necessary.

We have all heard this afternoon from some of the opponents of this amendment a hue and cry that this will do so much damage to the civil rights bill. Those of you who were in the House in 1957 will remember that, at that time, we considered an amendment to allow women to serve on Federal juries. That amendment was offered on the floor. At that time the hue and cry went out from these same partisans to the effect that it would ruin the bill. It did not ruin that bill.

I fail to see any logic in the argument that this amendment would do any damage to the legislation.

I thank the gentleman from Virginia for yielding.

Mr. WATSON. Mr. Chairman, will the gentleman yield?

Mr. SMITH of Virginia. I yield to the gentleman from South Carolina.

Mr. WATSON. Mr. Chairman, I commend my distinguished leader from Virginia for his foresight in presenting this splendid amendment. I join with him and others in wholehearted support of the amendment. I hope that it will pass to prove to everyone that we believe in equal rights for all people, and especially for the ladies of our Nation.

Mr. LINDSAY. Mr. Chairman, I move to strike the requisite number of words.

Mr. Chairman, I oppose the amendment, because I do not believe it belongs in this bill. I hope it will be voted down.

Mr. MATHIAS. Mr. Chairman, will the gentleman yield?

Mr. LINDSAY. I yield to the gentleman from Maryland.

Mr. MATHIAS. I concur fully with the gentleman from New York in opposition to the amendment.

Mrs. GREEN of Oregon. Mr. Chairman, will the gentleman yield?

Mr. LINDSAY. I yield to the gentlewoman from Oregon.

Mrs. GREEN of Oregon. I have been touched by the strong support of this legislation by some of my colleagues—for instance, the gentleman from Alabama [Mr. HUDDLESTON]. Could the gentleman tell me if he gave his support to the equal-pay-for-equal-work bill, considered a few months ago?

Mr. HUDDLESTON. Last year?

Mrs. GREEN of Oregon. Yes.

Mr. HUDDLESTON. I supported that legislation, and I also supported the amendment in the 1957 civil rights bill to allow women to serve on Federal juries. I intend to support the amendment this afternoon.

Mrs. GREEN of Oregon. I am glad the gentleman did. However, many of the people who are most ardent in support of this amendment today were among those who appeared before our committee and who talked to me on the floor and who were the strongest in their opposition to a very simple bill to provide equal pay for equal work for women.

Because of biological differences between men and women, there are different problems which will arise in regard to employment. These should be carefully considered by the Committee. There will be new problems for business, for managers, for industrial concerns. These should be taken into consideration before any vote is made in favor of the amendment without any hearings at all on the legislation.

Mr. ROOSEVELT. Mr. Chairman, will the gentleman yield?

Mr. LINDSAY. I yield to the gentleman from California.

Mr. ROOSEVELT. Mr. Chairman, I thank the gentleman for yielding. I want to quote from the President's Commission on Opportunities for Women of which, as I previously said, my mother was the Chairman. There are the fol-

lowing words in that report, and I hope you will all read them:

Actually situations vary far too much to make generalizations applicable and more information is needed on rates of quits, layoffs, absenteeism, and illness among women workers and on the qualifications of women for responsible supervisory or executive positions.

This is a clear indication that responsible women themselves recognize the problems that are inherent in any such approach as has now been proposed. I shall have to vote against the proposition.

Mr. CELLER. Mr. Chairman, will the gentleman yield?

Mr. LINDSAY. I yield to the gentleman from New York.

Mr. CELLER. I ask for this time in order to ask the gentleman from California if he will furnish some of the names of the women members and the organizations that are represented on that President's Commission of which your late lamented mother was Chairman.

Mr. ROOSEVELT. I do not want to take the time of the Committee to read all of them, but there are Dr. Mary I. Bunting, president, Radcliffe College; Mrs. Mary E. Callahan, member, executive board, International Union of Electrical, Radio & Machine Workers; Miss Dorothy Height, president, National Council of Negro Women, Inc.; Miss Margaret Hickey, public affairs editor, Ladies' Home Journal; Mrs. Viola H. Hymes, president, National Council of Jewish Women, Inc.; Miss Margaret J. Mealey, executive director, National Council of Catholic Women; Mr. William F. Schnitzler, secretary-treasurer, American Federation of Labor and Congress of Industrial Organizations; Dr. Cynthia C. Wedel, assistant general secretary for program, National Council of the Churches of Christ in the U.S.A.

I shall ask later for the privilege of inserting the entire list.

The list of all members of the Commission follows:

MEMBERS OF THE COMMISSION

The names of the men and women appointed to the Commission, and the posts they occupied at the time of their appointment, were:

Mrs. Eleanor Roosevelt, Chairman (deceased).

Mrs. Esther Peterson, Executive Vice Chairman, Assistant Secretary of Labor.

Dr. Richard A. Lester, Vice Chairman, Chairman, Department of Economics, Princeton University.

The Attorney General, Hon. Robert F. Kennedy.

The Secretary of Agriculture, Hon. Orville L. Freeman.

The Secretary of Commerce, Hon. Luther H. Hodges.

The Secretary of Labor, Hon. Arthur J. Goldberg, Hon. W. Willard Wirtz.

The Secretary of Health, Education, and Welfare, Hon. Abraham A. Ribicoff, Hon. Anthony L. Celebrezze.

Hon. George D. Aiken, U.S. Senate.

Hon. Maurine B. Neuberger, U.S. Senate.

Hon. Edith Green, U.S. House of Representatives.

Hon. Jessica M. Weis (deceased), U.S. House of Representatives.

The Chairman of the Civil Service Commission, Hon. John W. Macy, Jr.

Mrs. Macon Boddy, Henrietta, Tex.

Dr. Mary I. Bunting, president, Radcliffe College.

Mrs. Mary E. Callahan, member, executive board, International Union of Electrical, Radio & Machine Workers.

Dr. Henry David, president, New School for Social Research.

Miss Dorothy Height, president, National Council of Negro Women, Inc.

Miss Margaret Hickey, public affairs editor, Ladies' Home Journal.

Mrs. Viola H. Hymes, president, National Council of Jewish Women, Inc.

Miss Margaret J. Mealey, executive director, National Council of Catholic Women.

Mr. Norman E. Nicholson, administrative assistant, Kaiser Industries Corp., Oakland, Calif.

Miss Marguerite Rawalt, attorney; past president: Federal Bar Association, National Association of Women Lawyers, National Federation of Busines & Professional Women's Clubs, Inc.

Mr. William F. Schnitzler, secretary-treasurer, American Federation of Labor and Congress of Industrial Organizations.

Dr. Caroline F. Ware, Vienna, Va.

Dr. Cynthia C. Wedel, assistant general secretary for program, National Council of the Churches of Christ in the U.S.A.

The CHAIRMAN. The time of the gentleman from New York has expired.

Mr. GATHINGS. Mr. Chairman, I ask unanimous consent to extend my remarks at this point in the RECORD.

The CHAIRMAN. Is there objection to the request of the gentleman from Arkansas?

There was no objection.

Mr. GATHINGS. Mr. Chairman, the amendment of the gentleman from Virginia [Mr. SMITH] to protect the employment rights of all women should be agreed to. There can be no plausible reason that a white woman should be deprived of an equal opportunity to get a job simply because of her sex and a colored woman obtain that position because of her preferential rights as contained in this bill. Title VII seeks to make it an unlawful employment practice for an employer to fail or refuse to hire or to discharge or otherwise discriminate against any individual because of race, color, religion, or national origin. The language covers all employees, or would-be employees, except white women. I do not want to discriminate against a job applicant because of her sex and I hope that Members of this body will approve the amendment of the gentleman from Virginia.

The CHAIRMAN. The question is on the amendment offered by the gentleman from Virginia [Mr. SMITH].

Mrs. GRIFFITHS. Mr. Chairman, on that I demand tellers.

Tellers were ordered, and the Chairman appointed as tellers Mr. CELLER and Mrs. GRIFFITHS.

The Committee divided, and the tellers reported that there were—ayes 168, noes 133.

So the amendment was agreed to.

(material omitted)

63

c. Questions on the Legislative History of the Sex Discrimination Amendment

1. The floor debate on the sex discrimination amendment constitutes the entire record on congressional consideration of whether to add sex discrimination to Title VII. When Rep. Smith offers his amendments, is he operating in good faith? How can you tell? What does Rep. Green say that is relevant to the issue of Smith's motives?

2. How does Rep. Smith vote on final passage of the Civil Rights Act? How do Reps. Griffith and St. George vote on final passage of the Act? Assume for the sake of argument that the amendment adding a prohibition against sex discrimination would not have been approved without the support of numerous members who hoped it would be a "poison pill" for the bill as a whole: does that make the provision prohibiting sex discrimination less weighty than the provision prohibiting race discrimination? Why?

3. The Casebook authors describe Rep. Celler (at page 15) as "shocked [and] flustered" as he rose to speak against the Smith amendment. Based on the House floor debate passage you have read, is this an accurate statement?

4. What arguments do Celler and other liberals offer against the Smith amendment? Do you think his arguments are sincere or simply instrumental and political? Are Celler's arguments against the amendment entitled to special weight because he is floor manager of the bill?

5. As a general matter, is there any reason for courts to trust statements made by supporters of a bill (or amendment) more than statements from those who voted against the bill or amendment? Be prepared to defend your answer.

6. The history of the sex discrimination amendment is an extreme example of the way statutes are developed during the legislative process. What changes that have occurred since 1964 might make the kind of strategic voting engaged in by Southern Democrats less likely to occur today?

III. Vote in the House: Committee of the Whole Rises; H.R. 7152 is passed (February 10, 1964)

(material omitted)

House stopsacting as a whole

The CHAIRMAN. Under the rule, the Committee rises.

Accordingly, the Committee rose; and the Speaker having resumed the chair, Mr. KEOGH, Chairman of the Committee of the Whole House on the State of the Union, reported that that Committee having had under consideration the bill (H.R. 7152) to enforce the constitutional right to vote, to confer jurisdiction upon the district courts of the United States to provide injunctive relief against discrimination in public accommodations, to authorize the Attorney General to institute suits to protect constitutional rights in education, to establish a Community Relations Service, to extend for 4 years the Commission on Civil Rights, to prevent discrimination in federally assisted programs, to establish a Commission on Equal Employment Opportunity, and for other purposes, pursuant to House Resolution 616, he reported the bill back to the House with sundry amendments adopted by the Committee of the Whole.

The SPEAKER. Under the rule, the previous question is ordered.

The question is on the amendment.

Under the terms of House Resolution 616 a separate vote may be demanded on any amendment adopted in the Committee of the Whole.

Mr. WILLIAMS. Mr. Speaker, I demand a separate vote on the amendment that was offered by the gentleman from Virginia [Mr. SMITH] having to do with adding the word "sex" to the bill, and also the amendment offered by the gentleman from Ohio [Mr. ASHBROOK] dealing with the subject of atheism.

The SPEAKER. The Clerk will report the first amendment on which a separate vote has been demanded.

The Clerk read as follows:

On page 68, line 23, after the word "religion," insert the word "sex."
On page 69, line 10, after the word "religion," insert the word "sex."
On page 69, line 17, after the word "religion," insert the word "sex."
On page 70, line 1, after the word "religion," insert the word "sex."
On page 71, line 5, after the word "religion," insert the word "sex."

The SPEAKER. The question is on the amendment.

Mr. GROSS. Mr. Speaker, on that I demand the yeas and nays.

The yeas and nays were refused.

The amendment was agreed to.

The SPEAKER. The Clerk will report the next amendment on which a separate vote is demanded.

The Clerk read as follows:

On page 70, line 10, after the word "enterprise" insert a new section:

"(f) Notwithstanding any other provision of this title, it shall not be an unlawful employment practice for an employer to refuse to hire and employ any person because of said person's atheistic practices and beliefs."

The SPEAKER. The question is on the amendment.

The amendment was agreed to.

The SPEAKER. The question is on the Committee substitute as amended.

The Committee substitute as amended was agreed to.

The SPEAKER. The question is on the engrossment and third reading of the bill.

The bill was ordered to be engrossed and read a third time, and was read the third time.

Mr. CRAMER. Mr. Speaker, I offer a motion to recommit the bill.

The SPEAKER. Is the gentleman opposed to the bill?

Mr. CRAMER. I am, Mr. Speaker.

The SPEAKER. The Clerk will report the motion to recommit.

The Clerk read as follows:

Mr. CRAMER of Florida moves to recommit the bill, H.R. 7152, to the Committee on the Judiciary.

Mr. CELLER. Mr. Speaker, I move the previous question on the motion to recommit.

The previous question was ordered.

The SPEAKER. The question is on the motion to recommit.

The motion to recommit was rejected.

The SPEAKER. The question is on the passage of the bill.

Mr. WILLIAMS. Mr. Speaker, on that I demand the yeas and nays.

The yeas and nays were ordered.

The question was taken; and there were—yeas 290, nays 130, not voting 11, as follows:

[Roll No. 32]

YEAS—290

Abele
Adair
Addabbo
Albert
Anderson
Andrews, N. Dak.
Arends
Ashley
Aspinall
Auchincloss
Avery
Ayres
Baldwin
Barrett
Barry
Bass
Bates
Becker
Bell
Bennett, Mich.
Betts
Blatnik
Boland
Bolling
Bolton, Frances P.
Bolton, Oliver P.
Bow
Brademas
Bray
Bromwell
Brooks
Broomfield
Brotzman
Brown, Calif.
Brown, Ohio
Bruce
Buckley
Burke
Burkhalter
Burton
Byrne, Pa.
Byrnes, Wis.
Cahill
Cameron
Cannon
Carey
Cederberg
Celler
Chamberlain
Chenoweth
Clancy
Clark
Clausen, Don H.
Cleveland
Cohelan
Collier
Conte
Corbett
Corman
Cunningham
Curtin
Curtis
Daddario
Dague
Daniels
Dawson
Delaney
Dent
Denton
Derounian
Derwinski
Devine
Diggs
Dingell
Dole
Donohue
Dulski
Duncan
Dwyer
Edmondson
Edwards
Ellsworth
Fallon
Farbstein
Feighan
Findley
Finnegan
Fino
Flood
Fogarty
Ford
Fraser
Frelinghuysen
Friedel
Fulton, Pa.
Fulton, Tenn.
Gallagher
Garmatz
Giaimo
Gilbert
Gill
Glenn
Gonzalez
Goodell
Goodling
Grabowski
Gray
Green, Oreg.
Griffin
Griffiths
Grover
Gubser
Hagen, Calif.
Halleck
Halpern
Hanna
Hansen
Harding
Harsha
Harvey, Ind.
Harvey, Mich.
Hawkins
Hays
Healey
Hechler
Hoeven
Holifield
Holland
Horton
Hosmer
Ichord
Joelson
Johnson, Calif.
Johnson, Pa.
Johnson, Wis.
Karsten
Karth
Kastenmeier
Keith
Kelly
Keogh
King, Calif.
King, N.Y.
Kirwan
Kluczynski
Kunkel
Kyl
Laird
Langen
Latta
Leggett
Libonati
Lindsay
Lloyd
Long, Md.
McClory
McCulloch
McDade
McDowell
McFall
McIntire
McLoskey
Macdonald
MacGregor
Madden
Mailliard
Martin, Mass.
Martin, Nebr.
Mathias
Matsunaga
May
Michel
Miller, Calif.
Miller, N.Y.
Milliken
Minish
Minshall
Monagan
Montoya
Moore
Moorhead
Morgan
Morris
Morse
Morton
Mosher
Moss
Multer
Murphy, Ill.
Murphy, N.Y.
Nedzi
Nelsen
Nix
Norblad
O'Brien, N.Y.
O'Hara, Ill.
O'Hara, Mich.
Olsen, Mont.
Olson, Minn.
O'Neill
Osmers
Ostertag
Patten
Pepper
Perkins
Philbin
Pickle
Pike
Pillion
Pirnie
Powell
Price
Pucinski
Quie
Randall
Reid, Ill.
Reid, N.Y.
Reifel
Reuss
Rhodes, Pa.
Rich
Riehlman
Rivers, Alaska
Robison
Rodino
Rogers, Colo.
Rooney, N.Y.
Rooney, Pa.
Roosevelt
Rosenthal
Rostenkowski
Roudebush
Roush
Roybal
Rumsfeld
Ryan, Mich.
Ryan, N.Y.
St. George
St Germain
St. Onge
Saylor
Schadeberg
Schenck
Schneebeli
Schweiker
Schwengel
Secrest
Senner
Sheppard
Shriver
Sibal
Sickles
Sisk
Skubitz
Slack
Smith, Iowa
Springer
Staebler
Stafford
Staggers
Steed
Stinson
Stratton
Sullivan
Taft
Talcott
Teague, Calif.
Thomas
Thompson, N.J.
Thomson, Wis.
Toll
Tollefson
Tupper
Udall
Ullman
Van Deerlin
Vanik
Wallhauser
Weaver
Westland
Whalley
Wharton
White
Widnall
Wilson, Bob
Wilson, Charles H.
Wilson, Ind.
Wydler
Younger
Zablocki

NAYS—130

Abbitt
Abernethy
Alger
Andrews, Ala.
Ashbrook
Ashmore
Baring
Battin
Beckworth
Beermann
Belcher
Bennett, Fla.
Berry
Boggs
Bonner
Brock
Broyhill, N.C.
Broyhill, Va.
Burleson
Casey
Chelf
Clawson, Del
Colmer
Cooley
Cramer
Davis, Ga.
Dorn
Dowdy
Downing
Elliott
Everett
Evins
Fascell
Fisher
Flynt
Foreman
Forrester
Fountain
Fuqua
Gary
Gathings
Gibbons
Grant
Gross
Gurney
Hagan, Ga.
Haley
Hall
Hardy
Harris
Harrison
Hébert
Hemphill
Henderson
Herlong
Huddleston
Hull
Hutchinson
Jarman
Jennings
Jensen
Johansen
Jonas
Jones, Ala.
Jones, Mo.
Kilburn
Kilgore
Knox
Kornegay
Landrum
Lennon
Lesinski
Lipscomb
Long, La.
McMillan
Mahon
Marsh
Martin, Calif.
Matthews
Meader
Mills
Morrison
Murray
Natcher
Passman
Patman
Pilcher
Poage
Poff
Pool
Purcell
Quillen
Rains
Rhodes, Ariz.
Rivers, S.C.
Roberts, Ala.
Roberts, Tex.
Rogers, Fla.
Rogers, Tex.
Scott
Selden
Short
Sikes
Smith, Calif.
Smith, Va.

Snyder	Utt	Wickersham
Stephens	Van Pelt	Williams
Stubblefield	Vinson	Willis
Taylor	Waggonner	Winstead
Teague, Tex.	Watson	Wright
Thompson, La.	Watts	Wyman
Trimble	Weltner	Young
Tuck	Whitener	
Tuten	Whitten	

NOT VOTING—11

Davis, Tenn.	Lankford	Shipley
Hoffman	O'Brien, Ill.	Siler
Horan	O'Konski	Thompson, Tex.
Kee	Pelly	

So the bill was passed.

The Clerk announced the following pairs:

On this vote:

Mr. Shipley with Mr. Hoffman.

Mrs. Kee with Mr. Horan.

Until further notice:

Mr. O'Brien of Illinois for, with Mr. Siler against.

Mr. Pelly for, with Mr. Davis of Tennessee against.

The result of the vote was announced as above recorded.

The title was amended so as to read:

A bill to enforce the constitutional right to vote, to confer jurisdiction upon the district courts of the United States to provide injunctive relief against discrimination in public accommodations, to authorize the Attorney General to institute suits to protect constitutional rights in public facilities and public education, to extend the Commission on Civil Rights, to prevent discrimination in federally assisted programs, to establish a Commission on Equal Employment Opportunity, and for other purposes.

A motion to reconsider was laid on the table.

Mr. CELLER. Mr. Speaker, I want to express my gratitude for this, shall I say ovation; I deeply appreciate the kindness and courtesy of all the ladies and gentlemen who participated in this cause. It did warm the cockles of my heart. I want to state that the result would not have been the way it was were it not for the wholehearted support and most earnest and dedicated cooperation of my distinguished colleague and counterpart on the Judiciary Committee, the gentleman from Ohio [Mr. McCULLOCH].

Mr. McCULLOCH. Mr. Speaker and Members of the House, seldom, if ever, has anyone had the help and cooperation of able, devoted and sincere people as we have had during the debate and passage of this legislation.

Mr. Speaker, it has been indeed a pleasure for me to work with the chairman of the Committee on the Judiciary many long, difficult, trying days, and nights too, if you please. However, the result has more than justified all those difficult times.

Mr. Speaker, I am really deeply appreciative of this help and assistance from everyone of my colleagues, both the majority and the minority. Mr. Speaker, I am sure that in the 16-odd years that I have been a Member of the House no committee has ever had a more able, more effective, more devoted staff than has the Committee on the Judiciary. Mr. Speaker, I want to thank them, too.

Mr. CELLER. Mr. Speaker, also I must express my admiration for those in the minority, and state that they have been most dignified and most statesmanlike in their defeat. A tribute is due them even in their defeat.

GENERAL LEAVE TO EXTEND REMARKS

Mr. CELLER. Mr. Speaker, I ask unanimous consent that all Members may have 5 legislative days in which to extend their remarks in the RECORD on the bill just passed.

The SPEAKER. Is there objection to the request of the gentleman from New York?

There was no objection.

TRIBUTE TO CHAIRMAN OF THE COMMITTEE OF THE WHOLE

Mr. McCULLOCH. Mr. Speaker, I should like to, not only for myself, but I am sure for the chairman, if he has not already done so, say a word for the fair, able, and judicious manner in which the Chairman of the Committee of the Whole presided over these deliberations for so many days. No one has done a better job.

I WOULD HAVE VOTED "AYE"

Mr. TUPPER. Mr. Speaker, I ask unanimous consent that the gentleman from Wisconsin [Mr. O'KONSKI] may extend his remarks at this point in the RECORD and include extraneous matter.

The SPEAKER. Is there objection to the request of the gentleman from Maine?

There was no objection.

Mr. O'KONSKI. Mr. Speaker, due to illness in the family, I regret I could not be here to vote on the civil rights bill. I tried to get a live pair but could not get anyone to do so. If I were present to vote, I would have voted "aye" on the civil rights bill.

IMPRESSED BY THE DIGNITY OF THE CONGRESS

Mr. TUPPER. Mr. Speaker, I ask unanimous consent that the gentleman from California [Mr. TALCOTT] may extend his remarks at this point in the RECORD and include extraneous matter.

The SPEAKER. Is there objection to the request of the gentleman from Maine?

There was no objection.

Mr. TALCOTT. Mr. Speaker, although I disagreed with the opponents of this bill on most points, I was most favorably impressed with the gentility and dignity with which they comported themselves during the long, strenuous debate. Their conduct was a credit to the Congress of the United States. The image and stature of the House of Representatives was enhanced by them in defeat.

(material omitted)

(material omitted)

IV. Debate in the Senate

An important argument southern opponents of Title VII raised was that the civil rights bill, if enacted into law, would force employers to abandon business criteria and tests that screened out workers of color. As evidence that this would happen, opponents cited the hearing examiner's opinion in an Illinois (state) fair employment practices administrative proceeding. The "Motorola Case" (after the defendant company) became a focus of intense Senate debate, as it provided a reason for Senators sympathetic to businesses (especially small businesses) to oppose a bill they otherwise might support. A lot of pro-civil rights Republicans were strongly opposed to any kind of "socialist" government pressure telling businessmen what criteria they should be using to make decisions about hiring, promotion, and the like. Such Republicans favored legislation telling employers not to consider race, but opposed legislation telling employers they could not use professionally designed tests and other merits-based criteria.

Thus, it was important for supporters of the civil rights bill to refute the argument that Title VII would be interpreted to impose federal tests and other standards onto businesses. Notice the various arguments developed by the bill's supporters. Keep this in mind when the issue of employer tests and standards lands in the courts afterwards.

a. 110 Cong. Rec. 6415-16 (Bill is taken up and debate begins; discussing the purpose of Title VII)

(material omitted)

SENATE

THURSDAY, MARCH 26, 1964

(Legislative day of Monday, March 9, 1964)

(material omitted)

CIVIL RIGHTS ACT OF 1963

The Senate resumed the consideration of the motion of Mr. MANSFIELD that the Senate proceed to consider the bill (H.R.

7152) to enforce the constitutional right to vote, to confer jurisdiction upon the district courts of the United States to provide injunctive relief against discrimination in public accommodations, to authorize the Attorney General to institute suits to protect constitutional rights in public facilities and public education, to extend the Commission on Civil Rights, to prevent discrimination in federally assisted programs, to establish a Commission on Equal Employment Opportunity, and for other purposes.

Mr. MANSFIELD. Mr. President, there will be no morning business this morning.

What is the pending question?

The ACTING PRESIDENT pro tempore. The question is on agreeing to the motion of the Senator from Montana [Mr. MANSFIELD] that the Senate proceed to the consideration of House bill 7152, the Civil Rights Act of 1963.

Mr. MANSFIELD. Mr. President, I suggest the absence of a quorum.

The ACTING PRESIDENT pro tempore. The clerk will call the roll.

The Chief Clerk called the roll, and the following Senators answered to their names:

[No. 100 Leg.]

Aiken	Hartke	Morse
Bartlett	Hayden	Morton
Bayh	Hickenlooper	Mundt
Beall	Hill	Muskie
Bible	Holland	Neuberger
Boggs	Hruska	Pastore
Brewster	Humphrey	Pell
Burdick	Inouye	Prouty
Byrd, Va.	Jackson	Proxmire
Byrd, W. Va.	Javits	Ribicoff
Cannon	Johnston	Robertson
Carlson	Jordan, N.C.	Russell
Case	Jordan, Idaho	Saltonstall
Clark	Keating	Scott
Cooper	Kennedy	Smathers
Cotton	Kuchel	Smith
Dirksen	Lausche	Sparkman
Dodd	Long, Mo.	Stennis
Dominick	Long, La.	Symington
Douglas	Magnuson	Talmadge
Eastland	Mansfield	Thurmond
Edmondson	McCarthy	Walters
Ellender	McClellan	Williams, N.J.
Ervin	McGee	Williams, Del.
Fong	McGovern	Yarborough
Fulbright	McIntyre	Young, N. Dak.
Gore	Mechem	Young, Ohio
Gruening	Metcalf	
Hart	Miller	

Mr. HUMPHREY. I announce that the Senator from Idaho [Mr. CHURCH], the Senator from Michigan [Mr. McNAMARA], the Senator from Oklahoma [Mr. MONRONEY], the Senator from Utah [Mr. MOSS], and the Senator from Wisconsin [Mr. NELSON] are absent on official business.

I also announce that the Senator from New Mexico [Mr. ANDERSON] and the Senator from California [Mr. ENGLE] are necessarily absent.

I further announce that the Senator from West Virginia [Mr. RANDOLPH] is absent because of illness.

Mr. KUCHEL. I announce that the Senator from Colorado [Mr. ALLOTT] and the Senator from Kansas [Mr. PEARSON] are absent on official business.

The Senator from Utah [Mr. BENNETT], the Senator from Nebraska [Mr. CURTIS], the Senator from Wyoming [Mr. SIMPSON], and the Senator from Texas [Mr. TOWER] are necessarily absent.

The Senator from Arizona [Mr. GOLDWATER] is detained on official business.

The ACTING PRESIDENT pro tempore. A quorum is present.

Mr. CASE. Mr. President, during the course of the debate on the motion to take up the civil rights bill, there have been a number of allusions to the Myart against Motorola, Inc., case. The significance of this finding of a hearing examiner of the Illinois Fair Employment Practices Commission has, to say the least, been greatly exaggerated.

In the first place, the decision is merely that of an examiner and, as the chairman of the Illinois Commission made clear in a letter to the New York Times on March 25, the Illinois Commission "has not taken any stand of any kind at any time on the issue of the use of tests in employment."

Even were the Illinois Commission to follow the recommendation of the examiner, an assumption for which there is no basis, the action would have no relevance to the bill now coming before us.

To clear away misconceptions on this whole case, I have had prepared a memorandum which makes clear, I believe, that it would not be possible for a decision such as the finding of the examiner in the Motorola case to be entered by a Federal agency against an employer under title VII.

This is so, first, because the Equal Employment Opportunities Commission established by title VII would have no adjudicative functions and no authority to issue enforcement orders.

Second, title VII clearly would not permit even a Federal court to rule out the use of particular tests by employers because they do not "equate inequalities and environmental factors among the disadvantaged and culturally deprived groups."

Mr. President, I ask that the text of the letter from Charles W. Gray, chairman of the State of Illinois Fair Employment Practices Commission, and of the memorandum to which I have referred be printed in full at this point in the RECORD.

There being no objection, the letter and memorandum were ordered to be printed in the RECORD, as follows:

[From the New York Times, Mar. 25, 1964]

ILLINOIS FEPC—COMMISSIONER DONISS TAKING STAND ON USE OF TESTS IN HIRING

To the EDITOR:

Arthur Krock, writing in the Times of March 13, states that the Illinois Fair Employment Practices Commission has ruled on an issue involving the use of preemployment tests by Motorola.

The facts are these. The law establishing the Illinois Fair Employment Practices Commission provides that in the event a private conciliation conference between a respondent and a complainant fails to produce a mutually acceptable settlement, it shall be set for a public hearing.

The public hearing is conducted by a hearing examiner, who must be a lawyer. The hearing examiner is appointed by the commission, but is in no way an employee of the commission, and, therefore, certainly not a political appointee.

The findings of the hearing examiner are just that—not a ruling of the commission, nor are they necessarily the opinion or judgment of the commission.

NO POSITION ON FINDING

The Illinois Fair Employment Practices Commission has not acted on the Motorola finding, has issued no orders and has taken no position on whether the hearing examiner's finding will be the order of the commission.

The protection of both parties that our law provides is such that it is highly unlikely that this commission, or any other commission so constituted, could seize the kind of autocratic control of which Mr. Krock writes.

The hearing examiner's finding will be carefully considered by the commission. It will then issue an order which may or may not include the recommended conclusion of the hearing examiner. Once the commission rules on the matter, the ruling can be appealed directly to the courts under the Administrative Review Act in the statutes of the State of Illinois.

This commission has not taken any stand of any kind at any time on the issue of the use of tests in employment. Until we do so, it is totally inappropriate for anyone or any publication to make assumptions about the outcome of this matter.

CHARLES W. GRAY,
Chairman, State of Illinois Fair Employment Practices Commission.
CHICAGO, *March 17, 1964.*

MYART v. MOTOROLA, INC.

The decision of a hearing examiner in *Myart* v. *Motorola, Inc.*, a case under the Illinois Fair Employment Practices Act (CONGRESSIONAL RECORD, Mar. 19, 1964, pp. 5662–5664), has been the subject of some recent discussion.

In that case, the hearing examiner found that an employment test administered by respondent Motorola to a Negro job applicant was "obsolete" because "its norm was derived from standardization on advantaged groups," apparently meaning that persons coming from underprivileged or less well educated groups were less likely to be able to pass the test. He said that "in the light of current circumstances and the objectives of the spirit as well as the letter of the law, this test does not lend itself to equal opportunity to qualify for the hitherto culturally deprived and the disadvantaged groups." Accordingly, in addition to the relief he directed for the complainant, the hearing examiner ordered that Motorola cease to employ the test in question, and that if it chose to use any test, it should adopt one "which shall reflect and equate inequalities and environmental factors among the disadvantaged and culturally deprived groups." There is no description of the test in the hearing examiner's report, and no further discussion of why the test was considered unfair.

Of course, it should be noted, and indeed emphasized, that the decision in the Motorola case was merely an initial or preliminary decision of a part-time hearing examiner,[1] that this decision is subject to review by the full Illinois Fair Employment Practices Commission, and that any commission decision is subject to review by the Illinois courts. Consequently, no one can say with any degree of certainty at this time that the examiner's decision is a correct interpretation of the Illinois law.

It has been suggested, nevertheless, that the decision by the hearing examiner should be taken as indicative of the kinds of decisions which might be expected to be made by

[1] Hearing examiners are apparently not full-time employees of the commission. A panel of attorneys residing throughout the State, including at least two from each of the five supreme court districts, are designated as hearing examiners. Article VIII, Rules and Regulations of Procedure of the Illinois Fair Employment Practices Commission.

Federal bureaucrats if title VII of the pending civil rights bill were enacted. Of course, this is completely wrong. It would definitely not be possible for a decision like Motorola to be entered by a Federal agency against an employer under title VII. This is so for two very basic reasons.

First, unlike the Illinois commission, the Equal Employment Opportunities Commission established by title VII would have no adjudicative functions and no authority to issue enforcement orders. Its duties would be to receive and investigate complaints, to attempt to resolve disputes and to achieve compliance with the act through voluntary methods, and, where conciliation fails, to bring suit to obtain compliance in Federal court. Only a Federal court would have the authority to determine whether or not a practice is in violation of the act and only the court could enforce compliance. The Commisison not only could issue no enforcement orders, it could make no determination as to whether or not the act has been violated. Thus, enactment of title VII would not allow a Federal administrative agency to issue any compliance orders, much less one paralleling that of the Illinois hearing examiner.

Second, it is perfectly clear that title VII would not permit even a Federal court to rule out the use of particular tests by employers because they do not "equate inequalities and environmental factors among the disadvantaged and culturally deprived groups." Of course, it is not appropriate to comment here on whether the Motorola decision is correct as a matter of Illinois law. This is for the State commission and the State courts to determine. It is enough to note that the result seems questionable. There is no doubt, however, that such a result would be unmistakably improper under the proposed Federal law. The Illinois case is based on the apparent premise that the State law is designed to provide equal opportunity to Negroes, whether or not as well qualified as white job applicants.

The hearing examiner in the Motorola case wrote: "The task (of personnel executives) is one of adapting procedures within a policy framework to fit the requirements of finding and employing workers heretofore deprived because of race, color, religion, national origin, or ancestry. Selection techniques may have to be modified at the outset in the light of experience, education, or attitudes of the group. * * * The employer may have to establish in-plant training programs and employ the heretofore culturally deprived and disadvantaged persons as learners, placing them under such supervision that will enable them to achieve job success."

Whatever its merit as a socially desirable objective, title VII would not require, and no court could read title VII as requiring, an employer to lower or change the occupational qualifications he sets for his employees simply because proportionally fewer Negroes than whites are able to meet them. Thus, it would be ridiculous, indeed, in addition to being contrary to title VII, for a court to order an employer who wanted to hire electronic engineers with Ph. D.'s to lower his requirements because there were very few Negroes with such degrees or because prior cultural or educational deprivation of Negroes prevented them from qualifying. And unlike the hearing examiner's interpretation of the Illinois law in the Motorola case, title VII most certainly would not authorize any requirement that an employer accept an unqualified applicant or a less qualified applicant and undertake to give him any additional training which might be necessary to enable him to fill the job.

Title VII says merely that a covered employer cannot refuse to hire someone simply because of his color, that is, because he is

a Negro. But it expressly protects the employer's right to insist that any prospective applicant, Negro or white, must meet the applicable job qualifications. Indeed, the very purpose of title VII is to promote hiring on the basis of job qualifications, rather than on the basis of race or color. Title VII would in no way interfere with the right of an employer to fix job qualifications and any citation of the Motorola case to the contrary as precedent for title VII is wholly wrong and misleading.

Mr. MANSFIELD. Mr. President, I ask for the yeas and nays on my motion.

The yeas and nays were ordered.

Mr. MANSFIELD. I ask the Chair to call the roll.

(material omitted)

b. 110 Cong. Rec. 6548-53 (Sen. Humphrey discussing the purpose of Title VII)

6548   CONGRESSIONAL RECORD — SENATE   *March 30*

(material omitted)

Mr. HUMPHREY. Mr. President, title VII provides a very moderate and reasonable remedy for problems of racial discrimination in employment. Unlike most State fair employment laws it vests all enforcement powers in the courts, rather than in an administrative agency. This is an important difference. Ample time for adjustment is afforded by the provision that it will not become effective at all for 1 year, and will not become fully effective for 4 years. Again the doctrine of reasonableness has been applied to his bill. There is no effort suddenly to impose on the economy vast new legislation, in an effort to arrive at an immediate solution to a long-range problem.

Title VII would establish a five-member bipartisan Equal Employment Opportunities Commission, which would be responsible for receiving and investigating complaints of unlawful employment practices and for seeking to bring about voluntary compliance with the requirements of the title. However, the Commission will not have any responsibility for adjudicating complaints or any power to issue enforcement orders. In this respect the title is a departure from the usual statutory scheme for independent regulatory agencies.

DESCRIPTION OF PROCEDURE UNDER TITLE VII

The first step in any proceeding under title VII is the filing with the Commission of a charge of discrimination. The charge may be filed by the person allegedly discriminated against or by someone on his behalf. In either case the charge must be in writing and under oath. A written charge may also be filed by a member of the Commission where he has reasonable cause to believe that an unlawful act of discrimination has occurred. In any case where the alleged act of discrimination arises in a State which has an effective equal employment opportunity law, and the Commission has pursuant to section 708(b) entered into an agreement with the State authorities providing for exclusive State jurisdiction of such cases, the charge would be turned over to the State agency to be handled under State procedures.

Assuming that an agreement applicable to the charge in question is not in effect, the Commission, upon receipt of the charge, shall furnish a copy of the charge to the respondent—that is, the employer, employment agency, or labor organization accused of discrimination; and the Commission shall investigate the charge. How thorough an investigation is made at this stage will depend on the facts of the case. Presumably the respondent will be questioned and perhaps his records examined. However, the Commission and its investigators must and do have discretionary power to cut short an investigation where preliminary inquiry indicates no basis to the charge.

When the charge has been investigated, presumably by the Commission staff, it will be referred to the Commission, or perhaps to a panel of the Commission. If, at this stage, at least two members of the Commission conclude that there is reasonable cause to believe the charge is true, the Commission shall endeavor to eliminate the discrimination by informal means of conciliation and persuasion. If, on the other hand, after an investigation which the Commission believes adequate, at least two members do not conclude that such reasonable cause exists, the matter will be dropped. The Commission is intended to have considerable flexibility in designing procedures to screen cases at this stage. For example, the requirement that at least two Commission members conclude that reasonable cause exists does not mean necessarily that all five Commission members must review the results of each investigation. A panel of three members might be set up. If none or only one of the panel concludes that reasonable cause exists the proceeding could be dropped, or the Commission might reasonably provide that where one member out of the three on the panel reaches this conclusion, the remaining two should also consider the matter. Inevitably, much will depend on the Commission's caseload.

Assuming that two members have found reasonable cause, the Commission will proceed to attempt to conciliate the dispute. This procedure is wholly voluntary. A respondent cannot be compelled to participate in these procedures; and if he does so, his statements and actions in the course of conciliation cannot be used as evidence in a subsequent proceeding. The experience in the States with fair employment practice laws indicates that such informal procedures are the most effective means of bringing about compliance with requirements for nondiscrimination.

If the Commission is unable through its conciliation procedures to obtain voluntary compliance, it must again consider whether on the basis of all the information available to it, reasonable cause exists to believe the respondent has engaged in an unlawful discriminatory practice and whether a suit should be brought to compel compliance. If

CX——412

the Commission, that is to say, a majority of the members, decides that reasonable cause does exist, ordinarily a suit for preventive relief would be brought in a Federal district court in the judicial district in which the unlawful employment practice allegedly occurred or in the judicial district in which the respondent has his principal office. However, the Commission members may, by an affirmative vote, decide not to bring suit in a given case.

So this is not a harsh section; instead, it is a moderate section. It profits from the experience with some 25 State statutes and with long hearings before committees of the House of Representatives and of the Senate during the 15 years that I have been a Member of the Senate.

If the Commission at this stage of the proceeding decides not to sue, or if at any earlier stage it decides to proceed no further because of absence of reasonable cause, the party allegedly discriminated against may bring his own suit in Federal court, provided he obtains the written permission of one member of the Commission. However, the party would have to bear his own costs in such litigation, just like any other private plaintiff in a civil action.

The suit against the respondent, whether brought by the Commission or by the complaining party, would proceed in the usual manner for litigation in the Federal courts. It would not be in any sense a suit for judicial review of Commission action, but would be a trial de novo. This, too, is very significant. The respondent, now the defendant, would have a full opportunity to make his defense and the plaintiff would have the burden of proving that discrimination had occurred. The suit would ordinarily be heard by the judge sitting without a jury in accordance with the customary practice for suits for preventive relief. However, the judge is authorized to refer the case to a master, to hear testimony and submit a report and recommended order, which then would be reviewed by the judge.

The relief sought in such a suit would be an injunction against future acts or practices of discrimination, but the court could order appropriate affirmative relief, such as hiring or reinstatement of employees and the payment of back pay. This relief is similar to that available under the National Labor Relations Act in connection with unfair labor practices, 29 United States Code 160(b). No court order can require hiring, reinstatement, admission to membership, or payment of back pay for anyone who was not fired, refused employment or advancement or admission to a union by an act of discrimination forbidden by this title. This is stated expressly in the last sentence of section 707(e), which makes clear what is implicit throughout the whole title; namely, that employers may hire and fire, promote and refuse to promote for any reason, good or bad, provided only that individuals may not be discriminated against because of race, religion, sex, or national origin.

I hope this presentation will set to rest the doubts about this bill which have been voiced by many union members

across the country. This bill is not an instrument to abolish seniority or unions themselves, as some have charged. The only standard which the bill establishes for unions and management alike is that race will not be used as a basis for discriminatory treatment. The full rights and privileges of union membership, as protected by other Federal laws and court decisions, will in no way be impaired. As a longstanding friend of the American worker, I would not support this fair and reasonable equal employment opportunity provision if it would have any harmful effect on unions. The truth is that this title forbids discriminating against anyone on account of race. This is the simple and complete truth about title VII.

The able Senators in charge of title VII [Mr. CLARK and Mr. CASE] will comment at greater length on this matter.

Contrary to the allegations of some opponents of this title, there is nothing in it that will give any power to the Commission or to any court to require hiring, firing, or promotion of employees in order to meet a racial "quota" or to achieve a certain racial balance.

That bugaboo has been brought up a dozen times; but it is nonexistent. In fact, the very opposite is true. Title VII prohibits discrimination. In effect, it says that race, religion and national origin are not to be used as the basis for hiring and firing. Title VII is designed to encourage hiring on the basis of ability and qualifications, not race or religion.

In title VII we seek to prevent discriminatory hiring practices. We seek to give people an opportunity to be hired on the basis of merit, and to release the tremendous talents of the American people, rather than to keep their talents buried under prejudice or discrimination.

Racial prejudice in employment is one of the most wasteful practices for the economy. Senators and Members of the House of Representatives who are worried about waste would do well to see to it that this monstrous waste is eliminated. We seek to eliminate it by means of this title—and not merely by force of law, but also by the informal procedures of conference, conciliation, and mediation. We seek to use State statutes and local statutes and ordinances wherever they exist.

Every bit of evidence we have in connection with fair employment practice laws indicates that such a statute not only is good law, good morals, and good labor-management practice, but it also is good economics. When all of that can be put into one package, certainly it deserves our very serious consideration.

The present President, Lyndon B. Johnson, took great pride as Vice President in telling the American people and the Congress of the encouraging results which were obtained in hundreds of companies throughout the United States during his tenure as Chairman of the President's Committee on Equal Employment Opportunity. What was the result? Did it jeopardize security? Did it reduce income? Did it threaten the

6550   CON ATE

production line with stability and work stoppages? Did it result in favoritism? Did it result in all the worries that some of the opponents of title VII have?

The answer is "No." The answer is that the program that was utilized by the then Vice President, and now the President of the United States, worked; and it worked for the national interest. It worked for business interests. It worked for domestic tranquility. It worked for individual well being.

No State which has passed a fair employment practices law has repealed it. No President since the time of Franklin Delano Roosevelt has recommended anything less than fair employment practice for Federal employees and Federal contracts. There is a compelling case for title VII. Full protections are written into the title. The Commission itself would have no enforcement power. The most it could do would be to investigate the complaints of an aggrieved party, and, if the person who brings the complaint has a justifiable case, to take that case to a Federal court and to seek some remedy through the processes of law.

* * * *

[6552]   *March 30*

that some Members of the other body wanted a bill that they felt was stronger; while others wanted a bill that made a more modest beginning. Still others wanted no bill at all. H.R. 7152 is a compromise between these points of view. The bill embodies the thinking of literally hundreds of men of good will.

It is my earnest hope that Senators will respect and appreciate this precious investment, that they will realize what a great achievement it is to have brought this bill to its present place on the legislative schedule, and that they will honor the importance of the issue and the good faith of the bill's architects by passing H.R. 7152 as it now stands.

MISREPRESENTING THE CIVIL RIGHTS BILL

The goals of this bill are simple ones: To extend to Negro citizens the same rights and the same opportunities that white Americans take for granted. These goals are so obviously desirable that the opponents of this bill have not dared to dispute them. No one has claimed that Negroes should not be allowed to vote. No one has said that they should be denied equal protection of the laws. No one has said that Negroes are inherently unacceptable is places of public accommodation. No one has said that they should be refused equal opportunity in employment.

This bill cannot be attacked on its merits. Instead, bogeymen and hobgoblins have been raised to frighten well-meaning Americans.

A bill endorsed by hundreds of prominent attorneys and professors of law is called by the opponents unconstitutional.

A bill endorsed by every major religious denomination in America is called Communist inspired.

A bill passed by an overwhelming majority of 290 Members of the House of Representatives to 130 for the opposition—Democrats and Republicans alike—is called socialistic.

Good Americans, like the Speaker of the House, Mr. McCORMACK, the majority leader of the House, Mr. ALBERT, the minority leader of the House, Mr. HALLECK, the chairman of the Judiciary Committee, Mr. CELLER, who deserves a special note of tribute, and the ranking Republican member of the Judiciary Committee, Mr. McCULLOCH, who also deserves a special note of tribute on the floor of the Senate, formulated the bill and carried it through in the other body. I know that 290 Members of the other body are not Socialists. I know they are not Communists. I reject that kind of smokescreen attack upon a sensible piece of legislation.

It is said that the bill would make the Attorney General a dictator, when in fact the only power he is given is the authority to introduce lawsuits to give some American citizens their constitutional rights and require other Americans to obey the law.

It is called a force bill, when in fact it places first reliance on conciliation and voluntary action, and authorizes legal action only as a last resort.

It is called an attack on State government, when in fact the bill specifically directs that State and local offi-

[6553]   CO
1964

cials and agencies will be used wherever feasible, and appeals to the States to perform States' rights rather than States' wrongs.

It is claimed that the bill would produce a gigantic Federal bureaucracy, when in fact it will result in creating about 400 permanent new Federal jobs.

It is claimed that it would impair a property owner's ability to sell or rent his home, when in fact there is nothing in the bill pertaining to housing.

It is claimed that the bill would require racial quotas for all hiring, when in fact it provides that race shall not be a basis for making personnel decisions.

As I have said, the bill has a simple purpose. That purpose is to give fellow citizens—Negroes—the same rights and opportunities that white people take for granted. This is no more than what was preached by the prophets, and by Christ Himself. It is no more than what our Constitution guarantees.

One hundred and ninety years have passed since the Declaration of Independence, and 100 years since the Emancipation Proclamation. Surely the goals of this bill are not too much to ask of the Senate of the United States.

* * * *

c. 110 Cong. Rec. 7212-18 (Sens. Clark and Case's interpretive memorandum)

(material omitted)

Mr. CLARK. I conclude by saying that objection to the constitutionality of title VII can be nothing other than frivolous and not worthy of serious consideration.

I turn now to the provisions of the title.

The Senator from New Jersey [Mr. CASE], who will follow me, and I have had prepared an interpretive memorandum of title VII which we are jointly submitting to our colleagues in the Senate.

I ask unanimous consent that the memorandum may be printed in full at this point in my remarks.

There being no objection, the memorandum was ordered to be printed in the RECORD, as follows:

INTERPRETATIVE MEMORANDUM OF TITLE VII OF H.R. 7152 SUBMITTED JOINTLY BY SENATOR JOSEPH S. CLARK AND SENATOR CLIFFORD P. CASE, FLOOR MANAGERS

GENERAL

Title VII deals with discrimination in employment. It would make it an unlawful employment practice for employers of more than 25 persons, employment agencies, or labor organizations with more than 25 members to discriminate on account of race, color, religion, sex, or national origin in connection with employment, referral for employment, membership in labor organizations, or participation in apprenticeship or other training programs. An Equal Employment Opportunity Commission would be created to enforce the title through investigation of complaints of discrimination, conciliation of disputes, and where necessary, suits in Federal court to compel compliance with the provisions of the title.

COVERAGE

Title VII covers discriminatory practices by employers engaged in industries affecting commerce, as defined in the title, by employ-ment agencies which procure employees for such employers, and by labor organizations in industries affecting commerce. "Commerce" is, generally speaking, interstate commerce, but includes commerce within U.S. possessions and the District of Columbia. It is, in short, that commerce to which the regulatory power of Congress extends under the Constitution, a familiar concept which has been employed in other Federal statutes. The term "affecting commerce" is also familiar, since this is the standard of coverage employed in the National Labor Relations Act, 29 United States Code 152 (6), (7), and the Labor-Management Reporting and Disclosure Act of 1959, 29 United States Code 402(c).

Employers and labor organizations are not covered, however, if their employees or membership fall below certain minimum figures. When title VII is fully effective it will cover employers engaged in industries affecting commerce who have 25 or more employees, and labor organizations with 25 or more members. This coverage will not be reached until 4 years after the enactment of the title. During the first year after enactment the prohibitions of the title are not in effect. During the second year the title will cover employers and labor organizations with 100 or more employees or members, during the third year employers and labor organizations with 75 or more employees or members, and during the fourth year employers and labor organizations with 50 or more employees or members. An employer or labor organization is covered while its employment or membership is above the applicable minimum figure and ceases to be covered when employment or membership drops below the applicable minimum. This means that where employment fluctuates, an employer may be under a duty to avoid discriminating at some times but not at others. Since the principal purpose of the Commission's processing complaints is to obtain future compliance, it may be assumed that in the case of an employer who is intermittently subject to the title the Commission would seek compliance only where there was a prospect for meaningful relief.

There are specific exemptions for the Federal Government and for any State or political subdivision thereof, including governmental agencies, such as civil service commissions establishing standards and conditions for employment, promotion, and retirement but excluding the U.S. employment services and those State and local employment services which receive Federal assistance. There are also exemptions for tax exempt, bona fide private membership clubs, religious corporations, associations and societies, and for employers with respect to the employment of aliens abroad.

DISCRIMINATION

Sections 704 and 705 defined the employment practices prohibited by the title. It would be an unlawful employment practice for an employer to refuse to hire or to discharge any individual or otherwise to discriminate against him with respect to compensation or terms or conditions of employment because of such individual's race, color, religion, sex, or national origin, or to segregate or classify employees in any way on the basis of race, color, religion, sex, or national origin in such a way as to deprive them of employment opportunities or otherwise affect adversely their employment status. Employment agencies would be forbidden to classify, to refer for employment or to refuse to refer for employment, or otherwise to discriminate against any individual because of race, color, religion, sex, or national origin. Labor organizations would be forbidden to deny membership to any individual on the basis of his race, color, religion, sex, or national origin, or to segregate or classify its membership in any way which would deprive any individual of employment opportunities or adversely affect his status as an employee or an applicant for employment on the basis of that individual's race, color, religion, sex, or national origin. In addition, labor organizations would be forbidden to cause or to attempt to cause an employer to violate the section. Finally, it would be an unlawful employment practice for employers, labor organizations, or joint labor-management committees controlling apprenticeship or other training programs to discriminate against any individual in connection with admission to apprenticeship or other training on the basis of that individual's race, color, religion, sex, or national origin.

Those are the basic prohibitions of the title, but section 704 creates certain limited exceptions from these prohibitions. First, it would not be an unlawful employment practice to hire or employ employees of a particular religion, sex, or national origin in those situations where religion, sex, or national origin is a bona fide occupational qualification for the job. This exception must not be confused with the right which all employers would have to hire and fire on the basis of general qualifications for the job, such as skill or intelligence. This exception is a limited right to discriminate on the basis of religion, sex, or national origin where the reason for the discrimination is a bona fide occupational qualification. Examples of such legitimate discrimination would be the preference of a French restaurant for a French cook, the preference of a professional baseball team for male players, and the preference of a business which seeks the patronage of members of particular religious groups for a salesman of that religion. A second exception would permit religiously affiliated educational institutions to discriminate in employment on grounds of religion. The bill would also permit an employer to discriminate against an individual because of the individual's atheistic practices and beliefs. While this provision appears to us of doubtful constitutionality, it is clearly severable from the rest of the title (sec. 716), and if it is held invalid, it would not affect the broad obligation not to discriminate on religious grounds.

The House also provided an exception (sec. 704(g)) for actions taken with respect to an individual who is a member of the Communist Party or another Communist organization. Since discrimination on the basis of political beliefs or affiliations is not prohibited by the title, this subsection has no substantive effect.

With the exception noted above, therefore, section 704 prohibits discrimination in employment because of race, color, religion, sex, or national origin. It has been suggested that the concept of discrimination is vague. In fact it is clear and simple and has no hidden meanings. To discriminate is to make a distinction, to make a difference in treatment or favor, and those distinctions or differences in treatment or favor which are prohibited by section 704 are those which are based on any five of the forbidden criteria: race, color, religion, sex, and national origin. Any other criterion or qualification for employment is not affected by this title.

There is no requirement in title VII that an employer maintain a racial balance in his work force. On the contrary, any deliberate attempt to maintain a racial balance, whatever such a balance may be, would involve a violation of title VII because maintaining such a balance would require an employer to hire or to refuse to hire on the basis of race. It must be emphasized that discrimination is prohibited as to any individual. While the presence or absence of other members of the same minority group in the work force may be a relevant factor in determining whether in a given case a

decision to hire or to refuse to hire was based on race, color, etc., it is only one factor, and the question in each case would be whether that individual was discriminated against.

There is no requirement in title VII that employers abandon bona fide qualification tests where, because of differences in background and education, members of some groups are able to perform better on these tests than members of other groups. An employer may set his qualifications as high as he likes, he may test to determine which applicants have these qualifications, and he may hire, assign, and promote on the basis of test performance.

Title VII would have no effect on established seniority rights. Its effect is prospective and not retrospective. Thus, for example, if a business has been discriminating in the past and as a result has an all-white working force, when the title comes into effect the employer's obligation would be simply to fill future vacancies on a nondiscriminatory basis. He would not be obliged—or indeed, permitted—to fire whites in order to hire Negroes, or to prefer Negroes for future vacancies, or, once Negroes are hired, to give them special seniority rights at the expense of the white workers hired earlier. (However, where waiting lists for employment or training are, prior to the effective date of the title, maintained on a discriminatory basis, the use of such lists after the title takes effect may be held an unlawful subterfuge to accomplish discrimination.)

In addition to the discrimination forbidden by section 704, there are ancillary prohibitions in section 705. Section 705(a) prohibits discrimination by an employer or labor organization against persons for opposing discriminatory practices, and for bringing charges before the Commission or otherwise participating in proceedings under the title. Section 705(b) prohibits discriminatory advertising by employers, employment agencies and labor organizations. There is an appropriate exception where the discrimination is based on a bona fide occupational qualification. It should be noted that the prohibition does not extend to the newspaper or other publication printing the advertisement. It runs solely to the sponsoring firm or organization.

(material omitted)

* * * *

[Sen. Clark reads into the record a memorandum responding to questions previously raised by Sen. Dirksen]

Question. If an employer obtains his employees from a union hiring hall through operation of his labor contract, is he in fact the true employer from the standpoint of discrimination because of race, color, religion, or national origin when he exercises no choice in their selection? If the hiring hall sends only white males, is the employer guilty of discrimination within the meaning of this title? If he is not, then further safeguards must be provided to protect him from endless prosecution under the authority of this title.

Answer. An employer who obtains his employees from a union hiring hall through operation of a labor contract is still an employer. If the hiring hall discriminates against Negroes, and sends him only whites, he is not guilty of discrimination—but the union hiring hall would be.

Question. Would the same situation prevail in respect to promotions, when that management function is governed by a labor contract calling for promotions on the basis of seniority? What of dismissals? Normally, labor contracts call for "last hired, first fired." If the last hired are Negroes, is the employer discriminating if his contract requires they be first fired and the remaining employees are white?

Answer. Seniority rights are in no way affected by the bill. If under a "last hired, first fired" agreement a Negro happens to be the "last hired," he can still be "first fired" as long as it is done because of his status as "last hired" and not because of his race.

Question. If an employer is directed to abolish his employment list because of discrimination what happens to seniority?

Answer. The bill is not retroactive, and it will not require an employer to change existing seniority lists.

Question. Does an unfair practice arise as a result of the operation of this discrimination provision in title VII?

Answer. Nothing in this act affects the determination of what an "unfair labor practice" would be under the National Labor Relations Act.

Question. Now I turn to discrimination on account of sex. Frankly, I always like to discriminate in favor of the fairer sex. I hope that the might of the Federal Government will not enjoin me from such discrimination. But let us look further at this provision. Historically, discrimination because of sex has been a protective discrimination because we do not believe that women should do heavy manual labor of the sort which falls to the lot of some men. This is not true, of course, in some other countries where we see pictures of women working on the roads and in the mines. Then, too, we discriminate in favor of women because of nimble abilities in many fields, such as the assembly of radios and delicate instruments and machines. Where the discrimination is not in the best interest of the fairer sex we have approached the problem by specific prohibitions such as the requirement of equal pay for women doing the same work as men.

Answer. Wherever sex is a bona fide qualification or disqualification for a particular job, title VII does not require that equal job opportunity be given to both sexes.

(material omitted and repaginated)

Mr. CLARK. Mr. President, during the course of this debate, a number of objections have been raised to various provisions of title VII. I believe, rather than to deal with them seriatim, and to an empty Chamber, it would be wiser to have them printed in the RECORD, where they can be perused at leisure by Senators—there may be one or two who still read this debate in the CONGRESSIONAL RECORD. Accordingly, I ask unanimous consent that a series of objections which have been raised by opponents of the bill, either on or off the floor, to title VII, and the answers to these objections may be printed in full in the RECORD at this point in my remarks.

There being no objection, the statement was ordered to be printed in the RECORD, as follows:

* * * *

* * * *

Objection: The language of the statute is vague and unclear. It may interfere with the employers' right to select on the basis of qualifications.

Answer: Discrimination is a word which has been used in State FEPC statutes for at least 20 years, and has been used in Federal statutes, such as the National Labor Relations Act and the Fair Labor Standards Act, for even a longer period. To discriminate is to make distinctions or differences in the treatment of employees, and are prohibited only if they are based on any of the five forbidden criteria (race, color, religion, sex or national origin); any other criteria or qualification is untouched by this bill.

* * * *

Objection: The bill would require employers to establish quotas for nonwhites in proportion to the percentage of nonwhites in the labor market area.

Answer: Quotas are themselves discriminatory.

* * * *

d. Questions on Senate Legislative History Readings

1. What role did Senators Clark and Case have in the legislative process of the 1964 Civil Rights Act? Does their Interpretive Memorandum deserve any more weight or attention than the floor statements made by other Senators?

2. For whom are Senators Clark and Case speaking: Just themselves? Or the broader coalition?

3. Who was the intended audience of the Memorandum?

4. What was the strategic purpose of the Memorandum: that is, what strategic goal were Senators Clark and Case trying to achieve, and how were they seeking to achieve that goal?

5. Examine the Memorandum language with respect to its understanding of "discriminate." What are other meanings of "discriminate" that the Memorandum is implicitly rejecting? Or is the Memorandum not rejecting any other meaning?

6. Assuming the Memorandum is entitled to some weight from a reviewing court, does it specify unequivocally that race may never be a relevant factor favoring members of the class protected under Title VII?

e. 110 Cong. Rec. 13327 (The Senate Votes on Cloture)

1964   CONGRESSIONAL RECORD — SENATE   **13327**

(material omitted)   *(material omitted)*

Mechem	Pell	Stennis
Metcalf	Prouty	Symington
Miller	Proxmire	Talmadge
Monroney	Randolph	Thurmond
Morse	Ribicoff	Tower
Morton	Robertson	Walters
Moss	Russell	Williams, N.J.
Mundt	Saltonstall	Williams, Del.
Muskie	Scott	Yarborough
Nelson	Simpson	Young, N. Dak.
Neuberger	Smathers	Young, Ohio
Pastore	Smith	
Pearson	Sparkman	

The ACTING PRESIDENT pro tempore. A quorum is present.

The Sergeant at Arms is admonished that the only persons who may remain in the Chamber are those who have the privilege of the floor. Again, the Chair calls attention to the rule that clerks and members of the staffs of committees and Senators are allowed on the floor only to assist Senators in the actual discharge of their official duties.

The Senate is now approaching a vote. The present occupant of the Chair does not see how clerks and members of the staff can come under the rule of the privilege of the floor.

A quorum being present, the Chair submits to the Senate, without debate, the question: Is it the sense of the Senate that the debate shall be brought to a close?

The yeas and nays are required by the rule; and the Secretary will call the roll.

The Chief Clerk called the roll.

The yeas and nays resulted—yeas 71, nays 29, as follows:

[No. 281 Leg.]

YEAS—71

Aiken	Gruening	Monroney
Allott	Hart	Morse
Anderson	Hartke	Morton
Bartlett	Hickenlooper	Moss
Bayh	Hruska	Mundt
Beall	Humphrey	Muskie
Boggs	Inouye	Nelson
Brewster	Jackson	Neuberger
Burdick	Javits	Pastore
Cannon	Jordan, Idaho	Pearson
Carlson	Keating	Pell
Case	Kennedy	Prouty
Church	Kuchel	Proxmire
Clark	Lausche	Randolph
Cooper	Long, Mo.	Ribicoff
Cotton	Magnuson	Saltonstall
Curtis	Mansfield	Scott
Dirksen	McCarthy	Smith
Dodd	McGee	Symington
Dominick	McGovern	Williams, N.J.
Douglas	McIntyre	Williams, Del.
Edmondson	McNamara	Yarborough
Engle	Metcalf	Young, Ohio
Fong	Miller	

NAYS—29

Bennett	Hayden	Simpson
Bible	Hill	Smathers
Byrd, Va.	Holland	Sparkman
Byrd, W. Va.	Johnston	Stennis
Eastland	Jordan, N.C.	Talmadge
Ellender	Long, La.	Thurmond
Ervin	McClellan	Tower
Fulbright	Mechem	Walters
Goldwater	Robertson	Young, N. Dak.
Gore	Russell	

The ACTING PRESIDENT pro tempore. Two-thirds of the Senators present having voted in the affirmative, the motion is agreed to.

(material omitted)

The ACTING PRESIDENT pro tempore. The time of the Senator from Illinois has expired. All time has expired.

One hour having elapsed since the convening of the Senate today, the Chair, under the rule, lays before the Senate the pending cloture motion, and directs the Secretary to call the roll, to ascertain the presence of a quorum.

The Sergeant at Arms is directed to enforce the provisions of rule XXXIII, which provides for those who have the privilege of the floor. The Sergeant at Arms is admonished that clerks to the Senate and clerks to Senators and to committees are allowed the privilege of the floor only when they are in the actual discharge of their duties. All those who have not the privilege of the floor under rule XXXIII will immediately leave the Chamber. The Sergeant at Arms is directed to carry out the order of the Chair.

The clerk will call the roll.

The Chief Clerk called the roll, and the following Senators answered to their names:

[No. 280 Leg.]

Aiken	Dirksen	Humphrey
Allott	Dodd	Inouye
Anderson	Dominick	Jackson
Bartlett	Douglas	Javits
Bayh	Eastland	Johnston
Beall	Edmondson	Jordan, N.C.
Bennett	Ellender	Jordan, Idaho
Bible	Engle	Keating
Boggs	Ervin	Kennedy
Brewster	Fong	Kuchel
Burdick	Fulbright	Lausche
Byrd, Va.	Goldwater	Long, Mo.
Byrd, W. Va.	Gore	Long, La.
Cannon	Gruening	Magnuson
Carlson	Hart	Mansfield
Case	Hartke	McCarthy
Church	Hayden	McClellan
Clark	Hickenlooper	McGee
Cooper	Hill	McGovern
Cotton	Holland	McIntyre
Curtis	Hruska	McNamara

f. 110 Cong. Rec. 13492-93 (Sen. Tower's Title VII Amendment and the *Motorola* Case)

(material omitted)

Mr. TOWER. Mr. President, I call up my amendment No. 605, and ask that it be read.

The PRESIDING OFFICER. The amendment will be stated.

The LEGISLATIVE CLERK. On page 35, after line 20, insert the following new subsection:

(h) Notwithstanding any other provision of this title, it shall not be an unlawful employment practice for an employer to give any professionally developed ability test to any individual seeking employment or being considered for promotion or transfer, or to act in reliance upon the results of any such test given to such individual, if—

(1) in the case of any individual who is seeking employment with such employer, such test is designed to determine or predict whether such individual is suitable or trainable with respect to his employment in the particular business or enterprise involved, and such test is given to all individuals seeking similar employment with such employer without regard to the individual's race, color, religion, sex, or national origin; or

(2) in the case of any individual who is an employee of such employer, such test is designed to determine or predict whether such individual is suitable or trainable with respect to his promotion or transfer within such business or enterprise, and such test is given to all such employees being considered for similar promotion or transfer by such employer without regard to the employee's race, color, religion, sex, or national origin.

Mr. TOWER. Mr. President, I yield myself 9 minutes. First, may we have order.

The PRESIDING OFFICER. The Senate will be in order.

Mr. TOWER. Mr. President, I hope my colleagues in the Senate will give very careful attention to the amendment. I believe the proponents of the bill realize that this is not an effort to weaken the bill. It is an effort to protect the system whereby employers give general ability and intelligence tests to determine the trainability of prospective employees. The amendment arises from my concern about what happened in the Motorola FEPC case. I have discussed the case in great detail in the Senate, and I shall not repeat my argument.

Let me say, only, in view of the finding in the Motorola case, that the Equal Employment Opportunity Commission, which would be set up by the act, operating in pursuance of title VII, might attempt to regulate the use of tests by employers.

Senators will recall that in the Motorola case the FEPC examiner found that the test used to select employees was discriminatory to culturally deprived or disadvantaged groups, in the words of the FEPC examiner.

Since the determination in that case, it has been clearly stated by psychiatrists and testing experts that the test was not designed to make a selection from any cultural group, and that the tests are both fair and extremely useful. There is no professional evidence to the contrary.

My amendment is quite simple. It provides that an employer may give any professionally developed ability test to any individual seeking employment or being considered for promotion or transfer or to act in reliance upon the result of any such test.

Senators will note that I carefully provided in my amendment that the employer must give such tests to all concerned individuals; that is, to all applicants, without regard to the individual's color, religion, sex, or national origin. Thus every one would get the same fair test, and everyone would get the same fair chance.

The bill is supposed to be designed to assure that a fair chance is obtained by everyone. Therefore it is in this spirit that I offer the amendment.

In the Motorola case a test was given which had been in use since 1949, a test that was devised by trained, professional, reputable psychologists, a test which was available to other corporations. A Negro taking that test was denied employment as the result of that test.

Motorola hires many people of many different national origins. It also hires many Negroes. It has had a very good record of nondiscriminatory practices. It has had pretty good labor relations. The FEPC examiner stated that the test could not be used; that the test was a denial of a fair employment opportunity, because it discriminated against what he vaguely called culturally deprived or disadvantaged groups.

This is highly unreasonable, because if title VII were administered in this fashion, it would mean that an employer would be denied the means of determining the trainability and competence of a prospective employee, or the competence of one who is currently employed and who is being considered for promotion.

My amendment provides that everyone who applies must be allowed to take the test regardless of his race, color, national origin, sex, or creed. It provides that the test must be fairly administered so that there will not be any discriminatory practices because of color.

If we should fail to adopt language of this kind, there could be an Equal Employment Opportunity Commission ruling which would in effect invalidate tests of various kinds of employees by both private business and Government to determine the professional competence or ability or trainability or suitability of a person to do a job.

I point out that college entrance examinations discriminate against culturally deprived and disadvantaged persons. Civil service examinations discriminate. Various examintions given by the Federal Government for civil service positions requiring special abilities could be ruled to be discriminatory. Bar examinations could be ruled to be discriminatory to the culturally deprived and disadvantaged. A State medical examination could be held to be discriminatory.

The amendment is reasonable. It is one which the proponents of the bill should accept. It is one which merits careful consideration by the Senate.

Let me point out what the amendment provides:

(h) Notwithstanding any other provision of this title, it shall not be an unlawful employment practice for an employer to give any professionally developed ability test to any individual seeking employment or being considered for promotion or transfer, or to act in reliance upon the results of any such test given to such individual, if—

(1) in the case of any individual who is seeking employment with such employer, such test is designed to determine or predict whether such individual is suitable or trainable with respect to his employment in the particular business or enterprise involved, and such test is given to all individuals seeking similar employment with such employer without regard to the individual's race, color, religion, sex, or national origin, or

(material omitted)

(material omitted)

Mr. TOWER. Mr. President, I yield back the remainder of my time.

Mr. CASE. Mr. President, I feel certain that no Member of the Senate disagrees with the views of the Senator from Texas concerning the Motorola case finding by the referee or examiner. However, it has no relation to the provisions that would be enacted by the bill. The Motorola case could not happen under the bill the Senate is now considering.

However, I object to the amendment suggested by the Senator from Texas because, first, it is unnecessary; second,

(continued on next page)

the amendment would tend to complicate and make more difficult dealing with cases of actual discrimination and the elimination of them by persuasion as well as by enforcement procedures provided by the act.

If this amendment were enacted, it could be an absolute bar and would give an absolute right to an employer to state as a fact that he had given a test to all applicants, whether it was a good test or not,. so long as it was professionally designed. Discrimination could actually exist under the guise of compliance with the statute. The amendment is unnecessary and would make much more difficult the elimination of discrimination, which is the purpose of the bill.

I hope the Senate will reject the amendment.

Mr. HUMPHREY. Mr. President, I yield myself 30 seconds to say that the substance of this amendment was given the most careful consideration at the time the leadership group met to perfect the so-called package substitute. Needless to say, the amendment was of grave concern to us because it refers to a case in the State of Illinois, and that matter was well represented by none other than the distinguished minority leader.

Every concern of which this amendment seeks to take cognizance has already been taken care of in title VII, as amended, and presented in the substitute. These tests are legal. They do not need to be legalized a second time. They are legal unless used for the purpose of discrimination. The amendment is unnecessary. It would only complicate the package amendment, which has been carefully drawn and represents the considered views on the part of those concerned about title VII.

Mr. TOWER. Mr. President, I yield myself 2 additional minutes.

My purpose was not to be capricious.

Mr. HUMPHREY. I understand.

Mr. TOWER. Or to burden the bill with provisions that are redundant or unnecessary. As I read the measure, I see nothing that would prohibit this type of finding by the Equal Employment Opportunities Commission. I know that the Senator from Illinois [Mr. DIRKSEN] has given much thought to this problem. But I was thinking not only in terms of the State of Illinois, but also as an example of what might happen.

I am not commenting on the merits of that case because, as I understand, the FEPC has yet to make a report based on the finding of the examiner.

My amendment is so drawn that the test could not be used in a manner such as literacy tests are used in some States. It would have to be administered honestly and fairly and applied to all racial groups alike.

Mr. HUMPHREY. There is no power in the FEPC, in the bill before us, to take any administrative action. The most the Commission can do is to investigate. The most it can do, if it finds a pattern or practice of discrimination, is to recommend to the Attorney General that there be enforcement. That is a far cry from the original bill, under which the Commission could have taken administrative remedial action.

I think the amendment is redundant. I regret to say that it is unnecessary. It would only complicate our situation. I hope it will be rejected.

Mr. LAUSCHE. The Senator from Minnesota said that title VII contains provisions which cover the proposal submitted by the Senator from Texas. Will the Senator from Minnesota read the language in title VII that would make these tests valid and not subject to the charge of being discriminatory against applicants for jobs and applicants for promotions?

Mr. HUMPHREY. The point the Senator from Minnesota was making was that the National FEPC has no enforcement power; the test upon which this amendment is based related to Commission action that has enforcibility.

All that the National Commission could do under the substitute amendment—I regret to say this; I do not like it—would be to investigate. Nothing would be done in terms of enforcement other than to recommend to the Attorney General, if there were a large pattern of discrimination. Then the Attorney General might want to take some action. So the language of this provision is a far cry from the Illinois case.

Mr. LAUSCHE. If title VII contains no provision declaring under what circumstances such tests shall be valid, where in the bill are there provisions to make these tests valid, if the Senator can answer that question?

Mr. HUMPHREY. The Senator from Minnesota will be more than happy to do so. It is based on the experience in the States and upon the fact that there has been no declaration that they are invalid. Such tests are considered to be legal; there has never been a denial of that. The only point is that the test that is used for purposes of discrimination would be declared illegal.

It is not possible to write into the bill every action that will govern the conduct of an agency. The Senator's amendment would be much more pertinent and relevant if it were directed to a commission that had enforcement powers. But this Commission does not.

If a bill reported by the Committee on Labor and Public Welfare were directed to title VII of the House bill, it would have some effect and some direct purpose to serve. But the most a national commission could do under the bill would be to take testimony and investigate. It could not enjoin; it could not in any way take remedial action.

Mr. TOWER. Mr. President, I yield myself 15 seconds.

My amendment would not legalize discriminatory tests. It would not make discriminatory tests permissive.

Mr. HUMPHREY. I understand that.

Mr. CASE. Mr. President, I yield myself 15 seconds.

I want it to be clearly understood, so far as I am concerned—and I believe I speak for all members of the committee, the captains, and the leadership—that our position against this amendment and the vote we shall cast against it do not mean approval of the Motorola case or that the bill embodies anything like the action taken by the examiner

in that case. It is not necessary to have this amendment adopted in order to permit that result. Nothing in the bill authorizes such action as in the Motorola case. It would complicate the bill and possibly weaken the effectiveness of it.

Mr. MILLER. Mr. President, will the Senator yield for a question on my time?

Mr. CASE. I am happy to yield.

Mr. MILLER. Is it the position of the managers of the bill, particularly those in charge of this title, that the opportunity and the right to give the tests that are covered by the amendment of the Senator from Texas would be authorized under subparagraph (h), on page 44? The reason I ask the question is that I know something about the amendment and its reference. I believe that during the development of the amendment, the question of its not being an unfair labor practice for an employer to provide for the furnishing of employment pursuant to a bona fide seniority or merit system, or a system which measures earnings was discussed. Would not a test such as is covered by the amendment have to be included in the concept of such a system as I have mentioned?

Mr. HUMPHREY. That is correct. That amendment was one that was added after the original substitute package had been tentatively agreed upon. We reviewed the entire Motorola case, and then added that particular section.

Mr. MILLER. Let me say that I feel very strongly, as all other Senators do, about the Motorola case. When the amendment to which I have referred was drawn up, I was satisfied that such a situation would be prevented by the new language.

Mr. HUMPHREY. I believe the Senator spoke to me about that, at the time when the new language was added to the bill.

Mr. LAUSCHE. Mr. President, I yield myself 30 seconds.

The PRESIDING OFFICER. The Senator from Ohio is recognized for 30 seconds.

Mr. LAUSCHE. Let me ask whether the Senator from Iowa implied that his reading of the language he has just read was an answer to my question, which was as follows: Where in the bill are there provisions to insure that tests such as the one in the Motorola case are allowed?

Mr. MILLER. It is my interpretation—and that is why I wanted to clear this with the leadership, because I understood that during the drafting of this title, this was the intention—that the Motorola case was discussed——

Mr. HUMPHREY. The Motorola case was discussed, discussed, and cussed.

Mr. LAUSCHE. Mr. President, in whose time is the Senator from Minnesota speaking?

Mr. HUMPHREY. Mr. President, I ask the Senator to yield briefly to me.

Mr. MILLER. I yield.

Mr. HUMPHREY. It was the reason for some of the provisions of title VII. That is why I said I did not think the proposed new language was necessary.

The PRESIDING OFFICER. The question is on agreeing to the amendment of the Senator from Texas. [Putting the question.]

Mr. TOWER. Mr. President, have not the yeas and nays been ordered on the question of agreeing to this amendment?

The PRESIDING OFFICER. The yeas and nays have not yet been requested.

Mr. TOWER and other Senators requested the yeas and nays.

The PRESIDING OFFICER. Is there a sufficient second?

The yeas and nays were ordered.

The PRESIDING OFFICER. The yeas and nays have been ordered on the question of agreeing to the amendment of the Senator from Texas [Mr. TOWER]. The clerk will call the roll.

The legislative clerk proceeded to call the roll.

Mr. MANSFIELD (when his name was called). On this vote, I have a live pair with the Senator from Arkansas [Mr. FULBRIGHT]. If the Senator from Arkansas [Mr. FULBRIGHT] were present and voting, he would vote "yea." If I were at liberty to vote, I would vote "nay." I withhold my vote.

Mr. SYMINGTON (when his name was called). On this vote, I have a pair with the senior Senator from Louisiana [Mr. ELLENDER]. If the senior Senator from Louisiana [Mr. ELLENDER] were present and voting, he would vote "yea." If I were at liberty to vote, I would vote "nay." I withhold my vote.

The rollcall was concluded.

Mr. HUMPHREY. I announce that the Senator from Maryland [Mr. BREWSTER], the Senator from Oklahoma [Mr. EDMONDSON], the Senator from Louisiana [Mr. ELLENDER], the Senator from Arkansas [Mr. FULBRIGHT], the Senator from Alaska [Mr. GRUENING], the Senator from Virginia [Mr. ROBERTSON] and the Senator from Tennessee [Mr. WALTERS] are absent on official business.

I also announce that the Senator from California [Mr. ENGLE] is absent because of illness.

I further announce that, if present and voting, the Senator from Oklahoma [Mr. EDMONDSON] would vote "nay."

On this vote, the Senator from Virginia [Mr. ROBERTSON] is paired with the Senator from Maryland [Mr. BREWSTER]. If present and voting, the Senator from Virginia would vote "yea" and the Senator from Maryland would vote "nay."

Mr. KUCHEL. I announce that the Senator from Delaware [Mr. BOGGS] and and the Senator from Massachusetts [Mr. SALTONSTALL] are necessarily absent and, if present and voting, would each vote "nay."

The Senator from Vermont [Mr. PROUTY] is absent on official business, and, if present and voting, would vote "nay."

The result was announced—yeas 38, nays 49, as follows:

[No. 302 Leg.]

YEAS—38

Allott	Dominick	Hruska
Bennett	Eastland	Johnston
Byrd, Va.	Ervin	Jordan, N.C.
Byrd, W. Va.	Goldwater	Jordan, Idaho
Carlson	Gore	Lausche
Cooper	Hickenlooper	Long, La.
Cotton	Hill	McClellan
Curtis	Holland	Mechem
Morton	Smathers	Tower
Mundt	Sparkman	Williams, Del.
Pearson	Stennis	Yarborough
Russell	Talmadge	Young, N. Dak.
Simpson	Thurmond	

NAYS—49

Aiken	Hayden	Monroney
Anderson	Humphrey	Morse
Bartlett	Inouye	Moss
Bayh	Jackson	Muskie
Beall	Javits	Nelson
Bible	Keating	Neuberger
Burdick	Kennedy	Pastore
Cannon	Kuchel	Pell
Case	Long, Mo.	Proxmire
Church	Magnuson	Randolph
Clark	McCarthy	Ribicoff
Dirksen	McGee	Scott
Dodd	McGovern	Smith
Douglas	McIntyre	Williams, N.J.
Fong	McNamara	Young, Ohio
Hart	Metcalf	
Hartke	Miller	

NOT VOTING—13

Boggs	Fulbright	Saltonstall
Brewster	Gruening	Symington
Edmondson	Mansfield	Walters
Ellender	Prouty	
Engle	Robertson	

So Mr. TOWER's amendment was rejected.

(material omitted)

g. 110 Cong. Rec. 13724 (Revised Tower Amendment Accepted, becomes §703(h))

13724   CONGRESSIONAL RECORD — SENATE   *June 13*

(material omitted and repaginated)

Mr. TOWER. Mr. President, I call up my amendment No. 952, which I ask to have modified. I send to the desk the modification and ask that it be stated. It is my understanding that under a previous agreement, a Senator may be allowed to modify his own amendment.

The PRESIDING OFFICER. The amendment will be stated, as modified.

The legislative clerk read as follows:

On page 44, line 15, insert the following after the word "origin"; nor shall it be an unlawful employment practice for an employer to give and to act upon the results of any professionally developed ability test provided that such test, its administration or action upon the results is not designed, intended, or used to discriminate because of race, color, religion, sex, or national origin.

Mr. TOWER. Mr. President, I yield myself 1 minute.

This is similar to an amendment which I offered a day or two ago, and which was, I believe, agreed upon in principle.

But the language was not drawn as carefully as it should have been.

It is my understanding that the present language has been cleared through the Attorney General, the leadership, and the proponents of the bill.

I therefore urge its adoption. I ask for the yeas and nays.

Mr. HUMPHREY. Mr. President, will the Senator yield?

Mr. TOWER. I yield.

Mr. HUMPHREY. Mr. President, I think it should be noted that the Senators on both sides of the aisle who were deeply interested in title VII have examined the text of this amendment and have found it to be in accord with the intent and purpose of that title.

I do not think there is any need for a rollcall. We can expedite it. The Senator has won his point.

I concur in the amendment and ask for its adoption.

Mr. TOWER. Mr. President, I withdraw my request for the yeas and nays.

The PRESIDING OFFICER. The question is on agreeing to amendment No. 952 offered by the Senator from Texas [Mr. TOWER].

The amendment was agreed to.

Mr. TOWER. Mr. President, I move to reconsider the vote by which the amendment was agreed to.

Mr. HUMPHREY. Mr. President, I move to lay that motion on the table.

The motion to lay the motion to reconsider on the table was agreed to.

---

h. 110 Cong. Rec. 14239 (The Mansfield-Dirksen Amendment)

1964   CONGRESSIONAL RECORD — SENATE   **14239**

(material omitted and repaginated)

HUMPHREY STATEMENT ON CERTAIN PROVISIONS OF TITLES II AND VII

Mr. President, in the course of discussion of the package substitute for H.R. 7152, questions have arisen concerning two provisions of the substitute and a number of requests for additional explanation of these provisions have been received.

Concern has been expressed because the Attorney General must show "resistance to the full enjoyment of any of the rights secured by this title" before prevailing by him in cases brought by him under titles II and VII. This concern is unfounded. This language is adopted to conform with the change that limits the Attorney General to cases involving a pattern or practice of violations of rights protected by these titles. It is meant to exclude action in sporadic instances of violation of rights, which will be left to correction by individual complainants under other sections of these titles. It would be clear that an establishment or employer that consistently or avowedly denies rights under these titles is engaged in a "pattern or practice of resistance."

Section 703(g) of the bill has been widely misinterpreted. Some statements have been made indicating that employers could, merely by invoking national security, exempt themselves from coverage of the equal employment provisions of the act. This, of course, is not so. This provision must be applied equally without regard to race, color, religion, or national origin. An employer could not deny employment to a qualified Negro on the ground that he does not have security clearance and employ a white person without clearance. Nor could an employer prefer one employee

Negro on the ground that he does not have security clearance and employ a white person without clearance. Nor could an employer prefer one employee or applicant over another by seeking security clearance for him while refusing to request clearance for another, if such preference is based on discriminatory considerations. Since it is not likely that the Government will process a security clearance request except for a person who has been hired, the employer would generally make his decision as to whom he will employ before the security issue can be raised, and the issue of discrimination can be decided on the basis of the facts at that time. This amendment, in effect, is basically one of a clarifying nature. Even without it, employers would not, and could not, ignore valid national security regulations if they are engaged in governmental work involving the application of these regulations.

As floor manager of this bill, I thought this clarification of these two sections of titles II and VII would be helpful and appropriate.

The PRESIDING OFFICER. The question is on agreeing to the Mansfield-Dirksen substitute, amendment No. 1052, as amended. On this question, the yeas and nays have been ordered, and the clerk will call the roll.

The legislative clerk proceeded to call the roll.

Mr. MANSFIELD (when his name was called). On this vote I have a pair with the distinguished Senator from Virginia [Mr. ROBERTSON]. If he were present and voting, he would vote "nay." If I were at liberty to vote, I would vote "yea." I withhold my vote.

Mr. TOWER (when his name was called). On this vote I have a pair with

the distinguished junior Senator from Arizona [Mr. GOLDWATER]. If he were present and voting, he would vote "yea." If I were at liberty to vote, I would vote "nay." Therefore I withhold my vote.

The rollcall was concluded.

Mr. HUMPHREY. I announce that the Senator from Virginia [Mr. ROBERTSON] is absent on official business.

I also announce that the Senator from California [Mr. ENGLE] is absent because of illness.

I further announce that, if present and voting, the Senator from California [Mr. ENGLE] would vote "yea."

Mr. KUCHEL. I announce that the Senator from Arizona [Mr. GOLDWATER] and the Senator from Iowa [Mr. HICKENLOOPER] are detained on official business.

If present and voting, the Senator from Iowa [Mr. HICKENLOOPER] would vote "yea."

The pair of the Senator from Arizona [Mr. GOLDWATER] has been previously announced.

The result was announced—yeas 76, nays 18, as follows:

* * * *

So the Mansfield-Dirksen substitute (amendment No. 1052), as amended, was agreed to.

Mr. HUMPHREY. Mr. President, I move to reconsider the vote by which the amendment was agreed to.

Mr. KUCHEL. Mr. President, I move to lay that motion on the table.

The motion to lay on the table was agreed to.

The PRESIDING OFFICER. The question is on the engrossment of the amendment and the third reading of the bill.

The amendment was ordered to be engrossed, and the bill to be read a third time.

V. Vote in the Senate: The Amended Bill Is Passed (June 19, 1964)

    a. 110 Cong. Rec. 14506-11 (June 19, 1964)

(material omitted)

THE CIVIL RIGHTS ACT

Mr. McCARTHY. Mr. President, I yield myself such time as I may require.

The ACTING PRESIDENT pro tempore. The Senator from Minnesota may proceed.

Mr. McCARTHY. Mr. President, the Senate of the United States is about to approve the Civil Rights Act of 1964. This is not an action which is being taken without thorough consideration and study and reflection, as some have charged. It is not an action in which the will of the people is not fully and adequately known, as some Members of the Senate have suggested. It is not an action which is beyond the responsibility of the Federal Government, and hence not beyond the responsibility of the legislative branch of that Government, as some have suggested.

The need for this action has been demonstrated in the depth of over 100 years of American history and it has also been demonstrated in the breadth of contemporary America. It has been petitioned not only in words but also in the actions, even the sufferings, and in some cases by the death of American citizens.

The legislatures of the majority of States of the Union have shown their will and judgment through the years in passing laws against discrimination. The courts of the land have not only struck down segregation laws, but have also ruled against the practice of discrimination. Teachers and educators, who know that discrimination cannot be reconciled with the truths which they teach, have called upon us for action; and religious leaders have asked us to sustain in the law of this land the moral principles and precepts of reason and also of faith. Artists and those who are students of the arts have demonstrated and declared that excellence and creative ability are not the quality of a race but rather the quality of the individual.

Four Presidents of the United States have asked the Congress to close the gap between executive actions, the decisions of the courts, and the statutes of this land. We are here today taking action to close that gap, and to meet our responsibilities. Finally, there are those who have in person in the North and South, and in the East and West, given public demonstration that they believe in human dignity and in equality. Their leaders, more than any others, have called upon us to take action here today.

This long debate in the Senate has been in the best tradition of American disagreement and political controversy. The leaders on both sides have demonstrated their realization that this is a historic decision of great moral and cultural importance—as well as political significance. They have known that they dealt in the very substance of the democratic life of the United States, and that what was being tested was not just the reality and the practice of American democracy, but the fundamental principles on which this democracy has been built.

Those who have opposed the passage of this proposed legislation, or who have advocated that it be significantly modified, have not questioned the strength and the appropriateness of the Bill of Rights and the 14th and 15th amendments. On the contrary, they have, for the most part, raised practical questions as to the lines of authority between the Federal Government and State governments, as to the limitations of the authority of the Federal Government and of the executive branch of that Government; and they have raised honest questions as to whether the new procedures would be effective and as to whether the execution of this law might not result in the impairment or loss of other rights and privileges.

Certainly these are proper questions to raise—and these are questions which have been properly and adequately answered.

Why, some have asked, should the Federal Government now intervene in areas which traditionally have been State and local areas of responsibility; and why, they ask, should accepted or established arrangements—arrangements which have existed without disturbance for 50 years or more—now be declared not only to be unlawful, but also immoral?

The answer to these questions is to be found, in part, in principle and belief, and in part, also, in the very context of history itself. The search for freedom and for a world in which freedom and equality can be enjoyed has been the preoccupation of civilized people throughout the history of the world. Certainly, it has been the preoccupation of Americans since this country was first settled. One man has said: once we have declared for liberty and for freedom and for equality, we have declared for an unending war in an unending revolution. Certainly, we in the United States have declared more often, more consistently and more loudly, for equality, for liberty and freedom; and, consequently, we must bear the burden of that revolution and give the example.

The Declaration of Independence and the rights of that Declaration were not based on any reference to a papal bull or any kind of royal grant, nor of any ancient scroll which had been found.

These rights were not claimed because the people of this continent were once English, or because they were Christian, or because they were white, or because they were North Americans. These rights were claimed on the basis of the nature of man and the nature of a person. All of these rights to which we now refer today, on another occasion were declared to be the inalienable rights of all men. These civil rights do not derive because of law but, rather, derive from the very nature of man himself. They have their basis and they rest in that nature. We have made these basic human rights civil rights, and we have sought to guarantee and protect them through the Constitution of the United States and of the States, and through the laws of the land.

The moral basis of these civil rights and of this pending civil rights bill is expressed most clearly in the Declaration of Independence and in the Constitution, and affirmatively included in the moral and religious principles which the great majority of the citizens of the United States have accepted and do accept.

The formalization of these beliefs and of these principles in law has been a progressive one, depending upon events and the movement of history itself. The Constitution, we know, recognized slavery; the Emancipation Proclamation and the 13th amendment abolished it.

No new rights are created by this bill. The debate has not been over an abstract list of rights but over those changes in procedures and in law which may be necessary to facilitate and, in some cases, to insure the enjoyment of fundamental human rights.

It means little to speak about inalienable rights of life, liberty, and the pursuit of happiness, if there exist no opportunities for education or for useful employment—if those who speak of them or in whom these rights theoretically inhere do not have a chance to vote or to be educated or to participate in the economic efforts of the country, and on the basis of that participation to establish their claim to a share of the goods of that system.

Any venture of law in the field of human relations is a difficult and a dangerous one. This is a dangerous venture. The enactment of this law will not solve all problems of this kind. But this is, nonetheless, a necessary and an all-important law.

This is an imperfect law, as is any law which ventures into the difficult area of human relations. It is a law which will be subject to review by the courts and again by the Congress—perhaps again and again by the Congress. It is a law which, if it is to be reasonably effective, will depend for administration upon dedicated and prudent men.

It is a law, I insist, which is not directed against the people of any one region of this country, but one which calls for moral and intellectual response from all the people of the United States.

It is a law which could not be postponed, for both principle and the movement of history itself cry out for its passage in this year of 1964.

Mr. President, I reserve the remainder of my time.

Mr. CARLSON. Mr. President, I yield myself such time as I may need.

After weeks of debate, we are approaching a final vote on probably the most significant proposal to be considered by the Congress in this generation.

It is most difficult to legislate in the field of civil rights because of the emotional nature of the issues involved.

Many of the citizens of Kansas—both proponents and opponents—have written to me of their sincere concern about many of the provisions of the bill and its effect on the rights of citizens of our Nation.

To them I say that the bill is not as bad as its enemies claim; nor will it produce the benefits the proponents anticipate. In my opinion, the amendments approved by the Senate have made this a constitutional and effective civil rights bill.

In the final analysis, governmental coercion through legislation will not of itself bring an end to discrimination and insure equality of treatment to every citizen.

The end of discrimination and inequality of treatment among our citizens will come only when all of us are willing to lay aside bigotry and prejudice and give full credence to the Golden Rule.

I shall vote for this bill with some misgivings, but with the hope that it will bring about closer cooperation and good will among our citizens.

Mr. COOPER. Mr. President, we have spent many days in debating this important bill. At this late hour there is little that anyone can add to the long debate.

It is true that there are provisions in the bill which do not meet with the approval of many Senators, both those who support the bill, as well as those who oppose it. I respect the convictions of those who oppose the bill. I am led to say, however, that I do not know how Congress could agree upon any civil rights bill which could receive the approval of more Members unless it were so diluted that it would be ineffective.

I have some understanding of the problems of the Southern States. Having lived my entire lifetime in the border State of Kentucky, I know the emotions and the convictions and, I may say, the prejudices which are bound up in the issue of civil rights.

If I had lived in one of those States and were speaking and voting tonight, I could not say that I would hold the same position that I do, although I hope that I would. For years ago I reached the conviction that these great issues of human rights must be faced and must be solved within the framework of law. Time and again in this debate concern has been voiced about the incidents of violence which have grown in our land in recent years. I have been concerned about the trend toward violence. If it should become a practice in our country to employ violence to settle great governmental questions, it would seriously alter a distinguishing characteristic of our country—that of change and progress by the processes of law. Nevertheless, I know that protests, which sometimes lead to violence, are generally the constitutional demonstrations of men and women who are objecting, and objecting rightfully, because they are being denied their constitutional rights. These demonstrations will not end until these rights are assured by law, and not offered as a matter of grace.

This bill in three of its major sections, titles I, II, and IV deals with rights that have been declared constitutional rights by the Bill of Rights, and by the courts. If the titles against which complaint has been made—title II and title VII—have not yet been judged to be constitutional rights, nevertheless they are rights of equal opportunity, they are moral rights and rights of decency which should be accorded every citizen of this land. If they are not accorded, we will deny the promise of this land, the promise which our country has held for its people and the people of the world, as a country of freedom and justice.

Consent is a necessary element to law. Consent to law comes through education and through the leadership of those who govern; it comes through the leadership of people in every walk of life; but it must also come from a willingness to accept law, and from enforcement of the law.

Consent develops as Justice Frankfurter in the famous case, Cooper against Aaron, once declared, with the help of men who are charged with the responsibility of official power, as used in the leadership of people.

In speaking of consent, Justice Frankfurter said:

Local customs, however hardened by time, are not decreed in heaven. Habits and the feelings they engender may be counteracted and moderated. Experience attests that such local habits and feelings will yield, gradually though this be, to law and education. And educational influences are exerted not only by explicit teaching. They vigorously flow from the fruitful exercise of the responsibility of those charged with political official power, and from the almost unconsciously transforming actualities of living under law.

I believe that Congress, in passing this civil rights bill, will exercise its responsibility to assure the rights and opportunities of all of its citizens. We have placed these rights, as the great Justice said, in the "transforming actualities of living under law."

This is the final hour of decision. It is an hour which requires us, now that the bill is to be passed, to put our hands to the plow and to work together in the days ahead as men of good faith, and with faith in our system of law, which protects the equal rights of all our citizens.

Mr. THURMOND. Mr. President, I yield myself such time as I may use.

This bill is the greatest grasp of Executive power conceived in the 20th century. It will make of the President a czar and of the Attorney General a Rasputin.

This bill is drafted with the clear, deliberate intent to destroy every effective constitutional limitation upon the extension of Federal Executive power over individuals and States. While the Federal controls created by the bill apply primarily to discrimination on the grounds of race, color, religion, sex, or national origin, they would set a precedent for the expansion of Federal dictation into almost every phase of business and individual relationship.

The powers given to the Attorney General under the bill are enormous. The bill would grant to the Attorney General unprecedented authority to file suits against property owners, to file suits against plain citizens, to file suits against State and local officials, even though the supposed grievant has not filed suit. The Attorney General would become the grievant's lawyer at the taxpayer's expense.

The bill grants to the Attorney General the unprecedented power to shop around for a judge that he prefers to hear a voting suit; the right to sue an owner of public accommodations before the owner is accused of a discriminatory practice; the right to sue State and local officials concerning public facilities and against local school boards, although no suit has been filed by any schoolchild, parent, or any other person.

The bill would give unprecedented power to the Federal Government to withhold funds that are justly due the States or their political subdivisions. I again remind Senators that title VI of the bill amends every Federal law—and that means more than 100—that deals with financing, to require each Federal agency to issue regulations defining for itself "discrimination," and, "race, color, religion, or national origin." Subject to ineffective limitations, each agency is permitted to set up its own controls, sanctions and penalties, including "termination of, or refusal to grant or to continue assistance," and, "any other means authorized by law."

Mr. President, how much time have I remaining?

The ACTING PRESIDENT pro tempore. The Senator has 1 minute remaining.

Mr. THURMOND. Mr. President, I wish again to remind the Senate that this bill is clearly unconstitutional.

It would seek to permit Congress to establish qualifications for voting, although this power is reserved to the States under the Constitution. This is in violation of section 2 of article I, and the 10th and 17th amendments.

The bill attempts to apply the provisions of the 14th amendment to "private actions" although it is applicable on its very face only to State action. This bill is in direct conflict with the 1883 Civil Rights cases, and the 1959 Howard Johnson case.

The bill would deny the right of trial by jury in a criminal prosecution in violation of the sixth amendment.

The bill would deprive a person of property without due process, in violation of the fifth amendment. The bill would deprive a person of property without just compensation in violation of the fifth amendment.

The bill makes an offense of speaking or writing against the objects sought to be accomplished by the bill. This is a violation of the first amendment.

The bill seeks to regulate businesses which are solely local in character. This is in violation of section 8 of article I, which regulates commerce among the several States.

The bill seeks to subject citizens to "involuntary servitude" by making them render personal services against their own choice, in violation of the 13th amendment.

The bill attempts to delegate legislative powers to the Attorney General and other officials of the executive branch in violation of section 1 of article I of the Constitution.

Mr. President, I hope that the Senate will defeat the bill.

THIS THING THAT WE DO

Mr. PROUTY. Mr. President, 103 years ago—when the House of this Nation was divided—to serve the cause of freedom and to make our people one, a man came out of Illinois.

One hundred and three years later, to open the doors of our National House and to serve the cause of freedom, another man has come out of Illinois.

True it may be that no one man was responsible for the abolition of slavery. True it may be that no man is responsible for our statute to prohibit discrimination. But, without Lincoln there would have been no Emancipation Proclamation, and without DIRKSEN there would have been no civil rights bill.

From Jefferson to Johnson, from Lincoln to Dirksen, the roads are long and the journeys arduous.

Twice an assassin's bullet struck down the guiding spirit of liberty and twice the Nation moved on.

Frederick Douglass, Abraham Lincoln, John Fitzgerald Kennedy—all these are gone. How I wish they could know that in 1964 when there was heard the cry "freedom now," the Congress answered "ever more."

"Ever more" is the solemn pledge we make this day. It is ours to keep—it is ours to bequeath to the yet unborn.

History will long remember the sturdy stewards of this undertaking—DIRKSEN, MANSFIELD, HUMPHREY, KUCHEL, and all the rest—but the journey will go on. Indignities will not end in this generation, nor in the next, but let it go out to all the world that we have begun their undoing.

One hundred years ago man in bondage was set loose. Perhaps 100 years hence man in prejudice will be set free—free in every inch and corner of this vast earth; free in full measure; free for all ages and times. These are the aims of a mighty and majestic people.

Mr. President, I have often wondered during the course of these proceedings whether there was present some hand more splendid than our own. For, if not, even the falling of a sparrow could escape His note. I expect that He observes our feeble endeavors to restore what He intended and which man has taken away.

This thing that we do—if it be an act for vengence or gain—will surely fail. But if it be an act of love—it will surely succeed.

May our aim be noble and our law just, and may we have the touch of His blessing for "Except the Lord build the house, we labor in vain that build it."

Mr. MANSFIELD. Mr. President, I yield myself 10 minutes or less.

The ACTING PRESIDENT pro tempore. The Senator from Montana is recognized for 10 minutes.

Mr. MANSFIELD. Mr. President, this is the first anniversary of the late President John F. Kennedy's submission of the present legislation to Congress. In presenting it, President Kennedy asked for a law to provide "reasonable men with the reasonable means" to soothe the Nation's racial malady "however long it may take and however troublesome it may be."

Mr. President, the Senate is about to fulfill its responsibilities in the resolution of the most divisive issue in our history. The attainment of this moment, in my judgment, is perhaps of even greater significance than the outcome of the vote itself, for it underscores, once again, the basic premise of our Government—that a people of great diversity can resolve even its most profound differences, under the Constitution, through the processes of reason, restraint, and reciprocal understanding. And what has been done in the Senate on the issue of civil rights can and must be done throughout the Nation. The differences on civil rights run as deep in this body as elsewhere; but no blood has been shed in this Chamber, and blood need not be shed elsewhere.

Like other exceptional accomplishments of this body, this moment is the work, not of one, but of both parties. The course of the entire debate makes clear that there has existed, as the paramount consideration on both sides of the aisle, an awareness of a paramount need of the Nation.

This moment belongs to the Senate as a whole. Senators of the Republic have put aside personal inclinations. All Senators have endured frustrations, disappointments, and inconveniences along the arduous trail which has led to this vote.

But I want to say, in particular, of the distinguished Senator from Illinois, the minority leader [Mr. DIRKSEN], that this is his finest hour.

His concern for the welfare of the Nation, above personal and party concern, has been revealed many times in the Senate, but never before in so vital and difficult a context. The Senate and the whole country are in the debt of the Senator from Illinois.

And we are in debt, too, to the distinguished majority whip, the Senator from Minnesota [Mr. HUMPHREY]. He has rendered a great service under difficult personal circumstances, to the Senate and the Nation through his patience and dedication. He has performed Herculean feats in maintaining the Democratic share of a quorum day after day and night after night, in acting as the principal exponent and defender of the bill in debate, and in general floor management. He has served with a deep understanding of the Senate's ways and with the tremendous energy, intelligence, skill, and good humor which have characterized him in many other situations.

Others, too, have done exceptional service in these critical months. There has been the work of the distinguished minority whip, the Senator from California [Mr. KUCHEL], who filled the job of floor leader for the Republicans. The floor captains, both Democratic and Republican, made the major speeches to explain and to defend in detail the particular titles, and served long hours on the floor. There has been the good sense of the Senator from Vermont [Mr. AIKEN], the Senator from Massachusetts [Mr. SALTONSTALL], the Senator from Kentucky [Mr. COOPER], the Senator from Washington [Mr. MAGNUSON], the Senator from Rhode Island [Mr. PASTORE], the Senator from Michigan [Mr. HART], the Senator from Pennsylvania [Mr. CLARK], the Senator from Illinois, [Mr. DOUGLAS], the Senator from Hawaii [Mr. INOUYE], the Senator from Colorado [Mr. ALLOTT], the Senator from Kansas [Mr. CARLSON], the Senators from New York [Mr. JAVITS and Mr. KEATING], the Senator from Pennsylvania [Mr. SCOTT], the Senator from New Jersey [Mr. CASE], and other Senators—all others—who worked long and hard in conferences and on the floor. And I should like to note, too, the contribution of the Senator from Iowa [Mr. HICKENLOOPER], and certain of his Republican colleagues who, despite personal reservations, in the end, found the route to agreement which made cloture possible. In so doing, they placed the demeanor and responsibility of the Senate, as an institution, above personal feelings. The courage and dedication displayed by Senator CLAIR ENGLE were contributions, too, which should not and will not be forgotten.

And finally, Mr. President, there has been the insistence of the opposition on prolonged debate. It was learned and thorough, and it played an essential role in refining the provisions of the bill. But, in my judgment, its most important function was to discourage self-righteousness on the part of the majority. There is no room for unwarranted sentiments of victory if the legislation we have molded is to be given constructive meaning for the Nation in the years ahead. If we are about to enter upon a second Reconstruction—as the Senator from Georgia [Mr. RUSSELL] called it—then it must be a reconstruction of the heart, a reconstruction involving, not one section, but all sections of the Nation. The dimensions of the problem with which we have been struggling these past months stretch the length and breadth of the Nation. An accurate appraisal of them leads, not to a sense of triumph over the passage of this bill, but to a profound humility. No one, let me say, understood this reality better than the late President John Fitzgerald Kennedy. This, indeed, is his moment, as well as the Senate's.

Mr. President, William H. Stringer wrote an excellent article, entitled "The Senators' Creed," which was published earlier this week in the Christian Science Monitor. I quote from the article by Mr. Stringer:

> One of the observations that Americans can proudly make about the Senate's battle over cloture was that vituperation was held in check.

> Nearly everyone seemed to recognize that this was a solemn, poignant moment in the history of the United States—this struggle over a far-reaching civil rights bill, this wrenching change in the customs of proud people—and the Senators conducted themselves honorably.

> This is a behavior in American politics that needs to be cherished and cultivated. Politics is not always as practiced in heated election campaigns. But the Senate—that "gentlemen's club"—usually sets a standard.

Mr. President, it will soon be time to call the roll, to record the yeas and nays, and then to proceed to the other business of the Nation, which, of necessity, we have put aside for so long.

Mr. DIRKSEN. Mr. President, we are on the threshold of what I suppose everyone will consider a historic vote.

I am deeply grateful to the majority leader [Mr. MANSFIELD] for his patience, his tolerance, and his sense of self-effacement in all the tedious struggle that has gone on for nearly 100 days; and I am truly grateful to the deputy majority leader [Mr. HUMPHREY], because of the attributes he has brought to this struggle. He has been fair, tolerant, and just, and always has brought to this problem an understanding heart.

To my revered assistant, the distinguished whip on the minority side [Mr. KUCHEL], I say with equal accolade how grateful I am for the way he stood by under every circumstance and for the rare patience he has displayed in all this difficult time.

Mr. President, it has been a tedious matter. It has been a long labor, indeed. On looking back, I think a little of the rather popular television program called "That Was the Week That Was." I think tonight we can say, "That was the year that was," because it was a year ago this June that we first started coming to grips with this very challenging controversy on civil rights.

On the 5th of June, my own party, after 2 days of labor and conference, came forward with a consensus to express its views on the subject. That consensus is printed in the CONGRESSIONAL RECORD. I shall read only a portion of what we said in the course of that statement. Before I do so, I wish to say that prior to the conference I had worked out on a portable typewriter what I thought

was a general and acceptable statement of principle. In the course of the conference, a word was removed, and then it was restored; a phrase was removed, and then it was restored. Finally, we came up with a declaration of which I think we can all be proud, for among other things, the statement included the following:

> It is the consensus of the Senate Republican conference that: "The Federal Government, including the legislative, executive, and judicial branches, has a solemn duty to preserve the rights, privileges, and immunities of citizens of the United States in conformity with the Constitution, which makes every native-born and naturalized person a citizen of the United States, as well as the State in which he resides. Equality of rights and opportunities has not been fully achieved in the long period since the 14th and 15th amendments to the Constitution were adopted, and this inequality and lack of opportunity and the racial tensions which they engender are out of character with the spirit of a nation pledged to justice and freedom."

I recite one other paragraph from that statement of principle:

> The Republican Members of the U.S. Senate, in this 88th Congress, reaffirm and reassert the basic principles of the party with respect to civil rights, and further affirm that the President, with the support of Congress, consistent with its duties as defined in the Constitution, must protect the rights of all U.S. citizens regardless of race, creed, color, or national origin.

Mr. President, that conference took place on June 5, 1963, and this is June of 1964. So with a sense of propriety I can say for the bone pickers who will be setting it down on the history books that "this is the year that was."

After this statement of principle came the conferences at the White House. Those also occurred in the month of June. I remember how patient the late President of the United States was when he met first with the joint leadership, and then with individual Members, and then with the minority Members in the hope that his message and his bill to be presented to both branches of the Congress could be scheduled for early action.

I recited once before that I and my party had chided the late President of the United States for his dereliction in the matter, and said that there was a promise and a pledge that when a new Congress began in 1961 there would be early action on the civil rights issue.

When that action was not forthcoming, we were unsparing, of course, in our criticism, until at long last that bill was submitted.

Then came the grinding of the legislative mill. That mill grinds slowly but it grinds exceedingly fine. What has happened in "the year that was" is a tribute to the patience and understanding of the country, to the Senate, and generally the people of this Republic. It was marked, of course, by demonstrations and marches, and on occasion by some outbursts of violence. But the mills have ground before, Mr. President, where a moral issue was involved, and it is not too far from fact and reason to assert that they will continue to grind in the history of this blessed and continuing Republic.

For example, I mention that in the field of child labor, when even President Wilson observed, years ago, that the Beveridge bill was obviously absurd, the mill continued to grind, and at long last the Congress undertook to prevent the shipment in interstate commerce of goods that had been produced by the sweated toil of children. There was a moral issue.

In 1906, after the reports of Harvey Wiley—President McKinley had gone before—there were fulminations on the Senate floor. The speeches that were delivered about the intrusion of Federal power sound absolutely incredible today when we undertake to reread them. But there was an inexorable force. In the past 30 years, while I have been here, I have not seen a single Congress that has not added to the Pure Food, Drug, and Cosmetic Act.

I mentioned on the floor of the Senate once before that when the legislature in New York State inhibited work in the bake shops of that State beyond 10 hours a day and 6 days a week, the law was stricken down by the highest tribunal in the land. Then in the Wilson administration came the Adamson law, which provided for an 8-hour workday on the railroads. Today who will stand in his place and quarrel with those limitations upon the workday and the workweek?

I was in the House of Representatives in 1934 when the Social Security Act was placed upon the statute books. I remember the fulminations, the castigations, and the averments that the act was unconstitutional. But it is on the books and it is accepted; and all the trenchant editorials, all of the truculent statements, and all the speeches on the floor of the House and Senate were swept away by some inexorable force. I do not remember the beginning, but I mentioned before that in 1888, when a group of crusaders went to Chicago to enlarge, if they could, an interest in the civil service system, there were only six people who attended the meeting, but it required only one bullet—a bullet from an assassin—to reach President Garfield's heart to completely change the mood of the country and, as a result, in 1883 the Pendleton Act went on the books.

Will any Senator stand in his place today in this or any other body and undertake to sweep it aside and call for repeal of the civil service system?

Theodore Roosevelt and Gifford Pinchot argued and worked to get into the public domain great quantities of ground for the benefit of the people, and were met by every barricade and obstacle.

But truth and righteousness and a sense of justice prevailed, and it required no constitutional amendment to bring it about. Nor did it require a constitutional amendment to bring about these forward thrusts in the interest of the people and in the interest of the expansion of enjoyment for the living of our people.

The same thing can be said about the minimum wage. I had my fingers crossed about it many times. My friend from West Virginia nods his head in approval. He remembers very well when we were on a subcommittee together. We accepted that proposal as a matter of course.

These are programs that touch people. Today they are accepted because they are accepted as a part of the forward thrust in the whole efforts of mankind to move forward.

I reemphasize the fact that it required no constitutional change to bring this about, because it appeared there was latitude enough in that document, the oldest written constitution on the face of the earth, to embrace within its four corners these advances for human brotherhood.

It leads us—it leads me, certainly—to the conclusion that in the history of mankind there is an inexorable moral force that carries us forward.

No matter what statements may be made on the floor, no matter how tart the editorials in every section of the country, no matter what the resistance of people who do not wish to change, it will not be denied. Mankind ever forward goes. There have been fulminations to impede, but they have never stopped that thrust. As I think of it, it is slow. It is undramatic. Somebody once said that progress is the intelligent, undramatic application of life on what is here.

It is a good definition. When I think of the word dramatic I think of what Woodrow Wilson said in World War I. I was in uniform on the Western Front. There was a movement in this country to send Theodore Roosevelt there to head a division. That suggestion had great appeal. Letters by the hundred of thousands moved into the White House. Woodrow Wilson settled the issue with a single sentence. He said, "The answer is 'No' because the business in hand is undramatic."

This is not dramatic business. Here we are dealing with a moral force that carries us along.

Argue and fuss and utter all the extreme opinions one will, Mr. President—our people still go forward, and we will not be worthy of our trust if we do not give heed to the great, mobile force that carries humankind along its path.

There was a time when the attributes of life, when life itself, when all those things we hope for a human being, did not count too much in the scale of everyday values. When Peter the Great went to Poland on a visit, he was told, "We have invented a new torture machine. We put a body on the rack and tear it asunder." He said "I would like to have a demonstration." He was told, "We have nobody in prison on whom to demonstrate." He said, "It is all right. Take one of my retinue and break his body."

That is all life amounted to only a few hundred years ago.

There was a queen named Marie Antoinette. History records that as she was going through the countryside she saw groveling peasants trying to subsist on roots and herbs and whatever nature had to offer them. One of the servants said to her, "They are groveling peasants, without bread to eat." History records the cynical answer that she gave in response. She said, "Let them eat cake."

What an answer. But history would not accept that answer, because the thrust of humankind has been ever forward and upward.

I remember the day when I sat with General Eisenhower in his office. I saw a picture on the wall. I said, "That looks like Marshall Zhukov to me." He said, "It is. I want to tell you a story about him and when they gave me my decoration"—I forget whether it was the Red Star, or the Order of Lenin. He said, "You know, he is a great general, and he is an intriguing fellow, but he is very cynical. He has little regard for human life on the battlefield. When I told him of one of our forays and I told him we sent a minesweeper into the area so our soldiers could proceed, Zhukov said, 'Oh, you sent in your minesweepers? We do not do that. One life—what is it? One thousand lives—what are they? Ten thousand lives—what are they? Poof.'" That shows a disregard for human life and for all the attributes that go with it.

So today we come to grips finally with a bill that advances the enjoyment of living; but, more than that, it advances the equality of opportunity.

I do not emphasize the word "equality" standing by itself. It means equality of opportunity in the field of education. It means equality of opportunity in the field of employment. It means equality of opportunity in the field of participation in the affairs of government, and the day in the life of a citizen when he can go to the polls, under a representative system, to select the person for whom to vote, who is going to stay in that position for a period of years, whether it is at the local, State, or National level?

That is it.

Equality of opportunity, if we are going to talk about conscience, is the mass conscience of mankind that speaks in every generation, and it will continue to speak long after we are dead and gone.

Every generation, of course, must march up to the unfinished tasks of the generation that has gone before. Often times I have puzzled about the Tower of Babel which stood on the Plain of Shinar—that great work on which they labored in the hope that all those in that area might wander afield. Always there was a high beckoning tower to bring them back to the point of orientation. But then came the confusion of tongues, for that is exactly what "babel" means. That is the greatest unfinished project in the history of mankind. There probably will be greater, unfinished projects, and every generation will have to confront them.

They will also be found in the domain of freedom. They will be found in the pursuit of happiness as the Declaration of Independence asserts. They will be found in expanded living for people, for that is one of the goals of mankind. They will be found in the field of equal opportunity. They will be the unfinished work of every generation.

Mr. President, I must add a personal note, because on occasion a number of the "boys" up in the gallery have asked me, "How have you become a crusader in this cause?"

It is a fair question, and it deserves a fair answer.

That question was asked me once before. It was many years ago. I was then in the House of Representatives. I went to a meeting, and I listened to a Chinese doctor from the front at the time of the Japanese invasion of China come in and plead for money, for bandages, for medicine, in order to carry on. There was one line he used in his plea that seared itself indelibly into my memory.

He said, "They scream, but they live."

I carried those words with me for days and weeks, and when finally I was requested to go into the country for a number of speeches in the interest of Chinese relief, I did so.

A friend said to me, "Why do you waste your time on so remote a project? After all they are people with yellow skins, 12,000 miles from home. You are wasting time which you might well devote to your own constituents."

I said, "My friend, as an answer, there occurs to me a line from an English poet, whose name was John Donne. He left what I believe was a precious legacy on the parchments of history. He said, 'Any man's death diminishes me, because I am involved in mankind.'"

I am involved in mankind, and whatever the skin, we are all involved in mankind. Equality of opportunity must prevail if we are to complete the covenant that we have made with the people, and if we are to honor the pledges we made when we held up our hands to take an oath to defend the laws and to carry out the Constitution of the United States.

Eight times I did it in the House of Representatives.

Three times—God willing—my people have permitted me to do it in the Senate of the United States.

There is involved here the citizenship of people under the Constitution who, by the 14th amendment, are made not only citizens of the State where they reside, but also citizens of the United States of America.

That is what we deal with here. We are confronted with the challenge, and we must reckon with it.

I was heartened by a telegram dated June 10—I do not know whether other Senators received copies of it—datelined Cleveland, Ohio. It was addressed to me. I read it to the Senate:

We, the 40 undersigned Governors of the United States of America record our conviction that the prompt enactment of civil rights legislation by the Congress of the United States is urgently in the national interest and that the civil rights legislation pending before the Senate of the United States should be voted upon and approved, and that copy of this statement of principle be transmitted to the President.

Who were those Governors?

I shall not spell out the list in detail.

The Governors of Alaska, Ohio, and Connecticut.

The Governors of Pennsylvania, Hawaii, and Kansas.

The Governors of Indiana, South Dakota, and Kentucky.

The Governors of Wyoming, Massachusetts, and Maine.

The Governors of Missouri, Nevada, and Michigan.

The Governors of New Jersey, North Dakota, and Washington.

The Governors of Wisconsin, Guam, and California.

The Governors of Colorado, Delaware, and Rhode Island.

The Governors of Illinois, Oregon, and Iowa.

The Governors of Idaho, Maryland, and Utah.

The Governors of Minnesota, Arizona, and Nebraska.

The Governors of New Hampshire, Oklahoma, and New Mexico.

The Governors of Vermont, West Virginia, and American Samoa.

The Governor of the Virgin Islands.

There they are—40 of them.

What did they say?

Quick approval of the pending bill.

That is what they suggested to the Senate of the United States.

I believe that this telegram should be made a part of the RECORD, and I ask unanimous consent that the telegram be printed in the RECORD as a part of my remarks.

There being no objection, the telegram was ordered to be printed in the RECORD, as follows:

GOVERNORS' CONFERENCE—BIPARTISAN STATE-
MENT OF PRINCIPLE
CLEVELAND, OHIO,
June 10, 1964.

Senator EVERETT DIRKSEN,
Senate Office Building,
Washington, D.C.:

We, the 40 undersigned Governors of the United States of America, record our conviction that the prompt enactment of civil rights legislation by the Congress of the United States is urgently in the national interest and that the civil rights legislation now pending before the Senate of the United States should be voted upon and approved, and that copy of this statement of principle be transmitted to the President of the United States and to each Member of the Senate of the United States.

Gov. William A. Egan, Alaska; Gov. James A. Rhodes, Ohio; Gov. John Dempsey, Connecticut; Gov. William W. Scranton, Pennsylvania; Gov. John A. Burns, Hawaii; Gov. John Anderson, Jr., Kansas; Gov. Matthew E. Welsh, Indiana; Gov. Archie Gubbrud, South Dakota; Gov. Edward T. Breathitt, Kentucky; Gov. Clifford P. Hansen, Wyoming; Gov. Endicott Peabody, Massachusetts; Gov. John H. Reed, Maine; and Gov. John M. Dalton, Missouri; Gov. Grant Sawyer, Nevada; Gov. George Romney, Michigan; Gov. Richard J. Hughes, New Jersey; Gov. William L. Guy, North Dakota; Gov. Albert D. Rosellini, Washington; Gov. John W. Reynold, Wisconsin; Gov. Manuel Flores Leon Guerrero, Guam; Gov. Edmund G. Brown, California; Gov. John A. Love, Colorado; Gov. Elbert N. Carvel, Delaware; Gov. John H. Chafee, Rhode Island; Gov. Otto Kerner, Illinois; Gov. Mark O. Hatfield, Oregon; Gov. Harold E. Hughes, Iowa; Gov. Robert E. Smylie, Idaho; Gov. J. Millard Tawes, Maryland; Gov. George D. Clyde, Utah; Gov. Karl F. Rolvaag, Minnesota; Gov. Paul Fannin, Arizona; Gov. Frank B. Morrison, Nebraska; Gov. John W. King, New Hampshire; Gov. Henry Bellmon, Oklahoma; Gov. Jack M. Campbell, New Mexico; Gov. Philip H. Hoff, Vermont; Gov. William W. Barron, West Virginia; Gov. H. Rex Lee, American Samoa; Gov. Ralph M. Paiewonsky, Virgin Islands.

Mr. DIRKSEN. Mr. President, in line with the sentiment offered by the poet, "Any man's death diminishes me, because I am involved in mankind," so every denial of freedom, every denial of equal opportunity for a livelihood, for an education, for a right to participate in representative government diminishes me.

There is the moral basis for our case.

It has been long and tedious; but the mills will continue to grind, and, whatever we do here tonight as we stand on the threshold of a historic rollcall, those mills will not stop grinding.

So, Mr. President, I commend this bill to the Senate, and in its wisdom I trust that in bountiful measure it will prevail.

I close by expressing once more my gratitude to the distinguished majority leader for the tolerance that he has shown all through this long period of nearly 100 days.

But standing on the pinnacle of this night, looking back, looking around, looking forward, as an anniversary occasion requires, this is "the year that was," and it will be so recorded by the bone pickers who somehow put together all the items that portray man's journey through time that is history. I am prepared for the vote.

The ACTING PRESIDENT pro tempore. The bill having been read the third time, the question is, Shall it pass? The yeas and nays have been ordered, and the clerk will call the roll.

The legislative clerk called the roll.

The result was announced—yeas 73, nays 27, as follows:

[No. 436 Leg.]

YEAS—73

Aiken	Gruening	Morse
Allott	Hart	Morton
Anderson	Hartke	Moss
Bartlett	Hayden	Mundt
Bayh	Hruska	Muskie
Beall	Humphrey	Nelson
Bennett	Inouye	Neuberger
Bible	Jackson	Pastore
Boggs	Javits	Pearson
Brewster	Jordan, Idaho	Pell
Burdick	Keating	Prouty
Cannon	Kennedy	Proxmire
Carlson	Kuchel	Randolph
Case	Lausche	Ribicoff
Church	Long, Mo.	Saltonstall
Clark	Magnuson	Scott
Cooper	Mansfield	Smith
Curtis	McCarthy	Symington
Dirksen	McGee	Williams, N.J.
Dodd	McGovern	Williams, Del.
Dominick	McIntyre	Yarborough
Douglas	McNamara	Young, N. Dak.
Edmondson	Metcalf	Young, Ohio
Engle	Miller	
Fong	Monroney	

NAYS—27

Byrd, Va.	Hickenlooper	Russell
Byrd, W. Va.	Hill	Simpson
Cotton	Holland	Smathers
Eastland	Johnston	Sparkman
Ellender	Jordan, N.C.	Stennis
Ervin	Long, La.	Talmadge
Fulbright	McClellan	Thurmond
Goldwater	Mechem	Tower
Gore	Robertson	Walters

So the bill (H.R. 7152) was passed.

[Applause in the galleries.]

The ACTING PRESIDENT pro tempore. The guests in the galleries will refrain from conversation and comment. The Senate will be in order.

Mr. DIRKSEN. Mr. President, I move that the Senate reconsider the vote by which the bill was passed.

Mr. MANSFIELD. I move to lay that motion on the table.

The motion to lay on the table was agreed to.

Mr. HUMPHREY. Mr. President, I ask unanimous consent that the bill as amended by the Senate be printed.

The ACTING PRESIDENT pro tempore. Without objection, it is so ordered.

LEGISLATIVE PROGRAM — ORDER FOR ADJOURNMENT UNTIL MONDAY

Mr. DIRKSEN. Mr. President, I should like to query the majority leader with regard to the schedule for next week. I would like to know whether the Senate will adjourn until Monday.

Mr. MANSFIELD. Mr. President, in view of the circumstances, there will not be the usual Saturday session.

I ask unanimous consent that at the conclusion of business today, the Senate stand in adjournment until 12 noon, on Monday next.

The ACTING PRESIDENT pro tempore. Without objection, it is so ordered.

Mr. MANSFIELD. Mr. President, for the information of the Senate, in response to the question asked by the distinguished minority leader, it is anticipated that on Monday the Senate will start consideration of the Interior appropriation bill, to be followed, although not necessarily in this order, by the Treasury and Post Office appropriation bill, the atomic energy authorization bill, the National Aeronautics and Space authorization bill.

I would also, for the information of the Senate, state that after consulting with the distinguished minority leader— and I would hope with the concurrence of the Senate—we would be allowed to pass a number of unobjected-to items on the calendar. They are items which have been cleared. We would like to do it this evening.

The ACTING PRESIDENT pro tempore. The Senator from Illinois is recognized.

(material omitted)

b. 110 Cong. Rec. 15998 (1964): Comparative Analysis of the Two Versions of the Civil Rights Bill (H.R. 7152)

15998	CONGRESSIONAL RECORD — SENATE	*July 6*

COMPARATIVE ANALYSIS OF TWO VERSIONS OF CIVIL RIGHTS BILL (H.R. 7152)

Mr. DIRKSEN. Mr. President, Representative WILLIAM M. McCULLOCH, of Ohio, who had much to do with the passage and also the preparation of the civil rights bill, has prepared a comparative analysis of the House version and the Senate version of H.R. 7152. I believe this analysis is highly informative.

Mr. President, I ask unanimous consent as a special request, that in printing this comparative analysis in the REC-ORD, it be set forth in parallel columns, in order to show in every case the differences in the sections and in the titles. Mr. President, I ask unanimous consent that this be done.

The ACTING PRESIDENT pro tempore. Without objection, it is so ordered.

The tabulation follows.

1964	CONGRESSIONAL RECORD — SENATE	16001

(material omitted)

TITLE VII—EQUAL EMPLOYMENT OPPORTUNITY

1. Employers having 25 or more employees, labor organizations having 25 or more members, and commercial employment agencies are prohibited from discriminating against any individual in any phase of employment or union membership (including advertisement for employment) on the ground of race, color, religion, sex or national origin. (During the first year after the effective date of the act, only employers and labor organizations having 100 or more employees or members, respectively, shall be covered; during the second year only 75 or more employees, or members, respectively; and during the third year only 50 or more employees or members, respectively.)

Excluded from coverage are: (1) The United States, a corporation wholly owned by the Government of the United States, or a State or political subdivision thereof; (2) a bona fide private membership club (other than a labor organization). The U.S. Employment Service is covered, however, as well as the system of State and local employment services receiving Federal assistance.

2. Discrimination is also prohibited in apprenticeship or other training or retraining programs, including on-the-job training, by employers, labor organizations or joint labor-management committees.

3. Exemptions or limitations.

(a) The title shall not apply to the employment of aliens outside any State or employment by a religious corporation, association or society of individuals of a particular religion to perform work connected with the carrying on of religious activities.

(b) It shall not be an unlawful employment practice for an employer to advertise or employ employees of a particular religion, sex or national origin where such is a bona fide occupational qualification reasonably necessary to the normal operation of a particular business.

(c) It shall not be an unlawful employment practice for an institution of learning to hire or employ employees of a particular religion if such institution is owned, supported, controlled or managed by a particular religion or a particular religious organization, or if the curriculum of such institution is directed toward the "propagation" of a particular religion.

(d) It shall not be an unlawful employment practice for an employer to refuse to employ any person who holds atheistic practices and beliefs.

(e) The title shall not apply to any employment practice of an employer, labor organization, employment agency or joint labor-management committee with respect to an individual who is a member of the Communist Party or other subversive organization.

---

1. Same except that an employer will only be covered if he has 25 or more employees for each working day in each of 20 or more calendar weeks in a current or preceding calendar year. In addition, a labor organization is covered if it operates a hiring hall, while Indian tribes are excluded from coverage. But, it is provided that it shall be the policy of the United States to insure equal employment opportunities for Federal employees without discrimination because of race, color, religion, sex or national origin and the President shall utilize his existing authority to effectuate this policy.

2. Same.

3.—

(a) Same. In addition, the title shall not apply to an educational institution with respect to the employment of individuals to perform work connected with the educational activities of such institution.

(b) Same. In addition, labor organizations, employment agencies, and joint labor-management committees controlling apprenticeship or other training or retraining programs are granted the same exemption.

(c) Same.

(d) Deleted.

(e) Same.

TITLE VII—EQUAL EMPLOYMENT OPPORTUNITY—continued

House version	*Senate version*
(f) No such provision.	(f) It shall not be an unlawful employment practice for an employer to refuse to hire or to discharge an individual; or for a labor organization or employment agency to fail or refuse to refer an individual for employment if the position to be filled requires a Government security clearance and the individual has not obtained such clearance.
(g) No such provision.	(g) It shall not be an unlawful employment practice for an employer to apply different standards of compensation, or different terms, conditions or privileges of employment, pursuant to a bona fide seniority or merit system, to employees who work in different locations, provided that such differences are not the result of an intention to discriminate because of race, color, religion, sex, or national origin.
3. (h) No such provision.	3. (h) It shall not be an unlawful employment practice for an employer to give and act upon the results of any professionally developed ability test—provided that such test, its administration or action upon the results is not designed, intended, or used to discriminate because of race, color, religion, sex, or national origin.
(i) No such provision.	(i) It shall not be an unlawful employment practice for an employer to differentiate upon the basis of sex in determining the amount of wages or compensation paid to or to be paid to employees of the employer if the differentiation is authorized by the provisions of the Fair Labor Standards Act.
(j) No such provision.	(j) The title shall not apply to any business or enterprise on or near an Indian reservation with respect to any publicly announced employment practice of such business or enterprise under which preferential treatment is given to an Indian living on or near a reservation.
(k) No such provision.	(k) The title shall not be interpreted to require any employer, employment agency, labor organization, or joint labor-management committee to grant preferential treatment to any individual or to any group because of race, color, religion, sex, or national origin on account of an imbalance which may exist with respect to the total number or percentage of persons of any race, color, religion, sex, or national origin employed by an employer, referred or classified for employment by an employment agency or labor organization, or admitted to or employed in any apprenticeship or other training program, in comparison with the total number or percentage of persons of such race, color, religion, sex, or national origin in any community, State, section, or other area, or in the available work force in any community, State, section or other area.

c. Additional Questions on Senate Legislative History Readings

1. Looking back to the Clark-Case Memorandum at pp. 73-75, should this Memorandum be interpreted as prohibiting affirmative action under what is now § 703(j)? (Listed as (k) on p. 16002 above.)

2. When was § 703(j) added to the bill? How can you tell? Does the 'Comparative Analysis' document printed in the Congressional Record on July 6 shed any light on this matter?

VI. H.R. 7152 is Presented to the President for his Signature (July 2, 1964)

(material omitted)

BILLS PRESENTED TO THE PRESIDENT

Mr. BURLESON, from the Committee on House Administration, reported that that committee did on this day present to the President, for his approval, bills of the House of the following titles:

H.R. 7152. An act to enforce the constitutional right to vote, to confer jurisdiction upon the district courts of the United States to provide injunctive relief against discrimination in public accommodations; to authorize the Attorney General to institute suits to protect constitutional rights in public facilities and public education, to extend the Commission on Civil Rights, to prevent discrimination in federally assisted programs, to establish a Commission on Equal Employment Opportunity, and for other purposes; and

H.R. 10433. An act making appropriations for the Department of the Interior and related agencies for the fiscal year ending June 30, 1965, and for other purposes.

---

a. The President Signs the Bill (July 2, 1964)

MESSAGE FROM THE PRESIDENT

A message in writing from the President of the United States was communicated to the House by Mr. Ratchford, one of his secretaries, who also informed the House that on the following dates the President approved and signed bills and joint resolutions of the House of the following titles:

On July 2, 1964:

H.R. 3348. An act to amend section 318 of the Social Security Amendments of 1958 to extend the time within which teachers and other employees covered by the same retirement system in the State of Maine may be treated as being covered by separate retirement systems for purposes of the old-age, survivors, and disability insurance program;

H.R. 3496. An act to further amend the Reorganization Act of 1949, as amended, so that such act will apply to reorganization plans transmitted to the Congress at any time before June 1, 1965;

H.R. 6041. An act to amend the prevailing wage section of the Davis-Bacon Act, as amended, and related sections of the Federal Airport Act, as amended; and the National Housing Act, as amended;

H.R. 7152. An act to enforce the constitutional right to vote, to confer jurisdiction upon the district courts of the United States to provide injunctive relief against discrimination in public accommodations, to authorize the Attorney General to institute suits to protect constitutional rights in public facilities and public education, to extend the Commission on Civil Rights, to prevent discrimination in federally assisted programs, to establish a Commission on Equal Employment Opportunity, and for other purposes; and

H.R. 8459. An act to amend the Federal Credit Union Act to allow Federal credit unions greater flexibility in their organizations and operations;

(material omitted)

b. Lyndon Johnson's "Radio and Television Remarks Upon Signing the Civil Rights Bill"

---

[445]   July 2   *Public Papers of the Presidents*

(material omitted)

446   Radio and Television Remarks Upon Signing the
          Civil Rights Bill. *July 2, 1964*
[Broadcast from the East Room at the White House at 6:45 p.m.]

My fellow Americans:

I am about to sign into law the Civil Rights Act of 1964. I want to take this occasion to talk to you about what that law means to every American.

One hundred and eighty-eight years ago this week a small band of valiant men began a long struggle for freedom. They pledged their lives, their fortunes, and their sacred honor not only to found a nation, but to forge an ideal of freedom—not only for political independence, but for personal liberty—not only to eliminate foreign rule, but to establish the rule of justice in the affairs of men.

That struggle was a turning point in our history. Today in far corners of distant continents, the ideals of those American patriots still shape the struggles of men who hunger for freedom.

This is a proud triumph. Yet those who founded our country knew that freedom would be secure only if each generation fought to renew and enlarge its meaning. From the minutemen at Concord to the soldiers in Viet-Nam, each generation has been equal to that trust.

Americans of every race and color have died in battle to protect our freedom. Americans of every race and color have worked to build a nation of widening opportunities. Now our generation of Americans has been called on to continue the unending search for justice within our own borders.

We believe that all men are created equal. Yet many are denied equal treatment.

We believe that all men have certain unalienable rights. Yet many Americans do not enjoy those rights.

We believe that all men are entitled to the blessings of liberty. Yet millions are being deprived of those blessings—not because of their own failures, but because of the color of their skin.

The reasons are deeply imbedded in history and tradition and the nature of man. We can understand—without rancor or hatred—how this all happened.

But it cannot continue. Our Constitu-

842

tion, the foundation of our Republic, forbids it. The principles of our freedom forbid it. Morality forbids it. And the law I will sign tonight forbids it.

That law is the product of months of the most careful debate and discussion. It was proposed more than one year ago by our late and beloved President John F. Kennedy. It received the bipartisan support of more than two-thirds of the Members of both the House and the Senate. An overwhelming majority of Republicans as well as Democrats voted for it.

It has received the thoughtful support of tens of thousands of civic and religious leaders in all parts of this Nation. And it is supported by the great majority of the American people.

The purpose of the law is simple.

It does not restrict the freedom of any American, so long as he respects the rights of others.

It does not give special treatment to any citizen.

It does say the only limit to a man's hope for happiness, and for the future of his children, shall be his own ability.

It does say that there are those who are equal before God shall now also be equal in the polling booths, in the classrooms, in the factories, and in hotels, restaurants, movie theaters, and other places that provide service to the public.

I am taking steps to implement the law under my constitutional obligation to "take care that the laws are faithfully executed."

First, I will send to the Senate my nomination of LeRoy Collins to be Director of the Community Relations Service. Governor Collins will bring the experience of a long career of distinguished public service to the task of helping communities solve problems of human relations through reason and commonsense.

Second, I shall appoint an advisory committee of distinguished Americans to assist Governor Collins in his assignment.

Third, I am sending Congress a request for supplemental appropriations to pay for necessary costs of implementing the law, and asking for immediate action.

Fourth, already today in a meeting of my Cabinet this afternoon I directed the agencies of this Government to fully discharge the new responsibilities imposed upon them by the law and to do it without delay, and to keep me personally informed of their progress.

Fifth, I am asking appropriate officials to meet with representative groups to promote greater understanding of the law and to achieve a spirit of compliance.

We must not approach the observance and enforcement of this law in a vengeful spirit. Its purpose is not to punish. Its purpose is not to divide, but to end divisions—divisions which have all lasted too long. Its purpose is national, not regional.

Its purpose is to promote a more abiding commitment to freedom, a more constant pursuit of justice, and a deeper respect for human dignity.

We will achieve these goals because most Americans are law-abiding citizens who want to do what is right.

This is why the Civil Rights Act relies first on voluntary compliance, then on the efforts of local communities and States to secure the rights of citizens. It provides for the national authority to step in only when others cannot or will not do the job.

This Civil Rights Act is a challenge to all of us to go to work in our communities and our States, in our homes and in our hearts, to eliminate the last vestiges of injustice in our beloved country.

So tonight I urge every public official, every religious leader, every business and

843

professional man, every workingman, every housewife—I urge every American—to join in this effort to bring justice and hope to all our people—and to bring peace to our land.

My fellow citizens, we have come now to a time of testing. We must not fail.

Let us close the springs of racial poison. Let us pray for wise and understanding hearts. Let us lay aside irrelevant differ-ences and make our Nation whole. Let us hasten that day when our unmeasured strength and our unbounded spirit will be free to do the great works ordained for this Nation by the just and wise God who is the Father of us all.

Thank you and good night.

NOTE: The Civil Rights Act of 1964 is Public Law 88-352 (78 Stat. 241).

(material omitted)

844

ADMINISTRATIVE INPUT: DEFINING "DISPARATE IMPACT"

I. Overview: The Road to Disparate Impact Argumentation

Once the EEOC had been founded, a significant challenge arose in identifying how to use Title VII's terms to demonstrate findings of discrimination. A series of compromises before the Act's enactment left a substantially weaker charge than was first conceived, particularly because of efforts to demonstrate it was not a "quota bill." One of the most significant developments of the EEOC's early years, then, was the development of the disparate impact argument, an interpretive strategy seen in its completed form in *Griggs*. Disparate impact allowed the EEOC to make use of statistics to challenge facially neutral employment practices without reference to quotas.[1]

The first recorded articulation of the strategy came in a 1966 memo written by Sonia Pressman, the first female attorney in the EEOC general counsel's office, **reproduced below**.[2] The memo came in response to General Counsel Charles T. Duncan's request for an analysis of the interpretive options available given the current status of EEO law.[3] Pressman found instances where courts had upheld the use of statistical probability as evidence of "a pattern or practice of discrimination," including in jury selection, voter registration, and wage disparities.[4] She suggested that similar data could be used as evidence in civil suits and to supply the "facts" that Title VII's Section 706(a) required to be included in a Commissioner's charge.[5]

Within three months, Pressman's strategy had acquired a name. In *Guidelines on Employment Testing Procedures*, issued August 24, 1966, the EEOC mentioned that tests resulting in a demonstrated "adverse impact" were not allowed. The EEOC declined however to explain the term, planning instead to rely on the case law soon to be developed. Commission member Samuel C. Jackson shared the basic outline of the strategy with the NAACP in *The Crisis* just over a year later:

> EEOC has taken its interpretation of Title VII a step further than other agencies have taken their statutes. It has reasoned that in addition to discrimination in employment, it is also an unlawful practice to fail or refuse to hire, to discharge or to compensate unevenly, or to limit, segregate and classify employees on criteria which *prove to have a demonstrable racial effect* without a clear and convincing business motive.[6]

Jackson also offered some examples of specific promotion policies that were discriminatory.[7]

On July 2, 1968, Title VII became fully effective.[8] EEOC decisions from 1969 and 1970 embraced adverse impact, applying it most frequently to the question of testing (Document 3). For example, the Commission concluded that requiring a sixth grade education for a labor position was discriminatory, because the company could not show it was necessary to do the job, and the measure had a disproportionate impact on black workers.

In its 1970 *Guidelines on Employee Selection Procedures*, **reproduced below**, the EEOC refined the notion of disparate impact. The Guidelines provided more specific definitions of the types of proof necessary to establish the legality of hiring practices, and explained the process by which employment tests could be validated and what criteria must

---

1   EEOC, "Shaping Employment Discrimination Law: The Disparate Impact Theory of Discrimination." Available at http://www.eeoc.gov/abouteeoc/35th/1965-71/shaping.html. Hugh Davis Graham does an excellent job outlining these developments as well in Graham, *The Civil Rights Era* 244-54 (1990).

2   Pressman's career is outlined in her autobiography, Sonia Pressman Fuentes, *Eat First, You Don't Know What They'll Give You* (1999).

3   Graham 244.

4   Memorandum from Sonia Pressman to Charles T. Duncan 1-2 (May 31, 1966).

5   Ibid. 4.

6   Samuel C. Jackson, "EEOC vs. Discrimination, Inc." *The Crisis* January 1968, 16-17.

7   Ibid. 18-19.

8   Graham 251.

be considered. By stating that procedures with a disparate impact will have the presumption of being discriminatory, and that even a validated test cannot be used as a mechanism of disparate treatment (for example, by requiring only one group to take the test), the Guidelines created a significant burden for employers. The only question left was whether the argument underpinning these expectations would be accepted in decisions external to the Commission.

Thus, the EEOC was committed to the theory that institutional practices violated Title VII's anti-discrimination rule if they had a disparate impact preserving patterns of workforce segregation and no sufficient business justification. Because the 1964 Act vested interpretive authority in the federal courts, and not in the agency, the important question was whether judges would agree with the EEOC's theory of the statute.

Most federal court of appeals judges agreed with the EEOC. In *Local 189, United Papermakers v. United States*, 416 F.2d 980, 988-89 (5th Cir. 1969), the Fifth Circuit followed the EEOC's approach and ruled that seniority arrangements could be invalidated if they had a discriminatory effect that could not be justified by business necessity. Judge John Minor Wisdom's widely-praised opinion for the court reasoned that Title VII's integrative purpose would be thwarted if employers could adopt purportedly "neutral" practices that in fact preserved largely segregated workforces.

In *Griggs v. Duke Power Co.*, 420 F.2d 1225 (4th Cir. 1970), **reproduced in Chapter 1 of the Casebook**, the Fourth Circuit rejected the EEOC's approach and declined to follow Judge Wisdom's lead. The case involved an education requirement for blue collar jobs that, plaintiffs claimed, disqualified most black workers from better manual jobs, and without any genuine business reason. Judge Boreman's opinion for the court relied heavily on the Senate's ultimate acceptance of the Tower Amendment, relating to employment tests. Reread the materials above on the Tower Amendment: Do they support Judge Boreman's conclusion—or does Judge Soboloff's dissenting opinion have the better arguments?

Relying on the arguments made by Judges Wisdom and Soboloff, the NAACP's Inc. Fund filed an appeal with the Supreme Court—and the Nixon Administration's Solicitor General Erwin Griswold filed an important brief supporting a grant of *certiorari*. Given the Administration's arguments, the EEOC's views, and the split in the circuits, this was an easy grant. In *Griggs v. Duke Power Co.*, 401 U.S. 424 (1971), the Court unanimously reversed the Fourth Circuit and followed the argumentation of Griswold's *amicus* brief on the merits. "The objective of Congress," Chief Justice Burger reasoned, "was to achieve equality of employment opportunities and remove barriers that have operated in the past to favor an identifiable group of white employees over other employees." Thus, "practices, procedures, or tests neutral on their face, and even neutral in terms of intent, cannot be maintained if they operate to 'freeze' the status quo of prior discriminatory employment practices." Id. at 429-30. Burger's opinion explicitly deferred to the views of the agency, which guided employers in their efforts to comply with the statute.

II. "Use of Statistics in Title VII Proceedings," Memorandum from Sonia Pressman, Staff Attorney, to Charles T. Duncan, General Counsel, Equal Employment Opportunity Commission (May 31, 1966)

UNITED STATES GOVERNMENT

Memorandum

EQUAL EMPLOYMENT OPPORTUNITY COMMISSION

TO   :   Charles T. Duncan

DATE: May 31, 1966

In reply refer to:

FROM   :   Sonia Pressman

SUBJECT: Use of Statistics in Title VII Proceedings

The purpose of this memorandum will be (1) to review the use of statistical information by administrative agencies and courts in the area of job discrimination, [1] as well as other types of discrimination; and (2) to discuss the application of such rulings to Title VII cases.

It has frequently been recognized that proof of discrimination presents particular problems. Discrimination involves complex matters of the mind and heart not susceptible to objective or quantitative standards of proof, [2] and it is often pursued by means elusive, subtle and devious. [3] Courts, recognizing the difficulty of establishing discrimination on an individual basis, have placed particular emphasis on the use of statistics to prove discriminatory patterns and practices. "In the problem of racial discrimination, statistics often tell much, and Courts listen." [4]

Two types of statistical evidence has been relied upon in prior administrative and judicial proceedings: figures over a period of time in the past which indicate a continuous pattern of discrimination, and figures as to a current situation.

Evidence of statistical probability to infer the existence of a pattern or practice of discrimination has been used in the following situations: the Supreme Court and lower courts in numerous cases have found that the habitual absence of Negroes from juries, coupled with the presence in the district of Negroes qualified to serve, was ground for retrial when the state failed to introduce evidence of nondiscriminatory reasons therefor; [5] the courts have relied on

BUY U.S. SAVINGS BONDS REGULARLY ON THE PAYROLL SAVINGS PLAN

2.

statistical evidence to infer discrimination in the
registration of Negro voters, 6/ and to find a constitutional violation when a pattern of lower wages
for Negro school teachers was established; 7/ the
National Labor Relations Board, with court approval, has
inferred anti-union discrimination when the proportion
of union members laid off exceeded the proportion existing in the group from which selection was made; 8/ the
New York State Commission for Human Rights, in a decision
affirmed by the court, has relied on statistics to. establish discrimination against Negroes in the designation
and approval of applicants for sheet metal apprenticeship
training; 9/ and an arbitrator, dealing with a nondiscrimination provision of a collective bargaining contract,
found discrimination where the employer gave no consideration to Negro applicants at a time when substantial numbers
of inexperienced white employees were being hired. 10/

On the issue of the under-utilization of minority group
members, however, there is some language in the recent
Swain case, supra, 11/ which bears special consideration.

> Venires drawn from the jury box . . . unques-
> tionably contained a smaller proportion of the
> Negro community than of the white community. But
> a defendant in a criminal case is not constitu-
> tionally entitled to demand a proportionate number
> of his race on the jury which tries him nor on the
> venire or jury roll from which petit jurors are
> drawn. . . . Neither the jury roll nor the venire
> need be a perfect mirror of the community or accurate-
> ly reflect the proportionate strength of every iden-
> tifiable group. "Obviously the number of races and
> nationalities appearing in the ancestry of our citizens
> would make it impossible to meet a requirement of
> proportional representation. Similarly, since there
> can be no exclusion of Negroes as a race and no dis-
> crimination because of color, proportional limitation
> is not permissible." Cassell v. State of Texas,

3.

339 S. Ct. 282, 286-287, 70 S. Ct. 629, 631-632
(opinion of Mr. Justice Reed, announcing judgment.)
We cannot say that purposeful discrimination based
on race alone is satisfactorily proved by showing
that an identifiable group in a community is underrepresented by as much as 10%. . . . The overall
percentage disparity has been small, 12/ and reflects
no studied attempt to include or exclude a specific
number of Negroes. Undoubtedly the selection of
prospective jurors was somewhat haphazard and little
effort was made to ensure that all groups in the
community were fully represented. But an imperfect
system is not equivalent to purposeful discrimination
based on race.

The courts have relied on statistical information even
where the statistics supplied were only "reasonably correct
and reliable." 13/

Usually, the case will contain various other types of
evidence, including historical and sociological background, 14/
but in at least one case, Byrd v. Brice, supra, note 6, at
443, the court stated:

The record of this case shows that there are well
over 9,000 white registered voters in the Parish
and not a single colored one. This is enough,
taken arithmetically, to give the plaintiffs the
injunction they seek. (Emphasis supplied.) 15/

In some of these cases, there was evidence that qualified
Negroes were available or had applied for jury service or
had sought to register to vote, but proof of qualified
discriminatees is not always necessary to a finding of
discrimination. 16/

Frequently, the courts in some of these cases talk in
terms of the evidence being sufficient to establish a
prima facie case, because evidence negating the inference

4.

of discrimination is peculiarly within the knowledge of the defendant. [17]

With regard to Title VII, statistical evidence would be relevant in the following three principal ways:

1. To supply the "facts" referred to in Section 706(a) which form the basis for a Commissioner's charge.

2. To support a finding by the Commission of reasonable cause that a charge is true.

3. As evidence in civil suits brought either by the aggrieved person or by the Attorney General in a "pattern or practice" case.

Various problems present themselves in applying the administrative and judicial rulings discussed above to Title VII proceedings. Firstly, the voter registration, jury selection, and teacher pay cases discussed above involve conduct which was always violative of the United States Constitution. Accordingly, statistical information as to present disparities coupled with that of discriminatory past practices warranted a finding of a continuous pattern of discrimination. However, discrimination in employment was not a violation of Federal law prior to July 2, 1965, although in some instances it may have amounted to a violation of state law, and a contractual violation under state and Federal government contracts. Disparities in an employer's current work force would not necessarily indicate discrimination practiced since July 2, 1965, as most or all of the hires and promotions involved in establishing such disparities may very well have occurred prior to passage of the Act. Furthermore, evidence that an employer discriminated prior to July 2, 1965, standing alone, would not justify an inference that he continued to do so subsequent to passage of a statute making such discrimination unlawful. [18]

Under the literal language of Title VII, the only actions required by a covered employer are to post notices, and not to discriminate subsequent to July 2, 1965. By the explicit terms of Section 703(j), [19] an employer is not required to redress an imbalance in his work force which is the result of past discrimination.

The Commission should therefore attempt at some stage of
the proceedings to secure employment information on the
employer's personnel complement both prior and subsequent to July 2, 1965. It may be useful in future
report forms to request information on the employer's
hiring of new employees, transfers and promotions, since
July 2, 1965, instead of merely seeking information on
the employer's current complement.

It would appear that statistical evidence as to the
employer's current work force would be sufficient to
warrant issuance of a Commissioner's charge.[20/] During
the investigation, however, the investigator should attempt
to secure information on the employer's work force on
July 2, 1965, and on his personnel actions thereafter,
so as to ascertain whether there was a past pattern of
discrimination, and, if so, whether it has been continued
or discontinued since passage of Title VII.

While statistical information including pre-and post-
July 2, 1965, conduct may be sufficient to warrant the
issuance of a Commissioner's charge, more will be required to warrant the finding of cause that a Commissioner's
or an aggrieved person's charge is true,[21/] and more
evidence still will be needed to justify a judicial decision that the Act has been violated. [22/]

With regard to findings of cause in Commission Decisions,
a problem will be raised when the Commission's sole
evidence consists of statistics as to the employer's
current work force, and the employer refuses to cooperate
by revealing what personnel actions were taken prior to
and subsequent to July 2, 1965. It is questionable whether
a finding of reasonable cause could be based on such evidence alone. In such instances, the Commission may wish
to make a demand for access to the employer's past records,
or it may need to secure additional nonstatistical evidence of discrimination. Such additional evidence, plus
the statistical information, might then support a finding
of reasonable cause.

6.

Such evidence would likewise seem sufficient to establish a prima facie case in an administrative or judicial proceeding.

The language in _Swain_, _supra_ note 5, with regard to the fact that a minority group does not have the right to proportional representation also bears study with regard to Title VII charges. _Swain_ indicates that an employer cannot be found in violation of Title VII simply because his use of minority groups does not mirror their representation in the community. [23] However, the fact that an employer's personnel complement need not be an accurate reflection of the community does not mean that an employer is free to follow a discriminatory policy. Thus, when statistics are used, they should not be used to buttress the argument that the employer has a racially-imbalanced work force, or is underutilizing a minority group, but rather to establish the proposition that the employer is following a discriminatory policy with regard to hire, promotion, etc.

Where the statistics evidence gross disparities between the utilization of whites and Negroes, they will constitute strong evidence of such a discriminatory policy. However, where employers are more subtle, and employ token numbers of minority group members, the use of statistics will become more difficult and more complex. In such instances it may be necessary to refer to publications on chance and probability. [24]

Statistics may be used as evidence in Title VII cases to support two different types of charges: (1) that the employer is pursuing a discriminatory policy towards a minority group or one of the two sexes in general; and (2) that the employer has discriminated with regard to a particular individual or individuals.

Evidence of statistical disproportion in a work force or union does not necessarily support the inference that a pattern of discrimination exists. The decisions in the administrative and judicial cases not involving employment

-7-

referred to above cannot automatically be applied to
Title VII. There are, for example, many more variable
factors in the employment situation than in the jury selection
cases. Jurors are conscripted and the estimation of how
many of a district's Negroes meet the relatively simple
standards imposed upon jurors is far easier than calculating the number of Negroes in an area competent
to perform jobs of a certain difficulty. Furthermore, it
may be necessary in employment cases to also consider
the number of Negro applicants and the rate of job turnover.
Where a large company in an area with a diverse population
has no Negro employees even though it hires new employees
regularly and has standard job requirements, the inference
of discrimination may be reasonable, whereas a similar
inference in the case of a small company with limited
hiring may not be justified. Because of these variables,
it will be preferable, wherever possible, to support
statistical evidence of a Title VII violation with other
evidence.

It has been stated that the evidence tending to establish
that an employer has discriminated against an individual
can be divided into three categories: (1) evidence of the
employer's general discriminatory employment patterns and
practices; (2) evidence that the charging party is qualified for the job (where there is a specific charging
party); or evidence that there are members in the group
allegedly discriminated against who would be qualified
for the positions in question; and (3) evidence showing
that the reasons given by the employer for his actions
are unsubstantiated or pretextual. .. It is hoped that,
to the extent possible, considering the limitations of
time and staff, Commission investigators would attempt
to secure evidence on all three of these points. Wherever
possible, Commission investigators should be instructed
to attempt to secure information as to the employer's
utilization of minority members; 24/ as to his past practices; as to whether the employer is a federal or state
government contractor; as to whether qualified minority
group members have applied for positions with the employer;
whether there are qualified minority group members in the
community who may not have applied because the employer's

8.

or the community's discriminatory practices are well
known; and information as to whether the employer has
taken any action since July 2, 1965, to inform his employees,
prospective employees and members of the community of the
fact that he is pursuing an equal employment opportunity
policy. This would be of particular significance in
those instances where an employer has, prior to passage
of Title VII, pursued a policy of discrimination. 26/

With regard to the production of evidence, it has long been
recognized, as the Supreme Court stated in 1957, that "the
ordinary rule, based on considerations of fairness, does
not place the burden upon a litigant of establishing
facts peculiarly within the knowledge of his adversary."27/
Thus, the doctrine of the prima facie case has come into
play: the plaintiff need only supply a certain quantum
of evidence, after which the burden of going forward,
and of offering rebuttal to that which has been presented,
shifts to the respondent. This doctrine has been found
applicable in a wide range of cases 28/ and has already
been referred to above with regard to proof of discrimination in non-employment situations. It has been suggested
by several writers in the field 29/ that this doctrine is
also applicable to job discrimination proceedings. While
the quantum of evidence necessary to constitute a prima facie
case in Title VII proceedings will ultimately be determined by the courts, one of these writers 30/ has discussed
the matter as follows:

> Several factors must be considered: the nature
> of the charge, the type of action brought, and the
> remedy sought. For example, the Supreme Court's
> willingness to recognize a prima facie case in the
> jury-selection cases can be explained in part at
> least by the fact that the remedy sought is an
> impeachment of a verdict and not a criminal punishment
> or direct or indirect financial recovery. Likewise
> where a general injunction is sought, less certainty
> in the proof would be necessary than where affirmative
> action is the remedy desired. In the case of discrim-
> ination against a group, the showing of the general

9.

equality of the group to other groups plus the showing
of unequal treatment accorded to the group should
be sufficient to raise a prima facie case, while
in the case of discrimination against an individual,
the equality of the particular individual in question
to other individuals differently treated should be
demonstrated. Nevertheless, in the latter situation
as well, if the job applicant could show that he
possessed the objective qualifications for the job
in question, the burden could reasonably be placed
on the employer to justify his actions as not being
discriminatory. 31/

The use of statistics in discrimination cases, and the
litigation of such cases in general, will always be open
to the danger that in a particular case a personnel decision
was made not for unlawful reasons but for reasons personal
to the employer and the applicant. As has been stated in
a related context, 32/ almost any job applicant has "some
characteristic which may support a claim that he is unde-
sirable, or at least invite dispute, since human beings
are not wholly faultless." The only solution to the
problem of differentiating between unlawful and permissible
discrimination is for the Commission to be ever mindful
of the variables in this field, to conduct as complete
an investigation as is possible within the limitations
of time and staff, and then to strive for an equitable
result based on the facts at hand.

As has been stated:

> "The conflict between free choice and equality
> which is created by the enactment of and the enforce-
> ment of anti-discrimination measures will exist
> as long as racial, religious, and other forms of
> group prejudices endure in our society. While the
> fact that discrimination is not susceptible of certain
> proof may heighten this conflict, a judicious est-
> ablishment of the requirements of proof and a skillful
> manipulation of the burdens created by these require-
> ments may serve to prevent the engulfing of either
> ideal by the other." 33/

(endnotes omitted)

III. Guidelines on Employee Selection Procedures, Equal Employment Opportunity Commission (1970)

RULES AND REGULATIONS   12333

(material omitted)

[F.R. Doc. 70-9967; Filed, July 31, 1970; 8:46 a.m.]

Title 29—LABOR

Chapter XIV—Equal Employment Opportunity Commission

PART 1607—GUIDELINES ON EMPLOYEE SELECTION PROCEDURES

By virtue of the authority vested in it by section 713 of title VII of the Civil Rights Act of 1964, 42 U.S.C., section 2000e–12, 78 Stat. 265, the Equal Employment Opportunity Commission hereby issues Title 29, Chapter XIV, § 1607 of the Code of Federal Regulations.

These Guidelines on Employee Selection Procedures supersede and enlarge upon the Guidelines on Employment Testing Procedures, issued by the Equal Employment Opportunity Commission on August 24, 1966. Because the material herein is interpretive in nature, the provisions of the Administrative Procedure Act (5 U.S.C. 553) requiring notice of proposed rule making, opportunity for public participation, and delay in effective date are inapplicable. The Guidelines shall be applicable to charges and cases presently pending or hereafter filed with the Commission.

Sec.
1607.1   Statement of purpose.
1607.2   "Test" defined.
1607.3   Discrimination defined.

Sec.
1607.4   Evidence of validity.
1607.5   Minimum standards for validation.
1607.6   Presentation of validity evidence.
1607.7   Use of other validity studies.
1607.8   Assumption of validity.
1607.9   Continued use of tests.
1607.10 Employment agencies and employment services.
1607.11 Disparate treatment.
1607.12 Retesting.
1607.13 Other selection techniques.
1607.14 Affirmative action.

AUTHORITY: The provisions of this Part 1607 issued under Sec. 713, 78 Stat. 265, 42 U.S.C. sec. 2000e–12.

§ 1607.1   Statement of purpose.

(a) The guidelines in this part are based on the belief that properly validated and standardized employee selection procedures can significantly contribute to the implementation of nondiscriminatory personnel policies, as required by title VII. It is also recognized that professionally developed tests, when used in conjunction with other tools of personnel assessment and complemented by sound programs of job design, may significantly aid in the development and maintenance of an efficient work force and, indeed, aid in the utilization and conservation of human resources generally.

(b) An examination of charges of discrimination filed with the Commission and an evaluation of the results of the Commission's compliance activities has revealed a decided increase in total test usage and a marked increase in doubtful testing practices which, based on our experience, tend to have discriminatory effects. In many cases, persons have come to rely almost exclusively on tests as the basis for making the decision to hire, transfer, promote, grant membership, train, refer or retain, with the result that candidates are selected or rejected on the basis of a single test score. Where tests are so used, minority candidates frequently experience disproportionately high rates of rejection by failing to attain score levels that have been established as minimum standards for qualification.

It has also become clear that in many instances persons are using tests as the basis for employment decisions without evidence that they are valid predictors of employee job performance. Where evidence in support of presumed relationships between test performance and job behavior is lacking, the possibility of discrimination in the application of test results must be recognized. A test lacking demonstrated validity (i.e., having no known significant relationship to job behavior) and yielding lower scores for classes protected by title VII may result in the rejection of many who have necessary qualifications for successful work performance.

(c) The guidelines in this part are designed to serve as a workable set of standards for employers, unions and employment agencies in determining whether their selection procedures conform with the obligations contained in title VII of the Civil Rights Act of 1964. Section 703 of title VII places an affirmative obligation upon employers, labor unions, and employment agencies, as defined in section 701 of the Act, not to discriminate because of race, color, religion, sex, or national origin. Subsection (h) of section 703 allows such persons "* * * to give and to act upon the results of any professionally developed ability test provided that such test, its administration or action upon the results is not designed, intended or used to discriminate because of race, color, religion, sex or national origin."

§ 1607.2 "Test" defined.

For the purpose of the guidelines in this part, the term "test" is defined as any paper-and-pencil or performance measure used as a basis for any employment decision. The guidelines in this part apply, for example, to ability tests which are designed to measure eligibility for hire, transfer, promotion, membership, training, referral or retention. This definition includes, but is not restricted to, measures of general intelligence, mental ability and learning ability; specific intellectual abilities; mechanical, clerical and other aptitudes; dexterity and coordination; knowledge and proficiency; occupational and other interests; and attitudes, personality or temperament. The term "test" includes all formal, scored, quantified or standardized techniques of assessing job suitability including, in addition to the above, specific qualifying or disqualifying personal history or background requirements, specific educational or work history requirements, scored interviews, biographical information blanks, interviewers' rating scales, scored application forms, etc.

§ 1607.3 Discrimination defined.

The use of any test which adversely affects hiring, promotion, transfer or any other employment or membership opportunity of classes protected by title VII constitutes discrimination unless: (a) the test has been validated and evidences a high degree of utility as hereinafter described, and (b) the person giving or acting upon the results of the particular test can demonstrate that alternative suitable hiring, transfer or promotion procedures are unavailable for his use.

§ 1607.4 Evidence of validity.

(a) Each person using tests to select from among candidates for a position or for membership shall have available for inspection evidence that the tests are being used in a manner which does not violate § 1607.3. Such evidence shall be examined for indications of possible discrimination, such as instances of higher rejection rates for minority candidates than nonminority candidates. Furthermore, where technically feasible, a test should be validated for each minority group with which it is used; that is, any differential rejection rates that may exist, based on a test, must be relevant to performance on the jobs in question.

(b) The term "technically feasible" as used in these guidelines means having or obtaining a sufficient number of minority individuals to achieve findings of statistical and practical significance, the opportunity to obtain unbiased job performance criteria, etc. It is the responsibility of the person claiming absence of technical feasibility to positively demonstrate evidence of this absence.

(c) Evidence of a test's validity should consist of empirical data demonstrating that the test is predictive of or significantly correlated with important elements of work behavior which comprise or are relevant to the job or jobs for which candidates are being evaluated.

(1) If job progression structures and seniority provisions are so established that new employees will probably, within a reasonable period of time and in a great majority of cases, progress to a higher level, it may be considered that candidates are being evaluated for jobs at that higher level. However, where job progression is not so nearly automatic, or the time span is such that higher level jobs or employees' potential may be expected to change in significant ways, it shall be considered that candidates are being evaluated for a job at or near the entry level. This point is made to underscore the principle that attainment of or performance at a higher level job is a relevant criterion in validating employment tests only when there is a high probability that persons employed will in fact attain that higher level job within a reasonable period of time.

(2) Where a test is to be used in different units of a multiunit organization and no significant differences exist between units, jobs, and applicant populations, evidence obtained in one unit may suffice for the others. Similarly, where the validation process requires the collection of data throughout a multiunit organization, evidence of validity specific to each unit may not be required. There may also be instances where evidence of validity is appropriately obtained from more than one company in the same industry. Both in this instance and in the use of data collected throughout a multiunit organization, evidence of validity specific to each unit may not be required: Provided, That no significant differences exist between units, jobs, and applicant populations.

§ 1607.5 Minimum standards for validation.

(a) For the purpose of satisfying the requirements of this part, empirical evidence in support of a test's validity must be based on studies employing generally accepted procedures for determining criterion-related validity, such as those described in "Standards for Educational and Psychological Tests and Manuals" published by American Psychological Association, 1200 17th Street NW., Washington, D.C. 20036. Evidence of content or construct validity, as defined in that publication, may also be appropriate where criterion-related validity is not feasible. However, evidence for content or construct validity should be accompanied by sufficient information from job analyses to demonstrate the relevance of the content (in the case of job knowledge or proficiency tests) or the construct (in the case of trait measures). Evidence of content validity alone may be acceptable for well-developed tests that consist of suitable samples of the essential knowledge, skills or behaviors composing the job in question. The types of knowledge, skills or behaviors contemplated here do not include those which can be acquired in a brief orientation to the job.

(b) Although any appropriate validation strategy may be used to develop such empirical evidence, the following minimum standards, as applicable, must be met in the research approach and in the presentation of results which constitute evidence of validity:

(1) Where a validity study is conducted in which tests are administered to applicants, with criterion data collected later, the sample of subjects must be representative of the normal or typical candidate group for the job or jobs in question. This further assumes that the applicant sample is representative of the minority population available for the job or jobs in question in the local labor market. Where a validity study is conducted in which tests are administered to present employees, the sample must be representative of the minority groups currently

included in the applicant population. If it is not technically feasible to include minority employees in validation studies conducted on the present work force, the conduct of a validation study without minority candidates does not relieve any person of his subsequent obligation for validation when inclusion of minority candidates becomes technically feasible.

(2) Tests must be administered and scored under controlled and standardized conditions, with proper safeguards to protect the security of test scores and to insure that scores do not enter into any judgments of employee adequacy that are to be used as criterion measures. Copies of tests and test manuals, including instructions for administration, scoring, and interpretation of test results, that are privately developed and/or are not available through normal commercial channels must be included as a part of the validation evidence.

(3) The work behaviors or other criteria of employee adequacy which the test is intended to predict or identify must be fully described; and, additionally, in the case of rating techniques, the appraisal form(s) and instructions to the rater(s) must be included as a part of the validation evidence. Such criteria may include measures other than actual work proficiency, such as training time, supervisory ratings, regularity of attendance and tenure. Whatever criteria are used they must represent major or critical work behaviors as revealed by careful job analyses.

(4) In view of the possibility of bias inherent in subjective evaluations, supervisory rating techniques should be carefully developed, and the ratings should be closely examined for evidence of bias. In addition, minorities might obtain unfairly low performance criterion scores for reasons other than supervisors' prejudice, as, when, as new employees, they have had less opportunity to learn job skills. The general point is that all criteria need to be examined to insure freedom from factors which would unfairly depress the scores of minority groups.

(5) Differential validity. Data must be generated and results separately reported for minority and nonminority groups wherever technically feasible. Where a minority group is sufficiently large to constitute an identifiable factor in the local labor market, but validation data have not been developed and presented separately for that group, evidence of satisfactory validity based on other groups will be regarded as only provisional compliance with these guidelines pending separate validation of the test for the minority group in question. (See § 1607.9). A test which is differentially valid may be used in groups for which it is valid but not for those in which it is not valid. In this regard, where a test is valid for two groups but one group characteristically obtains higher test scores than the other without a corresponding difference in job performance, cutoff scores must be set so as to predict the same probability of job success in both groups.

(c) In assessing the utility of a test the following considerations will be applicable: .

(1) The relationship between the test and at least one relevant criterion must be statistically significant. This ordinarily means that the relationship should be sufficiently high as to have a probability of no more than 1 to 20 to have occurred by chance. However, the use of a single test as the sole selection device will be scrutinized closely when that test is valid against only one component of job performance.

(2) In addition to statistical significance, the relationship between the test and criterion should have practical significance. The magnitude of the relationship needed for practical significance or usefulness is affected by several factors, including:

(i) The larger the proportion of applicants who are hired for or placed on the job, the higher the relationship needs to be in order to be practically useful. Conversely, a relatively low relationship may prove useful when proportionately few job vacancies are available;

(ii) The larger the proportion of applicants who become satisfactory employees when not selected on the basis of the test, the higher the relationship needs to be between the test and a criterion of job success for the test to be practically useful. Conversely, a relatively low relationship may prove useful when proportionately few applicants turn out to be satisfactory;

(iii) The smaller the economic and human risks involved in hiring an unqualified applicant relative to the risks entailed in rejecting a qualified applicant, the greater the relationship needs to be in order to be practically useful. Conversely, a relatively low relationship may prove useful when the former risks are relatively high.

§ 1607.6   Presentation of validity evidence.

The presentation of the results of a validation study must include graphical and statistical representations of the relationships between the test and the criteria, permitting judgments of the test's utility in making predictions of future work behavior. (See § 1607.5(c) concerning assessing utility of a test.) Average scores for all tests and criteria must be reported for all relevant subgroups, including minority and nonminority groups where differential validation is required. Whenever statistical adjustments are made in validity results for less than perfect reliability or for restriction of score range in the test or the criterion, or both, the supporting evidence from the validation study must be presented in detail. Furthermore, for each test that is to be established or continued as an operational employee selection instrument, as a result of the validation study, the minimum acceptable cutoff (passing) score on the test must be reported. It is expected that each operational cutoff score will be reasonable and consistent with normal expectations of proficiency within the work force or group on which the study was conducted.

§ 1607.7   Use of other validity studies.

In cases where the validity of a test cannot be determined pursuant to § 1607.4 and § 1607.5 (e.g., the number of subjects is less than that required for a technically adequate validation study, or an appropriate criterion measure cannot be developed), evidence from validity studies conducted in other organizations, such as that reported in test manuals and professional literature, may be considered acceptable when: (a) The studies pertain to jobs which are comparable (i.e., have basically the same task elements), and (b) there are no major differences in contextual variables or sample composition which are likely to significantly affect test validity. Any person citing evidence from other validity studies as evidence of test validity for his own jobs must substantiate in detail job comparability and must demonstrate the absence of contextual or sample differences cited in paragraphs (a) and (b) of this section.

§ 1607.8   Assumption of validity.

(a) Under no circumstances will the general reputation of a test, its author or its publisher, or casual reports of test utility be accepted in lieu of evidence of validity. Specifically ruled out are: assumptions of validity based on test names or descriptive labels; all forms of promotional literature; data bearing on the frequency of a test's usage; testimonial statements of sellers, users, or consultants; and other nonempirical or anecdotal accounts of testing practices or testing outcomes.

(b) Although professional supervision of testing activities may help greatly to insure technically sound and nondiscriminatory test usage, such involvement alone shall not be regarded as constituting satisfactory evidence of test validity.

§ 1607.9   Continued use of tests.

Under certain conditions, a person may be permitted to continue the use of a test which is not at the moment fully supported by the required evidence of validity. If, for example, determination of criterion-related validity in a specific setting is practicable and required but not yet obtained, the use of the test may continue: Provided: (a) The person can cite substantial evidence of validity as described in § 1607.7 (a) and (b); and (b) he has in progress validation procedures which are designed to produce, within a reasonable time, the additional data required. It is expected also that the person may have to alter or suspend test cutoff scores so that score ranges broad enough to permit the identification of criterion-related validity will be obtained.

§ 1607.10   Employment agencies and employment services.

(a) An employment service, including private employment agencies, State employment agencies, and the U.S. Training and Employment Service, as defined in section 701(c), shall not make applicant or employee appraisals or referrals based on the results obtained from any psychological test or other selection standard

12336   RULES AND REGULATIONS

not validated in accordance with these guidelines.

(b) An employment agency or service which is requested by an employer or union to devise a testing program is required to follow the standards for test validation as set forth in these guidelines. An employment service is not relieved of its obligation herein because the test user did not request such validation or has requested the use of some lesser standard than is provided in these guidelines.

(c) Where an employment agency or service is requested only to administer a testing program which has been elsewhere devised, the employment agency or service shall request evidence of validation, as described in the guidelines in this part, before it administers the testing program and/or makes referral pursuant to the test results. The employment agency must furnish on request such evidence of validation. An employment agency or service will be expected to refuse to administer a test where the employer or union does not supply satisfactory evidence of validation. Reliance by the test user on the reputation of the test, its author, or the name of the test shall not be deemed sufficient evidence of validity (see § 1607.8(a)). An employment agency or service may administer a testing program where the evidence of validity comports with the standards provided in § 1607.7.

§ 1607.11   Disparate treatment.

The principle of disparate or unequal treatment must be distinguished from the concepts of test validation. A test or other employee selection standard— even though validated against job performance in accordance with the guidelines in this part—cannot be imposed upon any individual or class protected by title VII where other employees, applicants or members have not been subjected to that standard. Disparate treatment, for example, occurs where members of a minority or sex group have been denied the same employment, promotion, transfer or membership opportunities as have been made available to other employees or applicants. Those employees or applicants who have been denied equal treatment, because of prior discriminatory practices or policies, must at least be afforded the same opportunities as had existed for other employees or applicants during the period of discrimination. Thus, no new test or other employee selection standard can be imposed upon a class of individuals protected by title VII who, but for prior discrimination, would have been granted the opportunity to qualify under less stringent selection standards previously in force.

§ 1607.12   Retesting.

Employers, unions, and employment agencies should provide an opportunity for retesting and reconsideration to earlier "failure" candidates who have availed themselves of more training or experience. In particular, if any applicant or employee during the course of an interview or other employment pro- cedure claims more education or experience, that individual should be retested.

§ 1607.13   Other selection techniques.

Selection techniques other than tests, as defined in § 1607.2, may be improperly used so as to have the effect of discriminating against minority groups. Such techniques include, but are not restricted to, unscored or casual interviews and unscored application forms. Where there are data suggesting employment discrimination, the person may be called upon to present evidence concerning the validity of his unscored procedures as well as of any tests which may be used, the evidence of validity being of the same types referred to in §§ 1607.4 and 1607.5. Data suggesting the possibility of discrimination exist, for example, when there are differential rates of applicant rejection from various minority and nonminority or sex groups for the same job or group of jobs or when there are disproportionate representations of minority and nonminority or sex groups among present employees in different types of jobs. If the person is unable or unwilling to perform such validation studies, he has the option of adjusting employment procedures so as to eliminate the conditions suggestive of employment discrimination.

§ 1607.14   Affirmative action.

Nothing in these guidelines shall be interpreted as diminishing a person's obligation under both title VII and Executive Order 11246 as amended by Executive Order 11375 to undertake affirmative action to ensure that applicants or employees are treated without regard to race, color, religion, sex, or national origin. Specifically, the use of tests which have been validated pursuant to these guidelines does not relieve employers, unions or employment agencies of their obligations to take positive action in affording employment and training to members of classes protected by title VII.

The guidelines in this part are effective upon publication in the FEDERAL REGISTER.

Signed at Washington, D.C., 21st day of July 1970.

[SEAL]   WILLIAM H. BROWN III,
                              Chairman.

[F.R. Doc. 70–9962; Filed, July 31, 1970;
          8:46 a.m.]

(material omitted)

(material omitted)

AFFIRMATIVE ACTION: 1965-1972

I. Overview

Although use of the term "affirmative action" in American law predates the civil rights era by at least forty years, the first time it was used in connection to ending racial discrimination was by John F. Kennedy in his Executive Order No. 10925, issued March 6, 1961. There, the president decreed that federal contractors "will take affirmative action to ensure that applicants are employed, and that employees are treated during employment, without regard to their race, creed, color, or national origin."[1] Lyndon B. Johnson, vice president at the time, is credited with much of the Order's drafting.[2]

After the Civil Rights Act was passed, Johnson, now president, realized that the charge of the original Order needed to be updated so that it could capitalize on the new legislation. In 1965, he issued Executive Order No. 11246, **reproduced below**. It stated that "[t]he policy of equal opportunity applies to every aspect of Federal employment policy and practice," and consequently that every government contract would include a provision promising "affirmative action" to prevent discrimination.[3] The text of the provision was taken directly from Order No. 10925.

The affirmative action stipulation attracted little public notice at the time, in part because neither order specified just what affirmative action would entail. The task of shaping the details was left to the EEOC and later the Labor Department's Office of Federal Contract Compliance (OFCC). An August 1965 White House Conference included a panel on affirmative action, where EEOC member Charles Wilson explained that affirmative action was needed to counter the remnants of institutional racism. He insisted, however, that no quotas or preferences would be used to achieve that purpose. In fact, instituting such features would have proven nearly impossible at the time, since it was not until 1966 that federal agencies were required to maintain records of their employees' races – such record-keeping was initially regarded as inherently perverse.[4] The EEOC continued to hold annual conferences on affirmative action techniques through 1971, focusing in particular on trade associations. Simultaneously, the OFCC concentrated its attention on federal construction projects, initiating pilot programs in various U.S. cities to test the feasibility of mandating an increase in the hiring of racial minorities.

Richard Nixon's ascension to the presidency in 1969 ushered in an aggressive new era for affirmative action. The Philadelphia Plan, which developed out of the OFCC's pilot programs, required detailed tables for how many minorities were included in each sector of skilled construction union members with specific goals and deadlines. The Plan had first been attempted in 1967, but when union leaders opposed it, and members of Congress claimed it violated Title VII, it was abandoned. Two years later, Nixon encouraged the issuance of a Revised Philadelphia Plan penned by Labor Undersecretary Arthur Fletcher, **reproduced below**.[5] The new language stressed broad goals and good faith efforts rather than strict minimums, but the core of the model remained proportional racial representation. After five months of hearings and negotiations, Congress approved the plan on December 22, 1969.[6] The Philadelphia Plan expired four years later, but it and a string of derivative programs demonstrated the viability of the new civil rights strategy as an executive policy. Affirmative action had essentially become a quota by another name.[7]

---

1   Executive Order No. 10925, 3 C.F.R. 448 (1959-1963) (1961).

2   Graham 28.

3   Executive Order No. 11236, 3 C.F.R. 167 (1965 Supp.) (1965).

4   Graham 197-200.

5   35 Fed. Reg. 2586-2590 (5 February 1970). The plan was later revised to include sex discrimination as well. 35 Fed. Reg. 8888-8889 (9 June 1970).

6   For the history of the Philadelphia Plan with special attention to labor relations, see David Hamilton Golland, "Only Nixon Could Go to Philadelphia," Paper presented at the CUNY Race and Labor Matters Conference (Dec. 4-5, 2003) (available at http://journey-zone.com/Only_Nixon.pdf).

7   Philip F. Rubio, *A History of Affirmative Action 1619-2000* (Jackson: University Press of Mississippi, 2001), pp. 153-54.

II. *Executive Order 11246: Equal Employment Opportunity (Sept. 24, 1965)*

E. O. 11245   Title 3--Chapter II   E. O. 11246

(material omitted)

Executive Order 11246
EQUAL EMPLOYMENT OPPORTUNITY

Under and by virtue of the authority vested in me as President of the United States by the Constitution and statutes of the United States, it is ordered as follows:

PART I—NONDISCRIMINATION IN GOVERNMENT EMPLOYMENT

SECTION 101. It is the policy of the Government of the United States to provide equal opportunity in Federal employment for all qualified persons, to prohibit discrimination in employment because of race, creed, color, or national origin, and to promote the full realization of equal employment opportunity through a positive, continuing program in each executive department and agency. The policy of equal opportunity applies to every aspect of Federal employment policy and practice.

SEC. 102. The head of each executive department and agency shall establish and maintain a positive program of equal employment opportunity for all civilian employees and applicants for employment within his jurisdiction in accordance with the policy set forth in Section 101.

SEC. 103. The Civil Service Commission shall supervise and provide leadership and guidance in the conduct of equal employment opportunity programs for the civilian employees of and applications for employment within the executive departments and agencies and shall review agency program accomplishments periodically. In order to facilitate the achievement of a model program for equal employment opportunity in the Federal service, the Commission may consult from time to time with such individuals, groups, or organizations as may be of assistance in improving the Federal program and realizing the objectives of this Part.

167

E. O. 11246   Title 3--Chapter II   E. O. 11246

Sec. 104. The Civil Service Commission shall provide for the prompt, fair, and impartial consideration of all complaints of discrimination in Federal employment on the basis of race, creed, color, or national origin. Procedures for the consideration of complaints shall include at least one impartial review within the executive department or agency and shall provide for appeal to the Civil Service Commission.

Sec. 105. The Civil Service Commission shall issue such regulations, orders, and instructions as it deems necessary and appropriate to carry out its responsibilities under this Part, and the head of each executive department and agency shall comply with the regulations, orders, and instructions issued by the Commission under this Part.

Part II—Nondiscrimination in Employment by Government Contractors and Subcontractors

Subpart A—Duties of the Secretary of Labor

Sec. 201. The Secretary of Labor shall be responsible for the administration of Parts II and III of this Order and shall adopt such rules and regulations and issue such orders as he deems necessary and appropriate to achieve the purposes thereof.

Subpart B—Contractors' Agreements

Sec. 202. Except in contracts exempted in accordance with Section 204 of this Order, all Government contracting agencies shall include in every Government contract hereafter entered into the following provisions:

"During the performance of this contract, the contractor agrees as follows:

"(1) The contractor will not discriminate against any employee or applicant for employment because of race, creed, color, or national origin. The contractor will take affirmative action to ensure that applicants are employed, and that employees are treated during employment, without regard to their race, creed, color, or national origin. Such action shall include, but not be limited to the following: employment, upgrading, demotion, or transfer; recruitment or recruitment advertising; layoff or termination; rates of pay or other forms of compensation; and selection for training, including apprenticeship. The contractor agrees to post in conspicuous places, available to employees and applicants for employment, notices to be provided by the contracting officer setting forth the provisions of this nondiscrimination clause.

"(2) The contractor will, in all solicitations or advertisements for employees placed by or on behalf of the contractor, state that all qualified applicants will receive consideration for employment without regard to race, creed, color, or national origin.

"(3) The contractor will send to each labor union or representative of workers with which he has a collective bargaining agreement or other contract or understanding, a notice, to be provided by the agency contracting officer, advising the labor union or workers' representative of the contractor's commitments under Section 202 of Executive Order No. 11246 of September 24, 1965, and shall post copies of the notice in conspicuous places available to employees and applicants for employment.

"(4) The contractor will comply with all provisions of Executive Order No. 11246 of Sept. 24, 1965, and of the rules, regulations, and relevant orders of the Secretary of Labor.

168

"(5) The contractor will furnish all information and reports required by Executive Order No. 11246 of September 24, 1965, and by the rules, regulations, and orders of the Secretary of Labor, or pursuant thereto, and will permit access to his books, records, and accounts by the contracting agency and the Secretary of Labor for purposes of investigation to ascertain compliance with such rules, regulations, and orders.

"(6) In the event of the contractor's noncompliance with the nondiscrimination clauses of this contract or with any of such rules, regulations, or orders, this contract may be cancelled, terminated or suspended in whole or in part and the contractor may be declared ineligible for further Government contracts in accordance with procedures authorized in Executive Order No. 11246 of Sept. 24, 1965, and such other sanctions may be imposed and remedies invoked as provided in Executive Order No. 11246 of September 24, 1965, or by rule, regulation, or order of the Secretary of Labor, or as otherwise provided by law.

"(7) The contractor will include the provisions of Paragraphs (1) through (7) in every subcontract or purchase order unless exempted by rules, regulations, or orders of the Secretary of Labor issued pursuant to Section 204 of Executive Order No. 11246 of Sept. 24, 1965, so that such provisions will be binding upon each subcontractor or vendor. The contractor will take such action with respect to any subcontract or purchase order as the contracting agency may direct as a means of enforcing such provisions including sanctions for noncompliance: *Provided, however,* That in the event the contractor becomes involved in, or is threatened with, litigation with a subcontractor or vendor as a result of such direction by the contracting agency, the contractor may request the United States to enter into such litigation to protect the interests of the United States."

SEC. 203. (a) Each contractor having a contract containing the provisions prescribed in Section 202 shall file, and shall cause each of his subcontractors to file, Compliance Reports with the contracting agency or the Secretary of Labor as may be directed. Compliance Reports shall be filed within such times and shall contain such information as to the practices, policies, programs, and employment policies, programs, and employment statistics of the contractor and each subcontractor, and shall be in such form, as the Secretary of Labor may prescribe.

(b) Bidders or prospective contractors or subcontractors may be required to state whether they have participated in any previous contract subject to the provisions of this Order, or any preceding similar Executive order, and in that event to submit, on behalf of themselves and their proposed subcontractors, Compliance Reports prior to or as an initial part of their bid or negotiation of a contract.

(c) Whenever the contractor or subcontractor has a collective bargaining agreement or other contract or understanding with a labor union or an agency referring workers or providing or supervising apprenticeship or training for such workers, the Compliance Report shall include such information as to such labor union's or agency's practices and policies affecting compliance as the Secretary of Labor may prescribe: *Provided,* That to the extent such information is within the exclusive possession of a labor union or an agency referring workers or providing or supervising apprenticeship or training and such labor union or agency shall refuse to furnish such information to the contractor, the contractor shall so certify to the contracting agency as part of its Compliance Report and shall set forth what efforts he has made to obtain such information.

169

(d) The contracting agency or the Secretary of Labor may direct that any bidder or prospective contractor or subcontractor shall submit, as part of his Compliance Report, a statement in writing, signed by an authorized officer or agent on behalf of any labor union or any agency referring workers or providing or supervising apprenticeship or other training, with which the bidder or prospective contractor deals, with supporting information, to the effect that the signer's practices and policies do not discriminate on the grounds of race, color, creed, or national origin, and that the signer either will affirmatively cooperate in the implementation of the policy and provisions of this Order or that it consents and agrees that recruitment, employment, and the terms and conditions of employment under the proposed contract shall be in accordance with the purposes and provisions of the Order. In the event that the union, or the agency shall refuse to execute such a statement, the Compliance Report shall so certify and set forth what efforts have been made to secure such a statement and such additional factual material as the contracting agency or the Secretary of Labor may require.

SEC. 204. The Secretary of Labor may, when he deems that special circumstances in the national interest so require, exempt a contracting agency from the requirement of including any or all of the provisions of Section 202 of this Order in any specific contract, subcontract, or purchase order. The Secretary of Labor may, by rule or regulation, also exempt certain classes of contracts, subcontracts, or purchase orders (1) whenever work is to be or has been performed outside the United States and no recruitment of workers within the limits of the United States is involved; (2) for standard commercial supplies or raw materials; (3) involving less than specified amounts of money or specified numbers of workers; or (4) to the extent that they involve subcontracts below a specified tier. The Secretary of Labor may also provide, by rule, regulation, or order, for the exemption of facilities of a contractor which are in all respects separate and distinct from activities of the contractor related to the performance of the contract: *Provided*, That such an exemption will not interfere with or impede the effectuation of the purposes of this Order: *And provided further*, That in the absence of such an exemption all facilities shall be covered by the provisions of this Order.

(material omitted)

170

PART III—NONDISCRIMINATION PROVISIONS IN FEDERALLY ASSISTED
CONSTRUCTION CONTRACTS

SEC. 301. Each executive department and agency which administers a program involving Federal financial assistance shall require as a condition for the approval of any grant, contract, loan, insurance, or guarantee thereunder, which may involve a construction contract, that the applicant for Federal assistance undertake and agree to incorporate, or cause to be incorporated, into all construction contracts paid for in whole or in part with funds obtained from the Federal Government or borrowed on the credit of the Federal Government pursuant to such grant, contract, loan, insurance, or guarantee, or undertaken pursuant to any Federal program involving such grant, contract, loan, insurance, or guarantee, the provisions prescribed for Government contracts by Section 202 of this Order or such modification thereof, preserving in substance the contractor's obligations thereunder, as may be approved by the Secretary of Labor, together with such additional provisions as the Secretary deems appropriate to establish and protect the interest of the United States in the enforcement of those obligations. Each such applicant shall also undertake and agree (1) to assist and cooperate actively with the administering department or agency and the Secretary of Labor in obtaining the compliance of contractors and subcontractors with those contract provisions and with the rules, regulations, and relevant orders of the Secretary, (2) to obtain and to furnish to the administering department or agency and to the Secretary of Labor such information as they may require for the supervision of such compliance, (3) to carry out sanctions and penalties for violation of such obligations imposed upon contractors and subcontractors by the Secretary of Labor or the administering department or agency pursuant to Part II, Subpart D, of this Order, and (4) to refrain from entering into any contract subject to this Order, or extension or other modification of such a contract with a contractor debarred from Government contracts under Part II, Subpart D, of this Order.

SEC. 302. (a) "Construction contract" as used in this Order means any contract for the construction, rehabilitation, alteration, conversion, extension, or repair of buildings, highways, or other improvements to real property.

(b) The provisions of Part II of this Order shall apply to such construction contracts, and for purposes of such application the administering department or agency shall be considered the contracting agency referred to therein.

(c) The term "applicant" as used in this Order means an applicant for Federal assistance or, as determined by agency regulation, other program participant, with respect to whom an application for any grant, contract, loan, insurance, or guarantee is not finally acted upon prior to the effective date of this Part, and it includes such an applicant after he becomes a recipient of such Federal assistance.

174

Sec. 303. (a) Each administering department and agency shall be responsible for obtaining the compliance of such applicants with their undertakings under this Order. Each administering department and agency is directed to cooperate with the Secretary of Labor, and to furnish the Secretary such information and assistance as he may require in the performance of his functions under this Order.

(b) In the event an applicant fails and refuses to comply with his undertakings, the administering department or agency may take any or all of the following actions: (1) cancel, terminate, or suspend in whole or in part the agreement, contract, or other arrangement with such applicant with respect to which the failure and refusal occurred; (2) refrain from extending any further assistance to the applicant under the program with respect to which the failure or refusal occurred until satisfactory assurance of future compliance has been received from such applicant; and (3) refer the case to the Department of Justice for appropriate legal proceedings.

(c) Any action with respect to an applicant pursuant to Subsection (b) shall be taken in conformity with Section 602 of the Civil Rights Act of 1964 (and the regulations of the administering department or agency issued thereunder), to the extent applicable. In no case shall action be taken with respect to an applicant pursuant to Clause (1) or (2) of Subsection (b) without notice and opportunity for hearing before the administering department or agency.

Sec. 304. Any executive department or agency which imposes by rule, regulation, or order requirements of nondiscrimination in employment, other than requirements imposed pursuant to this Order, may delegate to the Secretary of Labor by agreement such responsibilities with respect to compliance standards, reports, and procedures as would tend to bring the administration of such requirements into conformity with the administration of requirements imposed under this Order: *Provided*, That actions to effect compliance by recipients of Federal financial assistance with requirements imposed pursuant to Title VI of the Civil Rights Act of 1964 shall be taken in conformity with the procedures and limitations prescribed in Section 602 thereof and the regulations of the administering department or agency issued thereunder.

175

PART IV—MISCELLANEOUS

SEC. 401. The Secretary of Labor may delegate to any officer, agency, or employee in the Executive branch of the Government, any function or duty of the Secretary under Parts II and III of this Order, except authority to promulgate rules and regulations of a general nature.

SEC. 402. The Secretary of Labor shall provide administrative support for the execution of the program known as the "Plans for Progress."

SEC. 403. (a) Executive Orders Nos. 10590 (January 19, 1955), 10722 (August 5, 1957), 10925 (March 6, 1961), 11114 (June 22, 1963), and 11162 (July 28, 1964), are hereby superseded and the President's Committee on Equal Employment Opportunity established by Executive Order No. 10925 is hereby abolished. All records and property in the custody of the Committee shall be transferred to the Civil Service Commission and the Secretary of Labor, as appropriate.

(b) Nothing in this Order shall be deemed to relieve any person of any obligation assumed or imposed under or pursuant to any Executive Order superseded by this Order. All rules, regulations, orders, instructions, designations, and other directives issued by the President's Committee on Equal Employment Opportunity and those issued by the heads of various departments or agencies under or pursuant to any of the Executive orders superseded by this Order, shall, to the extent that they are not inconsistent with this Order, remain in full force and effect unless and until revoked or superseded by appropriate authority. References in such directives to provisions of the superseded orders shall be deemed to be references to the comparable provisions of this Order.

SEC. 404. The General Services Administration shall take appropriate action to revise the standard Government contract forms to accord with the provisions of this Order and of the rules and regulations of the Secretary of Labor.

SEC. 405. This Order shall become effective thirty days after the date of this Order.

LYNDON B. JOHNSON

THE WHITE HOUSE,
September 24, 1965.

176

III. Order No. 4, "The Revised Philadelphia Plan," 35 Fed. Reg. 2586 (Feb. 6, 1970)

2586   **RULES AND REGULATIONS**

(material omitted)

Chapter 60—Office of Federal Contract Compliance, Equal Employment Opportunity, Department of Labor

PART 60-2—AFFIRMATIVE ACTION PROGRAMS

Pursuant to Executive Order 11246, sections 201, 205, 211 (30 F.R. 12319), and 41 CFR 60-1.6, 60-1.28, 60-1.29, 60-1.40, Title 41 of the Code of Federal Regulations is hereby amended by adding a new Part 60-2 to read as set forth below:

Subpart A—General

Sec.
60-2.1   Title, purpose and scope.
60-2.2   Agency action.

Subpart B—Required Contents of Affirmative Action Programs

60-2.10   Purpose of affirmative action program.
60-2.11   Required utilization analysis and goals.
60-2.12   Additional required ingredients of affirmative action programs.
60-2.13   Compliance status.

Subpart C—Suggested Methods of Implementing the Requirements of Subpart B

60-2.20   Development or reaffirmation of the equal employment opportunity policy.

RULES AND REGULATIONS   2587

AUTHORITY: The provisions of this Part 60-2 issued pursuant to sec. 201, E.O. 11246 (30 F.R. 12319).

Subpart A—General

§ 60-2.1 Title, purpose and scope.

This part shall also be known as "Order No. 4," and shall cover nonconstruction contractors. Section 60-1.40 of this chapter, Affirmative Action Compliance Programs, requires that within 120 days from the commencement of a contract each prime contractor or subcontractor with 50 or more employees and a contract of $50,000 or more develop a written affirmative action compliance program for each of its establishments. A review of agency compliance surveys indicates that many contractors do not have affirmative action programs on file at the time an establishment is visited by a compliance investigator. This part details the agency review procedure and the results of a contractor's failure to develop and maintain an affirmative action program and then sets forth detailed guidelines to be used by contractors and Government agencies in developing and judging these programs as well as the good faith effort required to transform the programs from paper commitments to equal employment opportunity.

§ 60-2.2 Agency action.

(a) Any contractor required by § 60-1.40 to develop an affirmative action program at each of his establishments who has not complied fully with that section is not in compliance with Executive Order 11246 (30 F.R. 12319). Until such programs are developed and found to be acceptable in accordance with the standards and guidelines set forth in §§ 60-2.10 through 60-2.31, the contractor is unable to comply with the equal employment opportunity clause.

(b) If, in determining such contractor's responsibility for an award of a contract it comes to the contracting officer's attention, through sources within his agency or through the Office of Federal Contract Compliance or other Government agencies, that the contractor has not developed an acceptable affirmative action program at each of his establishments, the contracting officer shall declare the contractor-bidder nonresponsible unless he can otherwise affirmatively determine that the contractor is able to comply with his equal employment obligations: Provided, That during the preaward conferences provided for in § 60-1.6(d)(3), every effort shall be made through the processes of conciliation, mediation and persuasion to develop an acceptable affirmative action program meeting the standards and guidelines set forth in §§ 60-2.10 through 60-2.31 so that, in the performance of his contract, the contractor is able to meet his equal employment obligations in accordance with the equal opportunity clause and applicable rules, regulations and orders: Provided further, That when the contractor-bidder is declared nonresponsible more than once for inability to comply with the equal employment opportunity clause a notice setting a timely hearing date shall be issued concurrently with the second nonresponsibility determination in accordance with the provisions of § 60-1.26 proposing to declare such contractor-bidder ineligible for future contracts and subcontracts.

(c) Immediately upon finding that a contractor has no affirmative action program or that his program is not acceptable the contracting officer shall notify officials of the appropriate compliance agency and the Office of Federal Contract Compliance of such fact. The compliance agency shall issue a notice to the contractor giving him 30 days to show cause why enforcement proceedings under section 209(b) of Executive Order 11246, as amended, should not be instituted.

(1) If the contractor fails to show good cause for his failure or fails to remedy that failure by developing and implementing an acceptable affirmative action program within 30 days, the compliance agency, upon the approval of the Director, shall issue a notice of proposed cancellation or termination of existing contracts or subcontracts and debarment from future contracts and subcontracts pursuant to § 60-1.26(b), giving the contractor 10 days to request a hearing. If a request for hearing has not been received within 10 days from such notice, such contractor will be declared ineligible for future contracts and current contracts will be terminated for default.

(2) During the "show cause" period of 30 days every effort shall be made by the compliance agency through conciliation, mediation and persuasion to resolve the deficiencies which led to the determination of noncompliance or nonresponsibility. If satisfactory adjustments designed to bring the contractor into compliance are not concluded, the compliance agency, with the prior approval of the Director, shall promptly commence formal proceedings leading to the cancellation or termination of existing contracts or subcontracts and debarment from future contracts and subcontracts under § 60-1.26(b).

(d) During the "show cause" period and formal proceedings, each contracting agency must continue to determine the contractor's responsibility in considering whether or not to award a new or additional contract.

Subpart B—Required Contents of Affirmative Action Programs

§ 60-2.10 Purpose of affirmative action program.

An affirmative action program is a set of specific and result-oriented procedures to which a contractor commits himself to apply every good faith effort. The objective of those procedures plus such efforts is equal employment opportunity. Procedures without effort to make them work are meaningless; and effort, undirected by specific and meaningful procedures, is inadequate. An acceptable affirmative action program must include an analysis of areas within which the contractor is deficient in the utilization of minority groups and, further, goals and timetables to which the contractor's good faith efforts must be directed to correct the deficiencies and, thus to increase materially the utilization of minorities at all levels and in all segments of his work force where deficiencies exist.

§ 60-2.11 Required utilization analysis and goals.

Affirmative action programs must contain the following information:

(a) An analysis of all major job categories at the facility, with explanations if minorities are currently being underutilized in any one or more job categories (job "category" herein meaning one or a group of jobs having similar content, wage rates and opportunities). "Underutilization" is defined as having fewer minorities in a particular job category than would reasonably be expected by their availability. In determining whether minorities are being underutilized in any job category, the contractor will consider at least all of the following factors:

(1) The minority population of the labor area surrounding the facility;

(2) The size of the minority unemployment force in the labor area surrounding the facility;

(3) The percentage of minority work force as compared with the total work force in the immediate labor area;

(4) The general availability of minorities having requisite skills in the immediate labor area;

(5) The availability of minorities having requisite skills in an area in which the contractor can reasonably recruit;

(6) The availability of promotable minority employees within the contractor's organization;

(7) The anticipated expansion, contraction and turnover of and in the work force;

(8) The existence of training institutions capable of training minorities in the requisite skills; and

(9) The degree of training which the contractor is reasonably able to undertake as a means of making all job classes available to minorities.

(b) Goals, timetables and affirmative action commitments must be designed to correct any identifiable deficiencies.

Where deficiencies exist and where numbers or percentages are relevant in developing corrective action, the contractor shall establish and set forth specific goals and timetables. Such goals and timetables, with supporting data and the analysis thereof shall be a part of the contractor's written affirmative action program and shall be maintained at each establishment of the contractor. Where the contractor has not established a goal his written affirmative action program must specifically analyze each of the factors listed in "a" above and must detail his reason for a lack of a goal. In establishments with over 1,000 employees, or where otherwise appropriate, goals and timetables may be presented by organizational unit. The goals and timetables should be attainable in terms of the contractor's analysis of his deficiencies and his entire affirmative action program. Thus, in establishing his goals and timetables the contractor should consider the results which could be reasonably expected from his good faith efforts to make his overall affirmative action program work. If he does not meet his goals and timetables, the contractor's "good faith efforts" shall be judged by whether he is following his program and attempting to make it work toward the attainment of his goals.

(c) Support data for the above analysis and program shall be compiled and maintained as part of the contractor's affirmative action program. This data should include progression line charts, seniority rosters, applicant flow data, and applicant rejection ratios indicating minority status.

(d) Based upon the Government's experience with compliance reviews under the Executive order programs and the contractor reporting system, over the past eight (8) years, minority groups are most likely to be underutilized in the following six (6) categories as defined by the Employer's Information Report, EEO-1: officials and managers, professionals, technicians, sales workers, office and clerical, and craftsmen (skilled). Therefore, the contractor shall direct special attention to these categories in his analysis and goal setting.

§ 60-2.12 Additional required ingredients of affirmative action programs.

Effective affirmative action programs shall contain, but not necessarily be limited to, the following ingredients:

(a) Development or reaffirmation of the contractor's equal employment opportunity policy in all personnel actions.

(b) Formal internal and external dissemination of the contractor's policy.

(c) Establishment of responsibilities for implementation of the contractor's affirmative action program.

(d) Identification of problem areas (deficiencies) by organizational units and job categories.

(e) Establishment of goals and objectives by organizational units and job category, including timetables for completion.

(f) Development and execution of action oriented programs designed to eliminate problems and further designed to attain established goals and objectives.

(g) Design and implementation of internal audit and reporting systems to measure effectiveness of the total program.

(h) Active support of local and national community action programs.

§ 60-2.13 Compliance status.

No contractor's compliance status shall be judged alone by whether or not he reaches his goals and meets his timetables. Rather each contractor's compliance posture shall be reviewed and determined by reviewing the contents of his program, the extent of his adherence to his program, and his good faith efforts to make his program work toward the realization of the program's goals within the timetables set for completion. There follows an outline of suggestions and examples of procedures that contractors and federal agencies may use as guidelines for establishing, implementing, and judging an acceptable affirmative action program.

Subpart C—Suggested Method of Implementing the Requirements of Subpart B

§ 60-2.20 Development or reaffirmation of the equal employment opportunity policy.

(a) The contractor's policy statement should indicate the chief executive officers' attitude on the subject matter, assign overall responsibility and provide for a reporting or monitoring procedure. Specific items to be mentioned should include, but not limited to:

(1) Recruit, hire, and promote all job classifications without regard to race, color, religion, sex, or national origin, except where sex is a bona fide occupational qualification.

(2) Base decisions on employment so as to further the principle of equal employment opportunity.

(3) Insure that promotion decisions are in accord with principles of equal employment opportunity by imposing only valid requirements for promotional opportunities.

(4) Insure that all other personnel actions such as compensation, benefits, transfers, layoffs, return from layoff, company sponsored training, education, tuition assistance, social and recreation programs, will be administered without regard to race, color, religion, sex, or national origin, except where sex is a bona fide occupational qualification.

(b) The contractor should periodically conduct analyses of all personnel actions to insure equal opportunity.

§ 60-2.21 Dissemination of the policy.

(a) The contractor should disseminate his policy internally as follows:

(1) Include it in contractor's policy manual.

(2) Publicize it in company newspaper, magazine, annual report, and other media.

(3) Conduct special meetings with executive, management, and supervisory personnel to explain intent of policy and individual responsibility for effective implementation, making clear the chief executive officer's attitude.

(4) Schedule special meetings with all other employees to discuss policy and explain individual employee responsibilities.

(5) Discuss the policy thoroughly in both employee orientation and management training programs.

(6) Meet with union officials to inform them of policy, and request their cooperation.

(7) Include nondiscrimination clauses in all union agreements, and review all contractual provisions to ensure they are nondiscriminatory.

(8) Publish articles covering EEO programs, progress reports, promotions of minority employees, etc., in company publications.

(9) Post the policy on company bulletin boards.

(10) When employees are featured in product or consumer advertising, both minority and nonminority employees should be pictured.

(b) The contractor should disseminate his policy externally as follows:

(1) Inform all recruiting sources verbally and in writing of company policy, stipulating that these sources actively recruit and refer minorities for all positions listed.

(2) Incorporate the Equal Opportunity clause in all purchase orders, leases, contracts, etc., covered by Executive Order 11246, as amended, and its implementing regulations.

(3) Notify minority organizations, community agencies, community leaders, secondary schools and colleges, of company policy, preferably in writing.

(4) When employees are pictured in consumer or help wanted advertising, both minorities and nonminorities should be shown.

(5) Send written notification of company policy to all subcontractors, vendors and suppliers requesting appropriate action on their part.

§ 60-2.22 Responsibility for implementation.

(a) An executive of the contractor should be appointed as director or manager of company Equal Opportunity Programs. Depending upon the size and geographical alignment of the company, this may be his sole responsibility. He should be given the necessary top management support and staffing to execute his assignment. His responsibilities should include, but not necessarily be limited to:

(1) Developing policy statements, affirmative action programs, internal and external communication techniques.

(2) Assisting in the identification of problem areas.

(3) Assisting line management in arriving at solutions to problems.

(4) Designing and implementing audit and reporting systems that will:

(i) Measure effectiveness of the contractor's program.

RULES AND REGULATIONS

(ii) Indicate need for remedial action.

(iii) Determine the degree to which the contractor's goals and objectives have been attained.

(5) Serve as liaison between the contractor and enforcement agencies, minority organizations, and community action groups.

(6) Keep management informed of latest developments in the entire equal opportunity area.

(b) Line responsibilities should include, but not be limited to, the following:

(1) Assistance in the identification of problem areas and establishment of local and unit goals and objectives.

(2) Active involvement with local minority organizations and community action groups.

(3) Periodic audit of hiring and promotion patterns to remove impediments to the attainment of goals and objectives.

(4) Regular discussions with local managers, supervisors and employees to be certain the contractor's policies are being followed.

(5) Review of the qualifications of all employees to insure minorities are given full opportunities for transfers and promotions.

(6) Career counseling for all employees.

(7) Periodic audit to insure that each location is in compliance in areas such as:

(i) Posters are properly displayed.

(ii) All facilities including company housing, are in fact desegregated, both in policy and in use.

(iii) Minority employees are afforded a full opportunity and are encouraged to participate in all company sponsored educational, training, recreational and social activities.

(8) Supervision should be made to understand that their work performance is being evaluated on the basis of their equal employment opportunity efforts and results, as well as other criteria.

§ 60–2.23 Identification of problem areas by organizational unit and job categories.

(a) An in-depth analysis of the following should be made, paying particular attention to apprentices and those categories listed in § 60–2.11(d):

(1) Racial composition of the work force.

(2) Racial composition of applicant flow.

(3) The total selection process including position descriptions, man specifications, application forms, interview procedures, test administration, test validity, referral procedures, final selection process, and similar factors.

(4) Transfer and promotion practices.

(5) Facilities, company sponsored recreation and social events, and special programs such as educational assistance.

(6) Seniority practices and seniority provisions of union contracts.

(7) Apprenticeship programs.

(8) All company training programs, formal and informal.

(9) Work force attitude.

(10) Technical phases of compliance, such as poster and notification to labor unions, retention of applications, notification to subcontractors, etc.

(b) If any of the following items are found in the analysis, special corrective action should be appropriate.

(1) An "underutilization" of minorities in specific work classifications.

(2) Lateral and/or vertical movement of minority employees occurring at a lesser rate (compared to work force mix) than that of nonminority employees.

(3) The selection process eliminates a higher percentage of minorities than nonminorities.

(4) Application and related preemployment forms not in compliance with local, State, or Federal legislation.

(5) Position descriptions inaccurate in relation to actual functions and duties.

(6) Man specifications not validated in relation to position requirements and job performance.

(7) Test forms not validated by location, work performance and inclusion of minorities in sample.

(8) Referral ratio of minorities to the hiring supervisor or manager indicates an abnormal percentage are being rejected as compared to nonminority applicants.

(9) Minorities are excluded from or are not participating in company sponsored activities or programs.

(10) De facto segregation still exists at some facilities.

(11) Seniority provisions contribute to overt or inadvertent discrimination, i.e., a racial disparity exists between length of service and types of jobs held.

(12) Nonsupport of company policy by managers, supervisors, or employees.

(13) Minorities underutilized or underrepresented in apprenticeship programs or other training or career improvement programs.

(14) No formal techniques established for evaluating effectiveness of EEO programs.

(15) Lack of access to suitable housing inhibits employment of qualified minorities for professional and management positions.

(16) Lack of suitable transportation (public or private) to the workplace inhibits minority employment.

(17) Labor unions and subcontractors not notified of their responsibilities.

(18) Purchase orders do not contain EEO clause.

(19) Posters not on display.

§ 60–2.24 Establishment of goals and timetables.

(a) The goals and timetables developed by the contractor should be attainable in terms of the contractor's analysis of his deficiencies and his entire affirmative action program. Thus, in establishing the size of his goals and the length of his timetables, the contractor should consider the results which could reasonably be expected from his putting forth every good faith effort to make his overall affirmative action program work. In determining levels of goals, the contractor should consider at least the factors listed in § 60–2.11(a).

(b) Involve personnel relations staff, department and division heads, and local and unit managers in the goal setting process.

(c) Goals should be significant, measurable and attainable.

(d) Goals should be specific for planned results, with timetables for completion.

(e) Goals may not be rigid and inflexible quotas which must be met, but must be targets reasonably attainable by means of applying every good faith effort to make all aspects of the entire affirmative action program work.

§ 60–2.25 Development and execution of programs.

(a) The contractor should conduct detailed analyses of position descriptions to insure that they accurately reflect position functions, and are consistent for the same position from one location to another.

(b) The contractor should validate man specifications by division, department, location, or other organizational unit and by job category using job performance criteria. Special attention should be given to academic, experience and skill requirements to insure that the requirements in themselves do not constitute inadvertent discrimination. Specifications should be consistent for the same job classification in all locations and should be free from bias as regards to race, color, religion, sex, or national origin, except where sex is a bona fide occupational qualification. Where requirements screen out a disproportionate number of minorities, such requirements should be professionally validated to job performance.

(c) Approved position descriptions and man specifications, when used by the contractor, should be made available to all members of management involved in the recruiting, screening, selection and promotion process. Copies should also be distributed to all recruiting sources.

(d) The contractor should evaluate the total selection process to insure freedom from bias and, thus, aid the attainment of goals and objectives.

(1) All personnel involved in the recruiting, screening, selection, promotion, disciplinary, and related processes should be carefully selected and trained to insure elimination of bias in all personnel actions.

(2) The contractor should validate all selection criteria (Note Department of Labor Order of Sept. 9, 1968) (33 F.R. 44392, Sept. 24, 1968) covering the validation of Employment Tests and Other Selection Techniques by Contractors and Subcontractors Subject to the Provisions of Executive Order 11246.

(3) Selection techniques other than tests may also be improperly used so as to have the effect of discriminating against minority groups. Such techniques include but are not restricted to, unscored interviews, unscored application forms, arrest records, and credit checks.

2590

RULES AND REGULATIONS

Where there exists data suggesting that such unfair discrimination or exclusion of minorities exists, the contractor should analyze his unscored procedures and eliminate them if they are not objectively valid.

(e) Suggested techniques to improve recruitment and increase the flow of minority applicants follow:

(1) Certain organizations such as the Urban League, Job Corps, Equal Opportunity Programs, Inc., Concentrated Employment Programs, Neighborhood Youth Corps, Secondary Schools, Colleges, and City Colleges with high minority enrollment, the State Employment Service, specialized employment agencies, Aspira, LULAC, SER, the G.I. Forum, the Commonwealth of Puerto Rico are normally prepared to refer qualified minority applicants. In addition, community leaders as individuals shall be added to recruiting sources.

(2) Formal briefing sessions should be held, preferably on company premises, with representatives from these recruiting sources. Plant tours, presentations by minority employees, clear and concise explanations of current and future job openings, position descriptions, man specifications, explanations of the company's selection process, and recruiting literature should be an integral part of the briefings. Formal arrangements should be made for referral of applicants, follow-up with sources, and feedback on disposition of applicants.

(3) Minority employees, using procedures similar to (2) above, should be actively encouraged to refer applicants.

(4) A special effort should be made to include minorities on the Personnel Relations staff.

(5) Minority employees should be made available for participation in Career Days, Youth Motivation Programs, and related activities in their communities.

(6) Active participation in "Job Fairs" is desirable. Company representatives so participating should be given authority to make on-the-spot commitments.

(7) Active recruiting programs should be carried out at secondary schools, junior colleges, and colleges with minority enrollments.

(8) Special employment programs should be undertaken whenever possible. Some possible programs are:

(i) Technical and nontechnical co-op programs with the predominantly Negro colleges.

(ii) "After school" and/or work-study jobs for minority youths.

(iii) Summer jobs for underprivileged youth.

(iv) Summer work-study programs for faculty members of the predominantly minority schools and colleges.

(v) Motivation, training and employment programs for the hard-core unemployed.

(9) When recruiting brochures pictorially present work situations, the minority members of the work force should be included.

(10) Help wanted advertising should be expanded to include the minority news media on a regular basis.

(f) The contractor should insure that minority employees are given equal opportunity for promotion. Suggestions for achieving this result include:

(1) An inventory of current minority employees to determine academic, skill and experience level of individual employees.

(2) Initiating necessary remedial, job training and work-study programs.

(3) Developing and implementing formal employee evaluation programs.

(4) Being certain "man specifications" have been validated on job performance related criteria. (Minorities should not be required to posses higher qualifications than those of the lowest qualified incumbent.)

(5) When apparently qualified minorities are passed over for upgrading, require supervisory personnel to submit written justification.

(6) Establish formal career counseling programs to include attitude development, education aid, job rotation, buddy system, and similar programs.

(7) Review seniority practices and seniority clauses in union contracts to insure such practices or clauses are nondiscriminatory and do not have a discriminatory effect.

(g) Make certain facilities and company-sponsored social and recreation activities are desegregated. Actively encourage minority employees to participate.

§ 60-2.26 Internal audit and reporting systems.

(a) The contractor should monitor records of referrals, placements, transfers, promotions and terminations at all levels to insure nondiscriminatory policy is carried out.

(b) The contractor should require formal reports from unit managers on a schedule basis as to degree to which corporate or unit goals are attained and time tables met.

(c) The contractor should review report results with all levels of management.

(d) The contractor should advise top management of program effectiveness and submit recommendations to improve unsatisfactory performance.

§ 60-2.27 Support of action programs.

(a) The contractor should appoint key members of management to serve on Merit Employment Councils, Community Relations Boards and similar organizations.

(b) The contractor should encourage minority employees to actively participate in National Alliance of Businessmen programs for youth motivation.

(c) The contractor should support Vocational Guidance Institutes, Vestibule Training Programs and similar activities.

(d) The contractor should assist secondary schools and colleges with significant minority enrollment in programs designed to enable graduates of these institutions to compete in the open employment market on a more equitable basis.

(e) The contractor should publicize achievements of minority employees in local and minority news media.

(f) The contractor should support programs developed by the National Alliance of Businessmen, the Urban Coalition and similar organizations.

Subpart D—Miscellaneous

§ 60-2.30 Use of goals.

The purpose of a contractor's establishment and use of goal is to insure that he meet his affirmative action obligation. It is not intended and should not be used to discriminate against any applicant or employee because of race, color, religion, sex or national origin.

§ 60-2.31 Supersedure.

This part is an amplification of and supersedes a previous "Order No. 4" from this Office dated November 20, 1969.

Effective date. This part is effective January 30, 1970.

Signed at Washington, D.C. this 30th day of January 1970.

GEORGE P. SHULTZ,
Secretary of Labor.

JOHN L. WILKS,
*Director, Office of
Federal Contract Compliance.*

[F.R. Doc. 70-1411; Filed, Feb. 4, 1970; 8:50 a.m.]

(material omitted)

CONGRESS RESPONDS TO *GRIGGS* & EXECUTIVE ORDER 11246: THE EQUAL EMPLOYMENT OPPORTUNITY ACT OF 1972

I. Overview

Both disparate impact liability and Executive Order 11246 were executive department strategies to speed up the pace of workforce desegregation. Lower federal court judges, notably Judge Wisdom in the Fifth Circuit and Judge Soboloff in the Fourth Circuit, maintained that both responses were consistent with, and required by, the integrative purpose of the 1964 Act and of the Equal Protection Clause as construed in the school desegregation cases. The Supreme Court explicitly adopted the EEOC's disparate impact theory in *Griggs*, but did not address the more controversial Executive Order or President Nixon's Philadelphia Plan (which was okayed by lower court judges).

Civil rights groups and progressives were strongly supportive of disparate impact liability and affirmative action pressure from the Office of Federal Contract Compliance (OFCC, the primary enforcement agency for the executive order)—but most employers and unions were not enthusiastic. They had their chance for a push-back when Congress revisited Title VII in 1971-72. The occasion for a new legislative initiative was that the original jobs title did not apply to federal, state, and municipal employees, a huge chunk of the nation's workforce. Civil rights groups complained that governmental workforces were slow to integrate and that constitutional rules were not sufficient to root out indirect discrimination. This legislative initiative, of course, opened the door to new political debates in response to *Griggs* and Executive Order 11246.

After extensive hearings, the Labor Committees in both chambers agreed with civil rights groups that governmental discrimination was both serious and pervasive. Even the federal Civil Service Commission had not been sufficiently aggressive, because it erroneously "assume[d] that employment discrimination in the Federal Government is solely a matter of malicious intent on the part of individuals" and "ha[d] not fully recognized that the general rules and procedures that it had promulgated may in themselves constitute systemic barriers to minorities and women." S. Rep. No. 92-415, at 14 (1971); accord, H.R. Rep. No. 92-238, at 24 (1971). The Committees also found that "widespread discrimination against minorities exists in state and local government employment"; the "existence of this discrimination is perpetuated by the presence of both institutional and overt discriminatory practices." Id. at 17. Both Committee Reports explicitly endorsed *Griggs* as foundational to Title VII. Id. at 8; S. Rep., at 15.

Unlike 1964, when the House of Representatives followed the Judiciary Committee's lead and voted for its version of the bill with few major amendments (the addition of "sex" to Title VII being the primary amendment), the House in 1971 narrowly rejected the Labor Committee's reported bill, in favor of a substitute proposed by Representative John Erlenborn (R-IL). Also unlike 1964, the Senate supported a more progressive, pro-civil rights bill than the House—but like 1964 the Senate engaged in more debate and considered a wider array of amendments.

No Senate amendment took direct aim at *Griggs*, but there were open attacks on Executive Order 11246. Senator Sam Ervin (D-NC) proposed the following amendment: "Nothing contained in this title or in Executive Order No. 11246, or in any other law or Executive Order, shall be interpreted to require any employer . . . to grant preferential treatment to any individual." 118 Cong. Rec. 1676 (1972). As the floor managers of the Title VII amendments recognized, e.g., 118 Cong. Rec. 1664-65 (1972), this was an attack on the Philadelphia plan and they urged its rejection for that reason; the Senate did indeed reject the Ervin Amendment, a fate shared by other such proposals in both the House and the Senate. *E.g.*, Subcomm. on Labor of the Senate Comm. on Labor and Public Welfare, *Legislative History of Equal Employment Opportunity Act of 1972*, at 1844 (1972) (subcommittee consensus that the Title VII amendments accepted the validity of decisions upholding remedial plans in response to OFCC pressure).

II. *Congress Ratifies Courts' Interpretation of Affirmative Action Plans*

a. Senator Ervin's Amendment, 118 Cong. Rec. 1676 (Jan. 28, 1972)

1662	CONGRESSIONAL RECORD — SENATE	*January 28, 1972*

(material omitted and repaginated)

Mr. ERVIN. Mr. President, I find that I was mistaken with respect to the draft of the modification. I send to the desk the amendment as modified and ask that it be stated in full.

The PRESIDING OFFICER. The clerk will state the amendment as modified.

The assistant legislative clerk read as follows:

Add a new section at the end of the bill appropriately numbered and reading as follows: "No department, agency, or officer of the United States shall require an employer to practice discrimination in reverse by employing persons of a particular race, or a particular religion, or a particular national origin, or a particular sex in either fixed or variable numbers, proportions, percentages, quotas, goals, or ranges. If any department, agency, officer, or employee of the United States violates or attempts or threatens to violate the provisions of the preceding sentence, the employer or employee aggrieved by the violation, or attempted or threatened violation, may bring a civil action in the United States District Court in the District in which he resides or in which the violation occurred, or is attempted or threatened, or in which the enterprise affected is located, and the District Court shall grant him such relief by way of temporary interlocutory or permanent injunctions as may be necessary to redress the consequences of the violation, or to prevent the attempted or threatened violation.

---

b. Congressional Debate on Ervin's Amendment, 118 Cong. Rec. 1664-65 (1972)

* * * *

[Sen. Ervin, recounting one of Aesop's fables:]

When the satyr was accompanying the man to the satyr's home, the man's hands were so cold that he blew on his hands, and the satyr asked the man, "Why are you blowing on your hands?" The man said, "I am blowing on my hands to keep them warm."

After the satyr and the man got to the satyr's habitation, the satyr prepared an evening meal, which consisted in the main of hot porridge. The porridge was particularly hot, and the man blew his breath on his porridge.

The satyr asked, "Why are you blowing your breath on the porridge?"

The man replied, "I am blowing my breath on the porridge to make the porridge cold."

The satyr said, "Out with you. I will have nothing to do with a man who blows hot and cold with the same breath."

That is precisely what the Office of Federal Contract Compliance of the Department of Labor and the EEOC have been doing in their alleged efforts to enforce Executive Order 11246 and title VII of the Civil Rights Act of 1964, respectively, which prohibit discrimination in employment on account of race, religion, national origin, or sex. These authorities, in case after case, have entered orders requiring employers to practice discrimination in reverse by employing persons of a particular race or a particular religion or a particular national origin or a particular sex, either in fixed or variable numbers, proportions, percentages, quotas, goals, or ranges. I do not believe you can enforce laws against discrimination in employment by commanding and requiring discrimination in employment. The two concepts are irreconcilable and repugnant to each other.

So I appeal to every Member of the Senate who does not think that the Office of Federal Contract Compliance and the EEOC should be permitted to blow hot and cold with the same breath to support this particular amendment.

Mr. President, I reserve the remainder, if any, of the time in support of this amendment.

The PRESIDING OFFICER. Who yields time?

Mr. WILLIAMS. Mr. President, I suggest the absence of a quorum.

The PRESIDING OFFICER. On whose time?

Mr. WILLIAMS. It will be on my time.

The PRESIDING OFFICER. The clerk will call the roll.

The second assistant legislative clerk proceeded to call the roll.

Mr. ERVIN. Mr. President, will the Senator consent to the withdrawing of his order for a moment? I just want to ask that the section of the Civil Rights Act of 1964 that I referred to be printed in the RECORD.

Mr. WILLIAMS. Mr. President, I ask unanimous consent that the order for the quorum call be rescinded.

The PRESIDING OFFICER. Without objection, it is so ordered.

Mr. ERVIN. I yield myself such time as I may use at this moment.

Mr. President, I ask unanimous consent that subsection (j) of section 703 of title VII of the Civil Rights Act of 1964 be printed in the RECORD at this point.

There being no objection, the statute was ordered to be printed in the RECORD, as follows:

(j) Nothing contained in this title shall be interpreted to require any employer, employment agency, labor organization, or joint labor-management committee subject to this title to grant preferential treatment to any individual or to any group because of the race, color, religion, sex, or national origin of such individual or group on account of an imbalance which may exist with respect to the total number or percentage of persons of any race, color, religion, sex, or national origin employed by any employer, referred or classified for employment by any employment agency or labor organization, admitted to membership or classified by any labor organization, or admitted to, or employed in, any apprenticeship or other training program, in comparison with the total number or percentage of persons of such race, color, religion, sex, or national origin in any community, State, section, or other area, or in the available work force in any community, State, section, or other area.

Mr. WILLIAMS. Mr. President, I suggest the absence of a quorum.

The PRESIDING OFFICER. The clerk will call the roll.

The second assistant legislative clerk proceeded to call the roll.

Mr. JAVITS. Mr. President, I ask unanimous consent that the order for the quorum call be rescinded.

The PRESIDING OFFICER (Mr. MONTOYA). Without objection, it is so ordered.

Mr. JAVITS. Mr. President, the amendment which is before us—

The PRESIDING OFFICER. How much time does the Senator yield himself?

Mr. JAVITS. Will the Senator from New Jersey yield me 10 minutes?

Mr. WILLIAMS. Such time as the Senator requires, yes.

Mr. JAVITS. Mr. President, the amendment which is before us affects both the problem of dealing with Government contractors in the Office of Contract Compliance, to which we have voted in the Department of Labor, and with remedies available under title 7. This amendment seeks to set a standard by which remedies shall be determined on the part of the United States.

Now, all we see in the wording of the amendment which is largely contained in its first sentence, is the tip of the iceberg because what this first sentence purports to restrain is a department, agency, or officer of the United States. But a department, agency, or officer of the United States may move respecting a given situation for or upon the order of the court. We do not have to specify in this amendment that it applies to the seeking or enforcing orders of a court because a court usually does not itself require anything of an employer but acts on motion of an officer or employee of the United States. Therefore, the depth of this amendment is much greater than is

apparent on the surface because it would purport not only to inhibit in given respects the officers of the United States but also the courts of the United States through whom, once they make a finding or a judgment, the officers of the United States are moved.

I make that analysis because it is clear that what is sought to be reached is, first the Philadelphia plan and similar plans in other cities, and beyond that, the whole concept of "affirmative action" as it has been developed under Executive Order 11246 and as a remedial concept under Title VII.

Philadelphia-type plans are based on the Federal Government's power to require its own contractors or contractors on projects to which it contributes—for example, State projects with a Federal contribution—to take affirmative action to enlarge the labor pool to the maximum extent by promoting full utilization of minority-group employees, and by making certain requirements for those who hire as well as majority employees and also to correct discrimination on its face which has persisted over a long period of time. The courts have sustained such requirements. The Philadelphia plan itself was sustained by the Court of Appeals for the Third Circuit in the case of *Contractors Association of Eastern Pennsylvania* v. *the Secretary of Labor*, 442 F. 2d 159. Certiorari was recently denied by the Supreme Court. The basis of sustaining it was really upon two critical points: First, the Government, as part of its procurement function, has the right to encourage full utilization of all minority-group employees as a method of insuring the availability of a broad manpower pool to support procurement efforts, and second, the plan was upheld as a proper way to remedy past discrimination in the six building trades covered by the plan.

Thus, with respect to procurement, the court—I am reading from page 171 of 442 Fed. 2d, if anyone is following the actual decision—stated:

In direct procurement the federal government has a vital interest in assuring that the largest possible pool of qualified manpower be available for the accomplishment of its projects.

Therefore, it was held that the Philadelphia plan requirement that construction contractors agree to use good-faith efforts to meet goals pertaining to the employment of minority-group employees in certain trades was entirely appropriate in terms of authority by the Federal Government.

The court also held that there was nothing inconsistent between the Philadelphia plan and section 703(j) of title VII of the Civil Rights Act because the Philadelphia plan was issued under an Executive order, rather than title VII of the Civil Rights Act, and that section 703(j) was a limitation only on title VII. The decision also implied that the words of the Civil Rights Act themselves apply to the matter of setting quotas for correction of imbalance in the percentage of people in any race, in comparison to the percentage in the available work

January 28, 1972   CONGRESSIONAL RECORD — SENATE   **1665**

force in the area, whereas the Philadelphia plan was applicable to the available work force in certain specific trades.

Finally, the court also held that the Civil Rights Act of 1964 does not prohibit specific relief requiring an employer to be "color conscious" to remedy the effects of past discrimination.

The court, on page 173, held:

Clearly the Philadelphia Plan is color-conscious. Indeed the only meaning which can be attributed to the "affirmative action" language which since March of 1961 has been included in successive Executive Orders is that Government contractors must be color-conscious. Since 1941 the Executive Order program has recognized that discriminatory practices exclude available minority manpower from the labor pool. In other contexts color-consciousness has been deemed to be an appropriate remedial posture. Porcelli v. Titus, 302 F. Supp. 726 (D.N.J. 1969), aff'd, 431 F.2d 1254 (3d Cir. 1970); Norwalk CORE v. Norwalk Redevelopment Agency, 395 F.2d 980, 931 (2d Cir. 1968); Offermann v. Nitkowski, 378 F.2d 22, 24 (2d Cir. 1967). It has been said respecting Title VII that "Congress did not intend to freeze an entire generation of Negro employees into discriminatory patterns that existed before the Act." Quarles v. Philip Morris, Inc., *supra*, 279 F. Supp. at 514. The *Quarles* case rejected the contention that existing, nondiscriminatory seniority arrangements were so sanctified by Title VII that the effects of past discrimination in job assignments could not be overcome. We object the contention that Title VII prevents the President acting through the Executive Order program from attempting to remedy the absence from the Philadelphia construction labor of minority tradesmen in key trades.

Therefore, that the Government had a right, under the Philadelphia plan, to order affirmative action which would overcome that past discrimination without transgressing the Civil Rights Act of 1964.

The court sealed that in on page 177 of the opinion, which states:

The Philadelphia Plan is valid Executive action designed to remedy the perceived evil that minority tradesmen have not been included in the labor pool available for the performance of construction projects in which the federal government has a cost and performance interest. The Fifth Amendment does not prohibit such action.

So, Mr. President, the courts have rejected much of the argument that we should—what in effect this amendment does—preclude preferential treatment under any and all circumstances, because it runs afoul of section 703(j).

I would also like to cite in that regard the opinion in the *United States* v. *Ironworkers Local No. 86,* 443 F.2d 544, decided in the Ninth Circuit Court of Appeals as recently as May of 1971, in which the court held, in a title VII "pattern or practice" case, that there was an affirmative duty for minority recruitment where it was shown that there was past discrimination which now required correction, and that the court could order that correction affirmatively without violating section 703(j) relating to preferential treatment of individuals of any group, and so forth, where there had been illegality. The court would not allow a respondent to profit from his own illegality under cover of section 703(j).

Now, Mr. President, I am told, and I believe the information to be reliable, that under the decision made last week by Judge Bonsal in New York, in the Steamfitters case, an affirmative order was actually entered requiring a union local to take in a given number of minority-group apprentices.

What this amendment seeks to do is to undo the Philadelphia plan and those court decisions. Incidentally, I take great pride in the fact that when the legality of the Philadelphia plan was argued here, and we had an opinion of the Attorney General which held it lawful pitted against an opinion of the Comptroller General's Office which held it unlawful, I think I was the principal Senator who sustained the doctrine of legality. And I am very grateful, naturally, that the courts took that view.

So, here I believe that the amendment does two things, both of which should be equally rejected.

First, it would undercut the whole concept of affirmative action as developed under Executive Order 11246 and thus preclude Philadelphia-type plans.

Second, the amendment, in addition to the dismantling the Executive order program, would deprive the courts of the opportunity to order affirmative action under title VII of the type which they have sustained in order to correct a history of unjust and illegal discrimination in employment and thereby further dismantle the effort to correct these injustices.

So, for both reasons, Mr. President, I believe that the amendment should be rejected, and I hope very much that the Senate will do that.

Mr. President, I ask unanimous consent that the two opinions which I have cited in this discussion be printed in the RECORD.

(material omitted)

c. Ervin Amendment is Rejected, 118 Cong. Rec. 1672 (Jan. 28, 1972)

1676   CONGRESSIONAL RECORD — SENATE   *January 28, 1972*

(material omitted)   *(material omitted)*   *(material omitted)*

The result was announced—yeas 22, nays 44, as follows:

[No. 19 Leg.]

YEAS—22

Allen	Ellender	Jordan, Idaho
Bible	Ervin	Long
Byrd, Va.	Fannin	Spong
Byrd, W. Va.	Fulbright	Talmadge
Cannon	Gurney	Tower
Chiles	Hollings	Young
Cotton	Hruska	
Curtis	Jordan, N.C.	

NAYS—44

Aiken	Griffin	Percy
Allott	Hart	Proxmire
Anderson	Hughes	Randolph
Bayh	Humphrey	Ribicoff
Beall	Inouye	Roth
Bennett	Javits	Saxbe
Brooke	Mansfield	Schweiker
Burdick	McGee	Scott
Case	McIntyre	Smith
Church	Mondale	Stafford
Cook	Montoya	Stevens
Cooper	Moss	Symington
Cranston	Nelson	Weicker
Dole	Pastore	Williams
Fong	Pell	

NOT VOTING—34

Baker	Hansen	Mundt
Bellmon	Harris	Muskie
Bentsen	Hartke	Packwood
Boggs	Hatfield	Pearson
Brock	Jackson	Sparkman
Buckley	Kennedy	Stennis
Dominick	Magnuson	Stevenson
Eagleton	Mathias	Taft
Eastland	McClellan	Thurmond
Gambrell	McGovern	Tunney
Goldwater	Metcalf	
Gravel	Miller	

So Mr. ERVIN's amendment was rejected.

(material omitted)

Mr. WILLIAMS. Mr. President, I do not believe that it is the intent of the Senator from North Carolina to deny to the judicial and executive branches of Government all power to remedy the evils of job discrimination; but I am afraid—I am desperately afraid—that this amendment would strip title VII of the Civil Rights Act of 1964 of all its basic fiber. It can be read to deprive even the courts of any power to remedy clearly proven cases of discrimination.

That statement follows right on examples of situations cited by the Senator from New York of the kind of situation that could be affected adversely.

I have listened intently to the debates on this bill. Not one Member of this body has spoken against providing some method for enforcing the law. This amendment raises the real threat of destroying any potential for effective law enforcement. If this amendment is accepted, I earnestly suggest that we will have a law, but there will be little chance for order under the law again if this amendment should prevail.

Mr. JAVITS. Mr. President, will the Senator yield?

Mr. WILLIAMS. I yield.

Mr. JAVITS. I am authorized to state that the Secretary of Labor is directly opposed to this amendment.

Mr. WILLIAMS. That is to say that the administration opposes this amendment?

Mr. JAVITS. That is correct.

Mr. WILLIAMS. I do not always speak for the administration. I am happy to.

Mr. ERVIN. It is not very surprising that a public official would object to anything which robs him of the power to be a tyrant. That is not surprising at all.

Mr. WILLIAMS. Moderately, may I say that I disagree with the tempestuous language of the Senator from North Carolina.

Mr. President, if any further time remains, I yield it back.

Mr. ERVIN. If any further time remains on our side, I should like to add to the Senator's statement—"tempestuous and truthful."

The PRESIDING OFFICER (Mr. MONTOYA). All time has now expired.

III. Conference Report on H.R. 1746, 118 Cong. Rec. 6643-6648 (March 2, 1972)

March 2, 1972

[page 6643:]

CONFERENCE REPORT ON H.R. 1746, EQUAL EMPLOYMENT OPPORTUNITY ACT OF 1972

Mr. PERKINS submitted the following conference report and statement on the bill (H.R. 1746) to further promote equal employment opportunities for American workers:

CONFERENCE REPORT (H. REPT. No. 92–899)

(material omitted)

[page 6646:]　　*March 2, 1972*

JOINT EXPLANATORY STATEMENT OF MANAGERS AT THE CONFERENCE ON H.R. 1746 TO FURTHER PROMOTE EQUAL EMPLOYMENT OPPORTUNITIES FOR AMERICAN WORKERS

The managers on the part of the House and Senate at the conference on the disagreeing votes of the two Houses on the amendment of the Senate to the bill (H.R. 1746) an Act to further promote equal employment opportunities for American workers, submit the following joint statement to the House and Senate in explanation of the effect of the action agreed upon by the managers and recommended in the accompanying conference report.

The points in disagreement and the conference resolution of them are as follows:

(material omitted)

* * * *

[Page 6648:]

The Senate amendment established an Equal Employment Opportunity Coordinating Council. The House bill had no such provision. The House receded.

The Committee of Conference believes that there are instances in which more than one agency may have legitimate interests in the employment standards applicable to a number of employees. So for example, the merit system standards of the Civil Service Commission should be considered by the Coordinating Council in relation to their effect on the conciliation and enforcement efforts of the Equal Employment Opportunity Commission and the Attorney General with respect to employees of governments, governmental agencies or political subdivisions.

The Senate amendment provided that all personnel actions involving Federal employees be free from discrimination. This policy was to be enforced by the United States Civil Service Commission. Each agency of the Federal Government would be responsible for establishing an internal grievance procedure and programs to train personnel so as to enable them to advance under the supervision of the Civil Service Commission. If final action had been taken by an agency or the Civil Service Commission, an aggrieved party could bring a civil action under the provisions of section 706. The House bill did not cover Federal employees. The House receded. In providing the statutory basis for such appeal or court access, it is not the intent of the Committee to subordinate any discretionary authority or final judgment now reposed in agency heads by, or under, statute for national security reasons in the interests of the United States.

The Senate amendment required consultation among the Executive branch agencies on Equal Employment matters. The House bill had no similar provision. The Senate receded in light of the action of the Conferees in establishing the Equal Employment Opportunity Coordinating Council.

The Senate amendment provided the Commission with authorization for an additional 10 positions at GS–16, GS–17, and GS–18 level. The House bill had no such provision. The House receded.

The Senate amendment provided that the new enforcement provisions of section 706 apply to charges pending before the Commission on enactment. The House bill was silent. The House receded.

The Senate amendment provided that no Government contract, whether subject to Executive Order 11246 or any other equal employment opportunity law such as section 3 of the Housing and Urban Development Act of 1968, as amended, could be terminated, denied, or withheld without a full hearing, where the employer had an affirmative action plan previously accepted within the past twelve months. The House bill had no such provision. The House receded.

CARL D. PERKINS,
JOHN H. DENT,
AUGUSTUS F. HAWKINS,
PATSY T. MINK,
PHILLIP BURTON,
WM. L. (BILL) CLAY,
JOSEPH M. GAYDOS,
WILLIAM D. FORD,
MARIO BIAGGI,
ROMANO L. MAZZOLI,
ROMAN C. PUCINSKI,
JOHN BRADEMAS,
ALBERT H. QUIE,
JOHN N. ERLENBORN,
ALPHONZO BELL,
MARVIN L. ESCH,
EARL F. LANDGREBE,
ORVAL HANSEN,
WILLIAM A. STEIGER,
JACK KEMP,
Managers on the Part of the House.

HARRISON A. WILLIAMS,
JENNINGS RANDOLPH,
CLAIBORNE PELL,
GAYLORD NELSON,
THOMAS F. EAGLETON,
ADLAI E. STEVENSON,
HAROLD E. HUGHES,
JACOB K. JAVITS,
RICHARD S. SCHWEIKER,
BOB PACKWOOD,
ROBERT TAFT, Jr.,
ROBERT T. STAFFORD,
Managers on the Part of the Senate.

* * *

AFFIRMATIVE ACTION, 1972-1979

I. Overview

The 1970s was the heyday of affirmative action in the workplace, with state and local governments joining the federal government in promoting "remedial" race-based hiring to create better racial balance in the workplace. The EEOC and OFCC consciously pressed employers to create more balanced workforces; national agreements involving the telephone, steel, and aluminum industries created quota programs to achieve such balance. The 1972 Amendments contributed to this process in a tangible manner, creating the Equal Employment Opportunity Coordinating Council to work with the EEOC, the Labor Department (where OFCC was located), the Justice Department, and other agencies to create a coherent federal affirmative action policy. In a 1976 policy directive, **excerpted below**, the Council provided guidance for "Affirmative Action Programs for State and Local Government Agencies" as well.

The issue of race-based affirmative action was one that was sure to reach the Supreme Court, because the issue posed—what is "discrimination"?—is one that was at once deeply political, increasingly emotional, and classically legal. In the early 1970s, the Supreme Court was able to duck the constitutional issue. Thus, in *Morton v. Mancari*, (1972), **excerpted in Chapter 8 of the Casebook**, the Court allowed hiring preferences for Native Americans in the agency administering Indian lands, but the opinion rested on bland statutory analysis and did not address constitutional concerns. In *DeFunis v. Odegaard*, (1973), the Court ruled that an equal protection challenge to a law school quota-admissions program was mooted by the graduation of the student challenging the program.

The Court's first big constitutional affirmative action decision came in *Regents of the University of California v. Bakke*, 438 U.S. 265 (1978). Alan Bakke had challenged an affirmative action quota program for admission to a state medical school. Although this was a challenge to a state program, Wade McCree, the Solicitor General of the United States, realized that Executive Order 11246 and some federal laws would be imperiled if the Court subjected race-based remedial quota programs to strictest scrutiny. The *amicus* brief for the United States started: "Congress and the Executive Branch have concluded that race must sometimes be taken into account in order to achieve the goal of equal opportunity." Although the Supreme Court did not accept McCree's arguments that remedial race-based quotas should not be subjected to strict scrutiny and that the medical school plan in *Bakke* was permissible, his impressive amicus brief probably affected the Court's disposition of the case.

Five Justices (William Brennan, Byron White, Thurgood Marshall, Harry Blackmun, and Lewis Powell) agreed that Title VI of the Civil Rights Act of 1964, barring the use of federal funds in governmental programs discriminating because of race, should be interpreted the same as the Equal Protection Clause. Id. at 284-87 (Powell, J., delivering the judgment of the Court); id. at 328-50 (Brennan, J., joined by White, Marshall & Blackmun, J.J., concurring in part). Among the five in that majority, Justice Powell found the quota program for admission to state schools to be a violation of the Fifth Amendment, and therefore also of Title VI. But Justice Powell opined that the Equal Protection Clause permitted race-based affirmative action if it was narrowly tailored to serve educational diversity. Id. at 311-15 (Powell, J.). Because four other Justices (Warren Burger [the Chief Justice], Potter Stewart, William Rehnquist, and John Paul Stevens) believed that the legislative history of Title VI evidenced a congressional judgment that even voluntary affirmative action or quota programs could not be supported by federal monies, the Court majority overturned the quota program followed by the public medical school. Id. 295-321 (Powell, J.); id. at 408-21 (Stevens, J., concurring in the judgment in part and dissenting in part).

Because of the severely fractured Court, *Bakke* settled nothing—and the next Term the same issue returned to the Court in the context of remedial quota programs assertedly in violation of Title VII. Taking the same approach it had adopted in *Bakke*, the Solicitor General again filed an *amicus* brief, urging the Supreme Court to allow remedial quotas under Title VII and to uphold the OFCC's program of pressuring federal contractors and subcontractors to achieve racially balanced workforces under Executive Order 11246. Unlike *Bakke*, the Court in *United Steelwork-*

ers of America v. Weber, 443 U.S. 183 (1979), **excerpted in Chapter 1 of the Casebook**, agreed with the bottom line posed by the Solicitor General (the Kaiser-Steelworkers quota program was legal) but declined to adopt the government's theory that if an employer or union were "arguably" in violation of *Griggs* it had leeway to adopt a quota program that would rectify the "arguable" violation.

The key brief in *Weber* was that written by Michael Gottesman, representing the Steelworkers. Based upon an exhaustive legislative history of the 1964 Act, Gottesman argued that Congress intended to give employers and unions a wide berth to remedy segregated workplaces on a voluntary basis, and that the bar to race-based preferences in § 703(j) was limited to programs *compelled* by the federal government and by implication allowed employers and unions to adopt *voluntary* programs. Like the majority, the dissenting opinion took all of its legislative history references from Gottesman's brief, but spun the arguments to focus on Congress's reluctance to sanction race-based job quotas. The dissent also complained that OFCC pressure on Kaiser to remedy its imbalanced craft forces made *Weber* more like a government-compulsion case than a pure voluntary affirmative action case.

II. Equal Employment Opportunity Coordinating Council: Affirmative Action Programs for State and Local Government Agencies (Sept. 13, 1976)

(material omitted)

EQUAL EMPLOYMENT OPPORTUNITY COORDINATING COUNCIL

AFFIRMATIVE ACTION PROGRAMS FOR STATE AND LOCAL GOVERNMENT AGENCIES

Policy Statement

The Equal Employment Opportunity Coordinating Council was established by Act of Congress in 1972, and charged with responsibility for developing and implementing agreements and policies designed, among other things, to eliminate conflict and inconsistency among the agencies of the Federal government responsible for administering Federal law prohibiting discrimination on grounds of race, color, sex, religion, and national origin. This statement is issued as an initial response to the requests of a number of State and local officials for clarification of the Government's policies concerning the role of affirmative action in the overall equal employment opportunity program. While the Coordinating Council's adoption of this statement expresses only the views of the signatory agencies concerning this important subject, the principles set forth below should serve as policy guidance for other Federal agencies as well.

1. Equal employment opportunity is the law of the land. In the public sector of our society, this means that all persons, regardless of race, color, religion, sex, or national origin shall have equal access to positions in the public service limited only by their ability to do the job. There is ample evidence in all sectors of our society that such equal access frequently has been denied to members of certain groups because of their sex, racial, or ethnic characteristics. The remedy for such past and present discrimination is twofold.

On the one hand, vigorous enforcement of the laws against discrimination is essential. But equally, and perhaps even more important, are affirmative, voluntary efforts on the part of public employers to assure that positions in the public service are genuinely and equally accessible to qualified persons, without regard to their sex, racial or ethnic characteristics. Without such efforts equal employment opportunity is no more than a wish. The importance of voluntary affirmative action on the part of employers is underscored by Title VII of the Civil Rights Act of 1964, Executive Order 11246, and related laws and regulations—all of which emphasize voluntary action to achieve equal employment opportunity.

As with most management objectives, a systematic plan based on sound organizational analysis and problem identification is crucial to the accomplishment of affirmative action objectives. For this reason, the Council urges all State and local governments to develop and implement results oriented affirmative action plans which deal with the problems so identified.

The following paragraphs are intended to assist State and local governments by illustrating the kinds of analyses and activities which may be appropriate for a public employer's voluntary affirmative action plan. This statement does not address remedies imposed after a finding of unlawful discrimination.

2. Voluntary affirmative action to assure equal employment opportunity is appropriate at any stage of the employment process. The first step in the construction of any affirmative action plan should be an analysis of the employer's work force to determine whether percentages of sex, race or ethnic groups in individual job classifications are substantially similar to the percentages of those groups available in the work force in the relevant job market who possess the basic job related qualifications.

When substantial disparities are found through such analyses, each element of the overall selection process should be examined to determine which elements operate to exclude persons on the basis of sex, race, or ethnic group. Such elements include, but are not limited to, recruitment, testing, ranking, certifica-

tion, interview, recommendations for selection, hiring, promotion, etc. The examination of each element of the selection process should at a minimum include a determination of its validity in predicting job performance.

3. When an employer has reason to believe that its selection procedures have the exclusionary effect described in paragraph 2 above, it should initiate affirmative steps to remedy the situation. Such steps, which in design and execution may be race, color, sex or ethnic "conscious," include, but are not limited to, the following:

The establishment of a long term goal, and short range, interim goals and timetables for the specific job classifications, all of which should take into account the availability of basically qualified persons in the relevant job market;

A recruitment program designed to attract qualified members of the group in question;

A systematic effort to organize work and re-design jobs in ways that provide opportunities for persons lacking "journeyman" level knowledge or skills to enter and, with appropriate training, to progress in a career field;

Revamping selection instruments or procedures which have not yet been validated in order to reduce or eliminate exclusionary effects on particular groups in particular job classifications;

The initiation of measures designed to assure that members of the affected group who are qualified to perform the job are included within the pool of persons from which the selecting official makes the selection;

A systematic effort to provide career advancement training, both classroom and on-the-job, to employees locked into dead end jobs; and

The establishment of a system for regularly monitoring the effectiveness of the particular affirmative action program, and procedures for making timely adjustments in this program where effectiveness is not demonstrated.

4. The goal of any affirmative action plan should be achievement of genuine equal employment opportunity for all qualified persons. Selection under such plans should be based upon the ability of the applicant(s) to do the work. Such plans should not require the selection of the unqualified, or the unneeded, nor should they require the selection of persons on the basis of race, color, sex, religion or national origin. Moreover, while the Council believes that this statement should serve to assist State and local employers, as well as Federal agencies, it recognizes that affirmative action cannot be viewed as a standardized program which must be accomplished in the same way at all times in all places.

Accordingly, the Council has not attempted to set forth here either the minimum or maximum voluntary steps that employers may take to deal with their respective situations. Rather, the Council recognizes that under applicable authorities, State and local employers have flexibility to formulate affirmative action plans that are best suited to their particular situations. In this manner, the Council believes that affirmative action

programs will best serve the goal of equal employment opportunity.

Respectfully submitted,

HAROLD R. TYLER, JR.,
Deputy Attorney General and Chairman of the Equal Employment Coordinating Council.

MICHAEL H. MOSKOW,
Under Secretary of Labor.

ETHEL BENT WALSH,
Acting Chairman, Equal Employment Opportunity Commission.

ROBERT E. HAMPTON,
Chairman, Civil Service Commission.

ARTHUR S. FLEMMING,
Chairman, Commission on Civil Rights.

Because of its equal employment opportunity responsibilities under the State and Local Government Fiscal Assistance Act of 1972 (the revenue sharing act), the Department of Treasury was invited to participate in the formulation of this policy statement; and it concurs and joins in the adoption of this policy statement.

Done, this 26th day of August 1976.

RICHARD ALBRECHT,
General Counsel, Department of the Treasury.

[FR Doc.76-26675 Filed 9-10-76;8:45 am]

(material omitted)

REAGAN-BUSH ERA PUSHBACK AGAINST *WEBER* AND *GRIGGS*, 1981-91

In some circles, *Weber* was subject to savage critique. On remand, usually a routine matter, Judge Gee wrote an opinion complaining that the Supreme Court's disposition was lawless—albeit not so "evil" that he felt compelled to defy the mandate. *Weber v. Kaiser Alum. & Chem. Co.*, 611 F.2d 132, 133 (5th Cir. 1980). Many voters considered race-based affirmative action to be quite evil, and this was an important issue that former Governor Ronald Reagan deployed adroitly to defeat President Jimmy Carter in 1980. Conservative quota-hating Republicans controlled the Presidency for the next twelve years, the Senate for the next six years, and a majority of the Supreme Court by 1988. The 1980s was one where affirmative action, and ultimately the disparate impact cause of action, came under fire.

Shortly after Reagan's election, Senator Orrin Hatch (R-UT) held hearings to publicize his proposed constitutional amendment to override both *Weber* and *Bakke* in favor of a strict colorblind understanding of the anti-discrimination principle. Senator Hatch griped that President Reagan's Department of Justice did not show up to bury *Bakke* and *Weber*—and indeed the Reagan Administration itself moved very cautiously and below the radar whenever possible on these issues. Although President Reagan never revoked Executive Order 11246, he did manage to savage the OFCC's budget and phased out back-pay awards from the agency's enforcement arsenal. See Philip F. Rubio, *A History of Affirmative Action, 1619-2000*, at 164 (2001). The EEOC also lost much of its budget, and its enforcement of disparate impact claims fell off markedly in the 1980s.

Even more effectively, President Reagan's Department of Justice planted "landmines" throughout the federal judiciary, as the President appointed true believers in conservative values as Article III vacancies occurred. See Terry H. Eastland, *The Pursuit of Fairness: A History of Affirmative Action* 176-77 (2004). His first three Supreme Court appointments—Sandra Day O'Connor (1982), William Rehnquist (Chief, 1986), and Antonin Scalia (1986)—were skeptical of race-based affirmative action. But the Court remained fractured. E.g., *Wygant v. Jackson Board of Education*, 476 U.S. 267 (1986) (no majority opinion, but five Justices supported the reversal of a school's board's policy of laying off non-minority teachers first, regardless of seniority).

Statutory affirmative action returned to the Court in *Johnson v. Transportation Agency, Santa Clara County*, 480 U.S. 616 (1987), **excerpted in Chapter 1 of the Casebook.** At issue was a public employment policy allowing sex and racial diversity to be considered as a "plus." Notwithstanding the Reagan appointments, Justice Brennan held together a five-Justice majority, as he had in *Weber*. Indeed, the new majority not only reaffirmed but expanded *Weber* to include remedies for sex-segregated workplaces and to allow employer discretion to adopt preferential policies any time there was a "manifest imbalance" or underrepresentation of a protected class under Title VII, (such as racial minorities or women) in a particular work category. Id. at 631-33. The case fractured the Justices in odd ways. Justice Stevens joined the Brennan opinion for reasons of *stare decisis*, even though he confessed he would have dissented in *Weber*. Id. at 644. In contrast, Brennan lost Justice White, who urged that *Weber* be overruled, apparently because White felt the earlier case reflected a serious effort "to remedy the intentional and systematic exclusion of blacks by the employer and the unions from certain job categories," while subsequent cases simply reflected employer deployment of racial preferences for their own sake. Id. at 647. Justice O'Connor concurred in the judgment. Following the equal protection approach Justice Powell had suggested in an earlier case, Justice O'Connor indicated that sex- or race-based preferences were allowable under Title VII so long as they employer had a "firm basis" to believe that it might be liable for *Griggs* violations. Id. at 647-56.

Justice Scalia, joined by Chief Justice Rehnquist and to a great extent by Justice White, dissented in *Johnson*. Although indicating that Justice Rehnquist's *Weber* dissent had "convincingly demonstrated" that any kind of racial preferences were illegal under Title VII, Justice Scalia focused on the majority's refusal to follow the plain meaning of section 703(a) and, indeed, its "inversion" of the rule in section 703(j). Oddly, Justice Scalia made no effort to defend his view that "discriminate" had only the broad meaning that Brian Weber had advanced a decade earlier. Notwithstanding Justice Scalia's blistering attack on *Weber*, and its abandonment by Justice White, six Justices reaffirmed it as binding precedent in 1987.

Despite *Johnson*, however, the Court was still moving to the right on workplace diversity issues. When centrist Justice Powell retired, Brennan lost his fifth *Johnson* vote, and the ultimate replacement was Judge Anthony Kennedy, another Reaganite skeptical of race-based affirmative action. Bush 41 Solicitor General Charles Fried pressed the friendly Court to be more aggressive in the affirmative action cases and had immediate success. In *City of Richmond v. Croson*, 488 U.S. 469 (1988), Fried filed an *amicus* brief urging the Court to hold that "benign" race-based classifications are suspect and thus must be narrowly tailored to serve a compelling state interest. Writing for the four Reagan-appointed Justices and Justice White, Justice O'Connor wrote an opinion for the Court holding precisely that, and the Court struck down a municipal program that was remedial but race-based. Extending *Croson's* strict scrutiny to federal programs using race for benign or remedial purposes, Justice O'Connor wrote for the Court again in *Adarand* U.S. (1995).

At the same time he was taking aim at *Bakke* and *Weber*, Solicitor General Fried also took aim at *Griggs*. The same Term the Solicitor General's Office urged the Court to apply strict scrutiny in *Croson*, it urged the Court to cut back *Griggs*. In *Wards Cove Packing Co. v. Atonio*, 490 U.S. 642 (1989), Justice White wrote for himself and the four Reagan appointees to accept the Solicitor General's invitation to impose a higher burden of proof on disparate impact plaintiffs. In a remarkable opinion, Justice White evaluated a *Griggs* claim against a classic "plantation" set up, where less desirable sweat jobs were held mainly by nonwhite workers, while the better jobs almost always went to white workers recruited through an old-boys network. Overturning the lower court, Justice White ruled that the plaintiffs had not made out a prima facie case under *Griggs* because they had not shown that there were a comparable number of nonwhites available for the better jobs nor had they shown any formal barrier to applications from nonwhites. The Court remanded for more proceedings but imposed a further burden on the plaintiffs: even if they are able to make out a prima facie case, they *also* have the burden of persuasion that the defendant did *not* have a business justification for its challenged practices.

In dissent, Justice Blackmun was astonished that the majority not only massively revised *Griggs* and effectively overruled subsequent decisions laying out the proof burdens in disparate impact cases, but also seemed oblivious to the discriminatory features of the plantation-like hiring and promotion practices followed by the packing company. "One wonders whether the majority still believes that race discrimination—or, more accurately, race discrimination against nonwhites—is a problem in our society, or even remembers that it ever was." 490 U.S. at 662. Was this the end of *Griggs*? And could *Weber* survive the overruling of *Griggs*?

THE CIVIL RIGHTS ACT OF 1991

I. Overview

Raising the bar for disparate impact plaintiffs to high, litigation-discouraging levels, the Supreme Court's opinion in *Wards Cove* created a huge public controversy. As explained in some detail in the **Casebook** (pp.116-118), the Supreme Court handed down five other decisions during this same 1989 Term that gave a narrow construction to Title VII and related statutes. These six decisions, along with three earlier procedural and fee-shifting decisions in civil rights cases from 1986 and 1987, created a number of practical difficulties for litigants challenging discriminatory employment prac tices.

Congress responded to this barrage of Supreme Court decisions with the Civil Rights Act of 1990. Despite compromises negotiated by the bill's key supporters, President Bush vetoed the bill and the Senate override vote failed by one vote: 65-34 (Casebook, 118).

On January 3, 1991, the bill that had come so close in 1990 was reintroduced as the Civil Rights and Women's Equity in Employment Act of 1991, H.R. 1, 102d Cong., 1st Sess. (1991). Hearings were held before the Education & Labor and the Judiciary Committees in February and March 1991, the Committees turned back Republican amendments and reported a very liberal bill, and the House passed H.R. 1 on June 5, 1991. See 137 Cong. Rec. H3924–25 (daily ed. June 5, 1991). It was a bill certain to be vetoed.

As before, once the bill reached the Senate floor, ongoing negotiations among liberal Democrats, moderate Republicans, and the Bush Administration intensified. Negotiations yielded a new bipartisan compromise bill, the Danforth-Kennedy substitute, S. 1745, which significantly rewrote the House bill. On the *Wards Cove* issues, S. 1745 simplified the burdens of proof in disparate impact cases (by adding new § 703(k)(1)(A)), generally required that plaintiffs link specific employer practices to their claimed disparate impact (see new § 703(k)(1)(B)), and abandoned prior efforts to define "business necessity" and left the definition to pre-*Wards Cove* caselaw (see § 3(2) of the Act).

There was still substantial doubt whether there would be civil rights legislation in 1991, because the Administration remained publicly unpersuaded that it was not a "quota bill" and because it was not clear how many Republicans would support the bill (eleven GOP Senators voted to override the 1990 veto). Allegedly, the key event was a meeting between President Bush and several GOP Senators who had voted to sustain the 1990 veto (most notably, Senator John Warner of Virginia) but warned the President that their votes to sustain a veto could no longer be taken for granted. (These and other Republicans were also concerned with addressing workplace sexual harassment in the wake of the confirmation hearings of Justice Clarence Thomas earlier that year.) After the meeting, President Bush discovered that the slightly altered bill was no longer a "quotas bill" and announced he would sign the legislation. See Helen Dewar, "President Endorses Rights Compromise; Two Senate Leaders Predict Quick Passage," Wash. Post, Oct. 26, 1991, at A1.

After overwhelming bipartisan votes in both chambers, the President signed the Civil Rights Act on November 21, 1991, Pub.L.No.102–166, 105 Stat.1071.The Act not only overrode most of the Supreme Court decisions targeted in 1990, but two more handed down by divided Courts in 1991, see *EEOC v. Arabian Am.Oil Co.*, 499 U.S. 244 (1991) (refusing to apply Title VII to foreign offices of American companies); *West Virginia Univ. Hosps., Inc. v. Casey*, 499 U.S.83 (1991) (refusing to provide expert fees in civil rights fee-shifting statute).

II. The Civil Rights Act of 1990: At First, the Presidential Veto is Successful

a. The Conference Bill Reaches the Senate (Sen. Kennedy discussing *Griggs*)

(material omitted)

CIVIL RIGHTS ACT OF 1990—CONFERENCE REPORT

Mr. KENNEDY. Mr. President, I submit a report of the committee of conference on S. 2104 and ask for its immediate consideration.

The ACTING PRESIDENT pro tempore. The report will be stated.

The bill clerk read as follows:

The committee of conference on the disagreeing votes of the two Houses on the amendment of the House to the bill (S. 2104) to amend the Civil Rights Act of 1964 to restore and strengthen civil rights laws that ban discrimination in employment, and for other purposes, having met, after full and free conference, have agreed to recommend and do recommend to their respective Houses this report, signed by a majority of the conferences.

The ACTING PRESIDENT pro tempore. Without objection, the Senate will proceed to the consideration of the conference report.

(The conference report is printed in the House proceedings of the RECORD of October 12, 1990.)

Mr. KENNEDY. Mr. President, the Civil Rights Act of 1990 ranks with the most important measures this Congress has addressed. Many Senators on both sides of the aisle have worked closely together for many months to fashion legislation to respond to an unfortunate series of recent Supreme Court decisions which have significantly undermined the Nation's civil rights laws banning job discrimination.

I believe that this conference report, reconciling the measures passed by the Senate and House of Representatives, achieves that goal, while scrupulously responding to every legitimate concern raised by the administration and the business community.

It is not yet clear whether President Bush will sign this legislation—but he should, if he shares our commitment to civil rights and to equal opportunity in employment.

Contrary to the view of some of the President's advisers, this is not a quota bill. In the course of the Senate and House debates and in the conference committee, we have adopted numerous modifications and refinements to ensure that nothing—absolutely nothing—in this legislation puts pressure on any employer to resort to quotas in hiring or promoting employees. We have prepared an antidiscrimination bill, not a quota bill.

One of the principal purposes of this legislation is to overrule the Supreme Court's decision in the Wards Cove case, in which the Court rejected the unanimous ruling by Chief Justice Burger in 1971 in the landmark case of Griggs versus Duke Power. In hundreds of antidiscrimination cases in the past two decades, the Griggs rule had been used to strike down the subtle and not-so-subtle practices that kept minorities and women from participating fully and fairly in our economy.

The Supreme Court decision in Wards Cove effectively overruled the Griggs decision. The new standard established by the Court in Wards Cove makes it far more difficult and expensive for victims of discrimination to challenge the barriers they face. The Civil Rights Act of 1990 restores the standard in Griggs, which served the country well for nearly two decades, and deserves to be reinstated.

The President's advisers persist in spreading the false charge that our response to the Wards Cove decision will lead to quotas. The conference report restores the Griggs rule; and in all the 18 years it was in effect, the Griggs rule did not force employers to resort to quotas. Raising the false hue and cry of quotas, as the Attorney General continues to do, does not make this a quota bill.

In fact, the revisions made by the conference committee remove any reasonable doubt about quotas.

The standards set forth in the bill for determining whether an employment practice is required by business necessity are virtually identical to those the administration itself indicated a willingness to accept in July.

The conference committee makes six important modifications in the legislation.

First, the bill addresses concerns about the definition of "business necessity." Where an employer's practices do not involve job performance or selection or where they concern methadone, alcohol, or tobacco use, an employer can avoid charges of discrimination by proving that the practices have a "significant relationship to a manifest business objective."

Second, the bill specifies additional types of evidence that a court may consider on this issue, including "testimony of individuals with knowledge of the practice."

Third, the bill provides expressly that nothing in the measure should be interpreted even "to encourage" employers to adopt quotas, let alone require them to do so.

Fourth, the bill requires the plaintiff to prove which specific practices are responsible for a disparate impact in all cases, except where the employer does not have the relevant records or has concealed, destroyed or refused to make them available.

Fifth, the conference report includes the text of the amendment proposed on the Senate floor by Senator PRYOR, confirming that the mere existence of a statistical imbalance in an employer's work force on account of race, color, religion, sex, or national origins does not create a violation of title VII.

Sixth, the conference committee bill includes a proposal made by Senator BOREN to limit punitive damages against any employer under title VII to $150,000, or the amount of compensatory damages, and backpay, whichever is greater.

There is no valid objection based on quotas to this legislation. The Attorney General's charge is simply a pretext for those who reject the principle of equal job opportunity for all Americans.

Next, the bill responds to the decision in Martin versus Wilks, in which the Supreme Court held that consent decrees settling job discrimination cases may be reopened in future lawsuits, even by people who sat on their hands while the Court considered the decree. In the months since that decision, new suits challenging long-settled decrees have been filed in more than a dozen cities. These cases are having a devastating impact on employers and communities who thought they had long ago turned their backs on discrimination.

The Civil Rights Act of 1990 provides a mechanism that allows finality to be achieved in such cases. It sets up procedures to ensure that interested persons can challenge proposed decrees before they are adopted, while limiting endless litigation and ensuring that fairly settled cases stay settled. These procedures recognize the right of every individual to due process of law, and the need of businesses and communities to bring an end to litigation. At the same time, the conference committee bill will enable more people to challenge consent decrees in job discrimination cases in the future, and it strengthens the notice requirements for such decrees.

The bill also fills a serious gap in Federal law caused by the lack of effective remedies for women and religious minorities in job discrimination cases. Under title VII, there is no adequate remedy for victims of intentional sex discrimination. Employers who engage in such reprehensible discrimination can walk out of court scot-free—and even send a bill for court costs to their victims. The remedies available under current law are often completely inadequate to vindicate the right of working women to be free from sex harassment in the workplace or from discrimination in basic employment decisions such as hiring, firing, and promotion. Those who suffer from religious discrimination are under a similar disadvantage.

The Civil Rights Act of 1990 provides meaningful remedies, granting victims of intentional sex and religious discrimination the right to recover compensatory damages. In particularly flagrant cases, punitive damages of up to the greater of $150,000 or the amount of compensatory damages and backpay may be awarded.

In addition, the conference agreement includes a specific provision to make clear that the bill is not intended to overrule existing cases involving "comparable worth."

This change is intended to allay concerns that this bill will require courts to adopt the "comparable worth" theory in cases alleging pay discrimination.

Further, the bill revises the "mixed motive" provision by eliminating both compensatory and punitive damages where an employer proves that the same job action would have taken place, even in the absence of discrimination.

The bill also provides that when an unsuccessful challenge to a court order or consent decree is brought by a third party, the court will have discretion to determine how attorney's fees should be assessed.

The bill also overrules the Patterson decision, in which the Supreme Court nullified the only Federal antidiscrimination law applicable to the 11 million workers in the 3.7 million firms with fewer than 15 employees.

That decision, with its devastating impact on minority workers, must be overturned, and the Civil Rights Act of 1990 overturns it. It permits victims of race discrimination in the workplace to sue for on-the-job harassment as well as for discrimination in hiring, promotion, and firing.

In addition, the bill corrects other problems caused by the Supreme Court's recent interpretations of Federal civil rights statutes. These problems concern a variety of issues, including seniority systems, attorney fees, and statutes of limitation. These are serious concerns, affecting large numbers of minorities and women, and they need to be addressed.

We have repeatedly modified this legislation in an attempt to meet the concerns of the administration. So far, however, the Attorney General continues to recommend a veto. I hope that President Bush will take an independent look at this legislation and the many good faith efforts we have made to go the extra mile and meet every reasonable objection of the White House. If he does, I believe he will sign this legislation, because he will see that it is an antidiscrimination bill, not a quota bill.

I urge my colleagues to vote for the Civil Rights Act of 1990, and I urge President Bush to sign it.

(material omitted)

b. President Bush Vetoes The Civil Rights Act of 1990

Veto message on S. 2104 entitled "Civil Rights Act of 1990."

The veto message is as follows:

To the Senate of the United States:

I am today returning without my approval S. 2104, the "Civil Rights Act of 1990." I deeply regret having to take this action with respect to a bill bearing such a title, especially since it contains certain provisions that I strongly endorse.

Discrimination, whether on the basis of race, national origin, sex, religion, or disability, is worse than wrong. It is a fundamental evil that tears at the fabric of our society, and one that all Americans should and must oppose. That requires rigorous enforcement of existing antidiscrimination laws. It also requires vigorously promoting new measures such as this year's Americans with Disabilities Act, which for the first time adequately protects persons with disabilities against invidious discrimination.

One step that the Congress can take to fight discrimination right now is to act promptly on the civil rights bill that I transmitted on October 20, 1990. This accomplishes the stated purpose of S. 2104 in strengthening our Nation's laws against employment discrimination. Indeed, this bill contains several important provisions that are similar to provisions in S. 2104:

—Both shift the burden of proof to the employer on the issue of "business necessity" in disparate impact cases.

—Both create expanded protections against on-the-job racial discrimination by extending 42 U.S.C. 1981 to the performance as well as the making of contracts.

—Both expand the right to challenge discriminatory seniority systems by providing that suit may be brought when they cause harm to plaintiffs.

—Both have provisions creating new monetary remedies for the victims of practices such as sexual harassment. (The Administration bill allows equitable awards up to $150,000.00 under this new monetary provision, in addition to existing remedies under Title VII.)

Both have provisions ensuring that employers can be held liable if invidious discrimination was a motivating factor in an employment decision.

—Both provide for plaintiffs in civil rights cases to receive expert witness fees under the same standards that apply to attorneys fees.

—Both provide that the Federal Government, when it is a defendant under Title VII, will have the same obligation to pay interest to compensate for delay in payment as a nonpublic party. The filing period in such actions is also lengthened.

—Both contain a provision encouraging the use of alternative dispute resolution mechanisms.

The congressional majority and I are on common ground regarding these important provisions. Disputes about other, controversial provisions in S. 2104 should not be allowed to impede the enactment of these proposals.

Along with the significant similarities between my Administration's bill and S. 2104, however, there are crucial differences. Despite the use of the term "civil rights" in the title of S. 2104, the bill actually employs a maze of highly legalistic language to introduce the destructive force of quotas into our Nation's employment system. Primarily through provisions governing cases in which employment practices are alleged to have *unintentionally* caused the disproportionate exclusion of members of certain groups, S. 2104 creates powerful incentives for employers to adopt hiring and promotion quotas. These incentives are created by the bill's new and very technical rules of litigation, which will make it difficult for employers to defend legitimate employment practices. In many cases, a defense against unfounded allegations will be impossible. Among other problems, the plaintiff often need not even show that any of the employer's practices caused a significant statistical disparity. In other cases, the employer's defense is confined to an unduly narrow definition of "business necessity" that is significantly more restrictive than that established by the Supreme Court in *Griggs* and in two decades of subsequent decisions. Thus, unable to defend legitimate practices in court, employers will be driven to adopt quotas in order to avoid liability.

Proponents of S. 2104 assert that it is needed to overturn the Supreme Court's *Wards Cove* decision and restore the law that had existed since the *Griggs* case in 1971. S. 2104, however, does not in fact codify *Griggs* or the Court's subsequent decisions prior to *Wards Cove*. Instead, S. 2104 engages in a sweeping rewrite of two decades of Supreme Court jurisprudence, using language that appears in no decision of the Court and that is contrary to principles acknowledged even by Justice Steven's *dissent* in *Wards Cove:* "The opinion in *Griggs* made it clear that a neutral practice that operates to exclude minorities is nevertheless lawful if it serves a valid business purpose."

I am aware of the dispute among lawyers about the proper interpretation of certain critical language used in this portion of S. 2104. The very fact of this dispute suggests that the bill is not codifying the law developed by the Supreme Court in *Griggs* and subsequent cases. This debate, moreover, is a sure sign that S. 2104 will lead to years—perhaps decades—of uncertainty and expensive litigation. It is neither fair nor sensible to give the employers of our country a difficult choice between using quotas and seeking a clarification of the law through costly and very risky litigation.

S. 2104 contains several other unacceptable provisions as well. One section unfairly closes the courts, in many instances, to individuals victimized by agreements, to which they were not a party, involving the use of quotas. Another section radically alters the remedial provisions in Title VII of the Civil Rights Act of 1964, replacing measures designed to foster conciliation and settlement with a new scheme modeled on a tort system widely acknowledged to be in a state of crisis. The bill also contains a number of provisions that will create unnecessary and inappropriate incentives for litigation. These include unfair retroactivity rules; attorneys fee provisions that will discourage settlements; unreasonable new statutes of limitation; and a "rule of construction" that will make it extremely difficult to know how courts can be expected to apply the law. In order to assist the Congress regarding legislation in this area, I enclose herewith a memorandum from the Attorney General explaining in detail the defects that make S. 2104 unacceptable.

Our goal and our promise has been equal opportunity and equal protection under the law. That is a bedrock principle from which we cannot retreat. The temptation to support a bill—any bill—simply because its title includes the words "civil rights" is very strong. This impulse is not entirely bad. Presumptions have too often run the other way, and our Nation's history on racial questions cautions against complacency. But when our efforts, however well intentioned, result in quotas, equal opportunity is not advanced but thwarted. The very commitment to justice and equality that is offered as the reason why this bill should be signed requires me to veto it.

Again, I urge the Congress to act on my legislation before adjournment. In order truly to enhance equal opportunity, however, the Congress must also take action in several related areas. The elimination of employment discrimination is a vital element in achieving the American dream, but it is not enough. The absence of discrimination will have little concrete meaning unless jobs are available and the members of all groups have the skills and education needed to qualify for those jobs. Nor can we expect that our young people will work hard to prepare for the future if they grow up in a climate of violence, drugs, and hopelessness.

In order to address these problems, attention must be given to measures

c. The Override Fails

[Page 33379:]

October 24, 1990

that promote accountability and parental choice in the schools; that strengthen the fight against violent criminals and drug dealers in our inner cities; and that help to combat poverty and inadequate housing. We need initiatives that will empower individual Americans and enable them to reclaim control of their lives, thus helping to make our country's promise of opportunity a reality for all. Enactment of such initiatives, along with my Administration's civil rights bill, will achieve real advances for the cause of equal opportunity.

GEORGE BUSH.
THE WHITE HOUSE, *October 22, 1990.*

(material omitted)

[Page 33404:]

CONGRESSIONAL RECORD—SENATE   *October 24, 1990*

Mr. MITCHELL. Mr. President and Members of the Senate, race has been the most divisive issue in American history.

Race was at the heart of our Nation's most devastating war, the Civil War. Race discrimination distorted the development of democratic systems in many States for more than a century after that war. Race discrimination deformed the lives of millions of Americans, black and white, for many decades.

Today, overt racism is rare. The vast majority of Americans believe that each of us should be judged on the basis of our efforts and our abilities, not on the basis of our skin color or our ancestry.

But the legacy of our racial history remains a potent force for exploitation. It is a sad truth that in the past decade relations between the races in our country have deteriorated.

It is also a sad truth that there have been some, black and white, who have chosen to exacerbate those tensions for their own purposes.

A decade of accumulated race-baiting on both sides has injured our society. Americans have been encouraged to blame national problems on each other, rather than to join together to search for solutions.

The President's veto of the Civil Rights Act of 1990 is deeply regrettable. It rejects a modest legislative proposal that would reverse the tragic trend of recent years.

The President's veto is also a rejection of the aspirations of American women. In recent decades, women have entered the work force by the millions, for the most part because of economic need. For the most part, the workplace has welcomed them. Their skills have helped our economy grow. Their wages have helped lift their families' living standards.

But in some ways, the workplace has created barriers to the entry and promotion of women as it long did for black Americans. That is why the goal of civil rights enforcement today is a multiracial goal. The civil rights of white working women as well as black men and women and other minorities all depend on the protection of our laws.

But with his veto, the President has rejected that fact. He has turned his back on working men and women, white and black whose rights would be protected by this bill.

The Civil Rights Act of 1990 would restore to the law the interpretation of job-place discrimination which was the law of the land from 1971 to 1989. It would restore explicitly to the law the understanding that a contract cannot be honored in the making and broken in the performance. And it explicitly instructs the courts that it is not to be construed to require any form of quota.

Under the 1971 Griggs ruling by the Supreme Court, which was the effective law of this land for nearly 20 years, no quotas were imposed, no unseen quotas were covertly implemented, no major additional costs to the business community accrued.

Yet this measure, which restores the law to its prior condition, a condition where no quotas existed, has been vetoed on the pretext that it would require quotas.

That allegation is disheartening.

It is discouraging that almost 40 years after the Supreme Court ruling in Brown versus Board of Education, a full quarter-century after passage of the Voting Rights Act and the Civil Rights Act, a full quarter century since America's conscience was awakened by the use of attack dogs and firehoses against peacefully assembled American citizens—it is discouraging to learn that we have come so far in time but so short a distance in understanding.

The bill the President vetoed does not constitute a major shift in civil rights law. It does not grant discontented employees carte blanche to harass their employers. It requires the same stiff burdens of proof that were required before 1989. It grants no novel relief to those who are able to meet these substantial requirements.

Yet, despite months of protracted negotiations to meet the President's stated goal of wanting a bill that would reverse these Supreme Court rulings, we were still met with a veto.

The reasoning for a veto is faulty. The bill does not require quotas. Indeed, it explicitly rejects quotas.

The President says he supports the goal of the legislation—workplaces free of the practices that lead to race-based or gender-based discrimination. He claimed he wanted to sign such a bill.

But when Congress gave him the opportunity to sign such a bill he chose to veto it instead.

The vetoed bill explicitly instructed the courts that no quota-style employment action is required or condoned by this law.

It retained the defense of business necessity with which employers have successfully defended against these suits for almost 20 years. It created no novel causes of action against employers. It did not impose novel demands on corporate employment practices. It did not require quotas. It would not result in quotas. It did not deserve a veto.

It deserved support because it restored to this area of law the most fundamental American value: equality of opportunity.

The bill would not have mandated equal results. It simply required that everyone get a fair chance. That is the goal and the promise of our system: That every American is entitled to fair treatment, every single American.

It is one of our proudest boasts that in America, no matter who your parents, no matter if they were rich or poor, black or white, Asian or Hispanic, you have a fair chance, an equal opportunity to compete with the most well-born, the best-connected, the most fortunate people in our society.

That fair chance was given to so many of us in past decades. We are now trying to ensure it for others in the future, those who face barriers of a different kind, barriers of race or sex or ethnic origin.

It is the most basic American promise. It is a promise we cannot deny to some Americans unless we want to see it eroded for all Americans.

If today we suggest that a certain degree of unfairness in the workplace is acceptable, if we suggest that reflexive prejudices should not necessarily be penalized, then how long will it be before we accept the claim that segregated workplaces or segregated neighborhoods or segregated schools reflect free choices which we should not disrupt?

If we accept the idea that a little bit of discrimination does not matter much in the larger scheme of things, then when that discrimination is turned against us, what will be our protection?

It has been much too long since an American leader reminded us that we are one Nation; that the laws we depend upon must serve all of us, not just the favored few; that the fair chance we seek for ourselves must also be available to our neighbor; that our neighbor is an American deserving of the same freedoms and rights we take for granted.

Abraham Lincoln said that a nation cannot endure half-slave and half free. He was right, although it took a ruinous war to prove it.

It took the civil rights marches of the 1960's to remind us that the rule of law cannot endure when the protection it guarantees to all is systematically denied to some.

Today we face no immediate crisis, no civil war, no civil disobedience, but the challenge is no less critical.

It is the fundamental challenge of America: to assure every American a fair chance; the equal opportunity promised by our Constitution. The Civil Rights Act of 1990 is designed to meet that challenge. It seeks to assure all Americans, those who are black, Asian, Hispanic, and women that in the workplace, they will be judged on their skills and their work, not on their skin color or their gender.

Yet we have a veto by a President who says he wants a civil rights bill. We have a veto justified by vague speculative fears of a very specific and precise bill.

It is hard to avoid the conclusion that this veto has little to do with the content of this legislation and much to do with political perceptions. That is a shame.

It is a rejection of the harsh history through which all Americans, black and white together, have come in the last quarter century.

We fought segregation by law and action. We fought discrimination based on fears and silent hatreds. We sought to give all Americans, black and white, the economic and personal security that would allow them to see each other as fellow Americans, not as potential threats.

The racial tragedy of America has been that our history is bound together and we will succeed or fail together, but that is also our great hope.

Ours will never be, like South Africa, two nations inhabiting the same continent. We will always strive for the goal of a unified nation, with liberty, justice, opportunity and respect for all.

We have come a long way toward that goal. But now we see that the road still stretches far ahead of us.

The promise of our Constitution and our law is so great. It has been such an inspiration to other nations and other societies.

In the past year, there have been stirring events abroad, as the people of Eastern Europe come to grips with the distortions communism forced upon their societies for 40 years. The peoples of the Soviet Union now struggle with the deformations that communism brought to their societies for 70 years.

We know that none of these societies will be able to escape their history, however unsought, however unfair.

Unlike those societies, America does not have to overcome 40 or 70 years of repression. But, like them, we are not free of our own history. In that history, the relations of the races have been a central fact.

The legacy of our national history is something none of us can escape. That legacy has left Americans of all colors with responsibilities as well as rights.

One of those responsibilities is to create the conditions in our society and in the hearts and minds of our children which will prevent for all time a recurrence of the darkest days of racial conflict in the past. That is a responsibility for parents, teachers, and leaders of all races. Sadly, for the past decade, our leaders have not fulfilled this responsibility. In the black community, some voices that should have spoken of constructive action have turned instead to recrimination. In the white community, some leaders who should have reminded us of our moral responsibilities sought, instead, to remind us of our differences.

That is why the Civil Rights Act of 1990 is so important. It seeks to restore the common American understanding that ours is a nation based on equality, on fairness, and on justice for all. The President's veto of this bill does him and his office no honor.

The veto does not reflect a President of all the people, a President whose vision of a kinder and gentler nation restored American spirits and hopes. The veto does not reflect a President who sees our society brightened by a thousand points of light.

The bill deserved the strong support it received from the Congress last week. The President's veto of the bill deserves our equally strong rejection and override.

I urge every one of my colleagues to vote to override the President's unwise veto of this important civil rights bill.

Mr. President, I yield the remainder of my time.

The PRESIDING OFFICER. All time having been yielded back, under the previous order there will be about 1 minute until the vote would begin.

Several Senators addressed the Chair.

Mr. HATCH. Have the yeas and nays been ordered?

The PRESIDING OFFICER. The yeas and nays are automatically ordered on override.

The Chair recognizes the Senator from Illinois.

Mr. SIMON. I have 1 minute. I ask unanimous consent to address the Senate for 1 minute.

The PRESIDING OFFICER. Without objection, it is so ordered.

Mr. SIMON. Mr. President, let me point out one thing that happened in conference. Because we went out of our way to meet the objections of the President on this matter of quotas, this language that keeps coming up, and we bent over backward, two of the African-American members of that conference committee voted against it in conference. We had gone so far. A majority voted for it.

But I just mention this because we have an opportunity to see that opportunity is here for all Americans. I note the presence of some members of the Congressional Black Caucus. We ought to be listening to them as we listen to our conscience in voting on this veto override. I hope we do the right thing.

Mr. MITCHELL addressed the Chair.

The PRESIDING OFFICER. The majority leader.

Mr. MITCHELL. Under the previous order, Mr. President, a rollcall vote on final passage of the foreign operations appropriations bill was scheduled to occur immediately following this vote.

In an effort to accommodate the interests of the schedule of some Senators, I ask unanimous consent that that vote now occur following the first rollcall vote on the NEA amendments to the Interior appropriations bill, which will be the pending business following completion of this vote.

The PRESIDING OFFICER. Is there objection to the unanimous-consent request?

If not, without objection it is so ordered.

Mr. MITCHELL. Mr. President, I want to take a moment to extend my sincere gratitude to Senator LEAHY, the manager of the foreign operations bill, for the relentless and tireless effort he made to get that bill cleared of the many complications which it had as it now commences to proceed to a rollcall vote on it early this afternoon.

The PRESIDING OFFICER. The hour of 11:50 having arrived, the question is, Shall the bill pass, the objections of the President of the United States to the contrary notwithstanding? The yeas and nays are required.

The clerk will call the roll.

The assistant legislative clerk called the roll.

The PRESIDING OFFICER (Mr. GRAHAM). Are there any other Senators in the Chamber who desire the vote?

The result was announced—yeas 66, nays 34, as follows:

[Rollcall Vote No. 304 Leg.]

YEAS—66

Adams	Breaux	Danforth
Akaka	Bryan	Daschle
Baucus	Bumpers	DeConcini
Bentsen	Burdick	Dixon
Biden	Byrd	Dodd
Bingaman	Chafee	Domenici
Boren	Cohen	Durenberger
Boschwitz	Conrad	Exon
Bradley	Cranston	Ford
Fowler	Kerrey	Pell
Glenn	Kerry	Pryor
Gore	Kohl	Reid
Graham	Lautenberg	Riegle
Harkin	Leahy	Robb
Hatfield	Levin	Rockefeller
Heflin	Lieberman	Sanford
Heinz	Metzenbaum	Sarbanes
Hollings	Mikulski	Sasser
Inouye	Mitchell	Shelby
Jeffords	Moynihan	Simon
Johnston	Nunn	Specter
Kennedy	Packwood	Wirth

NAYS—34

Armstrong	Helms	Pressler
Bond	Humphrey	Roth
Burns	Kassebaum	Rudman
Coats	Kasten	Simpson
Cochran	Lott	Stevens
D'Amato	Lugar	Symms
Dole	Mack	Thurmond
Garn	McCain	Wallop
Gorton	McClure	Warner
Gramm	McConnell	Wilson
Grassley	Murkowski	
Hatch	Nickles	

The PRESIDING OFFICER. The Chair would remind the galleries that expressions of approval or disapproval are not permitted under the rules of the Senate.

On rollcall vote 304, the veto override of S. 2104, the yeas are 66, the nays are 34. Two-thirds of the Senators voting, a quorum being present, not having voted in the affirmative, the bill on reconsideration fails to pass over the President's veto.

(material omitted)

III. Civil Rights Act of 1991: Congress Succeeds at Amending Title VII

a. Debate in the Senate (Sen. Danforth discussing Justice Scalia's view of legislative history)

(material omitted and repaginated)

Mr. DANFORTH. Mr. President, I would like to say a word this morning on the difficult, contentious subject of legislative history, what its limitations are, and how the issue of legislative history is one that is now before the Senate.

Justice Scalia has taken the position that the Supreme Court should not get into the business of interpreting legislative history but that instead the

[page 28856]

Court should attempt to construe legislative language as it appears in statutes themselves.

I think that the odyssey of the present legislation is a strong argument for Justice Scalia's position. One of the interesting things about this particular bill is that where as with much controversial legislation when a compromise is reached, all kinds of people say we really do not like this bill but we are not going to be able to do any better, therefore, we will support it.

This bill is different in that a whole variety of people have come forward and have expressed support and even enthusiasm for the bill. People as diverse as the administration, on one hand, Senator DOLE, Senator HATCH and, on the other hand, for example, Senator KENNEDY, Senator MITCHELL— all have expressed support. They have all said there is a lot to be said for this legislation.

One of the reasons that this is possible is that there are slightly different interpretations among Members of the Senate and between the Senate and the administration on the precise meaning of some of the provisions in the law. That is not unusual. What courts are for are to interpret what is meant by the Congress in passing laws.

It is very common for Members of the Senate to try to affect the way in which a court will interpret a statute by putting things into the CONGRESSIONAL RECORD. Sometimes statements are made on the floor of the Senate. Sometimes the Senator will say, but for such and such a provision, which I interpret in such and such a way, I never would support this bill. That is one method of trying to doctor the legislative history and influence the future course of litigation.

Another way to do it is to put interpretive memoranda in the CONGRESSIONAL RECORD. These memoranda typically are not read on the floor of the Senate. They are just stuck into the RECORD.

Another way to do it is for agreed colloquies to be signed by various Senators and for those to be stuck into the RECORD. This is what is happening with respect to this bill.

Last Friday, Senator KENNEDY made a speech on the floor of the Senate. He stated his views of what the bill does. Senator HATCH has just made a very extensive speech on the floor. He stated his views of what the bill does.

My guess, Mr. President, is that if Senator KENNEDY would give us his analysis of Senator HATCHs' position, he would disagree with it. If Senator HATCH would give us his analysis of Senator KENNEDY's position, Senator HATCH would disagree with Senator KENNEDY. I might disagree with both of them. I anticipate that I am going to have an interpretive memorandum which will be put into the RECORD signed by the other original six Republican cosponsors for the legislation. That will be our interpretation of various provisions, but it may not be the interpretation of Senator HATCH or Senator KENNEDY or anybody else.

So what I am saying is that Justice Scalia, I think, had a good point in stating that it is risky business to try to piece together from floor statements or from agreed memoranda legislative history which is informative to the court in interpreting the meaning of a statute.

Mr. HATCH. Will the Senator yield for just 1 minute?

Mr. DANFORTH. Of course.

Mr. HATCH. What I have been talking about is not trying to talk about legislative history. I have been talking about the actual word changes and how important they are and basically why the President has come on this bill.

I agree with the distinguished Senator. The Court in this particular matter needs to look at the words that we have agreed to, and I think if they do, they will find that they are significantly different from the predecessor bills.

Mr. DANFORTH. Mr. President, I will simply continue. I see the Republican leader is on the floor and if he wishes to speak, fine, I am not going to take very long.

But I do want to say this: That whatever is said on the floor of the Senate about a bill is the view of a Senator who is saying it. And if it is not written into legislative language, it does not necessarily bind and probably does not bind anybody else, including the 30-some odd cosponsors of the legislation.

We put into the RECORD an interpretive memorandum last Friday afternoon and the interpretive memorandum is said to cover Wards Cove—business necessity, cumulation, alternative business practice. It is said to constitute exclusive legislative history. But yesterday it appeared that we had a difference of opinion among people who had agreed to this as to what the meaning of this is and that the word "cumulation" that was used in the heading of this interpretive memorandum is subject to at least two interpretations.

All agree that cumulation covers the so-called Dothard case relating to combined requirements, such as height and weight. The administration believes that this agreed-to interpretive memorandum precludes further discussion on the floor or further weight being given to people's expressed position on the so-called black box issue; that is, what do you do when you do not really know what is on an employer's mind, or the lost and destroyed records issue.

So the administration thinks that this interpretive memorandum covers those issues.

I do not happen to agree with that analysis of what it means. I think that it does not cover those issues. But what I am saying is that this legislation, the bill itself has a history that goes back over maybe a year and a half. It has been enormously complex putting together legislative language, much less trying to get agreement on the floor of the Senate about legislative history or about interpretive matters that are put into the RECORD.

I believe, Mr. President, we should go ahead and pass the bill. I believe that it will be passed. But I simply want to state that a court would be well advised to take with a large grain of salt floor debate and statements placed into the CONGRESSIONAL RECORD which purport to create an interpretation for the legislation that is before us.

b. President Bush Again Opposes the Bill (Statement by Press Secretary Fitzwater)
2 PUBLIC PAPERS OF THE PRESIDENTS OF THE UNITED STATES: GEORGE BUSH 1991, at 613

Administration of George Bush, 1991 / June 5

Statement by Press Secretary Fitzwater on Civil Rights Legislation
June 5, 1991

Although the President has indicated that the Democratic leadership's civil rights bill passed by the House of Representatives today is a quota bill that he intends to veto, we are gratified by the number of votes in opposition to the legislation. The 273–158 vote indicates strong support for sustaining a Presidential veto.

We are disappointed that the President's civil rights legislation was not approved Tuesday evening. It is a comprehensive bill that fights discrimination and offers the Nation the best chance to ensure equal opportunity in the workplace. The President remains hopeful that antidiscrimination legislation which does not produce quotas is enacted by Congress this year. We hope that the President's proposed legislation will receive more comprehensive consideration as this issue moves to the Senate.

(material omitted)

613

c. President Bush Signs The Civil Rights Act of 1991 (remarks and signing statement)
2 PUBLIC PAPERS OF THE PRESIDENTS OF THE UNITED STATES: GEORGE BUSH 1991, at 1502

Nov. 20 / Administration of George Bush, 1991

(material omitted)

Remarks on Signing the Civil Rights Act of 1991
November 21, 1991

Welcome to the White House. And may I salute the members of the Cabinet who are here today, Members of the Congress, many Members of Congress, distinguished guests.

Today we celebrate a law that will fight the evil of discrimination while also building bridges of harmony between Americans of all races, sexes, creeds, and backgrounds. For the past few years, the issue of civil rights legislation has divided Americans. No more. From day one, I told the American people that I wanted a civil rights bill that advances the cause of equal opportunity. And I wanted a bill that advances the cause of racial harmony. And I wanted a bill that encourages people to work together. And today I am signing that bill, the Civil Rights Act of 1991.

Discrimination, whether on the basis of race, national origin, sex, religion, or disability, is worse than wrong. It's an evil that strikes at the very heart of the American ideal. This bill, building on current law, will help ensure that no American will discriminate against another.

For these reasons, this is a very good bill. Let me repeat: This is a very good bill. Last year, back in May of 1990 in the Rose Garden, right here with some of you present, I appealed for a bill I could sign. And I said that day that I cannot and will not sign a quota bill. Instead, I said that the American people deserved a civil rights bill that, number one, insisted that employers focus on equal opportunity, not on developing strategies to avoid litigation. Number two, they deserved a bill that was based upon fundamental principles of fairness, that anyone who believes their rights have been violated is entitled to their day in court and that the accused are innocent until proved guilty. And number three, they deserved a bill that provided adequate deterrent against harassment based upon race, sex, religion, or disability.

I also said, that day back in 1990, that this administration is committed to action that is truly affirmative, positive action in every sense, to strike down all barriers to advancement of every kind for all people. And in that same spirit, I say again today: I support affirmative action. Nothing in this bill overturns the Government's affirmative action programs.

And unlike last year's bill, a bill I was forced to veto, this bill will not encourage quotas or racial preferences because this bill will not create lawsuits on the basis of numbers alone. I oppose quotas because they incite tensions between the races, between the sexes, between people who get trapped in a numbers game.

1502

This bill contains several important innovations. For example, it contains strong new remedies for the victims of discrimination and harassment, along with provisions capping damages that are an important model to be followed in tort reform. And it encourages mediation and arbitration between parties before the last resort of litigation. Our goal and our promise is harmony, a return to civility and brotherhood, as we build a better America for ourselves and our children.

We had to work hard for this agreement. This bill passed both Houses of Congress overwhelmingly with broad support on both sides of the aisle. A tip of the hat goes to Senator Kennedy and former Congressman Hawkins, who, way back in February of 1990, got the ball rolling. And I congratulate and thank particularly Senators Dole, Danforth, and Hatch, Congressmen Michel, Goodling, and Hyde for ensuring that today's legislation fulfills those principles that I outlined in the Rose Garden last year.

No one likes to oppose a bill containing the words "civil rights," especially me. And no one in Congress likes to vote against one, either. I owe a debt of gratitude to those who stood with us against counterproductive legislation last year and again earlier this year, as well as to those who led the way toward the important agreement we've reached today. I'm talking about Democrats, I'm talking about Republicans, and those outside the Congress who played a constructive role. And to all of you, I am very, very grateful because I believe this is in the best interest of the United States.

But to the Congress I also say this: The 1991 civil rights bill is only the first step. If we seek—and I believe that every one of us does—to build a new era of harmony and shared purpose, we must make it possible for all Americans to scale the ladder of opportunity. If we seek to ease racial tensions in America, civil rights legislation is, by itself, not enough. The elimination of discrimination in the workplace is a vital element of the American dream, but it is simply not enough.

I believe in an America free from racism, free from bigotry.

I believe in an America where anyone who wants to work has a job.

I believe in an America where every child receives a first-rate education, a place where our children have the same chance to achieve their goals as everyone else's kids do.

I believe in an America where all people enjoy equal protection under the law, where everyone can live and work in a climate free from fear and despair, where drugs and crime have been banished from our neighborhoods and from our schools.

And I believe in an America where everyone has a place to call his own, a stake in the community, the comfort of a home.

I believe in an America where we measure success not in dollars and lawsuits but in opportunity, prosperity, and harmony. I believe in the ideals we all share, ideals that made America great: Decency, fairness, faith, hard work, generosity, vigor, and vision.

The American dream rests on the vision of life, liberty, and the pursuit of happiness. In our workplaces, in our schools, or on our streets, this dream begins with equality and opportunity. Our agenda for the next American century, whether it be guaranteeing equal protection under the law, promoting excellence in education, or creating jobs, will ensure for generations to come that America remains the beacon of opportunity in the world.

Now with great pride, and thanks to so many people here in the Rose Garden today, especially the Members of Congress with us, with great pride I will sign this good, sound legislation into law. Thank you very much.

Note: The President spoke at 1:18 p.m. in the Rose Garden at the White House. S. 1745, approved November 21, was assigned Public Law No. 102–166.

1503

Statement on Signing the Civil Rights Act of 1991
November 21, 1991

Today I am pleased to sign into law S. 1745, the "Civil Rights Act of 1991." This historic legislation strengthens the barriers and sanctions against employment discrimination.

Employment discrimination law should seek to prevent improper conduct and foster the speedy resolution of conflicts. This Act promotes the goals of ridding the workplace of discrimination on the basis of race, color, sex, religion, national origin, and disability; ensuring that employers can hire on the basis of merit and ability without the fear of unwarranted litigation; and ensuring that aggrieved parties have effective remedies. This law will not lead to quotas, which are inconsistent with equal opportunity and merit-based hiring; nor does it create incentives for needless litigation.

Most of this Act's major provisions have been the subject of a bipartisan consensus. Along with most Members of the Congress, for example, I have favored expanding the right to challenge discriminatory seniority systems; expansion of the statutory prohibition against racial discrimination in connection with employment contracts; and the creation of meaningful monetary remedies for all forms of workplace harassment outlawed under Title VII of the Civil Rights Act of 1964. Similarly, my Administration has concurred in proposed changes to authorize expert witness fees in Title VII cases; to extend the statute of limitations and authorize the award of interest against the U.S. Government; and to cure technical defects with respect to providing notice of the statute of limitations under the Age Discrimination in Employment Act of 1967. I am happy to note that every one of these issues is addressed in the Act that becomes law today.

It is regrettable that enactment of these worthwhile measures has been substantially delayed by controversies over other proposals. S. 1745 resolves the most significant of these controversies, involving the law of "disparate impact," with provisions designed to avoid creating incentives for employers to adopt quotas or unfair preferences. It is extremely important that the statute be properly interpreted—by executive branch officials, by the courts, and by America's employers—so that no incentives to engage in such illegal conduct are created.

Until now, the law of disparate impact has been developed by the Supreme Court in a series of cases stretching from the *Griggs* decision in 1971 to the *Watson* and *Wards Cove* decisions in 1988 and 1989. Opinions by Justices Sandra Day O'Connor and Byron White have explained the safeguards against quotas and preferential treatment that have been included in the jurisprudence of disparate impact. S. 1745 codifies this theory of discrimination, while including a compromise provision that overturns *Wards Cove* by shifting to the employer the burden of persuasion on the "business necessity" defense. This change in the burden of proof means it is especially important to ensure that all the legislation's other safeguards against unfair application of disparate impact law are carefully observed. These highly technical matters are addressed in detail in the analyses of S. 1745 introduced by Senator Dole on behalf of himself and several other Senators and of the Administration (137 Cong. Rec. S15472–S15478 (daily ed. Oct. 30, 1991); 137 Cong. Rec. S15953 (daily ed. Nov. 5, 1991)). These documents will be treated as authoritative interpretive guidance by all officials in the executive branch with respect to the law of disparate impact as well as the other matters covered in the documents.

Another important source of the controversy that delayed enactment of this legislation was a proposal to authorize jury trials and punitive damages in cases arising under Title VII. S. 1745 adopts a compromise under which "caps" have been placed on the amount that juries may award in such cases. The adoption of these limits on jury awards sets an important precedent, and I hope to see this model followed as part of an initiative to reform the Nation's tort

1504

system.

In addition to the protections provided by the "caps," section 118 of the Act encourages voluntary agreements between employers and employees to rely on alternative mechanisms such as mediation and arbitration. This provision is among the most valuable in the Act because of the important contribution that voluntary private arrangements can make in the effort to conserve the scarce resources of the Federal judiciary for those matters as to which no alternative forum would be possible or appropriate.

Finally, I note that certain provisions in Title III, involving particularly requirements that courts defer to the findings of fact of a congressional body, as well as some of the measures affecting individuals in the executive branch, raise serious constitutional questions.

Since the Civil Rights Act was enacted in 1964, our Nation has made great progress toward the elimination of employment discrimination. I hope and expect that this legislation will carry that progress further. Even if such discrimination were totally eliminated, however, we would not have done enough to advance the American dream of equal opportunity for all. Achieving that dream will require bold action to reform our educational system, reclaim our inner cities from violence and drugs, stimulate job creation and economic growth, and nurture the American genius for voluntary community service. My Administration is strongly committed to action in all these areas, and 1 look forward to continuing the effort we celebrate here today.

GEORGE BUSH

The White House,
November 21, 1991.

Note: S. 1745, approved November 21, was assigned Public Law No. 102–166.

(material omitted)

1505

THE CURT FLOOD ACT OF 1998 AND *FLOOD V. KUHN*

I. Overview and Questions

As the Casebook indicates (p. 642), Congress enacted the Curt Flood Act 26 years after the Court's decision in *Flood v. Kuhn* and one year after Flood died of cancer at the age of 59. We reproduce below the brief floor debates from the Senate and House; the Senate passed the bill by unanimous consent and the House followed pursuant to a suspension of its rules.

Apart from noting Senator Leahy's unintentionally ironic celebration of the home run displays of Mark McGwire and Sammy Sosa, consider the following questions as you review the Senate and House floor debates.

1. What does the Curt Flood Act change about the application of the antitrust exemption to baseball? What does it leave unchanged?

2. Justice Blackmun in *Flood v. Kuhn* concluded that "professional baseball is a business and it is engaged in interstate commerce." After this Act becomes law, does the antitrust exemption extend to aspects of the business other than player-management labor relations? In formulating your response, consider the floor statements by Rep. Conyers (a Democrat and principal bill sponsor) and Rep. Bunning (a Republican and member of the baseball Hall of Fame)

3. What explains Senator Wellstone's effort to "clarify legislative intent" as part of a colloquy with Senators Hatch and Leahy? [This colloquy is reproduced by Rep. Luther toward the end of the House debate.] The cases Wellstone cites are a 1994 Florida Supreme Court decision (*Butterworth*) and a 1993 federal district court case (*Piazza*), each holding that baseball's antitrust exemption, as carried forward by the Supreme Court in *Flood*, extends only to the major league player reserve system and specifically does not cover decisions involving the sale or relocation of franchises.

4. The Act's text (section 3) declares that the Act "does not create, permit, or imply a cause of action by which to ... apply the antitrust laws to any conduct, acts, practices, or agreements" other than those that "directly relate to or affect employment of major league baseball players." Does this language unambiguously point toward a neutral scope regarding antitrust coverage for all other aspects of the business of baseball?

5. Should a court or agency take account of the Wellstone-Hatch-Leahy colloquy? Is an exchange like this entitled to more weight when floor managers from both parties embrace the Wellstone position? Would your response be different if the bill had passed the Senate by 52-48 rather than by unanimous consent?

II. *144 Cong. Rec. S9494 (July 30, 1998)*

(material omitted)

nothing in this subsection shall be construed as providing the basis for any negative inference regarding the caselaw concerning the applicability of the antitrust laws to minor league baseball.

"*(b) Nothing contained in subsection (a) of this section shall be deemed to change the application of the antitrust laws to the conduct, acts, practices, or agreements by, between, or among persons engaging in, conducting, or participating in the business of organized professional baseball, except the conduct, acts, practices, or agreements to which subsection (a) of this section shall apply. More specifically, but not by way of limitation, this section shall not be deemed to change the application of the antitrust laws to—*

"*(1) the organized professional baseball amateur draft, the reserve clause as applied to minor league players, the agreement between organized professional major league baseball teams and the teams of the National Association of Professional Baseball Leagues, commonly known as the 'Professional Baseball Agreement', the relationship between organized professional major league baseball and organized professional minor league baseball, or any other matter relating to professional organized baseball's minor leagues;*

"*(2) any conduct, acts, practices, or agreements of persons in the business of organized professional baseball relating to franchise expansion, location or relocation, franchise ownership issues, including ownership transfers, and the relationship between the Office of the Commissioner and franchise owners;*

"*(3) any conduct, acts, practices, or agreements protected by Public Law 87–331 (15 U.S.C. 1291 et seq.) (commonly known as the 'Sports Broadcasting Act of 1961'); or*

"*(4) the relationship between persons in the business of organized professional baseball and umpires or other individuals who are employed in the business of organized professional baseball by such persons.*

"*(c) As used in this section, 'persons' means any individual, partnership, corporation, or unincorporated association or any combination or association thereof.*".

CURT FLOOD ACT OF 1997

Mr. JEFFORDS. Mr. President, I ask unanimous consent that the Senate proceed to the immediate consideration of Calendar 231, S. 53.

The PRESIDING OFFICER. Without objection, it is so ordered. The clerk will report.

The legislative clerk read as follows:

A bill (S. 53) to require the general application of the antitrust laws to major league baseball, and for other purposes.

The Senate proceeded to consider the bill which has been reported from the Committee on the Judiciary, with an amendment to strike all after the enacting clause and inserting in lieu thereof the following:

SECTION 1. SHORT TITLE.

This Act may be cited as the "Curt Flood Act of 1997".

SEC. 2. PURPOSE.

It is the purpose of this legislation to clarify that major league baseball players are covered under the antitrust laws (i.e., that major league players will have the same rights under the antitrust laws as do other professional athletes, e.g., football and basketball players), along with a provision that makes it clear that the passage of this Act does not change the application of the antitrust laws in any other context or with respect to any other person or entity.

SEC. 3. APPLICATION OF THE ANTITRUST LAWS TO PROFESSIONAL MAJOR LEAGUE BASEBALL.

The Clayton Act (15 U.S.C. 12 et seq.) is amended by adding at the end the following new section:

"*SEC. 27. (a) The conduct, acts, practices, or agreements of persons in the business of organized professional major league baseball relating to or affecting employment to play baseball at the major league level are subject to the antitrust laws to the same extent such conduct, acts, practices, or agreements would be subject to the antitrust laws if engaged in by persons in any other professional sports business affecting interstate commerce: Provided, however, That*

AMENDMENT NO. 3479

Mr. JEFFORDS. Senator HATCH has a substitute amendment at the desk. I ask for its consideration.

The PRESIDING OFFICER. The clerk will report.

The assistant legislative clerk read as follows:

The Senator from Vermont [Mr. JEFFORDS], for Mr. HATCH, proposes an amendment numbered 3479.

The amendment is as follows:

Strike all after the enacting clause and insert in lieu thereof the following:

SECTION 1. SHORT TITLE.

This Act may be cited as the "Curt Flood Act of 1998".

SEC. 2. PURPOSE.

It is the purpose of this legislation to state that major league baseball players are covered under the antitrust laws (i.e., that major league baseball players will have the same rights under the antitrust laws as do other professional athletes, e.g., football and basketball players), along with a provision that makes it clear that the passage of this Act does not change the application of the antitrust laws in any other context or with respect to any other person or entity.

SEC. 3. APPLICATION OF THE ANTITRUST LAWS TO PROFESSIONAL MAJOR LEAGUE BASEBALL.

The Clayton Act (15 U.S.C. §12 et seq.) is amended by adding at the end the following new section:

"Sec. 27(a) Subject to subsections (b) through (d) below, the conduct, acts, practices or agreements of persons in the business of organized professional major league baseball directly relating to or affecting employment of major league baseball players to play baseball at the major league level are subject to the antitrust laws to the same extent such conduct, acts, practices or agreements would be subject to the antitrust laws if engaged in by persons in any other professional sports business affecting interstate commerce.

"(b) No court shall rely on the enactment of this section as a basis for changing the application of the antitrust laws to any conduct, acts, practices or agreements other than those set forth in subsection (a). This section does not create, permit or imply a cause of action by which to challenge under the antitrust laws, or otherwise apply the antitrust laws to, any conduct, acts, practices or agreements that do not directly relate to or affect employment of major league baseball players to play baseball at the major league level, including but not limited to:

"(1) any conduct acts, practices or agreements of persons engaging in, conducting or participating in the business of organized professional baseball relating to or affecting employment to play baseball at the minor league level, any organized professional baseball amateur or first-year player draft, or any reserve clause as applied to minor league players.

"(2) the agreement between organized professional major league baseball teams and the teams of the National Association of Professional Baseball Leagues, commonly known as the "Professional Baseball Agreement," the relationship between organized profession major league baseball and organized professional minor league baseball, and organized professional minor league baseball, or any other matter relating to organized professional baseball's minor leagues;

"(3) any conduct, acts, practices or agreements of persons engaging in, conducting or participating in the business of organized professional baseball relating to or affecting franchise expansion, location or relocation, franchise ownership issues, including ownership transfers, the relationship between the Office of the Commissioner and franchise owners, the marketing or sales of the entertainment product of organized professional baseball and the licensing of intellectual property rights owned or held by organized professional baseball teams individually or collectively;

"(4) any conduct, acts, practices or agreements protected by Public Law 87–331 (15 U.S.C. §1291 et seq.) (commonly known as "the Sports Broadcasting Act of 1961");

"(5) the relationship between persons in the business of organized professional baseball and umpires or other individuals who are employed in the business of organized professional baseball by such persons; or

"(6) any conduct, acts, practices or agreements of persons not in the business of organized professional major league baseball.

"(c) Only a major league baseball player has standing to sue under this section. For the purposes of this section, a major league baseball player is:

"(1) a person who is a party to a major league player's contract, or is playing baseball at the major league level; or

"(2) a person who is a party to a major league player's contract or playing baseball at the major league level at the time of the injury that is the subject of the complaint; or

"(3) a person who has been a party to a major league player's contract or who has played baseball at the major league level, and who claims he has been injured in his efforts to secure a subsequent major league player's contract by an alleged violation of the antitrust laws, provided however, that for the purposes of this paragraph, the alleged antitrust violation shall not include any conduct, acts, practices or agreements of persons in the business of organized professional baseball relating to or affecting employment to play baseball at the minor league level, including any organized professional baseball amateur or first-year player draft, or any reserve clause as applied to minor league players; or

"(4) a person who was a party to a major league player's contract or who was playing baseball at the major league level at the conclusion of the last full championship season immediately preceding the expiration of the last collective bargaining agreement between persons in the business of organized professional major league baseball and the exclusive collective bargaining representative of major league baseball players.

"(d)(1) As used in this section, "person" means any entity, including an individual, partnership, corporation, trust or unincorporated association or any combination or association thereof. As used in this section, the National Association of Professional Baseball Leagues, its member leagues and the clubs of those leagues, are not "in the business of organized professional major league baseball."

"(2) In cases involving conduct, acts, practices or agreements that directly relate or affect both employment of major league baseball players to play baseball at the major league level and also relate to or affect any other aspect of organized professional baseball, including but not limited to employment to play baseball at the minor league level and the other areas set forth in subsection (b) above, only those components, portions or aspects of such conduct, acts, practices or agreements that directly relate to or affect employment of major league baseball players to play baseball at the major league level.

"(3) As used in subsection (a), interpretation of the term 'directly' shall not be governed by any interpretation of 29 U.S.C. §151 et seq. (as amended).

"(4) Nothing in this section shall be construed to affect the application to organized professional baseball of the nonstatutory labor exemption from the antitrust laws.

"(5) The scope of the conduct, acts, practices or agreements covered by subsection (b) shall not be strictly or narrowly construed.

Mr. HATCH. Mr. President, today I offer on behalf of myself and Senator LEAHY, the Ranking Member of the Judiciary Committee, an amendment in the nature of a substitute to S. 53, the Curt Flood Act of 1997. This bill, which was reported out of the Judiciary Committee on July 31, 1998, by a vote of 12–6, clarifies that the antitrust laws apply to labor relations at the major league level, but does not have any affect on any other persons or circumstances. Given our limited time, I will only make a few brief comments, and would ask unanimous consent that my full statement be entered into the RECORD.

In a baseball season that is likely to set records in a number of different categories, I am extremely pleased to be able to report that a truly historic milestone in the history of professional baseball has been reached. People said it would never happen, but today I can tell you that major league baseball players, along with both major and minor league club owners, have reached an agreement on a bill clarifying that the antitrust laws apply to major league professional baseball labor relations. This agreed upon language is reflected in the substitute we are offering today.

With this historic agreement, I am confident that Congress will, once and for all, make clear that professional baseball players have the same rights as other professional athletes, and will help assure baseball fans across the United States that our national pastime will not again be interrupted by strikes. With the home run battles and exciting pennant races, baseball is enjoying a resurgence. And, as fans are returning to the ballparks, they deserve to know that players will be on the field, not mired in labor disputes. I am pleased that Congress will, it now appears, be able to help guarantee that this is the case.

Due to an aberrant Supreme Court decision in 1922, labor relations in major league baseball have not been subject to antitrust laws, unlike any other industry in America. In every other professional sport, antitrust laws serve to stabilize relations between the team owners and players unions. That is one of the principal reasons why, in recent years, baseball has experienced more work stoppages, including the disastrous strike of 1994–95, than professional basketball, hockey and football combined.

In the 103d Congress, the House Judiciary Committee took the first important step by approving legislation which would have ensured that the antitrust laws apply to major league baseball labor relations, without impacting the minor leagues or team relocation issues. During the 104th Congress, the Senate Judiciary Committee approved and reported S. 627, The Major League Baseball Antitrust Reform Act, to apply federal antitrust laws to major league baseball labor relations. None of these bills were passed, however, as many Members of Congress were reluctant to take final action while there was an ongoing labor dispute.

With the settling of the labor dispute and with the signing of a long term agreement between the major league baseball team owners and the players union, the time was right this Congress finally to address this matter. In fact, in the new collective bargaining agreement, the owners pledged to work with the players to pass legislation that makes clear that major league baseball is subject to the federal antitrust laws with regard to owner-player relations.

At the beginning of this Congress, we introduced S. 53, a bill which was specifically supported by both the players and owners and which was reported out of the Judiciary Committee almost exactly one year ago. At the Committee markup, however, several Members indicated a concern that the bill might

S9496 CONGRESSIONAL RECORD — SENATE *July 30, 1998*

inadvertently have a negative impact on the Minor Leagues. Although both Senator LEAHY and myself were firmly of the view that the bill as reported adequately protected the minor leagues against such a consequence, we pledged to work with the minor leagues' representatives, in conjunction with the major league owners and players, to make certain that their concerns were fully addressed.

Although this process took much longer, and much more work, than I had anticipated, I am pleased to report that it has been completed. I have in my hand a letter from the minor leagues, and a letter co-signed by Don Fehr and Bud Selig, indicating that the major league players, and major and minor league owners, all support a new, slightly amended version of S. 53. I ask unanimous consent that these letters be printed in the RECORD.

There being no objection, the letters were ordered to be printed in the RECORD, as follows:

NATIONAL ASSOCIATION OF
PROFESSIONAL BASEBALL LEAGUES, INC.,
Washington, DC, July 27, 1998.
Re baseball legislation.

Hon. ORRIN HATCH,
Chairman, Senate Judiciary Committee, U.S. Senate, Senate Dirksen Office Building, Washington, DC.

DEAR MR. CHAIRMAN: As you know, the National Association of Professional Baseball Leagues, Inc. ("NAPBL") objected to S. 53 as it was reported out of the Judiciary Committee last year. Since that time, we have been consulted about proposals to amend the bill to assure the continued survival of minor league baseball. We understand that a draft of an amended bill has been put forth by the major leagues and the Players' Association (copy attached) that I believe addresses the concerns of the NAPBL which we support in its final form.

Respectfully yours,

Stanley M. Brand.

July 21, 1998.
Hon. ORRIN HATCH, *Chairman,*
Hon. PATRICK LEAHY,
Ranking Member, Senate Judiciary Committee, U.S. Senate, Washington, DC.

DEAR SENATOR HATCH AND SENATOR LEAHY: As requested by the Committee, the parties represented below have met and agreed to the attached substitute language for S. 53. In particular, we believe the substitute language adequately addresses the concerns expressed by some members of the Judiciary Committee that S. 53, as reported, did not sufficiently protect the interests of the minor leagues. We understand that the minor leagues will advise you that they agree with our assessment by a separate letter.

We thank you for your leadership and patience. Although, obviously, you are under no obligation to use this language in your legislative activities regarding S. 53, we hope that you will look favorably upon it in light of the agreement of the parties and our joint commitment to work together to ensure its passage.

If you have any questions or comments, please do not hesitate to contact us.

Sincerely,

DONALD M. FEHR,
Executive Director, Major League Baseball Players Association.

ALLAN H. "BUD" SELIG,
Commissioner, Major League Baseball.

OFFICE OF THE COMMISSIONER,
MAJOR LEAGUE BASEBALL,
July 21, 1998.

DONALD M. FEHR, ESQUIRE,
Executive Director and General Counsel, Major League Baseball Players Association, New York, NY.

DEAR DON: As you know, in our efforts to address the concerns of the minor leagues with S. 53, as reported by the Senate Judiciary Committee, several changes in the bill were agreed to by the parties, i.e., the Major League Clubs, the Major League Baseball Players Association and the National Association of Professional Baseball Leagues (minor leagues). Among those changes was the addition of the word "directly" immediately before "relating to" in new subsection (a) of the bill.

This letter is to confirm our mutual understanding that the addition of that word was something sought by the Minor leagues and is intended to indicate that this legislation is not meant to allow claims by non major league players. By using "directly" we are not limiting the application of new subsection (a) to matters which would be considered mandatory subjects of bargaining in the collective bargaining context. Indeed, that is the reason we agreed to add paragraph (d)(3). There is no question that, under this Act, major league baseball players may pursue such actions as could be brought by athletes in professional football and basketball with respect to their employment at the major league level.

I trust you concur with this intent and interpretation.

Very truly yours,

ALLAN H. SELIG,
Commissioner of Baseball.

Mr. HATCH. This new bill specifically precludes courts from relying on the bill to change the application of the antitrust laws in areas other than player-owner relations; clarifies who has standing under the new law; and adds several provisions which ensure that the bill will not harm the minor leagues.

Senator LEAHY and I have incorporate these changes into our substitute, which, given its support across the board, we hope and expect to be passed today without objection. I urge my colleagues to adopt this substitute.

This amendment, while providing major league players with the antitrust protections of their colleagues in the other professional sports, such as basketball and football, is absolutely neutral with respect to the state of the antitrust laws between all entities and in all circumstances other than in the area of employment as between major league owners and players. Whatever the law was the day before this bill passes in those other areas it will continue to be after the bill passes. Let me emphasize that the bill affects no pending or decided cases except to the extent a court would consider exempting major league clubs from the antitrust laws in their dealings with major league players.

But because of the complex relationship between the major leagues and their affiliated minor leagues, it was necessary to write the bill in a way to direct a court's attention to only those practices, or aspects of practices, that affect major league players. It is for that reason, that a bill that ought to be rather simple to write goes to such lengths to emphasize its neutrality. And, although much of the Report filed by the Committee with respect to S. 53 is still applicable to this substitute, there have been some changes.

Section 2 states the bill's purpose. As originally contained in S. 53, the purpose section used the word "clarify" instead of the word "state" as used in this substitute. That language had been taken verbatim from the collective bargaining agreement signed in 1997 between major league owners and major league players. When the minor leagues entered the discussions, they objected to the use of the word "clarify" on the grounds that using this term created an inference regarding the current applicability of the antitrust laws to professional baseball. The parties therefore agreed to insert in lieu thereof the word "state." Both the parties and the Committee agree that Congress is taking no position on the current state of the law one way or the other. It is also for that reason that subsection (b) was inserted, as will be discussed.

Section 3 amends the Clayton Act to add a new section 27. As was the case with S.53, as reported, new subsection 27(a) states that the antitrust laws apply to actions relating to professional baseball players' employment to play baseball at the major league level and as in S.53 is intended to incorporate the entire jurisprudence of the antitrust laws, as it now exists and as it may develop.

In order to accommodate the concerns of the minor leagues however, new subsection (a) has been changed by adding the word "directly" immediately before the phrase "relating to or affecting employment" and the phrase "major league players" has been added before the phrase "to play baseball." These two changes were also made at the behest of the minor leagues in order to ensure that minor league players, particularly those who had spent some time in the major leagues, did not use new subsection (a) as a bootstrap by which to attack conduct, acts, practices or agreements designed to apply to minor league employment. This is in keeping with the neutrality sought by the Committee with respect to parties and circumstances not between major league owners and major league players.

Additionally, the new draft adds a new paragraph (d)(3) that states that the term directly is not to be governed by interpretations of the labor laws. This paragraph was added to ensure that no court would use the word "directly" in too narrow a fashion and limit matters covered in subsection (a) to those that would otherwise be known as mandatory subjects of bargaining in the labor law context. The use of directly is related to the relationship between the major leagues and the minor leagues, not the relationship between major league owners and players. Mr. President, I have a letter from the Commissioner of Baseball, Mr. Allan H. "Bud" Selig, to the Executive Director of the Major League Baseball Players Association, confirming this interpretation of the use of the word "directly" and I ask unanimous consent that it be inserted in the RECORD at this time.

As in S. 53, as reported, new subsection (b) is the subsection which implements the portion of the purpose section stating that the "passage of the Act does not change the application of the antitrust laws in any other context or with respect to any other person or entity." In other words, with respect to areas set forth in subsection (b), whatever the law was before the enactment of this legislation, it is unchanged by the passage of the legislation. With the exception of the express statutory exemption in the area of television rights recognized in paragraph (d)(4), each of the areas set forth depend upon judicial interpretation of the law. But Congress at this time seeks only to address the specific question of the application of the antitrust laws in the context of the employment of major league players at the major league level.

Thus, as to any matter set forth in subsection (b), a plaintiff will not be able to allege an antitrust violation by virtue of the enactment of this Act. Nor can the courts use the enactment of this Act to glean congressional intent as to the validity or lack thereof of such actions.

New subsection "c" deals specifically with the issue of standing. Although normally standing under such an act would be governed by the standing provision of the antitrust laws, 15 U.S.C. Sec. 15, the minor leagues again expressed concern that without a more limited standing provision, minor league players or amateurs would be able to attack what are in reality minor league issues by bootstrapping under this Act through subsection (a). The subsection sets forth the zone of persons to be protected from alleged antitrust violations by major league owners under this Act.

New paragraph (d)(1) defines "person" for the purposes of the Act, but includes a provision expressly recognizing that minor league clubs and leagues are not in the business of major league baseball. This addition was requested by the minor leagues to ensure that they would not be named as party defendants in every action brought against the major leagues pursuant to subsection (a).

New paragraph (d)(2) was added to give the courts direction in cases involving matters that relate to both matters covered by subsection (a) and to those matters as to which the Act is neutral as set forth in subsection (b). In such a case, the acts, conducts or agreements may be challenged under this Act as they directly relates to the employment of major league players at the major league level, but to the extent the practice is challenged as to its effect on any issue set forth in subsection (b), it must be challenged under current law, which may or may not provide relief.

New paragraph (d)(5) merely reflects the Committee's intention that a court's determination of which fact situations fall within subsection (b) should follow ordinary rules of statutory construction, and should not be subject to any exceptions or departures from these rules.

As stated in the Committee Report, nothing in this bill is intended to affect the scope or applicability of the "non-statutory" labor exemption from the antitrust laws. See, e.g., Brown v. Pro Football, 116 S.Ct. 2116 (1996).

Before yielding to my good friend from Vermont, I would like to thank him for his hard work on this bill. His bipartisan efforts have been vital to the process. I would also like to thank our original cosponsors, Senators THURMOND and MOYNIHAN. I urge the quick adoption of this bill, which will help restore stability to major league baseball labor relations.

Mr. LEAHY. Mr. President, this summer we are being treated to an exceptional season of baseball, from the record breaking pace of the New York Yankees and the resurgence of the Boston Red Sox, to a number of inspiring individual achievements, including the perfect game of David Wells and the home run displays of McGwire, Griffey and Sosa. Such are the exploits that childhood memories are made of—and which we all thought could be counted on, that is until the summer of 1994.

Now finally, after years of turmoil, major league baseball is just beginning to emerge from the slump it inflicted upon itself, by returning to that which makes the game great—the game and the players on the field. And, last weekend, Larry Doby and others at long last were inducted into the Baseball Hall of Fame. These are steps in the right direction.

Today, the Senate will give baseball another nudge in the right direction by passing S. 53, the "Curt Flood Act of 1998." Murray Chass, a gifted reporter writing for The New York Times noted that on this issue we have finally "moved into scoring position with a bill that would alter the antitrust exemption Major League Baseball has enjoyed since 1922."

I am gratified that 76 years after an aberrant Supreme Court decision, we are finally making it clear that with respect to the antitrust laws, major league baseball teams are no different than teams in any other professional sport. For years, baseball was the only business or sport, of which I am aware, that claimed an exemption from antitrust laws, without any regulation in lieu of those laws. The Supreme Court refused to undue its mistake with respect to major league baseball made in the 1922 case of Federal Baseball. Fi-

nally, in the most well-known case on the issue, Flood v. Kuhn, the Court reaffirmed the Federal Baseball case on the basis of the legal principle of stare decisis while specifically finding that professional baseball is indeed an activity of interstate commerce, and thereby rejecting the legal basis for the Federal Baseball case.

Mr. President, as a result of that and subsequent decisions, and with the end of the major league reserve clause as the result of an arbitrator's ruling in 1976, there has been a growing debate as to the continued vitality, if any, of any antitrust exemption for baseball. It is for precisely this reason that this bill is limited in its scope to employment relations between major league owners and major league players. That is what is at the heart of turmoil in baseball and what is at the heart of the breach of trust with the fans that marked the cancellation of the 1994 World Series. At least we can take this small step toward ensuring the continuity of the game and restoring public confidence in it.

When David Cone testified at our hearing three years ago, he posed a most perceptive question. He asked: If baseball were coming to Congress to ask us to provide a statutory antitrust exemption, would such a bill be passed? The answer to that question is a resounding no. Nor should the owners, sitting at the negotiating table in a labor dispute, think that their anticompetitive behavior cannot be challenged. That is an advantage enjoyed by no other group of employers.

The certainty provided by this bill will level the playing field, making labor disruptions less likely in the future. The real beneficiaries will be the fans. They deserve it.

Mr. President, I just wanted to comment briefly on a couple of changes made in the substitute from the bill as reported by the Committee. First, the changes in the language in subsection (a) are not intended to limit in any way the rights of players at the major league level as they would be construed under the language of the bill as reported by the Judiciary Committee last July. The additional language was added to ensure that a minor league player, or someone who had played at the major league level and returned to the minor leagues, cannot use subsection (a), concerned with play at the major league level, to attack what is really a minor league employment issue only. Alternatively, neither can the major leagues use the wording of subsection (a) and that of subsection (d) to subvert the purpose of subsection (a) merely by linking a major league practice with a minor league practice. That linkage itself may be an antitrust violation and be actionable under this Act. It cannot be used as a subterfuge by which to subject players at the major league level to acts, practices or agreements that teams or owners in other sports could not subject athletes to.

Finally, the practices set forth in subsection (b) are not intended to be affected by this Act. While this is true, it should be remembered that although the pure entrepreneurial decisions in this area are unaffected by the Act, if those decisions are made in such a way as to implicate employment of major league players at the major league level, once again, those actions may be actionable under subsection (a). More importantly, we are making no findings as to how, under labor laws, those issues are to be treated.

In closing, Mr. President, I would like to thank all those involved in this undertaking: Chairman HATCH, of course, without whose unfailing efforts this result would not be possible; our fellow cosponsors, Senators THURMOND and MOYNIHAN, and other members of our Committee; and JOHN CONYERS, the Ranking Democrat on the House Judiciary Committee, for making this bill a priority. And I want to commend the interested parties for working to find a solution they can all support. Not only have they done a service to the fans, but they may find, on reflection, that they have done a service to themselves by working together for the good of the game.

Finally, Mr. President, I would be remiss if I did not comment on the man for whom this legislation is named, Curt Flood. He was a superb athlete and a courageous man who sacrificed his career for perhaps a more lasting baseball legacy. When others refused, he stood up and said no to a system that he thought un-American as it bound one man to another for his professional career without choice and without a voice in his future.

I am sad that he did not live long enough to see this day. In deference to his memory and in the interests of every fan of this great game, I hope that Congress will act quickly on this bill. I am delighted that we are moving forward today and that we are finally able to enjoy the game once again.

Mr. JEFFORDS. I ask unanimous consent the amendment be considered as read and agreed to, the bill be considered read a third time and passed as amended, the motion to reconsider be laid upon the table, and that any statements relating to the bill be printed at the appropriate place in the RECORD.

The PRESIDING OFFICER. Without objection, it is so ordered.

The amendment (No. 3479) was agreed to.

The bill (S. 53), as amended, was considered read a third time and passed.

———

(material omitted)   *(material omitted)*

III. 144 Cong. Rec. H9942 (Oct. 7, 1998)

(material omitted)   * * * *

CURT FLOOD ACT OF 1998

Mr. HYDE. Mr. Speaker, I move to suspend the rules and pass the Senate bill (S. 53) to require the general application of the antitrust laws to major league baseball, and for other purposes.

The Clerk read as follows:

S. 53

Be it enacted by the Senate and House of Representatives of the United States of America in Congress assembled,

SECTION 1. SHORT TITLE.

This Act may be cited as the "Curt Flood Act of 1998".

SEC. 2. PURPOSE.

It is the purpose of this legislation to state that major league baseball players are covered under the antitrust laws (i.e., that major league baseball players will have the same rights under the antitrust laws as do other professional athletes, e.g., football and basketball players), along with a provision that makes it clear that the passage of this Act does not change the application of the antitrust laws in any other context or with respect to any other person or entity.

SEC. 3. APPLICATION OF THE ANTITRUST LAWS TO PROFESSIONAL MAJOR LEAGUE BASEBALL.

The Clayton Act (15 U.S.C. §12 et seq.) is amended by adding at the end the following new section:

"SEC. 27. (a) Subject to subsections (b) through (d), the conduct, acts, practices, or agreements of persons in the business of organized professional major league baseball directly relating to or affecting employment of major league baseball players to play baseball at the major league level are subject to the antitrust laws to the same extent such conduct, acts, practices, or agreements would be subject to the antitrust laws if engaged in by persons in any other professional sports business affecting interstate commerce.

"(b) No court shall rely on the enactment of this section as a basis for changing the application of the antitrust laws to any conduct, acts, practices, or agreements other than those set forth in subsection (a). This section does not create, permit or imply a cause of action by which to challenge under the antitrust laws, or otherwise apply the antitrust laws to, any conduct, acts, practices, or agreements that do not directly relate to or affect employment of major league baseball players to play baseball at the major league level, including but not limited to—

"(1) any conduct, acts, practices, or agreements of persons engaging in, conducting or participating in the business of organized professional baseball relating to or affecting employment to play baseball at the minor league level, any organized professional baseball amateur or first-year player draft, or any reserve clause as applied to minor league players;

"(2) the agreement between organized professional major league baseball teams and the teams of the National Association of Professional Baseball Leagues, commonly known as the 'Professional Baseball Agreement', the relationship between organized professional major league baseball and organized professional minor league baseball, or any other matter relating to organized professional baseball's minor leagues;

"(3) any conduct, acts, practices, or agreements of persons engaging in, conducting or participating in the business of organized professional baseball relating to or affecting franchise expansion, location or relocation, franchise ownership issues, including ownership transfers, the relationship between the Office of the Commissioner and franchise owners, the marketing or sales of the entertainment product of organized professional baseball and the licensing of intellectual property rights owned or held by organized professional baseball teams individually or collectively;

"(4) any conduct, acts, practices, or agreements protected by Public Law 87–331 (15 U.S.C. §1291 et seq.) (commonly known as the 'Sports Broadcasting Act of 1961');

"(5) the relationship between persons in the business of organized professional baseball and umpires or other individuals who are employed in the business of organized professional baseball by such persons; or

"(6) any conduct, acts, practices, or agreements of persons not in the business of organized professional major league baseball.

"(c) Only a major league baseball player has standing to sue under this section. For the purposes of this section, a major league baseball player is—

"(1) a person who is a party to a major league player's contract, or is playing baseball at the major league level; or

"(2) a person who was a party to a major league player's contract or playing baseball at the major league level at the time of the injury that is the subject of the complaint; or

"(3) a person who has been a party to a major league player's contract or who has played baseball at the major league level, and who claims he has been injured in his efforts to secure a subsequent major league player's contract by an alleged violation of the antitrust laws: *Provided however*, That for the purposes of this paragraph, the alleged antitrust violation shall not include any conduct, acts, practices, or agreements of persons in the business of organized professional baseball relating to or affecting employment to play baseball at the minor league level, including any organized professional baseball amateur or first-year player draft, or any reserve clause as applied to minor league players; or

"(4) a person who was a party to a major league player's contract or who was playing baseball at the major league level at the conclusion of the last full championship season immediately preceding the expiration of the last collective bargaining agreement between persons in the business of organized professional major league baseball and the exclusive collective bargaining representative of major league baseball players.

"(d)(1) As used in this section, 'person' means any entity, including an individual, partnership, corporation, trust or unincorporated association or any combination or association thereof. As used in this section, the National Association of Professional Baseball Leagues, its member leagues and the clubs of those leagues, are not 'in the business of organized professional major league baseball'.

"(2) In cases involving conduct, acts, practices, or agreements that directly relate to or affect both employment of major league baseball players to play baseball at the major league level and also relate to or affect any other aspect of organized professional baseball, including but not limited to employment to play baseball at the minor league level and the other areas set forth in subsection (b) above, only those components, portions or aspects of such conduct, acts, practices, or agreements that directly relate to or affect employment of major league players to play baseball at the major league level may be challenged under subsection (a) and then only to the extent that they directly relate to or affect employment of major league baseball players to play baseball at the major league level.

"(3) As used in subsection (a), interpretation of the term 'directly' shall not be governed by any interpretation of section 151 et seq. of title 29, United States Code (as amended).

"(4) Nothing in this section shall be construed to affect the application to organized professional baseball of the nonstatutory labor exemption from the antitrust laws.

"(5) The scope of the conduct, acts, practices, or agreements covered by subsection (b) shall not be strictly or narrowly construed.".

The SPEAKER pro tempore. Pursuant to the rule, the gentleman from Illinois (Mr. HYDE) and the gentleman from Michigan (Mr. CONYERS) each will control 20 minutes.

The Chair recognizes the gentleman from Illinois (Mr. HYDE).

(Mr. HYDE asked and was given permission to revise and extend his remarks.)

GENERAL LEAVE

Mr. HYDE. Mr. Speaker, I ask unanimous consent that all Members may have 5 legislative days within which to revise and extend their remarks on the bill under consideration.

The SPEAKER pro tempore. Is there objection to the request of the gentleman from Illinois?

There was no objection.

Mr. HYDE. Mr. Speaker, I yield myself such time as I may consume.

Mr. Speaker, I rise in support of S. 53, the Curt Flood Act of 1998. After years of disagreement, the baseball players, the baseball owners, and the minor leagues have reached an historic agreement on the application of the antitrust laws to labor relations in baseball. This agreement has already passed the Senate by unanimous consent, and I hope we will pass it today.

Mr. Speaker, let me just add, because we are talking about baseball, let me tip my cap to my good friend, the gentleman from Michigan (Mr. CONYERS) the ranking member of the Committee on the Judiciary. He has his own bill on this topic, H.R. 21, and he has led the charge on this issue in the House. I want to thank him for his outstanding work in bringing this bill to fruition.

I also want to thank my friends, Senators ORRIN HATCH and PAT LEAHY, chairman and ranking member of the Senate Committee on the Judiciary. They worked many long hours to negotiate the delicate compromise that this bill embodies. We are also indebted to them for their outstanding efforts in bringing this bill to passage. I am delighted to support this simple but important bill, and I ask my colleagues to do the same.

Mr. Speaker, I rise in support of S. 53, the "Curt Flood Act of 1998." After years of disagreement, the baseball owners, and the minor leagues have reached a historic agreement on the application of the antitrust laws to labor relations in baseball. This agreement has already passed the Senate by unanimous consent, and I hope that we will pass it today.

The Supreme Court first held that the business of baseball is exempt from the antitrust laws in 1922. *Federal Baseball Club of Baltimore, Inc.* v. *National League of Professional Baseball Clubs*, 259 U.S. 200 (1922). The Court, emphasizing organized baseball's longstanding reliance on that exemption, has twice declined to overrule its original 1922 decision. *Flood* v. *Kuhn*, 407 U.S. 258 (1972); *Toolson* v. *New York Yankees, Inc.*, 346 U.S. 356 (1953). Instead, the Court has left it to Congress to decide whether the baseball exemption should continue.

Given the agreement of the parties, Congress has now decided to legislate in this area, but we do so only in an extremely narrow manner. S. 53 leaves completely unchanged all aspects of the baseball exemption except for the narrow issue of the labor relations of major league players at the major league level as set out in detail in the new subsection 27(b) of the Clayton Act.

This bill originates from a compromise struck during the last round of collective bargaining between the major league owners and the major league players. After a lengthy labor dispute, these parties reached a collective bargaining agreement that, among other things, required negotiation to reach agreement on a limited repeal of baseball's antitrust exemption. They did so because the players' union argued that the antitrust exemption contributed to the labor disputes that have long marked its relationship with the owners. Specifically, the union asserted that it was disadvantaged in its labor negotiations with the owners because, unlike unions of other professional athletes, it

could not challenge allegedly unlawful employment terms under the antitrust laws.

The major league clubs, of course, disagreed with this view. They contended that the baseball exemption was irrelevant to their labor negotiations with the union. The clubs argued that, like every other multi-employer bargaining group, they were protected from antitrust challenges to their employment terms by the nonstatutory labor antitrust exemption. In that regard, I want to note that nothing in this bill will affect in any way the protections afforded to the major league clubs by the nonstatutory labor antitrust exemption.

As a result of this difference of opinion, both the players and the owners were willing to support the repeal of the specific and narrow portion of the baseball exemption covering labor relations between major league players and major league clubs. The bill was carefully drafted, however, to leave the remainder of the exemption intact.

Before this bill passed the Senate, several changes were adopted to address concerns raised by owners of the minor league teams—the members of the National Association of Professional Baseball Leagues. Minor league baseball owners were concerned that the original bill reported by the Senate Judiciary Committee might not adequately protect their interests. Specifically, the minor league clubs were concerned that the original version of S. 53 was not sufficiently clear to preserve antitrust protection for: (1) the relationship between the major league clubs and the minor league clubs and (2) those work rules and employment terms that arguably affect both major league and minor league baseball players.

Members of Congress agreed that this narrow legislation should not hurt the grass roots minor league baseball played in over 150 towns across the country. For that reason, the minor league clubs were invited into the discussion and given an opportunity to suggest changes to address their concerns, and those changes have been incorporated.

As a result of these three-way negotiations, the parties agreed to amend the bill in several significant ways. These amendments clarify the limited reach of the bill and the expansive nature of the continued protection the bill affords to minor league baseball. For instance, to accommodate the concerns of the minor league clubs, subsection (b) of the new section 27 of the Clayton Act was changed by adding the word "directly" immediately before the phrase "relating to or affecting employment" and the phrase "major league players" was added before the phrase "to play baseball." These changes were made to ensure that neither major league players nor minor league players could use new subsection (a) to attack conduct, acts, practices, or agreements designed to apply to minor league employment.

In addition, new subsection (c) was added to clarify that only major league players could sue under the new subsection (a). Again, the minor leagues were concerned that, without a narrow standing section, minor league players or amateurs might attempt to attack minor league issues by asserting that these issues also indirectly affected major league employment terms.

Therefore, the new subsection (c) carefully limits the zone of persons protected by the bill to only major league players by providing that "only a major league baseball player has

FLOOD v. KUHN

standing to sue under" this limited antitrust legislation. The standing provision gives major league baseball players the same right to sue under the antitrust laws over the major league employment terms that other professional athletes have. Of course, the United States has standing to sue to enjoin all antitrust violations under 15 U.S.C. §§ 4 and 25, and we do not intend subsection 27(c) to limit that broad authority.

This bill does not affect the application of the antitrust laws to anyone outside the business of baseball. In particular, it does not affect the application of the antitrust laws to other professional sports. The law with respect to the other professional sports remains exactly the same after this bill becomes law.

Because we are talking about baseball, let me tip my cap to my good friend, the Ranking Member of the Judiciary Committee, JOHN CONYERS. Mr. CONYERS has his own bill on this topic, H.R. 21, and he has led the charge on this issue in the House. I want to thank him for his outstanding work in bringing this bill to fruition.

I also want to thank my friends Senators ORRIN HATCH and PAT LEAHY, the Chairman and Ranking Member of the Senate Judiciary Committee. They worked many long hours to negotiate the delicate compromise that this bill embodies. We are also indebted to them for their outstanding efforts in bringing this bill to passage.

Mr. Speaker, I am delighted to support this simple, but important, bill, and I ask my colleagues to do the same. At this point, I will reserve the balance of my time.

Mr. Speaker, I reserve the balance of my time.

Mr. CONYERS. Mr. Speaker, I yield myself such time as I may consume.

(Mr. CONYERS asked and was given permission to revise and extend his remarks.)

Mr. CONYERS. Mr. Speaker, this Curt Flood Act is an important piece of legislation. I thank the gentleman from Illinois (Chairman HYDE) for his very charitable comments. As two baseball aficionados, we know that the right thing is being done as we move this to finality.

Professional baseball is the only industry in the United States exempt from the antitrust laws without being subject to regulatory supervision. This circumstance has resulted from a rather sorry Supreme Court decision in 1922 holding that baseball did not involve interstate commerce and was beyond the reach of antitrust laws.

□ 2145

For some reason, we in the Congress have failed to rectify this, despite subsequent court decisions holding that all the other professional sports were fully subject to these same laws that baseball claimed to be exempt from.

There may have been a time when baseball's unique treatment was a source of pride and distinction for many loyal fans who loved our national pastime. But with baseball suffering more work stoppages over the last century than all the other sports combined, including a 1994 strike which ended the possibility of a world series

for the first time in 90 years, and depriving many of our cities of tens of millions of dollars in tax revenues, we can now no longer afford to treat professional baseball in a manner enjoyed by no other professional sport. And that is what S. 53 and H.R. 21 attempt to do.

I am very pleased to be a major sponsor of this legislation, because concerns have been previously raised that by repealing the antitrust exemption we would somehow be disrupting the operation of the minor leagues. That, my colleagues will remember, was the defense that was always raised. An ugly specter. Or professional baseball's ability to limit franchise relocation might also occur. This legislation carefully eliminates these matters from the scope of new antitrust coverage.

In the past, some of us in this body objected to legislating in this area because of their hesitancy to take any action which could impact an ongoing labor dispute. But because the owners and the players have recently agreed to enter into a new collective bargaining agreement, that objection no longer exists. Additionally, the baseball owners are now in full support of this legislation, as of course the Major League Players Association has always been.

This bill was introduced by myself in honor of a very courageous and beautiful ball player, center fielder, Curt Flood, who passed away earlier this year, in January, and, unfortunately, is no longer with us to see the fruit of his work. Mr. Flood, one of the greatest players of his time, risked his career when he challenged baseball's reserve clause after he was traded from the St. Louis Cardinals to the Philadelphia Phillies. Although the Supreme Court rejected the 1972 challenge of Flood, we all owe a debt of gratitude for his willingness to challenge the baseball oligarchy. And he paid the price, too.

By the way, at his funeral in California, George Will, perhaps the supreme baseball nut of all, was there, and Reverend Jesse Jackson, Senior was there as well. It was a very touching event.

Now, this bill has gone through many changes over the years and was introduced originally in the 103rd Congress by our former beloved member of the Judiciary, Mike Synar, of Oklahoma.

In order to address the concern of the minor leagues, it contains many redundancies and, accordingly, a court may have questions about how the provisions of this bill will interrelate. Any court facing such questions would be advised, if I may dare suggest, to return to the purpose section of the bill for aid and interpretation. The purpose section states what Congress intends; that is, that it is no longer subject to question that major league baseball players have the same rights under antitrust laws as do other professional athletes.

This is a simple proposition, yet it is indeed startling that 26 years after this brave and eloquent player, Curt Flood, stood alone before the Supreme Court

to seek an answer to a question whose answer seemed obvious to him, that it is only just now being addressed by this branch of government. I am very proud of the Congress for this.

If a court has any doubt as to the meaning or purpose of any provision of this act, it should be guided by our purpose, which is, at long last, to give the answer that Mr. Flood indeed knew to be the correct one. The legislation is not intended to have an adverse effect on any ongoing litigation nor intended to limit the ability of the United States Government to bring antitrust actions.

It is overdue. I hope it will be quickly passed for the good of the game, which has once again demonstrated why we love it, why baseball is on a resurgence, and we are just delighted that now that McGwire and Sosa have brought new enjoyment and life to the game that we now have this legislation to accompany it.

Mr. Speaker, I reserve the balance of my time.

Mr. HYDE. Mr. Speaker, I yield 5 minutes to the gentleman from Kentucky (Mr. JIM BUNNING), a member of Baseball's Hall of Fame.

(Mr. BUNNING asked and was given permission to revise and extend his remarks.)

Mr. BUNNING. Mr. Speaker, I thank the gentleman from Illinois for yielding me this time.

Mr. Speaker, I rise in strong support of S. 53, the Curt Flood Act, named for the player who challenged the antitrust laws all the way to the Supreme Court.

Baseball is the only sport, and just about the only business in America, that is immune from the antitrust laws. Because of an outdated supreme court decision, major league baseball has been operating under a different set of rules than everyone else for the past 75 years. The legislation before us today is very simple: It provides for a limited repeal of that exemption when it comes to labor-management relations.

Baseball has had big troubles in recent years, and the antitrust exemption has been the root cause. There has been eight work stoppages in the last three decades, and it is no coincidence that baseball, the only sport that enjoyed such special treatment, has had more strikes and lockouts than all other sports combined.

After playing and managing in professional baseball for over 25 years, and serving on the Executive Board of the Players Association, I know firsthand how the exemption distorts player-owner relationships and has contributed to the turmoil in baseball. The exemption effectively removes a negotiating tool from the labor negotiating process and forces both sides to play hardball when it comes to bargaining over contracts. It removes a way for the players to push their grievances, and encourages the owners to take a hard line and reduces their incentive to compromise.

Personally, I think this exemption should be repealed altogether. Baseball is a multibillion dollar business that should have to play by the same rules as other sports and businesses. The exemption is anti-competitive and anti-American. But by passing this bill today, and partially repealing the exemption, we provide another avenue for the owners and the players to explore another way to vent steam before calling a strike or staging a lockout.

This is a bipartisan consensus bill that the Senate passed without opposition. It is supported by all of the affected parties in baseball, owners, players, and the minor leagues. Everyone agrees that it represents a positive step forward for our national pastime.

But most importantly, this legislation represents a win for the fans. Just 4 years ago the players were on strike. The world series was canceled. Baseball seemed doomed. But this year, as the gentleman from Michigan (Mr. CONYERS) has said, baseball has had a renaissance. Mark McGwire and Sammy Sosa thrilled us with the home run race. The playoffs are more exciting than ever before. And baseball is back.

Fans are returning to baseball, and passing this bill today will help ensure that the game does not spiral backwards, down into the abyss of labor strife. It will help ensure that the fans are not robbed of their right to the greatest game ever invented.

Mr. Speaker, I urge strong support for the bill.

Mr. CONYERS. Mr. Speaker, I yield myself such time as I may consume.

I neglected to mention that the gentleman from Kentucky (Mr. JIM BUNNING), Hall of Famer, worked diligently on this bill with myself and the gentleman from Illinois (Mr. HYDE), and he was also a Detroit Tiger, where his greatest playing took place, and we still claim him, although he represents the great State of Kentucky. And, Mr. Speaker, he has a baseball in his hand now, as we watch.

Mr. Speaker, I yield back the balance of my time.

Mr. HYDE. Mr. Speaker, I yield 2 minutes to the gentleman from Arkansas (Mr. HUTCHINSON).

Mr. HUTCHINSON. Mr. Speaker, I want to thank the chairman for yielding me this time, and I want to thank the gentleman from Kentucky (Mr. BUNNING) for signing my baseball and being such a great baseball hero.

I speak as a fan today. In Arkansas, we do not have major league baseball in the State, but we have minor league baseball and we have a great baseball tradition. This bill that is before us has been agreed to by the players and the owners, but, more importantly, in my judgment, it is a bill for the fans. The fans want to see the boys of summer out on the field. They want to see them play ball. This has been a great year for the fans and we want that to continue without interruption.

This bill, as has been explained, and so eloquently by the gentleman from Michigan (Mr. CONYERS), and also by the chairman, provides baseball players with the same rights already afforded the National Football League and the National Basketball Association players. So they can act as their counterparts do in other fields of endeavor. But this also recognizes the importance of an antitrust exemption for certain aspects of the game so team owners may continue to cooperate on issues such as league expansion, franchise location and broadcast rights, without fear of lawsuit. So it protects and helps minor league baseball that is important in my State.

Mr. Speaker, baseball is America's pastime and it is my State's as well. Arkansas has produced its share of baseball greats as well, men like Lou Brock, Dizzy Dean, George Kell, and Brooks Robinson, all Hall of Famers, that have made us proud as they have carried a little bit of Arkansas to the far corners of this country.

Mr. Speaker, this is a good bill for baseball, the players and owners alike; it is a good bill for the fans, and I urge my colleagues to support it.

Mr. HYDE. Mr. Speaker, I yield 2 minutes to the gentleman from New York (Mr. BOEHLERT).

(Mr. BOEHLERT asked and was given permission to revise and extend his remarks.)

Mr. BOEHLERT. Mr. Speaker, I rise in support of this conference report. I do so in my capacity as chairman of the Minor League Baseball Caucus. The common thread that unites all of us in this caucus is our love for America's pastime.

I am a little bit disappointed that the two gentlemen that preceded me in the well, the gentleman from Kentucky (Mr. BUNNING), who is a member of the Baseball Hall of Fame, when he talked about the great year of 1998, I am surprised that he, a great Hall of Fame pitcher, did not mention that David Wells pitched a perfect game for the New York Yankees. The gentleman from Kentucky knows more than most that good pitching beats good hitting all the time.

Mr. HYDE. Mr. Speaker, will the gentleman yield?

Mr. BOEHLERT. I yield to the gentleman from Illinois.

Mr. HYDE. I would like to point out to the gentleman that the gentleman from Kentucky (Mr. BUNNING) also pitched a perfect game when he was in the major leagues.

Mr. BOEHLERT. Reclaiming my time, Mr. Speaker, the gentleman is exactly right, and I was one of the great fans cheering him on when he pitched that perfect game.

And my colleague from Arkansas neglected to mention another great Hall of Famer from his home State. Arky Vaughn.

The fact of the matter is, one of the reasons why this settlement was delayed was the genuine concern for the future of minor league baseball. Because when all is said and done, while we are all thrilled by America's pastime, most people have to watch it on television. But across America, 35 million fans are going to the ball parks to see minor league baseball, in places like Syracuse, New York, and Utica, New York, and all over America. In Toledo, Ohio, the Mudhens. Who can forget them.

□ 2200

It is indeed America's pastime. The great concern that all of us had was the preservation of minor league baseball. I am pleased to report to my colleagues that the minor league baseball officials have worked cooperatively, and they do endorse this package. It is good for baseball at all levels.

Mr. LUTHER. Mr. Speaker, in an attempt to clarify the legislative intent of S. 53, I would like to place the following Senate colloquy between Senator PAUL WELLSTONE, Judiciary Committee Chairman ORRIN HATCH and Ranking Judiciary Committee Member PATRICK LEAHY in the House record.

CURT FLOOD ACT OF 1998

Mr. WELLSTONE. Mr. President, late last night (July 30, 1998), the Senate passed by unanimous consent S. 53. I have been contacted by the Attorney General of my State, Hubert H. Humphrey III, and asked to try to clarify a technical legal point about the effect of this legislation. The State of Minnesota, through the office of Attorney General, and the Minnesota Twins are currently involved in an antitrust-related investigation. It is my understanding that S. 53 will have no impact on this investigation or any litigation arising out of the investigation.

Mr. HATCH. That is correct. The bill simply makes it clear that major league baseball players have the same rights under the antitrust laws as do other professional athletes. The bill does not change current law in any other context or with respect to any other person or entity.

Mr. WELLSTONE. Thank you for that clarification. I also note that several lower courts have recently found that baseball currently enjoys only a narrow exemption from antitrust laws and that this exemption applies only to the reserve system. For example, the Florida Supreme Court in *Butterworth* v. *National League*, 644 So.2d 1021 (Fla. 1994), the U.S. District Court in Pennsylvania in *Piazza* v. *Major League Baseball*, 831 F. Supp. 420 (E.D. Pa. 1993) and a Minnesota State court in a case involving the Twins have all held the baseball exemption from antitrust laws is now limited only to the reserve system. It is my understanding that S. 53 will have no effect on the courts' ultimate resolution of the scope of the antitrust exemption on matters beyond those related to owner-player relations at the major league level.

Mr. HATCH. That is correct. S. 53 is intended to have no effect other than to clarify the status of major league players under the antitrust laws. With regard to all other context or other persons or entities, the law will be the same after passage of the Act as it is today.

Mr. LEAHY. I concur with the statement of the Chairman of the Committee. The bill affects no pending or decided cases except to the extent that courts have exempted major league baseball clubs from the antitrust laws in their dealings with major league players. In fact, Section 3 of the legislation makes clear that the law is unchanged with regard to issues such as relocation. The bill has no impact on the recent decisions in federal and state courts in Florida, Pennsylvania and

H9946   CONGRESSIONAL RECORD — HOUSE   *October 7, 1998*

Minnesota concerning baseball's status under the antitrust laws.

Mr. WELLSTONE. I thank the Senator. I call to my colleagues attention the decision in *Minnesota Twins v. State by Humphrey*, No. 62-CX-98-568 (Minn. dist. Court, 2d Judicial dist., Ramsey County April 20, 1998) reprinted in 1998-1 Trade Cases (CCH) 72,136.

Mr. BILIRAKIS. Mr. Speaker, I rise to support S. 53, the Curt Flood Act, which gives major league baseball players the same rights other professional athletes have under antitrust laws.

As a longtime proponent of lifting baseball's antitrust exemption, I have sponsored bills in the past to lift this exemption completely as it applies to all aspects of baseball's business. Although the bill we are considering now is more limited in scope, it is an important first step in correcting a seven decade-old mistake.

Federal antitrust laws prohibit businesses from taking actions that "unreasonably" constrain interstate commerce. However, many years ago Major League Baseball was singled out for a complete exemption from America's antitrust laws by the Supreme Court. The Court said baseball was an amusement and not a business, exempting it from antitrust laws. This exemption created a monopoly for baseball and established artificial barriers to league expansion. It sent the wrong signal to Americans that baseball did not have to comply with our country's antitrust laws.

In 1972, the Supreme Court called the situation an "anomaly" and an "aberration" which Congress should remedy. A 1976 report by the House Select Committee on Professional Sports concluded that there was no justification for baseball's special exemption. Unfortunately, no action was ever taken.

Mr. Speaker, baseball has seen a resurgence since the dark days of the 1994 strike. Who can forget Cal Ripken's triumphant lap around Camden Yards after breaking Lou Gehrig's Iron Man streak of consecutive games played? Or the incredible home run chase this year between Mark McGwire and Sammy Sosa that culminated in both players smashing the thirty-seven-year home run record held by Roger Maris?

I felt immense personal pride when I watched my hometown team, the Tampa Bay Devil Rays, take the field for their inaugural season at Tropicana field. The debut of a major league team in the Tampa-St. Petersburg area was delayed for years because Major League Baseball did not have to abide by our nation's antitrust laws.

I urge my colleagues to support S. 53 because it makes baseball live by the same laws as the fans who sit in the bleachers. It tells baseball fans that competition and fairness in baseball boardrooms is just as important as it is on the field. Let's give America its game back.

Mr. CHABOT. Mr. Speaker, the legislation before us today is the result of a negotiation resulting in a compromise among the union that represents major league players, the owners of major league baseball clubs, and by the owners of minor league baseball teams affiliated with major league clubs. The compromise addresses only the limited area of the labor relations of major league players at the major league level. The bill does not affect any other aspect of the organized baseball exemption. Also, the legislation does not change in any way the antitrust exemption for the major league players union or the major league clubs in the collective bargaining process provided by the nonstatutory labor antitrust exemption available to all unions and employers.

The legislation is a success because it has been carefully crafted to make clear that only major league baseball players, and no other party, can bring suit under this amendment to the Clayton Act.

This protection will help to ensure the continued viability of minor league baseball.

Minor league baseball owners were concerned that any legislation preserve the antitrust protections for the historic relationship between the major league clubs and the minor league clubs. The minor league owners were particularly concerned about the work rules and terms of employment that impact both major league and minor league baseball players. The language of the bill guarantee that neither major league players nor minor league players can use subsection (a) of new section 27 of the Clayton Act to attack conduct, acts, practices or agreements designed to apply only to minor league employment.

I believe the compromise is successful because it protects minor league baseball by barring minor league players or amateur players from using the antitrust laws to attack issues unique to the continued economic success of minor league baseball.

Mr. CLAY. Mr. Speaker, I rise in strong support of S. 53, the "Curt Flood Act of 1998." This is the Senate counterpart of H.R. 21, legislation I introduced in the each of the last two Congresses providing for the partial repeal of baseball's antitrust exemption. I'd like to thank Chairman Hyde for his leadership in seeing that this vital and long overdue legislation reached the House Floor.

Professional baseball is the only industry in the United States exempt from antitrust laws without being subject to alternative regulatory supervision. This circumstance resulted from an erroneous 1922 Supreme Court decision holding that baseball did not involve "interstate commerce" and was therefore beyond the reach of the antitrust laws. Congress has failed to overturn this decision despite subsequent court decisions holding that the other professional sports were fully subject to the antitrust laws.

There may have been a time when baseball's unique treatment was a source of pride and distinction for the many loyal fans who loved our national pastime. But with baseball suffering more work stoppages over the last 25 years than all of the other professional sports combined—including the 1994-95 strike which ended the possibility of a World Series for the first time in 90 years and deprived our cities of thousands of jobs and millions of dollars in tax revenues—we can no longer afford to treat professional baseball in a manner enjoyed by no other professional sport.

Because concerns have previously been raised that by repealing the antitrust exemption we could somehow be disrupting the operation of the minor leagues, or professional baseball's ability to limit franchise relocation, the legislation carefully eliminates these matters from the scope of the new antitrust coverage.

In the past, some in Congress had objected to legislating in this area because of their hesitancy to take any action which could impact the ongoing labor dispute. But because the owners and players have recently agreed to enter into a new collective bargaining agreement, this objection no longer exists. In addition, the baseball owners are now in full support of this legislation as are the Major League Players Association.

I originally introduced the House version of the bill as H.R. 21, in honor of the courageous center fielder, Curt Flood, who passed away earlier this year on January 21. Mr. Flood, one of the greatest players of his time, risked his career when he challenged baseball's reserve clause after he was traded from the St. Louis Cardinals to the Philadelphia Phillies. Although the Supreme Court rejected Flood's challenge in 1972, we all owe a debt of gratitude for his willingness to challenge the baseball oligarchy.

This bill has gone through many iterations over the years, beginning with its first enaction by the House Judiciary Committee at the end of the 103d Congress. That legislation was introduced by my former colleague Mike Synar.

In order to address the concern of the minor leagues, it contains many redundancies. Accordingly, a court may have questions about how the provisions of this bill interrelate. Any court facing such questions would be well-advised to return to the purpose section of the bill for aid in interpretation. The purpose section is the statement of what Congress intends the bundle of works now known as the "Curt Flood Act of 1998" to mean—that is, it is no longer subject to question that major league baseball players have the same rights under the antitrust laws as do other professional athletes. That is a simple proposition, yet it is indeed startling that 26 years after a brave and eloquent player stood alone before the Supreme Court to seek an answer that was obvious to him, it is only now being addressed directly by any branch of the United States government. If a court has any doubt as to the meaning or purpose of any provision of this new Act, it should be guided by our purpose which is at long last to give the answer Mr. Flood knew to be the correct one. This legislation is not intended to have any adverse effect on any ongoing litigation nor is it intended to limit the ability of the United States to bring antitrust actions.

Mr. Speaker, this bill is long overdue. I hope the House will act quickly to pass it for the good of the game, which has once again demonstrated why we love it, and for the good of the fans, who deserve to enjoy the national pastime without the continuous interruptions that have become nearly as predictable and plentiful, as McGwire or Sosa home runs.

Mr. HYDE. Mr. Speaker, I have no further requests for time, and I yield back the balance of my time.

The SPEAKER pro tempore (Mr. GUTKNECHT). The question is on the motion offered by the gentleman from Illinois (Mr. HYDE) that the House suspend the rules and pass the Senate bill, S. 53.

The question was taken; and (two-thirds having voted in favor thereof) the rules were suspended and the Senate bill was passed.

A motion to reconsider was laid on the table.

———

(material omitted)

THE 1885 CONTRACT LABOR LAW AND *HOLY TRINITY CHURCH*

I. Overview and Questions

The *Holy Trinity Church* decision is often cited as inaugurating the modern era of statutory interpretation by the courts. The decision construes the 1885 Contract Labor Law, a major immigration statute that was considered by the House primarily in June 1884 and by the Senate at the start of the following Congress in early 1885. At the time (and indeed well into the 20th century), the federal fiscal year ran from July 1 through June 30, and Congress strove mightily to complete each session's business on or shortly after July 1.

The late 1800s was a period of intense industrialization and urbanization in this country. Immigrants from China and southern and eastern Europe fulfilled a rising demand for cheap labor in mines and especially in factories. The waves of immigrants that flooded the country in the second half of the 19th century were widely perceived as allowing managers to depress wage rates for all American workers. Inspired by racial as well as economic fears, Congress responded from the mid-1870s onward with a series of restrictive immigration laws—aimed first at the Chinese and then at immigrants from parts of Europe as well.

The 1885 law was identified—at its introduction and final enactment—as "an act to prohibit the importation and migration of foreigners and aliens under contract to perform labor in the United States." The House Labor Committee reported out the 1884 contract labor bill in February of 1884. The full House debated the bill in June and passed it by a 102-17 vote on June 19. The Senate Education and Labor Committee reported out the bill on June 28: its report consisted of three brief paragraphs of explanation followed by a reprinting of the entire House report. The full Senate took up the bill on July 5, but agreed to postpone consideration after a short debate. The Senate returned to the bill in February 1885, and after several days of discussion—including the acceptance of some amendments and the rejection of others—it passed the amended bill by a 50-9 margin (17 members recorded as absent) on February 18. The House concurred in the Senate version without a recorded vote on February 23—one member expressed opposition at that time.

The legislative history excerpted below may be viewed as addressing two distinct aspects of the bill. The first involves evidence related to the bill's general purpose. There are numerous statements, in the House committee report and on both House and Senate floor, describing in some depth the perceived evil or mischief at which the law was aimed. The articulation of this public policy mischief reflects that members of Congress harbored strong beliefs about labor protectionism as well as some pronounced racist sentiments. The statute's general purpose or "spirit" may shed light on the likelihood that Congress meant for pastors to be among those restricted from entering the country.

The other focus for our legislative history excerpts involves evidence of Congress's possible specific intent with regard to pastors. The statute as finally enacted includes a list of exceptions and exemptions in section 5, identifying *inter alia* five particular occupations not covered by the act's restrictive provisions: professional actors, artists, lecturers, and singers, and also personal or domestic servants (see Casebook, p.700). The House committee reported out a version of this section, and the Senate in 1885 considered several amendments to modify its contents. The Senate accepted two proposed changes (adding personal or domestic servants and artists), rejected another (a proposal to add artisans), and also rejected a proposal to delete an exempted occupation (singers). There was no discussion of including pastors on this list. In addition, one might draw inferences related to Congress's specific intent with respect to pastors from certain substantive floor exchanges, such as the extended discussions between Senator Morgan (one of nine senators to vote No) and Senators Blair and Sherman, both strong supporters of the bill.

As you review this history, consider the following questions.

1. What is the general or overall purpose of the 1885 contract labor law? Does "contract labor" suggest or entail targeting groups of workers brought to the U.S. under certain conditions or arrangements? Could "contract labor" also be meant to cover individual contracted-for laborers?

2. Is Congress concerned about whether these contract laborers return to their home countries after the contract expires? Why might this be relevant to Congress's general purpose?

3. In light of the statute's general purpose, and the exceptions contained in section 5 of the law, can you argue that this is a law focused on manual labor?

4. Given that the Senate adds to the list of exceptions approved by the House, and also rejects certain proposed changes, is Congress's silence on pastors more significant? Should dancers or musicians be exempted from the Act's restrictions under section 5? What about doctors? Should these professions be treated any differently from pastors?

5. The Senate committee report states the committee would have preferred that the text be modified to replace "labor or service" with "'manual labor' or 'manual service' as sufficiently broad to accomplish the purposes of the bill." But it left the language unchanged on June 28, 1884, "believing that the bill in its present form will be [so] construed" and "in the hope that the bill may not fail of passage in the present session." Should the committee's belief carry any interpretive weight on this point? How hard would it have been to fix the language?

6. Does the Senate committee's reluctance to modify the language become more persuasive—or alternatively less persuasive—when in the next session of Congress (in early 1885), the Senate considers various floor amendments and adopts some, but does not add an amendment specifying "manual labor"?

7. Stepping back and considering the matter in more general terms, should failure to clarify language that has been noted as ambiguous or unfortunate in a committee report be regarded as significant? As suspicious?

II. Excerpts from H.R. Rep. No. 48-444 (Feb. 3, 1884)

| 48TH CONGRESS, 1st Session. | HOUSE OF REPRESENTATIVES. | REPORT No. 444. |

TO PROHIBIT THE IMPORTATION OF FOREIGN CONTRACT LABOR INTO THE UNITED STATES, ETC.

FEBRUARY 23, 1884.—Referred to the House Calendar and ordered to be printed.

Mr. FORAN, from the Committee on Labor, submitted the following

REPORT:
[To accompany bill H. R. 2550.]

The Committee on Labor, to whom were referred the bills (H. R. 2550 and H. R. 3313) to prohibit the importation and migration of foreigners and aliens under contract to perform labor in the United States, have had the same under consideration, and beg leave to report back bill H. R. 2550, and recommend its passage, with the following amendment, a substitute for both of said bills:

Add to section 5 the following: "Nor shall anything in this act be so construed as to prevent any person or persons, partnership or corporation from engaging under contract or agreement skilled workmen in foreign countries to perform labor in the United States in or upon any new industry not at present existing or established in the United States, provided skilled labor for that purpose cannot be otherwise obtained; nor shall the provisions of this act apply to professional actors, lecturers, or singers."

This recommendation is founded upon the investigations of the committee, and the conclusion to which the committee have come, based upon such investigation, that the evils complained of and sought to be remedied by the bill actually and to an alarming extent exist. The bill in no measure seeks to restrict free immigration. Such a proposition would be, and justly so, odious to the American people. The foreigner who voluntarily and from choice leaves his native land and settles in this country with the intention of becoming an American citizen, a part of the American body politic, has always been welcome to our shores. As a recent writer well said—

Such an immigrant by his coming to this country gives us a certain assurance as to his ability to take care of himself, and to hold up the standard of social well-being which he finds already existing among our working classes.

Such an immigrant comes here because the institutions of the country are in consonance with his social and political ideas, and because of the advantages and opportunities afforded by the extent of our domain and our material resources. He comes to better his social and financial condition, to take advantage of the facilities which he finds here; and as he comes of his own volition, by his own means, and from choice, he always exacts for his labor the highest rates which the market affords. No one is injured by his coming, and as he generally makes a good citizen the State is benefited by the acquisition. These immigrants are generally of a higher class, socially, morally, and intellectually, and

2   FOREIGN CONTRACT LABOR.

have aided largely in the development of our industries and the material progress of our people. With this class of immigrants this bill has no concern. Its object is to restrict and prohibit the immigration or rather the importation of an entirely different class of persons, the immigrant who does not come by "his own initiative, but by that of the capitalist." It seeks to restrain and prohibit the immigration or importation of laborers who would have never seen our shores but for the inducements and allurements of men whose only object is to obtain labor at the lowest possible rate, regardless of the social and material well-being of our own citizens and regardless of the evil consequences which result to American laborers from such immigration. This class of immigrants care nothing about our instutitions, and in many instances never even heard of them; they are men whose passage is paid by the importers; they come here under contract to labor for a certain number of years; they are ignorant of our social conditions, and that they may remain so they are isolated and prevented from coming into contact with Americans. They are generally from the lowest social stratum, and live upon the coarsest food and in hovels of a character before unknown to American workmen. Being bound by contract they are unable, even were they so disposed, to take advantage of the facilities afforded by the country to which they have been imported. They, as a rule, do not become citizens, and are certainly not a desirable acquisition to the body politic. When their term of contract servitude expires, their place is supplied by fresh importations. The inevitable tendency of their presence amongst us is to degrade American labor and reduce it to the level of the imported pauper labor.

The demand for the enactment of some restrictive measure of this character comes not alone from American workingmen, but also from employers of labor in America. The employers of labor, who from inability or from patriotic motives, employ only American workingmen, are unable to compete in the markets with the corporations who employ the cheap imported labor.

As an evidence of the truth of this proposition, the glass manufacturers of Pittsburgh, including all the large employers of labor in that industry, in January, 1880, denounced the action of the manufacturers west of Pittsburgh in importing European workmen in place of discharged American workmen.

This evil has become so extensive, alarming, and great, that the attention of our foreign consuls has been directed to it.

[p. 8:]

APPENDIX.

SUMMARY OF TESTIMONY TAKEN BY THE COMMITTEE.

* * * *

EMILE BOUILLET, of Zanesville, Ohio, W. G. W. A., said:

"I was hired at Antwerp by an agent of Dean F. Williams, of Zanesville, Ohio, who came for a set of men (sixty). When I went to see him I asked him why he came to Europe for men. He replied 'that men were scarce and work plenty in the United States.' I told him we would expect the same wages paid in the United States. He said 'they would pay the New York tariff.' When we arrived at Zanesville we discovered that the New York tariff was 25 per cent. less than the regular price. I complained to the company of this misrepresentation and they answered that 'they did not authorize the payment of more than what they were then paying.' At Kent the company did not pay the price agreed upon. They brought them to Kent on a contract for three years. The men were not permitted to associate with American workingmen lest they might find out the true state of affairs. Two of these men were arrested and put in jail for some days for violating this contract. When we arrived a friend of one of us was met by a man whom he knew in Europe. As soon as they commenced to talk the manager ordered the arrest of the party. When we arrived at Mansfield, Ohio, a member of the firm came into the car and inquired if any of us could speak English; I answered that 'my father and I could.' He then warned us not to talk to the men."

Question by member of committee. What is the difference between the wages paid these foreigners and Americans?

Answer by John Schlicker. Between 28 and 50 per cent.

Question. Did any of these people show a disposition to become citizens?

Answer. I think not.

10   FOREIGN CONTRACT LABOR.

(material omitted)

WILLIAM ASHTON, of Philadelphia, Pa., W. G. W. A., said:

"My information is in regard to importation of foreigners to Baltimore, Md. These men were brought under a contract; they were window-glass blowers. The first importation took place in 1879; forty-eight were then brought over by Swindell Bros. The following year Baker Bros. imported seventeen, King Bros. twenty-two, and Swindell Bros. twenty-three. The first importation occurred during a strike; there was no strike when the second importation occurred. Some of the foreigners refused to work and were arrested, but discharged before a hearing was had; their clothing was retained by the firm and it was weeks before they could secure it. They were kept locked in houses, when not working, and could not be seen by the Americans. Most of them have since returned home, some being sent by the glass-blowers' association, and some by the Belgian consul, who complained bitterly of the treatment they received. The effect of their importation was the reduction of wages about 12 per cent. An injunction was issued against the American workmen from interfering with them and made perpetual by Judge Brown, of Baltimore. * * * *

(material omitted)

[Page 12:]

Copies of agreements with foreign workmen, executed in Belgium.

No. 1.

(Original in English.)

Agreement made by and between the firm of Day, Williams & Co., of Kent, Ohio, of the first part, and each of the signers hereto of the second part, exactly as if a separate agreement were made between said firm and each of said signers.

Each of the signers of the second part agrees and promises to work for the said first party at the business of window-glass making for the term of three (3) consecutive years beginning January 1, 1880, and to faithfully perform his duties; shall be paid the wages currently paid by the New York State manufacturers. Said first party agrees that the wages of each flattener shall be not less than at the rate of sixty (60) dollars per calendar month, and that the wages of each cutter shall be not less than at the rate of (50) fifty dollars per calendar month for work actually performed, or during the fire. It is agreed that said first party shall retain ten (10) per cent. of the wages of each and every workman until the expiration of this contract, as a guaranty of its faithful performance; said ten (10) per cent. to be forfeited by each and every workman who shall fail to perform the conditions of this contract. It is also agreed that said first party shall advance the passage money of the party of the second part to Kent, Ohio, and that in case any workman shall fail to perform the conditions of this contract, he shall repay to said first party the amount of said passage money. It is also agreed that said first party shall have the right to discharge any workman who

FOREIGN CONTRACT LABOR.   13

shall neglect his work through drunkenness or idleness, or who shall attempt to create dissatisfaction among the workmen. The said Day, Williams & Co., its successors and assigns, however constituted, shall always be taken as the party of the first part.

Signed by said first party by its firm name and by each of the signers of the second party by his own name, as of this second day of December, 1879. It is agreed that the flatteners shall receive $30 (thirty dollars) per month for all work done other than flattening.

DAY, WILLIAMS & CO.
HENRY PIERRE.
ADOLPH BRESSON.
AUGUST COENEN.

No. 2.

(Original in German.)

Agreement between the firm of Swindell Bros. of the first part, and John Schmidt, gatherer, and Carl Wagner, blower, of the second part.

The undersigned, of the second part, covenants and agrees with the party of the first part that they will for two consecutive years, beginning January 1st, 1882, work and duly perform such duties as instructed by the party of the first part, or his superintendents. The party of the first part covenants and agrees to pay the undersigned, who may duly perform their duties, the price generally paid by Baltimore manufacturers for the size of 16 by 24 inches, and all sheets shall be estimated at a sheet of 36 by 54 in. for 100 square feet. The party of the first part covenants and agrees that the wages of each glass-blower shall be an average of $80 per calendar month, on condition that he makes 180 boxes of 100 square feet per calendar month.

The gatherer shall receive 65 per cent. of the sum paid the blower for wages per calendar month for actual work performed during the fire. It is agreed that the party of the first part shall retain 10 per cent. of the wages of each and every workman until the expiration of this contract as a guarantee of the faithful performance of the provisions of this contract. The aforesaid 10 per cent. shall be forfeited by each and every workman who shall fail to comply with the provisions of this contract.

It is further agreed that the party of the first part shall advance the passage money of the parties of the second part.

It is further agreed that the party of the first part have the right to discharge any of the workmen for drunkenness, or neglect of duty, or for disturbing the peace, or creating dissatisfaction among them, or for joining any association of American workmen.

The said Swindell Bros., their heirs and assigns, shall be considered the parties of the first part, and they agree to pay each blower $12 per week and the gatherer $9 per week, on condition that each perform his work faithfully at every blowing. The parties of the first part agrees to make monthly settlements with the parties of the second part, after the advances for passage, &c., shall have been repaid. Provided you faithfully perform your work for the term of contract (two years), we will pay back the passage money from Europe to America.

Antwerp, Dec. 15, 1882.

SWINDELL BROS.
YOHONN SCHMIDT,
Gatherer.
CARL WAGENER,
Blower.

III. *Excerpts from 15 Cong. Rec. 5349-71 (June 19, 1884)*

(material omitted)

The bill was reported by the Committee on Labor with the following amendments:

At the end of section 5 insert the following:

" Nor shall this act be so construed as to prevent any person, or persons, partnership, or corporation from engaging, under contract or agreement, skilled workmen in foreign countries to perform labor in the United States in or upon any new industry not at present established in the United States: *Provided,* That skilled labor for that purpose can not be otherwise obtained; nor shall the provisions of this act apply to professional actors, lecturers, or singers.

Add as a new section the following:

SEC. 6. That all laws or parts of laws conflicting herewith be, and the same are hereby, repealed.

Mr. HOPKINS. The bill just read was prepared by my colleague on the committee, the gentleman from Ohio [Mr. FORAN]. He has also made a very careful, elaborate, and able report on the subject. I yield the control of the debate and the floor to him, reserving to myself a few minutes at the conclusion if I should think it proper to say anything in reply to arguments against the bill.

Mr. FORAN. Mr. Speaker, before proceeding with my argument I desire to state that in printing this bill the word " parol" was by some mistake printed " paid." At the proper time the committee will move that the word " paid " be stricken out wherever it occurs and the word " parol" inserted. There are a few other clerical errors which will also be remedied.

Mr. Speaker, this bill in no manner seeks to restrict or prohibit voluntary or free immigration. The oppressed of all lands, the victims of tyrant misrule, those persecuted for the free expression of opinion, as well as those who from choice or love of our beneficent institutions have sought a shelter and home beneath our flag, have ever been welcome to our shores, and will no doubt be ever welcome until the time shall come when population begins to press upon the limits of subsistence and we find the public domain no more than sufficient for our own people.

With this class of immigrants this bill has no concern. Its object is to restrict and prohibit the importation of foreigners to this country under contract to perform labor here. That is, its object is to prevent and prohibit men whose love of self is above their love of country and humanity from importing into this country large bodies of foreign laborers to take the places of and crowd out American laborers. It also prohibits the importation of skilled workmen to take the places of American skilled artisans.

We claim it to be a fact, an admitted fact, that during the last five or six years American capitalists have repeatedly sent agents to Europe, who, under instructions from their principals, have contracted with skilled workmen there to perform labor here, and that the passage of these men has been paid to this country; that after being shipped here by the ship-load they have been given the places of American workmen of greater skill and efficiency; and that the American workmen have been thrown out of employment and compelled to seek other avocations or starve.

We also claim that American capitalists and corporations have imported and shipped into this country, as so many cattle, large numbers of degraded, ignorant, brutal Italians and Hungarian laborers. American citizens, men who pay our taxes and fight our battles, have been replaced by these foreign serfs. This is the class of persons, this the species of immigration with which this bill seeks to deal. These men do not come here of their own volition. Many perhaps had never heard of America; they certainly know nothing of our institutions, our customs, or of the habits and characteristics of our people.

They do not initiate their coming, they do not intend to stay, and if they did they would not be a desirable acquisition to our population. They are brought here precisely in the same manner that the Chinese were brought here by the Six Companies of California. They are not freemen, and very many of them have no conception of freedom; they are virtually the slaves of those greedy corporations who bring them here.

That a system of importation or modern white-slave trade exists to an alarming extent is now generally conceded. The committee had before it and took the testimony of gentlemen well informed on this subject from Pennsylvania, Indiana, Ohio, New York, New Jersey, Maryland, and Massachusetts. All this testimony was published with the report which I prepared on this bill. Gentlemen of the House have no doubt read this report and testimony, and further allusion to it would be unnecessary. In addition to this, the report of the Senate Committee on Education and Labor, that is, the testimony taken by that committee in the city of New York last year, conclusively demonstrates that this system of slave labor is rapidly growing in the United States.

(material omitted)

IMPORTATION OF LABOR UNDER CONTRACT.

The House proceeded to consider the special order, being the bill reported by Mr. FORAN from the Committee on Labor, a bill (H. R. 2550) to prohibit the importation and migration of foreigners and aliens under contract or agreement to perform labor in the United States, its Territories, and the District of Columbia.

The bill was read, as follows:

Be it enacted, &c., That from and after the passage of this act it shall be unlawful for any person, company, partnership, or corporation, in any manner whatsoever, to enter into an agreement or contract with any foreigner or foreigners, alien or aliens, to perform labor or service of any kind in the United States, its Territories, or the District of Columbia, or to prepay the transportation, or in any way assist or encourage the importation or migration of any alien or aliens, any foreigner or foreigners, into the United States, its Territories, or the District of Columbia, under contract or agreement, paid or special, expressed or implied, made previous to the importation or migration of such alien or aliens, foreigner or foreigners.

SEC. 2. That all contracts or agreements, expressed or implied, paid or special, which may hereafter be made by and between any person, company, partnership, or corporation, and doing business within the United States, and any foreigner or foreigners, alien or aliens, to perform labor or service of any kind in the United States, its Territories, or the District of Columbia, previous to the migration or importation of such persons into the United States, shall be utterly void and of no effect.

SEC. 3. That for every violation of any of the provisions of sections 1 and 2 of this act the person, partnership, company, or corporation violating the same, by assisting, encouraging or soliciting the migration or importation of any alien or aliens, foreigner or foreigners, into the United States, its Territories, or the District of Columbia, to perform labor or service of any kind under contract or agreement, expressed or implied, paid or special, with such alien or aliens, foreigner or foreigners, previous to becoming residents or citizens of the United States, shall forfeit and pay for every such offense the sum of $1,000, which may be sued for and recovered by any person, including any such alien or foreigner who may be a party to any such contract or agreement, who may choose to bring such suit, as debts of like amount are now recovered in the circuit courts of the United States; the one-half or moiety of said sum to be paid to the person bringing suit to recover the same, and the remaining half or moiety into the Treasury of the United States; and separate suits may be brought for each alien or foreigner being a party to such contract or agreement aforesaid.

SEC. 4. That the master of any vessel who shall knowingly bring within the United States on any such vessel, and land, or permit to be landed, from any foreign port or place, any alien laborer, mechanic, or artisan who, previous to embarkation on such vessel, had entered into contract or agreement, paid or special, expressed or implied, to perform labor or service in the United States, shall be deemed guilty of a misdemeanor, and, on conviction thereof, shall be punished by a fine of not less than $500 for each and every such alien laborer, mechanic, or artisan so brought as aforesaid, and may also be imprisoned for a term not exceeding six months.

SEC. 5. That nothing in this act shall be so construed as to prevent any citizen of any foreign country temporarily residing in the United States, either in private or official capacity, from engaging, under contract or otherwise, persons not residents or citizens of the United States to act as private secretaries, servants, or domestics for such foreigner temporarily residing in the United States as aforesaid.

5350   CONGRESSIONAL RECORD—HOUSE.   JUNE 19,

(material omitted)

Mr. BLOUNT. I do not like to interrupt my friend, but he has been reading the statistics of immigration through several years; and I would like to know whether these statistics disclose what part of those immigrants came here under contracts as laborers?

Mr. FORAN. The statement does not show that fact. On that question our statistics are silent. From the testimony taken by the committee we learn that about one hundred and ten window-glass blowers were brought in 1879 and 1880 under contract to Baltimore. There were eighty glass-bottle blowers imported under contract about the same time into the States west of Ohio. I can not state the number brought to Ohio. I think the number was about one hundred. But with regard to the unskilled labor I reason this way: I find in three years a little over 80,000 Italians have been landed on our shores, and of this number nearly 70,000 are males.

During the same time I find a Hungarian immigration of 26,993, and of this number over 20,000 are males. I think these facts demonstrate conclusively that this is a forced and assisted immigration. If these people came here of their own volition, with the intent and purpose of making a home here, it is reasonable to suppose they would bring with them their wives and families. But the fact is they come in droves of males; and that their passage is paid by persons on this side is beyond doubt or question.

The strongest reason urged against Chinese immigration was the fact that it was confined almost exclusively to males, and that being without families, they gave no "hostages to fortune." It is certainly true that the family is the only sure foundation upon which any government can rest.

* * * *

[Page 5351]

Mr. BLOUNT. Do any of these persons who come here under contract remain and become naturalized?

Mr. FORAN. Not to any extent. A few hundred dollars is to an Italian laborer a fortune upon which he can live in squalid magnificence in sunny Italy the balance of his days. They generally return after having accumulated what to them seems a large and princely fortune. But even if they did not, when we consider their intellectual status, it is questionable indeed whether they would make desirable citizens. We ought not to feel anxious on that score.

* * * *

That large numbers of inferior, unskilled, degraded laborers are annually imported under contract to perform labor in the United States is known to everybody. That the direct competition of these people with American laborers will either drive out the American or greatly

[Page 5352]

reduce his wages no one will undertake to deny; that a general reduction of wages will lower the moral, social, and intellectual tone of American labor is equally certain; that degraded, unskilled, pauperized labor results in decreased production and consequent loss of national wealth is an axiom understood and appreciated by every student in political economy; and that high rates of wages tend to elevate workingmen, render them more efficient, more skillful, more inventive, more productive, and beneficial to the community, has been conclusively demonstrated by the industrial history of the civilized world. These are the considerations that induce me to support this bill, and which prompted me to introduce it in this House.

* * * *

[Page 5355-56]
[Mr. CONNOLLY:]

During the present session a bill was introduced by the gentleman from Ohio [Mr. FORAN] and referred to the Committee on Labor, who have reported it favorably with amendments to the House. This bill aims to prohibit the importation and migration of foreigners and aliens under contract to perform labor in the United States. The necessity for legislation of this kind shows the existence of a most pernicious and dangerous system now in force in this country, a system by which American mechanics and laborers are made the mere slaves of their employers. By "American" I mean not only native but adopted citizens who have become a part of the body-politic and have adopted our manners and customs. The census reports show that of the persons engaged in manufactures and mechanical and mining industries in the United States in the year 1880 the nativity was:

United States	2,611,325
Ireland	284,175
Germany	368,110
Great Britain	225,730
Scandinavia	44,615
British America	153,935
Other countries	149,222

By this table it appears that of the persons engaged in manufactures and mechanical and mining industries in the year 1880 2,611,325 were natives and 1,225,787, or nearly one-third of the whole number engaged, were of foreign birth.

We must bear in mind also that a large percentage of those classed as natives are the children of foreign parents. Most of these men came here under the influence of the policy adopted at an early day in our history—a policy that encouraged *bona fide* immigration, and that had in view the adoption as citizens of the immigrants. That policy has succeeded in bringing to our shores millions of the most hardy, industrious, and respectable workingmen, mechanics, artisans, and farmers of Continental Europe. By the amalgamation of the races a people have grown up in this country the equals if not the superiors of any race in the world. So that it is not against the continued immigration of foreigners who come here of their own volition and for the purpose of becoming citizens of the Republic, with the settled purpose to subject themselves to our institutions and laws, that the proposed legislation is directed, but against that new and degraded class who are brought here by the agents of incorporated companies to work for whatever pay their employers wish to give them, who have no knowledge of or respect for our laws, and who do not know the meaning of the word citizen. It is against this "pauper labor" of Europe, brought to our doors by the men who have always been loudest in their profession of regard for the interests of American labor; this ignorant, servile, unskilled, and debased labor, whose direct tendency is to degrade and drag down to its own level the labor of this country, that we protest.

* * * *

* * * *

[Mr. FERRELL (NJ):]

The agitation now prevailing throughout the country is to prevent the fixed contract of laborers in Europe for a term of years to labor here, ostensibly for the purpose of reducing the established prices of wages for labor in the American market to that of the countries from which these people emigrate, as shown by the recent large importation of Hungarian, Belgian, and Italian laborers under special contracts by corporations and companies for the accomplishment of certain ends. The daily habits and wants of these people, who are becoming a source of great agitation in many parts of the country, are entirely different from those of our laborers and open to very severe criticism. Their wants are prescribed to correspond with their ability to purchase, the poorer classes living almost entirely on rice and vegetables, to which they add, when opportunity will permit, small pieces of meat, generally fish, because it costs nothing to produce it.

The article of clothing, which is a very important item with our people, is a mere bagatelle with these laborers. They use the cheapest kind of goods and the least number of pieces to cover them, and it is consequently an insignificant item in their expenditures. Thus a Chinaman or Hungarian could live where an American would starve, and it is to these conditions of life of these laborers from China and elsewhere, under their forms of government, as compared with the American laborer under the institutions of his Government, that they are able to underbid our workmen, and ofttimes reducing them to the same condition of life.

The large importation of Hungarians and Italians and Belgians from Europe under special contract to work in the coal mines and factories of Ohio, New York, Pennsylvania, Maryland, West Virginia, and New Jersey, and many other parts of the country, in the recent past has caused the agitation from all classes to assume giant proportions.

* * * *

[Page 5360]

The testimony of leading men in the labor ranks of our country who testified before the Committee on Labor and Education last year, and also before the Committee on Labor of this House recently, on this subject, unanimously agree that to cure this evil the passage of the bill we are now considering must be secured.

Ex-Mayor Powderly, of Scranton, whose testimony carries great weight, representing 500,000 workingmen, says:

These imported men show no disposition to become citizens of this country, but, on the contrary, seek to obtain a certain sum of money, which they consider a competence, and with it return to Italy or Hungary. I have seen eight of these people and one woman living in a small house, without beds or furniture, sleeping on the floor, and have been informed by reliable authority that these nine persons' expenses for one month was only $27. I have seen them in the Frostburg region of Maryland, where they had been brought by agents, who engaged them at Castle Garden, living in a wooden building, sleeping on bunks, this building being fenced in to prevent them being communicated with by the people whose places they had taken. The diet of these men was water and mush, with a small quantity of meat on Sunday. These men are brought into competition with skilled as well as unskilled labor, and it is fast becoming as bad as the competition of the Chinese in the West.

* * * *

[Page 5367]

Mr. O'NEILL, of Missouri. I yield five minutes to the gentleman from Maine [Mr. DINGLEY].

Mr. DINGLEY. While many of the provisions of the bill as it now stands are imperfect and unwise, yet the evil against which it is aimed is to my mind one which demands legislation. Voluntary immigration of foreigners who come here to improve their condition and make this country their home, immigration of men who land on our shores as freemen, at liberty to avail themselves of American opportunities and American wages, has always been considered wise and acceptable. Such immigration does not interfere with our protective system, which is designed to discourage the importation of the products of the cheaper labor of Europe and Canada and protect American industry and labor, because whenever a voluntary immigrant comes here free to make his own engagements on arrival and to become an American citizen he accepts not European but American wages and becomes identified with American interests.

The evil against which this measure is directed is not voluntary immigration, but the importation of foreign laborers, usually in large companies on contracts entered into abroad, under foreign conditions and at foreign wages. It is the importation of men who come here without freedom of action after they land, to serve under overseers who control their movements for a definite job or time, without an expectation of making a home here and generally without wife or family.

Such an importation of contract labor is contrary to a sound public policy, contrary to our ideas of freedom, and contrary to the best interests of our country. In the State which I have the honor in part to represent there was imported last year several hundred Italian laborers to construct a railroad at wages far below the American standard. They came not to become citizens, not to live as American laborers live, not to add their earnings to the wealth of the country; but they came as Italians, lived as Italian laborers of the lower sort, disturbed the peace and quiet of our State during their brief stay, and then left to return to Italy or to be contracted elsewhere by their overseer. It makes no difference what the nationality of such servile laborers may be, it is contrary to the best interests of our country to encourage or allow their importation under contract which renders them no longer freemen.

[Here the hammer fell.]

* * * *

[Page 5368]

Mr. CUTCHEON. Mr. Speaker, it is very little indeed that one can say on such a subject as this in the limited time accorded to me by the gentleman from Missouri [Mr. O'NEILL]; but I will avail myself of the permission granted to extend my remarks in the RECORD.

I desire simply to say that I am in hearty sympathy with the purpose of this bill, as I understand it. I think there are very serious imperfections in the draught of the bill, which I hope may be remedied by amendment. Some of the amendments already offered will, if adopted, remove some of these imperfections.

WHAT THE BILL MEANS.

As I understand this bill, it is designed to prevent the depressing influence upon American labor of the introduction from foreign lands of laborers who have previously entered into contract to work for less wages than the current wages of American labor in the same class of industry. With that purpose I am heartily in sympathy. It is a part of the great "American system" by which we seek to prevent the hurtful and destructive competition of the ignorant, half-paid, and half-civilized laborers of Asia and Europe with our own. It is supplementary to the legislation restrictive of Chinese immigration, and has in view the same object.

NOT TO PREVENT BONA FIDE IMMIGRATION.

This legislation is not designed to interfere with the usual and ordinary voluntary immigration of those foreigners who come in good faith to our shores seeking a new home and the blessings of a better civilization; who bring with them their earthly stores, be the same more or less; who set up here under new roof-trees the *lares* and *penates* which have made sacred the homes of their ancestors, with the purpose of casting here their lot, of building here new homes, and finding here their final resting-place after having served a true allegiance to the government of their adoption.

It is designed rather to exclude the degraded *lazzaroni* of Italy, the almost servile laborers of Hungary and other southern European countries who come here moved not by the healthy and normal impulse of migration, but incited and instigated by the mercenary agents of corporations whose only object is not the building up of an intelligent and manly laboring class, but only to procure the cheapest labor with which to wage war against those laborers who are seeking by associated effort to compel a more equitable division of the joint product of labor and capital and the maintenance of the American scale of wages for workingmen.

Foreigners who come to our shores in good faith, to seek more friendly skies, more favorable laws, higher civilization, freer schools for their children, better fortunes for themselves, and all the blessings of American citizenship, always have been and always should be welcome.

Not many of us would be able to trace our lineage very far back before we should find where we ourselves or our immediate ancestors were emigrants to these shores; and we should be alike false to ourselves and to our history, as well as false to our future, did we seek to prevent or to hamper *bona fide* and legitimate immigration.

THE GOTHS AND VANDALS.

But the laborers against whom this bill is directed are the Goths and Vandals of the modern era. They come only to lay waste, to degrade, and to destroy. They bring with them ignorance, degraded morals, a low standard of civilization, and no motive of intended American citizenship. Like the vast flights of grasshoppers and locusts that a few years since devastated our Western prairie States, they sweep down upon our fields of labor to devour and strip from us the benefit of our customs and of the laws protecting American labor, and then take their flight again back to the breeding places from which they came.

There is nothing in our history, nothing in our traditions, nothing in our laws or in our duties to the race that requires us longer to submit to these invasions.

* * * *

[Page 5371]

Mr. HOPKINS. I move the correction of the following clerical errors: Strike out "paid," wherever it occurs, and insert in lieu thereof the word "parol." Also strike out "expressed" and insert in lieu thereof "express." In section 3, line 2, strike out the words "and two." In section 4, line 9, strike out "less" and insert "more."

There was no objection, and the corrections were made accordingly.

The SPEAKER. The question now recurs on ordering the bill as amended to be engrossed and read a third time.

The House divided; and there were—ayes 102, noes 17.

Mr. DARGAN demanded the yeas and nays.

The yeas and nays were not ordered:

The bill was ordered to be engrossed and read a third time; and being engrossed, it was accordingly read the third time, and passed.

Mr. HOPKINS moved to reconsider the vote by which the bill was passed; and also moved that the motion to reconsider be laid on the table.

The latter motion was agreed to.

* * * *

IV. Excerpts from S. Rep. No. 48-820 at 1 (June 28, 1884)

48TH CONGRESS, }   SENATE.   { REPORT
1st Session. }   { No. 820.

IN THE SENATE OF THE UNITED STATES.

JUNE 28, 1884.—Ordered to be printed.

Mr. BLAIR, from the Committee on Education and Labor, submitted the following

REPORT:

[To accompany bill H. R. 2550.]

The Committee on Education and Labor, to whom was referred the bill (H. R. 2550) entitled "An act to prohibit the importation and migration of foreigners and aliens under contract or agreement to perform labor in the United States, its Territories, and the District of Columbia," have considered the same, and hereby report the bill back to the Senate favorably, and recommend its passage. The general facts and considerations which induce the committee to recommend the passage of this bill are set forth in the report of the committee of the House.

The committee report the bill back without amendment—although there are certain features thereof which might well be changed or modified —in the hope that the bill may not fail of passage during the present session. Especially would the committee have otherwise recommended amendments, substituting for the expression "labor and service" wherever it occurs in the body of the bill the words "manual labor" or "manual service" as sufficiently broad to accomplish the purposes of the bill, and that such amendments would remove objections which a sharp and perhaps unfriendly criticism may urge to the proposed legislation. The committee, however, believing that the bill in its present form will be construed as including only those whose labor or service is manual in character, and being very desirous that the bill become a law before the adjournment, have reported the bill without change.

The following is the report of the House committee. To the facts collected in the appendix may be added many more which can be found in the testimony taken during the recent investigation of your committee, by order of the Senate, upon the relations between labor and capital:

[House Report No. 444, Forty-eighth Congress, first session]

(material omitted)

V. Excerpts from 15 Cong. Rec. 6057-67 (July 5, 1884)

1884.	CONGRESSIONAL RECORD—SENATE.	6057

(material omitted)

perform labor in the United States, its Territories, and the District of Columbia.

The PRESIDENT *pro tempore.* The question is on the motion of the Senator from New Hampshire.

Mr. MORGAN. I ask that the bill be read for information.

The PRESIDENT *pro tempore.* The bill will be read for information if there be no objection. The Chair hears none, and it will be read.

The Secretary read the bill.

The PRESIDENT *pro tempore.* The question is on agreeing to the motion of the Senator from New Hampshire that this bill be now taken up for consideration. [Putting the question.] The noes appear to have it.

Mr. BLAIR. My attention was diverted by three or four Senators upon five or six different things, and I should like to understand what was the question just taken.

The PRESIDENT *pro tempore.* The question was on agreeing to the motion of the Senator from New Hampshire that this bill be now considered, on which the Chair announced that the noes appeared to prevail.

Mr. BLAIR. Before the vote is taken I ask unanimous consent to say a word.

The PRESIDENT *pro tempore.* The Senator from New Hampshire asks unanimous consent to speak on this question. Is there objection? The Chair hears none.

Mr. BLAIR. This is a bill which comes to us from the House of Representatives after considerable discussion and with practically a unanimous vote. I think I may be justified in stating that as bearing upon the question whether it is likely to consume a great length of time in its discussion at this late hour of the session. I am exceedingly anxious, as is the Committee on Education and Labor, who reported it unanimously, that it be considered and disposed of at this session. It is aimed at a practice that no individual as far as I know, certainly no party, in this country pretends to justify. Its object is to remove a great and rapidly growing public evil, an evil striking at the interests of millions of our countrymen, and those of our countrymen who can least bear the existence, much less any increase, of the evil of which they complain.

Of course it is well understood. I hardly need take the time of the Senate in stating the fact that the practice has grown up on the part of many of the employers of the country of sending their agents abroad to England, France, Italy, Hungary, Germany, Austria, and in fact to all European countries with hardly an exception, for the purpose of contracting with bodies of working people, paying their expenses of transportation to this country, in order that their cheap labor may be brought in competition with that of our own citizens. We claim to believe in protective tariffs, some of us, and we loudly proclaim to the people of this country, especially to the laboring people, that the protection of their labor is the primary object for which we institute those tariffs. That is the great general consideration which we who believe in a protective tariff allege as the one that justifies and demands of a patriotic American citizen that he maintain a tariff upon imported goods. The protection of American labor is the object, and to us the revenue which results from a tariff is a secondary consideration; while another great party in this country claims that revenue is the primary consideration, and I believe also alleges that in its adjustment the American laborer should be protected as far as possible from competition with foreign goods in our own markets. But it is obvious to any one, it has become now a great national fact, a national evil, too, that the higher wages we pay to our American laborers are more endangered by the practice which has been initiated and which is increasing, of bringing the foreign laborer directly in contact within our own borders with the American laborer under a contract to receive the compensation which he might have received in his own country in the manufacture of the same goods. Thus it is that by the importation of the living laborer a vastly greater evil is likely to be done than by the importation of the production of that same labor expended in its own country.

The object of this bill is to extinguish that evil. It has been a subject of great complaint for many years. The House of Representatives have sent us what I conceive to be a very well-matured bill, which if adopted and enforced will eradicate the evil. I do not think that it is susceptible of any reasonable or rational objection. It is very true that in slight particulars in the forms of expression employed it might be somewhat limited. I would not object to verbal amendments in several of the sections. In fact, if the bill is considered I shall ask that such amendments be made as will I think absolutely remove any of the objections which have been raised by an adverse, hostile criticism to the bill.

I trust the Senate under these circumstances will not dispose of this bill in quite so abrupt a fashion as to refuse it any consideration whatever. Nothing is immediately pressing upon the Senate. No conference reports are now here. The work of the Senate is now being transacted by conference committees. The fact that I have unanimous consent to make these remarks shows that there is nothing pressing upon the Senate at this time. Therefore I respectfully and earnestly appeal to the Senate to give this bill consideration. Of course it can be interrupted if more important business shall be placed before the Senate.

FOREIGN CONTRACT LABOR.

Mr. BLAIR. I now move that the Senate proceed to consider Order of Business 863, being the bill (H. R. 2550) to prohibit the importation and migration of foreigners and aliens under contract or agreement to

)The conference committees always have the floor." But I do ask the Senate that this bill may receive such consideration as under its rules it may properly claim.

The PRESIDENT *pro tempore.* The question is on agreeing to the motion of the Senator from New Hampshire that this bill be now considered.

Mr. HAWLEY. Is that motion debatable?

The PRESIDENT *pro tempore.* It is not debatable. The Senator from New Hampshire was speaking by unanimous consent.

Mr. BLAIR. If the Senator wishes to say anything I hope he may have consent.

The question being put, it was declared that the noes appeared to prevail.

Mr. BLAIR. I ask for a division.

The question being put, there were on a division—ayes 4, noes 8; no quorum voting.

Mr. BLAIR. There is a quorum in the Capitol. I do not like to yield this point, and I ask for the yeas and nays.

The yeas and nays were ordered.

Mr. BLAIR. I am informed by Senators that to insist upon this call will probably disclose the absence of a quorum and interrupt the further transaction of business.

The PRESIDENT *pro tempore.* The absence of a quorum is already disclosed. No further business can be done until a quorum appears.

Mr. BLAIR. Very well.

The PRESIDENT *pro tempore.* The roll will be called.

The Secretary proceeded to call the roll.

* * * *

[Page 6065]

FOREIGN-LABOR CONTRACTS.

Mr. BLAIR. Mr. President——

The PRESIDENT *pro tempore.* The pending order will be laid before the Senate.

The CHIEF CLERK. "A bill (H. R. 2550) to prohibit the importation and migration of foreigners and aliens under contract or agreement to perform labor in the United States, its Territories, and the District of Columbia."

Mr. BLAIR. I ask that the reading of the report be continued.

The PRESIDENT *pro tempore.* The reading of the report will be continued.

Mr. BROWN. As this is a very important measure, and as it is very difficult to keep a quorum, and as we can not discuss a great question of this character at the close of the session as we would have to do and as we ought to do if we mean to consider it properly, I move that the further consideration of the bill be postponed until the third Thursday in December next.

Mr. BLAIR. I hope the Senator, if the question is to be taken, will change the time to the first Monday of December, at 2 o'clock.

Mr. BROWN. I think there have been other bills put down for that day.

Mr. BLAIR. No; later than that Thursday.

Mr. BROWN. I only want to avoid having the same time fixed for other measures.

Mr. BLAIR. I do not think that time is fixed for any measure, but I can not say in regard to that. The Secretary will be able to inform us whether other measures have been postponed to an earlier part of the month. I think as this is caught between heaven and earth and about half discussed and half not discussed, half passed and half not passed, it ought to receive attention earlier than any other if it is postponed, and therefore I wish that it be taken up substantially as the unfinished business at the commencement of the next session.

Mr. BROWN. My motion now is for the second Thursday in December.

The PRESIDENT *pro tempore.* The Senator from Georgia moves that the further consideration of this bill be postponed until the second Thursday of December next.

Mr. BLAIR. I gather the impression that a majority of the Senate is in favor of postponing this bill; but I would ask unanimous consent that the remainder of the report, which was about half or two-thirds read, may be printed in connection with what is already spread upon the record. ["No objection!"]

The PRESIDENT *pro tempore.* Pending the motion of the Senator from Georgia, the Senator from New Hampshire asks unanimous consent that the residue of the report not yet read be printed in the RECORD. Is there objection? The Chair hears none.

The matter ordered to be printed in the RECORD is as follows:

* * * *

[Page 6067]

The PRESIDENT *pro tempore.* The question is on agreeing to the motion of the Senator from Georgia, that the further consideration of the bill be postponed until the second Thursday of December next.

The question being put, it was declared that the ayes appeared to prevail.

Mr. BLAIR. I ask for the yeas and nays. ["No!" "No!"] I withdraw the call on the suggestion that it may disable us from doing business.

The PRESIDENT *pro tempore.* The yeas have it, and the motion to postpone is agreed to.

* * * *

VI. Excerpts from 16 Cong. Rec. 1621-35 (Feb. 13, 1885)

1885.	CONGRESSIONAL RECORD—SENATE.	1621

(material omitted)   *(material omitted)*

FOREIGN-LABOR CONTRACTS.

The Senate, as in Committee of the Whole, proceeded to consider the bill (H. R. 2550) to prohibit the importation and migration of foreigners and aliens under contract or agreement to perform labor in the United States, its Territories, and the District of Columbia.

Mr. BLAIR. My intimation to the Senate was that I did not desire to be heard in a set speech on the general subject; but I wish to have a few amendments made, which are chiefly formal.

In section 1, lines 9 and 10, I move that the words "to perform service or labor" be stricken out. They seem to be superfluous.

The amendment was agreed to.

Mr. BLAIR. In section 2, line 6, after the word "service," I move to insert the words "or having reference to the performance of service or labor by any person."

The amendment was agreed to.

Mr. BLAIR. In section 2, line 8, I move to strike out the words "such persons" and to insert "the person or persons whose labor or service is contracted for."

The amendment was agreed to.

Mr. BLAIR. In section 3, line 12, after the word "person," I move to insert the words "who shall first bring his action therefor."

The amendment was agreed to.

Mr. BLAIR. In section 3, line 14, I move to strike out the words "who may choose to bring such suit."

The amendment was agreed to.

Mr. BLAIR. In section 5, line 15, after the word "singers," I move to insert the words, "nor to persons employed strictly as personal or domestic servants."

The amendment was agreed to.

The PRESIDING OFFICER (Mr. ALLISON in the chair). The Chair suggests a verbal correction in line 8 of section 3. The word "poral" is printed instead of "parol." That change will be made.

Mr. BLAIR. They are retained.

Mr. McPHERSON. In the eleventh and twelfth lines?

Mr. BLAIR. Certainly.

Mr. McPHERSON. I understood the Senator's amendment to strike out all the words "to perform service or labor" in the section, in lines 9 and 10 and in lines 11 and 12.

Mr. BLAIR. I thought the Senator must have misapprehended it. I failed to make myself understood. I gave as a reason for striking out the words in the ninth and tenth lines the fact that they were in the eleventh and twelfth lines.

Mr. McPHERSON. I am entirely wrong, for I supposed the Senator's amendment included the striking out of the words in the eleventh and twelfth lines.

Mr. BLAIR. No. With those words retained the section has precisely the effect which the Senator understands it to have had originally in the way of the protection of American labor.

I hardly know whether it is worth while to engage in any discussion. I had not contemplated it. This bill has been before the country for a long time and the subject-matter to which it relates has been much discussed. I had supposed the measure to be entirely in consonance with the principles of the Declaration of Independence and the rights of mankind. I certainly would not have purposely made an assault upon the muniments of American liberty or of human liberty. I am willing, I am really if I know myself anxious, that all men should have a chance; that poor men should have a chance, and that the poor classes in all parts of the world should get up a little, step after step, and rise to the full dignity of freedom and of individual sovereignty; that every man should be a king, and that every man should have all the rights that any other man has.

The bill is aimed at slavery rather than freedom. It is designed to prevent substantially the cooly practices which have been initiated and carried on to a considerable extent between America and Europe, and which we have undertaken to prohibit not alone in the forum of general public sentiment, but in the legislation which both parties and the majorities in both branches of Congress have seen fit to enact.

The bill does not aim to prohibit the natural flow of immigration from any other land to the United States. It leaves all natural laws, business laws, social laws, industrial laws to their natural effect and operation. But it does undertake to prohibit the efforts of corporations and of individuals, of capitalists, which have been put forth to some extent in this country to introduce into it the cheap and servile labor of foreign lands, and, when it is not necessary to do so for the good of the American people and the promotion of American industries, the skilled labor of other countries, because that labor, as we know, can be commanded at very greatly reduced wages as compared with what we pay to the working people of our own country.

There have been repeated instances in all the great industries of this country where such importation has been made for the purpose of effecting a reduction of the natural rate of wages in this country such as our working people seem to be entitled to, such as are indispensable in order that they may participate by purchase (for we have nothing that we do not pay for with money in this world) in their due and just proportion of the benefits of civilization and of the principles of American liberty realized. It was in evidence before the committee of the House, and I was so informed personally by some of the leading representatives of the laboring element of the glass industry in this country, that the introduction of skilled glass workmen from the old countries by the practice which is prohibited by the bill—that is, by contracts made in advance for the services of skilled laborers abroad—had the effect to reduce at least 25 per cent. the previously existing rates and the natural rates of wages to those workmen who were engaged in that industry. That is one illustration.

I suppose it is not necessary to quote the newspapers of the country to show that the tremendous difficulties, disturbances, dangers not alone to capital but to life, and affording a most dangerous example to the country at large, in the Hocking Valley mines in Ohio, are attributed by the laboring people there to precisely the same practice that the bill is designed to prohibit; and I have seen it recently stated that already the pecuniary loss to that valley is upward of $4,000,000, and when the trouble is to end and how it is to end is beyond the prophetic vision of any man.

In regard to the suggestion that Patrick can not send for Mike, his relative and friend in the old country, it would almost seem to be trifling with the general framework and purposes of the bill. There is an express provision that this measure shall not be held to interfere with any individual assisting any member of his family or any relative to migrate from any foreign country to the United States.

It would be utterly impossible, probably, to fashion a bill which could not be subjected to some criticism. It would probably be utterly impossible to so frame this bill that in some direction, to some extent, it might not by an adverse and unfriendly spirit of interpretation, be claimed that it verged somewhat in the direction of an impairment of individual rights. But here is an evil which in the estimation of those who are interested in this bill is a very great one, and we must so frame our legislation as to reach the evil. If it should be found in its practical working that further legislation should be had to relieve it of some of its harsher operations, if evils shall be developed in its operation, then that can be remedied. It is comparatively a new field of legislation.

The bill has been prepared with a great deal of care and thought; and by those who have suffered from the evil and who are interested in the Declaration of Independence as much as the Senator from Connecticut or as myself, it has been thought to reach with its remedial provisions the evil under which they suffer. I am not averse to any criticism or discussion of the bill nor to any amendment of it which seems to be consistent with the principles of the Declaration of Independence and not subversive of the general purposes of the bill.

(material omitted)

(material omitted)

Mr. HAWLEY. Mr. President, I do not share the apprehensions of the Senator from Kansas [Mr. INGALLS] as to the future of this country, socially or politically. I am aware that there are many disturbing elements; but I see abundant signs of hope and comfort. These are but merely wrinkles on the great body of politics—little local humors. I am satisfied that the great and generous influences of civilization and of Christianity are abundantly capable of coping with them. I know there are some ranting men who talk about a forcible distribution of property, who pose all over the country as the enemies of property; but there is no land in which there is so general a distribution of wealth as here. Any man who has saved a hundred dollars or obtained for himself a cabin, however humble, or five acres of the sand and pine lands of the South, has given bonds to society against these pernicious errors. He is on the side of law and order; he is not ready to divide what he has. If he is worth $500 he is much more likely to take a musket and fall in at the command of the governor and the sheriff to repress riots than the millionaire who, perhaps, takes his yacht and escapes the danger, having bought foreign exchange. The safety of the country is in the hands of the poor men who have something or who mean to save something, if you omit any respect for their moral and Christian principles.

But, sir, indiscriminate legislation of the kind proposed here, a prohibition of immigration to poor men, would not tend to correct the evils against which the Senator warns us. The dynamite conspirator or the roaring socialist who would destroy all the natural rights, as we consider them, of property, can easily raise money enough to pay the twenty-five or thirty or forty dollars needed for transportation. The professional agitator will not be excluded by any bills like this. I am not willing to put a brand upon immigration by the wholesale. The dangerous men are not alone those who come from abroad, not those ill-informed and ill-educated poor laborers who came from other lands. The dangerous men have some money either from their own resources or by levying upon others, and have a good deal of education, such as it may be. They do not lack for intellectual acumen; they do not lack for the facility of expressing their ideas in common language. They are the men who make the trouble.

I acknowledge freely the evils. I want to correct them. I object to going carelessly and recklessly and too sweepingly at the work. The contracts that bring a body of poor laborers over here, paying their transportation under an agreement that they shall work not alone till they have paid their fare, but shall work for months and years for wage below those of the ordinary American laborer—those contracts are shameful, they are criminal, they are wrong, they are against natural right, against American law and the spirit of our institutions. They ought not to be permitted. They endeavor to establish a new system of slavery here. As I said substantially in my first remarks, they attempt to introduce a peasantry, a class of peons, a degraded class, to be considered as permanently belonging as the basis of society underneath those who may rule and govern the land. I would repress those evils. I would forbid them by all reasonable legislation. At the same time I would be very careful not to interfere with honest immigration; I would be very careful not to affix the brand of crime to deeds that are not only naturally right but exceedingly commendable; and that is what I fear this bill may do. I have specified the class of deeds that under this bill may be fined heavily, fined a thousand dollars, and which of themselves actually reflect great credit upon the men committing the deeds. I do think that a criminal law, a law making that a crime which is not by nature a crime, ought to be very carefully drawn; that is all. I denounce the evils, but I will not hurt the right by reckless and sweeping legislation.

* * * *

[Pages 1630-31]

* * * *

Mr. MORGAN. Will the Senator from New Hampshire allow me to inquire whether he puts laborers who are coming here from Europe, for instance the Irish and Germans and Italians, upon a footing with the Chinese? Does he think they are not better people than the Chinese?

Mr. BLAIR. If they come here by virtue of a contract of this kind by which their compensation is to be restricted to a lower rate of wages than the natural rate of wages which they would obtain in fair competition with our own laboring people, the effect upon American labor is precisely that which we undertook to remedy and to prohibit by the anti-Chinese act.

Mr. MORGAN. My relations with foreign people both by affinity and by blood are of such a character that I could scarcely admit that the English people, the Irish people, the Welsh people, the Scotch people, the German people, or the Italian people are to be placed by the people of the United States in the same category that we place the Chinese. It is very true that we found ourselves necessitated to pass "cooly laws" to exclude cooly labor from this country, and those laws apply to all countries in Asia where the cooly system obtains.

If you will look over our statutes you will find that there is no definition of what is a cooly. We go to the East for that definition. We find it there in a social caste. A cooly in the East is a man whose business in life it is to labor under employment, having a master or a supervisor, or, as we call it in this country, a boss, who manages all of his affairs, hires him out, receives his wages, and doles out to him a part of it after having taken out his brokerage or his commission. That system obtains in India and in China, and through that system we were getting into this country, as they were doing also into Cuba and elsewhere, a large number of very inferior and very degraded people, people that belonged to a different class from those that possess the Anglo-Saxon blood; and we thought it was our duty, for the protection of our race, to legislate against the introduction of those coolies.

It was not merely a labor question, it was a social question, a question of the infusion of lower blood into the social element in this country. So we pass laws to restrain the importation of coolies. We went on afterward, when we found that the Pacific coast was being swarmed with Chinese, a very inferior and disagreeable and repulsive class of people, and we passed law after law for their exclusion. Some of these laws were vetoed by the President of the United States on the ground that they were in conflict with the Burlingame treaty. None of them, I believe, were vetoed because we were doing violence to any national public policy in their enactment, but those of us who sustained these laws I think were largely if not entirely actuated by the idea that it was a very false and dangerous policy to introduce this lower race into this country at all. We were not solely actuated by the idea of their competition with our home laborers, but it was more a question of race than anything else.

Some of us were born and raised in the slave States. We had received as an inheritance from our ancestors that crime, as it has been called a crime, which was perpetrated by the people of the North upon this country, and by whom it was inflicted upon the people of the South. It was something that we were born to as an inheritance; we had no agency at all in starting it up; and having seen the difficulties that it produced in the land, having seen the bloodshed that it led to through the strife between sections as well as between races, we thought that it was a proper thing to do to exclude the coming in of any more of the inferior Asiatic or African races into this land. So we voted for the laws prohibiting the Chinese from coming here.

That cooly system has been two or three times alluded to to-day by the Senator from New Hampshire as a justification of this line of enactment that we are now proceeding with. That includes necessarily the proposition that the men whom we are excluding by this law from migrating must be put on the same basis as the coolies. I object to that. I object to it in the name of those men who assisted us in winning our independence. I object to it in the name of those men who assisted us in winning our second independence from Great Britain in the war of 1812. I object to it in the name of those people who are represented to-day on this floor in the persons of Scotchmen, Irishmen, and Englishmen who are here. There are men on this floor to-day who came as laborers to this country, some as ordinary mechanics, and some who were diggers in mines are Senators on this floor. The law that you propose to enact, that the Senator from New Hampshire proposes now to spread all over the country except New Hampshire and Vermont and the Northeast, would have excluded these Senators from coming here unless they had the manhood to work their passage, or had the friends abroad, not in this country, to have advanced them money enough to pay their expenses to get here.

I am opposed on principle, I am opposed in deference to the traditions of this country, and I am opposed from a sense of respect for the work that these men have done in this country, to placing these people who are coming from abroad, under contracts to do labor in this land, upon the basis of the coolies. I do not want to extend the cooly system to them. I do not want to disgrace and dishonor them in that way, and I shall never vote for it.

(material omitted)

[Pages 1632-33:]

* * * *

I do not propose to engage in any class legislation while I am here. There is nothing in the bill that is not directed expressly to class legislation. The classes legislated for and protected by the bill are not the agriculturists, they are not the house-builders and the ordinary mechanics of the country. They are almost wholly and exclusively the miners, the men who delve about the iron-works, and the men who do the ruder sorts of work about the manufacturing establishments of this land. When any Senator will take the bill and analyze it, and submit it to the quiet judgment of his mind, he must be convinced that the whole purpose of it is class legislation.

It is not legislation for the people of the United States at large. Certain particular classes—not named, I grant you, but nevertheless as clearly designated as if they had been named—are provided for in the bill, and no others. In that sense it is vicious legislation; vicious because it is class legislation; vicious because it violates the traditions of the Anglo-Saxon race in legislation by converting the ordinary and natural rights to make a contract into a crime; vicious in that, even in the admission of people into this country, it discriminates in favor of professional actors, lecturers, or singers. It makes an express exception and provision for professional actors, lecturers, and singers, leaving out all the other classes of professional men.

Mr. BLAIR. Not at all; personal or domestic servants are also excepted. That has been put in by an amendment.

Mr. MORGAN. Yes, personal or domestic servants. "Nor shall the provisions of this act apply to professional actors, lecturers, or singers," and, says the Senator from New Hampshire, "nor shall it apply to body servants."

Mr. BLAIR. "Personal or domestic servants."

Mr. MORGAN. Personal or domestic servants are excepted; that is to say, a gentleman who has got the money can come here and bring his personal or domestic servants with him from abroad; but if he happens to be a lawyer, an artist, a painter, an engraver, a sculptor, a great author, or what not, and he comes under employment to write for a newspaper, or to write books, or to paint pictures, as we are informed that a recent Secretary of State sent abroad for an artist to paint his picture, he comes under the general provisions of the bill.

Mr. BLAIR. The Senator will observe that it is only the importation of such people under contract to labor that is prohibited.

Mr. MORGAN. Of course; I understand.

Mr. BLAIR. If that class of people are liable to become the subject-matter of such importation, then the bill applies to them. Perhaps the bill ought to be further amended.

Mr. MORGAN. People who can instruct us in morals and religion and in every species of elevation by lectures and by acting plays in the theaters and by singing are not prohibited. The Senator wants to introduce those people into this country free; there is to be no tariff on them, no prohibitory duty. Let them come and act and sing and play as much as they please for the enlightenment of humanity on this side of the Atlantic Ocean. Chinese singers and Japanese players can come over here. They can come from any quarter, provided they fall within these honorable and distinguished and exempt provisions.

Now, I shall propose when we get to it to put an amendment in there. I want to associate with the lecturers and singers and actors, painters, sculptors, engravers, or other artists, farmers, farm laborers, gardeners, orchardists, herders, farriers, druggists and druggists' clerks, shopkeepers, clerks, book-keepers, or any person having special skill in any business, art, trade, or profession. I should like to be permitted without getting into the penitentiary to go abroad, if I were engaged in some of these trades and industries, and employ men particularly skilled, and I should like it especially if they happened to be any kin to me or those who are very dear to me.

If I were an Irishman or an Englishman and located in this country, and if I knew of some nice relative, it might be a lady who was capable of being a clerk in a dry-goods store, I should like to bring her in; but no, says the Senator from New Hampshire, "you can not bring her in if she does not sing, or lecture, or act on the stage," and therefore she can not come. If I were an Irishman who had been here only about a month and filed my naturalization papers before this proposed law was passed, I might like to send a little money back to my brother perhaps or to my son in Ireland and say, "I have established the business here of a hatter or a shoemaker, and I propose to carry it on, and if you will come and join me I will give you so much money to pay your expenses, or advance it to you so that you may come to this free and good country and share in its blessings."

Mr. BLAIR. The Senator can send to Ireland for all the relatives he may have there, or to any foreign country where they happen to be, as he will see by the provision of the bill.

Mr. MORGAN. I have failed to find it.

Mr. BLAIR. If the Senator will read the bill, perhaps he will criticise it with less severity.

Mr. MORGAN. I have read it and reread it.

Mr. BLAIR. The Senator will observe, since it seems he has not read the bill, that the very next clause after the one with which he is now dealing is:

That nothing in this act shall be construed as prohibiting any individual from assisting any member of his family or any relative to migrate from any foreign country to the United States.

Mr. MORGAN. "Migrate;" but before you migrate or while you are migrating you must not have a contract to labor in this country. It only shows that the gentleman who drew the bill for the committee outside of the Senate did not very carefully weigh the words of it.

(material omitted)

Mr. SHERMAN. The Senator from Alabama [Mr. MORGAN] made some statements interesting in their character which I think ought to be answered if they can be. He stated that the Chinese bill, as it was called, was adopted upon certain principles. If the Chinese bill was a mere bill to discriminate against a man on account of color because he was of a copper color, or on account of his race because he was Chinese or Japanese or Indian—if that was the object of the bill it was very different from what I supposed. I supposed the object of that legislation was to exclude a class of men who came to this country not the owners of themselves, but owned by others, owned by corporations, who had contracted away their liberty, their manhood, before they came here—a class who were quasi servants and serfs, and that was the objection to that kind of immigration.

I voted against the Chinese bill because I thought it was dangerous to depart from the established policy of the American Government to open our doors to laboring men from all lands and from all climes. As I understand, the friends of that bill pressed it upon the ground that the men who came here under contracts as coolies were not free men. It was not because they were Chinese, or because their color was different from ours, but because they were not free men, because they came here as slaves to work against and to compete with free men in their labor. Still, even upon that claim I was opposed to the Chinese bill, and I was very sorry indeed that it passed.

Although I have often been severely criticised on account of my vote, I would stand by that vote now. I was opposed to restrictions upon the immigration of men who come to our country to better their condition, and I thought it was better to submit to the evils even of cooly contract labor than to undertake to interfere with our time-honored American policy. But when I was overruled in that particular, and Congress by a large majority, I think supported by the general public opinion, thought it was best to exclude those people, not because of their race and color, but because they were not free men, because they were owned by others, I yielded at once to that principle, and that became the law of the land and will not be changed.

The same rule ought to be applied to the same class of people of any other race or of any other color, or else I have not learned my theory of this Government aright. You can not base a discrimination of this kind upon race or color, but you must base it upon the condition of the people. We may properly refuse to allow slaves to be brought into this country, as our forefathers did when they prohibited the slave trade, not because they were black, but because they were slaves, and they were excluded on that ground. When slavery was abolished we regarded that the great thing accomplished was that those men were all made free, not that they were slaves and should be made white, or that they were made white by our emancipation, but that they were made free, the owners of themselves, their wives, and their children, hoping that in time, by education and association with our race they would become strong, self-reliant, self-governing. That was my idea of this class of legislation.

I have not considered the bill much. I suppose it would pass by common consent, as it did, I am told, in the other House. I supposed that the bill was in the line of the other legislation, to discriminate against a class, I do not care of what race or of what color, but a class of people who do not own themselves, who are brought here by corporations or by wealthy persons to compete in mines, manufactures, and establishments of various kinds with the free labor of free men, against hardy miners, mechanics, manufacturers, and even farmers; and that the objection to their coming here, whether they are Irishmen, or Englishmen, or Frenchmen, or Italians, is not on account of their race or their color, but simply because they are not in a condition to share with us in the civilization which has been founded by free men and which is to be perpetuated by the free intelligent laboring men of this country.

I know there was a demand in my own State that the laboring men of that region should be freed from this kind of competition. They do not object to the incoming into this country of any man from any country of Europe or from anywhere else, but they object to these men brought by corporations under special contracts, to be fed as they were fed in Europe, to be brought up without the opportunity of education or means of improvement, and that they should not be compelled while they are working away at their hard toil to compete with that kind of contract labor.

* * * *

* * * *

* * * *

Mr. SHERMAN. Our land laws to which the Senator from Delaware refers were all based upon the idea that the immigration to this country was the immigration of industrious independent men. The whole theory of our land laws, which are the most liberal ever offered in the world, was founded upon the experience of the immigration to this country from 1820, because it did not commence much until after the war of 1812.

Mr. BAYARD. Will not my friend look at the language of the bill? It is confined to persons who are to perform labor or service.

Mr. SHERMAN. All these laws were based on the kind of immigration that came to this country from 1820 to 1870. Down to that time the idea of contract labor described in the bill was not thought of.

Mr. BAYARD. It may be the idea, but it is not the letter.

Mr. SHERMAN. It is the letter.

Mr. BAYARD. The letter is simply encouragement; it is to encourage migration.

Mr. SHERMAN. I will answer that. I say our land laws were made generous and liberal because they applied to a class of men who were worthy of that favor and who when they came upon the land at once contributed to our national wealth. But take the men who come here under these contracts to labor at a specific place and for a specific price; would you give them land? They do not want land; they do not come here for land; they do not come here for home or for family.

Mr. MORGAN. Will the Senator from Ohio now allow me to ask him a question?

The PRESIDENT pro tempore. Senators will please address the Chair.

Mr. SHERMAN. I will hear the Senator from Alabama as soon as I answer the Senator from Delaware, if he will allow me a moment further. Look at the language of the bill. The bill prohibits the encouragement of what? The assisting and encouraging of the importation or migration of any alien or aliens. If it stopped there I would say it would be seriously subject to the objection made by the Senator from Delaware, but it goes on, "under contract or agreement." I leave out the words "parol or special, express or implied." I do not think they ought to be there.

Under contract or agreement made previous to the importation or migration of such alien or aliens, foreigner or foreigners, to perform labor or service of any kind in the United States, its Territories, or the District of Columbia.

Take the first section in connection with the exceptions contained in the fifth section. That describes the importation of men who come here under special contracts, mostly in large numbers, to work at largely reduced pay for the benefit of corporations and companies. If the definition is not correctly given, if the kind of people aimed at by the bill is not correctly defined, then as a matter of course the Senator from Delaware and the Senator from Alabama can suggest the correction. What I intend to vote for when I vote for the bill is to prevent this organized corporate importation, not of laboring men, but of bought men, to come here and compete with our laboring men, with our mechanics and miners. That is what I mean by it; that is the intention of the bill; and that importation ought to be prohibited in my judgment. Now I will hear the Senator from Alabama, if I have not already answered him.

Mr. MORGAN. I wanted to inquire of the Senator whether, if the party employed came here with the intention on his own part of remaining and becoming a citizen of the United States, he would then punish a man for having invited him to come or having paid his expenses?

Mr. SHERMAN. The bill does not propose to punish such a man. If a man comes here and enters into any of the ordinary avocations of life without regard to his contract it does not even prohibit his migration hither. The bill does not operate upon the man who migrates, but only upon the man who imports or encourages the migration of contract labor. That is the difference.

If a man comes here under one of these contracts and goes out and claims the benefit of our pre-emption law, and thus becomes an independent citizen, I do not see how he can be punished; but the man who entices him, the shysters, the fellows who are sent off by corporations to gather up a gang of a hundred or a thousand men to come here and drive out an equal number of hardy, industrious miners and laborers, it is that kind whom it is proposed to punish by severe penalties, and also corporations who do it, and the owners or masters of the ships that bring them over knowingly and willfully. That is the class who are to be punished.

Mr. MORGAN. Will the Senator allow me to ask him, if a farmer desired to bring over laborers to work on his farm in the West and he should make a contract with them that he would employ them for a year, and should say to them, "In addition to my contract to employ you for a year and to pay you for your service the Government of the United States will give you one hundred and sixty acres of land under her laws if you come," would the Senator consider that a violation of the public policy of the country or a violation of this proposed statute?

Mr. SHERMAN. All that would be done in that case would be that this bill would declare such a contract null and void unless it came within the exceptions embraced in the fifth section. There is no such kind of migration. We all know, the Senator knows as well as any one, that the kind of immigration which comes to this country which adds to our wealth and strength is that immigration which comes first from the adventurers who land here and start homes, who write back to the fatherland that here they can earn a dollar or a dollar and a half a day, and perhaps that information is accompanied with a twenty-dollar or a thirty-dollar contribution, saying, "Come here and share in the blessings of this great and free country." Those are the little influences and motives which have drawn to our country the great mass of our foreign immigration, and those are healthy in their character. They come here without contract, without arrangement, they take their chances with the rest of the laboring men in the country. The contracts described by the bill are contracts for organized labor which comes in competition with the free men who have thus been brought over in driblets in the ordinary course of migration.

Mr. MORGAN. But still, if the Senator will allow me, that would be encouraging the migration of those people into this country, and the bill denounces that.

Mr. SHERMAN. For one, if the Senator from Alabama can point out to me language more meet than the language contained in the first section to express what I want to prohibit, I will try to join with him in not prohibiting any more than we really desire to prohibit in order to accomplish the policy I have indicated. It may be that the language is not such as I would have used if I had framed the bill, and there are a good many things in it that I should have left out.

Mr. MORGAN. If the Senator will excuse me, I can scarcely be called upon to frame language to except people he wants to prohibit from coming here; he can frame it himself.

Mr. SHERMAN. I do not profess to reorganize all the bills that are brought here. I find here a bill that I believe aims at a good purpose. If in practice any defect should occur in its execution, just like the Chinese bill, which was very bad and faulty in the first instance and which was amended by subsequent legislation, so if this legislation is faulty it can be hereafter easily corrected by amendment.

* * * *

VII. *Excerpts from 16 Cong. Rec. 1778-1797 (Feb. 17, 1885)*

1778   CONGRESSIONAL RECORD—SENATE.   FEBRUARY 17,

(material omitted)

Mr. MILLER, of New York. Mr. President, I was necessarily absent from the Senate several days ago when the bill was under discussion. I do not intend to detain the Senate at any length at the present time.

I desire to say that I am in full sympathy with the object of the bill, which is the prevention of the bringing into this country of foreigners under contract to compete in the labor market of the United States. Looking over the debate had upon this question the other day, I find that it was participated in by Senators on the other side of the Chamber who, two sessions ago, when we were discussing the tariff questions, and when the Senators upon this side were in favor of a protective tariff and legislating in that direction, met us with the taunting question whether we were in favor of protection to labor, charging that we were only in favor of protection to the manufacturers, the property-owners of the country, but that we proposed to leave and did leave the labor market of the country entirely open to foreign competition. I supposed from the questions then put to us, from the arguments they then made, that if a bill of this kind should come before the Senate they would be the first in its defense, and in advocacy of such a measure. I regret to find, however, that such is not the case; that several of the gentlemen who put that question to us at that time have now by their speeches placed themselves in opposition to this proposition, and have made extensive arguments here against it.

I believe that the system of bringing into this country labor under contract is entirely vicious. While the United States Government opens its doors to all voluntary immigration, it should most unequiv-

ocally close its doors against all involuntary immigration, or against any immigration which comes in here under contracts to labor for a period of years. Such immigration, such labor, is to all intents and purposes slave labor, and it can under no circumstances do anything else than degrade and debase free American labor.

You will remember, Mr. President, that during the colonial times much of this kind of labor came into some of the colonies, particularly into Pennsylvania, and under the laws which then prevailed there was absolutely white slavery in this country. Large numbers of white emigrants were brought here under contract for a term of years, and the owners of their labor were able to sell that labor and pass it from hand to hand.

I wish to say as a manufacturer myself that the manufacturers of this country do not desire to have this kind of labor brought into the country, that so far as my knowledge goes one and all are opposed to it. If skilled labor, manufacturing labor, desires to come to this country, let it come intelligently and voluntarily, and when it is here it will then be upon an equality and a par with American labor. Those laborers can make, as all free men can make, their own contracts. They may go and come as they please. But we have seen within the past few years, and see at the present time, when large numbers of American laborers are being thrown out of the market, that organizations and companies have been formed in this country which have brought in large numbers of ignorant and degraded foreigners to work in our mines and upon our railroads. It is in these two industries chiefly that the contract labor brought in from Europe is to-day employed. In the mines of Pennsylvania, and in some other portions of the country, this labor has been introduced, and it has brought with it crime and misery: It has driven out of employment large numbers of free American citizens, voters like ourselves, who have their rights as American citizens. They have been driven from their employment by the bringing in of cheap foreign labor under contract.

Large numbers of these contract laborers have been brought from Hungary. Still larger numbers have come from Italy. There has been and still exists, I believe, in the city of New York a regular organization, a regular company I may say, of Italians who have brought into New York within the past few years many thousands of Italian laborers, and they have been put upon our railroads and public works under contract, and always at prices ranging from 50 to 75 per cent. only of the ordinary wages paid to American citizens in the same localities where this labor has been employed.

Large amounts of this labor have been employed in my own State. I now particularly recall the conditions under what is known as the West Shore Railroad was built. The great majority of all the labor used upon that road for three or four years was Italian contract labor. The men came in gangs. They were not able to speak our language. The contracts were made with their masters or foreman, who staid with them and controlled them upon the works. They lived in rude huts or in dilapidated barns and houses which were found along the road. I will not here go into any description of the squalor and filth which was found in those habitations, or the manner in which they lived. Even at the reduced wages of not more than from 50 to 75 per cent. of ordinary wages, they expended upon their living, on an average, not more than 25 cents a day, and yet each laborer accumulated a sum ranging from $400 to $800. They have gone back to sunny Italy, there to enjoy the little competence which they obtained here, thus taking away from this country our money and at the same time depriving American citizens of labor. Of the fifty-odd million dollars which was put into the construction of the West Shore Railroad a very large portion has been carried out of the country by Italians, and is to-day in Italy. If this labor had not been brought here under contract it would not have come at all. The average Italian laborer who is brought here under contract has not sufficient intelligence or education to enable him to come to this country for himself and to make contracts or find labor for himself. It was done in all cases by an organized company, which sent their agents to Italy, there collected together the labor of that country, brought it here, and, by making favorable contracts, made large profits for themselves.

I believe this whole thing to be vicious. The result has been that in my part of the country where this road has been built the better portion of the Italian labor has gone back to Italy, but it left all through our counties the paupers and the criminals who came with it. They have filled our almshouses and our jails; and in my own county I think, at the present time, one or two of them are under indictment for murder, or at least they were. Very much of crime and of misery and of pauperism was brought with them, and everywhere they threw American labor out of employment, for Americans would not work at the wages which the Italians were willing to take.

The bill gives us a perfect remedy for that condition of things. It says that there shall no longer be white slavery in this country, and that the labor of our country shall be open only to the competition of free men, each one acting for himself and not controlled by any company or any master.

(material omitted)

(material omitted)

[Mr. MORGAN:]

What is the pretext now that has been urged for the bill? Let us look at it in the light of honest truth. It is that some Hungarians and Italians have been brought here by railway and coal-mining companies and perhaps by a few of the rougher manufacturing companies in large numbers under contracts of hire; that they come, and they are a filthy, dirty set; they remain but a short time until they work out their contract, and then they take their money, as the Chinese used to do, and they go back home. Instead of coming right to the question that we met in the case of the Chinese and saying to the Hungarian Government and to the Italian Government, "Your lazzaroni and your paupers and your criminals are being collected and sent to this country under labor contracts, under a sort of boss or cooly system; we object and protest against it, and we are going to legislate them out of this country," the President of the United States will recommend, or if he does not some Senator will recommend by a bill he introduces, that Hungarians and Italians shall be excluded from the United States for

[Page 1793:]

the reason that I state, that after having tried them experimentally we find that they are an unfit class of people to come into this land. Senators in their eagerness to gratify a supposed desire on the part of certain influential people or societies to control the labor market of this country, instead of confining the application of their law to the evil which they mention, spread it over all foreign immigration, and old Scotland, Wales, England, Germany, and France, that have furnished us millions of our most enlightened and excellent people, are put under the ban by this legislation along with Italy and Hungary. We find in the evil which came in from Italy and from Austria a pretext for attacking all the foreign immigration to this country and putting every bit of it on the same footing with the cooly system.

That is all that is complained of here. Why not bring in your bill to attack the very people you complain of? Why spread it all over foreign countries when you admit that the evil exists only in certain localities and in reference to certain people?

I beg to remind Senators that while they are insulting the Irish people, and the English, and the Scotch, and the Welsh, and the Germans, and the French, by this measure, they need not lock themselves up in the security that they may feel that they are pandering to a sentiment which will support them for offices hereafter. No, sir, the reaction will come from those great masses of population, and they will make the Senate of the United States feel their weight when they come to resent this insult to great states and communities and races of men, because the Senate has not got the courage to pick out the people that it wants to attack.

Mr. President, I appreciate the peril that I put myself in by daring to attack anything at all that appears to have the sanction of the great masses of certain classes of people who are organized in societies in this country; but I appeal to their honor and to their sense of justice. When they come to realize that Senators are here willing to serve them at the expense of justice and reason, they will turn to me with a welcome hand as they turn their back coldly upon those who are afraid to do what they know is right.

There is but one way to manage a matter of this kind, and that is to find where the evil is, and to strike at that, get through with the business, and then let it alone. It is quite a disagreeable thing to do under any circumstances; but when it is admitted on all hands that we are not suffering from Ireland, or England, or Wales, or Scotland, or Germany, or France, but that we are suffering only from Hungary and Italy, let us reduce our attack to the point from whence the injury comes, and not include all classes of people abroad on that account.

* * * *

Mr. HAWLEY. Mr. President, can the amendment be divided?
Mr. MILLER, of California. Certainly.
The PRESIDENT *pro tempore*. The Chair thinks the amendment is capable of division after the word "States." Does the Senator desire that it be divided?
Mr. HAWLEY. I ask that it be divided.
The PRESIDENT *pro tempore*. The question will be first put on the first branch of the amendment, which will be read.
The Chief Clerk read as follows:

This act shall not apply to any agent of a State, acting under the authority of law, who shall induce immigration to such State from any country in Europe, or from Great Britain, Canada, Mexico, or any Central or South American state.

* * * *

[Page 1797:]

The result was announced—yeas 18, nays 24; as follows:

YEAS—18.

Beck,	Coke,	Jonas,	Slater,
Brown,	Colquitt,	McPherson,	Vest,
Butler,	Hampton,	Maxey,	Williams.
Call,	Harris,	Morgan,	
Cockrell,	Jackson,	Saulsbury,	

NAYS—24.

Blair,	Frye,	McMillan,	Platt,
Cameron of Wis.,	George,	Manderson,	Plumb,
Conger,	Harrison,	Mitchell,	Sawyer,
Cullom,	Hoar,	Morrill,	Sewell,
Dawes,	Ingalls,	Palmer,	Sherman,
Edmunds,	Jones of Nevada,	Pike,	Wilson.

ABSENT—34.

Aldrich,	Farley,	Kenna,	Ransom,
Allison,	Garland,	Lamar,	Riddleberger,
Bayard,	Gibson,	Lapham,	Sabin,
Bowen,	Gorman,	Logan,	Vance,
Camden,	Groome,	Mahone,	Van Wyck,
Cameron of Pa.,	Hale,	Miller of Cal.,	Voorhees,
Chace,	Hawley,	Miller of N. Y.,	Walker.
Dolph,	Hill,	Pendleton,	
Fair,	Jones of Florida,	Pugh,	

So the first branch of the amendment was rejected.

* * * *

Mr. HARRIS. What is the remainder of the amendment?
The PRESIDING OFFICER. It will be read.
The Secretary read as follows:

Nor shall it apply to any person who in good faith shall assist persons or families to come from any of those countries for the purpose of permanent settlement in any State or Territory of the United States.

* * * *

The roll-call having been concluded, the result was announced—yeas 17, nays 23; as follows:

YEAS—17.

Beck,	Colquitt,	Lapham,	Vest,
Brown,	Hampton,	McPherson,	Williams.
Butler,	Harris,	Maxey,	
Call,	Jackson,	Morgan,	
Coke,	Jonas,	Slater,	

NAYS—23.

Blair,	George,	McMillan,	Platt,
Cameron of Wis.,	Harrison,	Manderson,	Plumb,
Conger,	Hill,	Mitchell,	Sewell,
Cullom,	Hoar,	Morrill,	Sherman,
Dawes,	Ingalls,	Palmer,	Wilson.
Edmunds,	Jones of Nevada,	Pike,	

ABSENT—36.

Aldrich,	Fair,	Jones of Florida,	Ransom,
Allison,	Farley,	Kenna,	Riddleberger,
Bayard,	Frye,	Lamar,	Sabin,
Bowen,	Garland,	Logan,	Saulsbury,
Camden,	Gorman,	Mahone,	Sawyer,
Cameron of Pa.,	Gibson,	Miller of Cal.,	Vance,
Chace,	Groome,	Miller of N. Y.,	Van Wyck,
Cockrell,	Hale,	Pendleton,	Voorhees,
Dolph,	Hawley,	Pugh,	Walker.

So the second division of the amendment was rejected.

* * * *

VIII. Excerpts from 16 Cong. Rec. 1837-1840 (Feb. 18, 1885)

---

* * * *

Mr. LAPHAM. I gave notice of an amendment to strike out the words "or singers," in section 5, line 15. I think the worst form of tyranny is found in the case of the Italian children who are brought over here and who go about our streets singing, and who are whipped every night when they go home if they do not bring in a certain sum of money. I do not want to have the bill so framed that its prohibition will not apply to that class of cases.

Mr. BLAIR. The clause refers to professional singers.

The PRESIDENT *pro tempore*. The amendment proposed by the Senator from New York will be reported.

The CHIEF CLERK. In section 5, line 15, it is proposed to strike out the words "or singers;" so as to read:

Nor shall the provisions of this act apply to professional actors or lecturers, nor persons employed strictly as personal or domestic servants.

The amendment was rejected.

* * * *

Mr. PLUMB. In section 5, line 14, after the word "actors," I move to insert the word "artists;" so as to read:

Nor shall the provisions of this act apply to professional actors, artists, lecturers, or singers.

The amendment was agreed to.

Mr. MORGAN. In section 5, line 14, before the word "professional," I move to insert "artisans;" so as to read:

Nor shall the provisions of this act apply to artisans, professional actors, artists, ecturers, &c.

The amendment was rejected.

* * * *

[Page 1839:]

(*material omitted*)

The bill was read the third time.

The PRESIDENT *pro tempore*. The bill having been read three times the question is, Shall it pass?

Mr. BLAIR. I call for the yeas and nays.

The yeas and nays were ordered, and the Secretary proceeded to call the roll.

Mr. COKE (when his name was called). I am paired on this bill with the Senator from Massachusetts [Mr. HOAR]. If he were here, I should vote "nay."

Mr. DAWES (when Mr. HOAR's name was called). My colleague [Mr. HOAR] is paired upon this bill with the Senator from Texas [Mr. COKE]. If my colleague were here, he would vote "yea."

Mr. MANDERSON (when his name was called). I am paired with the Senator from Florida [Mr. JONES]. If he were here, I should vote for the bill.

Mr. WALKER (when his name was called). I am paired generally with the Senator from Virginia [Mr. RIDDLEBERGER]. Believing that he would vote in the affirmative, as I would, I therefore vote. I vote "yea."

The roll-call was concluded.

Mr. RANSOM. I am paired with the Senator from Illinois [Mr. LOGAN], but I am informed by his colleague that he would vote "yea." I vote "yea."

Mr. MITCHELL. My colleague [Mr. CAMERON, of Pennsylvania] has been absent some days on account of illness. He is paired with the Senator from California [Mr. FARLEY]. If he were present, I have no doubt my colleague would vote "yea."

The result was announced—yeas 50, nays 9; as follows:

YEAS—50.

Aldrich,	Fair,	Lamar,	Pugh,
Allison,	Frye,	Lapham,	Ransom,
Blair,	George,	McMillan,	Sabin,
Bowen,	Gibson,	McPherson,	Sawyer,
Brown,	Gorman,	Mahone,	Sewell,
Call,	Hale,	Miller of Cal.,	Sherman,
Camden,	Harris,	Miller of Cal.,	Van Wyck,
Cameron of Wis.,	Harrison,	Miller of N. Y.,	Vest,
Chace,	Ingalls,	Mitchell,	Voorhees,
Conger,	Jackson,	Morrill,	Walker,
Cullom,	Jonas,	Palmer,	Wilson.
Dawes,	Jones of Nevada,	Pike,	
Dolph,	Kenna,	Platt,	
		Plumb,	

NAYS—9.

Butler,	Hawley,	Morgan,	Vance,
Groome,	Maxey,	Saulsbury,	Williams.
Hampton,			

[Page 1840:]

ABSENT—17.

Bayard,	Colquitt,	Hoar,	Riddleberger,
Beck,	Edmunds,	Jones of Florida,	Slater.
Cameron of Pa.,	Farley,	Logan,	
Cockrell,	Garland,	Manderson,	
Coke,	Hill,	Pendleton,	

So the bill was passed.

Mr. BLAIR. I move that the bill be printed as it has passed the Senate.

The PRESIDENT *pro tempore*. The question is on the motion to print.

The motion was agreed to.

* * * *

IX. 16 Cong. Rec. 2032 (Feb. 23, 1885)

2032   CONGRESSIONAL RECORD—HOUSE.   FEBRUARY 23,

(material omitted)

Mr. HOPKINS. It prohibits the importation under contract of all classes with the exceptions named in the bill.

Mr. MILLS. I am opposed to the bill.

The amendments of the Senate were concurred in.

Mr. HOPKINS moved to reconsider the vote by which the Senate amendments were concurred in; and also moved to lay the motion to reconsider on the table.

The latter motion was agreed to.

* * * *

IMPORTATION AND IMMIGRATION OF ALIENS.

Mr. HOPKINS. I ask unanimous consent to take from the Speaker's table for the purpose of disposing of the Senate amendments the bill (H. R. 2550) to prohibit the importation and immigration of foreigners and aliens under contract or agreement to perform labor in the United States, its Territories, and the District of Columbia.

The amendments of the Senate were read, as follows:

Page 1, lines 7 and 8, strike out "to perform service or labor."
Page 1, lines 14 and 15, strike out "and doing business within the United States."
Page 1, line 10, after the word "service," insert "or having reference to the performance of labor or service by any person."
Page 1, line 16, strike out the words "of any kind."
Page 1, line 18, strike out the words "such persons" and insert "the person or persons whose labor or service is contracted for."
Page 1, line 22, after "by" insert "knowingly."
Page 2, line 8, after the word "recovered," insert "by the United States or."
Page 2, line 8, after "person," insert "who shall first bring his action therefor."
Page 2, lines 9 and 10, strike out "who may choose to bring such suit."
Page 2, strike out all after "United States" in line 11, down to and including "moiety," in line 13, and insert "the proceeds to be paid."
Page 2, after the end of line 15, insert "and it shall be the duty of the district attorney of the proper district to prosecute every such suit at the expense of the United States."
Page 2, line 27, after the word "citizen," insert "or subject."
Page 3, line 11, after the word "actors," insert "artists."
Page 3, line 11, after "singers," insert "nor to persons employed strictly as personal or domestic servants."
Page 3, line 13, after "relative," insert "or personal friends."
Page 3, line 14, after "United States," insert "for the purpose of settlement here."

Mr. KEIFER. Mr. Speaker, is it proposed to concur in these amendments?

The SPEAKER. The Chair does not know what motion the gentleman from Pennsylvania [Mr. HOPKINS] proposes to make.

Mr. KEIFER. I will ask the gentleman from Pennsylvania [Mr. HOPKINS] whether he proposes that the House shall concur in these Senate amendments?

Mr. HOPKINS. That is my motion, Mr. Speaker—to concur in the amendments of the Senate. They are mostly verbal amendments.

Mr. KEIFER. I think they are pretty important.

Mr. MILLS. I will ask the gentleman from Pennsylvania [Mr. HOPKINS] whether this bill proposes to prohibit the introduction of agricultural laborers?

THE 1976 CIVIL RIGHTS ATTORNEYS' FEES AWARDS ACT AND THE *CASEY* DECISION

I. *Overview and Questions*

The *Casey* decision appears in summary form in the Casebook (pp.790-91). We include the majority and dissenting opinions here because they provide an important, and highly accessible, example of how textualist and legal process justices at the top of their game approach the uses of plain meaning, textual structure, and legislative history. *Casey* is the first of two Supreme Court decisions treated in this Supplement to address the Civil Rights Attorneys' Fees Awards Act of 1976 (our discussion of *Blanchard v. Bergeron* appears below at pp. 262-269). In addition to the *Casey* opinions, we provide excerpts from the Senate and House committee reports and floor debates preceding enactment of the 1976 statute.

Consider the following questions, keyed to the legislative history as well as the two opinions:

1. Justice Scalia's majority opinion relies heavily on Congress's use of the terms "attorney's fees" and "expert fees" in other federal statutes. Which other statutes are most persuasive in this regard and why? Does it matter at all if other statutes were drafted by different committees than the one that produced the Civil Rights Attorneys' Fees Awards Act? Are differences in subject matter among these statutes relevant to Scalia's argument?

2. Does Justice Scalia see any role for legislative history in his majority opinion?

3. What is the basic thrust of the 1976 statute? Is it aimed at covering only attorneys' fees? Or does the mischief aimed at by Congress encompass other expenses related to what an attorney must do to prevail in a civil rights case? Do the floor statements of Senators Scott and Mathias (p.31471) shed any light on these questions? What about the statement by Senator Tunney (pp.33313-14)? What is the relevance of Rep. Drinan's observation (p.35123) that "the phrase 'attorney's fee' would include the values of the legal services provided by counsel, *including all incidental and necessary expenses incurred in furnishing effective and competent representation*" (emphasis added)?

4. The Senate Committee report states (p.2) that "citizens must have the opportunity to recover what it costs them to vindicate these [civil] rights in court." Assume the report added that this includes recovering all costs that go into the attorney's preparation and presentation of the case, including the use of paralegals, experts, telecommunications, and photocopying. Would that addition change Justice Scalia's analysis or conclusion? Should it?

5. Justice Stevens in dissent notes that the Senate Committee report refers with approval to "*all of the cases contained in*" the 1973 Judiciary Committee hearings on legal fees, including many cases that permitted the shifting of expert witness fees. Were these hearings from the same Congress as the one that passed the statute? Does this matter at all when assessing the weight to be given such a committee reference?

6. The cases noted with approval from earlier Hearings are identified in a string cite that is part of a footnote in the Senate committee report (p.4, n.3). Are such citations at all probative when considering what attorney-related expenses committee members meant for the statute to cover?

7. Reframe the questions in #5 and #6 above, from the standpoint of a judge needing guidance. What might make the report's discussion of this Hearings testimony and analysis *more* probative than the discussion invoked by Justice Stevens, assuming arguendo that the Hearings had taken place in the same Congress, conducted by the same committee that later reported out the bill?

8. Justice Stevens concludes that "we [the Court] do the country a disservice when we needlessly ignore persuasive evidence of Congress's actual purpose and require it 'to take the time to revisit the matter.'" What is the disservice to which Stevens refers?

II. *West Virginia University Hospitals v. Casey, 499 U.S. 83 (1991)*

Supreme Court of the United States

WEST VIRGINIA UNIVERSITY HOSPITALS, INC., Petitioner

v.

Robert CASEY, Governor of Pennsylvania, et al.

No. 89-994.

Argued Oct. 9, 1990.

Decided March 19, 1991.

Justice SCALIA delivered the opinion of the Court.

This case presents the question whether fees for services rendered by experts in civil rights litigation may be shifted to the losing party pursuant to 42 U.S.C. § 1988, which permits the award of "a reasonable attorney's fee."

I

Petitioner West Virginia University Hospitals, Inc. (WVUH), operates a hospital in Morgantown, W.Va., near the Pennsylvania border. The hospital is often used by Medicaid recipients living in southwestern Pennsylvania. In January 1986, Pennsylvania's Department of Public Welfare notified WVUH of new Medicaid reimbursement schedules for services provided to Pennsylvania residents by the Morgantown hospital. In administrative proceedings, WVUH unsuccessfully objected to the new reimbursement rates on both federal statutory and federal constitutional grounds. After exhausting administrative remedies, WVUH filed suit in Federal District Court under 42 U.S.C. § 1983. Named as defendants (respondents here) were Pennsylvania Governor Robert Casey and various other Pennsylvania officials.

Counsel for WVUH employed Coopers & Lybrand, a national accounting firm, and three doctors specializing in hospital finance to assist in the preparation of the lawsuit and to testify at trial. WVUH prevailed at trial in May 1988. The District Court subsequently awarded fees pursuant to 42 U.S.C. § 1988, [FN1] including over $100,000 in fees attributable to expert services. The District Court found these services to have been "essential" to presentation of the case-a finding not disputed by respondents.

FN1. ☐ Title 42 U.S.C. § 1988 provides in relevant part: "In any action or proceeding to enforce a provision of sections 1981, 1982, 1983, 1985, and 1986 of this title, title IX of Public Law 92-318 ..., or title VI of the Civil Rights Act of 1964 ..., the court, in its discretion, may allow the prevailing party, other than the United States, a reasonable attorney's fee as part of the costs."

Respondents appealed both the judgment on the merits and the fee award. The Court of Appeals for the Third Circuit affirmed as to the former, but reversed as to the expert fees, disallowing them except to the extent that they fell within the $30-per-day fees for witnesses prescribed by 28 U.S.C. § 1821(b). 885 F.2d 11 (1989). WVUH petitioned this Court for review of that disallowance; we granted certiorari, 494 U.S. 1003, 110 S.Ct. 1294, 108 L.Ed.2d 472 (1990).

II

[1] Title 28 U.S.C. § 1920 provides:

"A judge or clerk of any court of the United States may tax as costs the following:

"(1) Fees of the clerk and marshal;

"(2) Fees of the court reporter for all or any part of the stenographic transcript necessarily obtained for use in the case;

"(3) Fees and disbursements for printing and witnesses;

"(4) Fees for exemplification and copies of papers necessarily obtained for use in the case;

"(5) Docket fees under section 1923 of this title;

"(6) Compensation of court appointed experts, compensation of interpreters, and salaries, fees, expenses, and costs of special interpretation services under section 1828 of this title."

Title 28 U.S.C. § 1821(b) limits the witness fees authorized by § 1920(3) as follows: "A witness shall be paid an attendance fee of $30 per day for each day's attendance. A witness shall also be paid the attendance fee for the time necessarily occupied in going to and returning from the place of attendance...." [FN2] In *Crawford Fitting Co. v. J.T. Gibbons, Inc.,* 482 U.S. 437, 107 S.Ct. 2494, 96 L.Ed.2d 385 (1987), we held that these provisions define the full extent of a federal court's power to shift litigation costs absent express statutory authority to go further. "[W]hen," we said, "a prevailing party seeks reimbursement for fees paid to its own expert witnesses, a federal court is bound by the limits of § 1821(b), absent contract or explicit statutory authority to the contrary." *Id.,* at 439, 107 S.Ct., at 2496. "We will not lightly infer that Congress has repealed §§ 1920 and 1821, either through [Federal Rule of Civil Procedure] 54(d) or any other provision not referring explicitly to witness fees." *Id.,* at 445, 107 S.Ct., at 2499.

FN2. Section 1821(b) has since been amended to increase the allowable per diem from $30 to $40. See Judicial Improvements Act of 1990, Pub.L. 101-650, § 314.

As to the testimonial services of the hospital's experts, therefore, *Crawford Fitting* plainly requires, as a prerequisite to reimbursement, the identification of "explicit statutory authority." WVUH argues, however, that some of the expert fees it incurred in this case were unrelated to expert *testimony,* and that as to those fees the § 1821(b) limits, which apply only to witnesses in attendance at trial, are of no consequence. We agree with that, but there remains applicable the limitation of § 1920. *Crawford Fitting* said that we would not lightly find an implied repeal of § 1821 *or* of § 1920, which it held to be an express limitation upon the types of costs which, absent other authority, may be shifted by federal courts. 482 U.S., at 441, 107 S.Ct., at 2497. None of the categories of expenses listed in § 1920 can reasonably be read to include fees for services rendered by an expert employed by a party in a nontestimonial advisory capacity. The question before us, then, is-with regard to both testimonial and nontestimonial expert fees-whether the term "attorney's fee" in § 1988 provides the "explicit statutory authority" required by *Crawford Fitting.*[FN3]

FN3. Justice STEVENS suggests that the expert fees requested here might be part of the "costs" allowed by § 1988 even if they are not part of the "attorney's fee." We are aware of no authority to support the counter-intuitive assertion that "[t]he term 'costs' has a different and broader meaning in fee-shifting statutes than it has in the cost statutes that apply to ordinary litigation," *post*, at 1150. In *Crawford Fitting* we held that the word "costs" in Federal Rule of Civil Procedure 54(d) is to be read in harmony with the word "costs" in 28 U.S.C. § 1920, see 482 U.S., at 441, 445, 107 S.Ct., at 2497, 2499, and we think the same is true of the word "costs" in § 1988. We likewise see nothing to support Justice STEVENS' speculation that the court below or the parties viewed certain disbursements by the hospital's attorneys as "costs" within the meaning of the statute. Rather, it is likely that these disbursements (billed directly to the client) were thought subsumed within the phrase "attorney's fee." See, *e.g.*, *Northcross v. Board of Ed. of Memphis Schools*, 611 F.2d 624, 639 (CA6 1979) ("reasonable out-of-pocket expenses incurred by the attorney" included in § 1988 "attorney's fee" award).

III

[2] The record of statutory usage demonstrates convincingly that attorney's fees and expert fees are regarded as separate elements of litigation cost. While some fee-shifting provisions, like § 1988, refer only to "attorney's fees," see, *e.g.*, Civil Rights Act of 1964, 42 U.S.C. § 2000e-5(k), many others explicitly shift expert witness fees *as well as* attorney's fees. In 1976, just over a week prior to the enactment of § 1988, Congress passed those provisions of the Toxic Substances Control Act, 15 U.S.C. §§ 2618(d), 2619(c)(2), which provide that a prevailing party may recover "the costs of suit and reasonable fees for attorneys *and expert witnesses.*" (Emphasis added.) Also in 1976, Congress amended the Consumer Product Safety Act, 15 U.S.C. §§ 2060(c), 2072(a), 2073, which as originally enacted in 1972 shifted to the losing party "cost[s] of suit, including a reasonable attorney's fee." see 86 Stat. 1226. In the 1976 amendment, Congress altered the fee-shifting provisions to their present form by adding a phrase shifting expert witness fees *in addition to* attorney's fees. See Pub.L. 94-284, § 10, 90 Stat. 506, 507. Two other significant Acts passed in 1976 contain similar phrasing: the Resource Conservation and Recovery Act of 1976, 42 U.S.C. § 6972(e) ("costs of litigation (including reasonable attorney and expert witness fees)"), and the Natural Gas Pipeline Safety Act Amendments of 1976, 49 U.S.C.App. § 1686(e) ("costs of suit, including reasonable attorney's fees and reasonable expert witnesses fees").

Congress enacted similarly phrased fee-shifting provisions in numerous statutes both before 1976, see, *e.g.*, Endangered Species Act of 1973, 16 U.S.C. § 1540(g)(4) ("costs of litigation (including reasonable attorney and expert witness fees)"), and afterwards, see, *e.g.*, Public Utility Regulatory Policies Act of 1978, 16 U.S.C. § 2632(a)(1) ("reasonable attorneys' fees, expert witness fees, and other reasonable costs incurred in preparation and advocacy of [the litigant's] position"). These statutes encompass diverse categories of legislation, including tax, administrative procedure, environmental protection, consumer protection, admiralty and navigation, utilities regulation, and, significantly, civil rights: The Equal Access to Justice Act (EAJA), the counterpart to § 1988 for violation of federal rights by federal employees, states that " 'fees and other expenses' [as shifted by § 2412(d)(1)(A)] includes the reasonable expenses of expert witnesses ... and reasonable attorney fees." 28 U.S.C. § 2412(d)(2)(A). At least 34 statutes in 10 different titles of the United States Code explicitly shift attorney's fees *and* expert witness fees.

The laws that refer to fees for nontestimonial expert services are less common, but they establish a similar usage both before and after 1976: Such fees are referred to *in addition to* attorney's fees when a shift is intended. A provision of the Criminal Justice Act of 1964, 18 U.S.C. § 3006A(e), directs the court to reimburse appointed counsel for expert fees necessary to the defense of indigent criminal defendants-even though the immediately preceding provision, § 3006A(d), already directs that appointed defense counsel be paid a designated hourly rate plus "expenses reasonably incurred." WVUH's position must be that expert fees billed to a client through an attorney are "attorney's fees" because they are to be treated as part of the expenses of the attorney; but if this were normal usage, they would have been reimbursable under the Criminal Justice Act as "expenses reasonably incurred"-and subsection 3006A(e) would add nothing to the recoverable amount. The very heading of that subsection, "Services *other than* counsel" (emphasis added), acknowledges a distinction between services provided by the attorney himself and those provided to the attorney (or the client) by a nonlegal expert.

To the same effect is the 1980 EAJA, which provides: " 'fees and other expenses' [as shifted by § 2412(d)(1)(A)] includes the reasonable expenses of expert witnesses, *the reasonable cost of any study, analysis, engineering report, test, or project* which is found by the court to be necessary for the preparation of the party's case, and reasonable attorney fees." 28 U.S.C. § 2412(d)(2)(A) (emphasis added). If the reasonable cost of a "study" or "analysis"-which is but another way of describing nontestimonial expert services-is by common usage already included in the "attorney fees," again a significant and highly detailed part of the statute becomes redundant. The Administrative Procedure Act, 5 U.S.C. § 504(b)(1)(A) (added 1980), and the Tax Equity and Fiscal Responsibility Act of 1982, 26 U.S.C. § 7430(c)(1), contain similar language. Also reflecting the same usage are two railroad regulation statutes, the Regional Rail Reorganization Act of 1973, 45 U.S.C. §§ 726(f)(9) ("costs and expenses (including reasonable fees of accountants, experts, and attorneys) actually incurred"), and the Railroad Revitalization and Regulatory Reform Act of 1976, 45 U.S.C. § 854(g) ("costs and expenses (including fees of accountants, experts, and attorneys) actually and reasonably incurred").[FN5]

FN5. WVUH cites a House Conference Committee Report from a statute passed in 1986, stating: "The conferees intend that the term 'attorneys' fees as part of the costs' include reasonable expenses and fees of expert witnesses and the reasonable costs of any test or evaluation which is found to be necessary for the preparation of the ... case." H.R.Conf.Rep. No. 99-687, p. 5 (1986) (discussing the Handicapped Children's Protection Act of 1986, 20 U.S.C. § 1415(e)(4)(B)). In our view this undercuts rather than supports WVUH's position: The specification would have been quite unnecessary if the ordinary meaning of the term included those elements. The statement is an apparent effort to *depart* from ordinary meaning and to define a term of art.

We think this statutory usage shows beyond question that attorney's fees and expert fees are distinct items of expense. If, as WVUH argues, the one includes the other, dozens of statutes referring to the two separately become an inexplicable exercise in redundancy.

IV

WVUH argues that at least in pre-1976 *judicial* usage the phrase "attorney's fees" included the fees of experts. To support this proposition, it relies upon two historical assertions: first, that pre-1976 courts, when exercising traditional equitable discretion in shifting attorney's fees, taxed as an element of such fees the expenses related to expert services; and second, that pre-1976 courts shifting attorney's fees pursuant to statutes identical in phrasing to § 1988 allowed the recovery of expert fees. We disagree with these assertions. The judicial background against which Congress enacted § 1988 mirrored the statutory background: expert fees were regarded not as a subset of attorney's fees, but as a distinct category of litigation expense.

* * * *

V

WVUH suggests that a distinctive meaning of "attorney's fees" should be adopted with respect to § 1988 because this statute was meant to overrule our decision in *Alyeska Pipeline Service Co. v. Wilderness Society,* 421 U.S. 240, 95 S.Ct. 1612, 44 L.Ed.2d 141 (1975). As mentioned above, prior to 1975 many courts awarded expert fees and attorney's fees in certain circumstances pursuant to their equitable discretion. In *Alyeska,* we held that this discretion did not extend beyond a few exceptional circumstances long recognized by common law. Specifically, we rejected the so-called "private attorney general" doctrine recently created by some lower federal courts, see, *e.g., La Raza Unida v. Volpe,* 57 F.R.D. 94, 98-102 (ND Cal.1972), which allowed equitable fee shifting to plaintiffs in certain types of civil rights litigation. 421 U.S., at 269, 95 S.Ct., at 1627. WVUH argues that § 1988 was intended to restore the pre- *Alyeska* regime-and that, since expert fees were shifted then, they should be shifted now.

Both chronology and the remarks of sponsors of the bill that became § 1988 suggest that at least some members of Congress viewed it as a response to *Alyeska.* See, *e.g.,* S.Rep. No. 94-1011,

pp. 4, 6 (1976). It is a considerable step, however, from this proposition to the conclusion the hospital would have us draw, namely, that § 1988 should be read as a reversal of *Alyeska* in all respects.

By its plain language and as unanimously construed in the courts, § 1988 is both broader and narrower than the pre- *Alyeska* regime. Before *Alyeska,* civil rights plaintiffs could recover fees pursuant to the private attorney general doctrine only if private enforcement was necessary to defend important rights benefiting large numbers of people, and cost barriers might otherwise preclude private suits. *La Raza Unida, supra,* at 98-101. Section 1988 contains no similar limitation-so that in the present suit there is no question as to the propriety of shifting WVUH's *attorney's* fees, even though it is highly doubtful they could have been awarded under pre- *Alyeska* equitable theories. In other respects, however, § 1988 is not as broad as the former regime. It is limited, for example, to violations of specified civil rights statutes-which means that it would not have reversed the outcome of *Alyeska* itself, which involved not a civil rights statute but the National Environmental Policy Act of 1969, 42 U.S.C. § 4321 *et seq.* Since it is clear that, in many respects, § 1988 was not meant to return us precisely to the pre- *Alyeska* regime, the objective of achieving such a return is no reason to depart from the normal import of the text.

WVUH further argues that the congressional purpose in enacting § 1988 must prevail over the ordinary meaning of the statutory terms. It quotes, for example, the House Committee Report to the effect that "the judicial remedy [must be] full and complete," H.R.Rep. No. 94-1558, p. 1 (1976), and the Senate Committee Report to the effect that "[c]itizens must have the opportunity to recover what it costs them to vindicate [civil] rights in court," S.Rep. No. 94-1011, *supra,* at 2. As we have observed before, however, the purpose of a statute includes not only what it sets out to change, but also what it resolves to leave alone. See *Rodriguez v. United States,* 480 U.S. 522, 525-526, 107 S.Ct. 1391, 1393-1394, 94 L.Ed.2d 533 (1987). The best evidence of that purpose is the statutory text adopted by both Houses of Congress and submitted to the President. Where that contains a phrase that is unambiguous-that has a clearly accepted meaning in both legislative and judicial practice-we do not permit it to be expanded or contracted by the statements of individual legislators or committees during the course of the enactment process. See *United States v. Ron Pair Enterprises, Inc.,* 489 U.S. 235, 241, 109 S.Ct. 1026, 1030, 103 L.Ed.2d 290 (1989) ("[W]here, as here, the statute's language is plain, 'the sole function of the court is to enforce it according to its terms' "), quoting *Caminetti v. United States,* 242 U.S. 470, 485, 37 S.Ct. 192, 194, 61 L.Ed. 442 (1917). Congress could easily have shifted "attorney's fees and expert witness fees," or "reasonable litigation expenses," as it did in contemporaneous statutes; it chose instead to enact more restrictive language, and we are bound by that restriction.

WVUH asserts that we have previously been guided by the "broad remedial purposes" of § 1988, rather than its text, in a context resolving an "analogous issue": In *Missouri v. Jenkins,* 491 U.S. 274, 285, 109 S.Ct. 2463, 2470, 105 L.Ed.2d 229

(1989), we concluded that § 1988 permitted separately billed paralegal and law clerk time to be charged to the losing party. The trouble with this argument is that *Jenkins* did *not* involve an "analogous issue," insofar as the relevant considerations are concerned. The issue there was not, as WVUH contends, whether we would permit our perception of the "policy" of the statute to overcome its "plain language." It was not remotely plain in *Jenkins* that the phrase "attorney's fee" did not include charges for law clerk and paralegal services. Such services, like the services of "secretaries, messengers, librarians, janitors, and others whose labor contributes to the work product," *id.,* at 285, 109 S.Ct., at 2470, had traditionally been included in calculation of the lawyers' hourly rates. Only recently had there arisen "the 'increasingly widespread custom of separately billing for [such] services,' " *id.,* at 286, 109 S.Ct., at 2471 (quoting from *Ramos v. Lamm,* 713 F.2d 546, 558 (CA10 1983)). By contrast, there has never been, to our knowledge, a practice of including the cost of expert services within attorneys' hourly rates. There was also no record in *Jenkins*-as there is a lengthy record here-of statutory usage that recognizes a distinction between the charges at issue and attorney's fees. We do not know of a single statute that shifts clerk or paralegal fees separately; and even those, such as the EAJA, which comprehensively define the assessable "litigation costs" make no separate mention of clerks or paralegals. In other words, *Jenkins* involved a respect in which the term "attorney's fees" (giving the losing argument the benefit of the doubt) was genuinely ambiguous; and we resolved that ambiguity not by invoking some policy that supersedes the text of the statute, but by concluding that charges of this sort had traditionally been included in attorney's fees and that separate billing should make no difference. The term's application to expert fees is not ambiguous; and if it were the means of analysis employed in *Jenkins* would lead to the conclusion that since such fees have not traditionally been included within the attorney's hourly rate they are not attorney's fees.

WVUH's last contention is that, even if Congress plainly did not include expert fees in the fee-shifting provisions of § 1988, it would have done so had it thought about it. Most of the pre-§ 1988 statutes that explicitly shifted expert fees dealt with environmental litigation, where the necessity of expert advice was readily apparent; and when Congress later enacted the EAJA, the federal counterpart of § 1988, it explicitly included expert fees. Thus, the argument runs, the 94th Congress simply forgot; it is our duty to ask how they would have decided had they actually considered the question. See *Friedrich v. Chicago,* 888 F.2d 511, 514 (CA7 1989) (awarding expert fees under § 1988 because a court should "complete ... the statute by reading it to bring about the end that the legislators would have specified had they thought about it more clearly").

This argument profoundly mistakes our role. Where a statutory term presented to us for the first time is ambiguous, we construe it to contain that permissible meaning which fits most logically and comfortably into the body of both previously and subsequently enacted law. See 2 J. Sutherland, Statutory Construction § 5201 (3d F. Horack ed.1943). We do so not because that precise accommodative meaning is what the lawmakers must have had in mind (how could an earlier Congress know what a later Congress would enact?), but because it is our role to make sense rather than nonsense out of the *corpus juris.* But where, as here, the meaning of the term prevents such accommodation, it is not our function to eliminate clearly expressed inconsistency of policy and to treat alike subjects that different Congresses have chosen to treat differently. The facile attribution of congressional "forgetfulness" cannot justify such a usurpation. Where what is at issue is not a contradictory disposition within the same enactment, but merely a difference between the more parsimonious policy of an earlier enactment and the more generous policy of a later one, there is no more basis for saying that the earlier Congress forgot than for saying that the earlier Congress felt differently. In such circumstances, the attribution of forgetfulness rests in reality upon the judge's assessment that the later statute contains the *better* disposition. But that is not for judges to prescribe. We thus reject this last argument for the same reason that Justice Brandeis, writing for the Court, once rejected a similar (though less explicit) argument by the United States:

"[The statute's] language is plain and unambiguous. What the Government asks is not a construction of a statute, but, in effect, an enlargement of it by the court, so that what was omitted, presumably by inadvertence, may be included within its scope. To supply omissions transcends the judicial function." *Iselin v. United States,* 270 U.S. 245, 250-251, 46 S.Ct. 248, 250, 70 L.Ed. 566 (1926).[FN7]

FN7. WVUH at least asks us to guess the preferences of the *enacting* Congress. Justice STEVENS apparently believes our role is to guess the desires of the *present* Congress, or of Congresses yet to be. "Only time will tell," he says, "whether the Court, with its literal reading of § 1988, has correctly interpreted the will of Congress," *post,* at 1156. The implication is that today's holding will be proved wrong if Congress amends the law to conform with his dissent. We think not. The "will of Congress" we look to is not a will evolving from Session to Session, but a will expressed and fixed in a particular enactment. Otherwise, we would speak not of "interpreting" the law but of "intuiting" or "predicting" it. Our role is to say what the law, as hitherto enacted, *is;* not to forecast what the law, as amended, *will be.*

* * * *

For the foregoing reasons, we conclude that § 1988 conveys no authority to shift expert fees. When experts appear at trial, they are of course eligible for the fee provided by § 1920 and § 1821-which was allowed in the present case by the Court of Appeals.

The judgment of the Court of Appeals is affirmed.

It is so ordered.

* * * *

Justice STEVENS, with whom Justice MARSHALL and Justice BLACKMUN join, dissenting.

Since the enactment of the Statute of Wills in 1540, careful draftsmen have authorized executors to pay the just debts of the decedent, including the fees and expenses of the attorney for the estate. Although the omission of such an express authorization in a will might indicate that the testator had thought it unnecessary, or that he had overlooked the point, the omission would surely not indicate a deliberate decision by the testator to forbid any compensation to his attorney.

In the early 1970's, Congress began to focus on the importance of public interest litigation, and since that time, it has enacted numerous fee-shifting statutes. In many of these statutes, which the majority cites at length, see ante, at 1141-1143, Congress has expressly authorized the recovery of expert witness fees as part of the costs of litigation. The question in this case is whether, notwithstanding the omission of such an express authorization in 42 U.S.C. § 1988, Congress intended to authorize such recovery when it provided for "a reasonable attorney's fee as part of the costs." In my view, just as the omission of express authorization in a will does not preclude compensation to an estate's attorney, the omission of express authorization for expert witness fees in a fee-shifting provision should not preclude the award of expert witness fees. We should look at the way in which the Court has interpreted the text of *this statute* in the past, as well as *this statute's* legislative history, to resolve the question before us, rather than looking at the text of the many other statutes that the majority cites in which Congress expressly recognized the need for compensating expert witnesses.

I

Under either the broad view of "costs" typically assumed in the fee-shifting context or the broad view of "a reasonable attorney's fee" articulated by this Court, expert witness fees are a proper component of an award under § 1988. Because we are not interpreting these words for the first time, they should be evaluated in the context that this and other courts have already created.

The term "costs" has a different and broader meaning in fee-shifting statutes than it has in the cost statutes that apply to ordinary litigation. The cost bill in this case illustrates the point. Leaving aside the question of expert witness fees, the prevailing party sought reimbursement for $45,867 in disbursements, see App. to Pet. for Cert. C-1, which plainly would not have been recoverable costs under 28 U.S.C. § 1920. These expenses, including such items as travel and long-distance telephone calls, were allowed by the District Court and were not even questioned by respondents. They were expenses that a retained lawyer would ordinarily bill to his or her client. They were accordingly considered proper "costs" in a case of this kind.

The broad construction typically given to "costs" in the fee-shifting context is highlighted by THE CHIEF JUSTICE's contrasting view in Missouri v. Jenkins, 491 U.S. 274, 109 S.Ct. 2463, 105 L.Ed.2d 229 (1989), in which he argued that paralegal and law clerk fees could not even be awarded as "costs" under 28 U.S.C. § 1920. One of the issues in *Jenkins* was the *rate* at which the services of law clerks and paralegals should be compensated. The State contended that actual cost, rather than market value, should govern. It did not, however, even question the propriety of reimbursing the prevailing party for the work of these nonlawyers. Only THE CHIEF JUSTICE-in a lone dissent the reasoning of which is now endorsed by the Court-advanced a purely literal interpretation of the statute. He wrote:

"I also disagree with the State's suggestion that law clerk and paralegal expenses incurred by a prevailing party, if not recoverable at market rates as 'attorney's fees' under § 1988, are nonetheless recoverable at actual cost under that statute. The language of § 1988 expands the traditional definition of 'costs' to include 'a reasonable attorney's fee,' but it cannot fairly be read to authorize the recovery of all other out-of-pocket expenses actually incurred by the prevailing party in the course of litigation. Absent specific statutory authorization for the recovery of such expenses, the prevailing party remains subject to the limitations on cost recovery imposed by Federal Rule of Civil Procedure 54(d) and 28 U.S.C. § 1920, which govern the taxation of costs in federal litigation where a cost-shifting statute is not applicable. Section 1920 gives the district court discretion to tax certain types of costs against the losing party in any federal litigation. The statute specifically enumerates six categories of expenses which may be taxed as costs: fees of the court clerk and marshal; fees of the court reporter; printing fees and witness fees; copying fees; certain docket fees; and fees of court-appointed experts and interpreters. We have held that this list is exclusive. *Crawford Fitting Co. v. J. T. Gibbons, Inc.*, 482 U.S. 437 [107 S.Ct. 2494, 96 L.Ed.2d 385] (1987). Since none of these categories can possibly be construed to include the fees of law clerks and paralegals, I would also hold that reimbursement for these expenses may not be separately awarded at actual cost." 491 U.S., at 297-298, 109 S.Ct., at 2476-2477.

Although THE CHIEF JUSTICE argued that charges for the work of paralegals and law clerks were not part of the narrowly defined "costs" that were reimbursable under § 1920, nor were they part of an "attorney's fee" reimbursable under § 1988, the Court did not reach THE CHIEF JUSTICE's point about costs because it held in *Jenkins* that such expenses were part of a "reasonable attorney's fee" authorized by § 1988, and thus could be reimbursed at market rate. In the Court's view, a "reasonable attorney's fee" referred to "a reasonable fee for the work product of an attorney," *Id.*, at 285, 109 S.Ct., at 2470. We explained:

"[T]he fee must take into account the work not only of attorneys, but also of secretaries, messengers, librarians, janitors, and others whose labor contributes to the work product for which an attorney bills her client; and it must also take account of other expenses and profit. The parties have suggested no reason why the work of paralegals should not be similarly compensated, nor can we think of any. We thus take as our starting point the self-evident proposition that the 'reasonable attorney's fee' provided for by statute should compensate the work of paralegals, as well as that of attorneys." *Ibid.*

In *Jenkins*, the Court acknowledged that the use of paralegals instead of attorneys reduced the cost of litigation, and " 'by reducing the spiraling cost of civil rights litigation, further[ed] the policies underlying civil rights statutes.' " *Id.*, at 288, 109 S.Ct., at 2471. If attorneys were forced to do the work that paralegals could just as easily perform under the supervision of an attorney, such as locating and interviewing witnesses or compiling statistical and financial data, then "it would not be surprising to see a greater amount of such work performed by attorneys themselves, thus increasing the overall cost of litigation." *Id.*, at 288, n. 10, 109 S.Ct., at 2472, n. 10.

This reasoning applies equally to other forms of specialized litigation support that a trial lawyer needs and that the client customarily pays for, either directly or indirectly. Although reliance on paralegals is a more recent development than the use of traditional expert witnesses, both paralegals and expert witnesses perform important tasks that save lawyers' time and enhance the quality of their work product. In this case, it is undisputed that the District Court correctly found that the expert witnesses were "essential" and "necessary" to the successful prosecution of the plaintiff's case, and that their data and analysis played a pivotal role in the attorney's trial preparation. Had the attorneys attempted to perform the tasks that the experts performed, it obviously would have taken them far longer than the experts and the entire case would have been far more costly to the parties. As Judge Posner observed in a comparable case:

"The time so spent by the expert is a substitute for lawyer time, just as paralegal time is, for if prohibited (or deterred by the cost) from hiring an expert the lawyer would attempt to educate himself about the expert's area of expertise. To forbid the shifting of the expert's fee would encourage underspecialization and inefficient trial preparation, just as to forbid shifting the cost of paralegals would encourage lawyers to do paralegals' work. There is thus no basis for distinguishing *Jenkins* from the present case so far as time spent by these experts in educating the plaintiffs' lawyer is concerned...." *Friedrich v. Chicago*, 888 F.2d 511, 514 (CA7 1989).

In *Jenkins*, we interpreted the award of "a reasonable *attorney's fee*" to cover charges for paralegals and law clerks, even though a paralegal or law clerk is not an attorney. Similarly, the federal courts routinely allow an attorney's travel expenses or long-distance telephone calls to be awarded, even though they are not literally part of an "attorney's *fee*," or part of "costs" as defined by 28 U.S.C. § 1920. To allow reimbursement of these other categories of expenses, and yet not to include expert witness fees, is both arbitrary and contrary to the broad remedial purpose that inspired the fee-shifting provision of § 1988.

II

The Senate Report on the Civil Rights Attorney's Fees Awards Act of 1976 explained that the purpose of the proposed amendment to 42 U.S.C. § 1988 was "to remedy anomalous gaps in our civil rights laws created by the United States Supreme

Court's recent decision in *Alyeska Pipeline Service Co. v. Wilderness Society*, 421 U.S. 240, 95 S.Ct. 1612, 44 L.Ed.2d 141 (1975), and to achieve consistency in our civil rights laws." [FN7] S.Rep. No. 94-1011, p. 1 (1976), 1976 U.S.Code Cong. & Admin. News 5909. The Senate Committee on the Judiciary wanted to level the playing field so that private citizens, who might have little or no money, could still serve as "private attorneys general" and afford to bring actions, even against state or local bodies, to enforce the civil rights laws. The Committee acknowledged that "[i]f private citizens are to be able to assert their civil rights, and if those who violate the Nation's fundamental laws are not to proceed with impunity, then citizens must have the opportunity to recover *what it costs them* to vindicate these rights in court." *Id.*, at 2, 1976 U.S.Code Cong. & Admin.News 5910 (emphasis added). According to the Committee, the bill would create "no startling new remedy," but would simply provide "the technical requirements" requested by the Supreme Court in *Alyeska*, so that courts could "continue the practice of awarding attorneys' fees which had been going on for years prior to the Court's May decision." *Id.*, at 6, 1976 U.S.Code Cong. & Admin.News 5913.

FN7. In *Alyeska Pipeline Service Co. v. Wilderness Society*, 421 U.S. 240, 95 S.Ct. 1612, 44 L.Ed.2d 141 (1975), the Court held that courts were not free to fashion new exceptions to the American Rule, according to which each side assumed the cost of its own attorney's fees. The Court reasoned that it was not the Judiciary's role "to invade the legislature's province by redistributing litigation costs ...," *id.*, at 271, 95 S.Ct., at 1628, and that it would be "inappropriate for the Judiciary, without legislative guidance, to reallocate the burdens of litigation...." *Id.*, at 247, 95 S.Ct., at 1616.

To underscore its intention to return the courts to their pre-*Alyeska* practice of shifting fees in civil rights cases, the Senate Committee's Report cited with approval not only several cases in which fees had been shifted, but also all of the cases contained in Legal Fees, Hearings before the Subcommittee on Representation of Citizen Interests of the Senate Committee on the Judiciary, 93d Cong., 1st Sess., pt. 3, pp. 888-1024, 1060-1062 (1973) (hereinafter Senate Hearings). See S.Rep. No. 94-1011, at 4, n. 3. The cases collected in the 1973 Senate Hearings included many in which courts had permitted the shifting of costs, including expert witness fees. At the time when the Committee referred to these cases, though several were later reversed, it used them to make the point that prior to *Alyeska*, courts awarded attorney's fees and costs, including expert witness fees, in civil rights cases, and that they did so in order to encourage private citizens to bring such suits.[FN8] It was to this pre-*Alyeska* regime, in which courts could award expert witness fees along with attorney's fees, that the Senate Committee intended to return through the passage of the fee-shifting amendment to § 1988.

The House Report expressed concerns similar to those raised by the Senate Report. It noted that "[t]he effective enforcement of Federal civil rights statutes depends largely on the efforts of private citizens" and that the House bill was "designed to give such persons effective access to the judicial process...." H.R.Rep. No. 94-1558, p. 1 (1976). The House Committee on the Judiciary concluded that "civil rights litigants were suffering very severe hardships because of the *Alyeska* decision," and that the case had had a "devastating impact" and had created a "compelling need" for a fee-shifting provision in the civil rights context. *Id.*, at 2-3.

According to both Reports, the record of House and Senate subcommittee hearings, consisting of the testimony and written submissions of public officials, scholars, practicing attorneys, and private citizens, and the questions of the legislators, makes clear that both committees were concerned with preserving access to the courts and encouraging public interest litigation.[FN9]

FN9. A frequently expressed concern was the need to undo the damage to public interest litigation caused by *Alyeska.* See, *e.g.,* Awarding of Attorneys' Fees, Hearings before the Subcommittee on Courts, Civil Liberties, and the Administration of Justice of the House Committee on the Judiciary, 94th Cong., 1st Sess., 2, 41, 42, 43, 54, 82-85, 87, 90-92, 94, 103, 119-121, 123-125, 134, 150, 153-155, 162, 182-183, 269, 272-273, 370, 378-395, 416-418 (1975) (hereinafter House Hearings). Many who testified expressed the view that attorneys needed fee-shifting provisions so that they could afford to work on public interest litigation, see, *e.g., id.,* at 66-67, 76, 78-79, 80, 89, 124-125, 137-142, 146, 158-159, 276-277, 278-280, 306-308; see also *id.,* at 316-326; Senate Hearings, pt. 3, pp. 789-790, 855-857, 1115, and private citizens needed fee-shifting provisions so that they could be made whole again, see, *e.g.,* House Hearings, pp. 60, 189, 192, 254-255, 292, 328; see also *id.,* at 106-111, 343-345, 347-349. For example, the private citizen who was brought into court by the Government and who later prevailed would still not be made whole, because he had to bear the costs of his own attorney's fees. The Senate Hearings also examined the average citizen's lack of access to the legal system. See, *e.g.,* Senate Hearings, pts. 1, 2, pp. 1-2, 3-4, 273 (addressing question whether coal miners were receiving adequate legal coverage); *id.,* pt. 2, at 466, 470-471, 505-509, 515 (addressing question whether veterans were denied legal assistance by $10 contingent fee); *id.,* pt. 3, at 789, 791-796, 808-810 (Indians' access to lawyers); *id.,* pt. 3, at 1127, 1253-1254 (average citizen cannot afford attorney).

It is fair to say that throughout the course of the hearings, a recurring theme was the desire to return to the pre-*Alyeska* practice in which courts could shift fees, including expert witness fees, and make those who acted as private attorneys general whole again, thus encouraging the enforcement of the civil rights laws.

The case before us today is precisely the type of public interest litigation that Congress intended to encourage by amending § 1988 to provide for fee shifting of a "reasonable attorney's fee as part of the costs." Petitioner, a tertiary medical center in West Virginia near the Pennsylvania border, provides services to a large number of Medicaid recipients throughout Pennsylvania. In January 1986, when the Pennsylvania Department of Public Welfare notified petitioner of its new Medicaid payment rates for Pennsylvania Medicaid recipients, petitioner believed them to be below the minimum standards for reimbursement specified by the Social Security Act. Petitioner successfully challenged the adequacy of the State's payment system under 42 U.S.C. § 1983.

This Court's determination today that petitioner must assume the cost of $104,133 in expert witness fees is at war with the congressional purpose of making the prevailing party whole. As we said in *Hensley v. Eckerhart,* 461 U.S. 424, 435, 103 S.Ct. 1933, 1940, 76 L.Ed.2d 40 (1983), petitioner's recovery should be "fully compensatory," or, as we expressed in *Jenkins,* petitioner's recovery should be "comparable to what 'is traditional with attorneys compensated by a fee-paying client.' S.Rep. No. 94-1011, p. 6 (1976), U.S.Code Cong. & Admin. News 1976, pp. 5908, 5913." 491 U.S., at 286, 109 S.Ct., at 2470-2471.

III

In recent years the Court has vacillated between a purely literal approach to the task of statutory interpretation and an approach that seeks guidance from historical context, legislative history, and prior cases identifying the purpose that motivated the legislation. Thus, for example, in *Christiansburg Garment Co. v. EEOC,* 434 U.S. 412, 98 S.Ct. 694, 54 L.Ed.2d 648 (1978), we rejected a "mechanical construction," *id.,* at 418, 98 S.Ct., at 699, of the fee-shifting provision in § 706(k) of Title VII of the Civil Rights Act of 1964 that the prevailing defendant had urged upon us. Although the text of the statute drew no distinction between different kinds of "prevailing parties," we held that awards to prevailing plaintiffs are governed by a more liberal standard than awards to prevailing defendants. That holding rested entirely on our evaluation of the relevant congressional policy and found no support within the four corners of the statutory text. Nevertheless, the holding was unanimous and, to the best of my knowledge, evoked no adverse criticism or response in Congress.

On those occasions, however, when the Court has put on its thick grammarian's spectacles and ignored the available evidence of congressional purpose and the teaching of prior cases construing a statute, the congressional response has been dramatically different. It is no coincidence that the Court's literal reading of Title VII, which led to the conclusion that disparate treatment of pregnant and nonpregnant persons was not discrimination on the basis of sex, see *General Electric Co. v. Gilbert,* 429 U.S. 125, 97 S.Ct. 401, 50 L.Ed.2d 343 (1976), was repudiated by the 95th Congress; that its literal reading of the "continuous physical presence" requirement in § 244(a)(1) of the Immigration and Nationality Act, which led to the view that the statute did not permit even temporary or inadvertent absences from this country, see *INS v. Phinpathya,* 464 U.S. 183, 104 S.Ct. 584, 78 L.Ed.2d 401 (1984), was rebuffed by the 99th Congress; that its literal reading of the word "program" in Title IX of the Education Amendments of 1972, which led to the Court's gratuitous limit on the scope of the antidiscrimination provisions of Title IX, see *Grove City College v. Bell,* 465 U.S. 555, 104 S.Ct. 1211, 79 L.Ed.2d 516 (1984), was rejected by the 100th Congress; or that its refusal to accept the teaching of earlier decisions in *Wards Cove Packing Co. v. Atonio,* 490 U.S. 642, 109 S.Ct. 2115, 104 L.Ed.2d 733 (1989) (reformulating order of proof and weight of parties' burdens in disparate-impact cases), and *Patterson v. McLean Credit Union,* 491 U.S. 164, 109 S.Ct. 2363, 105 L.Ed.2d 132 (1989) (limiting scope of 42 U.S.C. § 1981 to the making and enforcement of contracts), was overwhelmingly rejected by the 101st Congress, and its refusal to accept the widely held view of lower courts about the scope of fraud, see *McNally v. United States,* 483 U.S. 350, 107 S.Ct. 2875, 97 L.Ed.2d 292 (1987) (limiting mail fraud to protection of property), was quickly corrected by the 100th Congress.

In the domain of statutory interpretation, Congress is the master. It obviously has the power to correct our mistakes, but we do the country a disservice when we needlessly ignore persuasive evidence of Congress' actual purpose and require it "to take the time to revisit the matter" and to restate its purpose in more precise English whenever its work product suffers from an omission or inadvertent error. As Judge Learned Hand explained, statutes are likely to be imprecise.

"All [legislators] have done is to write down certain words which they mean to apply generally to situations of that kind. To apply these literally may either pervert what was plainly their general meaning, or leave undisposed of what there is every reason to suppose they meant to provide for. Thus it is not enough for the judge just to use a dictionary. If he should do no more, he might come out with a result which every sensible man would recognize to be quite the opposite of what was really intended; which would contradict or leave unfulfilled its plain purpose." L. Hand, How Far Is a Judge Free in Rendering a Decision?, in The Spirit of Liberty 103, 106 (I. Dilliard ed.1952).

The Court concludes its opinion with the suggestion that disagreement with its textual analysis could only be based on the dissenters' preference for a "better" statute, *ante,* at 1148. It overlooks the possibility that a different view may be more faithful to Congress' command. The fact that Congress has consistently provided for the inclusion of expert witness fees in fee-shifting statutes when it considered the matter is a weak reed on which to rest the conclusion that the omission of such a provision represents a deliberate decision to forbid such awards. Only time will tell whether the Court, with its literal reading [FN19] of § 1988, has correctly interpreted the will of Congress with respect to the issue it has resolved today.

FN19. Seventy years ago, Justice Cardozo warned of the dangers of literal reading, whether of precedents or statutes:

"[Some judges'] notion of their duty is to match the colors of the case at hand against the colors of many sample cases spread out upon their desk. The sample nearest in shade supplies the applicable rule. But, of course, no system of living law can be evolved by such a process, and no judge of a high court, worthy of his office, views the function of his place so narrowly. If that were all there was to our calling, there would be little of intellectual interest about it. The man who had the best card index of the cases would also be the wisest judge. It is when the colors do not match, when the references in the index fail, when there is no decisive precedent, that the serious business of the judge begins." The Nature of the Judicial Process, at 20-21.

I respectfully dissent.

III. S. Rep. No. 94-1011, at 1-5 (June 29, 1976)

Calendar No. 955

94TH CONGRESS 2d Session	SENATE	REPORT No. 94–1011

CIVIL RIGHTS ATTORNEYS' FEES AWARDS ACT

JUNE 29 (legislative day, JUNE 18), 1976.—Ordered to be printed

---

Mr. TUNNEY, from the Committee on the Judiciary,
submitted the following

REPORT

[To accompany S. 2278]

The Committee on the Judiciary, to which was referred the bill (S. 2278) to amend Revised Statutes section 722 (42 U.S.C. § 1988) to allow a court, in its discretion, to award attorneys' fees to a prevailing party in suits brought to enforce certain civil rights acts, having considered the same, reports favorably thereon and recommends that the bill do pass.

The text of S. 2278 is as follows:

S. 2278

Revised Statutes section 722 (42 U.S.C. Sec. 1988) is amended by adding the following: "In any action or proceeding to enforce a provision of sections 1977, 1978, 1979, 1980 and 1981 of the Revised Statutes, or Title VI of the Civil Rights Act of 1964, the court, in its discretion, may allow the prevailing party, other than the United States, a reasonable attorney's fee as part of the costs.".

PURPOSE

This amendment to the Civil Rights Act of 1866, Revised Statutes Section 722, gives the Federal courts discretion to award attorneys' fees to prevailing parties in suits brought to enforce the civil rights acts which Congress has passed since 1866. The purpose of this amendment is to remedy anomalous gaps in our civil rights laws created by the United States Supreme Court's recent decision in *Alyeska Pipeline Service Co.* v. *Wilderness Society*, 421 U.S. 240 (1975), and to achieve consistency in our civil rights laws.

57–010

2

HISTORY OF THE LEGISLATION

The bill grows out of six days of hearings on legal fees held before the Subcommittee on the Representation of Citizen Interests of this Committee in 1973. There were more than thirty witnesses, including Federal and State public officials, scholars, practicing attorneys from many areas of expertise, and private citizens. Those who did not appear were given the opportunity to submit material for the record, and many did so, including the representatives of the American Bar Association and the Bar Associations of 22 States and the District of Columbia. The hearings, when published, included not only the testimony and exhibits, but numerous statutory provisions, proposed legislation, case reports and scholarly articles.

In 1975, the provisions of S. 2278 were incorporated in a proposed amendment to S. 1279, extending the Voting Rights Act of 1965.

The Subcommittee on Constitutional Rights specifically approved the amendment on June 11, 1975, by a vote of 8–2, and the full Committee favorably reported it on July 18, 1975, as part of S. 1279. Because of time pressure to pass the Voting Rights Amendments, the Senate took action on the House-passed version of the legislation. S. 1279 was not taken up on the Senate floor; hence, the attorneys' fees amendment was never considered.

On July 31, 1975, Senator Tunney introduced S. 2278, which is identical to the amendment to S. 1279 which was reported favorably by this Committee last summer.

Shortly thereafter, similar legislation was introduced in the House of Representatives, including H.R. 9552, which is identical to S. 2278 except for one minor technical difference. The Subcommittee on Courts, Civil Liberties and the Administration of Justice of the House Judiciary Committee has conducted three days of hearings at which the witnesses have generally confirmed the record presented to this Committee in 1973. H.R. 9552, the counterpart of S. 2278, has received widespread support by the witnesses appearing before the House Subcommittee.

STATEMENT

The purpose and effect of S. 2278 are simple—it is designed to allow courts to provide the familiar remedy of reasonable counsel fees to prevailing parties in suits to enforce the civil rights acts which Congress has passed since 1866. S. 2278 follows the language of Titles II and VII of the Civil Rights Act of 1964, 42 U.S.C. §§ 2000a–3(b) and 2000e–5(k), and section 402 of the Voting Rights Act Amendments of 1975, 42 U.S.C. § 1973l(e). All of these civil rights laws depend heavily upon private enforcement, and fee awards have proved an essential remedy if private citizens are to have a meaningful opportunity to vindicate the important Congressional policies which these laws contain.

In many cases arising under our civil rights laws, the citizen who must sue to enforce the law has little or no money with which to hire a lawyer. If private citizens are to be able to assert their civil rights, and if those who violate the Nation's fundamental laws are not to proceed with impunity, then citizens must have the opportunity to recover what it costs them to vindicate these rights in court.

S.R. 1011

192

3

Congress recognized this need when it made specific provision for such fee shifting in Titles II and VII of the Civil Rights Act of 1964:

> When a plaintiff brings an action under [Title II] he cannot recover damages. If he obtains an injunction, he does so not for himself alone but also as a "private attorney general," vindicating a policy that Congress considered of the highest priority. If successful plaintiffs were routinely forced to bear their own attorneys' fees, few aggrieved parties would be in a position to advance the public interest by invoking the injunctive powers of the Federal courts. Congress therefore enacted the provision for counsel fees—* * * to encourage individuals injured by racial discrimination to seek judicial relief under Title II." *Newman* v. *Piggie Park Enterprises, Inc.*, 390 U.S. 400, 402 (1968).

The idea of the "private attorney general" is not a new one, nor are attorneys' fees a new remedy. Congress has commonly authorized attorneys' fees in laws under which "private attorneys general" play a significant role in enforcing our policies. We have, since 1870, authorized fee shifting under more than 50 laws, including, among others, the Securities Exchange Act of 1934, 15 U.S.C. §§ 78i(c) and 78r(a), the Servicemen's Readjustment Act of 1958, 38 U.S.C. § 1822(b), the Communications Act of 1934, 42 U.S.C. § 206, and the Organized Crime Control Act of 1970, 18 U.S.C. § 1964(c). In cases under these laws, fees are an integral part of the remedy necessary to achieve compliance with our statutory policies. As former Justice Tom Clark found, in a union democracy suit under the Labor-Management Reporting and Disclosure Act (Landrum-Griffin),

> Not to award counsel fees in cases such as this would be tantamount to repealing the Act itself by frustrating its basic purpose. * * * Without counsel fees the grant of Federal jurisdiction is but an empty gesture * * *. *Hall* v. *Cole*, 412 U.S. 1 (1973), quoting 462 F. 2d 777, 780–81 (2d Cir. 1972).

The remedy of attorneys' fees has always been recognized as particularly appropriate in the civil rights area, and civil rights and attorneys' fees have always been closely interwoven. In the civil rights area, Congress has instructed the courts to use the broadest and most effective remedies available to achieve the goals of our civil rights laws.[1] The very first attorneys' fee statute was a civil rights law, the Enforcement Act of 1870, 16 Stat. 140, which provided for attorneys' fees in three separate provisions protecting voting rights.[2]

Modern civil rights legislation reflects a heavy reliance on attorneys' fees as well. In 1964, seeking to assure full compliance with the Civil Rights Act of that year, we authorized fee shifting for private suits establishing violations of the public accommodations and equal employment provisions. 42 U.S.C. §§ 2000a–3(b) and 2000e–5(k). Since 1964, every major civil rights law passed by the Congress has included, or has been amended to include, one or more fee provisions.

---

[1] For example, the Civil Rights Act of 1866 directed Federal courts to "use that combination of Federal law, common law and State law as will be best adapted to the object of the civil rights laws." *Brown* v. *City of Meridian, Mississippi*, 356 F. 2d 602, 605 (5th Cir. 1966). See 42 U.S.C. § 1988; *Lefton* v. *City of Hattiesburg, Mississippi*, 333 F. 2d 280 (5th Cir. 1964).

[2] The causes of action established by these provisions were eliminated in 1894. 28 Stat. 36.

S.R. 1011

4

E.g., Title VIII of the Civil Rights Act of 1968, 42 U.S.C. § 3612(c); the Emergency School Aid Act of 1972, 20 U.S.C. § 1617; the Equal Employment Amendments of 1972, 42 U.S.C. § 2000e–16(b); and the Voting Rights Act Extension of 1975, 42 U.S.C. § 1973*l*(e).

These fee shifting provisions have been successful in enabling vigorous enforcement of modern civil rights legislation, while at the same time limiting the growth of the enforcement bureaucracy. Before May 12, 1975, when the Supreme Court handed down its decision in *Alyeska Pipeline Service Co.* v. *Wilderness Society*, 421 U.S. 240 (1975), many lower Federal courts throughout the Nation had drawn the obvious analogy between the Reconstruction Civil Rights Acts and these modern civil rights acts, and, following Congressional recognition in the newer statutes of the "private attorney general" concept, were exercising their traditional equity powers to award attorneys' fees under early civil rights laws as well.[3]

These pre-*Alyeska* decisions remedied a gap in the specific statutory provisions and restored an important historic remedy for civil rights violations. However, in *Alyeska*, the United States Supreme Court, while referring to the desirability of fees in a variety of circumstances, ruled that only Congress, and not the courts, could specify which laws were important enough to merit fee shifting under the "private attorney general" theory. The Court expressed the view, in dictum, that the Reconstruction Acts did not contain the necessary congressional authorization. This decision and dictum created anomalous gaps in our civil rights laws whereby awards of fees are, according to *Alyeska*, suddenly unavailable in the most fundamental civil rights cases. For instance, fees are now authorized in an employment discrimination suit under Title VII of the 1964 Civil Rights Act, but not in the same suit brought under 42 U.S.C. § 1981, which protects similar rights but involves fewer technical prerequisites to the filing of an action. Fees are allowed in a housing discrimination suit under Title VIII of the Civil Rights Act of 1968, but not in the same suit brought under 42 U.S.C. § 1982, a Reconstruction Act protecting the same rights. Likewise, fees are allowed in a suit under Title II of the 1964 Civil Rights Act challenging discrimination in a private restaurant, but not in suits under 42 U.S.C. § 1983 redressing violations of the Federal Constitution or laws by officials sworn to uphold the laws.

This bill, S. 2278, is an appropriate response to the *Alyeska* decision. It is limited to cases arising under our civil rights laws, a category of cases in which attorneys fees have been traditionally regarded as appropriate. It remedies gaps in the language of these civil rights laws by providing the specific authorization required by the Court in *Alyeska*, and makes our civil rights laws consistent.

It is intended that the standards for awarding fees be generally the same as under the fee provisions of the 1964 Civil Rights Act. A party seeking to enforce the rights protected by the statutes covered by S. 2278, if successful, "should ordinarily recover an attorney's fee unless special circumstances would render such an award unjust." *Newman* v. *Piggie Park Enterprises, Inc.*, 390 U.S. 400, 402 (1968).[4]

---

[3] These civil rights cases are too numerous to cite here. See, e.g., *Sims* v. *Amos* 340 F. Supp. 691 (M.D. Ala. 1972), aff'd, 409 U.S. 942 (1972); *Stanford Daily* v. *Zurcher*, 366 F. Supp. 18 (N.D. Cal. 1973); and cases cited in *Alyeska Pipeline, supra*, at n. 46. Many of the relevant cases are collected in "Hearings on the Effect of Legal Fees on the Adequacy of Representation Before the Subcom. on Representation of Citizen Interests of the Senate Comm. on the Judiciary," 93d Cong., 1st sess., pt. III, at pp. 888–1024, and 1060–62.

[4] In the large majority of cases the party or parties seeking to enforce such rights will be the plaintiffs and/or plaintiff-intervenors. However, in the procedural posture of some cases, the parties seeking to enforce such rights may be the defendants and/or defendant-intervenors. See, e.g., *Shelley* v. *Kraemer*, 334 U.S. 1 (1948).

5

Such "private attorneys general" should not be deterred from bringing good faith actions to vindicate the fundamental rights here involved by the prospect of having to pay their opponent's counsel fees should they lose. *Richardson v. Hotel Corporation of America*, 332 F. Supp. 519 (E.D. La. 1971), aff'd, 468 F. 2d 951 (5th Cir. 1972). (A fee award to a defendant's employer, was held unjustified where a claim of racial discrimination, though meritless, was made in good faith.) Such a party, if unsuccessful, could be assessed his opponent's fee only where it is shown that his suit was clearly frivolous, vexatious, or brought for harassment purposes. *United States Steel Corp. v. United States*, 385 F. Supp. 346 (W.D. Pa. 1974), aff'd, 9 E.P.D. ¶ 10,225 (3d Cir. 1975). This bill thus deters frivolous suits by authorizing an award of attorneys' fees against a party shown to have litigated in "bad faith" under the guise of attempting to enforce the Federal rights created by the statutes listed in S. 2278. Similar standards have been followed not only in the Civil Rights Act of 1964, but in other statutes providing for attorneys' fees. E.g., the Water Pollution Control Act, 1972 U.S. Code Cong. & Adm. News 3747; the Marine Protection Act, Id. at 4249–50; and the Clean Air Act, Senate Report No. 91–1196, 91st Cong., 2d Sess., p. 483 (1970). See also *Hutchinson v. William Barry, Inc.*, 50 F. Supp. 292, 298 (D. Mass. 1943) (Fair Labor Standards Act).

(material omitted)

IV. *122 Cong. Rec. 31471 (Sept. 21, 1976)*

September 21, 1976   CONGRESSIONAL RECORD — SENATE   31471

So Mr. ROBERT C. BYRD's motion was agreed to.

CLOTURE MOTION

Mr. ROBERT C. BYRD. Mr. President, I send a cloture motion to the desk.

The PRESIDING OFFICER. The cloture motion having been presented under rule XXII, the Chair, without objection, directs the clerk to read the motion.

The legislative clerk read as follows:

CLOTURE MOTION

We, the undersigned Senators, in accordance with the provisions of Rule XXII of the Standing Rules of the Senate, hereby move to bring to a close the debate upon S. 2278, the Civil Rights Attorneys' Fees Awards Act of 1975.

Hubert H. Humphrey, Birch Bayh, Quentin N. Burdick, Alan Cranston, Robert C. Byrd, Patrick J. Leahy, William D. Hathaway, Dick Clark, Edward M. Kennedy, James Abourezk, Hugh Scott, Harrison A. Williams, John A. Durkin, James B. Pearson, Bob Packwood, Frank E. Moss, Jacob K. Javits, William Proxmire, Henry M. Jackson, Lowell P. Weicker, Mark O. Hatfield.

CIVIL RIGHTS ATTORNEYS' FEES AWARDS ACT

The Senate continued with the consideration of the bill (S. 2278) relating to the Civil Rights Attorneys' Fees Awards Act of 1975.

Mr. HUGH SCOTT. Mr. President, I rise in support of S. 2278.

I believe it ranks among the most important measures we will act on this year. Simply stated, S. 2278 is designed principally to allow the courts to award attorneys fees to prevailing plaintiffs in civil rights cases. Such a provision would greatly aid the cause of human rights in this country, would cost the Government nothing, and would make the civil rights laws almost self-enforcing.

If we pass this worthwhile measure, we will do a great service in the continuing battle to eradicate discrimination in the United States. And we will do so without an increase in the Federal budget or in the bureaucracy.

Each of the provisions covered by S. 2278 relies upon private enforcement. Recently, spiraling court costs have created an absolute necessity of attorney's fee provisions in those civil rights statutes which contain citizen suit provisions. Congress should encourage citizens to go to court in private suits to vindicate its policies and protect their rights. To do so, Congress must insure that they have the means to go to court and to be effective once they get there. This is particularly true in the civil rights area, where those men and women whom the laws protect are rarely, if ever, in a financial position to undertake the costly task of enforcement of their rights.

The enactment of S. 2278 is needed to assure that attorney's fees will be available in suits brought under the reconstruction-era civil rights laws, title VI of the 1964 Civil Rights Act, and title IX of the Education Amendments of 1972 in the same fashion and to the same extent as the statutes presently provide in cases brought under title VII of the 1964 Civil Rights Act. Mr. President, as a nation of laws, and as a government of laws, we should welcome citizen suits which succeed in enforcing the laws. Attorney's fees have proven to be a singularly effective and flexible way to encourage private enforcement of public rights, and I strongly urge this body to accept S. 2278.

My one regret is that the distinguished Senator from Michigan (Mr. PHILIP A. HART), who has been at my side so often in the past fighting for the cause of civil rights, cannot be with us for the last battle of this final campaign. His efforts on behalf of the bill earlier in the session proved decisive, however. Without his powerful intellect and moral suasion, the bill would have languished in committee. I know he too joins us in urging its passage.

Mr. MATHIAS. Mr. President, as a supporter of civil rights for all Americans, I support S. 2278, the Civil Rights Attorneys' Fees Awards Act.

The goal of S. 2278 is clear and compelling—to insure that the high cost of litigation does not bar the Federal courts to citizens who seek to enforce their rights under our civil rights laws. By passing S. 2278, the Senate can transform this goal into a reality.

The need for this bill arises from a recent Supreme Court decision which has erected a formidable financial barrier against those seeking access to Federal courts and has consequently dealt a serious blow to the effective enforcement of our civil rights laws. Specifically, in *Alyeska Pipeline Service Co. v. Wilderness Society*, 421 U.S. 240 (1975) the Supreme Court held that Congress, not the judiciary, should authorize the award of attorney fees in cases arising under Federal laws. The Court found that in the absence of clear statutory language the courts were powerless to award attorney's fees.

Given the often staggering costs of litigation, this decision has predictably slowed the number of private suits brought to enforce federally mandated rights, including cases premised upon our civil rights laws. Alyeska presented Congress with an opportunity to enact legislation to help insure that one's financial resources need not be a prerequisite to access to Federal court.

I believe that S. 2278 constitutes a much needed response to Alyeska and is necessary to guarantee the proper enforcement of our civil rights laws which the Congress has so earnestly labored for in the past. Unless the Congress enacts S. 2278, one of the groups of potential litigants most severely affected by Alyeska—those persons seeking to assert their rights under Federal civil rights statutes—will frequently be denied access to Federal courts.

Mr. President, we must bear in mind at all times that rights that cannot be enforced through the legal process are valueless; such a situation breeds cynicism about the basic fairness of our judicial system. Consequently, Congress must be vigilant to insure that our legal rights are not hollow ones.

This vigilance is especially important at a time when access of individuals to our Federal courts has been severely limited by several recent Supreme Court decisions interpreting Federal statutes. Mr. Justice Brennan poignantly described in inequities flowing from such restrictive judicial rulings:

A series of decisions have shaped the doctrines of jurisdiction, justiciability and remedy, so as to increasingly bar the federal courthouse door in the absence of showings probably impossible to make. It is true of course that there has been an increasing amount of litigation of all types filling the calendars of virtually every state and federal court. But a solution that shuts the courthouse door in the face of a litigant with a legitimate claim for relief, particularly a claim for a deprivation of a constitutional right, seems to be not only the wrong tool, but a dangerous tool for solving the problem. The victims of the use of that tool are most often the litigants in need of judicial protection of their rights: the poor, the underprivileged, the deprived minorities. The very life blood of courts is the popular confidence that they mete out evenhanded justice and any discrimination that denies these groups access to the courts for resolution of their meritorious claims, unnecessary risks loss of that confidence.

I fully concur with the views expressed by Justice Brennan and I urge my colleagues to keep his eloquent words in mind when considering S. 2278 and related legislation.

Mr. President, I believe that it is incumbent upon Congress to do its part to insure the proper enforcement of our civil rights laws. By providing for reasonable counsel fees to prevailing parties in civil rights cases, the Congress can take a giant step in that direction by minimizing the formidable barrier erected by the Court's decision. I urge my colleagues to act favorably upon S. 2278.

UP AMENDMENT NO. 469

(Subsequently numbered amendment 2347)

Mr. KENNEDY. Mr. President, I send to the desk an amendment and ask for its immediate consideration.

The PRESIDING OFFICER. The amendment will be stated.

The legislative clerk read as follows:

The Senator from Massachusetts (Mr. KENNEDY) proposes an unprinted amendment numbered 469:

Strike out all after the enacting clause and insert in lieu thereof the following:

That this Act may be cited as "The Civil Rights Attorneys' Fees Awards Act of 1976".

SEC. 2. That the Revised Statutes section 722 (42 U.S.C. 1988) is amended by adding the following: "In any action or proceeding to enforce a provision of sections 1977, 1978, 1979, 1980, and 1981 of the Revised Statutes, title IX of Public Law 92-318, or title VI of the Civil Rights Act of 1964, the court, in its discretion, may allow the prevailing party, other than the United States, a reasonable attorney's fee as part of the costs.".

Mr. KENNEDY. Mr. President, I yield for a unanimous-consent request to the Senator from Maine without losing my right to the floor.

The PRESIDING OFFICER. Is there objection?

Mr. MUSKIE addressed the Chair.

Mr. ALLEN. Mr. President, there will be no unanimous-consent requests granted in the Senate until this matter has been disposed of as long as I am on the floor. I object.

The PRESIDING OFFICER. Objection is heard.

The Senator from Massachusetts has the floor.

Mr. KENNEDY. Then, Mr. President,

V. 122 Cong. Rec. 33313-15 (Sept. 29, 1976)

than to prevailing plaintiffs, and these apply equally in tax cases and in actions brought to enforce the civil rights laws. Awarding fees to prevailing defendants is intended to protect parties from being harassed by unjustifiable lawsuits. It is not, however, intended to deter plaintiffs from seeking to enforce the protections afforded by our civil rights laws, or in this instance to deter the Government from instituting legitimate tax cases by threatening it with the prospect of having to pay the defendant's counsel fees should it lose. Were Congress or the courts to provide otherwise, it would have a substantial chilling effect on the bringing of genuinely meritorious actions. I am sure that none of us would want to inhibit responsible lawsuits brought by the United States to enforce the tax laws of our country.

It should be clear, then, that a provision authorizing fee awards in tax cases has a fundamentally different purpose from one authorizing awards in lawsuits brought by private citizens to enforce the protections of our civil rights laws. In enacting the basic civil rights attorneys fees awards bill, Congress clearly intends to facilitate and to encourage the bringing of actions to enforce the protections of the civil rights laws. By authorizing awards of fees to prevailing defendants in cases brought under the Internal Revenue Code, however, Congress merely intends to protect citizens from becoming victims of frivolous or otherwise unwarranted lawsuits. Enactment of this amendment should in no way be understood as implying that Congress intends to discourage the Government from initiating legitimate lawsuits under the tax laws.

That Congress must act to provide means for citizens to enforce laws that are enacted for their protection can no longer be disputed. It has already included provisions for awards of attorneys fees in over 50 statutes. I was pleased to see that on Tuesday the Senate adopted the conference report on the Toxic Substances Act, which contains several attorneys' fees provisions. The debate on the Senate floor during the past week has underscored the importance of including attorneys' fees provisions in all of our civil rights laws. I think the adoption of Senator ALLEN's amendment complements the legislation we are now considering, and I would very much hope that we would move to its immediate passage.

Mr. President, a parliamentary inquiry.

The PRESIDING OFFICER. The Senator will state it.

Mr. KENNEDY. I believe that the yeas and nays have been ordered on the amendment. Am I correct?

The PRESIDING OFFICER. The Senator is correct.

Mr. KENNEDY. It seems to me that we have voted basically on this principle when we voted on the Allen amendment, and I would be glad to have a voice vote so we could get to passage of the measure, unless there will be objection.

I ask unanimous consent that the order for the yeas and nays be vitiated, so that we can go to third reading and passage.

The PRESIDING OFFICER. Is there

objection? Without objection, it is so ordered.

Mr. ABOUREZK. Mr. President, I ask unanimous consent that the vote on passage be limited to 10 minutes.

Mr. ROBERT C. BYRD. Mr. President, I hope the Senator, in this instance, will not ask for a 10-minute rollcall. There are certain Senators who are attending a reception for PHIL HART, and I am afraid they would miss that vote.

Mr. ABOUREZK. I withdraw the request.

Mr. STENNIS. What was the announcement, Mr. President?

Mr. ABOUREZK. I withdraw my request for a 10-minute vote.

Mr. ROBERT C. BYRD. I ask for the yeas and nays.

The PRESIDING OFFICER. Is there a sufficient second? There is a sufficient second.

The yeas and nays were ordered.

The PRESIDING OFFICER. The question is on agreeing to the amendment of the Senator from Massachusetts, as amended.

The amendment, as amended, was agreed to.

Mr. KENNEDY. I move to reconsider the vote by which the amendment was agreed to.

Mr. ABOUREZK. I move to lay that motion on the table.

The motion to lay on the table was agreed to.

Mr. ALLEN. Mr. President, will the Senator now accept my amendment designating this bill the Kennedy-Tunney-Abourezk lawyers relief bill?

Mr. ABOUREZK. Mr. President, may I be recognized on that?

The PRESIDING OFFICER. No.

[Laughter.]

Mr. ABOUREZK. What if I said please?

Several Senators addressed the Chair.

The PRESIDING OFFICER. The question is on the engrossment and third reading of the bill.

The bill was ordered to be engrossed for a third reading, and was read the third time.

Mr. ABOUREZK. If I said please, could I be recognized?

I just want to make a response to the question of Senator ALLEN as to whether we would accept a name change.

I think, in view of the fact that the Senate has accepted his amendment on it, it ought to be called the Kennedy-Tunney- Abourezk- Allen- Thurmond-Helms-Scott amendment.

[Laughter.]

The PRESIDING OFFICER. The question is, Shall the bill pass?

Mr. TUNNEY. Mr. President, before we vote, I would like to say to my colleagues how deeply I appreciate the Senator from South Dakota's (Mr. ABOUREZK) floor management of the bill, which was my legislation, and also how much I appreciate the very hard work of the majority whip in making sure this legislation stays on track, and the work of Senator KENNEDY and the others who played a part. I, unfortunately, was not able to be present during the major part of the consideration of this legislation, but it was in extraordinarily good hands in the hands of Sen-

ator ABOUREZK. I thank him personally for having floor-managed the bill.

Mr. President, the Senate is nearing enactment of S. 2278—legislation that is vitally important to the enforcement of our Nation's civil rights laws.

As we all know, the last 7 days have been difficult—the bill's fate unclear during much of the time.

It is clear to me that without the determination and care shown by the junior Senator from South Dakota, and ample help from a bipartisan group of Senators and the Acting Majority Leader, this bill would have died.

Instead, it survived and we can be very hopeful that it will be enacted into law this session.

I am proud to have been its initial sponsor.

I see it as a cornerstone of legislation developed by the Subcommittee on Constitutional Rights, which I chair, on the subject of access to justice.

The problem of unequal access to the courts in order to vindicate congressional policies and enforce the law is not simply a problem for lawyers and courts. Encouraging adequate representation is essential if the laws of this Nation are to be enforced. Congress passes a great deal of lofty legislation promising equal rights to all.

Although some of these laws can be enforced by the Justice Department or other Federal agencies, most of the responsibility for enforcement has to rest upon private citizens, who must go to court to prove a violation of the law. This fact has been recognized in statutes specifically giving private citizens the right to go to court to redress grievances, and by court decisions which have broadly expanded the concepts of private causes of action and standing to sue. But without the availability of counsel fees, these rights exist only on paper. Private citizens must be given not only the rights to go to court, but also the legal resources. If the citizen does not have the resources, his day in court is denied him; the congressional policy which he seeks to assert and vindicate goes unvindicated; and the entire Nation, not just the individual citizen, suffers.

Unless effective ways are found to provide equal legal resources, the Nation must expect its most basic and fundamental laws to be objectively repealed by the economic fact of life that the people these laws are meant to benefit and protect cannot take advantage of them. Attorneys' fees have proved one extremely effective way to provide these equal legal resources, and are, in fact, an obvious and logical complement to citizen suit provisions.

When Congress calls upon citizens—either explicitly or by construction of its statutes—to go to court to vindicate its policies and benefit the entire Nation, Congress must also ensure that they have the means to go to court, and to be effective once they get there. No one expects a policeman, or an officeholder, to pay for the privilege of enforcing the law. It should be no different for a private citizen, as the first circuit realized in the 1972 case of Knight against Auciello:

The violation of an important public policy may involve little by way of actual damages, so far as a single individual is concerned, or little in comparison with the cost of vindication. . . . If a defendant may feel that the cost of litigation, and, particularly, that the financial circumstances of an injured party may mean that the chances of suit being brought, or continued in the face of opposition, will be small, there will be little brake upon deliberate wrongdoing.

We cannot hope for vigorous enforcement of our civil rights laws unless we, in the words of the Knight court, "remove the burden from the shoulders of the plaintiff seeking to vindicate the public right." That is what this bill does, and why it is so vital.

Mr. KENNEDY. Mr. President, I want to take a moment to address the charge, made by certain opponents of S. 2278, that this is a lawyers' relief bill. That could not be further from the truth.

The lawyer who undertakes to represent a client alleging a violation of the civil rights statutes covered by this bill faces significant uncertainty of payment, even where he has a strong case. For there is often important principles to be gained in such litigation, and rights to be conferred or enforced, but just as often no large promise of monetary recovery lies at the end of the tunnel. So civil rights cases—unlike tort or antitrust cases—do not provide the prevailing plaintiff with a large recovery from which he can pay his lawyer. That is why Congress has already decided in many recent civil rights laws to include provisions for recovery of attorneys' fees, in order to insure that the rights guaranteed by the laws are not lost through the inability of those who are supposed to benefit to obtain judicial enforcement of those rights.

Even with enactment of this bill, the lawyer who undertakes to represent a client will face more uncertainty of payment than one involved in a usual contingency fee case. His fee is contingent not only upon his success, but also upon the discretion of the judge before whom he appears.

Even if he wins his case, and the judge decides he has won a fee as well, his rate of compensation is fixed not by a grateful client, but by a disinterested judge. In the traditional contingency case, the lawyer is assured of a high percentage of a monetary award should he win. If the proponents of this bill were interested in creating a relief fund for lawyers, they would surely have gone about it in a different fashion.

No, this bill is not for the purpose of aiding lawyers. The purpose of this bill is to aid civil rights. Before the Alyeska case of last year, the Federal courts throughout the country were assuming that their traditional equity jurisdiction covered the granting of fees, and were awarding attorneys' fees under the statutes included in this bill. This practice was reviving the older civil rights statutes and increasing tremendously the enforcement of the rights involved. In Alyeska the Supreme Court said that, no matter how beneficial this practice might be in certain areas of the law, only Congress, and not the courts, had the power to decide which areas of the law deserved the additional inducement of attorneys' fees for enforcement. Civil rights is one of those areas.

The provisions covered by this bill are laws, since they protect the most basic civil rights. There are laws which we have learned, sadly, are prone to be violated, and which require the utmost vigilance by private enforcement if they are not to be rendered useless.

Mr. President, a short glance at a few cases under these laws may be instructive. These are all cases which were made possible by counsel fee awards before Alyeska, and which could probably not be brought today. They are but a few of the many examples of the need for this bill.

In one case, a veteran of the U.S. Army died, and his family was told he could not be buried in the local cemetery because his skin was black. *Terry v. Elmwood Cemetery,* 307 F. Supp. 369 (N.D. Ala. 1969). In other cases, black citizens had been systematically kept off the jury lists in many counties for years, thus denying justice. *Ford v. White,* 430 F.2d 951 (5th Cir. 1970). In one case, a musician was repeatedly followed by police, stopped, harassed and arrested—again because of his skin color. *Lyle v. Teresi,* 327 F. Supp. 683 (D. Minn. 1971). Then there was a case in which doctors who participated in a program of medical assistance to black citizens were denied any privileges in a local hospital. *Blumenthal v. Lee Memorial Hospital* (E.D. Ark. August 6, 1971). And a case where a highway was planned specifically to go through a black neighborhood and displace its residents, while carefully skirting around white neighborhoods. *La Raza Unida v. Volpe,* 57 F.R.D. 94 (N.D. Cal. 1973).

Then there was the case about the housing project which had separate rent scales, incredibly charging higher rents to those tenants who were on welfare. *Hammond v. Housing Authority,* 328 F. Supp. 586 (D. Ore. 1971). Another housing case involved a housing authority—unfortunately one of many—which operated separate projects which it kept rigidly segregated by race. *Taylor v. City of Millington,* 476 F.2d 599 (6th Cir. 1973). Another black citizen had to go to court against a housing development which actually sent out thousands of handbills advertising it was "white only." *Lee v. Southern Home Sites,* 444 F.2d 143 (5th Cir. 1971). In a case now pending, officials accepted Social Security Act funds for years for certain medical screening programs when in fact they had no such programs in most of the State. *Bond v. Stanton,* 528 F.2d 688 (7th Cir. 1976). Perhaps the saddest, most tragic case of all is the one in which mental patients, guilty of no crime or wrongdoing, were forced into involuntary, unpaid labor. *Downs v. Department of Public Welfare,* 65 F.R.D. 557 (E.D. Pa. 1974).

Mr. President, I could go on and on, with examples of conduct which this bill would help redress. Unfortunately, in each of these cases, the victim—or, as in some cases, like the deceased war veteran, the victim's family—had to go to court to enforce the rights promised by Congress or the Constitution. In the aftermath of Alyeska, violations like these will go unredressed without enactment of this bill.

I do not believe that those who oppose this bill really want our laws violated, but defeat of this measure would, until enactment in the next Congress, at least, rob our citizens of the ability to enforce their most basic civil rights. The net effect is to tell law violators that we will tolerate their lawlessness. We cannot do that, we should not do that. We must give our people the tools to avoid it.

This legislation is vitally necessary and proper to carry out not only the laws covered, but all the provisions of the Constitution, including the 13th and 14th amendments. I hope we can get on with the business of passing S. 2278 without more delay.

Mr. ABOUREZK. Mr. President, the Senate tonight, with the passage of S. 2278, the Civil Rights Attorneys' Fees Award Act of 1976, has acted in a true spirit of compromise. I want to thank the distinguished Senator from Alabama for his good judgment and support this evening. In passing this worthwhile measure, we have done a great service to the continuing struggle to eradicate discrimination in this country. We have assured that attorneys' fees will be available, in the discretion of the court, to successful litigants in suits brought under the reconstruction era civil rights laws, title VI of the 1964 Civil Rights Act, title IX of the education amendments of 1972, and certain Internal Revenue Code suits brought by the Government.

The many statutes covered by this bill are all major civil rights provisions, and the Senate report which my colleague from Alabama is so fond of quoting, said no differently. The report said that the major civil rights bills passed since 1964 included fee provisions. Five of the seven provisions covered by this bill were passed prior to 1964; two of the remaining three provisions covered by the bill are included in bills which contain at least one fee provision in other sections. These are major civil rights laws, and we have an obligation to guarantee their fullest enforcement.

All of these laws depend heavily upon private parties for enforcement. If Congress wants these laws enforced—and I assume we would not have passed them if we did not—then we must provide some mechanism for insuring their enforcement. The fee-shifting mechanism has proved a particularly equitable and efficient means of enforcing the law by enlisting private citizens as law enforcement officials. It is a mechanism which increases law enforcement without increasing the Federal budget or bureaucracy.

The Civil Rights Attorneys' Fees Awards Act authorizes Federal courts to award attorneys' fees to a prevailing party in suits presently pending in the Federal courts. The application of this Act to pending cases is in conformity with the unanimous decision of the Supreme Court in *Bradley v. School Board of City of Richmond,* 416 U.S. 696 (1974).

This application is necessary to fill the gap created by the Alyeska decision and thus avoid the inequitable situation of an award of attorneys' fees turning on the date the litigation was commenced, or the date legal services were rendered.

It will also result in a significant saving of judicial resources. At present, due to the Alyeska decision, a court must analyze a party's actions to determine bad faith in order to award attorneys' fees. This is a complex, time-consuming process often requiring an extensive evidentiary hearing. The enactment of this legislation will make such an evidentiary hearing unnecessary in the many civil rights cases presently pending in the Federal courts.

In enacting this legislation we are acting pursuant to section 2 of the 13th amendment and section 5 of the 14th amendment. See Fitzpatrick against Bitzer, 96 S. Ct. 2666 (June 28, 1976). This legislation is intended to cover cases based on both constitutional and statutory rights, including supremacy clause cases. See 42 U.S.C. § 1983.

In conclusion, I would like to say that I am proud of this body for taking this necessary step to insure that "equal protection under the law" is achieved.

The PRESIDING OFFICER. The question is, Shall the bill pass?

Mr. ABOUREZK. Mr. President, I yield myself 1 minute. I wish to express my thanks to Senator ROBERT C. BYRD for his assistance, to Senator DURKIN for his help while this proceeding was going on, to the other members of the committee who helped, to the staff, and also to all the Members of the Senate for their patience in going through this entire filibuster procedure. It was very much appreciated by those of us working on the measure.

Mr. ROBERT C. BYRD. Mr. President, I thank the Senator very much.

The PRESIDING OFFICER. The question is, Shall the bill pass? The yeas and nays have been ordered, and the clerk will call the roll.

Mr. ROBERT C. BYRD. Mr. President, no debate is in order, but this is not the last rollcall today.

The second assistant legislative clerk called the roll.

Mr. ROBERT C. BYRD. I announce that the Senator from Texas (Mr. BENTSEN), the Senator from Virginia (Mr. HARRY F. BYRD, JR.), the Senator from Nevada (Mr. CANNON), the Senator from Florida (Mr. CHILES), the Senator from Idaho (Mr. CHURCH), the Senator from California (Mr. CRANSTON), the Senator from Michigan (Mr. PHILIP A. HART), the Senator from Indiana (Mr. HARTKE), the Senator from Wyoming (Mr. McGEE), the Senator from Minnesota (Mr. MONDALE), the Senator from New Mexico (Mr. MONTOYA), the Senator from West Virginia (Mr. RANDOLPH), the Senator from Connecticut (Mr. RIBICOFF), and the Senator from Georgia (Mr. TALMADGE) are necessarily absent.

I further announce that the Senator from Ohio (Mr. GLENN), the Senator from Montana (Mr. MANSFIELD), the Senator from South Dakota (Mr. McGOVERN), and the Senator from Hawaii (Mr. INOUYE) are absent on official business.

I further announce that, if present and voting, the Senator from West Virginia (Mr. RANDOLPH) would vote "yea."

Mr. GRIFFIN. I announce that the Senator from Maryland (Mr. BEALL) the Senator from Oklahoma (Mr. BELLMON), the Senator from Tennessee (Mr. BROCK), the Senator from New York (Mr. BUCKLEY), the Senator from Kansas

(Mr. DOLE), the Senator from Arizona (Mr. GOLDWATER), the Senator from Vermont (Mr. STAFFORD), the Senator from South Carolina (Mr. THURMOND), and the Senator from Texas (Mr. TOWER) are necessarily absent.

I also announce that the Senator from Virginia (Mr. WILLIAM L. SCOTT) is absent on official business.

I further announce that, if present and voting, the Senator from South Carolina (Mr. THURMOND) would vote "nay."

The result was announced—yeas 57, nays 15, as follows:

[Rollcall Vote No. 677 Leg.]

YEAS—57

Abourezk	Haskell	Nunn
Baker	Hatfield	Packwood
Bayh	Hathaway	Pastore
Biden	Hollings	Pearson
Brooke	Huddleston	Pell
Bumpers	Humphrey	Percy
Burdick	Jackson	Proxmire
Byrd, Robert C.	Javits	Roth
Case	Johnston	Schweiker
Clark	Kennedy	Scott, Hugh
Culver	Leahy	Sparkman
Domenici	Magnuson	Stevens
Durkin	Mathias	Stevenson
Eagleton	McIntyre	Stone
Fong	Metcalf	Symington
Ford	Morgan	Taft
Gravel	Moss	Tunney
Griffin	Muskie	Weicker
Hart, Gary	Nelson	Williams

NAYS—15

Allen	Garn	Long
Bartlett	Hansen	McClellan
Curtis	Helms	McClure
Eastland	Hruska	Stennis
Fannin	Laxalt	Young

NOT VOTING—28

Beall	Cranston	Mondale
Bellmon	Dole	Montoya
Bentsen	Glenn	Randolph
Brock	Goldwater	Ribicoff
Buckley	Hart, Philip A.	Scott,
Byrd,	Hartke	William L.
Harry F., Jr.	Inouye	Stafford
Cannon	Mansfield	Talmadge
Chiles	McGee	Thurmond
Church	McGovern	Tower

So the bill (S. 2278), as amended, was passed, as follows:

Be it enacted by the Senate and House of Representatives of the United States of America in Congress assembled, That this Act may be cited as "The Civil Rights Attorney's Fees Awards Act of 1976".

SEC. 2. That the Revised Statutes section 722 (42 U.S.C. 1988) is amended by adding the following: "In any action or proceeding to enforce a provision of sections 1977, 1978, 1979, 1980, and 1981 of the Revised Statutes, title IX of Public Law 92–318, or in any civil action or proceeding, by or on behalf of the United States of America, to enforce, or to charge a violation of, a provision of the United States Internal Revenue Code, or title VI of the Civil Rights Act of 1964, the court, in its discretion, may allow the prevailing party, other than the United States, a reasonable attorney's fee as part of the costs.".

Mr. ALLEN. Mr. President——

Mr. ABOUREZK. Mr. President, I move to reconsider the vote by which the bill was passed.

Mr. DURKIN. I move to lay that motion on the table.

The motion to lay on the table was agreed to.

Mr. MORGAN. Mr. President, I voted for the attorney's fees bill on final passage but only after a significant amendment was accepted by the Senate broadening it to cover attorney fees for prevailing defendants in actions brought

against citizens by the Internal Revenue Service.

I was taught in law school that the awarding of attorney fees by the courts was against public policy, as such awards tend to "stir up" or "promote" litigation. Nevertheless, the Federal courts, and some State courts, have in recent years strayed far from this principle—sometimes with the authority of statutory laws and sometimes without any authority. This became a regular practice in the Fourth Circuit Court of Appeals.

Whether the public policy was correct or not, though in most cases I think it was, the question is now almost moot since so many exceptions have been made.

The proponents of the original bill had the votes to prevail as evidenced by the vote on many amendments. The compromise made by accepting the amendment concerning IRS fees makes the bill more palatable and represents the best the opponents could accomplish.

During consideration of this bill my colleague, Mr. HELMS, offered an amendment which would have required the Federal Government to pay attorney fees to the prevailing defendants in all cases brought and lost by the Government. Because of the tendency of many agencies of Government to engage citizens and businesses in needless litigation it may be desirable to consider this issue again during the next Congress in order to discourage overzealous bureaucrats from hauling too many people into the courts.

Therefore, I have voted aye on the bill as a compromise—which after all most legislation is. I am fearful however, that the measure will be abused—so I hope that the Congress will monitor the results and review the entire field of law relating to the awarding of attorney fees.

NUCLEAR FUEL ASSURANCE ACT

Mr. ALLEN addressed the Chair.

The PRESIDING OFFICER. The Senator from Alabama is recognized.

Mr. ALLEN. Mr. President, without doubt, the most important bill on the calendar is H.R. 8401, the Nuclear Fuel Assurance Act. At the conclusion of my remarks and at the conclusion of answering any questions Senators might ask, I will, on behalf of myself and my distinguished senior colleague, Mr. SPARKMAN, move to proceed to the consideration of H.R. 8401.

This is the ideal time to make this motion, because there is no pending business. For the first time in many days, we are not operating under cloture and there is no pending business and no unfinished business. Therefore, it is appropriate that a motion be made.

Mr. President, I am not acting in opposition to the leadership in this matter. I call attention to the fact that many days ago, the distinguished majority leader, Mr. MANSFIELD, asked unanimous consent for a time limit on this bill, showing that he felt that the bill should have consideration in the Senate Chamber. The House has passed it. It was approved by the Joint Committee on Atomic Energy, and it is now

VI. *H.R. Rep. No. 94-1558, at 1-3 (Sept. 15, 1976)*

94TH CONGRESS 2d Session	HOUSE OF REPRESENTATIVES	REPORT No. 94–1558

THE CIVIL RIGHTS ATTORNEY'S FEES AWARDS ACT OF 1976

SEPTEMBER 15, 1976.—Committed to the Committee of the Whole House on the State of the Union and ordered to be printed

---

Mr. DRINAN, from the Committee on the Judiciary, submitted the following

REPORT

[Including cost estimate of the Congressional Budget Office]

[To accompany H.R. 15460]

The Committee on the Judiciary, to whom was referred the bill (H.R. 15460) to allow the awarding of attorney's fees in certain civil rights cases, having considered the same, report favorably thereon without amendment and recommend that the bill do pass.

PURPOSE OF THE BILL

H.R. 15460, the Civil Rights Attorney's Fees Awards Act of 1976, authorizes the courts to award reasonable attorney fees to the prevailing party in suits instituted under certain civil rights acts. Under existing law, some civil rights statutes contain counsel fee provisions, while others do not. In order to achieve uniformity in the remedies provided by Federal laws guaranteeing civil and constitutional rights, it is necessary to add an attorney fee authorization to those civil rights acts which do not presently contain such a provision.

The effective enforcement of Federal civil rights statutes depends largely on the efforts of private citizens. Although some agencies of the United States have civil rights responsibilities, their authority and resources are limited. In many instances where these laws are violated, it is necessary for the citizen to initiate court action to correct the illegality. Unless the judicial remedy is full and complete, it will remain a meaningless right. Because a vast majority of the victims of civil rights violations cannot afford legal counsel, they are unable to present their cases to the courts. In authorizing an award of reasonable attorney's fees, H.R. 15460 is designed to give such persons effective access to the judicial process where their grievances can be resolved according to law.

57–006

2.

STATEMENT

A. NEED FOR THE LEGISLATION

In *Alyeska Pipeline Service Corp* v. *Wilderness Society*, 421 U.S. 240 (1975), the Supreme Court held that federal courts do not have the power to award attorney's fees to a prevailing party unless an Act of Congress expressly authorizes it.[1] In the *Alyeska* case, the plaintiffs sought to prevent the construction of the Alaskan pipeline because of the damage it would cause to the environment. Although the plaintiffs succeeded in the early stages of the litigation, Congress later overturned that result by legislation permitting the construction of the pipeline. Nonetheless the lower federal courts awarded the plaintiffs their attorney's fees because of the service they had performed in the public interest. The Supreme Court reversed that award on the basis of the "American Rule": that each litigant, victorious or otherwise, must pay for its own attorney.

Although the *Alyeska* case involved only environmental concerns, the decision barred attorney fee awards in a wide range of cases, including civil rights. In fact the Supreme Court, in footnote 46 of the *Alyeska* opinion, expressly disapproved a number of lower court decisions involving civil rights which had awarded fees without statutory authorization. Prior to *Alyeska*, such courts had allowed fees on the theory that civil rights plaintiffs act as "private attorneys general" in eliminating discriminatory practices adversely affecting all citizens, white and non-white. In 1968, the Supreme Court had approved the "private attorney general" theory when it gave a generous construction to the attorney fee provision in Title II of the Civil Rights Act of 1964. *Newman* v. *Piggie Park Enterprises, Inc.*, 390 U.S. 400 (1968).[2] The Court stated:

> If (the plaintiff) obtains an injunction, he does so not for himself alone but also as a "private attorney general," vindicating a policy that Congress considered of the highest importance. *Id*. at 402.

However, the Court in *Alyeska* rejected the application of that theory to the award of counsel fees in the absence of statutory authorization. It expressly reaffirmed, however, its holding in *Newman* that, in civil rights cases where counsel fees are allowed by Congress, "the award should be made to the successful plaintiff absent exceptional circumstances." *Alyeska* case, *supra* at 262.

In the hearings conducted by the Subcommittee on Courts, Civil Liberties, and the Administration of Justice, the testimony indicated that civil rights litigants were suffering very severe hardships because of the *Alyeska* decision. Thousands of dollars in fees were automatically lost in the immediate wake of the decision. Representatives of the Lawyers Committee for Civil Rights Under Law, the Council

---

[1] The Court in *Alyeska* recognized three very narrow exceptions to the rule: (1) where a "common fund" is involved; (2) where the litigant's conduct is vexatious, harassing, or in bad faith; and (3) where a court order is willfully disobeyed.
[2] In *Trafficante* v. *Metropolitan Life Insurance Co.*, 409 U.S. 205 (1972), the Supreme Court applied the "private attorney general" theory in according broad "standing" to persons injured by discriminatory housing practices under the Federal Fair Housing Act. 42 U.S.C. 3601–3619.

3

for Public Interest Law, the American Bar Association Special Committee on Public Interest Practice, and witnesses practicing in the field testified to the devastating impact of the case on litigation in the civil rights area. Surveys disclosed that such plaintiffs were the hardest hit by the decision.[3] The Committee also received evidence that private lawyers were refusing to take certain types of civil rights cases because the civil rights bar, already short of resources, could not afford to do so. Because of the compelling need demonstrated by the testimony, the Committee decided to report a bill allowing fees to prevailing parties in certain civil rights cases.

It should be noted that the United States Code presently contains over fifty provisions for attorney fees in a wide variety of statutes. See Appendix A. In the past few years, the Congress has approved such allowances in the areas of antitrust, equal credit, freedom of information, voting rights, and consumer product safety. Although the recently enacted civil rights statutes contain provisions permitting the award of counsel fees, a number of the older statutes do not. It is to these provisions that much of the testimony was directed.

B. HISTORY OF H.R. 15460

At the time of the Subcomittee hearings on October 6 and 8, and Dec. 3, 1975, three bills were pending which dealt expressly with counsel fees in civil rights cases: H.R. 7828 (same as H.R. 8220); H.R. 7969 (same as H.R. 8742); and H.R. 9552. H.R. 7828 and H.R. 9552 would allow attorney fees to be awarded in cases brought under specific provisions of the United States Code, while H.R. 7969 would permit such awards in any case involving civil or constitutional rights, no matter what the source of the claim. H.R. 7828 was stated in mandatory terms; H.R. 9552 and H.R. 7969 allowed discretionary awards. The Justice Department, through its representative, Assistant Attorney General Rex Lee of the Civil Division, expressed its support of H.R. 9552. Hearings held in 1973 by the Senate Judiciary Subcommittee on the Representation of Citizen Interests also highlighted the need of the public for legal assistance in this and other areas.

In August, 1976, the Judiciary Subcommittee on Courts, Civil Liberties, and the Administration of Justice concluded that a bill to allow counsel fees in certain civil rights cases should be reported favorably in view of the pressing need. On August 26, 1976, the Subcommittee approved H.R. 9552 with an amendment in the nature of a substitute because it was similar to S. 2278, which had cleared the Senate Judiciary Committee and was awaiting action by the full Senate. The amendment in the nature of a substitute sought to conform H.R. 9552 technically to S. 2278; no substantive changes were made. It was then reported unanimously by the Subcommittee.

On September 2, 1976, the full Committee approved H.R. 9552, as amended, with an amendment offered by Congresswoman Holtzman and accepted by the Committee. That amendment added title IX of Public Law 92–318 to the substantive provisions under which successful litigants could be awarded counsel fees. The Committee then

---

[3] See *Balancing the Scales of Justice: Financing Public Interest Law in America* (Council for Public Interest Law, 1976), pp. 238, 364, D–2).

VII. Excerpts from 122 Cong. Rec. 35121-30 (Oct. 1, 1976)

October 1, 1976   **CONGRESSIONAL RECORD — HOUSE**   **35121**

ACTIONS ON REQUESTS FOR NEW BUDGET AUTHORITY CONSIDERED IN APPROPRIATION BILLS, 94TH CONG., 2D SESS.[1] (REVISED TO OCT. 1, 1976)—Continued

[This table excludes "backdoor" spending authority in legislative bills and permanent budget authority (Federal and Trust) available without further action by Congress.]

Bill and fiscal year	House				Senate			Congress	
	Budget requests considered	Reported by committee	Approved by House	Compared with budget requests considered by House	Budget requests considered	Approved by Senate	Compared with budget requests considered by Senate	Approved by Congress	Compared with budget request
10. Public Works [9] (P.L. 94–355).	9,220,095,000	9,551,209,000	9,645,609,000	+425,514,000	9,398,895,000	9,718,885,000	+319,990,000	9,703,713,000	+304,818,000
11. Public Works Employment (H.R. 15194)	[10] 1,138,300,000	[10] 1,138,300,000	+1,138,300,000		[10] 1,638,300,000	+1,638,300,000	[10] 1,418,300,000	+1,418,300,000
12. State-Justice-Commerce-Judiciary (P.L. 94–362).	6,297,119,000	6,382,828,000	6,541,128,000	+244,009,000	6,313,251,453	[7] 6,880,147,453	+566,896,000	[7] 6,680,314,453	+367,063,000
13. Transportation [3] (P.L. 94–387).	5,352,292,357	5,286,077,357	5,296,077,357	−56,215,000	5,268,892,357	5,411,139,357	+142,247,000	5,311,839,357	+42,947,000
14. Treasury-Postal Service-General Gov't (P.L. 94–363).	7,983,147,000	8,275,958,000	8,267,636,000	+284,489,000	8,004,892,000	8,301,470,000	+296,578,000	8,313,119,000	+308,227,000
15. Guam Typhoon Supplemental (H.J. Res. 1096) [8]					247,951,838	250,051,838	+2,100,000	250,051,838	+2,100,000
16. Continuing Resolution (H.J. Res. 1105)		12,000,000	12,000,000	+12,000,000	45,147,921	47,147,921	+2,000,000	47,147,921	+2,000,000
Total, bills for fiscal 1977	260,704,519,357	262,377,727,707	262,130,004,307	+1,425,484,950	263,054,809,334	264,936,100,786	+1,881,291,452	262,935,183,086	−119,626,248
B. Bills for fiscal 1976:									
1. District of Columbia (P.L. 94–333)	507,841,000	465,688,000	465,688,000	−42,153,000	507,841,000	464,364,700	−43,476,300	464,636,700	−43,204,300
2. Foreign Assistance (P.L. 94–330)	5,764,640,909	4,988,997,454	5,001,497,454	−763,143,455	5,789,640,909	5,328,640,909	−461,000,000	5,179,890,909	−609,750,000
3. Supplemental Railroad Appropriations (P.L. 94–252) [3]	404,100,000	404,100,000	464,100,000	+60,000,000	[4] 472,800,000	722,532,956	+249,732,956	587,000,000	+114,200,000
4. Legislative Branch Supplemental (P.L. 94–226)	33,000,000	33,000,000	33,000,000		33,000,000	33,000,000		33,000,000	
5. Further Continuing Appropriations (P.L. 94–254)	175,000		175,000		175,000	175,000		175,000	
6. Second Supplemental, 1976 (P.L. 94–303)	[6] 8,001,689,067	[6] 7,749,126,167	[6] 8,133,161,167	+131,472,100	9,920,681,850	9,716,514,420	−204,167,430	9,393,791,970	−526,889,880
7. Emergency Health Supplemental (P.L. 94–266)	[6] 2,275,364,000	[6] 1,513,764,000	[6] 1,942,384,000	−332,980,000	2,363,484,000	1,942,384,000	−421,100,000	1,942,384,000	−421,100,000
Total, bills for fiscal 1976, 2d Session	16,986,809,976	15,154,675,621	16,040,005,621	−946,804,355	19,087,622,759	18,207,611,985	−880,010,774	17,600,878,579	−1,486,744,180
C. Cumulative totals for the session to date:									
1. House	277,691,329,333	277,532,403,328	278,170,009,928	+478,680,595					
2. Senate					282,142,432,093	283,143,712,771	+1,001,280,678		
3. Enacted								280,536,061,665	−1,606,370,428

[1] Additionally, the Congress has taken action during this period, to rescind budget authority as follows:

Bills	Proposed rescissions considered	Approved by House	Approved by Senate	Approved by Congress	Compared with proposed rescissions
Third Budget Rescission Bill (P.L. 94–249)	$646,176,000	$12,431,000	$75,831,000	$75,831,000	−$570,345,000

[2] Includes advance funding for fiscal year 1978.
[3] Amounts for fiscal year 1976; additionally, there were amounts in the bill for the transition quarter, fiscal years 1978 and 1979.
[4] Includes $68,700,000 in budget estimates greater than those originally considered by the House and Senate because the Administration transmitted these estimates just prior to the House-Senate Conference. The Senate had recommended appropriations for the items affected in anticipation that the estimates would be transmitted before final congressional action on the Railroad Supplemental.
[5] In addition, there are budget requests and amounts approved to be made available in the transition period. For the House, the amounts are $189,000,000 and $163,073,000, respectively; for the Senate, the amounts are $689,000,000 and $615,312,000, respectively. The conference agreement for the transition period provides $622,033,000. In all, the bill provides $872,084,838 for both the transition period and fiscal year 1977. The conference agreement is $62,767,000 under the budget estimates.
[6] Originally, the House Committee on Appropriations had considered budget requests of $10,141,989,067, for the Second Supplemental. These included budget requests for several job-related items (Public Service jobs, Comprehensive Manpower Assistance, etc.). The Committee, in reporting the Second Supplemental, recommended almost $1.4 billion for these programs. In considering the Emergency Health Supplemental (the Swine Flu vaccine bill: P.L. 94–266), the Senate added $1.8 billion for the job items. The House agreed to these amendments to the Swine Flu bill, and removed the Second Supplemental as appropriate. In the above table the requests, reported, and approved amounts for the House have all been adjusted to show the practical effects of these changes, although the House actually approved only $135 million for the Swine Flu bill.
[7] These amounts include $375,000 and $340,000 for the Senate and Congress, respectively, that became available on July 1, 1976.

[8] Amounts exclude $20 million requested by the President (Sen. Doc. 92–224) and approved be the House and Senate for emergency aid to Guam, to become available upon enactment of thy Interior and related agencies appropriations bill.
[9] Amounts exclude $200 million for damages caused by the failure of the Teton River Dam, requested in a supplemental estimate for FY 1976 (H. Doc. 94–523), and approved by House and Senate to become available upon enactment of this appropriation bill.
[10] In addition, the bill contains $2,314,133,000 in new budget authority to be made available immediately upon enactment; in total, $3,452,433,000 in new budget authority is provided by the House bill; $3,952,433,000 by the Senate bill; $3,732,433,000 by the conference agreement.
[11] The $36,450,000 budget request shown in parentheses is also included in the amount considered by the Senate for the Interior appropriations bill; however, the request could not be funded in that bill. This amount was then recommended in the Senate version of Title I! of the District of Columbia and other activities appropriations bill (H.R. 15193), but was not approved in the final version of the bill.

Note: The Budget for 1977, as submitted Jan. 21, 1976, tentatively estimated total new budget authority for 1977 at $433,409,000,900 net ($495,777,327,000 gross, including $62,368,318,000 in intragovernmental transactions and certain so-called proprietary receipts handled as offsets for budget purposes only). An estimated $227.4 billion does not require current action by Congress, this amount includes permanent appropriations such as interest and various trust funds already provided in basic law. Virtually all of the remaining $268.4 b'llion is for consideration at this Session in the appropriation bills. About $5.9 billion of the $268.4 billion was shown in the January budget as being "for later transmittal" for supplemental requirements under present law, new legislation allowances and for contingencies and civilian pay raises.

The SPEAKER pro tempore. Is there objection to the request of the gentleman from Texas?

There was no objection.

A motion to reconsider was laid on the table.

GENERAL LEAVE

Mr. MAHON. Mr. Speaker, I ask unanimous consent that all Members may have 5 legislative days in which to revise and extend their remarks on the Senate amendments just agreed to and that I may insert extraneous matter with my remarks.

The SPEAKER. Is there objection to the request of the gentleman from Texas?

There was no objection.

CIVIL RIGHTS ATTORNEY'S FEES AWARDS ACT OF 1976

Mr. DRINAN. Mr. Speaker, pursuant to the rule I call up the bill (S. 2278) The Civil Rights Attorney's Fees Awards Act of 1976, and ask for its immediate consideration in the House.

The Clerk read the title of the bill.

Mr. DRINAN. Mr. Speaker, I ask unanimous consent to consider the bill as read and printed in the RECORD.

Mr. BAUMAN. Mr. Speaker, reserving the right to object.

The SPEAKER pro tempore. The gentleman from Massachusetts is recognized for 1 hour.

Mr. BAUMAN. Mr. Speaker, again I reserve the right to object.

The SPEAKER pro tempore. There was no request properly pending until I made that statement.

The gentleman from Massachusetts is recognized for 1 hour.

Mr. DRINAN. Mr. Speaker, this bill is similar to the bill H.R. 15460, which was reported out of the Judiciary Committee by voice vote on September 9, 1976.

Mr. BAUMAN. Mr. Speaker, I make a point of order. Does not the Constitution of the United States require the reading of legislation before us?

The SPEAKER pro tempore. The bill is read by title.

Mr. BAUMAN. I thank the Speaker.

The SPEAKER pro tempore. The gentleman from Massachusetts has been recognized for 1 hour.

Mr. DRINAN. Mr. Speaker, this bill is identical to H.R. 15460, which was reported out of the Judiciary Committee by voice vote on September 9, 1976—27 members of the committee were present. The only difference between the two bills is the Allen amendment, adopted by the Senate unanimously—79 to 0—on Tuesday, which I will discuss later. With the approval of the minority, the House bill had been placed on the suspension calendar for consideration on Tuesday, September 21. Unfortunately the House did not reach the bill because a number of suspensions had been carried over from the previous day.

Regarding the substance of the bill, let me begin by noting that the United States Code presently contains over 50 provisions which allow the awarding of attorney fees to prevailing parties. They span a wide range of subjects: perishable agricultural commodities, securities transactions, copyright—which we approved once again yesterday—antitrust, corporate reorganizations, and many other topics. I have a list of those statutory provisions which I am inserting in the RECORD at the conclusion of these remarks.

With respect to civil rights, Congress has provided for the award of a reasonable attorney's fee in recent statutes, such as the Federal Fair Housing Act of 1968 and the Voting Rights Act Amendments of 1975. In addition this week the House approved two conference reports on bills which have attorney fee provisions in their nondiscrimination sections: the LEAA authorization bill and the measure to extend the general revenue sharing program.

The purpose of S. 2278—and its House counterpart, H.R. 15460—is to authorize the award of a reasonable attorney's fee in actions brought in State or Federal courts, under certain civil rights statutes, which are presently contained in title 42 and title 20 of the United States Code. By permitting fees to be recovered under those statutes, we seek to make uniform the rule that a prevailing party, in a civil rights case, may, in the discretion of the court, recover counsel fees.

The Civil Rights Attorney's Fees Awards Act of 1976, S. 2278 (H.R. 15460) is intended to restore to the courts the authority to award reasonable counsel fees to the prevailing party in cases initiated under certain civil rights acts. The legislation is necessitated by the decision of the Supreme Court in Alyeska Pipeline Service Corp against Wilderness Society, 421 U.S. 240 (1975). In Alyeska, the Court held that attorney fees should not ordinarily be awarded to a prevailing party unless expressly authorized by act of Congress.

Prior to the Alyeska decision, the lower Federal courts had regularly awarded counsel fees to the prevailing party in a variety of cases instituted under the sections of the United States Code covered by S. 2278. Even though no express provision of law authorized such awards, the courts reasoned that, in these civil rights cases, the private plaintiff, in effect, acted as a "private attorney general" advancing the rights of the public at large, and not merely some narrow parochial interest. The Alyeska decision ended that practice, which this bill seeks to restore.

This bill would authorize State and Federal courts to award counsel fees in actions brought under specified sections of the United States Code relating to civil and constitutional rights. As I indicated earlier, over 50 Federal statutes presently provide for the awarding of fees in a wide variety of circumstances. In the past few years, Congress has approved such allowances in the areas of antitrust, equal credit, freedom of information, voting rights, and consumer product safety.

The attorney fee provision of this bill would apply to actions instituted under sections 1981, 1982, 1983, 1985, 1986, and 2000d of title 42, sections 1681–1686 of title 20, and the Internal Revenue Code. These sections generally prohibit the denial of civil and constitutional rights in a variety of areas, including contractual relationships, property transactions, and federally assisted programs and activities. It should be emphasized that S. 2278 would not make any substantive changes in these statutory provisions. Whatever is presently allowed or forbidden under them would continue to be permitted or proscribed.

Let me describe briefly the scope of the covered statutes. Section 1981 is frequently used to challenge discrimination in employment and recreational facilities. Under that section, the Supreme Court recently held that whites as well as non-whites could bring suit alleging discriminatory employment practices. Section 1982 prohibits discrimination in property transactions, including the purchase of a home. Both these sections afford victims of housing and employment discrimination remedies supplementary to title VII—employment—of the 1964 Civil Rights Act, and title VIII—housing—of the 1968 Civil Rights Act.

Section 1983 protects civil and constitutional rights from abridgement by state and local officials. The landmark case of Brown against Board of Education was initiated under this provision. Ironically, because that section does not authorize counsel fees, the plaintiffs in Brown could not have recovered their attorney fees, despite the importance of the decision in eliminating officially imposed racial segregation. Under applicable judicial decisions, Section 1983 authorizes suits against State and local officials based upon Federal statutory as well as constitutional rights. For example, Blue against Craig, 505 F.2d 830 (4th Cir. 1974). The closely related Sections 1985 and 1986 are employed to challenge conspiracies, both public and private, to deprive individuals of the equal protection of the laws:

The bill also covers any action, including suits by individuals, instituted under title IX of the Education Amendments of 1972, and title VI of the Civil Rights Act of 1964. These titles forbid the discriminatory use of Federal funds, and requires recipients to use such moneys in a nondiscriminatory fashion. Title VI is a general prohibition which applies to all federally assisted programs or activities, but is limited to discrimination on account of race, color, or national origin. Title IX covers certain education programs and proscribes discrimination based on sex, blindness, or visual impairment.

The only difference between S. 2278 and H.R. 15460 is the result of an amendment offered by Senator ALLEN and adopted unanimously by the Senate. Because the bills are identical, with the limited exception of the Allen amendment, it is intended that the courts will interpret S. 2278 in accordance with House Report No. 94–1558, together with the Senate report and the debates in both Houses.

The Allen amendment would allow the prevailing party to recover its counsel fees in any civil action brought by the United States to enforce the Internal Revenue Code. It would not apply to actions instituted against the Government by the taxpayer. Since S. 2278 does not allow the U.S. Government to recover its fees under any circumstances, the effect of the Allen amendment is to permit prevailing defendants in such cases to recover their attorney fees if they satisfy the criteria generally applicable under the bill to prevailing defendants, which I will discuss later at greater length.

Briefly, under settled judicial standards, prevailing defendants would recover their attorney fees only if they could prove that the United States brought the action to harass them, or if the suit is frivolous and vexatious. During the hearings last fall conducted by the Kastenmeier subcommittee on various attorney fee bills, the representative of the Justice Department testified that these were the only circumstances when he believed prevailing defendants should recover their fees in Government initiated suits.

I should note that the Allen amendment might involve an expense to the United States. However since awards of counsel fees under that amendment would occur only in the special circumstances I have described, it is fair to say that the total costs to the Government for fiscal year 1977 would be negligible.

The language of S. 2278 tracks the wording of attorney fee provisions in other civil rights statutes, such as section 706(k) of title VII—employment—of the Civil Rights Act of 1964. The phraseology employed has been reviewed, examined, and interpreted by the courts, which have developed standards for its application. The language contains three key features: first that it applies to any "prevailing party," whether a plaintiff or defendant; second, that it gives the court discretion to award fees; and third, that it permits only a "reasonable" fee to be imposed.

First, I wish to discuss the scope of the phrase "prevailing party." Under S. 2278, either the plaintiff or the defendant is eligible to receive attorney fees. Congress is not always that generous. About two-thirds of the statutes which provide counsel fees allow them only to the prevailing plaintiff. This bill takes the more modest approach of other civil rights statutes, allowing fees to any prevailing party.

There is a real danger, however, that allowing fees to any prevailing party might have a "chilling effect" on civil rights plaintiffs. Victims of discrimination may be reluctant to initiate legal action to protect their rights for fear that they may be required to pay the counsel fees of the defendant. To guard against this possible deterrent, the courts have developed a dual standard for awarding fees.

On two occasions, the Supreme Court has held that, where counsel fees are authorized in civil rights cases, a prevailing plaintiff should ordinarily recover his other attorney fees unless special circumstances would render such an award unjust. The Court adopted this view based on the important public interest served by the elimination of racial discrimination and the securing of other constitutional rights, matters which Congress has determined to be of the highest importance.

Of course, in proper cases, prevailing defendants may recover their counsel fees. To avoid the "chilling effect" which such fees might have on victims bringing suit, the courts have designed a different standard for awarding fees to prevailing defendants. Under the case law, such an award may be made only if the action is vexatious and frivolous, or if the plaintiff instituted it solely to harass the defendant. In Carrion versus Yeshiva University, for example, the Second Circuit Court of Appeals awarded the defendant attorney fees because the litigation was "motivated by malice and vindictiveness."

Second, I should note that the bill commits the award of fees to the discretion of the court. Congress has passed many statutes requiring that fees be awarded. Again this bill takes a more moderate approach, leaving the award to the discretion of the court guided by the case law.

Third, the bill permits the recovery only of a "reasonable" attorney fee. Here too the courts have identified a number of factors to determine the reasonableness of awards. In Johnson versus Georgia Highway Express, for example, the court enumerated 12 factors to be considered, including the time and labor required, the novelty and difficulty of the questions, the skill needed to present the case, the customary fee for similar work, and the amount received in damages, if any. These evolving standards should provide sufficient guidance to the courts in construing this bill which uses the same term. I should add that the phrase "attorney's fee" would include the values of the legal services provided by counsel, including all incidental and necessary expenses incurred in furnishing effective and competent representation.

The question has been raised whether allowing fees against State governments in suits properly brought under the covered statutes would violate the 11th amendment. That amendment limits the power of the Federal courts to entertain

actions against a State. This issue is no longer seriously in dispute after the recent Supreme Court decision in Fitzpatrick against Bitzer. Since this bill is enacted pursuant to the power of Congress under section 2 of the 13th amendment and section 5 of the 14th amendment, any question arising under the 11th amendment is resolved in favor of awarding fees against State defendants.

I should add also that, as the gentleman from Illinois (Mr. ANDERSON) observed during consideration of the resolution on S. 2278, this bill would apply to cases pending on the date of enactment. It is the settled rule that a change in statutory law is to be applied to cases in litigation. In Bradley versus Richmond School Board, the Supreme Court expressly applied that long-standing rule to an attorney fee provision, including the award of fees for services rendered prior to the effective date of the statute.

Finally it should be noted that civil rights attorneys and organizations have lost thousands of dollars in fees since the Alyeska decision. That case has greatly impaired citizen enforcement of the statutes covered by S. 2278. If Federal laws providing for the protection of civil and constitutional rights are to be fully enforced, Congress must provide effective remedies for the vindication of those guarantees. Authorizing the award of reasonable counsel fees is an important tool for effectuating that purpose.

I include the following:

APPENDIX [1]—FEDERAL STATUTES AUTHORIZING THE AWARD OF ATTORNEY FEES

1. Federal Contested Election Act, 2 U.S.C. 396.
2. Freedom of Information Act, 5 U.S.C. 552(a)(4)(E).
3. Privacy Act, 5 U.S.C. 552a(g)(3)(B).
4. Federal Employment Compensation For Work Injuries, 5 U.S.C. 8127.
5. Packers and Stockyards Act, 7 U.S.C. 210(f).
6. Perishable Agricultural Commodities Act, 7 U.S.C. 499g(b), (c).
7. Agricultural Unfair Trade Practices Act, 7 U.S.C. 2305(a), (c).
8. Plant Variety Act, 7 U.S.C. 2565.
9. Bankruptcy Act, 11 U.S.C. 104(a)(1).
10. Railroad Reorganization Act of 1935, 11 U.S.C. 205(c)(12).
11. Corporate Reorganization Act, 11 U.S.C. 641, 642, 643, and 644.
12. Federal Credit Union Act, 12 U.S.C. 1786(O).
13. Bank Holding Company Act, 12 U.S.C. 1975.
14. Clayton Act, 15 U.S.C. 15.
15. Unfair Competition Act (FTC), 15 U.S.C. 72.
16. Securities Act of 1933, 15 U.S.C. 77k(e).
17. Trust Indenture Act, 15 U.S.C. 77www(a).
18. Securities Exchange Act of 1934, 15 U.S.C. 78i(e), 78r(a).
19. Jewelers Hall-Mark Act, 15 U.S.C. 298(b), (c), and (d).
20. Truth-in-Lending Act (Fair Credit Billing Amendments), 15 U.S.C. 1640(a).
21. Fair Credit Reporting Act, 15 U.S.C. 1681(n).
22. Motor Vehicle Information and Cost Savings Act, 15 U.S.C. 1918(a), 1989(a)(2).

[1] This list is compiled from information submitted to the Judiciary Subcommittee by the Council for Public Interest Law and the Attorneys' Fee Project of the Lawyers' Committee for Civil Rights Under Law.

23. Consumer Product Safety Act, 15 U.S.C. 2072, 2073.
24. Federal Trade Improvements Act (Amendments), 15 U.S.C. 2310(a)(5)(d)(2).
25. Copyright Act, 17 U.S.C. 1116.
26. Organized Crime Control Act of 1970, 18 U.S.C. 1964(c).
27. Education Amendments of 1972, 20 U.S.C. 1617.
28. Mexican American Treaty Act of 1950, 22 U.S.C. 277d-21.
29. International Claim Settlement Act, 22 U.S.C. 1623(f).
30. Federal Tort Claims Act, 28 U.S.C. 2678.
31. Norris-LaGuardia Act, 29 U.S.C. 107.
32. Fair Labor Standards Act, 29 U.S.C. 216(b).
33. Employees Retirement Income Security Act, 29 U.S.C. 1132(g).
34. Labor Management Reporting and Disclosure Act, 29 U.S.C. 431(c), 501(b).
35. Longshoremen and Harbor Workers Compensation Act, 33 U.S.C. 928.
36. Water Pollution Prevention and Control Act, 33 U.S.C. 1365(d).
37. Ocean Dumping Act, 33 U.S.C. 1415(g)(4).
38. Deepwater Ports Act of 1974, 33 U.S.C. 1515.
39. Patent Infringement Act, 35 U.S.C. 285.
40. Servicemen's Group Life Insurance Act, 38 U.S.C. 784(g).
41. Servicemen's Readjustment Act, 38 U.S.C. 1822(b).
42. Veterans Benefit Act, 38 U.S.C. 3404(c).
43. Safe Drinking Water Act, 42 U.S.C. 300j-8(d).
44. Social Security Act (Amendments of 1965), 42 U.S.C. 405(b).
45. Clean Air Act (Amendments of 1970), 42 U.S.C. 1857h-2.
46. Voting Rights Act Amendments of 1975, 42 U.S.C. 19731(e).
47. Civil Rights Act of 1964, Title II, 42 U.S.C. 2000a-3(b).
48. Civil Rights Act of 1964, Title VII, 42 U.S.C. 2000e-5(k).
49. Legal Services Corporation Act, 42 U.S.C. 2996e(f).
50. Fair Housing Act of 1968, 42 U.S.C. 3612(c).
51. Noise Control Act of 1972, 42 U.S.C. 4911(d).
52. Railway Labor Act, 45 U.S.C. 153(p).
53. Merchant Marine Act of 1936, 46 U.S.C. 1227.
54. Communications Act of 1934, 47 U.S.C. 206.
55. Interstate Commerce Act, 49 U.S.C. 8, 16(2), 908(b), 908(e), and 1017(b)(2).

In the Alyeska decision the court held that attorneys' fees should not ordinarily be awarded to a prevailing party, unless expressly authorized by act of Congress.

Mr. WHITE. Mr. Speaker, will the gentleman yield?

Mr. DRINAN. I yield to the gentleman from Texas (Mr. WHITE).

Mr. WHITE. Mr. Speaker, I want to clear up some colloquy made earlier during the rule debate. The gentleman from Massachusetts has made an interesting point, that previous to the Alyeska case, the courts were awarding attorneys' fees to the prevailing side, but by reason of that case the courts have said they must have statutory authority prior to awarding attorneys' fees to either prevailing party.

Mr. DRINAN. The gentleman has stated the case very precisely.

(material omitted)

always, and I certainly can understand her point. I am not so much concerned about dampening enthusiasm for law suits. I agree that people ought to have their legal rights vindicated, but could we not imagine a situation in which a so-called public interest lawyer, who may be financed independently, would be inclined to file a suit not only to test a legal point but also in the hope that the court would grant his client plaintiffs' legal fees, and therefore his expenses?

It might well be in the nature of a harassing suit, and there are many of these filed across the country. It seems to me that this legislation and the hope of reimbursement it creates is going to encourage suits. It is most difficult to prove harassment or malicious intent on the part of a plaintiff and so defendants would be at a disadvantage.

Miss JORDAN. I can only say in response to the gentleman from Maryland, have faith in your judges. It is their discretion which will determine whether this party is entitled to attorneys' fees, and I know the gentleman has an abiding faith in the American judiciary.

Mr. SEIBERLING. Mr. Speaker, as the original congressional sponsor of legislation to authorize the awarding of attorneys' fees in civil rights cases, I rise in strong support of S. 2278.

Although the bill is entitled the Civil Rights Attorney's Fee Awards Act, it is not a lawyers' bill. Instead, it is legislation which is clearly needed—because of the Supreme Court's ruling last year in *Alyeska Pipeline Service Co. v. Wilderness Society*—if our civil rights laws are to be effective.

In the Alyeska case, the Supreme Court held that, with a few very narrow exceptions, the Federal courts have no inherent power to award attorneys' fees unless a statute expressly authorizes such awards.

The effect of that ruling on the civil rights laws is going to be devastating unless we enact this bill. In fact, a failure to authorize the awarding of attorneys' fees in civil rights cases will, as a practical matter, repeal the civil rights laws for most Americans.

Most Americans, Mr. Speaker, cannot afford to hire a lawyer if their constitutional rights are violated or if they are the victims of illegal discrimination. Most Americans simply cannot obtain free legal services, no matter how meritorious their case may be.

Right now, if someone violates your civil rights, you have the legal right to go to court and sue that person to make him stop violating your rights and also to make him pay you for any injury you have suffered. But—and this is important but—you have to pay the entire expense of hiring your lawyer, even if you win the case. So, what do you do if you cannot afford a lawyer and cannot get free legal services? The answer is that there is nothing you can do, because you will have become the victim of a legal system which is not very responsive to the majority of Americans who cannot find effective legal assistance and representation.

Unless you can get adequate legal representation, the civil rights laws are just a lot of words. But if you can obtain a lawyer's services, those civil rights laws are the vehicle for you to fight illegal and unconstitutional discrimination. If you have a meaningful opportunity to use the civil rights laws to protect yourself, then they are among the most important laws in the entire United States Code.

If the law does not authorize the awarding of attorneys' fees in meritorious civil rights cases, many potential plaintiffs will be deterred from bringing deserving cases to remedy violations of the Constitution, especially those cases in which the appropriate relief is primarily equitable or injunctive rather than monetary.

Mr. Speaker, neither the Constitution nor the civil rights laws are self-executing. Instead, they rely both on public or governmental and on private enforcement. The Government obviously does not have the resources to investigate and prosecute all possible violations of the Constitution, so a great burden falls directly on the victims to enforce their own rights. Our laws should facilitate that private enforcement, and should—within reasonable limits—encourage potential civil rights plaintiffs to bring meritorious cases.

Two weeks ago, Mr. Speaker, Congress completed action on a very important antitrust bill, the Hart-Scott-Rodino Antitrust Improvements Act. Yesterday the President signed it into law. That act contains a provision for attorneys' fees in purely private injunction cases under the antitrust laws. What we said in the Judiciary Committee report on that bill is worth repeating here:

> The antitrust laws clearly reflect the national policy of encouraging private parties . . . to help enforce the antitrust laws . . . Litigation by "private attorneys general" for monetary relief and for injunctive relief has frequently proved to be an effective enforcement tool. . . . Alyeska creates a significant deterrent to potential plaintiffs bringing and maintaining lawsuits to enjoin antitrust violations. Without the opportunity to recover attorneys' fees in the event of winning their cases, many persons and corporations would be unable to afford or unwilling to bring antitrust injunction cases.
> Indeed, the need for awarding of attorneys' fees in § 16 injunction cases is greater than the need in § 4 treble damage cases. In damage cases, a prevailing plaintiff recovers compensation, at least. In injunction cases, however, without the shifting of attorneys' fees, a plaintiff with a deserving case would personally have to pay the very high price of obtaining judicial enforcement of the law and of the important national policies the antitrust laws reflect. A prevailing plaintiff should not have to bear such an expense.

The meaning is very simple: when the cost of private enforcement actions becomes too great, there will be no private enforcement.

The civil rights laws are no less important than the antitrust laws, so we should give civil rights victims the same protections we give antitrust victims.

Of course, Congress has recognized that some civil rights laws are deserving of attorneys' fees awards. In reviewing one such law, the Supreme Court said the following:

> When the Civil Rights Act of 1964 was passed it was evident that enforcement would prove difficult and that the Nation would

have to rely in part upon private litigation as a means of securing broad compliance with the law. A Title II [of the 1964 Civil Rights Act, 42 U.S.C. § 2000a, *et seq.*] suit is thus private in form only. When a plaintiff brings an action under the Title, he cannot recover damages. If he obtains an injunction, he does so not for himself alone but also as a "private attorney general," vindicating a policy that Congress considered of the highest priority. If successful plaintiffs were routinely forced to bear their own attorneys' fees, few aggrieved parties would be in a position to advance the public interest by invoking the injunctive powers of the federal courts. Congress therefore enacted the provision for counsel fees—not simply to penalize litigants who deliberately advance arguments they know to be untenable but, more broadly, to encourage individuals injured by racial discrimination to seek judicial relief under Title II.
> "It follows that one who succeeds in obtaining an injunction under that Title should ordinarily recover an attorney's fee unless special circumstances would render such an award unjust . . . *Newman v. Piggie Park Enterprises, Inc.,* 390 U.S. 400, 401–02 (1968) (footnotes omitted).

One of the expert witnesses in the Judiciary Committee hearings, Armand Derfner of the Lawyers' Committee for Civil Rights Under Law, explained the anomoly created by Alyeska in the following manner:

> The *Alyeska* decision created an unexpected and anomalous gap in laws. For instance, fees are now authorized in an employment discrimination suit under Title VII of the 1964 Civil Rights Act, but not in the same case brought under 42 U.S.C. § 1981, which protects similar rights, but involves fewer technical prerequisites to the filing of an action. Fees are allowed in a suit under Title II of the 1964 Act challenging discrimination in a private restaurant, but not in suits under 42 U.S.C. § 1983 redressing violations of the Federal Constitution or laws by officials who are sworn to uphold the laws.

Mr. Speaker, the civil rights attorneys' fee legislation which I introduced—H.R. 8220, with 16 cosponsors—called for the mandatory award of attorneys' fees to prevailing plaintiffs, because I felt that the awards should be automatic except in the most extraordinary circumstances. I understand that S. 2278 will codify that view as to prevailing plaintiffs, following the Piggie Park guidelines.

I also felt that prevailing defendants should receive attorneys' fees only in the most extraordinary circumstances. Alyeska makes it very clear that the Federal courts have the inherent authority to award attorneys' fees to defendants if the plaintiffs has acted in bad faith, vexatiously, wantonly, or for oppressive reasons. And that is the standard which should be applied under S. 2278. It would be wholly inappropriate for the courts to regularly award attorneys' fees to defendants who prevail in these civil rights cases.

It is important that we understand that, while the bill authorizes awards to "any party" who substantially prevails, in the exercise of discretion under this bill, the courts are expected to apply the appropriate, and differing, standards applicable to plaintiffs and to defendants. Mary Frances Derfner of the Lawyers Committee for Civil Rights Under Law explained the reason for the difference in the following way:

The reasons for the different standards are obvious. Congress, having provided for attorneys' fees as a means of enabling aggrieved parties to bring enforcement suits, does not intend to deter those aggrieved parties. by making them face the prospect of paying their opponents' fees if the suit, though brought in good faith, is unsuccessful. Congress does, however, intend to deter frivolous and harassing litigation, and the availability of fees to prevailing defendants would definitely deter those plaintiffs who seek, for their own ends, to take advantage of citizen suit provisions. This theme has been repeatedly expressed in cases and legislative history.

Mr. Speaker, the House Judiciary Committee reported out a counterpart, H.R. 15460, to the bill before us, S. 2278. The Senate bill, however, contains an additional provision allowing the award of attorneys' fees to prevailing defendants in cases brought by the Government against persons alleged to have violated the Internal Revenue Code. In view of the possibility—and, unfortunately, the occasional actuality—of abuse by the Internal Revenue Service of the Government's powers to enforce the tax laws by bringing civil actions without foundation, in bad faith or for the purpose of harassing individual taxpayers, the Senate addition is a good one, which I strongly support.

Mr. Speaker, this bill deserves our overwhelming support. A vote for the bill is a vote for effective civil rights laws.

Mr. DRINAN. Mr. Speaker, I move the previous question on the Senate bill.

The previous question was ordered.

The Senate bill was ordered to be read a third time and was read the third time.

MOTION TO RECOMMIT OFFERED BY MR. ASHBROOK

Mr. ASHBROOK. Mr. Speaker, I offer a motion to recommit.

The Clerk read as follows:

The SPEAKER. Is the gentleman opposed to the bill?

Mr. ASHBROOK. I certainly am, Mr. Speaker.

The SPEAKER. The gentleman qualifies.

The Clerk read as follows:

Mr. ASHBROOK moves to recommit the bill, S. 2278, to the Committee on the Judiciary with instructions that the bill be reported back forthwith with the following amendment;

"SEC. 3. The provisions of this act shall take effect upon enactment and shall be applicable to cases filed only after the effective date of this act."

Mr. ASHBROOK. Mr. Speaker, I merely take this time—and I will not take more than a minute—but I think I can point out to the House, or at least to those who are here, the legislative travesty we find ourselves in. The gentleman from Massachusetts would not recognize anyone for an amendment. I think there are very important amendments to be offered.

Whatever problems we have with this bill, whatever fears we have, we will at least allay some of those fears if we exempt from the coverage of this act all of those hundreds of cases which are pending right now. That is one small step we can take to make this a more responsible piece of legislation.

Mr. Speaker, I certainly would urge adoption of this motion to recommit.

The SPEAKER. Without objection, the motion to recommit.

There was no objection.

The SPEAKER. The question is on the motion to recommit.

The question was taken; and the Speaker announced that the noes appeared to have it.

Mr. ASHBROOK. Mr. Speaker, I object to the vote on the ground that a quorum is not present and make the point of order that a quorum is not present.

The SPEAKER. Evidently a quorum is not present.

The Sergeant at Arms will notify absent Members.

The vote was taken by electronic device, and there were—yeas 104, nays 268, not voting 58, as follows:

[Roll No. 859]

YEAS—104

Abdnor	Ginn	Moorhead,
Ambro	Goldwater	Calif.
Anderson,	Goodling	Mottl
Calif.	Grassley	Myers, Ind.
Archer	Guyer	Nichols
Ashbrook	Haley	Paul
Bafalis	Hammer-	Poage
Bauman	schmidt	Rhodes
Beard, Tenn.	Hansen	Roberts
Bevill	Harsha	Robinson
Bowen	Hefner	Rousselot
Breaux	Henderson	Runnels
Brinkley	Hightower	Satterfield
Brooks	Holt	Schneebeli
Brown, Mich.	Jarman	Schulze
Brown, Ohio	Johnson, Pa.	Sebelius
Broyhill	Jones, N.C.	Shriver
Burleson, Tex.	Jones, Okla.	Shuster
Burlison, Mo.	Kasten	Sikes
Butler	Kelly	Skubitz
Cederberg	Kemp	Smith, Nebr.
Clawson, Del	Ketchum	Spence
Collins, Tex.	Kindness	Symms
Conlan	Landrum	Taylor, Mo.
Crane	Latta	Taylor, N.C.
Daniel, Dan	Levitas	Teague
Daniel, R. W.	Lloyd, Tenn.	Vander Jagt
Devine	Lott	Waggonner
Dickinson	Lujan	Wampler
Downing, Va.	McDonald	Whitehurst
Edwards, Ala.	Martin	Whitten
English	Mathis	Winn
Erlenborn	Michel	Wirth
Forsythe	Miller, Ohio	Young, Alaska
Fountain	Mitchell, N.Y.	Young, Fla.
Frey	Montgomery	

NAYS—268

Abzug	Burgener	Downey, N.Y.
Addabbo	Burke, Calif.	Drinan
Alexander	Burke, Mass.	Duncan, Oreg.
Allen	Burton, John	Duncan, Tenn.
Anderson, Ill.	Byron	Early
Andrews, N.C.	Carney	Eckhardt
Andrews,	Carr	Edgar
N. Dak.	Carter	Edwards, Calif.
Annunzio	Chappell	Eilberg
Ashley	Chisholm	Emery
Aspin	Clausen,	Evans, Ind.
AuCoin	Don H.	Fary
Badillo	Clay	Fascell
Baucus	Cleveland	Fenwick
Beard, R.I.	Cochran	Findley
Bedell	Cohen	Fish
Bell	Collins, Ill.	Fisher
Bennett	Conable	Fithian
Bergland	Conte	Flood
Biaggi	Corman	Florio
Biester	Cornell	Flowers
Bingham	Coughlin	Foley
Blanchard	D'Amours	Ford, Mich.
Blouin	Daniels, N.J.	Ford, Tenn.
Boggs	Danielson	Fraser
Boland	Davis	Frenzel
Bolling	de la Garza	Fuqua
Bonker	Delaney	Gaydos
Brademas	Dellums	Giaimo
Breckinridge	Dent	Gibbons
Brodhead	Derrick	Gilman
Broomfield	Derwinski	Gonzalez
Brown, Calif.	Diggs	Gradison
Buchanan	Dodd	Gude

Hagedorn	Metcalfe	Rostenkowski
Hall, Tex.	Mezvinsky	Roush
Hamilton	Miller, Calif.	Roybal
Hanley	Mills	Ruppe
Hannaford	Mineta	Russo
Harkin	Minish	St. Germain
Harrington	Mitchell, Md.	Santini
Harris	Moakley	Sarbanes
Hawkins	Mollohan	Schroeder
Hayes, Ind.	Moore	Seiberling
Hechler, W. Va.	Moorhead, Pa.	Sharp
Heckler, Mass.	Morgan	Shipley
Hestoski	Mosher	Simon
Hicks	Murphy, Ill.	Sisk
Holtzman	Murphy, N.Y.	Slack
Horton	Murtha	Smith, Iowa
Howard	Myers, Pa.	Solarz
Hubbard	Natcher	Staggers
Hughes	Neal	Stanton,
Hungate	Nedzi	J. William
Hutchinson	Nolan	Stanton,
Hyde	Nowak	James V.
Jeffords	Oberstar	Stark
Jenrette	Obey	Steed
Johnson, Calif.	O'Neill	Steiger, Wis.
Jones, Ala.	Ottinger	Stokes
Jones, Tenn.	Patten, N.J.	Stratton
Jordan	Patterson,	Stuckey
Karth	Calif.	Studds
Kastenmeier	Pattison, N.Y.	Sullivan
Kazen	Perkins	Symington
Koch	Pettis	Talcott
Krebs	Peyser	Thone
Krueger	Pickle	Thornton
LaFalce	Pike	Traxler
Lagomarsino	Pressler	Treen
Leggett	Preyer	Tsongas
Lehman	Price	Ullman
Lent	Pritchard	Van Deerlin
Lloyd, Calif.	Quie	Vander Veen
Long, La.	Railsback	Vanik
Long, Md.	Randall	Walsh
Lundine	Rangel	Waxman
McClory	Rees	Weaver
McCloskey	Regula	Whalen
McCormack	Reuss	White
McDade	Richmond	Wiggins
McEwen	Rinaldo	Wilson, Bob
McFall	Risenhoover	Wilson, Tex.
McHugh	Rodino	Wolff
McKay	Roe	Wydler
McKinney	Rogers	Wylie
Madden	Roncalio	Yates
Maguire	Rooney	Yatron
Mazzoli	Rose	Young, Tex.
Meeds	Rosenthal	Zablocki
Melcher		Zeferetti

NOT VOTING—58

Adams	Hinshaw	Passman
Armstrong	Holland	Pepper
Baldus	Howe	Quillen
Burke, Fla.	Ichord	Riegle
Burton, Phillip	Jacobs	Ryan
Clancy	Johnson, Colo.	Sarasin
Conyers	Keys	Scheuer
Cotter	McCollister	Snyder
Dingell	Madigan	Spellman
du Pont	Mahon	Steelman
Esch	Mann	Steiger, Ariz.
Eshleman	Matsunaga	Stephens
Evans, Colo.	Meyner	Thompson
Evins, Tenn.	Mikva	Udall
Flynt	Milford	Vigorito
Green	Mink	Wilson, C. H.
Hall, Ill.	Moffett	Wright
Hébert	Moss	Young, Ga.
Heinz	Nix	
Hillis	O'Hara	

The Clerk announced the following pairs:

Mrs. Meyner with Mr. Evins of Tennessee.
Mr. Pepper with Mr. Armstrong.
Mr. Thompson with Mr. Mahon.
Mr. Phillip Burton with Mr. Esch.
Mr. Cotter with Mr. Holland.
Mr Hébert with Mr. Hall of Illinois.
Mr. Matsunaga with Mr. Madigan.
Mr. Moss with Mr. du Pont.
Mr. Nix with Mr. Passman.
Mr. Mikva with Mr. Burke of Florida.
Mr. Ichord with Mr. Milford.
Mr. Conyers with Mr. Eshleman.
Mr. Adams with Mr. Moffett.
Mr. Green with Mr. Sarasin.
Mrs. Keys with Mr. Clancy.
Mr. Jacobs with Mr. Quillen.
Mr. Riegle with Mr. Howe.
Mrs. Spellman with Mr. McCollister.
Mr. Vigorito with Mr. Flynt.

35130   CONGRESSIONAL RECORD — HOUSE   *October 1, 1976*

Mr. Charles H. Wilson of California with Mr. Scheuer.

Mr. Young of Georgia with Mr. Steiger of Arizona.

Mr. Wright with Mr. Heinz.

Mr. Mann with Mr. Johnson of Colorado.

Mr. Evans of Colorado with Mr. Stephens.

Mr. Dingell with Mr. Hillis.

Mr. Baldus with Mr. O'Hara.

Mrs. Mink with Mr. Udall.

Mr. Ryan with Mr. Steelman.

Messrs. TALCOTT, QUIE, and HAGEDORN changed their vote from "'yea" to "nay."

So the motion to recommit was rejected.

The result of the vote was announced as above recorded.

The SPEAKER pro tempore (Mr. BOLLING). The question is on the passage of the bill.

The question was taken.

RECORDED VOTE

Mr. BUTLER. Mr. Speaker, I demand a recorded vote.

A recorded vote was ordered.

The vote was taken by electronic device, and there were—ayes 306, noes 68, not voting 56, as follow:

[Roll No. 860]

AYES—306

Abzug	Cornell	Harkin
Addabbo	Coughlin	Harrington
Alexander	D'Amours	Harris
Allen	Daniels, N.J.	Harsha
Anderson,	Danielson	Hawkins
Calif.	Davis	Hayes, Ind.
Anderson, Ill.	de la Garza	Hechler, W. Va.
Andrews, N.C.	Delaney	Heck'er, Mass.
Andrews,	Dellums	Hefner
N. Dak.	Dent	Helstoski
Annunzio	Derrick	Hicks
Armstrong	Derwinski	Holtzman
Ashley	Diggs	Horton
Aspin	Dodd	Howard
AuCoin	Downey, N.Y.	Hubbard
Badillo	Downing, Va.	Hughes
Baucus	Drinan	Hungate
Beard, R.I.	Duncan, Oreg.	Hu'chinson
Bedell	Duncan, Tenn.	Hyde
Bell	Early	Jenrette
Bennett	Eckhardt	Johnson, Calif.
Bergland	Edgar	Johnson, Pa.
Biaggi	Edwards, Ala.	Jones, Okla.
Biester	Edwards, Calif.	Jordan
Bingham	El'berg	Kasten
Blanchard	Emery	Kastenmeier
Blouin	English	Kazen
Boggs	Erlenborn	Kemp
Boland	Evans, Ind.	Koch
Bolling	Fary	Krebs
Bonker	Fascell	Krueger
Brademas	Fenwick	LaFalce
Breckinridge	Findley	Lagomarsino
Brodhead	Fish	Latta
Brooks	Fisher	Lehman
Broomfield	Fithian	Lent
Brown, Calif.	Flood	Levitas
Brown, Mich.	Florio	Lloyd, Calif.
Brown, Ohio	Flowers	Long, La.
Broyhill	Foley	Long, Md.
Buchanan	Ford, Mich.	Lujan
Burgener	Ford, Tenn.	Lundine
Burke, Calif.	Forsythe	McClory
Burke, Mass.	Fountain	McCloskey
Burton, John	Fraser	McCormack
Butler	Frenzel	McDade
Byron	Fuqua	McEwen
Carney	Gaydos	McFall
Carr	G'a'mo	McHugh
Carter	Gibbons	McKay
Cederberg	Gilman	McKinney
Chappell	Ginn	Madden
Chisholm	Go'dwater	Madigan
Clausen,	Gonzalez	Maguire
Don H.	Goodling	Mann
Clay	Gradison	Martin
C.eveland	Grassley	Mazzoli
Cochran	Gude	Meeds
Cohen	Guyer	Melcher
Collins, Ill.	Hagedorn	Metcalfe
Conable	Hamilton	Mezvinsky
Conte	Hanley	Miller, Calif.
Corman	Hannaford	Mills

Mineta	Rangel	Stark
Minish	Rees	Steiger, Wis.
Mitchell, Md.	Regula	Stokes
Mitchell, N.Y.	Reuss	Stratton
Moak.ey	Richmond	St.uckey
Mollohan	Rinaldo	Studds
Moore	Risenhoover	Sullivan
Moorhead, Pa.	Rodino	Symington
Morgan	Roe	Talcott
Mosher	Rogers	Teague
Murphy, Ill.	Roncalio	Thompson
Murphy, N.Y.	Rooney	Thone
Murtha	Rose	Thornton
Myers, Pa.	Rosenthal	Traxer
Natcher	Rostenkowski	Treen
Neal	Roush	Tsongas
Nedzi	Roybal	Ullman
No.an	Runnels	Van Deerlin
Nowak	Ruppe	Vander Jagt
Oberstar	Russo	Vander Veen
Obey	St Germain	Vanik
O'Brien	Santini	Walsh
O'Hara	Sarbanes	Wampler
O'Neill	Schroeder	Waxman
Ottinger	Schulze	Weaver
Patten, N.J.	Sebelius	Whalen
Patterson,	Seiberling	White
Calif.	Sharp	Whitehurst
Pattison, N.Y.	Shipley	Wiggins
Perkins	Shriver	Wilson, Bob
Pettis	Simon	Wilson, Tex.
Peyser	S'sk	Winn
Pickle	Skubitz	Wolff
Pike	S!ack	Wydler
Pressler	Smith, Iowa	Wylie
Preyer	Smith, Nebr.	Yates
Price	Solarz	Yatron
Pritchard	Spellman	Young, Tex.
Quie	Staggers	Zablocki
Railsback	Stanton,	Zeferetti
Randall	J. William	

NOES—68

Abdnor	Hansen	Paul
Ambro	Henderson	Poage
Archer	Hightower	Rhodes
Ashbrook	Holt	Roberts
Bafalis	Jarman	Robinson
Bauman	Jones, Ala.	Rousselot
Beard, Tenn.	Jones, N.C.	Satterfield
Bevill	Jones, Tenn.	Schneebeli
Bowen	Kelly	Shuster
Breaux	Ketchum	Sikes
Brinkley	Kindness	Spence
Burleson, Tex.	Landrum	Symms
Burlison, Mo.	Lloyd, Tenn.	Taylor, Mo.
Clawson, Del	Lott	Taylor, N.C.
Collins, Tex.	McDonald	Waggonner
Conlan	Mahon	Whitten
Crane	Mathis	Young, Alaska
Daniel, Dan	Michel	Young, Fla.
Daniel, R. W.	Milford	
Devine	Miller, Ohio	
Dickinson	Montgomery	
Frey	Moorhead,	
Haley	Calif.	
Hall, Tex.	Mottl	
Hammer-	Myers, Ind.	
schmidt	Nichols	

NOT VOTING—56

Adams	Hinshaw	Pepper
Baldus	Holland	Quillen
Burke, Fla.	Howe	Riegle
Burton, Phillip	Ichord	Ryan
Clancy	Jacobs	Sarasin
Conyers	Jeffords	Scheuer
Cotter	Johnson, Colo.	Snyder
Dingell	Karth	Stanton,
du Pont	Keys	James V.
Esch	Leggett	Steed
Eshleman	McCollister	Stee man
Evans, Colo.	Matsunaga	Steiger, Ariz.
Evins, Tenn.	Meyner	Stephens
Flynt	Mikva	Udall
Green	Mink	Vigorito
Hall, Ill.	Moffett	Wilson, C. H.
Hébert	Moss	Wirth
He'nz	Nix	Wright
Hillis	Passman	Young, Ga.

The Clerk announced the following pairs:

Mr. Wirth with Mr. Dingell.

Mrs. Meyner with Mr. Evins of Tennessee.

Mr. Pepper with Mr. Esch.

Mr. Cotter with Mr. Holland.

Mr. Phillip Burton with Mr. Hall of Illinois.

Mr. Matsunaga with Mr. du Pont.

Mr. Moss with Mr. Passman.

Mr. Nix with Mr. Burke of Florida.

Mr. Mikva with Mr. Eshleman.

Mr. Conyers with Mr. Heinz.

Mr. Adams with Mr. Sarasin.

Mr. Green with Mr. Clancy.

Mrs. Keys with Mr. Howe.

Mr. Jacobs with Mr. McCollister.

Mr. Riegle with Mr. Flynt.

Mr. Moffett with Mr. Scheuer.

Mr. Vigorito with Mr. Steiger of Arizona.

Mr. Charles H. Wilson of California with Mr. Stephens.

Mr. Young of Georgia with Mr. Hillis.

Mr. Wright with Mr. Steelman.

Mr. Evans of Colorado with Mr. Karth.

Mr. Baldus with Mr. Leggett.

Mrs. Mink with Mr. Ryan.

Mr. Hébert with Mr. Udall.

Mr. Steed with Mr. James V. Stanton.

Mr. Ichord with Mr. Jeffords.

Mr. Quillen with Mr. Johnson of Colorado.

So the Senate bill was passed.

The result of the vote was announced as above recorded.

A motion to reconsider was laid on the table.

GENERAL LEAVE

Mr. DRINAN. Mr. Speaker, I ask unanimous consent that all Members may have 5 legislative days in which to revise and extend their remarks on the Senate bill, S. 2278, just passed.

The SPEAKER pro tempore (Mr. BOLLING). Is there objection to the request of the gentleman from Massachusetts?

There was no objection.

MESSAGE FROM THE PRESIDENT

A message in writing from the President of the United States was communicated to the House by Mr. Heiting, one of his secretaries.

PERMISSION TO INCLUDE REPORT ON H.R. 15390 IN PERMANENT RECORD

Mr. FOUNTAIN. Mr. Speaker, H.R. 15390, a bill to establish an HEW Office of Inspector General which I sponsored, and which was cosponsored by other Members, was approved by the House on September 29 as an amendment to H.R. 11347. In order that an explanation of this legislation and its background may appear in the RECORD. I ask unanimous consent that House Report No. 94–1573, the report on H.R. 15390, be included in the permanent record following my remarks on H.R. 11347.

The SPEAKER pro tempore (Mr. BOLLING). Is there objection to the request of the gentleman from North Carolina?

There was no objection.

PROVIDING FOR CONVENING OF 1ST SESSIONS OF 95TH CONGRESS

Mr. O'NEILL. Mr. Speaker, I offer a privileged joint resolution (H.J. Res. 1119) to provide for the convening of the first session of the 95th Congress, and ask for its immediate consideration.

The SPEAKER pro tempore. Is there objection to the request of the gentleman from Massachusetts?

There was no objection.

The Clerk read the joint resolution as follows:

THE 1973 ENDANGERED SPECIES ACT AND THE *SWEET HOME* DECISION

I. *Overview and Questions*

The Endangered Species Act of 1973 is among the most comprehensive and far-reaching of more than twenty environmental statutes enacted during the 1970s. In his special environmental message to Congress in February 1972, President Nixon observed that "even the most recent act to protect endangered species, which dates only from 1969, simply does not provide the kind of management tools needed to act early enough to save a vanishing species. In particular, existing laws do not generally allow the Federal Government to control shooting, trapping, or other taking of endangered species." Nixon proposed legislation that *inter alia* "would make the taking of endangered species a Federal offense for the first time, and would permit protective measures to be undertaken before a species is so depleted that regeneration is difficult or impossible."

Congress responded with the landmark Endangered Species Act (ESA). Scientists and lawyers from the Executive Branch had substantial input in the drafting process. The House committee report conveyed some sense of the intensity with which Congress approached the situation:

> "Throughout the history of the world, as we know it, species of animals and plants have appeared, changed, and disappeared. The disappearance of a species is by no means a current phenomenon, nor is it an occasion for terror or panic.
>
> It is however, at the same time an occasion for caution, for self-searching and for understanding. Man's presence on the Earth is relatively recent, and his effective domination over the world's life-support systems has taken place within a few short generations. Our ability to destroy, or almost destroy, all intelligent life on the planet became apparent only in this generation. A certain humility, and a sense of urgency, seem indicated.
>
> From all evidence available to us, it appears that the pace of disappearance of species is accelerating. As we homogenize the habitats in which these plants and animals evolved, and as we increase the pressure for products that they are in a position to supply (usually unwillingly) we threaten their—and our own—genetic heritage.
>
> The value of this genetic heritage is, quite literally, incalculable."

The Senate approved its version of the ESA unanimously (92-0) on July 24, 1973. The House approved its version by a vote of 391-12 on September 18, 1973. The conference report was approved in late December 1973, and President Nixon signed the law on December 28. As enacted, the statute includes broad restrictions on the taking of endangered species. The meaning of the term "take," as understood by the enacting Congress as well as by the Congress that approved relevant amendments in 1982, is the focus of our legislative history excerpts—as it is the focus of the *Sweet Home* case.

We include portions of the 1973 Senate and House committee reports, excerpts from the 1973 Senate and House floor debates, and selections from the 1982 House committee report and the 1982 Conference committee report. After reviewing these excerpts, consider the following questions:

1. For the 1973 statute, Senator Tunney, the floor manager, added the verb "harm" on the Senate floor to the definition of "take" that appeared in the text of the bill reported by the Senate committee. This was an addition to the nine verbs included in the committee-reported definition of "take"; the change was part of a series of "technical and clarifying" amendments approved unanimously by the Senate (*see* 119 Cong Rec 25682-83). Senator Tunney called the amendment "technical in nature" but also "important." Does this addition clarify the Senate committee report explanation of "take"? In what way is it "important"?

2. Compare the 1973 House committee report explanation of the meaning of "take" with Rep. Sullivan's opening floor statement explaining the bill's approach to intentional or unintentional habitat destruction and the risk from those who seek to capture or kill endangered species. Are the committee and floor explanations entirely consistent? Does Rep. Sullivan's discussion carry any implications for the meaning of the term "take"?

3. According to Justice Scalia, Rep. Sullivan's floor statement signifies that the law addresses habitat destruction through its land acquisition program rather than through its prohibition on takings. Is this the only inference one can draw from Rep. Sullivan's statement? Can you offer an alternative reading?

4. The 1982 House and conference committee report excerpts address an amendment that gives the Secretary greater flexibility when regulating the "incidental taking" of endangered species. Does this amendment contemplate an intent-based or an effects-based approach to the term "taking"? Is your answer a function of the committees' approach to ordinary meaning? Their use of an illustrative example? Both?

5. In *Babbitt v. Sweet Home*, Justices Stevens and Scalia debate at some length the implications of the 1973 and 1982 legislative history with respect to the meaning of "take." In your view, which justice has the better of the argument? Is your response the same for 1973 and 1982?

II. Excerpts from S. Rep. No. 93-307 at 1-14 (July 1, 1973)

Calendar No. 289

93D CONGRESS }   SENATE   { REPORT
1st Session   No. 93–307

ENDANGERED SPECIES ACT OF 1973

JULY 1, 1973.—Ordered to be printed
Filed under authority of the order of the Senate of June 30, 1973

Mr. MAGNUSON, from the Committee on Commerce,
submitted the following

REPORT

[To accompany S. 1983]

The Committee on Commerce, to which was referred the bill (S. 1983) to provide for the conservation, protection, restoration, and propagation of species of fish, wildlife, and plants facing extinction, and for other purposes, having considered the same, reports favorably thereon with amendments and recommends that the bill do pass.

* * * *

SECTION-BY-SECTION ANALYSIS

* * * *

(3) *Section 3 (Definitions)*

* * * *

"Take" is defined in section 3(12) in the broadest possible manner to include every conceivable way in which a person can "take" or attempt to "take" any fish or wildlife.

* * * *

TEXT OF S. 1983, AS REPORTED

* * * *

(12) "Take" means to harass, pursue, hunt, shoot, wound, kill, trap, capture, or collect, or to attempt to engage in any such conduct.

III. Excerpts from119 Cong. Rec. 25668-83 (July 24, 1973)

(material omitted)   * * * *

the average, one species disappears every year.

This is an extremely disturbing trend. To allow the extinction of animal species is ecologically, economically, and ethically unsound. Each species provides a service to its environment; each species is a part of an immensely complicated ecological organization, the stability of which rests on the health of its components. At present, we are unsure of the total contribution of each species of fish and wildlife to the health of our ecology. To permit the extinction of any species which contributes to the support of this structure without knowledge of the cost or benefits of such extinction is to carelessly tamper with the health of the structure itself.

The existence of each species is also important to the growth of our scientific knowledge of man and his environment. Diversity of genetic types is necessary for thorough scientific knowledge. There is a yet unknown potential for investigation into these species' genetic structure which must remain unhindered if we wish to probe for further knowledge and the transfer of that knowledge into beneficial uses for man.

Finally, many of these animals simply give us esthetic pleasure. We like to view them in zoos and in their natural habitats. We, and our children, learn from these species about the diversity of our universe and the many forms of life which are necessary to support our bountiful and wonderful environment.

For these reasons, it is important that we adopt this act to protect our wildlife. In prior legislation we have taken several steps toward solution of the problem. In 1966 and in 1969, we provided the Secretary with the power to list species or subspecies of fish and wildlife that were threatened with extinction. Importation of these species from foreign countries was prohibited. Federal endangered wildlife reserves were encouraged by authorization of grants for land acquisition. However these provisions only gave limited protection to domestic endangered species; and the Federal grant program terminated last year. There is still no Federal prohibition against the taking of endangered species, still no widespread action to conserve and restore these animals, and the problem of the continuing extinction of species still exists.

The challenge before us now is to protect these species and their vital habitat and to restore their numbers to optimum levels. S. 1983 would accomplish this goal in several ways. First, it provides protection to a broader range of species by affording the Secretary the power to list animals which he determines are likely in the foreseeable future to become extinct, as well as those animals which are presently threatened with extinction. This gives the Secretary and the States which adopt endangered species management plans, the ability not only to protect the last remaining members of the species but to take steps to insure that species which are likely to be threatened with extinction never reach the state of being presently endangered.

The bill would thus, hopefully, prevent a crisis situation from occurring for a number of species which would otherwise come close to extinction in future years.

Mr. TUNNEY. Mr. President, the Endangered Species Act of 1973 is a vital piece of legislation which is absolutely necessary to provide protection to our Nation's species of wildlife that are threatened with extinction.

The goal of the Endangered Species Act is to conserve, protect, restore, and propagate species of fish and wildlife, that are in imminent danger of extinction or are likely to become endangered within the foreseeable future. This bill employs several mechanisms to insure the accomplishment of this goal. They include provision of greater authority to the Secretaries of Interior and Commerce to list endangered or threatened animals, encouragement of further international cooperation for the protection of these animals, provision for the acquisition of habitat useful for the purposes of this act, and incentives for the establishment of effective endangered species programs by the several States.

There is an urgent need for this type of protective legislation. In our country alone, there are 109 species listed as endangered by the Secretary of the Interior. On his foreign list, there are over 300 species. Furthermore, the situation continues to worsen. The rate of extinction has increased to a point where, on

The two levels of classification facilitate regulations that are tailored to the needs of the animal while minimizing the use of the most stringent prohibitions. Since most of our resources for restoring and propagating species lie with the States, they are encouraged to use their discretion to promote the recovery of threatened species and Federal prohibitions against taking must be absolutely enforced only for those species on the brink of extinction.

To aid in the delicate and highly specialized task of listing these animals, the Secretary is required to appoint an advisory committee to assist him in the designation of endangered and threatened species. To insure that the States that may be affected by the Secretary's designation are fully active through the listing process, the Secretary must consult with the States affected prior to listing any species. Furthermore, half the members of the advisory committee must be employed by State governments.

Many species have been inadvertently exterminated by a negligent destruction of their habitat. Their habitats have been cut in size, polluted, or otherwise altered so that they are unsuitable environments for natural populations of fish and wildlife. Under this bill, we can take steps to make amends for our negligent encroachment. The Secretary would be empowered to use the land acquisition authority granted to him in certain existing legislation to acquire land for the use of the endangered species programs. The bill also eliminates the restrictive ceiling which was placed on funds available to the Land and Water Conservation Fund Act by the Act of 1969. Through these land acquisition provisions, we will be able to conserve habitats necessary to protect fish and wildlife from further destruction.

Although most endangered species are threatened primarily by the destruction of their natural habitats, a significant portion of these animals are subject to predation by man for commercial, sport, consumption, or other purposes. The provisions in S. 1983 would prohibit the commerce in or the importation, exportation, or taking of endangered species except where permitted by the Secretary for scientific purposes in furtherance of the purpose of this act, or for the propagation of such species in captivity in a controlled habitat. Amendments which will be offered today, and which would greatly add to the purposes of this act would permit otherwise prohibited acts when they are undertaken to enhance the propagation or survival of the affected species or to prevent serious and otherwise unavoidable threats to human health or the environment.

(material omitted)

* * * *

[Page 25682:]

Mr. TUNNEY. Mr. President, I send to the desk a series of technical and clarifying amendments to S. 1973 and ask unanimous consent that they be considered en bloc.

The PRESIDING OFFICER. The amendments will be stated.

The legislative clerk proceeded to read the amendments.

Mr. TUNNEY. Mr. President, I ask unanimous consent that further reading of the amendments be dispensed with.

The PRESIDING OFFICER. Without objection, it is so ordered, and the amendments will be printed in the RECORD.

The text of the amendments is as follows:

On page 27, line 12, before the word "educational," insert the words "aesthetic, ecological,".

* * * *

On page 28, line 8, after the word "States" insert the words "and other interested parties,".

On page 31, line 6, delete the word "terrestrial".

On page 31, line 20, after the word "harass," and before the word "pursue", insert the word "harm,".

On page 33, delete lines 17–23.

On page 33, line 34, delete the number "3" and insert the number "2".

On page 35, line 9, delete the word "Secretary" and insert the word "Secretaries".

On page 36, lines 15–16, strike the words "endangered or".

On page 38, line 12, before the word "and" insert the word "propagation".

On page 38, line 18, after the word "has", insert the words "statutory and regulatory".

On page 39, line 13, strike the words "facing extinction" and, before the word "fish" strike the words "endangered and threatened".

On page 40, strike lines 13–17 and insert, in lieu thereof, the following:

"(B) the readiness of a State to proceed with a conservation and management program consistent with the objectives and purposes of this Act;

"(C) the number of endangered and threatened species within a State;

"(D) the potential for restoring endangered and threatened species within a State; and

"(E) the relative urgency to initiate a program to restore and protect an endangered or threatened species in terms of the survival of the species."

On page 40, line 19, after the word "year" insert the word "shall".

On page 40, line 20, after the period insert the words "Any funds remaining unobligated or unexpended at the close of the second fiscal year shall remain available to the Secretary for the purpose of this section."

On page 41, line 18, after the period, insert the words "For the purposes of this section, the non-federal share may, in the discretion of the Secretary, be in the form of real or personal property, the value of which will be determined by the Secretary, as well as money."

On page 41, line 23, after the word "appropriated" insert the words "through the fiscal year ending June 30, 1977."

On page 42, line 12, strike the word "of" and insert in lieu thereof the word "regarding".

On page 49, lines 19 and 20, delete the words "subsection (a)" and insert the words "paragraph (1) of this subsection".

On page 50, lines 20–22, strike the words "specimens or products processed or manufactured in whole or in part from specimens of any such species" and insert, in lieu thereof the words "any endangered species of fish or wildlife".

On page 51, lines 12–14, after the word "consumption" strike the words, "or taken for recreational purpose in waters under United States jurisdiction or on the high seas," and insert in lieu thereof the words ", or fish or wildlife taken for recreational purposes pursuant to applicable Federal or State laws and regulations in waters under United States jurisdiction or on the high seas".

On page 55, line 16, after the word "consumption" insert the words "within native villages or towns".

On page 59, line 14, after the word "revocation," insert the words "made pursuant to this section".

On page 68, line 11, strike the word "protection", and insert in lieu thereof the word "conservation".

On page 69, line 20, add a new subsection as follows:

"(f) Section 2(l) of the Federal Environmental Pesticide Control Act of 1972 (P. L. 92–516) is amended by striking out the words 'by the Secretary of the Interior under Public Law 91–135' and inserting in lieu thereof

the words 'or threatened by the Secretary pursuant to the Endangered Species Act of 1973'".

The PRESIDING OFFICER. Without objection, the amendments will be considered en bloc.

Mr. TUNNEY. Mr. President, I have submitted these technical and clarifying amendments to the Senator from Alaska (Mr. STEVENS) and he has indicated that he will support them. The amendments will help to achieve the purposes of the bill and will clarify some confusion caused by language remaining in the bill from earlier drafts or omitted from earlier drafts which went unnoticed during the final committee markup.

They are, as I indicate, technical in nature. They are important, however.

If there is a member of the minority on the floor now, I should like to move their adoption.

(material omitted)

* * * *

Mr. TUNNEY. Mr. President, as I understand it, the parliamentary situation is that I have an amendment pending. I have not yet yielded back the remainder of my time.

The PRESIDING OFFICER. The Senator is correct.

Mr. TUNNEY. I am prepared to yield back the remainder of my time. Is the designee of the minority leader prepared to yield back the remainder of his time?

Mr. COOK. Mr. President, I yield back the remainder of my time.

The PRESIDING OFFICER. The question is on agreeing to the amendment.

The amendment was agreed to.

(material omitted)

IV. Excerpts from H.R. Rep. No. 93-412 at 1-15 (July 27, 1973)

93D CONGRESS } HOUSE OF REPRESENTATIVES {   REPORT
   1st Session   }   { No. 93-412

ENDANGERED AND THREATENED SPECIES CONSERVATION ACT OF 1973

JULY 27, 1973.—Committed to the Committee of the Whole House on the State
of the Union and ordered to be printed

Mrs. SULLIVAN, from the Committee on Merchant Marine and
Fisheries, submitted the following

REPORT

[To accompany H.R. 37]

The Committee on Merchant Marine and Fisheries, to whom was referred the bill (H.R. 37) to provide for the conservation, protection, and propagation of species or subspecies of fish and wildlife that are threatened with extinction or likely within the foreseeable future to become threatened with extinction, and for other purposes, having considered the same, report favorably thereon with amendments and recommend that the bill as amended do pass.

The amendment to the text of the bill strikes out all after the enacting clause and inserts in lieu thereof a substitute which appears in the reported bill in italic type.

The other amendment modifies the title of the bill to make it conform to the changes made by the amendment to the text.

PURPOSE OF THE LEGISLATION

There is presently in effect a series of Federal laws designed to protect species of fish and wildlife which may face extinction without that protection. The first of these laws was passed in 1966 and the second in 1969; at the time they were enacted, they were adequate to meet the demands as they then existed.

Subsequent events, however, have demonstrated the need for greater flexibility in endangered species legislation, more closely designed to meet their needs. In response to this need, legislation was proposed in the last Congress, but failed of passage. The Congress is now in a position to move in this critical area.

H.R. 37, as amended, combines features of the Administration bill (H.R. 4758), and the original H.R. 37. It is designed to widen the protection which can be provided to endangered species under the laws now on the books.

(1)

2

The principal changes to be effected by the new legislation include:

1. It extends protection to animals which may become endangered, as well as to those which are now endangered.

2. It permits protection of animals which are in trouble in any significant portion of their range, rather than threatened with worldwide extinction.

3. It makes taking of such animals a Federal offense.

4. It eliminates existing dollar ceilings ($15 million, already consumed) on acquisition of critical habitat areas.

5. It gives management authority for marine species to the Department of Commerce.

6. It authorizes the use of counterpart funds, where proper.

7. It allows states to adopt more restrictive legislation than the Federal laws.

8. It clarifies and extends the authorities of the Department of Agriculture to assist landowners to carry out the purposes of the Act.

9. It directs a study of the problems involved in the domestic regulation of trade in endangered plants.

* * * *

[4]

BACKGROUND AND NEED FOR THE LEGISLATION

Throughout the history of the world, as we know it, species of animals and plants have appeared, changed, and disappeared. The disappearance of a species is by no means a current phenomenon, nor is it an occasion for terror or panic.

It is however, at the same time an occasion for caution, for self-searching and for understanding. Man's presence on the Earth is relatively recent, and his effective domination over the world's life support systems has taken place within a few short generations. Our ability to destroy, or almost destroy, all intelligent life on the planet became apparent only in this generation. A certain humility, and a sense of urgency, seem indicated.

From all evidence available to us, it appears that the pace of disappearance of species is accelerating. As we homogenize the habitats in which these plants and animals evolved, and as we increase the pressure for products that they are in a position to supply (usually unwillingly) we threaten their—and our own—genetic heritage.

The value of this genetic heritage is, quite literally, incalculable. The blue whale evolved over a long period of time and the combination of factors in its background has produced a certain code, found in its genes, which enables it to reproduce itself, rather than producing sperm whales, dolphins or goldfish. If the blue whale, the largest animal in the history of this world, were to disappear, it would not be possible to replace it—it would simply be gone. Irretrievably. Forever.

One might analogize the case to one in which one copy of all the books ever printed were gathered together in one huge building. The position in which we find ourselves today is that of custodians of this building, and our choice is between exercising our responsibilities and ignoring them. If these theoretical custodians were to permit a madman to enter, build a bonfire and throw in at random any volume he

5

selected, one might with justification suggest that others be found, or at least that they be censored and told to be more careful in the future. So it is with mankind. Like it or not, we are our brothers' keepers, and we are also keepers of the rest of the house.

From the most narrow possible point of view, it is in the best interests of mankind to minimize the losses of genetic variations. The reason is simple: they are potential resources. They are keys to puzzles which we cannot solve, and may provide answers to questions which we have not yet learned to ask.

To take a homely, but apt, example: one of the critical chemicals in the regulation of ovulation in humans was found in a common plant. Once discovered, and analyzed, humans could duplicate it synthetically, but had it never existed—or had it been driven out of existence before we knew its potentialities—we would never have tried to synthesize it in the first place.

Who knows, or can say, what potential cures for cancer or other scourges, present or future, may lie locked up in the structures of plants which may yet be undiscovered, much less analyzed? More to the point, who is prepared to risk being those potential cures by eliminating those plants for all time? Sheer self-interest impels us to be cautious.

The institutionalization of that caution lies at the heart of H.R. 37, as ordered reported to the Congress. Several scores of nations have similarly endorsed the need for comparable legislation within their own countries by signing the recent Convention which takes a giant step in this direction.

Man can threaten the existence of species of plants and animals in any of a number of ways, by excessive use, by unrestricted trade, by pollution or by other destruction of their habitat or range. The most significant of those has proven also to be the most difficult to control: the destruction of critical habitat.

Clearly it is beyond our capability to acquire all the habitat which is important to those species of plants and animals which are endangered today, without at the same time dismantling our own civilization. On the other hand, there are certain areas which are critical which can and should be set aside. It is the intent and purpose of this legislation to see that our ability to do so, at least within this country, is maintained. H.R. 37 articulates and enhances this purpose and ability.

[page 10:]

DEFINITIONS

Sec. 3. (1) "Convention" means the recently concluded Convention on International Trade in Endangered Species of Wild Fauna and Flora.

(2) The term "Endangered Species" means any species of fish or wildlife which is in danger of extinction throughout its entire range, or any portion of its range. This definition is a significant shift in the definition in existing law, which considers a species to be endangered only when it is threatened with worldwide extinction. It includes the possibility of declaring a species endangered within the United States where its principal range is in another country, such as Canada or Mexico, and members of that species are only found in this country insofar as they exist on the periphery of their range.

[page 10:]

(11) "Take" is defined broadly. It includes harassment, whether intentional or not. This would allow, for example, the Secretary to regulate or prohibit the activities of birdwatchers where the effect of those activities might disturb the birds and make it difficult for them to hatch or raise their young.

217

15

(material omitted)

PROHIBITED ACTS

Sec. 9. (a) Subparagraphs (1) through (5) of this paragraph spell
out a number of activities which are specifically prohibited with respect to endangered (not threatened) species for persons subject to the
jurisdiction of the United States. It includes, in the broadest possible
terms, restrictions on the taking, importation and exportation, and
transportation of such species, as well as other specified acts.

V. Excerpts from 119 Cong. Rec. 30162-63 (Sept. 18, 1973)

[Page 30162]

NGRESSIONAL RECORD — HOUSE   *September 18, 1973*

(material omitted)

Mrs. SULLIVAN. Mr. Speaker, H.R. 37 should be enacted at the earliest possible moment. It represents hours of intense committee consideration and of painstaking analysis by members and staff of the committee.

H.R. 37 revises and extends existing law—law which was proposed by this committee in earlier years. As far as it went, the earlier legislation has been valuable—even invaluable—but that law did not go far enough. That defect we hope to remedy today.

H.R. 37 comes on the heels of and implements, an important international convention, which produced a treaty providing for the protection and preservation of endangered species of plants and animals. That Convention, signed by the United States on March 3 of this year, has been submitted to the Congress for approval by the Senate and was in fact approved 5 months later. That is pretty fast action and I would hope that we can reciprocate by moving promptly on H.R. 37 today.

That additional protection for endangered species of plants and animals is necessary is indisputable. Within the past few years, it was necessary for the Department of the Interior to place eight species of whales on that list, and as many species of "spotted cats": leopards, tigers, cheetahs, et cetera.

For the most part, the principal threat to animals stems from the destruction of their habitat. The destruction may be intentional, as would be the case in clearing of fields and forests for development of resource extraction, or it may be unintentional, as in the case of the spread of pesticides beyond their target area. Whether it is intentional or not, however, the result is unfortunate for the species of animals that depend on that habitat, most of whom are already living on the edge of survival. H.R. 37 will meet this problem by providing funds for acquisition of critical habitat through the use of the land and water conservation fund. It will also enable the Department of Agriculture to cooperate with willing landowners who desire to assist in the protection of endangered species, but who are understandably unwilling to do so at excessive cost to themselves.

Another hazard to endangered species arises from those who would capture or kill them for pleasure or profit. There is no way that the Congress can make it less pleasurable for a person to take an animal, but we can certainly make it less profitable for them to do so. H.R. 37 makes it a Federal offense to violate the act or regulations published pursuant to the act, and prescribes penalties and fines of up to $20,000 for persons convicted of violations.

I should point out, however, that in our desire to create unpleasant consequences for those who violate the act, we have at the same time been very aware of the need to assure due process for anyone accused of violating the act. There are requirements for public hearings on violations, with a full opportunity for the defendants to review the evidence against them, and judicial review of decisions which are felt to be unjust.

Protection of endangered species is, as the gentleman from Michigan has already indicated, far more than a matter of esthetics. As our report on the bill points out, endangered species of plants and animals possess genetic characteristics which cannot be replaced or artificially reproduced. Once the passenger pigeon disappeared, it was gone. It will not, and cannot, ever be back. The loss of the passenger pigeon is unfortunate; it may or may not be tragic. The loss of the blue whale, on the other hand, might very well be tragic: It is possibly the largest mammal ever to have existed on the face of the Earth, and it may be the most efficient harvester of tiny marine life that exists today. In a protein-hungry world, the loss of huge potential sources of food is not an occasion which can be lightly considered.

When we threaten endangered species, we tinker with our own futures. We run risks whose magnitude we understand dimly, if at all. And we do so, for the most part, for reasons that can be described most charitably as trivial.

The purpose and intent of the bill before you is to bring into focus the costs of further endangering the plants and animals of this world. I believe that we have achieved this objective, and I support the bill strongly, and urge the support of my colleagues.

Mr. DINGELL. Mr. Speaker, I yield myself 3 minutes.

Mr. Speaker, I strongly urge enactment of H.R. 37, a bill to protect and encourage endangered and threatened species of fish and wildlife. This bill has been considered at length by our committee in the course of hearings during this and the previous Congress. It has been unanimously endorsed by members of our subcommittee and by members of the full Committee on Merchant Marine and Fisheries. It should be enacted today.

H.R. 37 amends and extends laws now on the books: Endangered species legislation enacted in 1966 and 1969. The existing laws are sound, as far as they go, but later events have shown that they do not go far enough. Present laws need to be made more flexible, to adapt themselves to the needs of the animals themselves and to deal with problems which did not exist until a few years ago.

[Page 30163]

September 18, 1973   CO

There is a further need, which enactment of this legislation will meet. In March of this year, representatives of 80 nations met in Washington, in response to an earlier congressional directive, and negotiated a comprehensive convention for the protection of endangered species of plants and animals. On August 3, that convention was approved by the Senate, making this country the first to approve the convention. That it will ultimately be in force—which will take place after the 10th ratification takes place—is not questioned by anyone. Enactment of H.R. 37 will take all the steps which must be taken by this country in order to fully implement the requirements of this convention. It will place us in the forefront of the nations of the world that expressed interest and concern for this problem.

The principal changes to be effected by passage of H.R. 37 are:

First, it extends protection to animals which may become endangered, as well as to those which are now endangered.

Second, it extends protection to animals which are in trouble in any significant portion of their range, rather than threatened, and they must now be, with worldwide extinction.

Third, it makes taking of such animals a Federal offense.

Fourth, it eliminates existing dollar ceilings on acquisition of critical habitat for such species. The present ceiling, which has been almost exhausted, is $15 million.

Fifth, it gives to the Department of Commerce the authority to manage endangered and threatened species which were transferred to them under Reorganization Plan No. 4 of 1970.

Sixth, it authorizes the use of counterpart funds for programs involving foreign countries, wherever this is appropriate.

Seventh, it authorizes and encourages the State governments to adopt and enforce laws and regulations which are consistent with those adopted by the Federal Government.

Eighth, it clarifies and extends the authority of the Department of Agriculture to assist landowners, wherever they are willing to carry out the purposes of the act.

Ninth, it directs that a study be made of the problems associated with the domestic regulation of trade in endangered species of plants.

For a more extended discussion of these and other changes which will be accomplished by passage of this bill, I invite the attention of the House to our committee's report on H.R. 37 (H. Rept. 93-412).

(material omitted)

VI.   Excerpts from H.R. Rep. No. 97-567 at 1, 31 (May 17, 1982)

97TH CONGRESS	HOUSE OF REPRESENTATIVES	REPT. 97–567
2d Session		Part 1

ENDANGERED SPECIES ACT AMENDMENTS

MAY 17, 1982.—Ordered to be printed

Mr. JONES of North Carolina, from the Committee on Merchant Marine and Fisheries, submitted the following

REPORT

together with

ADDITIONAL VIEWS

[To accompany H.R. 6133]

[Including cost estimate of the Congressional Budget Office]

The Committee on Merchant Marine and Fisheries, to whom was referred the bill (H.R. 6133) to authorize appropriations to carry out the Endangered Species Act of 1973, as amended, through fiscal year 1984, having considered the same, report favorably thereon with amendments and recommend that the bill as amended do pass.

The amendments are as follows:

(material omitted)

31

(material omitted)

SECTION 5—EXPERIMENTAL POPULATION AND OTHER EXEMPTIONS.

Section 5 of H.R. 6133 amends Section 10 of the Act in several important ways. It would add new provisions to facilitate the establishment of experimental populations, to give the Secretary more flexibility in regulating the incidental taking of endangered species, to facilitate the disposition of existing stocks of whale bone and teeth, and to provide for the establishment of experimental populations.

First, the legislation establishes a procedure whereby those persons whose actions may affect endangered or threatened species may receive permits for the incidental taking of such species if the action would not jeopardize the continued existence of the species. This provision addresses the concerns of private landowners who are faced with having otherwise lawful actions not requiring federal permits prevented by the Section 9 prohibitions against taking.

Section 10(a), as amended, would allow the Secretary to permit any taking otherwise prohibited by Section 9(a)(1)(B) if the taking is incidental to, and not the purpose of, an otherwise lawful activity. By use of the word "incidental" the Committee intends to cover situations in which it is known that a taking will occur if the other activity is engaged in but such taking is incidental to, and not the purpose of, the activity. An applicant for such a permit would submit to the Secretary a plan that would specify the number of species likely to be taken, what steps the applicant would take to minimize the takings, and what alternative actions that did not involve the takings were analyzed and why those alternatives were not adopted. The secretary would base his determination on whether or not to grant the permit under the same standard as found in Section 7(a)(2) of the Act, that is, whether or not the taking would jeopardize the continued existence of the species. To issue the permit, the Secretary would also have to find that the taking would be incidental to another activity and that the applicant would minimize the taking to the maximum extent practicable.

As with all Section 10 permits, the legislation provides that the Secretary shall prescribe terms and conditions to ensure that appropriate measures are taken by the applicant to minimize the takings and shall revoke the permit if the permittee is not complying with the terms and conditions of the permit.

(material omitted)

VII. Excerpts from H.R. Rep. No. 97-835 at 1, 19, 29-32 (Sept. 17, 1982)

| 97TH CONGRESS | HOUSE OF REPRESENTATIVES | REPORT |
| 2d Session | | No. 97–835 |

ENDANGERED SPECIES ACT AMENDMENTS OF 1982

SEPTEMBER 17, 1982.—Ordered to be printed

Mr. JONES of North Carolina, from the committee of conference,
submitted the following

CONFERENCE REPORT

[To accompany H.R. 6133]

The committee of conference on the disagreeing votes of the two
Houses on the amendments of the Senate to the bill (H.R. 6133) to
authorize appropriations to carry out the provisions of the Endangered Species Act of 1973 for fiscal years 1983, 1984, and 1985, and
for other purposes, having met, after full and free conference, have
agreed to recommend and do recommend to their respective Houses
as follows:

That the House recede from its disagreement to the amendment
of the Senate to the text of the bill and agree to the same with an
amendment as follows:

In lieu of the matter proposed to be inserted by the Senate
amendment insert the following:

*That this Act may be cited as the "Endangered Species Act Amend-
ments of 1982".*

(material omitted)

JOINT EXPLANATORY STATEMENT OF THE COMMITTEE OF CONFERENCE

The managers on the part of the House and the Senate at the conference on the disagreeing votes of the two Houses on the amendments of the Senate to the bill (H.R. 6133) to extend the authorization for appropriations for the Endangered Species Act of 1973, and for other purposes, submit the following joint statement to the House and the Senate in explanation of the effect of the action agreed upon by the managers and recommended in the accompanying conference report.

The Senate amendment to the text of the bill struck out all of the House bill after the enacting clause and inserted a substitute text.

The House recedes from its disagreement to the amendment of the Senate with an amendment which is a substitute for the House bill and the Senate amendment. The House also recedes from its disagreement to the title of the bill. The differences between the House bill, the Senate amendment, and the substitute agreed to in conference are noted below, except for clerical corrections, conforming changes made necessary by agreements reached by the conferees, and minor drafting and clarifying changes.

SECTION-BY-SECTION ANALYSIS

Section 1. Title

The short title of this bill is the "Endangered Species Act Amendments of 1982."

* * * *

[29:]

Section 6. Experimental populations and other exemptions

Section 6 of the Conference substitute amends section 10 of the Act. Sections 6 (1) and (2) give the Secretary more flexibility in regulating the incidental taking of endangered species. * * * *

Sections 6 (1) and (2) adopt, with amendments, a provision appearing in the House bill to give the Secretary more flexibility in regulating the incidental taking of endangered and threatened species. This provision establishes a procedure whereby those persons whose actions may affect endangered or threatened species may receive permits for the incidental taking of such species, provided the action will not jeopardize the continued existence of the species. This provision addresses the concerns of private landowners who are faced with having otherwise lawful actions not requiring Federal permits prevented by section 9 prohibitions against taking.

As amended, section 10(a) of the Act will authorize the Secretary to permit any taking otherwise prohibited by section 9(a)(1)(B) of the Act if the taking is incidental to, and not the purpose of, an otherwise lawful activity. An applicant for such a permit must submit to the Secretary a conservation plan that specifies the impacts which will likely result from such taking, what steps the applicant will take to minimize and mitigate those impacts, what other alternatives that would not result in the takings were analyzed, and why those alternatives were not adopted. * * * *

* * * *

[30:]

> To the maximum extent possible, the Secretary should utilize this authority under this provision to encourage creative partnerships between the public and private sectors and among governmental agencies in the interest of species and habitat conservation.
>
> A comprehensive conservation plan prepared pursuant to section 10(a) would be developed jointly between the appropriate Federal wildlife agency and the private sector or local or state governmental agencies. This provision is modeled after a habitat conservation plan that has been developed by three Northern California cities,

31

> the County of San Mateo, and private landowners and developers to provide for the conservation of the habitat of three endangered species and other unlisted species of concern within the San Bruno Mountain area of San Mateo County.

* * * *

> Because the San Bruno Mountain plan is the model for this long term permit and because the adequacy of similar conservation plans should be measured against the San Bruno plan, the Committee believes that the elements of this plan should be clearly understood. Large portions of the habitat on San Bruno Mountain are privately owned. Prior to the discovery of two species of endangered butterflies, the landowner planned to develop much of its

32

> land. The butterflies face threats to their existence, however, even in the absence of any development. The primary threats to the species consist of insufficient regulation of recreational activities and encroachment on the species' habitat by brush and exotic species.
>
> Prior to developing the conservation plan, the County of San Mateo conducted an independent exhaustive biological study which determined the location of the butterflies, and the location of their food plants. The biological study also developed substantial information regarding the habit and life cycles of the butterflies and other species of concern. The biological study was conducted over a two year period and at one point involved 50 field personnel.
>
> The San Bruno Mountain Conservation Plan is based on this extensive biological study. The basic elements of the plan are the following:
>
> 1. The Conservation Plan addresses the habitat throughout the area and preserves sufficient habitat to allow for enhancement of the survival of the species. The plan protects in perpetuity at least 87 percent of the habitat of the listed butterflies;
>
> 2. The establishment of a funding program which will provide permanent on-going funding for important habitat management and enhancement activities. Funding is to be provided through direct interim payments from landowners and developers and through permanent assessments on development units within the area;
>
> 3. The establishment of a permanent institutional structure to insure uniform protection and conservation of the habitat throughout the area despite the division of the habitat by the overlapping jurisdiction of various governmental agencies and the complex pattern of private and public ownership of the habitat; and
>
> 4. A formal agreement between the parties to the plan which ensures that all elements of the plan will be implemented.

THE 1968 GUN CONTROL ACT AND *MUSCARELLO*

I. Overview and Questions

Congress first enacted a version of what is now 18 U.S.C. § 924(c)(1) as part of the Gun Control Act of 1968. The provision was introduced in July 1968 as a floor amendment by Rep. Poff, a Republican from Virginia and Judiciary Committee member, who was modifying a colleague's earlier proposal. Debate on the Poff amendment took place less than six weeks after Senator Robert Kennedy's assassination. As enacted in 1968, the provision mandated an enhanced punishment for anyone who uses a firearm to commit a federal felony or carries a firearm unlawfully during the commission of a federal felony.

Congress amended this language as part of the Comprehensive Crime Control Act of 1984. The amended text deleted the modifier "unlawfully" after "carries a firearm"; this change eliminated the registered gun exception, extending enhanced penalty requirements to defendants who have a permit for their gun. The new text also changed the precursor crime from "any felony" to "any crime of violence." In 1988, Congress further amended the section by adding drug trafficking crimes to crimes of violence as precursor offenses triggering enhanced sentences for carrying a gun.

We include key excerpts from the 1968 House floor debate on the Poff amendment as well as a solitary observation from the 1968 Senate floor debate. We also include several pages from the Senate committee report accompanying the 1984 statute, as this excerpt explains in some detail the committee's motivation in modifying the 1968 statutory text.

After reviewing this legislative history, consider the following questions.

1. When explaining his amendment on the House floor (at 22231), Representative Poff states that "the effect of a mandatory minimum sentence ... is to persuade the man who is tempted to commit a Federal felony to leave his gun at home." Some other House members echo Poff's concern to have the criminal leave his gun at home (e.g., Rep. Meskill, at 22236; Rep. Randall at 22244). Does their motivation support a broader or narrower penal scope for the activity of carrying a firearm during commission of a felony? Should this motivation be imputed to the House as a whole?

2. Why do you suppose the 1968 Poff amendment limited the enhanced penalty provision to individuals carrying a firearm *unlawfully* during a felony? Does the exchange between Reps. Yates and Cellar at 21788 shed light on this question?

3. The 1983 Senate committee report explains its position on "carries" as follows (see p.235 below): "Evidence that the defendant had a gun in his pocket but did not display it, or refer to it, could still support a conviction for "carrying" a firearm in relation to the crime if from the circumstances or otherwise it could be found that the defendant intended to use the gun if a contingency arose or to make his escape .... [T]he requirement that the firearm's use or possession be "in relation to" the crime would preclude its application in a situation where its presence played no part in the crime, such as a gun carried in a pocket and never displayed or referred to in the course of a pugilistic barroom fight." Does this footnote explanation support Justice Breyer's approach to "carries" or Justice Ginsburg's?

4. The 1983 Senate committee explanation of the revised section 924(c)(1) appears at pp.312-314 of an 800-page committee report. The quoted language in question 3 appears at p.314, n.10. Should courts expect any member of Congress other than those most active on this bill to be aware of or influenced by explanatory statements buried in a footnote of a massively long committee report?

II. *114 Cong. Rec. 21788 (July 17, 1968)*

* * * *

Mr. YATES. Mr. Chairman, will the gentleman yield at that point?

Mr. CELLER. I yield to the gentleman from Illinois.

Mr. YATES. The Casey bill itself states:

That whoever during the commission of any robbery, assault, murder, rape, burglary, kidnaping, or homicide uses or carries any firearm which has been transported in interstate.

I direct the chairman's attention to the crime of assault. Suppose a policeman carrying a gun, as policemen do, were to slap somebody and it were found that he was not justified in doing so. Could he be indicted under this bill?

Mr. CELLER. I will say to the gentleman that the language is most imprecise. The language is rather broad and permits a number of unusual interpretations.

Mr. YATES. May I ask another question?

Mr. CELLER. I yield to the gentleman from Illinois.

Mr. YATES. Suppose a licensee is carrying a pistol, as he is authorized to do pursuant to his license, and pushes somebody or assaults somebody, and he does not use the pistol but carries it on his hip.

Mr. CELLER. He would come within the toils of the so-called Casey amendment.

Mr. YATES. He would be within it?

Mr. CELLER. He would suffer the mandatory punishments for the first offense, 10 years beyond what other punishment might be under the State law, and 25 more years for the second, third, fourth, and subsequent offenses.

Mr. YATES. May I ask the gentleman another question. Under this proposed bill, in prosecuting a crime, would not the district attorney have to prove that the gun was shipped in interstate commerce?

Mr. CELLER. That raises a serious question as to the constitutionality of the so-called Casey amendment. I do not know whether it would be or would not be impervious to an attack on its constitutionality. The only basis that I can see for its constitutionality would be the interstate commerce clause, but there should be some sequence between the date of the interstate shipment of the gun and the use or possession of the gun at the time of the crime.

Mr. YATES. Suppose the gun were shipped prior to the enactment of the so-called Casey bill—in the event it were enacted—and a person were indicted under the Casey bill, and proof made of the fact that the gun was shipped prior to that time. Could conviction be obtained, or would this be ex post facto?

Mr. CELLER. The gentleman raises some very ticklish and some very difficult questions to answer. There is nothing in the Casey amendment which says or does not say when the gun shall have been imported into the State where it is used unlawfully, and it does not indicate the time when it shall have been brought into the State. There is nothing in the Casey amendment which makes that manifest. It is very dangerous, to say the least.

This is a criminal statute and a crime must be clearly defined. The Federal crime certainly is not clearly defined. I wonder whether or not there is even due process under the Constitution under the present wording of this so-called Casey amendment.

Mr. YATES. Mr. Chairman, I thank the gentleman.

* * * *

* * * *

III. Excerpts from 114 Cong. Rec. 22231-44 (July 19, 1968)

(material omitted)   * * * *

alties. For the first offense, the penalty is a minimum of 1 year and a maximum of 10 years. For the second offense, the penalty is a minimum of 5 years and a maximum of 25 years. It will be said that the penalty structure in my substitute is less than that in the Casey amendment. While it is true that the minimum penalties are smaller, the substitute is not weaker. Indeed, the substitute is stronger. The substitute provides that the penalties cannot be suspended and that probation cannot be granted. The Casey amendment contains no such provision.

My substitute is also stronger in that it compels the court to impose the sentence to run consecutively upon the penalty previously imposed for the basic crime. The Casey amendment permits the court to make the two penalties run concurrently and to suspend any part or all of either or both.

It will also be argued in opposition to both the Casey amendment and my substitute that the minimum mandatory penalty is often counterproductive. Ordinarily, this is true for two reasons. First, when the prosecuting attorney feels that the minimum penalty is greater that the gravity of the offense in a particular case, he simply indicts for a lesser included offense or abandons prosecution altogether. If the accused is indicted and the jury feel that extenuating circumstances make the minimum penalty too harsh, they search diligently for reasonable doubt and acquit. In this particular context, however, the argument is not quite so valid. The effect of a minimum mandatory sentence in this case is to persuade the man who is tempted to commit a Federal felony to leave his gun at home. Any such person should understand that if he uses his gun and is caught and convicted, he is going to jail. He should further understand that if he does so a second time, he is going to jail for a longer time.

The Casey amendment applies to both Federal felonies and State felonies. My substitute is confined to Federal felonies. This is for three reasons.

* * * *

SUBSTITUTE AMENDMENT OFFERED BY MR. POFF FOR THE AMENDMENT OFFERED BY MR. CASEY

Mr. POFF. Mr. Chairman, I offer a substitute amendment for the amendment offered by the gentleman from Texas [Mr. CASEY].

The Clerk read as follows:

Amendment offered by Mr. POFF as a substitute for the amendment offered by Mr. CASEY: On page 28, after line 2, insert a new subsection as follows:

"(c) Whoever—

"(1) uses a firearm to commit any felony which may be prosecuted in a court of the United States, or

"(2) carries a firearm unlawfully during the commission of any felony which may be prosecuted in a court of the United States, shall be sentenced to a term of imprisonment for not less than one year nor more than ten years. In the case of his second or subsequent conviction under this subsection, such person shall be sentenced to a term of imprisonment for not less than five years nor more than twenty-five years. The execution or imposition of any term of imprisonment imposed under this subsection may not be suspended, and probation may not be granted. Any term of imprisonment imposed under this subsection may not be imposed to run concurrently with any term of imprisonment imposed for the commission of such felony."

And redesignate the following subsection accordingly.

(By unanimous consent, Mr. POFF was allowed to proceed for 5 additional minutes.)

Mr. POFF. Mr. Chairman, my amendment is a substitute for the Casey amendment, but it is not in derogation of the Casey amendment. Rather, it retains its central thrust and targets upon the criminal rather than the gun. In several particulars, the substitute strengthens the Casey amendment.

My substitute makes it a separate Federal crime to use a firearm in the commission of another Federal crime and invokes separate and supplemental pen-

[Pages 22234-35]

* * * *

Virginia first and this is certainly as it should be, because the gentleman from Virginia is a member of the Judiciary Committee which is handling this bill, and, according to the rules of the House, members of the committee handling the legislation should have priority in matters of this kind, and I certainly agree with this procedure.

The gentleman from Virginia is attempting to do what I have attempted to do in my amendment and in my proposed bill which I introduced dealing with this matter of crime and the use of firearms. The emphasis should be, and we are in agreement, on the user of the weapon, rather than the weapon itself. Certainly, if we are going to vigorously combat this problem of crime, we are going to have to have not only stricter measures dealing with the subject, but we are also going to have to require a vigorous prosecution of those measures and incarceration of the guilty, so as to provide the strongest deterrent to preclude the repetition of the crimes of violence and the unlawful use of firearms in their commission.

For too long now the emphasis, by judicial interpretation, has been placed on the "rights" of the criminal to the neglect of his responsibility as a member of society and to the neglect of the rights and privileges of the law-abiding citizen. Courts in many cases have been too promiscuous in their use of probation and too lenient in their exercise of judicial discretion and suspension of criminal penalties.

As I previously said, I had introduced a companion measure to the so-called Casey amendment, and yet while I strongly believe that his amendment is a step in the right direction, I am quick to realize that there are some problems with the provision that requires those merely having a gun in their possession to be subject to the same penalties as those who actually use that weapon in the commission of a crime. On the other hand, the situation is so abnormal and of such paramount interest to the welfare and security of our law-abiding citizens, I feel that we have to adopt stringent measures to remedy the situation. While I can see that the substitute of the gentleman from Virginia is a perfecting amendment and eliminates the possibility of probation or suspension of the mandatory minimum sentence for both first and second offenses, I regret that his substitute only covers the violation of Federal crimes. Unfortunately, this does not cover the bulk of crimes because most of them are violations of State laws. Hopefully, State legislatures will take the necessary action to cover these problems. Admittedly, police protection and law enforcement is a local matter, yet because of the gravity of the situation and its national scope, I think the Federal Government has a proper role to play in dealing with the problem.

Mr. Chairman, rather than to control guns, I think that the solution to this problem is to control crime. The criminal always finds a way to obtain a weapon and I fear that by legislation dealing with weapons, if we are not exceedingly careful, we may be providing the criminal with additional advantages over the law-abiding citizen and, rather than re-

Mr. HARSHA. Mr. Chairman, I rise to commend the gentleman from Virginia.

Mr. Chairman, I rise in support of the substitute amendment offered by the gentleman from Virginia. I had a similar substitute prepared to offer, but the Chair recognized the gentleman from

stricting the use and possession of weapons by criminals, we may wind up by prohibiting the lawful use of weapons by the law-abiding citizen.

Mr. Chairman, while my amendment is more restrictive and imposes more severe penalties than the amendment of the gentleman from Virginia, his is a much needed step in the right direction and I can certainly wholeheartedly support it. I would urge my colleagues to adopt this amendment so that if we are to have legislation dealing further with the use of guns, we can make that legislation meaningful and effective by placing the burden upon the criminal rather than on the law-abiding citizen.

(material omitted)

22236   CON SE   22239

(material omitted)

(material omitted)

Mr. MESKILL. Mr. Chairman, my amendment deletes one word from the Poff substitute. I want it understood that I support the Poff substitute, but the deletion of the word "unlawfully" will strengthen this substitute. I recognize the fact that the word is in the substitute for the purpose of protecting the police officer, but the immunity goes beyond the police officer. I wonder if we really want to create a double standard here.

We are concerned, as the gentleman from Virginia [Mr. POFF] said, with having the criminal leave his gun at home. I wonder if we want to create two classes of people, those with permits, or licenses to carry a firearm who can go out with firearms in their possession, commit Federal felonies, and be immune from the provisions of the Poff substitute. I do not think they should be immune. I think the provisions of the Poff substitute should apply to every person whether he carries a gun lawfully or unlawfully, if he commits a Federal felony while he has a firearm on his person.

I think my amendment will strengthen the Poff substitute. If my amendment does not pass, I shall support the Poff substitute, because it is a great improvement over the Casey amendment.

* * * *

Mr. PUCINSKI. Mr. Chairman, I rise in support of the amendment offered by the gentleman from Florida. I believe it will cure one of the defects raised by the chairman of the Judiciary Committee. As pointed out, if you tried to burden the Federal courts with the whole problem of handling these prosecutions, you would really overburden them.

It would be my hope, if the gentleman's amendment prevails, and the amendment offered by the gentleman from Texas [Mr. CASEY], is then approved by this House, that this legislation will prove to be the deterrent that this country needs to eliminate the large number of crimes that were cited by the chairman of this committee.

The chairman said there were 900,000-plus crimes committed in this country that would come under the purview of this act. It occurs to me that when we consider the 6,500 people killed in America by guns last year and compared with 36 people killed in England, the urgent need for this legislation becomes apparent. Certainly, Federal statutes and Federal prosecutions have some bearing and this is demonstrated not only in the lower incidence of Federal crimes in this country but in England as well.

I call attention again to the argument offered by some Member here a moment ago that only 16,000 crimes were prosecuted by the Federal Government last year involving the use of firearms. That is probably the best answer we can give here today for the legislation, for the gentleman's amendment and the Casey amendment. If indeed it is a fact that these criminals have greater fear of the Federal Government, then we ought to give the Federal Government the jurisdiction. I know that as an old police reporter, I recall that criminals always feared vastly more violating Federal laws than State laws.

It occurs to me that we can make a sufficient deterrent with this legislation. After all, what is the purpose of this legislation? If we are going to legislate here and then project a continuation of 900,000 crimes a year with 6,500 Americans killed annually, we might as well stop wasting our time. But if we are going to legislate here to provide sufficient and meaningful deterrents to crime, then, indeed, our mission here is worth while.

I suggest that the amendment offered by the gentleman from Florida [Mr. PEPPER] and the amendment offered by the gentleman from Texas [Mr. CASEY] can, for the first time, make a criminal who takes a gun in his hand realize that he is going to be prosecuted to the fullest extent of the Federal law. Nobody is going to bring that little grocer back to life who was slaughtered this morning in the District but perhaps he would not have been murdered in an attempted holdup of his store if the gunman knew the penalty that faced him for merely carrying a gun during a felony.

* * * *

(material omitted)   * * * *

Mr. CELLER. I doubt the power; yes.

Mr. RANDALL. Mr. Chairman, the gentleman from New York heard the gentleman from Florida a moment ago read from the U.S. Constitution saying the Congress can create inferior Federal courts and Congress may elect to confer jurisdiction on the State courts. Would the gentleman respond to these contentions, whether in his opinion they are valid?

Mr. CELLER. I do not know if it can be interpreted that way. That is probably taking it out of context. I will say now, I just do not know, and I have grave doubts. I do not think there is a man in this Chamber who can tell me beyond peradventure of doubt that there is jurisdiction in the Congress to do exactly what the amendment of the gentleman from Florida purports to do.

Mr. RANDALL. Mr. Chairman, while it is true our friend from New York states there is not a man in this Chamber who can say beyond peradventure of doubt that we in the Congress can do what the amendment of the gentlemen from Florida seeks to do, on the other hand, in none of these exchanges has he said it cannot be done. He has only said he has doubts or as he put it, grave doubts. On the other hand, his counterpart on the other side of the aisle has stated affirmatively, in his opinion, the Congress could assign the jurisdiction contained in the amendment of the gentlemen from Florida to the State courts.

While it appears both sides of the aisle believe the amendment may be unwise, one side reaches the conclusion the amendment is constitutional. The other side the chairman of the committee now makes an expression of doubt.

I came to the floor this afternoon intent upon supporting the Casey amendment. The only question I raise against his proposal is that the penalties for first and second offenses are not strong enough. I agree fully with the gentleman from Texas [Mr. CASEY], about the high cost of crime and I know many of the offenses are committed by repeaters. These repeat offenders do not stay in their cells much longer than it takes to apprehend them. Even if mandatory penalties should have the result of filling our prisons then it is money well spent to build more prisons and much better than to spend money to apprehend repeat offenders.

If I may respectfully say so, the Poff substitute to the Casey amendment while it rules out a suspended sentence, it is not strong enough and the penalties are not severe enough. In my opinion the Poff substitute may be a step in the right direction, but it will reach only a small percentage of the total number of crimes. As the gentleman from Texas stated it will cover only about 1,600 cases annually and there will remain outside the coverage of the Poff amendment about 90 percent of the total offenses committed with firearms.

Of course, what we are trying to do by these penalties is to persuade the criminal to leave his gun at home. If he knows he is convicted with a gun and is going to jail, it might serve as a deterrent. The facts are the Poff substitute would eliminate thousands of State

Mr. RANDALL. Well, of course, I was not asking the gentleman whether he was for or against the amendment but only whether in his opinion the Congress could confer this area of Federal jurisdiction upon the State courts.

Now I would like to ask the chairman, the gentleman from New York, substantially the same question. Is there any doubt about the power of the Congress to confer this jurisdiction on the State courts?

Mr. CELLER. I will say to the gentleman offhand I just do not know. I would like to have the opportunity to look into that question. I would not want to categorically say yes or no. I do not know. I do not think there is any man in this Chamber who knows at this moment This is pounced on us suddenly. I do not think we can decide a question as important as this, as paramount as this—to confer jurisdiction on the State courts— in a thrice, as it were, in 20 minutes or a half hour. You cannot do it.

Mr. RANDALL. Until now I thought you were of the opinion that the Pepper amendment to confer jurisdiction on State courts was just a departure from present practice. In other words, you were saying a while ago you thought it was unwise to assign to the State courts Federal questions. Now you say there is some doubt as to our power. Is that right?

IV. 114 Cong. Rec. 27144 (Sept. 17, 1968)

* * * *   * * * *   * * * *

Mr. MURPHY subsequently said: Mr. President, I have cosponsored amendment No. 958, introduced by my able colleagues from Colorado which allows, but does not require increased sentences, the length being left to the court's discretion, for those persons convicted of committing a felony while using or having a firearm in their possession.

I strongly support the purpose of this amendment, because I believe it speaks directly to the problem which we are trying to solve by our consideration of firearms legislation today.

Our intent obviously is to take guns out of the hands of criminals. I think there is little doubt but that the effective enforcement of an amendment such as that proposed by Senators ALLOTT and DOMINICK will make every criminal and would-be criminal think twice before using or even carrying a firearm.

However, Mr. President, that amendment, as it is drafted, does leave an opening which I would hope the courts will see fit to close. It states that the court may increase the sentence of the convicted criminal, but it does not say that the court must do so. I think the court should do its utmost so as to keep this provision from being an empty threat.

Now, Mr. President, the House of Representatives, by a vote of 412 to 11, included in its gun legislation a provision which will require the court to sentence any person committing any felony, as defined by this act, while using or carrying a firearm to an additional 1 to 10 years' imprisonment. For the second offense of such a nature it will require the term of imprisonment range between 5 and 25 years. In neither case can there exist a possibility of a suspended sentence, probation, or consideration being given to the sentence running concurrently with any term of incarceration imposed for the commission of the original felony.

Mr. President, I believe the amendment we are considering will allow a greater degree of flexibility for the court to utilize its just discretion in relation to the facts peculiar to the individual case involved. I think its passage is essential if we are truly concerned with the increase in the crime rate, the number of felonies which have been committed with firearms and have resulted in deaths and injuries, and the need for a peaceful society.

* * * *

V. S. Rep. No. 98-225 at 1, 312-14 (Sept. 14, 1983)

98TH CONGRESS *1st Session*	SENATE	REPORT No. 98-225

COMPREHENSIVE CRIME CONTROL ACT OF 1983

R E P O R T

OF THE

COMMITTEE ON THE JUDICIARY
UNITED STATES SENATE

ON

S. 1762

together with

ADDITIONAL AND MINORITY VIEWS

SEPTEMBER 14 (legislative day, SEPTEMBER 12), 1983.—Ordered to be printed

U.S. GOVERNMENT PRINTING OFFICE

24-038 O   WASHINGTON : 1983

PART D—MANDATORY PENALTY FOR THE USE OF A FIREARM IN A FEDERAL CRIME OF VIOLENCE

1. In general and present Federal law

Part D of title X is designed to impose a mandatory penalty without the possibility of probation or parole, for any person who uses or carries a firearm during and in relation to a Federal crime of violence. Although present Federal law, section 924(c) of title 18, appears to set out a mandatory minimum sentencing scheme for the use or unlawful carrying of a firearm during any Federal felony, drafting problems and interpretations of the section in recent Supreme Court decisions have greatly reduced its effectiveness as a deterrent to violent crime.

Section 924(c) sets out an offense distinct from the underlying felony and is not simply a penalty provision.[1] Hence, the sentence provided in section 924(c) is in addition to that for the underlying felony and is from one to ten years for a first conviction and from two to twenty-five years for a subsequent conviction. However, section 924(c) is drafted in such a way that a person may still be given a suspended sentence or be placed on probation for his first violation of the section, and it is ambiguous as to whether the sentence for a first violation may be made to run concurrently with that for the underlying offense. Some courts have held that a concurrent sentence may be given.[2] Moreover, even if a person is sentenced to imprisonment under section 924(c), the normal parole eligibility rules apply.

In addition to these problems with present section 924(c), the Supreme Court's decisions in *Simpson* v. *United States*,[3] and *Busic* v. *United States*,[4] have negated the section's use in cases involving statutes, such as the bank robbery statute[5] and assault on Federal officer statute[6] which have their own enhanced, but not mandatory, punishment provisions in situations where the offense is committed with a dangerous weapon. These are precisely the type of extremely dangerous offenses for which a mandatory punishment for the use of a firearm is the most appropriate.

In *Simpson*, the defendants had been convicted of armed bank robbery involving the use of a dangerous weapon or device in violation of 18 U.S.C. 2113 (a) and (d), and of using firearms to commit the robbery in violation of 18 U.S.C. 924(c). They were sentenced to maximum terms of 25 years in prison on the aggravated robbery count and to 10-year consecutive prison terms on the firearms

---

[1] *Simpson* v. *United States*, 435 U.S. 6, 10 (1978).
[2] *United States* v. *Sudduth*, 457 F.2d 1198 (9th Cir. 1972); *United States* v. *Gaines*, 594 F.2d 541 (7th Cir. 1979).
[3] *Supra*, note 1.
[4] 446 U.S. 398 (1980).
[5] 18 U.S.C. 2113.
[6] 18 U.S.C. 111.

(312)

313

count. The Supreme Court held that the statutory construction and legislative history of section 924(c) rendered it inapplicable in cases where the predicate felony statute contains its own enhancement provision for the use of a dangerous weapon.

In *Busic*, the two defendants had been convicted, among other things, of narcotics offenses, and of armed assault on Federal officers resulting from a shoot-out with agents of the Drug Enforcement Administration, in violation of 18 U.S.C. 111. In addition, one defendant had been convicted of using a firearm in the commission of a felony, in violation of 18 U.S.C. 924(c)(1) and the other of carrying a firearm in the commission of a felony, under section 924(c)(1). Each was sentenced to a total of 30 years of imprisonment, of which five years resulted from concurrent sentences on the narcotics charges, five were the result of the assault charges, and 20 were imposed for the section 924(c) violations. Relying on *Simpson*, the Supreme Court held that where the predicate felony statute contains its own enhancement provision, section 924(c) "may not be applied at all * * *"[7] Thus, the twenty-year sentence was nullified.

The Committee has concluded that subsection 924(c) should be completely revised to ensure that all persons who commit Federal crimes of violence, including those crimes set forth in statutes which already provide for enhanced sentences for their commission with a dangerous weapon,[8] receive a mandatory sentence, without the possibility of the sentence being made to run concurrently with that for the underlying offense or for any other crime and without the possibility of a probationary sentence or parole.

2. Provisions of the bill, as reported

Part D of title X represents a complete revision of subsection 924(c) of title 18 to overcome the problems with the present subsection discussed above. As amended by Part D, section 924(c) provides for a mandatory, determinate sentence for a person who uses or carries a firearm during and in relation to any Federal "crime of violence," including offenses such as bank robbery or assault on a Federal officer which provide for their own enhanced punishment if committed by means of a dangerous weapon.[9] In the case of a first conviction under the subsection, the defendant would be sentenced to imprisonment for five years. For a second or subsequent conviction he would receive a sentence of imprisonment for ten years. In either case, the defendant could not be given a suspended or probationary sentence, nor could any sentence under the revised subsection be made to run concurrently with that for the predicate crime or with that for any other offense. In addition, the Committee intends that the mandatory sentence under the revised subsection 924(c) be served prior to the start of the sentence for the underlying or any other offense. For example, a person convicted of

---

[7] *Supra*, note 4 at 407.

[8] These statutes include 18 U.S.C. 111, 112, 113, 2113, 2114 and 2231. Enhancement of sentences varies widely among these sections and the terms called for are generally less than the penalty under section 924(c).

[9] The term "crime of violence" is defined in Part A of this title and the discussion in the Report thereon should be consulted here. In essence the term includes any offenses in which the use of physical force is an element and any felony which carries a substantial risk of such force. Thus, the section expands the scope of predicate offenses, as compared with current law, by including some violent misdemeanors, but restricts it by excluding non-violent felonies.

314

armed bank robbery in violation of section 2113 (a) and (d) and of using a gun in its commission (for example by pointing it at a teller or otherwise displaying it whether or not it is fired) [10] would have to serve five years (assuming it was his first conviction under the subsection) less only good time credit for proper behavior in prison, before his sentence for the conviction under section 2113 (a) and (d) could start to run. Finally, a person sentenced under the new subsection 924(c) would not be eligible for parole.

---

[10] Evidence that the defendant had a gun in his pocket but did not display it, or refer to it, could nevertheless support a conviction for "carrying" a firearm in relation to the crime if from the circumstances or otherwise it could be found that the defendant intended to use the gun if a contingency arose or to make his escape. The requirement in present section 924(c) that the gun be carried unlawfully, a fact usually proven by showing that the defendant was in violation of a State or local law, has been eliminated as unnecessary. The "unlawfully" provision was added originally to section 924(c) because of Congressional concern that without it policemen and persons licensed to carry firearms who committed Federal felonies would be subjected to additional penalties, even where the weapon played no part in the crime, whereas the section was directed at persons who chose to carry a firearm as an offensive weapon for a specific criminal act. See *United States* v. *Howard*, 504 F.2d 1281, 1285–1286 (8th Cir. 1974). The Committee has concluded that persons who are licensed to carry firearms and abuse that privilege by committing a crime with the weapon, as in the extremely rare case of the armed police officer who commits a crime, are as deserving of punishment as a person whose possession of the gun violates a State or local ordinance. Moreover, the requirement that the firearm's use or possession be "in relation to" the crime would preclude its application in a situation where its presence played no part in the crime, such as a gun carried in a pocket and never displayed or referred to in the course of a pugilistic barroom fight.

THE 1974 NLRA NONPROFIT HOSPITALS AMENDMENT AND *CATHOLIC BISHOP*

I. *Overview and Questions*

Congress first addressed the issue of whether the NLRA should apply to nonprofit hospitals, schools, colleges and churches when it debated changes in the definition of a covered "employer" as part of the Taft Hartley Act in 1947. As our 1947 legislative history excerpts indicate, the House favored a broad exemption, the Senate a narrow one limited to hospitals. The conference committee adopted the Senate approach, excluding only nonprofit corporations and associations operating hospitals. There was no discussion of the First Amendment or religion: conferees' explanation for not excluding schools and churches from the Act's coverage reflected their anticipation that these other nonprofit institutions would only rarely be deemed to affect interstate commerce.

Congress in 1974 amended the NLRA to remove the exclusion for hospital employers. The House committee report explained that the National Labor Relations Board after the 1947 enactment had initially declined to exercise jurisdiction over nonprofit or charitable schools and colleges as well as hospitals. However, as growing numbers of employees at these institutions sought to unionize, there was a marked increase in recognition strikes and related labor unrest. The Labor Board came to assert jurisdiction over all nonprofits except hospitals so that the organizing campaigns would be resolved through secret ballot elections under the statute rather than through a proliferation of strikes. The goal of the 1974 legislation was to cover the one set of employers that in 1947 had been explicitly exempted from the Act's jurisdiction.

The 1974 floor debate excerpts address two amendments related to the religious employer issue. One is an amendment proposed by Senator Ervin to retain an exemption for religious hospitals even as Congress was moving to extend the law's coverage to nonprofit hospitals in general. That amendment was debated in the Senate and then defeated. The other involves an amendment proposed by Rep. Erlenborn to allow individuals with bona fide objections to joining or financially supporting unions to refrain from doing so—although the union and employer would be allowed to negotiate for such individuals to pay to a charity an equivalent "fair share" amount (i.e. equivalent to what bargaining unit members pay to their union). This amendment was agreed to just before final passage of the bill, despite opposition from the bill's floor manager Rep. Thompson.

As you review the excerpts from 1947 and 1974, consider the following questions.

1. The canon *expressio unius* suggests that when Congress in 1947 identified for exclusion one kind of nonprofit institution, it had no intention of excluding other nonprofit institutions that are not listed. In this instance, the conference committee expressly identifies the other non-listed institutions, including nonprofit schools, while suggesting they won't be covered often anyway. Under these circumstances, is it "fairly possible" to avoid the constitutional question of whether the Act covers religious schools?

2. Can it fairly be argued that Congress, by exempting one kind of nonprofit institution, meant for other nonprofits to fall outside the Labor Board's jurisdiction? Assuming arguendo that this was the conferees' expectation in 1947 given their understanding about the Commerce Clause, should that understanding—consciously omitted from text—carry any weight in 1974? in 1979?

3. Senator Ervin's 1974 Amendment to exempt church-operated hospitals drew opposition on the floor from Senators Cranston, Javits, and Williams. Given this debate, and the fact the amendment was rejected on a recorded vote, is it fairly possible to argue that the Senate understood the NLRA to exclude Board jurisdiction over church-operated schools?

4. The majority opinion in *Catholic Bishop* contends that acceptance of Rep. Erlenborn's 1974 amendment "reflects congressional sensitivity to First Amendment guarantees." (Casebook, p.914). Can you argue that the existence of this amendment accommodating employees' religious beliefs actually undermines the majority's position? Did Congress see the need for equivalent accommodation for religiously motivated employees and employers? Was Congress's approach to accommodation toward religiously motivated employees to exclude them altogether from the Act's coverage?

II. *H.R. Rep. No. 80-245 at 1, 12 (April 11, 1947)*

80TH CONGRESS } HOUSE OF REPRESENTATIVES { REPORT No. 245
1st Session

LABOR-MANAGEMENT RELATIONS ACT, 1947

APRIL 11, 1947.—Committed to the Committee of the Whole House on the State of the Union and ordered to be printed

Mr. HARTLEY, from the Committee on Education and Labor, submitted the following

REPORT

[To accompany H. R. 3020]

---

12   LABOR-MANAGEMENT RELATIONS ACT, 1947

(B) Under the old act, the term "employer" does not include the United States. The same exemption that applies to the Government should apply equally to instrumentalities of the Government. The bill therefore excludes "the United States or any instrumentality thereof" from the definition of "employer". Up to now, the Board, apparently has not applied the act to any of the many instrumentalities of the United States, but whether or not it should do so, Congress, not the Board, should decide.

(C) Churches, hospitals, schools, colleges, and societies for the care of the needy are not engaged in "commerce" and certainly not in interstate commerce. These institutions frequently assist local governments in carrying out their essential functions, and for this reason should be subject to exclusive local jurisdiction. The bill therefore excludes from the definition of "employer" institutions that qualify as charities under our tax laws. In this respect, the bill is consistent with similar laws in a number of States, notably New York, Pennsylvania, and Wisconsin. The bill does not exclude from the definition institutions organized for profit or those a substantial part of whose activities is carrying on propaganda or attempting to influence legislation.

III. H.R. 320, as it passed the House, in *1 Federal History of the Labor Management Relations Act, 1947 at 160-161 (1948)*

---

160   H. R. 3020, AS PASSED HOUSE   [3]

1   TITLE I—AMENDMENT OF NATIONAL LABOR

2   RELATIONS ACT

3   SEC. 101. The National Labor Relations Act is hereby

4   amended to read as follows:

5   "POLICY

6   *(material omitted)*

7

8

9

10

11

12

13

14   "DEFINITIONS

15   "SEC. 2. When used in this Act—

16   "(1) The term 'person' includes one or more indi-

17   viduals, partnerships, associations, corporations, labor organ-

18   izations, legal representatives, trustees, trustees in bank-

19   ruptcy, or receivers.

20   "(2) The term 'employer' includes any person acting

21   as an agent of an employer, directly or indirectly, but

22   shall not include the United States or any instrumentality

23   thereof, or any State or political subdivision thereof, or

24   any person subject to the Railway Labor Act, as amended

---

1 from time to time, or any labor organization (other than

2 when acting as an employer), or anyone acting in the

3 capacity of officer or agent of such labor organization, or

4 any corporation, community chest, fund, or foundation

5 organized and operated exclusively for religious, charitable,

6 scientific, literary, or educational purposes, or for the pre-

7 vention of cruelty to children or animals, no part of the

8 net earnings of which inures to the benefit of any private

9 shareholder or individual, and no substantial part of the

10 activities of which is carrying on propaganda, or otherwise

11 attempting to influence legislation.

(material omitted)

IV. 93 Cong. Rec. 4997 (May 12, 1947)

(material omitted)

Mr. TYDINGS. I did not want to interfere with the unanimous-consent request. If the Senator from Wisconsin will yield to me, I should like to submit an amendment.

Mr. WILEY. I yield.

Mr. TYDINGS. I ask that the amendment be stated.

The PRESIDING OFFICER. The clerk will state the amendment.

The CHIEF CLERK. On page 4, line 10, after the comma, it is proposed to insert the following: "or any corporation or association operating a hospital, if no part of the net earnings inures to the benefit of any private shareholder or individual."

Mr. TYDINGS. Mr. President, this amendment is designed merely to help a great number of hospitals which are having very difficult times. They are eleemosynary institutions; no profit is involved in their operations, and I understand from the Hospital Association that this amendment would be very helpful in their efforts to serve those who have not the means to pay for hospital service, enable them to keep the doors open and operate the hospitals. I do not believe the committee is opposed to the amendment. I do not believe the chairman of the committee, the Senator from Ohio [Mr. TAFT], is opposed to it, and I hope there will be no objection from any quarter.

The PRESIDING OFFICER. Does the Senator move the adoption of the amendment?

Mr. TYDINGS. I move that the amendment be agreed to.

The PRESIDING OFFICER. The question is on agreeing to the amendment offered by the Senator from Maryland.

Mr. TAFT. Mr. President, will the Senator from Wisconsin yield?

Mr. WILEY. I yield.

Mr. TAFT. The committee considered this amendment, but did not act on it, because it was felt it was unnecessary. The committee felt that hospitals were not engaged in interstate commerce, and that their business should not be so construed. We rather felt it would open up the question of making other exemptions. That is why the committee did not act upon the amendment as it was proposed.

Mr. TYDINGS. Mr. President, I appreciate the reasons given why the committee did not act on it. I think we all realize that hospitals that are working on a nonprofit basis are not engaged in interstate commerce, but I know they are having a hard time to keep going, and

I think it would be very helpful if the committee would put the specific language in the bill. They serve all mankind. I move the adoption of the amendment.

The PRESIDING OFFICER. The question is on agreeing to the amendment offered by the Senator from Maryland.

Mr. TAYLOR. Mr. President, will the Senator yield?

Mr. WILEY. For what purpose?

Mr. TAYLOR. I want to address an inquiry to the Senator from Maryland about the proposed amendment.

Mr. WILEY. I yield.

Mr. TAYLOR. What does the amendment do, may I ask the Senator from Maryland? Does it prevent hospital employees, particularly nurses, from organizing? Is that the sense of the amendment?

Mr. TYDINGS. It simply makes a hospital not an "employer" in the commercial sense of the term. It is not a business operating on a profit basis. It is a charitable institution which is kept open, and it is to lift it out of the category of ordinary business, and is to except such charitable institutions. It is, rather, to relieve them from the pressures that normally go with business. Such institutions cannot keep open, in certain cases, I may say to the Senator, unless relief is afforded. The people who are affected are the poor people of the country. The amendment affects only charitable institutions, which do not derive a cent of profit, but are maintained by donations almost entirely, except for a small amount of revenue received for services rendered.

Mr. TAYLOR. The Senator has made that clear, but I wanted to know what would be the effect if nurses in a hospital should decide to organize. Would it prevent their organization?

Mr. TYDINGS. I do not think it would.

Mr. TAYLOR. That is all I wanted to know.

Mr. TYDINGS. They should not have to come to the National Labor Relations Board, as in the case of ordinary business concerns. They are not in interstate commerce. A hospital is a local institution, quite often kept up by the donations of benevolent persons. I hope the Senate will let the amendment go to conference. Employees of such a hospital should not have to come to the National Labor Relations Board. A charitable institution is away beyond the scope of labor-management relations in which a profit is involved. No profit is involved in this work.

Mr. TAYLOR. That may be true, but nevertheless I have in mind that nursing is one of the most poorly paid professions in America; outside the profession of school teaching it is perhaps the poorest paid, in proportion to the service rendered to humanity. I do not want to place the nursing profession under any handicap in their efforts to obtain an improved standard of living.

Mr. TYDINGS. I do not think the amendment will affect them in the slightest way as to salaries. I will say to the Senator they can still protest, they can still walk out. The only thing it

does is to lift them out of commercial channels of labor-management where a profit is involved. The most of these institutions are maintained by the benevolence of thousands of people who contribute to community funds and so on, to keep them going. I am told it will be a big aid to the community if they are not brought in under the strict scope of labor-management commercial relations where profit is involved.

Mr. TAYLOR. I understand the Senator. These may not be profit-making institutions, but even so I feel that, simply because an institution, even one like the Red Cross, is kept up by popular subscription, the professional workers, even employees of the Red Cross, should be permitted a decent living and should not be hamstrung in their efforts to obtain it.

Mr. TYDINGS. I agree with the Senator.

Mr. TAYLOR. With that assurance, I shall not oppose it.

The PRESIDING OFFICER. The question is on the adoption of the amendment offered by the Senator from Maryland [Mr. TYDINGS].

Mr. KILGORE. Mr. President, will the Senator yield?

Mr. WILEY. I yield.

Mr. KILGORE. I wanted to ask the Senator from Maryland a question. Is the amendment so worded that it applies only to hospitals not operated for profit?

Mr. TYDINGS. Absolutely.

Mr. KILGORE. There are hospitals that are highly profitable.

Mr. TYDINGS. The specific language is, "that are operated with no effort to make a profit." The amendment applies to completely nonprofit organizations. There is not a penny of profit in it for anybody.

Mr. DONNELL. Mr. President, will the Senator yield?

Mr. WILEY. I yield.

Mr. DONNELL. May I ask the Senator from Maryland to tell us at what point the amendment is to be inserted?

Mr. TYDINGS. On page 4, line 10, after the comma.

Mr. DONNELL. What is the language, please?

Mr. TYDINGS. I do not have the language.

The PRESIDING OFFICER. The clerk will again state the amendment.

The LEGISLATIVE CLERK. On page 4, line 10, after the comma, it is proposed to insert "or any corporation or association operating a hospital, if no part of the net earnings inures to the benefit of any private shareholder or individual."

Mr. DONNELL. I thank the Senator.

The PRESIDING OFFICER. The question is on agreeing to the amendment offered by the Senator from Maryland.

The amendment was agreed to.

* * * *

V. H.R. Rep. No. 80-510 at 1, 3, 32 (June 3, 1947)

80TH CONGRESS 1st Session	HOUSE OF REPRESENTATIVES	REPORT No. 510

LABOR-MANAGEMENT RELATIONS ACT, 1947

JUNE 3, 1947.—Ordered to be printed

Mr. HARTLEY, from the committee of conference, submitted the following

CONFERENCE REPORT

[To accompany H. R. 3020]

The committee of conference on the disagreeing votes of the two Houses on the amendments of the Senate to the bill (H. R. 3020) to prescribe fair and equitable rules of conduct to be observed by labor and management in their relations with one another which affect commerce, to protect the rights of individual workers in their relations with labor organizations whose activities affect commerce, to recognize the paramount public interest in labor disputes affecting commerce that endanger the public health, safety, or welfare, and for other purposes, having met, after full and free conference, have agreed to recommend and do recommend to their respective Houses as follows:

That the House recede from its disagreement to the amendment of the Senate to the text of the bill and agree to the same with an amendment as follows:

In lieu of the matter proposed to be inserted by the Senate amendment insert the following:

(material omitted)

LABOR-MANAGEMENT RELATIONS ACT, 1947   3

* * * *

"DEFINITIONS

"Sec. 2. When used in this Act—

"(1) The term 'person' includes one or more individuals, labor organizations, partnerships, associations, corporations, legal representatives, trustees, trustees in bankruptcy, or receivers.

"(2) The term 'employer' includes any person acting as an agent of an employer, directly or indirectly, but shall not include the United States or any wholly owned Government corporation, or any Federal Reserve Bank, or any State or political subdivision thereof, or any corporation or association operating a hospital, if no part of the net earnings inures to the benefit of any private shareholders or individual, or any person subject to the Railway Labor Act, as amended from time to time, or any labor organization (other than when acting as an employer), or anyone acting in the capacity of officer or agent of such labor organization.

* * * *

32   LABOR-MANAGEMENT RELATIONS ACT, 1947

* * * *

The conference agreement follows the provisions of the House bill in the matter of agents of an employer, and follows the Senate amendment in the matter of exclusion of nonprofit corporations and associations operating hospitals. The other nonprofit organizations excluded under the House bill are not specifically excluded in the conference agreement, for only in exceptional circumstances and in connection with purely commercial activities of such organizations have any of the activities of such organizations or of their employees been considered as affecting commerce so as to bring them within the scope of the National Labor Relations Act.   * * * *

VI. S. Rep. No. 93-766 at 1-3 (April 2, 1974)

93D CONGRESS	}	SENATE	{	**Calendar No. 738**
2d Session				REPORT No. 93-766

COVERAGE OF NONPROFIT HOSPITALS UNDER THE NATIONAL LABOR RELATIONS ACT

APRIL 2, 1974—Ordered to be printed

Mr. CRANSTON, from the Committee on Labor and Public Welfare, submitted the following

REPORT

together with

INDIVIDUAL VIEWS

[To accompany S. 3203]

The Committee on Labor and Public Welfare to which was referred the bill (S. 3203) to amend the National Labor Relations Act to extend its coverage and protection to employees of nonprofit hospitals, and for other purposes, having considered the same, reports favorably thereon and recommends that the bill do pass.

SUMMARY

The National Labor Relations Act governs the collective bargaining relationship of millions of workers including employees of proprietary hospitals, proprietary nursing homes and nonprofit nursing homes. It specifically exempts from coverage employees of private nonprofit hospitals. This bill repeals the present exemption, establishes certain new procedures governing labor relations in health care institutions, and creates a new definition of health care institution to include hospitals, nursing homes, health maintenance organizations, extended care facilities, health and medical clinics and other similar institutions caring for the sick, infirm or aged. The bill also contains several additional special provisions designed to facilitate collective bargaining settlements and to provide advance notice of any strike or picketing involving a health care institution, as follows:

1. The requirement for notice of termination or expiration of a contract will be 90 days;

99-010—74——1

★(Star Print)

2

2. The Federal Mediation and Conciliation Service [FMCS] must be given 60 days notice of such termination or expiration;

3. In initial contract negotiation a 30 day notice of a dispute to FMCS will be required;

4. The health care institution and labor organization will be required to participate in mediation at the direction of the FMCS.

5. The health care institution must be given a 10 day notice by a labor organization before any picketing or strike (whether or not related to bargaining) can take place.

On February 7, 1973, S. 794 was introduced by Senators Cranston and Javits and on July 31, 1973, S. 2292 was introduced by Senator Taft. The Subcommittee on Labor conducted hearings on these bills on July 31, August 1, 2 and October 4, 1973.

During the course of these hearings testimony was received from a number of interested groups, including the U.S. Department of Labor; AFL-CIO; the Service Employees International Union, AFL-CIO; American Hospital Association; Industrial Union Department, AFL-CIO; Local 1199, Drug and Hospital Workers Union; American Nurses Association; Communication Workers of America, AFL-CIO; General Conference of Seventh-day Adventists; American Federation of State, County, and Municipal Employees, AFL-CIO; New Jersey Hospital Association; Committee of Interns and Residents of New York City; Colorado Hospital Association; Federation of American Hospitals; Catholic Hospital Association Board of Trustees; Commission on Economic and General Welfare of the American Nurses' Association; Hospital Association of Pennsylvania; Texas Hospital Association; Iowa Hospital Association; International Union of Operating Engineers; Ohio Hospital Association; Minnesota Hospital Association; National Right to Work Committee; Mt. Sinai Hospital; National Federation of Licensed Practical Nurses; Physicians National Housestaff Association; United States Industrial Council; California Hospital Association; New York University Medical Center; and Mount Sinai Medical Center.

On February 28, 1974, S. 3088 was introduced by Senator Taft and on March 13, 1974, the full Committee discharged the Subcommittee from further consideration of S. 794, S. 2292 and S. 3088. On March 20, 1974, S. 3203 was introduced by Senators Williams, Cranston, Javits, Taft, Stafford, Pell, Kennedy, Eagleton, Hughes, and Schweiker. The Committee considered the legislation in executive session on March 20, 1974, and ordered S. 3203 reported by voice vote.

During the executive session an amendment proposed by Senator Mondale was offered. It would have required the NLRB to cede jurisdiction to certain state agencies covering nonprofit hospitals where the state law was in existence prior to 1947. The amendment was defeated by voice vote.

BACKGROUND

Section 2(2) of the National Labor Relations Act defines the term "employer" as not to include "any corporation or association operating a hospital, if no part of the net earnings inures to the benefit of any private shareholder or individual."

3

The original Wagner Act of 1935 did not contain this exemption and in the only reported case relating to coverage of nonprofit hospitals, the NLRB and the Court of Appeals upheld the coverage.[1]

In 1947, the Wagner Act was amended by the Taft-Hartley Act. Included in these amendments was a provision, added as a floor amendment in the Senate, to exempt nonprofit hospitals. This amendment was retained in conference.

In 1972, the House passed H.R. 11357 which would have repealed the exemption. No action was taken by the Senate beyond hearings on the bill.

NEED FOR THE BILL

The bill removes the existing exemption in section 2(2) of the NLRA for employees of non-profit hospitals and extends the protections of the Act to such employees to the same extent as currently applicable to employees of nursing homes and proprietary hospitals.

The Committee could find no acceptable reason why 1,427,012 employees of these non-profit, non-public hospitals, representing 56% of all hospital employees, should continue to be excluded from the coverage and protections of the Act. In the Committee's deliberations on this measure, it was recognized that the needs of patients in health care institutions required special consideration in the Act including a provision requiring hospitals to have sufficient notice of any strike or picketing to allow for appropriate arrangements to be made for the continuance of patient care in the event of a work stoppage. In this respect the Committee believed that the special notice requirements should be extended to all proprietary and nonprofit hospitals, convalescent hospitals, health maintenance organizations, health or medical clinics, nursing homes, extended care facilities or other institutions devoted to the care of sick, infirm or aged persons. Accordingly this bill will provide the same procedures for employees of all health care institutions.

The Committee was also impressed with the fact, emphasized by many witnesses, that the exemption of nonprofit hospitals from the Act had resulted in numerous instances of recognition strikes and picketing. Coverage under the Act should completely eliminate the need for any such activity, since the procedures of the Act will be available to resolve organizational and recognition disputes.

(material omitted)

---

[1] *Central Dispensary and Emergency Hospital* 44 N L R B 533 (1942), 145 F. 2d 852 (1944), cert. den. 655 sup. ct. 564.

VII. Excerpts from 120 Cong. Rec. 12946-12968 (May 2, 1974)

CONGRESSIONAL RECORD — SENATE May 2, 1974

[Page 12946:]

(material omitted)

Mr. ROBERT C. BYRD. Mr. President, I ask unanimous consent that after the Senator from North Carolina (Mr. ERVIN) offers his amendment, the pending measure be temporarily laid aside and that the Senate proceed to the consideration of H.R. 12920, which is under a time limitation.

The PRESIDING OFFICER. Without objection, it is so ordered.

Mr. ERVIN. Mr. President, I send to the desk an amendment and ask to have it stated.

The PRESIDING OFFICER. The amendment will be stated.

The assistant legislative clerk read the amendment as follows:

On page 1, strike out the quotation on lines 4, 5, and 6, before the period, and insert in lieu thereof the following: 'or any corporation or association operating a hospital, if that hospital is owned, supported, controlled, or managed by a particular religion or by a particular religious corporation or association.' "

Mr. ERVIN. Mr. President, I understand the distinguished assistant majority leader has a motion to make, but I would like to state, very briefly, that I think the things that belong to Caesar should be given to Caesar and the things that belong to God should be left to God, unregulated by Caesar.

I have offered this amendment at the request of the Adventist Church, which conducts throughout this country many hospitals for the treatment of the sick and injured, and they feel like they are doing the work of the Lord, and I agree with them, and they ought not to be regulated by the National Labor Relations Board. I do not think the National Labor Relations Board has any ability to regulate the affairs of the Almighty, and I think they had better be confined to regulating the affairs of Caesar.

This amendment is to exempt from the provisions of the National Labor Relations Act the effort to bring under the jurisdiction of the National Labor Relations Act matters that belong to God rather than to Caesar.

If the Senator wishes to make his motion, I will yield temporarily.

* * * *

[Page 12950:]

COVERAGE AND PROTECTION FOR EMPLOYEES OF NONPROFIT HOSPITALS

Mr. ROBERT C. BYRD. Mr. President, I ask unanimous consent that the Senate now resume its consideration, until the hour of 1:30 p.m. today, of S. 3203.

The PRESIDING OFFICER. Without objection, it is so ordered.

Mr. ROBERT C. BYRD. And I ask unanimous consent that immediately following the disposition of the Peace Corps bill, on which the vote will occur at 1:30 p.m. today, the Senate again resume the consideration of S. 3203.

The PRESIDING OFFICER. Without objection, it is so ordered.

Mr. CRANSTON. Mr. President, I ask unanimous consent that Mike Mullen, of Senator BURDICK's staff, have the privilege of the floor during the consideration of this measure.

The PRESIDING OFFICER. Without objection, it is is ordered.

The bill will be stated by title.

The assistant legislative clerk read as follows:

A bill (S. 3203) to amend the National Labor Relations Act to extend its coverage and protection to employees of nonprofit hospitals, and for other purposes.

The PRESIDING OFFICER. The pending question is on agreeing to the amendment of the Senator from North Carolina (Mr. ERVIN).

Mr. ERVIN. Mr. President, this amendment would add a proviso at the end of line 6 on page 1 of S. 3203 reading as follows:

Provided, however, this act shall not apply to any corporation or association operating a hospital, if that hospital is owned, supported, controlled, or managed by a particular religion or by a particular religious corporation or association.

When this bill was pending before the committee, the Seventh Day Adventists, who object to being subjected to the regulations of the National Labor Relations Board, filed a brief with the committee. That brief makes the following statement:

THE PROBLEM

The Seventh Day Adventists operate numerous non-profit hospitals in nineteen states, and the District of Columbia.[1] These non-profit hospitals are regarded by the

---

[1] Arizona, California, Colorado, Florida, Georgia, Hawaii, Illinois, Kentucky, Maine, Maryland, Massachusetts, New Jersey, Ohio, Oklahoma, Oregon, Pennsylvania, Tennessee, Texas, Utah, and Washington, D.C.

[page 12950, continued:]

Church as an extension of the conscience of the Church.

For many years, and at present, the Church has taught and is teaching its members not to belong to or contribute support to a labor organization, and has based this teaching on passages in the Bible, thereby making this teaching part of the religious doctrine of the Church.

The prospect of having its non-profit hospitals placed under the National Labor Relations Act, as Amended,[2] poses the question of whether or not the Church will be required to choose between the Church's obligations to God, on the one hand, and its duty to obey the law, on the other hand. Is there an irreconcilable conflict between the Church's teachings and what its duties and obligations would be under the Act? If there is such a conflict, how does this come about?

THE ANSWER

There is no way the Church could remain steadfast in its teachings and properly discharge its duties under the Act, for the reasons set forth below:

THE ASSUMPTIONS

For purposes of the discussion below it is assumed that a union has been successful in its organizing drive and has demonstrated its majority status in an appropriate unit by means of an election conducted by the National Labor Relations Board (hereinafter called the Board).[3] It is assumed that the Board has issued its certification that the union is the majority representative in a unit appropriate for collective bargaining.

THE LEGAL DUTIES

On the summed fact, the Church would be required to (1) recognize the union as the exclusive representative of the employees in regard to anything pertaining to wages, hours, working conditions, or other conditions of employment, and (2) bargain with the union in good faith.[4] To meet its bargaining obligation the Church would be required to enter negotiations with a sincere purpose and intent to arrive at an agreement. It would not be allowed to "shadow box the union to a draw". Although "hard bargaining", as such, is permissible, the Church would be required to have a sincere intent to reach an agreement. While the Act provides that the obligation to bargain does not entail the granting of a concession or the making of a compromise, both the Board and the Courts will look to all the surrounding facts and circumstances to ascertain whether or not the party charged with a refusal to bargain entered negotiations with a sincere intent to arrive at an agreement, with a mind not "hermetically sealed" against discussion, and with no intent to reach an agreement under any circumstances.

The union's ultimate weapon at the bargaining table is a strike. There are two broad classes of strikes. One is called an economic strike, which is a strike over wages, hours, working conditions, or other conditions of employment. The other is called an unfair labor practice strike, which is a strike caused or prolonged by the unfair labor practices of an employer. The legal and economic consequences to an employer flowing from the type of strike are vastly different, as will be shown below:

If the Church refused recognition after the Board had issued its certification, and the union struck, this would be a strike caused by the unfair labor practice of the employer. When such a strike occurs, the employer is not entitled to hire permanent replacements for the strikers, and all strikers

---

[2] Hereinafter referred to as the Act.
[3] An election conducted by the Board is only one means by which a union may demonstrate a majority status. It may be done by authorization cards, by strike, etc.
[4] This obligation is imposed by Section 8(a)(5) of the Act.

[Page 12951:]

May 2, 1974   CONGRESSIONAL RECORD — SENATE   12955

have an almost absolute right to return to their jobs, even though such return means the discharge of employees hired to replace them. If the strikers are not so returned, the employer becomes liable for back pay, etc.

If the union strikes over economic issues, then, and in that event, the employer has the right to hire permanent replacements, and strikers are entitled, when they have been permanently replaced, to their jobs only when those jobs again become open.

THE RECOGNITION PROBLEM

At the outset, the Church would have to decide whether or not to recognize the union. If it recognized the union, it would have to do so in the face of its religious teachings that its members should not belong or contribute support to a labor organization.

If the church decided not to recognize the union, then its only legal course of action would be to cease to operate the hospital actually and completely. An employer may cease to do business for any reason, but the employer must really and actually cease doing business. For example, an employer may not merely shift orders from one of its many plants, while closing down the plant which has been unionized. Similarly, a hospital could not merely transfer its patients, doctors, nurses, etc., from one hospital to another hospital to avoid dealing with the union. It is conceivable that the Church might have to decide not to operate any non-profit hospitals at all, providing it decided that it could not in good conscience recognize or deal with the union.

THE BARGAINING PROBLEM

If the Church should decide that it could recognize the union, the bargaining obligation is fraught with difficulties. For example, in those states which do not have right-to-work laws, the Church would be required to bargain about a union security agreement, which is a form of compulsory union membership requiring employees to join the union after thirty days of employment or lose their jobs. While the Board does allow those persons having religious scruples against unionism, to merely pay the dues and initiation fees without actually joining the union, this exception still runs afoul of the Church's teachings that its members should not contribute support to a labor organization.

Should the union file a charge with the Board alleging a refusal to bargain, and should the General Counsel of the Board issue a complaint, the Church's teachings about labor organizations would be admissible evidence bearing on the Church's state of mind or attitude in the bargaining negotiations, and it would be almost impossible to defend against a charge of bad faith bargaining. The General Counsel could allege, and in all probability prove, that the Church's mind was "hermetically sealed" on the question of a union security agreement. The Church would be faced with prolonged, protracted, and expensive litigation, in which, in all probability, it would be unsuccessful.

CONCLUSION

It is my considered opinion that if the Church's nonprofit hospitals are placed under the Act, the Church must give serious consideration to not operating any hospitals at all. There is no way of reconciling its religious teachings with what its obligations would be if its hospitals are placed under the Act.[5]

This brief was prepared by Joseph Alton Jenkins of Dallas, Tex., as counsel for the Seventh-Day Adventist Church.

---

[5] For ready reference, there is attached hereto as Exhibit "A" a list of states in which Seventh Day Adventists maintain hospital facilities, and pertinent labor law provisions of said states.

I ask unanimous consent to have printed in the RECORD the statement of W. Melvin Adams, the director of the department of public affairs and religious liberty, North American division, general conference of Seventh-day Adventists, accompanied by Raymond L. Pelton, hospital administration, department of health, and Irwin J. Remboldt, president, Adventists Pacific Health Care Corp., Glendale, Calif., a statement offered before the committee by the Adventists Church in opposition to inclusion of nonprofit hospitals under the National Labor Relations Act.

There being no objection, the statement was ordered to be printed in the RECORD, as follows:

(material omitted)

(material omitted)

Mr. ERVIN. Mr. President, it seems to me that these people should be considered. Whether their religious beliefs are acceptable in this respect to a majority of the American people, they are entitled under the first amendment to their religious beliefs. The Constitution claims that Congress shall make no law forbidding the exercise of religious freedom. The Adventist Church feels that if they are placed under regulations of the National Labor Relations Act, it will be, in effect, placing their affairs relating to God under regulation. It does seem to me that a Federal agency should be able to restrain its greed for power and jurisdiction to the extent of recognizing that people have the right, under the first amendment, to their religious beliefs and not have to require them either to violate their religious beliefs or to go out of the business of administering to those who are sick and injured.

The Adventist Church in my county has done great work in the relief of the ill and the injured. It does seem to me that Congress should not place them under the jurisdiction of a secular body like the National Labor Relations Board.

We should have some respect left in this country for religious freedom and the right of the people to participate in the healing of the sick and the injured without being forced either to sacrifice their religious beliefs or to stop administering to the ill and the injured.

I, therefore, hope that my amendment will be acceptable. It applies only to church-operated institutions.

Mr. CRANSTON. Mr. President, I am always reluctant to differ with the distinguished Senator from North Carolina (Mr. ERVIN), whom I respect and love so very much, but I must oppose this amendment which would deny employees of religiously affiliated hospitals the basic rights and privileges which S. 3203 seeks to grant their nonsectarian counterparts.

In the early days of this country, institutions dealing with the provision of social services were few and far between.

Because governments in general were loath to accept responsibility for such services, and were otherwise preoccupied during the Nation's formative years, the burden fell almost completely to the only institutions both willing and capable to respond—those affiliated with organized religious groups. It was they who ministered to the sick, fed the hungry, and clothed and sheltered the poor. For so many years, no one else filled the breach of social responsibility. The various religious groups more often than not had to go it alone, so to speak—that is rely on their own resources, and the charitable instincts of the community, both in terms of personnel and funds.

It has only been in relatively recent times that the Government has acknowledged its own responsibility, and has been willing to commit significant resources in this area. No longer must religious organizations have to depend solely on their own resources to support their various social involvements.

Today, in the area of health, religiously affiliated hospitals are supported by a variety of Government subsidies and grants. In some instances, these institutions have had the entire cost of construction assumed by the Federal Government.

And so it seems to me that, as to Caesar and God and their observations, as so eloquently and forcefully stated by the distinguished Senator from North Carolina, they do not apply to this measure. This measure does not touch religious teaching or religious leaders. It does not touch religious interpretation. It does not touch philosophy in the realm of God. The hospitals which relate to religious orders in one way or another are conducted or owned or operated by them and are publicly regulated. They are touched by public policy, affected by public policy, and governed by public policy and law.

There is one institution near this Capitol which was built entirely with public funds and is simply operated by a religious order. At least one Seventh-Day Adventist hospital or nursing home has entered into a collective bargaining agreement with a union.

By and large, hospitals administered by religiously affiliated groups have already recognized this change. In many instances, except for architectural variations, religiously affiliated hospitals and nonreligiously affiliated hospitals are often indistinguishable. The objective of each is clearly the same—to achieve the highest standard of professional health care. Both must adhere to the same medical and health codes; both must follow local ordinances and laws to the same extent.

As for their respective employment relationships, each hospital must compete for the same labor market since religiously affiliated hospitals no longer depend on recruiting exclusively from members of their religious order or persuasion. Because of their markedly similar operating and administrative structure, both religious and nonreligiously affiliated hospitals draw upon the existing manpower pool to fill their ranks.

Likewise, people who work for a hospital, regardless of its affiliation, think of their jobs purely in nonsectarian occupational terms, not with respect to any particular religious ideology. Their concerns, their hopes, and their frustrations are no different than one would expect of other similarly situated employees. And because of this, these workers, who are often unable to press for economic advantage on their own, have sought to better themselves by organizing to bargain collectively—just as their peers in other sectors of the economy have done for many years, and just as their fellow hospital workers employed by nonsectarian employees will soon be able to do.

The fact is that many hospital administrators of religiously affiliated institutions throughout the country have recognized this desire of their employees, and have voluntarily agreed in one form or another to recognize the union as their bargaining representatives.

To exempt these institutions, who incidentally, as a group, have not asked for this type of special treatment, would result in a social and economic inequity of the highest magnitude.

I think it is important at this time to note that during the committee's deliberations, many letters were received from official representatives of a wide range of religious organizations in which the concept of collective bargaining for all hospital workers, including those employed by ones with religious affiliations, was either endorsed fully, or with the understanding that any bill granting such bargaining rights would include provisions for the maintenance of patient care. S. 3203 was, of course, specifically drafted with these considerations in mind.

Mr. President, I ask unanimous consent, that copies of some of these letters be printed in the RECORD.

There being no objection, the letters were ordered to be printed in the RECORD, as follows:

THE UNITED METHODIST CHURCH,
Washington, D.C., October 11, 1973.
Hon. HARRISON A. WILLIAMS,
*Chairman, Senate Subcommittee on Labor,
Dirksen Senate Office Building,
Washington, D.C.*

DEAR SENATOR WILLIAMS: I am writing in support of S. 794, a bill to amend the National Labor Relations Act to extend its coverage and protection to employees of nonprofit hospitals.

My reasons for supporting this bill grow out of my experience as an administrator in the church. The United Methodist Church operated 342 health and welfare agencies in 1972, serving 4,855,436 persons and with total budgets of over 792 million dollars. I have served as a trustee of two major hospitals in the past twelve years.

In recent years an unusual amount of strain and conflict has arisen in the labor market of nonprofit hospitals over the issue of union recognition. The terms of contract are not so difficult to bargain as is the prior question of who represents the workers. The result has been work stoppages in the flow of health services, the consequences of which can be severe for patients and for families. Public policy should regularize the process of determining worker representation in the health sector of the economy. Senate bill 794 accomplishes this, so it seems to me, without complicated amendments to the National Labor Relations Act. Once the question of recognition is determined, the terms of the contract can be achieved through the regular channels of collective bargaining.

A second reason for supporting this bill is that it fulfills a resolution passed by the General Conference of the United Methodist Church in 1972. The General Conference meets every four years and is the highest legislative body of the church and speaks authoritatively for the church to the church and society. Observing strain in particular labor markets, the General Conference said:

"Historically, the United Methodist Church has recognized and supported the right of workers to organize and bargain collectively over wages, hours, and conditions of labor. National policy since 1935 has codified procedures for the recognition of labor unions and for collective bargaining with the result of lessened conflict in the private industrial sector of the economy.

"However, several categories of employees were excluded from the coverage of the National Labor Relations Act including (1) federal employees or employees of any political subdivision such as state or school district, (2) employees of hospitals operated entirely on a nonprofit basis.

"Unfortunately, social strife in the occupational markets of nonprofit hospital workers and public employees has led to high social costs, including the tragedy of death. In view of this unresolved strain, the United Methodist Church requests the Congress to amend the National Labor Relations Act to include under its coverage (1) government employees, federal, state, and local, and (2) the employees of hospitals operated entirely on a nonprofit basis."

I wish to thank you for the opportunity of placing this letter in the record of the hearings on S. 794. Your Subcommittee on Labor is dealing with an issue that deeply affects the American public. I appreciate your interest and leadership in this matter.

Very sincerely yours,
JAMES K. MATHEWS.

NOVEMBER 2, 1973.
Hon. HARRISON A. WILLIAMS,
Senate Committee on Labor and Public Welfare, Senate Building, Washington, D.C.

DEAR SENATOR WILLIAMS: The Board of Global Ministries of The United Methodist Church at its annual meeting, October 23-27, 1973, in New Orleans, Louisiana, adopted the enclosed resolution on recommendation of its Health and Welfare Ministries Division. This Board represents the 80 acute care hospitals across the nation operated by The United Methodist Church.

We strongly oppose S. 794 which simply removes the not-for-profit hospital exemption from the National Labor Relations Act and support S. 2292 which includes special provisions applying to all health care institutions for dealing with collective bargaining impasses. We support the testimony of the American Hospital Association made before your committee on July 31, 1973.

May we encourage your support for this position to assure continuous and uninterrupted hospital care of patients?

Sincerely yours,
DONALD C. KRAUSHAAR,
Director, Department of Health Care Ministries.

FEBRUARY 26, 1973.
Senator HARRISON A. WILLIAMS,
*New Senate Office Building,
Washington, D.C.*

DEAR SENATOR WILLIAMS: For just a few moments of your time, I would like your undivided attention. I would like you to consider very carefully something that is of great concern to me. We, the staff of St. Elizabeth's and myself, are very much concerned about the outcome of the bill that your committee is presently considering, House Bill 1236. And, while I fully realize that you've heard many reactions to this bill from other sources, I would like, on behalf of our hospital, a chance to add our thoughts, and our feelings to those already voiced.

Our stand on this issue is a very clear, and yet a very forceful, one. We are opposed to any legislation that would remove the exemption from the Taft-Hartley Act that not-for-profit hospitals enjoy presently, unless and until such a legislative proposal contain a provision for uninterrupted life serving services. We wish to insure that any such legislation, which contains provision dealing with strikes, picketing, impasse resolution, and bargaining unit fragmentation, *will* insure the continuity of life serving services to patients. Our opinion, as you have now seen it, is in conjunction with our local organization of hospitals, The Catholic Hospital Association, and the national organization, The American Hospital Association.

It is our intent that the rights of employees and the rights of management be recognized and respected, but we are deeply concerned that the rights of patients also be recognized and respected. You may already be familiar with the "Patient's Bill of Rights" that has been approved by the Board of Trustees of the American Hospital Association. This document has been developed precisely in view of recognizing and protecting the rights of the persons we serve. And we want to insure their well-being regardless of the circumstances that may prevail in the hospital in question.

Enclosed with my letter, please find a copy of the statement by the Catholic Hospital Association in 1967, and with which I concur and do heartily support today.

Thank you for your kind attention.

Sincerely,

Sister MARY THOMAS,
Administrator.

THE CATHOLIC HOSPITAL ASSOCIATION,
St. Louis, Mo., August 20, 1973.
Hon. HARRISON A. WILLIAMS,
Chairman, Senate Committee of Labor and Public Welfare, Old Senate Office Building, Washington, D.C.

DEAR SENATOR WILLIAMS: I am writing to you as President of The Catholic Hospital Association, an association of over 850 hospitals and related health facilities in the United States. These health facilities consist of approximately 160,000 beds, and employ over 360,000 people who assisted in providing over 45 million patient days of care last year.

The purpose of this letter is to express the official position of The Catholic Hospital Association's Board of Trustees on S. 2292, a bill introduced by Senator Robert Taft, Jr. The Catholic Hospital Association has, as a matter of official policy, continuously recognized the right of hospital employees to form or join a union or association for purposes of collective bargaining and that hospitals should recognize this right of employees. At the same time, *The Catholic Hospital Association has advocated the need for certain protections for hospitals and the public if the not-for-profit hospital exemption is removed from the National Labor Relations Act* (Taft-Hartley). The Catholic Hospital Association believes that S. 2292 reflects the required protections. We urge that you favorably consider S. 2292 as a substitute bill for S. 794.

The primary and specific protections in S. 2292 which we believe adequately respond to our previously stated concerns are:

1. Jurisdictional strife and the potential for work stoppages over bargaining will be reduced by limiting the number of bargaining units in a hospital to four.

2. To increase the responsiveness of bargaining, the parties will be required to utilize the Federal Mediation and Conciliation Service. At the request of either party, there is a requirement to submit their impasse issues to nonbinding, factfinding.

3. For public protection, all strikes are prohibited except a strike for a contract following the exhaustion of a lengthy bargaining procedure. The institution is to be given advance notice of any strike so as to prepare for patient transfers, etc.

4. Immediate relief is provided by way of court injunction in the event of an unlawful strike or lockout.

We ask that you make this letter, which reflects The Catholic Hospital Association's support for S. 2292, a part of your committee's hearing record.

We are sending a copy of this letter to each member of the Senate Committee of Labor and Public Welfare.

Sincerely,

Rev. Msgr. JAMES T. McDONOUGH,
President.

Mr. CRANSTON. Mr. President, in addition, such an exemption for religiously affiliated hospitals would seriously erode the existing national policy which holds religiously affiliated institutions generally such as proprietary nursing homes, residential communities, and educational facilities to the same standards as their nonsectarian counterparts.

I would also like to raise one other area of concern. That is, simply what is the definition of a religiously affiliated institution. In today's contemporary society, the traditional definition of religion in many instances is not applicable. The hospital industry is in a state of flux vis-a-vis ownership. For many hospitals, the determination of whether or not it is religiously affiliated is indeed a difficult question.

In conclusion, one can truly say that this Nation owes religious groups throughout the country a debt of gratitude for these many years of selfless social service. But this debt cannot, and must not, include a subsidy from the workers themselves, which in effect is what this amendment would provide by denying them rights under the National Labor Relations Act.

I urge that the amendment be rejected.

Mr. JAVITS. Mr. President, I, too, would wish to—and also with great respect for the distinguished Senator from North Carolina (Mr. ERVIN) and with great respect for the institutions to which he has referred—be in opposition to the amendment.

Without repeating anything that Senator CRANSTON has just said as manager of the bill for the majority, I would simply state these points:

One, in practical terms, this would be a devastating blow because at least one-third of all nonprofit hospitals have some religious affiliations. So the impact of this amendment would be truly devastating.

Second, in my own State, which is perhaps a characteristic one, our hospital employees are subject to the State Labor Relations Act, whether or not the hospital is a religious affiliate. There has been no challenge to that. Their labor relations need stability and an orderly quality, just as that of any other hospital. No one in New York seems to have required or requested a special religious exemption from the law.

Third, in the Federal Establishment, these hospitals are subject to the Occupational Safety and Health Act, OSHA. They are subject to the minimum wage, workmen's compensation, unemployment compensation, and so forth.

Insofar as their relations with their employees are concerned, it certainly would not seem to me, especially in view of all these other precedents, that there would be any possible interference with first amendment rights if the employee relationship had this further element of regulation—to wit, the availability of the National Labor Relations Board and the law under which it operates to deal with labor-management relations in the field of hospitals which are nonprofit, though they happen to have religious affiliation.

For all those reasons, Mr. President, with great respect, I join in opposing the amendment.

Mr. WILLIAMS. Mr. President, I join my colleagues on the Committee on Labor and Public Welfare, the Senator from California and the Senator from New York, in opposition to the amendment offered by the Senator from North Carolina.

It should be pointed out that the hope and objective of this legislation is that in an area where there have been disruptions in vital services because of work stoppages related to disagreements between the workers and the management of hospitals, we want to bring a new order into the situation, which now, unfortunately, has a degree of chaos because there is no overriding orderly procedure under law. This measure would bring to hospitals the procedures that apply in other areas of our economy, and working people would have the opportunity to organize and to bargain out their objectives and differences, rather than being placed in a position, as at present, in which the only way they can be considered is to engage in work stoppages or strikes.

I ask unanimous consent to have printed in the RECORD at this point a list of the institutions that have religious affiliations, hospitals that have had work stoppages. These have occurred without the benefit of inclusion of these workers under the National Labor Relations Act.

There being no objection, the list was ordered to be printed in the RECORD, as follows:

(material omitted)

12958

CONGRESSIONAL RECORD — SENATE

12967

(material omitted)

(material omitted)

rollcall vote on the passage of the Peace Corps bill at 1:30 p.m. today. Senators may have scheduled their appointments accordingly, and they may not be anticipating a rollcall vote prior to 1:30.

I ask unanimous consent that the vote on the amendment by Mr. ERVIN occur immediately, back to back, following the vote on final passage of the Peace Corps bill.

The PRESIDING OFFICER. Is there objection? The Chair hears none, and it is so ordered.

Mr. HARRY F. BYRD, Jr. Mr. President, I ask unanimous consent that during the consideration of the pending bill, George Shanks, a member of my staff, be permitted the privilege of the floor.

The PRESIDING OFFICER. Without objection, it is so ordered.

* * * *

Mr. ERVIN. Mr. President, I ask for the yeas and nays on this amendment.

The yeas and nays were ordered.

Mr. CRANSTON. Mr. President, I ask for the yeas and nays on final passage of the bill.

The yeas and nays were ordered.

The PRESIDING OFFICER. The question is on the adoption of the amendment of the Senator from North Carolina.

Mr. ERVIN. Mr. President, I should like to speak to the Senators who were not in the Chamber when I presented my argument.

This is an amendment to modify the amendment which brings nonprofit hospitals under the jurisdiction of the National Labor Relations Board so as to exempt the church-supported hospitals from the coverage by the National Labor Relations Board.

I think it is pretty inconsistent, regardless of technicalities, but it is very inconsistent for an agency of Caesar to be regulating the work that is done in the name of God. And that is true of the Adventist Church.

Mr. ROBERT C. BYRD. Mr. President, the word has gone out from both cloakrooms to Senators that there will be a

COVERAGE AND PROTECTION FOR EMPLOYEES OF NONPROFIT HOSPITALS

The Senate continued with the consideration of the bill, S 3203, to amend the National Labor Relations Act to extend its coverage and protection to employees of nonprofit hospitals, and for other purposes.

Mr. ROBERT C. BYRD. Mr. President, I ask unanimous consent that the Senator from North Carolina may proceed for 2 minutes.

The PRESIDING OFFICER. Without objection, it is so ordered.

Mr. ERVIN. I just want to explain

what the next vote is on. It is on an amendment which I offered to continue in existence the exemption which church-supported hospitals have always enjoyed not to be under the jurisdiction of the National Labor Relations Board.

I think it is pretty bad to allow the regulations of Caesar to go to regulating the affairs of God, and therefore I urge the adoption of my amendment.

Mr. CRANSTON. Mr. President, I ask unanimous consent that I may speak for 2 minutes also.

The PRESIDING OFFICER. Without objection, it is so ordered.

Mr. CRANSTON. Mr. President, the committee position in opposition to this amendment is based upon the fact that many of the hospitals operated by religious orders of one sort or another were built by public funds, or there were public contributions to them under other programs, or they are thoroughly infected with the public interest and subject to various types of public regulation.

It is the feeling of the committee that if we permit an exemption, there will be other requests for other exemptions in other areas of activity. We have had support from a number of the religious groups in our country for inclusion under the NLRA and the workers of their hospitals are certainly entitled to the same protection as workers in all other hospitals would be provided under this bill.

The PRESIDING OFFICER (Mr. HATHAWAY). The question is on agreeing to the amendment of the Senator from North Carolina. On this question, the yeas and nays have been ordered, and the clerk will call the roll.

The legislative clerk called the roll.

Mr. ROBERT C. BYRD. I announce that the Senator from Delaware (Mr. BIDEN), the Senator from Idaho (Mr. CHURCH), the Senator from Arkansas (Mr. FULBRIGHT), the Senator from Alaska (Mr. GRAVEL), the Senator from Hawaii (Mr INOUYE), the Senator from Montana (Mr. METCALF), the Senator from Ohio (Mr. METZENBAUM), the Senator from Maine (Mr. MUSKIE), and the Senator from California (Mr. TUNNEY) are necessarily absent.

I further announce that, if present and voting, the Senator from Ohio (Mr. METZENBAUM) would vote "nay."

Mr. GRIFFIN. I announce that the Senator from Tennessee (Mr. BAKER), the Senator from Oklahoma (Mr. BELLMON), and the Senator from Utah (Mr. BENNETT) are necessarily absent.

I also announce that the Senator from North Dakota (Mr. YOUNG) is absent on official business.

I further announce that the Senator from Florida (Mr. GURNEY) is absent due to illness in the family.

The result was announced—yeas 36, nays 50, as follows:

[No. 173 Leg.]

YEAS—36

Allen, Bartlett, Bible, Brock, Buckley, Byrd, Harry F., Jr., Byrd, Robert C., Cannon, Cotton, Curtis, Dole, Domenici, Dominick, Eastland, Ervin, Pannin, Goldwater, Griffin, Hansen, Hatfield, Helms, Hruska, Johnston, Long, McClellan, McClure

McGee, Mondale, Moss, Nunn, Scott, William L., Sparkman, Stennis, Talmadge, Thurmond, Tower

NAYS—50

Abourezk, Aiken, Bayh, Beall, Bentsen, Brooke, Burdick, Case, Chiles, Clark, Cook, Cranston, Eagleton, Fong, Hart, Hartke, Haskell, Hathaway, Hollings, Huddleston, Hughes, Humphrey, Jackson, Javits, Kennedy, Magnuson, Mansfield, Mathias, McGovern, McIntyre, Montoya, Nelson, Packwood, Pastore, Pearson, Pell, Percy, Proxmire, Randolph, Ribicoff, Roth, Schweiker, Scott, Hugh, Stafford, Stevens, Stevenson, Symington, Taft, Weicker, Williams

NOT VOTING—14

Baker, Bellmon, Bennett, Biden, Church, Fulbright, Gravel, Gurney, Inouye, Metcalf, Metzenbaum, Muskie, Tunney, Young

So Mr. ERVIN's amendment was rejected.

Mr. JAVITS. Mr. President, I move that the vote by which the amendment was rejected be reconsidered.

Mr. CRANSTON. Mr. President, I move to lay that motion on the table.

The motion to lay on the table was agreed to.

(material omitted)

VIII. H.R. Rep. No. 93-1051 at 1-5 (May 20, 1974)

93D CONGRESS 2d Session	HOUSE OF REPRESENTATIVES	REPORT No. 93-1051

COVERAGE OF NONPROFIT HOSPITALS UNDER THE NATIONAL LABOR RELATIONS ACT

MAY 20, 1974.—Committed to the Committee of the Whole House on the State of the Union and ordered to be printed

---

Mr. THOMPSON, of New Jersey, from the Committee on Education and Labor, submitted the following

REPORT

together with

ADDITIONAL VIEWS

[To accompany H.R. 13678]

The Committee on Education and Labor, to whom was referred the bill (H.R. 13678) to amend the National Labor Relations Act to extend its coverage and protection to employees of nonprofit hospitals, and other purposes, having considered same, report favorably thereon with amendment and recommend that the bill as amended do pass.

The amendment is as follows:

At page 3, line 22, add the following:

(f) The amendments made herein to the Act shall take effect 30 days after the date of enactment of this bill.

PURPOSE OF H.R. 13678

The National Labor Relations Act governs the collective bargaining relationship of millions of workers including employees of proprietary hospitals, proprietary nursing homes and nonprofit nursing homes. It specifically exempts from coverage employees of private nonprofit hospitals. This bill repeals the present exemption, establishes certain new procedures governing labor relations in health care institutions, and creates a new definition of health care institution to include hospitals, nursing homes, health maintenance organizations, extended care facilities, health and medical clinics and other similar institutions caring for the sick, infirm or aged. The bill also contains several additional special provisions designed to facilitate collective

38-006

2

bargaining settlements and to provide advance notice of any strike or picketing involving a health care institution, as follows:

1. The requirement for notice of termination or expiration of a contract will be 90 days;

2. The Federal Mediation and Conciliation Service (FMCS) must be given 60 days notice of such termination or expiration;

3. In initial contract negotiations a 30 day notice of a dispute to FMCS will be required;

4. The health care institution and labor organization will be required to participate in mediation at the direction of the FMCS.

5. The health care institution must be given a 10 day notice by a labor organization before any picketing or strike (whether or not related to bargaining) can take place.

Legislative History of H.R. 13678

The Special Subcommittee on Labor, chaired by Representative Frank Thompson, Jr., conducted hearings during the 92d Congress on a bill, H.R. 11357, to strike the exemption of nonprofit hospitals as employers under the Act. That bill was unanimously ordered reported by voice vote by the full Education and Labor Committee on July 18, 1972, without amendment, and passed by the House, on the Suspension Calendar, by a vote of 285–95 on August 7, 1972.

No action beyond hearings was taken in the Senate.

An identical bill was introduced by Representatives Thompson and Ashbrook in the 93d Congress. Hearing were held on that bill, H.R. 1236, in Washington, D.C. on April 12th and 19th, 1973 by the Special Subcommittee on Labor.

H.R. 13678 was subsequently introduced by Representatives Thompson and Ashbrook on March 21, 1974. That bill was ordered reported by the full Education and Labor Committee, as amended, on May 14, 1974, voting unanimously.

Background and Need for Legislation

Section 2(2) of the National Labor Relations Act defines the term "employer" as not to include "any corporation or association operating a hospital, if no part of the net earnings inures to the benefit of any private shareholder or individual." This "exemption" was added to the original Wagner Act of 1935 in the Taft-Hartley Amendments of 1947 for reasons which are not altogether clear.

A. Decisions Under the Wagner Act

The Wagner Act of 1935 did not exclude the employees of nonprofit hospitals from the protections afforded most other employees, and the Board and the reviewing courts refused to create an exception by implication.

The only case reported under the Wagner Act is *Central Dispensary and Emergency Hospital* 44 NLRB 533 (1942). There, the Building Service and Maintenance Workers filed a petition to conduct an elec-

3

tion among certain employees at the Emergency Hospital in Washington, D.C. to determine whether or not they wished to be represented by the union. The Board agreed to conduct the election, and said the following:

> The hospital contends that it is a charitable institution but neither charitable institutions nor their employees are exempted from operation of the act by its terms, although certain other employers and employees are exempted. If Congress did not intend to exempt charities from the scope of the act, an exact determination of the hospital's status in this respect becomes immaterial * * * *employees of hospitals, like employees of automobile factories, must live upon their wages.* (Emphasis supplied.)

The Labor Board decision was appealed to the U.S. Court of Appeals for the District of Columbia. That court, in an opinion by Judge Thurman Arnold, wrote:

> Respondent (hospital) argues that the spirit or policy of the act is such that we should read into it an exemption of charitable hospitals * * * We are unable to follow the reasoning * * * We cannot understand what considerations of public policy deprive hospital employees of the privilege granted to the employees of other institutions . . . (*NLRB* v. *Central Disp. & E. Hosp.*, 145 F.2d 852 (1944), cert.den. 65 S.Ct.684).

B. THE TAFT-HARTLEY AMENDMENTS

In 1947 there were certain amendments made to the Wagner Act. The House version of the Taft-Hartley Act did not deal with the question of nonprofit hospitals as employers.

However, in the Senate, Senator Tydings offered a floor amendment to exclude from the term "employer" the nonprofit hospitals.

Senator Taft, in explaining the Tydings amendment, stated:

> The committee considered this amendment, but did not act on it, because we felt it was unnecessary. The committee felt that hospitals were not engaged in interstate commerce; and that their business should not be so construed. We felt it would open up the question of making further exemptions. That is why the committee did not act upon the amendment as it was proposed.

The remainder of the debate was very brief, and between Senators Taylor and Tydings:

> Mr. TAYLOR. What does the amendment do? Does it prevent hospital employees, particularly nurses, from organizing? Is that the sense of the amendment?
>
> Mr. TYDINGS. It simply makes a hospital not an "employer" in the commercial sense of the term * * *
>
> Mr. TAYLOR. Would nurses be prevented from organizing? They are poorly paid.

4

Mr. Tydings. I don't think so * * * They (the hospitals) should not have to come to the National Labor Relations Board * * * A charitable institution is away beyond the scope of labor management relations in which profit is involved.

Mr. Taylor. These may not be profitmaking institutions, but even so I feel that simply because an institution, even one like the Red Cross, is kept up by popular subscription, the professional workers being employees of the Red Cross, should be permitted a decent living and should not be hamstrung in their efforts to obtain it.

Mr. Tydings. I agree with the Senator.

The bill then passed the Senate. The conference committee accepted the Senate version, which is now part of section 2(2) of the National Labor Relations Act.

C. Experience Under the Exemption

The National Labor Relations Board, initially, extended the Taft-Hartley exemption to a host of other eleemosynary, charitable, educational and similar types of institutions.

Experience indicated, however, that the withholding of the Board's jurisdiction did not cut down on the number of strikes or labor unrest. There was in fact, evidence to the contrary: with the rapid development of the nonprofit hospital industry there were increasing numbers of recognitional strikes.

Accordingly, in recent years the Board began to assert jurisdiction over areas it had formerly left alone. Currently, the only broad area of charitable, eleemosynary, educational institutions wherein the Board does not now exercise jurisdiction concerns the nonprofit hospitals, explicitly excluded by section 2(2) of the Act.

D. Impact of H.R. 13678

The bill removes the existing Taft-Hartley exemption in section 2(2) of the Act. It restores to the employees of nonprofit hospitals the same rights and protections enjoyed by the employees of proprietary hospitals and most all other employees. Indeed, the Committee could find no reason why 1,427,012 employees of these nonprofit hospitals—representing 56% of all hospital employees—should continue to be excluded.

In the Committee's deliberations on this measure, it was recognized that the needs of patients in health care institutions required special consideration in the Act, including a provision requiring hospitals to have sufficient notice of any strike or picketing to allow for appropriate arrangements to be made for the continuance of patient care in the event of a work stoppage. In this respect the Committee believed that the special notice requirements should be extended to all proprietary and nonprofit hospitals, convalescent hospitals, health maintenance organizations, health or medical clinics, nursing homes, extended care facilities or other institutions devoted to the care of sick, infirm or aged persons. Accordingly this bill will provide the same procedures for employees of all health care institutions.

5

The Committee was also impressed with the fact, emphasized by many witnesses, that the exemption of non-profit hospitals from the Act had resulted in numerous instances of recognition strikes and picketing. Coverage under the Act should completely eliminate the need for any such activity, since the procedures of the Act will be available to resolve organizational and recognition disputes.

(material omitted)

IX. Excerpts from 120 Cong. Rec. 16900, 16914-915 (May 30, 1974)

(material omitted)

Mr. ASHBROOK. Mr. Chairman, I rise to support H.R. 13678, a bill which I have the pleasure of cosponsoring with my friend and colleague from New Jersey (Mr. THOMPSON). I support it for three basic reasons.

One, our hearings clearly established that recognition strikes are an outgrowth of the lack of NLRB jurisdiction. Nonprofit hospitals are not required by law to recognize or bargain with organizations representing their employees.

In a number of instances, hospitals have voluntarily chosen to recognize and bargain with representatives of such employees. Where they refuse, however, employees are often forced to strike—not for better wages or fringe benefits, but merely to obtain recognition. In effect, current law denies such employees access to election procedures of the National Labor Relations Board. This bill would grant such employees access to the NLRB's election process and should reduce if not eliminate the "recognition strike."

The second reason for my support of this bill is simply a question of equity. Why should we continue an unwarranted discrimination against this one category of employees—the employees of nonprofit hospitals? There is no justification for permitting nurses, nurses aides, and other hospital employees to be covered under the National Labor Relations Act if they are employed anywhere but in a nonprofit hospital.

My third reason is that this bill adequately protects both employee and patient. The former is given much-needed equity without sacrificing health care continuity for the latter.

Extended negotiations preceded our introduction of H.R. 13678, a bill to remove the present exemption of nonprofit hospitals from the National Labor Relations Act, with specific protections for health care institutions. We had originally introduced a bill providing only for the straight removal of the present exemption (H.R. 1236). Such a bill followed the precedent in the 92d Congress, where a similar bill reached the Floor of the House, and passed by a 285–95 vote. Because of this favorable reception by the House, we reintroduced the same bill in this session.

Following our introduction of H.R. 1236, we had 2 days of hearings where we heard testimony from both labor and employer hospitals. Similar activity followed on the Senate side, where the Subcommittee on Labor held 4 days of hearings. These hearings revealed that an accommodation was needed to balance the rights of employees in nonprofit hospitals against the rights of the public for uninterrupted health care delivery.

The need for granting representational and collective bargaining rights to employees of nonprofit hospitals is apparent when we consider that the hospital industry presently employs over 3 million workers, 1½ million in nonprofit hospitals—or about 56 percent of all hospital employees—in more than 7,000 hospitals in the United States. That is almost 10 times the number employed in 1947 when they were excluded from coverage under the NLRA. Congress has included them in coverage under other labor legislation, including social security and medicare. Furthermore, it is clear that the hospital industry is big business, and no longer community charitable-type institutions that Senator Tydings envisioned when he had nonprofit hospitals excluded from coverage in 1947.

Also, it should be noted that the NLRB presently takes jurisdiction over other types of "charitable institutions," if the gross income to those institutions meets the Board's jurisdictional standards, as well as having and presently exercising jurisdiction over proprietary hospitals, nonprofit and profit nursing homes, and other profitmaking health-care institutions.

Finally, there is no reason to exclude the employees in nonprofit hospitals from rights granted other employees in profit-making hospitals or other industries. Nonprofit hospital workers perform essentially the same functions as employees presently covered, and should not be excluded from the rights and benefits inuring to other employees in other American institutions.

When the hearings revealed a real concern for the public's right to uninterrupted patient care, apparently fearing strikes by employees of nonprofit hospitals, an accommodation was made, reflected in H.R. 13678. Accordingly, H.R. 13678 treats all health care institutions and their employees alike. There is no distinction between the procedures to be followed by labor organizations and nonprofit hospitals from procedures which proprietary hospitals or nursing homes and their labor organizations must follow. Those procedures, set out in H.R. 13678, take into account the public's right to health care delivery.

This bill provides for an extended notice period of an additional 30 days to both the other party and to mediation services in case of termination or modification of a collective-bargaining agreement; it provides, for the first time, a notice period in cases of initial negotiations; it provides, for the first time, for mandated mediation in cases of health care institutions; and it provides for a definite 10-day strike notice.

The mandated mediation and the 10-day strike notice provide protection to the public, involve the mediation services to help resolve disputes, and give the hospital ample warning should the dispute fail to be resolved. If the union or employees fail to observe the notice provisions, including the 10-day strike notice, they lose their status as employees. In other words, they can be dismissed for striking without giving the public the protection the bill provides.

If the unions, which supported this compromise, are also willing to abide by the procedures set forth in this bill, the public should be amply protected. It seems to me the unions have given up quite a bit to insure health care delivery.

Mr. Chairman, three amendments will be offered. I sympathize with the amendment of the gentleman from Minnesota (Mr. QUIE). It is true that Minnesota has a model law. However, on close examination, any of the worthwhile provisions of that law which have proved workable over the past quarter century in Minnesota can be included in any contract the parties would negotiate. I personally have opposed compulsory arbitration as a matter of principle and would not want to mandate it in this legislation. In the Minnesota law, there is a provision for compulsory arbitration. Many contracts throughout the country call for compulsory arbitration. I do not see H.R. 13678 in any way inhibiting the rights of the parties to contract on provisions which will assure continuity of medical care. I reluctantly oppose his amendment because of my high regard for him and his legislative record.

My colleague from Illinois (Mr. ERLENBORN) has given advance notice that he will offer two amendments. The one calls for an additional 60-day cooling off period. This would bring the time to 5 months. I think we have provided adequate time in the 90-day provision with 10-day advance notice for strikes. I oppose this amendment but do support his other amendment on exempting those with bona fide religious convictions from union membership. I will support this amendment when it comes to a vote.

* * * *

16914   CONGRESSIONAL RECORD — HOUSE   *May 30, 1974*

Mr. ERLENBORN. Mr. Chairman, I offer an amendment.

The Clerk read as follows:

Amendment offered by Mr. ERLENBORN: Page 3, after line 21, insert the following:

(f) Such Act is amended by adding immediately after section 18 thereof the following new section:

"INDIVIDUALS WITH RELIGIOUS CONVICTIONS

"SEC. 19. An employee of a health care institution who is a member of and adheres to tenets or teachings of a bona fide religion, body, or sect which has historically held conscientious objections to joining or financially supporting labor organizations shall not be required to join or financially support any labor organization as a condition of employment."

And strike out "(g)" in lien 22 and insert in lieu thereof "(h)".

Mr. DON H. CLAUSEN. Mr. Chairman, will the gentleman yield?

Mr. ERLENBORN. I yield to the gentleman from California (Mr. DON H. CLAUSEN).

Mr. DON H. CLAUSEN. Mr. Chairman, I rise to support the amendment now being offered by my friend from Illinois (Mr. ERLENBORN). Further, I want to compliment him for his understanding, sensitivity, and willingness to use his position of influence on the Education and Labor Committee to provide the leadership for this vital and important amendment. The central issue is the preservation of full religious liberty for the country and in particular, those religious organizations in our country who have consistently demonstrated strict adherence to those matters of conscience that are inherent in the accepted principle of full religious liberty as guaranteed by the first amendment to the Constitution.

Mrs. GREEN of Oregon has been a consistent champion of this cause throughout her distinguished service in the Congress. I would hope that someday this Congress would establish this guaranteed protection in perpetuity so we may remove the concern, once and for all for those dedicated religious organizations that provide some of the finest medical, educational, and religious programs in the country.

Mr. BUCHANAN. Mr. Chairman, will the gentleman yield?

Mr. ERLENBORN. I yield to the gentleman from Alabama.

Mr. BUCHANAN. Mr Chairman, I move to strike the requisite number of words and rise in strong support of the amendment offered by the gentleman and commend him for it.

Mr. ERLENBORN. Mr. Chairman, this is the religious freedom amendment. It has been described in letters sent to the office of every Member. In brief what this provides is if a person working in one of these health care facilities or hospitals belongs to a regular religious sect which holds as part of their regularly held belief that it is against their religion to belong to or pay dues to a labor union, this person would be exempt from the requirement of joining the labor union even though there be a union shop contract.

We have made it clear in the legislative history that this would not prevent and it would allow the union and employer to negotiate payment of a like sum to a charity in lieu of the union dues, but it would accommodate the religious beliefs of those who belong to a regular sect which holds these religious beliefs.

It is rather narrowly drawn, more narrowly drawn than the conscientious objector provision of the military draft law and it would affect only a very small number of people because there are only a few religions that do hold this religious belief. One such religion is the Seventh Day Adventists. They have a hospital in my district and they would be affected and they have asked me to sponsor this. I believe it is reasonable. They have 47 health care institutions across the country. Many of their members work in their institutions and they would be accommodated in their beliefs by the passage of this amendment.

Mr. Chairman, I hope the amendment will be supported and adopted.

Mr. THOMPSON of New Jersey. Mr. Chairman, I rise in opposition to the amendment.

Mr. Chairman, I recognize very deeply that this is an ancient and yet still valid question. Those with such religious convictions are in my considered judgment entitled to the exercise of those convictions. They are indeed a minority. Nowhere under the law or under the case law would they be required in the unlikely event of the organization of a union in a hospital for instance run and operated by the Seventh Day Adventists to join the union but they would indeed be required to pay what is called their fair share of the support of the union without violating their beliefs by becoming a member of it.

Mr. Chairman, the amendment is unnecessary. Since 1951 the Federal courts have held membership in a union cannot be compelled where sincere religious convictions are involved. *Union Starch & Refining Co. v. NLRB*, 186 F. 2d 1008 (1951).

If no one can be compelled to join a union, the question then becomes one of financial support.

Again, the Federal courts have addressed themselves to this issue. In *Railway Employee Department v. Hansel*, 351 U.S. 225 (1956), the Supreme Court held that the requirement of financial support of a union by those who receive its benefits does not violate either the first or fifth amendments.

And in a case decided several weeks ago, William F. Buckley against American Federation of Radio and Television Artists, the U.S. court of appeals for the second circuit declared that a required tolerance of "free riders" would result not only in flagrant inequity, but might eventually seriously undermine the union's ability to perform its bargaining function.

So, Mr. Chairman, while you cannot compel a person to join a union, you can make him pay his fair share of the costs of maintaining a collective bargaining agency.

The only thing this amendment would do would be to relieve employees who receive the benefits of collective bargaining from financially supporting its administrative costs.

"And that, to me, Mr. Chairman, does not seem fair.

This amendment also would discriminate against the millions of employees who do not work for health care institutions—what about their religious convictions? Is it right to single out one class of American workers for special treatment?

It seems to me that it clearly is neither fair nor right.

Further, this amendment would be difficult for the employer to administer and would burden the National Labor Relations Board and the courts with unneeded litigation.

What does the employer do when the union says deduct the dues and the individual claims sincere religious convictions?

What are "historically held conscientious objections"?

Since the draft cases do not require a belief in any particular God, would the courts apply the same rationale here? Who has the burden of proof in these matters?

Mr. Chairman, the courts and Constitution have always protected the religious beliefs of our citizens. But like all other rights, they must be balanced with other interests, in this case collective bargaining and industrial peace.

The first amendment rights are not absolute when a religious belief is translated into an act or refusal to act.

Were it otherwise, I am afraid, we would have many citizens with sincere religious convictions against paying their Federal income tax.

Mr. Chairman, it is already union policy and practice to fully recognize the religious convictions of individuals. The AFL–CIO Executive Council officially declared, nearly 10 years ago:

That unions should accommodate themselves to genuine individual scruples.

AFL–CIO affiliates were urged to "immediately adopt procedures for respecting sincere personal religious convictions as to union membership or activities."

Throughout the Nation unions have negotiated such provisions in their contracts with employers—including nonprofit hospitals, both religiously sponsored and nonsectarian. The question of an in lieu payment of union dues to a charity is a condition of employment that the parties can negotiate. At the same time, it is the committee's understanding that collective bargaining agreements would not contain substantive provisions relating to moral and religious precepts.

Further, Mr. Chairman, this issue was not raised during the hearings on this bill. We have no facts, no background information, no testimony.

This is an extremely complex and far-reaching proposal. I would suggest that the gentleman consider introducing legislation to effect this purpose so that we might properly examine the issue.

Finally, Mr. Chairman, the adoption of the amendment would place a great strain on this delicately balanced compromise bill—a bill, I am sure, that the gentleman from Illinois, agrees is much needed.

For these reasons I must urge my colleagues to vote "no."

Mrs. GREEN of Oregon. Mr. Chairman, I move to strike the last word.

Mr. Chairman, I rise in strong support of this amendment. It is very similar to one which I wanted to offer several years ago when we were debating 14(b) and for some interesting reason it was ruled nongermane at that time even though amendments to 14(b) were the basis for legislation that day.

I did look into this very carefully. There are seven religious groups, to the best of my knowledge, in this country which according to their religious teachings do not allow their members to belong to a union or to any other organization to which they must pay dues.

In seeking the exemption from union shop agreements, they cannot be called "freeloaders." When I talked with the representatives of these seven groups, they were perfectly willing to pay the full amount of initiation and the full amount of dues to a welfare group or a charity that was mutually acceptable to both the union and to the people who as a matter of conscience could not join the union.

If seems very wrong to me to have the Federal Government impose upon any individual at the end of 30 days either the loss of job or the violation of conscience.

At the time that I offered that amendment on the floor, I said then that the matter of individual conscience is something that should not be forced to give way to the rights of the state. Religious liberty has always been a matter of the highest priority and I have always thought of the highest importance to the Congress. We have made provision both in the Social Security Act and in the military conscription provision for allowing certain exemptions to certain religious groups. At the time I intended to offer an amendment to 14(b) very similar to the one now before us—I received from the National Council of Churches a letter, and let me read two parts, because they were rather eloquent:

We urge the Congress to take such steps as may be necessary to guarantee the religious liberty of those workers who as a matter of religious belief cannot join or support any organization other than their own church, except for the State.

Then they went on to say:

In our judgment it should be possible for the Congress to find a formula which simultaneously guarantees the legitimate rights of organized labor and the rights of those workers referred to above whose religious beliefs make it impossible for them to join or support a labor organization.

I would say to the Members of this House, Mr. Chairman, that I think it would be terribly wrong at any time to legislate nationally so that certain individuals of certain religious persuasions should have their economic livelihood placed in jeopardy. We should make sure that their religious convictions are protected under the guarantees of the Constitution.

I urge support for this amendment. I do not consider it an antiunion matter. In fact, in my judgment, the image of the unions would be greatly improved if they would lead the fight for such an amendment. I think it should not only

apply to the hospital workers that we are talking about today, but this conscience clause should become an integral part of 14(b).

The CHAIRMAN. The question is on the amendment offered by the gentleman from Illinois (Mr. ERLENBORN).

The amendment was agreed to.

The CHAIRMAN. Are there further amendments? If not, under the rule, the Committee rises.

Accordingly the Committee rose; and the Speaker having resumed the chair, Mr. GIAIMO, Chairman of the Committee of the Whole House on the State of the Union, reported that that Committee having had under consideration the bill (H.R. 13678) to amend the National Labor Relations Act to extend its coverage and protection to employees of nonprofit hospitals, and for other purposes, pursuant to House Resolution 1151, he reported the bill back to the House with sundry amendments adopted by the Committee of the Whole.

The SPEAKER. Under the rule, the previous question is ordered.

Is a separate vote demanded on any amendment? If not, the Chair will put them en gros.

The amendments were agreed to.

The SPEAKER. The question is on the engrossment and third reading of the bill.

The bill was ordered to be engrossed and read a third time, and was read the third time.

The SPEAKER. The question is on the passage of the bill.

Mr. THOMPSON of New Jersey. Mr. Speaker, on that I demand the yeas and nays.

The yeas and nays were ordered.

The vote was taken by electronic device, and there were—yeas 240, nays 58, answered "present" 1, not voting 134, as follows:

[Roll No. 260]

YEAS—240

Abdnor
Abzug
Addabbo
Anderson, Calif.
Anderson, Ill.
Annunzio
Arends
Ashbrook
Ashley
Badillo
Barrett
Bennett
Bergland
Bevill
Biester
Bingham
Blatnik
Boggs
Bolling
Brademas
Brasco
Bray
Breaux
Breckinridge
Brinkley
Brooks
Broomfield
Brown, Mich.
Burgener
Burke, Fla.
Burke, Mass.
Burlison, Mo.
Burton
Carney, Ohio
Carter
Cederberg
Chisholm
Clark
Clausen, Don H.
Clawson, Del
Clay
Cohen
Collier
Collins, Ill.
Conable
Corman
Coughlin
Culver
Danielson
Davis, Wis.
Delaney
Dellenback
Dellums
Dent
Drinan
Dulski
du Pont
Eckhardt
Edwards, Ala.
Edwards, Calif.
Eilberg
Erlenborn
Esch
Eshleman
Evans, Colo.
Fascell
Fish
Flowers
Ford
Frenzel
Frey
Froehlich
Fulton
Fuqua
Gaydos
Giaimo
Gilman
Ginn
Gonzalez
Grasso
Gray
Green, Oreg.
Green, Pa.
Grover
Gubser
Gunter
Guyer
Hamilton
Hanley
Hanrahan
Harrington
Harsha
Hastings
Hechler, W. Va.
Heckler, Mass.
Heinz
Hicks
Hillis
Hogan
Holifield
Holtzman
Horton
Hosmer
Huber
Hudnut
Hungate
Ichord
Johnson, Calif.
Johnson, Pa.
Jones, Okla.
Jones, Tenn.
Jordan
Karth
Kastenmeier
Kemp
King
Kluczynski
Koch
Lagomarsino
Landrum
Leggett
Long, La.
Long, Md.
Lujan
Luken
McClory
McCollister
McDade
McFall
McKinney
Macdonald
Madden
Mahon
Mallary
Maraziti
Matsunaga
Mayne
Mazzoli
Melcher
Metcalfe
Mezvinsky
Michel
Miller
Mills
Mink
Mitchell, Md.
Mitchell, N.Y.
Moakley
Mollohan
Moorhead, Pa.
Morgan
Mosher
Moss
Murphy, Ill.
Murtha
Myers
Natcher
Nedzi
Nichols
Nix
Obey
O'Brien
O'Hara
O'Neill
Passman
Patten
Pepper
Perkins
Peyser
Pickle
Pike
Powell, Ohio
Preyer
Price, Ill.
Pritchard
Quie
Randall
Rangel
Rees
Reuss
Riegle
Robison, N.Y.
Roncalio, Wyo.
Roncallo, N.Y.
Rostenkowski
Roush
Roybal
Runnels
Sandman
Sarasin
Sarbanes
Schroeder
Seiberling
Shipley
Shoup
Shriver
Shuster
Sikes
Skubitz
Slack
Staggers
Stanton, J. William
Stanton, James V.
Steed
Steiger, Wis.
Stephens
Stokes
Stratton
Studds
Sullivan
Symington
Talcott
Thompson, N.J.
Thomson, Wis.
Thone
Thornton
Tiernan
Towell, Nev.
Ullman
Van Deerlin
Vanik
Vigorito
Waldie
Walsh
White
Whitehurst
Widnall
Williams
Wilson, Bob
Wilson, Charles H., Calif.
Wolff
Wright
Wyatt
Wydler
Yates
Yatron
Young, Alaska
Young, Fla.
Young, Ill.
Zablocki

NAYS—58

Alexander
Archer
Bauman
Beard
Bowen
Broyhill, Va.
Buchanan
Burleson, Tex.
Butler
Byron
Casey, Tex.
Cleveland
Cochran
Collins, Tex.
Conlan
Crane
Daniel, Dan
Daniel, Robert W., Jr.
Dennis
Derwinski
Downing
Duncan
Flynt
Fountain
Goodling
Gross
Haley
Hammerschmidt
Henderson
Holt
Jarman
Jones, N.C.
Kazen
Landgrebe
Latta
Lott
Mann
Mathis, Ga.
Mizell
Montgomery
Poage
Rarick
Roberts
Robinson, Va.
Rose
Rousselot
Ruth
Satterfield
Sebelius
Spence
Steiger, Ariz.
Taylor, N.C.
Treen
Whitten
Winn
Wylie
Young, Tex.

ANSWERED "PRESENT"—1

Hunt

NOT VOTING—134

Adams
Andrews, N.C.
Andrews, N. Dak.
Armstrong
Aspin
Bafalis
Baker
Bell
Biaggi
Blackburn
Boland
Brotzman
Brown, Calif.
Brown, Ohio
Broyhill, N.C.
Burke, Calif.
Camp
Carey, N.Y.
Chamberlain
Chappell
Clancy
Conte
Conyers
Cotter
Cronin
Daniels, Dominick V.
Davis, Ga.
Davis, S.C.
de la Garza
Denholm
Devine
Dickinson
Diggs
Dingell
Donohue
Dorn
Evins, Tenn.
Findley
Fisher
Flood
Foley
Forsythe
Fraser
Frelinghuysen
Gettys
Gibbons
Goldwater
Griffiths
Gude
Hanna
Hansen, Idaho
Hansen, Wash.
Hawkins
Hays
Hébert
Helstoski
Hinshaw
Howard
Hutchinson
Johnson, Colo.
Jones, Ala.
Ketchum
Kuykendall
Kyros
Lehman
Lent
Litton
McCloskey
McCormack
McEwen
McSpadden
Madigan
Martin, Nebr.
Martin, N.C.
Mathias, Calif.
Meeds
Milford
Minish
Minshall, Ohio
Moorhead, Calif.
Murphy, N.Y.
Nelsen
Owens
Parris
Patman
Pettis
Podell
Price, Tex.
Quillen
Railsback
Regula
Reid
Rhodes
Rinaldo
Rodino
Roe
Rogers
Rooney, N.Y.
Rooney, Pa.
Rosenthal
Roy
Ruppe
Ryan
St Germain
Scherle
Schneebeli
Sisk
Smith, Iowa

X. H.R. Rep. No. 93-1175 at 1, 4 (July 3, 1974)

93D CONGRESS 2d Session	HOUSE OF REPRESENTATIVES	REPORT No. 93–1175

COVERAGE OF NONPROFIT HOSPITALS UNDER THE NATIONAL LABOR RELATIONS ACT

JULY 3, 1974.—Ordered to be printed

Mr. PERKINS from the committee of conference,
submitted the following

CONFERENCE REPORT

[To accompany S. 3203]

The committee of conference on the disagreeing votes of the two Houses on the amendment of the House to the bill (S. 3203) to amend the National Labor Relations Act to extend its coverage and protection to employees of nonprofit hospitals, and for other purposes, having met, after full and free conference, have agreed to recommend and do recommend to their respective Houses as follows:

That the Senate recede from its disagreement to the amendment of the House and agree to the same with an amendment as follows:

In lieu of the matter proposed to be inserted by the Senate amendment insert the following:

That (a) section 2(2) of the National Labor Relations Act is amended by striking out "or any corporation or association operating a hospital, if no part of the net earnings inures to the benefit of any private shareholder or individual,".

(material omitted)

★38–006

JOINT EXPLANATORY STATEMENT OF THE COMMITTEE OF CONFERENCE

The managers on the part of the House and the Senate at the conference on the disagreeing votes of the two Houses on the amendment of the House to the bill (S. 3203) to amend the National Labor Relations Act to extend its coverage and protection to employees of nonprofit hospitals, and for other purposes, submit the following joint statement to the House and the Senate in explanation of the effect of the action agreed upon by the managers and recommended in the accompanying conference report:

The House amendment struck out all of the Senate bill after the enacting clause and inserted a substitute text.

The Senate recedes from its disagreement to the amendment of the House with an amendment which is a substitute for the Senate bill and the House amendment. The differences between the Senate bill, the House amendment, and the substitute agreed to in conference are noted below, except for clerical corrections, conforming changes made necessary by agreements reached by the conferees, and minor drafting and clarifying changes.

BASIC PURPOSE OF THE SENATE BILL AND THE HOUSE AMENDMENT

Both Senate bill and the House amendment amended the National Labor Relations Act to remove the exemption for employees of nonprofit hospitals. Both the Senate bill and the House amendment establishes additional mediation and conciliation procedures for employees of all health care institutions including requirements for mandatory mediation and that a 10 day notice of any strike or picketing be given to a health care institution.

The language of the House amendment is identical to the Senate bill except in the following two respects:

INDIVIDUALS WITH RELIGIOUS CONVICTIONS

Subsection (g) of the first section of the House amendment amended the Act by adding at the end thereof a new section 19 (relating to individuals with religious convictions). The new section 19 provided that employees of health care institutions who object to joining or financially supporting labor organizations on religious grounds shall not be required to do so as a condition of employment. The Senate receded with a clarifying amendment under which, in recognition of the special humanitarian character of health care institutions, an employee may be required to make payments to a nonreligious charitable fund in lieu of periodic dues and initiation fees designated from among at least three funds pursuant to the collective bargaining agreement between the employer and the labor organization, or if the labor-management agreement fails to make such designation, to any nonreligious charitable fund selected by the employee.

(4)

H.R. 1175

THE 1976 CIVIL RIGHTS ATTORNEYS' FEES AWARDS ACT AND
THE *BLANCHARD* DECISION

I. *Overview and Questions*

Blanchard v. Bergeron is the second Supreme Court decision we address that interprets the short statute known as the Civil Rights Attorneys' Fees Award Act of 1976. (The first decision, *West Virginia Univ. Hospitals v. Casey*, is summarized at pp. 790-91 of the Casebook. We present the majority and dissenting opinions in *Casey*, along with legislative history related to the issue raised in that case, at pp.182-208 supra of this Supplement.)

In *Blanchard*, Justice White for the majority has several grounds for ruling in favor of the civil rights plaintiffs, and Justice Scalia endorses all of these except for reliance on legislative history. Justice White's invocation of legislative history is confined to a single paragraph at page six of a seven-page Senate committee report. We provide pages one and six of the Senate committee report here (for additional perspective, you may consult pages one through five of the report, included in the materials accompanying *W. Va. Univ. Hospitals v. Casey*). We also include some further legislative history, not invoked by Justice White, that offers relevant context: excerpts from the House committee report and from floor statements by the bill's Senate and House authors.

As you review this legislative history, consider the following questions:

1. Looking at the key paragraph that appears at page 6 of the seven-page Senate committee report, how persuasive is the majority's application of these case references? Does a fair reading of the Senate report language suggest that the committee regarded contingent fee arrangements as simply one factor among many, or that they were viewed as a potentially controlling factor? Be prepared to justify your response.

2. Justice Scalia's concurring opinion in *Blanchard* questions whether a single, modestly explained string-cite in a report from one House should be viewed as convincing evidence of what the voting members of Congress had in mind. Examine page 8 of the House committee report, and the floor statements by bill managers Senator Tunney (122 Cong. Rec. 31285) and Rep. Drinan (*id.* at 35123). Do these additional references suggest that contingent fee arrangements were viewed as having any special significance among the 12 factors? How might this additional history provide support for Justice White's reliance on the Senate committee report?

3. Assume that the Senate committee report paragraph also appears in *haec verba* in the House committee report, and assume further that the paragraph includes an explanation of the holdings in *Zurcher* and *Davis*—that contingent fee agreements are a factor but are not dispositive. Is this enough to render the committee report probative or reliable as an expression of what Congress meant when invoking the 12 *Johnson* factors?

4. Now assume that instead of the explanation for these court holdings, we have the Senate committee report paragraph accompanied by a statement in the report's minority views expressing disagreement with the majority's reliance on *Zurcher* and *Davis*, and urging Congress to treat contingency fee contracts as a ceiling on fee recovery. Does the presence of such minority views affect your position on whether the committee report is a reliable expression of congressional intent?

5. Courts frequently cite cases without explanation as a shorthand way to inform litigants about the substance of some authoritative doctrinal rule. Why assume, as Justice Scalia does, that legislators cannot do the same thing for one another?

6. If your answer to the preceding question involves the fact that many legislators are not lawyers—or that even those who are lawyers no longer read cases for a living—to what extent is it reasonable to assume that lawmakers are novices or naifs about the work of courts in general? For instance, should judges assume that legislators know nothing about language canons and how courts use them? Substantive canons?

II. Excerpts from S. Rep. No. 94-1011 (June 29, 1976)

Calendar No. 955

94TH CONGRESS 2d Session	SENATE	REPORT No. 94-1011

CIVIL RIGHTS ATTORNEYS' FEES AWARDS ACT

JUNE 29 (legislative day, JUNE 18), 1976.—Ordered to be printed

---

Mr. TUNNEY, from the Committee on the Judiciary,
submitted the following

REPORT

[To accompany S. 2278]

The Committee on the Judiciary, to which was referred the bill
(S. 2278) to amend Revised Statutes section 722 (42 U.S.C. § 1988)
to allow a court, in its discretion, to award attorneys' fees to a prevailing party in suits brought to enforce certain civil rights acts, having
considered the same, reports favorably thereon and recommends that
the bill do pass.

The text of S. 2278 is as follows:

S. 2278

Revised Statutes section 722 (42 U.S.C. Sec. 1988) is
amended by adding the following: "In any action or proceeding to enforce a provision of sections 1977, 1978, 1979,
1980 and 1981 of the Revised Statutes, or Title VI of the Civil
Rights Act of 1964, the court, in its discretion, may allow the
prevailing party, other than the United States, a reasonable
attorney's fee as part of the costs.".

PURPOSE

This amendment to the Civil Rights Act of 1866, Revised Statutes
Section 722, gives the Federal courts discretion to award attorneys'
fees to prevailing parties in suits brought to enforce the civil rights
acts which Congress has passed since 1866. The purpose of this amendment is to remedy anomalous gaps in our civil rights laws created by
the United States Supreme Court's recent decision in *Alyeska Pipeline
Service Co.* v. *Wilderness Society*, 421 U.S. 240 (1975), and to achieve
consistency in our civil rights laws.

57-010

6

It is intended that the amount of fees awarded under S. 2278 be governed by the same standards which prevail in other types of equally complex Federal litigation, such as antitrust cases and not be reduced because the rights involved may be nonpecuniary in nature. The appropriate standards, see *Johnson* v. *Georgia Highway Express*, 488 F. 2d 714 (5th Cir. 1974), are correctly applied in such cases as *Stanford Daily* v. *Zurcher*, 64 F.R.D. 680 (N.D. Cal. 1974); *Davis* v. *County of Los Angeles*, 8 E.P.D. ¶ 9444 (C.D. Cal. 1974); and *Swann* v. *Charlotte-Mecklenburg Board of Education*, 66 F.R.D. 483 (W.D.N.C. 1975). These cases have resulted in fees which are adequate to attract competent counsel, but which do not produce windfalls to attorneys. In computing the fee, counsel for prevailing parties should be paid, as is traditional with attorneys compensated by a fee-paying client, "for all time reasonably expended on a matter." *Davis, supra; Stanford Daily, supra,* at 684.

This bill creates no startling new remedy—it only meets the technical requirements that the Supreme Court has laid down if the Federal courts are to continue the practice of awarding attorneys' fees which had been going on for years prior to the Court's May decision. It does not change the statutory provisions regarding the protection of civil rights except as it provides the fee awards which are necessary if citizens are to be able to effectively secure compliance with these existing statutes. There are very few provisions in our Federal laws which are self-executing. Enforcement of the laws depends on governmental action and, in some cases, on private action through the courts. If the cost of private enforcement actions becomes too great, there will be no private enforcement. If our civil rights laws are not to become mere hollow pronouncements which the average citizen cannot enforce, we must maintain the traditionally effective remedy of fee shifting in these cases.

CHANGES IN EXISTING LAW MADE BY THE BILL ARE ITALICIZED

REVISED STATUTES § 722, 42 U.S.C. § 1988

"The jurisdiction in civil and criminal matters conferred on the district courts by the provisions of this chapter and Title 18, for the protection of all persons in the United States in their civil rights, and for their vindication, shall be exercised and enforced in conformity with the laws of the United States, so far as such laws are suitable to carry the same into effect; but in all cases where they are not adapted to the object, or are deficient in the provisions necessary to furnish suitable remedies and punish offenses against law, the common law, as modified and changed by the constitution and statutes of the State wherein the court having jurisdiction of such civil or criminal cause is held, so far as the same is not inconsistent with the Constitution and laws of the United States, shall be extended to and govern the said courts in the trial and disposition of the cause, and, if it is of a criminal nature, in the infliction of punishment on the party found guilty." *In any action or proceeding to enforce a provision of sections 1977, 1978, 1979, 1980 and 1981 of the Revised Statutes, or Title VI of the Civil Rights Act of 1964, the court, in its discretion, may allow the prevailing party, other than the United States, a reasonable attorney's fee as part of the costs.*

S.R. 1011

III. H.R. Rep. No. 94-1558, at 1, 8-9 (Sept. 15, 1976)

94TH CONGRESS *2d Session*	HOUSE OF REPRESENTATIVES	REPORT No. 94-1558

THE CIVIL RIGHTS ATTORNEY'S FEES AWARDS ACT OF 1976

SEPTEMBER 15, 1976.—Committed to the Committee of the Whole House on the State of the Union and ordered to be printed

Mr. DRINAN, from the Committee on the Judiciary, submitted the following

REPORT

[Including cost estimate of the Congressional Budget Office]

[To accompany H.R. 15460]

The Committee on the Judiciary, to whom was referred the bill (H.R. 15460) to allow the awarding of attorney's fees in certain civil rights cases, having considered the same, report favorably thereon without amendment and recommend that the bill do pass.

PURPOSE OF THE BILL

H.R. 15460, the Civil Rights Attorney's Fees Awards Act of 1976, authorizes the courts to award reasonable attorney fees to the prevailing party in suits instituted under certain civil rights acts. Under existing law, some civil rights statutes contain counsel fee provisions, while others do not. In order to achieve uniformity in the remedies provided by Federal laws guaranteeing civil and constitutional rights, it is necessary to add an attorney fee authorization to those civil rights acts which do not presently contain such a provision.

The effective enforcement of Federal civil rights statutes depends largely on the efforts of private citizens. Although some agencies of the United States have civil rights responsibilities, their authority and resources are limited. In many instances where these laws are violated, it is necessary for the citizen to initiate court action to correct the illegality. Unless the judicial remedy is full and complete, it will remain a meaningless right. Because a vast majority of the victims of civil rights violations cannot afford legal counsel, they are unable to present their cases to the courts. In authorizing an award of reasonable attorney's fees, H.R. 15460 is designed to give such persons effective access to the judicial process where their grievances can be resolved according to law.

57-006

8

Corcoran v. *Columbia Broadcasting System*, 121 F.2d 575 (9th Cir. 1941), as long as the other factors, noted earlier, governing awards to defendants are met. Finally the courts have also awarded counsel fees to a plaintiff who successfully concludes a class action suit even though that individual was not granted any relief. *Parham* v. *Southwestern Bell Telephone Co., supra; Reed* v. *Arlington Hotel Co., Inc.*, 476 F.2d 721 (8th Cir. 1973).

Furthermore, the word "prevailing" is not intended to require the entry of a *final* order before fees may be recovered. "A district court must have discretion to award fees and costs incident to the final disposition of interim matters." *Bradley* v. *Richmond School Board*, 416 U.S. 696, 723 (1974); see also *Mills* v. *Electric Auto-Lite Co.*, 396 U.S. 375 (1970). Such awards pendente lite are particularly important in protracted litigation, where it is difficult to predicate with any certainty the date upon which a final order will be entered. While the courts have not yet formulated precise standards as to the appropriate circumstances under which such interim awards should be made, the Supreme Court has suggested some guidelines. "(T)he entry of any order that determines substantial rights of the parties may be an appropriate occasion upon which to consider the propriety of an award of counsel fees. . . ." *Bradley* v. *Richmond School Board, supra* at 722 n. 28.

2. Judicial discretion

The second key feature of the bill is its mandate that fees are only to be allowed in the discretion of the court. Congress has passed many statutes *requiring* that fees be awarded to a prevailing party.[15] Again the Committee adopted a more moderate approach here by leaving the matter to the discretion of the judge, guided of course by the case law interpreting similar attorney's fee provisions. This approach was supported by the Justice Department on Dec. 31, 1975. The Committee intends that, at a minimum, existing judicial standards, to which ample reference is made in this report, should guide the courts in construing H.R. 15460.

3. Reasonable fees

The third principal element of the bill is that the prevailing party is entitled to "reasonable" counsel fees. The courts have enumerated a number of factors in determining the reasonableness of awards under similarly worded attorney's fee provisions. In *Johnson* v. *Georgia Highway Express, Inc.*, 488 F.2d 714 (5th Cir. 1974), for example, the court listed twelve factors to be considered, including the time and labor required, the novelty and difficulty of the questions involved, the skill needed to present the case, the customary fee for similar work, and the amount received in damages, if any. *Accord: Evans* v. *Sheraton Park Hotel*, 503 F.2d 177 (D.C. Cir. 1974); see also *United States Steel Corp.* v. *United States, supra.*

Of course, it should be noted that the mere recovery of damages should not preclude the awarding of counsel fees.[16] Under the anti-

---

[15] E.g., 7 U.S.C. 499a(b) (Perishable Agricultural Commodities Act); 15 U.S.C. 1640(a) (Truth-in-Lending Act); 46 U.S.C. 1277 (Merchant Marine Act of 1936); 47 U.S.C. 206 (Communications Act of 1934).

[16] Similarly, a prevailing party is entitled to counsel fees even if represented by an organization or if the party is itself an organization. *Incarcerated Men of Allen County* v. *Fair, supra; Torres* v. *Sachs*, 69 F.R.D. 343 (S.D.N.Y. 1975), aff'd. —— F.2d —— (2d Cir., June 25, 1976); *Fairley* v. *Patterson*, 493 F2d 598 (5th Cir. 1974).

9

trust laws, for example, a plaintiff may recover treble damages and still the court is required to award attorney fees. The same principle should apply here as civil rights plaintiffs should not be singled out for different and less favorable treatment. Furthermore, while damages are theoretically available under the statutes covered by H.R. 15460, it should be observed that, in some cases, immunity doctrines and special defenses, available only to public officials, preclude or severely limit the damage remedy.[17] Consequently awarding counsel fees to prevailing plaintiffs in such litigation is particularly important and necessary if Federal civil and constitutional rights are to be adequately protected. To be sure, in a large number of cases brought under the provisions covered by H.R. 15460, only injunctive relief is sought, and prevailing plaintiffs should ordinarily recover their counsel fees. *Newman* v. *Piggie Park Enterprises, Inc., supra; Northcross* v. *Memphis Board of Education, supra.*

The application of these standards will insure that reasonable fees are awarded to attract competent counsel in cases involving civil and constitutional rights, while avoiding windfalls to attorneys. The effect of H.R. 15460 will be to promote the enforcement of the Federal civil rights acts, as Congress intended, and to achieve uniformity in those statutes and justice for all citizens.

OVERSIGHT

Oversight of the administration of justice in the federal court system is the responsibility of the Committee on the Judiciary. The hearings on October 6 and 8 and Dec. 3, 1975, focused on specific pending legislation. However, they did have an oversight purpose, as well, since the impact of the Supreme Court's *Alyeska* decision on the public and the related issue of equal access to the courts were subjects of the hearing.

COMMITTE VOTE

H.R. 15460 was reported favorably by a voice vote of the Committee on September 9, 1976. Twenty-seven members of the Committee were present.

STATEMENT OF THE COMMITTE ON GOVERNMENT OPERATIONS

No statement has been received on the legislation from the House Committee on Government Operations.

STATEMENT OF THE CONGRESSIONAL BUDGET OFFICE

Pursuant to clause 7, rule XIII of the Rules of the House of Representatives and section 403 of the Congressional Budget Act of 1974, the Committee estimates there will be no cost to the federal government.

---

[17] *Wood* v. *Strickland,* 420 U.S. 308 (1975) ; *Scheuer* v. *Rhodes,* 416 U.S. 232 (1974) ; *Pierson* v. *Ray,* 386 U.S. 547 (1967).

IV. 122 Cong. Rec. 32185 (Sept. 23, 1976)

failure to reopen would be a serious administrative omission.

However, our most serious objection is to the concept itself—that taxpayers should be reimbursed by the Government for expenses incurred in the settlement of a tax dispute. The proposal will set a precedent which may lead to further and more costly demands for legislation extending the principle of reimbursement under other circumstances. For FY 1975, IRS audited 2.465 million tax returns and closed 2.9 million delinquent accounts. Once the concept of reimbursement is introduced, it will be very difficult to limit its application to a particular taxpayer or tax action.

It is hoped that the Congress would defer its action on this very important matter until it has been more thoroughly considered. We will be pleased to study this matter in greater depth and submit a report of our views if that is desired.

With kind regards,
Sincerely,
DONALD C. ALEXANDER,
Commissioner.

Mr. TUNNEY. Mr. President, on Tuesday of this week the junior Senator from Alabama asked rhetorically why I was not present in this Chamber if this bill, which I had introduced, the Civil Rights Attorney's Fees Awards Act, was so important to me. He then proceeded to answer his question. He stated that I was engaged in a tough fight for reelection but not withstanding my campaign battle, I would be present for this cloture vote today.

He was correct on both points: I am here and I am engaged in an extremely tough election. But every Senator realizes that the great issues involved in this bill do not involve granting relief to attorneys. Senator KENNEDY yesterday challenged Senator ALLEN to show a single case of a lawyer getting rich on civil rights cases. It just does not happen. In fact, a 1975 study undertaken by Leslie Helfman of the Antioch Law School indicates that of the 140 most recent cases decided prior to Alyeska, civil rights cases ranked near the bottom with fees averaging $37 per hour compared to $181 per hour for the highest ranking field of antitrust law.

If any relief is accorded by the passage of this bill, it will be granted to those individuals who have been unlawfully deprived of their constitutional rights. That is why a majority of the Senate has supported this bill through more than a dozen rollcall votes and have opposed the dilatory amendments that have been offered during the last 2 days of debate. That is why a dozen Senators believed that this bill was so important that they adjusted their schedules and canceled appointments in order to take turns managing this bill. Mr. President, I would like to express my deepest appreciation to Senators ROBERT C. BYRD, CRANSTON, ABOUREZK, BAYH, BROOKE, EAGLETON, GRAVEL, HATHAWAY, JAVITS, KENNEDY, MATHIAS, and HUGH SCOTT for their diligence and leadership in pressing for passage of this legislation.

I would also like to express my special thanks to Senator PHIL HART of Michigan for his solid work on behalf of this bill in the Judiciary Committee.

Mr. President, the action that I ask the Senate to take today is far from unique. Fifty-four Federal statutes presently authorize the award of attorney fees in areas as diverse as antitrust, freedom of information, consumer product safety, banking, international relations, and patents, to name only a few. S. 2278, when enacted, will close a loophole in our present civil rights enforcement laws.

In *Alyeska Pipeline Service Corp.* v. *Wilderness Society,* 421 U.S. 240 (1975), the Supreme Court expressly stated that the lower Federal courts had no inherent equity power to award attorney's fees in civil rights cases absent statutory direction. This bill creates the necessary authorization and is addressed to the key questions raised in the opinion. The bill states, in part,

The court, *in its discretion,* may allow the *prevailing party,* other than the United States, a *reasonable* attorney's fee as part of the costs. (Emphasis added.)

The award, Mr. President, must be reasonable and the courts have been exceptionally clear in stating their views on this aspect of the problem. In *Johnson* v. *Georgia Highway Express, Inc.,* 488 F. 2d 714 (5th Cir. 1974) the court of appeals listed 12 factors to be considered in computing the fees including the time and labor required, the novelty and difficulty of the question involved, the skill needed to present the case, the customary fee for similar work and the amount received in damages, if any.

S. 2278 also provides for awards to the prevailing party, a more moderate approach than limiting recovery to prevailing plaintiffs. This was designed to avoid bringing vexatious or harassing lawsuits by allowing the award of fees to prevailing defendants under those circumstances. *United States Steel Corp.* v. *United States,* 519 F. 2d 359, 364 (3rd Cir. 1975). At the same time, existing case law is clear on the point that prevailing plaintiffs "should ordinarily recover our attorney's fee unless special circumstances would render such an award unjust." *Newman* v. *Piggie Park Enterprises, Inc.,* 390 U.S. 400, 402 (1968) (per curiam).

Finally, S. 2278 states that the fees are to be allowed in the discretion of the court. That discretion has been included in the most recent civil rights statutes allowing attorneys' fees and the standards enunciated in *Newman* v. *Piggie Park Enterprises, Inc.,* 390 U.S. 400, 402 (1968) have been more than ample.

Thus, Mr. President, we have before us a moderate, rational plan carefully drafted to insure that the constitutional rights of our people may be adequately protected. I ask that the bill be passed.

REQUEST FOR ROUTINE MORNING BUSINESS

Mr. ROBERT C. BYRD. Mr. President, I do not believe there will be any vote on the motion to adjourn tonight; it is my understanding there is no one who plans to ask for the yeas and nays on that. Therefore, there will be no more rollcall votes today.

I ask unanimous consent that at this time there may be a brief period for the transaction of routine morning business.

The ACTING PRESIDENT pro tempore. Is there objection?

Mr. ALLEN. Mr. President, reserving the right to object, I object.

Mr. SPARKMAN. Mr. President, will the Senator from West Virginia yield to me for a brief question?

Mr. ROBERT C. BYRD. Yes.

Mr. SPARKMAN. The Senator knows that both Senator ALLEN and I have spoken to him and to Senator MANSFIELD with reference to the Nuclear Fuel Assurance Act. I think that number is H.R. 8401. And I know that it is included among "Subjects on the Table." I assume that means there definitely cannot be action during this session of Congress; is that right?

Mr. ROBERT C. BYRD. Not necessarily. A bill on that calendar may be called up by unanimous consent or by a motion just as can any measure on the regular calendar. It has been put on that calendar along with many other measures so as to clear the calendar of general orders of so many measures that are not likely to be called up.

Mr. SPARKMAN. As the leader knows, I have been greatly interested and concerned about this action. Many people in my State have been. If I understand correctly, the President wrote a letter to Senator MANSFIELD urging action on this bill before Congress adjourned. Therefore, I wanted to inquire just what the situation is with reference to it.

Mr. ROBERT C. BYRD. There are quite a number of measures that have been placed on the calendar entitled "Subjects On The Table." I may have asked unanimous consent to transfer them when I was directed to do so. The majority leader, I am sure, did ask unanimous consent that a good many of them go on that calendar, the purpose being to get them off the calendar of general orders. There is obviously a lot of opposition to them and in the opinion of the leadership—not me necessarily, because I am unaware of the contents of a good many of these measures, or of the nature of the opposition—they have been moved off the calendar of general orders and placed on the calendar of "Subjects On The Table," so as to clear the general orders calendar of measures that are going nowhere in this Congress before it adjourns.

We are trying to clean it up as much as possible. There are a good many other measures on the General Orders Calendar that really will not be acted on in this session and could just as well go on the Calendar of "Subjects on the Table," but, again in answer to the able Senator, the same unanimous-consent request can bring a measure off the "Subjects on the Table" Calendar or the same motion as with the Calendar of General Orders.

There is apparently very strong opposition to any measure that is on the Calendar of "Subjects on the Table."

Mr. SPARKMAN. I realized the situation, but I did wish to inquire, particularly if we are not going to be able to get action in this session, and I think I am ready to concede that we cannot hope for action during this session. I do hope that soon after the beginning of the new year we may have opportunity to bring it up and get a vote on it.

V. 122 Cong. Rec. 35123 (Oct. 1, 1976)

counsel fees allow them only to the prevailing plaintiff. This bill takes the more modest approach of other civil rights statutes, allowing fees to any prevailing party.

There is a real danger, however, that allowing fees to any prevailing party might have a "chilling effect" on civil rights plaintiffs. Victims of discrimination may be reluctant to initiate legal action to protect their rights for fear that they may be required to pay the counsel fees of the defendant. To guard against this possible deterrent, the courts have developed a dual standard for awarding fees.

On two occasions, the Supreme Court has held that, where counsel fees are authorized in civil rights cases, a prevailing plaintiff should ordinarily recover his other attorney fees unless special circumstances would render such an award unjust. The Court adopted this view based on the important public interest served by the elimination of racial discrimination and the securing of other constitutional rights, matters which Congress has determined to be of the highest importance.

Of course, in proper cases, prevailing defendants may recover their counsel fees. To avoid the "chilling effect" which such fees might have on victims bringing suit, the courts have designed a different standard for awarding fees to prevailing defendants. Under the case law, such an award may be made only if the action is vexatious and frivolous, or if the plaintiff instituted it solely to harass the defendant. In Carrion versus Yeshiva University, for example, the Second Circuit Court of Appeals awarded the defendant attorney fees because the litigation was "motivated by malice and vindictiveness."

Second, I should note that the bill commits the award of fees to the discretion of the court. Congress has passed many statutes requiring that fees be awarded. Again this bill takes a more moderate approach, leaving the award to the discretion of the court guided by the case law.

Third, the bill permits the recovery only of a "reasonable" attorney fee. Here too the courts have identified a number of factors to determine the reasonableness of awards. In Johnson versus Georgia Highway Express, for example, the court enumerated 12 factors to be considered, including the time and labor required, the novelty and difficulty of the questions, the skill needed to present the case, the customary fee for similar work, and the amount received in damages, if any. These evolving standards should provide sufficient guidance to the courts in construing this bill which uses the same term. I should add that the phrase "attorney's fee" would include the values of the legal services provided by counsel, including all incidental and necessary expenses incurred in furnishing effective and competent representation.

The question has been raised whether allowing fees against State governments in suits properly brought under the covered statutes would violate the 11th amendment. That amendment limits the power of the Federal courts to entertain

CXXII——2213——Part 27

actions against a State. This issue is no longer seriously in dispute after the recent Supreme Court decision in Fitzpatrick against Bitzer. Since this bill is enacted pursuant to the power of Congress under section 2 of the 13th amendment and section 5 of the 14th amendment, any question arising under the 11th amendment is resolved in favor of awarding fees against State defendants.

I should add also that, as the gentleman from Illinois (Mr. ANDERSON) observed during consideration of the resolution on S. 2278, this bill would apply to cases pending on the date of enactment. It is the settled rule that a change in statutory law is to be applied to cases in litigation. In Bradley versus Richmond School Board, the Supreme Court expressly applied that long-standing rule to an attorney fee provision, including the award of fees for services rendered prior to the effective date of the statute.

Finally it should be noted that civil rights attorneys and organizations have lost thousands of dollars in fees since the Alyeska decision. That case has greatly impaired citizen enforcement of the statutes covered by S. 2278. If Federal laws providing for the protection of civil and constitutional rights are to be fully enforced, Congress must provide effective remedies for the vindication of those guarantees. Authorizing the award of reasonable counsel fees is an important tool for effectuating that purpose.

I include the following:

APPENDIX 1—FEDERAL STATUTES AUTHORIZING THE AWARD OF ATTORNEY FEES

1. Federal Contested Election Act, 2 U.S.C. 396.
2. Freedom of Information Act, 5 U.S.C. 552(a) (4) (E).
3. Privacy Act, 5 U.S.C. 552a(g) (3) (B).
4. Federal Employment Compensation For Work Injuries, 5 U.S.C. 8127.
5. Packers and Stockyards Act, 7 U.S.C. 210(f).
6. Perishable Agricultural Commodities Act, 7 U.S.C. 499g (b), (c).
7. Agricultural Unfair Trade Practices Act, 7 U.S.C. 2305 (a), (c).
8. Plant Variety Act, 7 U.S.C. 2565.
9. Bankruptcy Act, 11 U.S.C. 104(a)(1).
10. Railroad Reorganization Act of 1935, 11 U.S.C. 205(c) (12).
11. Corporate Reorganization Act, 11 U.S.C. 641, 642, 643, and 644.
12. Federal Credit Union Act, 12 U.S.C. 1786(O).
13. Bank Holding Company Act, 12 U.S.C. 1975.
14. Clayton Act, 15 U.S.C. 15.
15. Unfair Competition Act (FTC), 15 U.S.C. 72.
16. Securities Act of 1933, 15 U.S.C. 77k(e).
17. Trust Indenture Act, 15 U.S.C. 77www (a).
18. Securities Exchange Act of 1934, 15 U.S.C. 78i(e), 78r(a).
19. Jewelers Hall-Mark Act, 15 U.S.C. 298 (b), (c), and (d).
20. Truth-in-Lending Act (Fair Credit Billing Amendments), 15 U.S.C. 1640(a).
21. Fair Credit Reporting Act, 15 U.S.C. 1681(n).
22. Motor Vehicle Information and Cost Savings Act, 15 U.S.C. 1918(a), 1989(a) (2).

¹ This list is compiled from information submitted to the Judiciary Subcommittee by the Council for Public Interest Law and the Attorneys' Fee Project of the Lawyers' Committee for Civil Rights Under Law.

23. Consumer Product Safety Act, 15 U.S.C. 2072, 2073.
24. Federal Trade Improvements Act (Amendments), 15 U.S.C. 2310(a) (5) (d) (2).
25. Copyright Act, 17 U.S.C. 1116.
26. Organized Crime Control Act of 1970, 18 U.S.C. 1964(c).
27. Education Amendments of 1972, 20 U.S.C. 1617.
28. Mexican American Treaty Act of 1950, 22 U.S.C. 277d–21.
29. International Claim Settlement Act, 22 U.S.C. 1623(f).
30. Federal Tort Claims Act, 28 U.S.C. 2678.
31. Norris-LaGuardia Act, 29 U.S.C. 107.
32. Fair Labor Standards Act, 29 U.S.C. 216(b).
33. Employees Retirement Income Security Act, 29 U.S.C. 1132(g).
34. Labor Management Reporting and Disclosure Act, 29 U.S.C. 431(c), 501(b).
35. Longshoremen and Harbor Workers Compensation Act, 33 U.S.C. 928.
36. Water Pollution Prevention and Control Act, 33 U.S.C. 1365(d).
37. Ocean Dumping Act, 33 U.S.C. 1415 (g) (4).
38. Deepwater Ports Act of 1974, 33 U.S.C. 1515.
39. Patent Infringement Act, 35 U.S.C. 285.
40. Servicemen's Group Life Insurance Act, 38 U.S.C. 784(g).
41. Servicemen's Readjustment Act, 38 U.S.C. 1822(b).
42. Veterans Benefit Act, 38 U.S.C. 3404(c).
43. Safe Drinking Water Act, 42 U.S.C. 300j–8(d).
44. Social Security Act (Amendments of 1965), 42 U.S.C. 406(b).
45. Clean Air Act (Amendments of 1970), 42 U.S.C. 1857h-2.
46. Voting Rights Act Amendments of 1975, 42 U.S.C. 1973l(e).
47. Civil Rights Act of 1964, Title II, 42 U.S.C. 2000a-3(b).
48. Civil Rights Act of 1964, Title VII, 42 U.S.C. 2000e-5(k).
49. Legal Services Corporation Act, 42 U.S.C. 2996e(f).
50. Fair Housing Act of 1968, 42 U.S.C. 3612(c).
51. Noise Control Act of 1972, 42 U.S.C. 4911(d).
52. Railway Labor Act, 45 U.S.C. 153(p).
53. Merchant Marine Act of 1936, 46 U.S.C. 1227.
54. Communications Act of 1934, 47 U.S.C. 206.
55. Interstate Commerce Act, 49 U.S.C. 8, 16(2), 908(b), 908(e), and 1017(b) (2).

In the Alyeska decision the court held that attorneys' fees should not ordinarily be awarded to a prevailing party, unless expressly authorized by act of Congress.

Mr. WHITE. Mr. Speaker, will the gentleman yield?

Mr. DRINAN. I yield to the gentleman from Texas (Mr. WHITE).

Mr. WHITE. Mr. Speaker, I want to clear up some colloquy made earlier during the rule debate. The gentleman from Massachusetts has made an interesting point, that previous to the Alyeska case, the courts were awarding attorneys' fees to the prevailing side, but by reason of that case the courts have said they must have statutory authority prior to awarding attorneys' fees to either prevailing party.

Mr. DRINAN. The gentleman has stated the case very precisely.

Mr. WHITE. Mr. Speaker, if the gentleman will yield further, in this case the bill suggests awarding attorneys' fees to the prevailing side, but on further

THE 1986 BANKRUPTCY LAW AMENDMENTS AND *IN RE SINCLAIR*

I. Overview and Questions

In *Shine v. Shine* (Casebook, pp.723-26), the First Circuit remarked that the final version of an earlier bankruptcy reform law, forging agreement between House and Senate versions, was produced in a "harried and hurried atmosphere" during the closing days of the 1978 Congress. Conference reports often are produced in the final days or weeks of a Congress, when members attempt to resolve disagreements between measures that may have been approved by one or both houses many months earlier. The predictable pressures associated with attempts to bridge differences of policy, doctrine, and language may well be exacerbated by the intensity of partisan divisions. This is because eleventh-hour House-Senate conference sessions are taking place during the final stages of biannual national election campaigns that affect all 435 House districts and one-third of the Senate seats.

The Conference Report for the 1986 bankruptcy law, which included the new provisions affecting family farms at issue in *In re Sinclair*, was completed October 2. In printed form, the conference report comprised 44 pages of text plus a 7-page joint explanatory statement signed by the conference committee members from both houses (10 from the House and 5 from the Senate). As is customary, the report was reproduced in full in the Congressional Record as part of the floor debates in the first chamber to take up the report. The 1986 law dealt with numerous bankruptcy-related issues apart from the family farm bankruptcies. We reproduce relevant excerpts from the floor debates in the House on October 2, and in the Senate on October 3. Consider the following questions, related to the distinct nature of conference committee reports as well as to Judge Easterbrook's analysis in *Sinclair*.

1. What differences do you see between standing committee reports you have previously studied and a conference report? Are standing committee reports signed by committee members? Are they printed in the congressional record? Are they voted on by the full Congress? How would you evaluate the reliability of a conference committee joint statement of managers compared to the views expressed in a standing committee report?

2. Based on the House and Senate floor discussions below, do you see any problems with Judge Easterbrook's view that this case involves a simple tension between clear text and clearly contrary legislative history? Is the text so clear? Is there only one "text"?

3. To which section or provision in the text does the conference report joint statement of managers refer at p.28144? How can you tell?

4. How would you describe the basic purpose of the new chapter 12 that is added to the Bankruptcy Code here? What reading of the text and legislative history best furthers that purpose?

5. How often would you expect family farmers to file for bankruptcy under chapter 11 after the effective date of this new law? What does your answer suggest regarding the meaning or primary application of "conversions" from chapter 11 to chapter 12?

II. Excerpts from 132 Cong. Rec. 28131-28148 (Oct. 2, 1986)

October 2, 1986

CONGRESSIONAL RECORD—HOU

[page 28131]

(material omitted)

□ 1645

CONFERENCE REPORT OF H.R. 5316, BANKRUPTCY JUDGES, UNITED STATES TRUSTEES, AND FAMILY FARMER BANKRUPTCY ACT OF 1986

Mr. EDWARDS of California submitted the following conference report and statement on the bill (H.R. 5316) to amend title 28 of the United States Code to provide for the appointment of additional bankruptcy judges, to provide for the appointment of United States trustees to serve in bankruptcy cases in judicial districts throughout the United States, to make certain changes with respect to the role of United States trustees in such cases, and for other purposes:

CONFERENCE REPORT (H. REPT. 99-958)

The committee of conference on the disagreeing votes of the two Houses on the amendment of the Senate to the bill (H.R. 5316) to amend title 28 of the United States Code to provide for the appointment of additional bankruptcy judges, to provide for the appointment of United States trustees to serve in bankruptcy cases in judicial districts throughout the United States, to make certain changes with respect to the role of United States trustees in such cases, and for other purposes, having met, after full and free conference, have agreed to recommend and do recommend to their respective Houses as follows:

That the House recede from its disagreement to the amendment of the Senate and agree to the same with an amendment as follows:

In lieu of the matter proposed to be inserted by the Senate amendment insert the following:

In lieu of the matter proposed to be inserted by the Senate amendment insert the following:

That this Act may be cited as the "Bankruptcy Judges, United States Trustees, and Family Farmer Bankruptcy Act of 1986".

TITLE I—AMENDMENTS TO TITLE 28 OF THE UNITED STATES CODE

(material omitted)

[page 28134]

TITLE II—AMENDMENTS TO TITLE 11 OF THE UNITED STATES CODE

Subtitle A—Activities of United States Trustees

(material omitted)

28136   CONGRESSIONAL RECORD—HOUSE   *October 2, 1986*

(material omitted)

(1) in paragraph (17) by inserting "(except when such term appears in the term 'family farmer')" after "means",

(2) by redesignating paragraphs (17) through (49) as paragraphs (19) through (51), respectively, and

(3) by inserting after paragraph (16) the following new paragraphs:

"(17) 'family farmer' means—

"(A) individual or individual and spouse engaged in a farming operation whose aggregate debts do not exceed $1,500,000 and not less than 80 percent of whose aggregate noncontingent, liquidated debts (excluding a debt for the principal residence of such individual or such individual and spouse unless such debt arises out of a farming operation), on the date the case is filed, arise out of a farming operation owned or operated by such individual or such individual and spouse, and such individual or such individual and spouse receive from such farming operation more than 50 percent of such individual's or such individual and spouse's gross income for the taxable year preceding the taxable year in which the case concerning such individual or such individual and spouse was filed; or

"(B) corporation or partnership in which more than 50 percent of the outstanding stock or equity is held by one family, or by one family and the relatives of the members of such family, and such family or such relatives conduct the farming operation, and

"(i) more than 80 percent of the value of its assets consists of assets related to the farming operation;

"(ii) its aggregate debts do not exceed $1,500,000 and not less than 80 percent of its aggregate noncontingent, liquidated debts (excluding a debt for one dwelling which is owned by such corporation or partnership and which a shareholder or partner maintains as a principal residence, unless such debt arises out of a farming operation), on the date the case is filed, arise out of the farming operation owned or operated by such corporation or such partnership; and

"(iii) if such corporation issues stock, such stock is not publicly traded;

"(18) 'family farmer with regular annual income' means family farmer whose annual income is sufficiently stable and regular to enable such family farmer to make payments under a plan under chapter 12 of this title;".

SEC. 252. APPLICABILITY OF CHAPTERS.

Section 103 of title 11, United States Code, is amended—

(1) in subsection (a) by striking out "or 13" and inserting in lieu thereof "12, or 13";

(2) by adding at the end thereof the following:

"(i) Chapter 12 of this title applies only in a case under such chapter.".

SEC. 253. WHO MAY BE A DEBTOR.

Section 109 of title 11, United States Code, is amended—

(1) in subsection (f)—

(A) by inserting "or family farmer" after "individual", and

(B) by redesignating such subsection as subsection (g), and

(2) by inserting after subsection (e) the following:

"(f) Only a family farmer with regular annual income may be a debtor under chapter 12 of this title.".

SEC. 254. INVOLUNTARY CASES.

Section 303(a) of title 11, United States Code, is amended by inserting ", family farmer," after "farmer".

SEC. 255. FAMILY FARMERS.

Title 11 of the United States Code is amended by inserting after chapter 11 the following new chapter:

"**CHAPTER 12—ADJUSTMENT OF DEBTS OF A FAMILY FARMER WITH REGULAR ANNUAL INCOME**

"**SUBCHAPTER I—OFFICERS, ADMINISTRATION, AND THE ESTATE**

"Sec.

"1201. Stay of action against codebtor.

"1202. Trustee.

"1203. Rights and powers of debtor.

"1204. Removal of debtor as debtor in possession.

"1205. Adequate protection.

"1206. Sales free of interests.

"1207. Property of the estate.

"1208. Conversion or dismissal.

"**SUBCHAPTER II—THE PLAN**

"1221. Filing of plan.

"1222. Contents of plan.

"1223. Modification of plan before confirmation.

"1224. Confirmation hearing.

"1225. Confirmation of plan.

"1226. Payments.

"1227. Effect of confirmation.

"1228. Discharge.

"1229. Modification of plan after confirmation.

"1230. Revocation of an order of confirmation.

"1231. Special tax provisions.

"**SUBCHAPTER I—OFFICERS, ADMINISTRATION, AND THE ESTATE**

"**§ 1201. Stay of action against codebtor**

"(a) Except as provided in subsections (b) and (c) of this section, after the order for relief under this chapter, a creditor may not act, or commence or continue any civil action, to collect all or any part of a consumer debt of the debtor from any individual that is liable on such debt with the debtor, or that secured such debt, unless—

"(1) such individual became liable on or secured such debt in the ordinary course of such individual's business; or

"(2) the case is closed, dismissed, or converted to a case under chapter 7 of this title.

"(b) A creditor may present a negotiable instrument, and may give notice of dishonor of such an instrument.

"(c) On request of a party in interest and after notice and a hearing, the court shall grant relief from the stay provided by subsection (a) of this section with respect to a creditor, to the extent that—

"(1) as between the debtor and the individual protected under subsection (a) of this section, such individual received the consideration for the claim held by such creditor;

"(2) the plan filed by the debtor proposes not to pay such claim; or

"(3) such creditor's interest would be irreparably harmed by continuation of such stay.

"(d) Twenty days after the filing of a request under subsection (c)(2) of this section for relief from the stay provided by subsection (a) of this section, such stay is terminated with respect to the party in interest making such request, unless the debtor or any individual that is liable on such debt with the debtor files and serves upon such party in interest a written objection to the taking of the proposed action.

"**§ 1202. Trustee**

"(a) If the United States trustee has appointed an individual under section 586(b) of title 28 to serve as standing trustee in

---

Subtitle B—Debtors Who Are Family Farmers

SEC. 251. DEFINITIONS.

Section 101 of title 11, United States Code, as amended by section 201 of this Act, is amended—

* * * *

hearing, the court may revoke such discharge only if—

"(1) such discharge was obtained by the debtor through fraud; and

"(2) the requesting party did not know of such fraud until after such discharge was granted.

"(e) After the debtor is granted a discharge, the court shall terminate the services of any trustee serving in the case.

"§1229. Modification of plan after confirmation

"(a) At any time after confirmation of the plan but before the completion of payments under such plan, the plan may be modified, on request of the debtor, the trustee, or the holder of an allowed unsecured claim, to—

"(1) increase or reduce the amount of payments on claims of a particular class provided for by the plan;

"(2) extend or reduce the time for such payments; or

"(3) alter the amount of the distribution to a creditor whose claim is provided for by the plan to the extent necessary to take account of any payment of such claim other than under the plan.

"(b)(1) Sections 1222(a), 1222(b), and 1223(c) of this title and the requirements of section 1225(a) of this title apply to any modification under subsection (a) of this section.

"(2) The plan as modified becomes the plan unless, after notice and a hearing, such modification is disapproved.

"(c) A plan modified under this section may not provide for payments over a period that expires after three years after the time that the first payment under the original confirmed plan was due, unless the court, for cause, approves a longer period, but the court may not approve a period that expires after five years after such time.

"§ 1230. Revocation of an order of confirmation

"(a) On request of a party in interest at any time within 180 days after the date of the entry of an order of confirmation under section 1225 of this title, and after notice and a hearing, the court may revoke such order if such order was procured by fraud.

"(b) If the court revokes an order of confirmation under subsection (a) of this section, the court shall dispose of the case under section 1207 of this title, unless, within the time fixed by the court, the debtor proposes and the court confirms a modification of the plan under section 1229 of this title.

"§ 1231. Special tax provisions

"(a) For the purpose of any State or local law imposing a tax on or measured by income, the taxable period of a debtor that is an individual shall terminate on the date of the order for relief under this chapter, unless the case was converted under section 706 of this title.

"(b) The trustee shall make a State or local tax return of income for the estate of an individual debtor in a case under this chapter for each taxable period after the order for relief under this chapter during which the case is pending.

"(c) The issuance, transfer, or exchange of a security, or the making or delivery of an instrument of transfer under a plan confirmed under section 1225 of this title, may not be taxed under any law imposing a stamp tax or similar tax.

"(d) The court may authorize the proponent of a plan to request a determination, limited to questions of law, by a State or local governmental unit charged with responsibility for collection or determination of a tax on or measured by income, of the tax effects, under section 346 of this title

and under the law imposing such tax, of the plan. In the event of an actual controversy, the court may declare such effects after the earlier of—

"(1) the date on which such governmental unit responds to the request under this subsection; or

"(2) 270 days after such request.".

SEC. 256. CONVERSION FROM CHAPTER 11 TO CHAPTER 12.

Section 1112(d) of title 11, United States Code, is amended—

(1) by inserting "12 or" before "13",

(2) in paragraph (1) by striking out "and" at the end thereof,

(3) in paragraph (2) by striking out the period at the end thereof and inserting "; and", and

(4) by inserting after paragraph (2) the following:

"(3) if the debtor requests conversion to chapter 12 of this title, such conversion is equitable.".

SEC. 257. CONFORMING AMENDMENTS.

(a) Title 11 of the United States Code is amended in the table of chapters by inserting after the item relating to chapter 11 the following new item:

(material omitted)

TITLE III—TRANSITION AND ADMINISTRATIVE PROVISIONS

SEC. 301. INCUMBENT UNITED STATES TRUSTEES.

(a) AREA FOR WHICH APPOINTED.—Notwithstanding any paragraph of section 581(a) of title 28, United States Code, as in effect before the effective date of this Act, a United States trustee serving in such office on the effective date of this Act shall serve the remaining term of such office as United States trustee for the region specified in a paragraph of such section, as amended by this Act, that includes the site at which the primary official station of the United States trustee is located immediately before the effective date of this Act.

(b) TERM OF OFFICE.—Notwithstanding section 581(b) of title 28, United States Code, as in effect before the effective date of this Act, the term of office of any United States trustee serving in such office on the date of the enactment of this Act shall expire—

(1) 2 years after the expiration date of such term of office under such section, as so in effect, or

(2) 4 years after the date of the enactment of this Act,

whichever occurs first.

SEC. 302. EFFECTIVE DATES; APPLICATION OF AMENDMENTS.

(a) GENERAL EFFECTIVE DATE.—Except as provided in subsections (b), (c), (d), (e), and (f), this Act and the amendments made by this Act shall take effect 30 days after the date of the enactment of this Act.

(b) AMENDMENTS RELATING TO BANKRUPTCY JUDGES AND INCUMBENT UNITED STATES TRUSTEES.—Subtitle A of title I, and sections 301 and 307(a), shall take effect on the date of the enactment of this Act.

(c) AMENDMENTS RELATING TO FAMILY FARMERS.—(1) The amendments made by subtitle B of title II shall not apply with respect to cases commenced under title 11 of the United States Code before the effective date of this Act.

(2) Section 1202 of title 11 of the United States Code (as added by the amendment made by section 255 of this Act) shall take effect on the effective date of this Act and before the amendment made by section 227 of this Act.

(3) Until the amendments made by subtitle A of title II of this Act become effective in a

(2) in accordance with the Federal Property and Administrative Services Act of 1949, the Office of Federal Procurement Policy Act, and title 31 of the United States Code.

(b) STUDY BY GENERAL ACCOUNTING OFFICE.—Not later than 1 year after the electronic case management system begins to operate in all of the judicial districts participating in the demonstration project carried out under subsection (a), the General Accounting Office shall conduct a study to compare the cost and effectiveness of such system with the cost and effectiveness of case management systems used in Federal judicial districts that are not participating in such project.

(c) TERM OF PROJECT.—The demonstration project required by subsection (a) shall be carried out until—

(1) the expiration of the 2-year period beginning on the date the electronic case management system begins to operate in all of the judicial districts participating in such project, or

(2) legislation is enacted to extend, expand, modify, or terminate the operation of such project,

whichever occurs first.

(material omitted)

* * * *

DON EDWARDS,
WILLIAM J. HUGHES,
MIKE SYNAR,
DAN GLICKMAN,
EDWARD F. FEIGHAN,
HAMILTON FISH, JR.,
E. CLAY SHAW, JR.,
CARLOS MOORHEAD,
HENRY J. HYDE,
Managers on the Part of the House.
STROM THURMOND,
ORRIN HATCH,
CHUCK GRASSLEY,
DENNIS DECONCINI,
HOWELL HEFLIN,
Managers on the Part of the Senate

JOINT EXPLANATORY STATEMENT OF THE
COMMITTEE OF CONFERENCE

The managers on the part of the House and the Senate at the conference on the disagreeing votes of the two Houses on the amendment of the Senate to the bill (H.R. 5316) to amend title 28 of the United States Code to provide for the appointment of additional bankruptcy judges, to provide for the appointment of United States trustees to serve in bankruptcy cases in judicial districts throughout the United States, to make certain changes with respect to the role of United States trustees in such cases, and for other purposes submit the following joint statement to the House and the Senate in explanation of the effect of the action agreed upon by the managers and recommended in the accompanying conference report:

The Senate amendment struck out all of the House bill after the enacting clause and inserted a substitute text.

The House recedes from its disagreement to the amendment of the Senate with an amendment which is a substitute for the House bill and the Senate amendment. The differences between the House bill, the Senate amendment, and the substitute agreed to in conference are noted below, except for clerical corrections, conforming changes made necessary by agreements reached by the conferees, and minor drafting and clarifying changes.

(material omitted)

And the Senate agree to the same.
PETER W. RODINO,

(material omitted)

(material omitted)

inordinately expensive and, in too many cases, unworkable.

Accordingly, this subtitle creates a new chapter of the Code—Chapter 12—to be used only by family farmers. It is designed to give family farmers facing bankruptcy a fighting chance to reorganize their debts and keep their land. It offers family farmers the important protection from creditors that bankruptcy provides while, at the same time, preventing abuse of the system and ensuring that farm lenders receive a fair repayment.

This new chapter is closely modeled after existing Chapter 13. At the same time, however, the new chapter alters those provisions that are inappropriate for family farmers—the requirement that the plan be filed within 15 days of the petitions; the requirement that plan payments start within 30 days of the plan confirmation; and the low debt limits found in Chapter 13.

Under this new chapter, it will be easier for a family farmer to confirm a plan of reorganization.

SUNSET PROVISION

A seven-year sunset is provided for Chapter 12. Because this is a new chapter aimed at a specific class of debtors. Congress will want to evaluate both whether the chapter is serving its purpose and whether there is a continuing need for a special chapter for the family farmer When it makes this evaluation, Congress will be able to determine whether or not to make this chapter permanent.

APPLICABILITY OF CHAPTER 12 TO PENDING CHAPTER 11 AND 13 CASES

It is not intended that there be routine conversion of Chapter 11 and 13 cases, pending at the time of enactment, to Chapter 12. Instead, it is expected that courts will exercise their sound discretion in each case, in allowing conversions only where it is equitable to do so.

Chief among the factors the court should consider is whether there is a substantial likelihood of successful reorganization under Chapter 12.

Courts should also carefully scrutinize the actions already taken in pending cases in deciding whether, in their equitable discretion, to allow conversion. For example, the court may consider whether the petition was recently filed in another chapter with no further action taken. Such a case may warrant conversion to the new chapter. On the other hand, there may be cases where a reorganization plan has already been filed or confirmed. In cases where the parties have substantially relied on current law, availability to convert to the new chapter should be limited.

USE OF CASH COLLATERAL

No debtor may use cash collateral unless the secured creditor consents, or the court, after notice and a hearing, authorizes such use.

The Conferees intend that courts will apply existing legal precedents, consistent with this legislation, when considering applications to use cash collateral.

SECTION 1204—DISPOSSESSION OF DEBTOR-IN-POSSESSION

In the event the Chapter 12 debtor is dispossessed and a trustee is substituted for the debtor in possession, the Conferees contemplate that the trustee, or the trustee's designee, will be responsible for operating the farm. This transfer of duties is modeled after provisions in Chapter 11. However, it is important to note that the Conferees do

OVERVIEW OF THE FAMILY FARM SUBTITLE OF THE CONFERENCE REPORT

Under current law, family farmers in need of financial rehabilitation may proceed under either Chapter 11 or Chapter 13 of the Bankruptcy Code. Most family farmers have too much debt to qualify as debtors under Chapter 13 and are thus limited to relief under Chapter 11. Unfortunately, family farmers have found Chapter 11 needlessly complicated, unduly time-consuming, not authorize the Chapter 12 trustee to file a plan of reorganization, as is the case in Chapter 11.

SECTION 1205—ADEQUATE PROTECTION

Under current law, the filing of a bankruptcy petition operates as an automatic stay against any act to create, perfect, or enforce an alien against property of the estate. The secured creditor must file a motion to have the stay lifted in order to proceed with foreclosure. The primary basis for lifting the stay is a lack of adequate protection. This term is not defined in the Bankruptcy Code, but examples of adequate protection are set out in 11 U.S.C. 361.

The Fourth and Ninth Circuits have held that adequate protection requires the debtor to compensate the secured creditor for so-called "lost opportunity costs" in those cases where the value of the collateral is less than the amount of debt secured by the collateral. *In re American mariner Industries, Inc.*, 734 F.2d 426 (9th Cir. 1984); *Grundy National Bank v. Tandem Mining Corp.*, 754 F.2d 1436 (4th Cir. 1985). The payment of lost opportunity costs requires the periodic payment of a sum of cash equal to the interest that the undercollateralized secured creditor might earn on an amount of money equal to the value of the collateral securing the debt.

Lost opportunity costs payments present serious barriers to farm reorganizations, because farmland values have dropped so dramatically in many sections of the country—making for many undercollaterialized secured lenders. Family farmers are usually unable to pay lost opportunity costs. Thus, family farm reorganizations are often throttled in their infancy upon motion to lift the automatic stay.

Accordingly, section 1205 of the conference report provides a separate test for adequate protection in Chapter 12 cases. It eliminates the need of the family farmer to pay lost opportunity costs, and adds another means for providing adequate protection for farmland—paying reasonable market rent. Section 1205 eliminates the "indubitable equivalent" language of 11 U.S.C. 361(3) and makes it clear that what needs to be protected is the value of property, not the value of the creditor's "interest" in property.

It is expected that this provision will reduce unnecessary litigation during the term of the automatic stay, and will allow the family farmer to devote proper attention to plan preparation.

SECTION 1206—SALES FREE OF INTEREST

Most family farm reorganizations, to be successful, will involve the sale of unnecessary property. This section of the Conference Report allows Chapter 12 debtors to scale down the size of their farming operations by selling unnecessary property.

This section modifies 11 U.S.C. 363(f) to allow family farmers to sell assets not needed for the reorganization prior to confirmation without the consent of the secured creditor, subject to approval of the court.

This section also explicitly makes clear that the creditor's interest (which includes a lien) would attach to the proceeds of the sale. Of course, the holders of secured claims would have the right to bid at the sale to the extent permitted under 11 U.S.C. 363(k).

SECTION 1224—CONFIRMATION HEARING

Section 1224 requires that Chapter 12 confirmation hearings be concluded within forty-five days after the filing of the plan.

The Conferees are aware that this imposes a burden on the bankruptcy courts. Therefore, an exception for cause is provided. While a backlog of cases is sufficient cause for an extension of the forty-five day requirement, the Conferees expect this exception to be used sparingly in order to facilitate the proper operation of Chapter 12—which proper operation depends on prompt action.

SECTION 1225—DISPOSABLE INCOME REQUIREMENT

Section 1225 defines "disposable income" as income which is not reasonably necessary to be expended for the maintenance or support of the debtor or a dependent of the debtor or for the payment of expenditures necessary for the continuation, preservation, and operation of the debtor's business.

The Conferees recognize that family farmers who are eligible for Chapter 12 may be involved in *minor* businesses not directly related to the farming operation. The Conferees intend that the term "debtor's business" in section 1225 include such businesses.

SECTION 1227—POST-CONFIRMATION CREDIT

The Conferees are concerned that farmers be able to obtain post confirmation credit. The Conferees are in agreement that current law allows Chapter 13 debtors to do so. Because section 1227 is modeled after section 1327, family farmers may provide in their plans for post-confirmation financing secured by assets that have revested in the debtor. The debtor may also use revested property to the extent it is not encumbered by the plan or order of confirmation to secure post-confirmation credit.

> PETER W. RODINO,
> DON EDWARDS,
> WILLIAM J. HUGHES,
> MIKE SYNAR,
> DAN GLICKMAN,
> EDWARD F. FEIGHAN,
> HAMILTON FISH, JR.,
> E. CLAY SHAW, JR.,
> CARLOS MOORHEAD,
> HENRY J. HYDE,
> *Managers on the Part of the House.*
> STROM THURMOND,
> ORRIN HATCH,
> CHUCK GRASSLEY,
> DENNIS DeCONCINI,
> HOWELL HEFLIN,
> *Managers on the Part of the Senate.*

Mr. EDWARDS of California. Mr. Speaker, I call up the conference report on the bill (H.R. 5316) to amend title 28 of the United States Code to provide for the appointment of additional bankruptcy judges, to provide for the appointment of U.S. trustees to serve in bankruptcy cases in judicial districts throughout the United States, to make certain changes with respect to the role of U.S. trustees in such cases, and for other purposes, and ask unanimous consent for its immediate consideration.

The Clerk read the title of the bill.

The SPEAKER pro tempore (Mr. GRAY of Illinois). Is there objection to the request of the gentleman from California?

Mr. FISH. Mr. Speaker, reserving the right to object, I just wish to say that we have no objection.

Mr. Speaker, I withdraw my reservation of objection.

The SPEAKER pro tempore. Is there objection to the request of the gentleman from California?

There was no objection.

The SPEAKER pro tempore. The Clerk will read the conference report.

The Clerk proceeded to read the conference report.

Mr. EDWARDS of California (during the reading). Mr. Speaker, I ask unanimous consent that the statement of the managers be read in lieu of the report.

The SPEAKER pro tempore. Is there objection to the request of the gentleman from California?

There was no objection.

The Clerk read the statement.

Mr. EDWARDS of California (during the reading). Mr. Speaker, I ask unanimous consent that the statement be considered as read.

The SPEAKER pro tempore. Is there objection to the request of the gentleman from California?

There was no objection.

The SPEAKER pro tempore. The gentleman from California [Mr. EDWARDS] will be recognized for 30 minutes and the gentleman from New York [Mr. FISH] will be recognized for 30 minutes.

The Chair recognizes the gentleman from California [Mr. EDWARDS].

Mr. EDWARDS of California. Mr. Speaker, I yield myself such time as I may consume.

Mr. Speaker, I am pleased to announce that an agreement has been reached with the other body on H.R. 5316, the Bankruptcy Judges, United States Trustees and Family Farmer Bankruptcy Act of 1986. I have filed the conference report on this measure with the House and urge its approval.

H.R. 5316 authorizes the creation of 52 additional bankruptcy judgeships across the country. This will help deal with the mounting bankruptcy caseload in many districts.

The bill establishes a new chapter 12 in the bankruptcy laws to help family farmers. Chapter 12 recognizes some of the problems that are unique to family farmers, while still protecting the rights of creditors. This new chapter will be implemented for a 7-year period.

H.R. 5316 also implements the United States Trustee Program of bankruptcy administration on a nationwide, self-funding basis—at no cost to the taxpayer. This program will separate the administrative functions in bankruptcy cases from judicial functions, and thus further one of the aims of the Bankruptcy Reform Act of 1978. U.S. Trustees will improve the administration of bankruptcy cases, and perform functions such as monitoring payment of witholding taxes by debtors and acting as watchdogs against fraud.

I urge the House to adopt the conference report.

Mr. Speaker, I certainly should mention that the distinguished chairman of the subcommittee and of the full Committee on the Judiciary, the gentleman from New Jersey [Mr. RODINO] did a splendid job, not only in guiding this bill through the House, but in the conference, which was, in many ways, not the easiest conference in the world. The gentleman from Oklahoma [Mr. SYNAR] was of immense help and offered invaluable advice and counsel throughout. And, of course, as always, the gentleman from New York [Mr. FISH] did a splendid job. We should all be very grateful to all the members of the subcommittee.

Mr. Speaker, I reserve the balance of my time.

Mr. FISH. Mr. Speaker, I yield myself such time as I may consume.

Mr. Speaker, I welcome this opportunity to speak in support of the conference report on H.R. 5316, legislation that authorizes additional bankruptcy judgeships, establishes a nationwide U.S. Trustee Program, and helps family farmers in financial distress. The conferees from the two bodies, in my judgment, fairly resolved the differences in the two versions of this bill and produced a product that can expedite bankruptcy adjudications, improve bankruptcy administration, and permit some family farmers to avoid liquidation.

The two bodies agreed on the need for additional bankruptcy judges to address a burgeoning bankruptcy caseload. The combined effect of dramatic increases in filings and petition termination rates that fall short of new filings has been a steady increase in the pending caseload—with bankruptcy judges falling further and further behind. An appropriate and limited response to the excessive demands on bankruptcy judges in a number of Federal judicial districts has been an objective of both bodies. The conferees agreed that the most heavily burdened judicial districts needed relief—and accepted this body's figure of 52 additional positions rather than the 49 judgeships favored by the other body.

The conference report incorporates a nationwide U.S. Trustee Program to supervise the administration of bankruptcy cases, a feature of both versions of this legislation. The nationwide program will build on the success of the pilot program currently operating in 18 of the 94 Federal judicial districts.

The U.S. Trustee Program is designed to be self-funding—with increases in bankruptcy filing fees and a new quarterly fee in reorganization cases covering the costs of the program. During our committee markup, I sponsored two amendments to improve the self-funding mechanism in an earlier version of this legislation. The first mandated transfer to the general fund of the Treasury of funds not needed for U.S. trustee operations. The second imposed the periodic fee in reorganization cases that varies depending on disbursements—a formula thoroughly studied by the committee. I am pleased that these two provisions are included in the conference committee's recommendation.

The conferees rejected a provision in the version adopted by the other body that would have allowed any Federal judicial district to elect not to participate in the U.S. Trustee Program and to have officers and employees of the courts perform U.S. trustee functions. A single, nationwide program for supervision of bankruptcy administration is essential to uniform application of our bankruptcy laws.

U.S. Trustees, located within the Department of Justice, can function as effective watchdogs of bankruptcy administration—uncovering abuses and providing guidance to private trustees. The National Bankruptcy Conference, in testimony before the Committee on the Judiciary, supported "retention of the (U.S. Trustee) program in the Department of Justice and vigorously oppose[d] its transfer (S.D.N.Y), a former U.S. trustee, emphasized that" it is of paramount importance that there be independence and a clear segregation of duties and responsibilities between the judicial aspects of a case and its administration.

The conferees did agree to an extended transition period for the States of Alabama and North Carolina as part of a compromise to drop the dual system of supervision of bankruptcy adminstration in the version passed by the other body. A possible delay in extending the U.S. Trustee Program to these two States is far preferable to a permanent, confusing dual system.

In concluding my discussion of the U.S. Trustee Program, Mr. Speaker, I would like to direct my colleagues' attention to a very important provision of the bill passed by this body and included in the conference committee's recommendation. The provision amends section 707(b) of the Bankruptcy Code to clarify that a motion for dismissal on the ground of substantial abuse may be offered by the U.S. trustee.

The 98th Congress had provided new authority in section 707(b) of title II to assure that debtors, primarily with consumer debts, would not be granted inappropriate relief under the bankruptcy laws. Section 706(b) specifies that the court, after notice and a hearing, can on its own motion, dismiss a case filed by an individual consumer debtor where it finds that granting relief would constitute a "substantial abuse" of chapter 7 provisions. Section 707(b) further stipulates that the court may not make such a dismissal "at the request or suggestion of any party in interest."

Mr. Speaker, this "substantial abuse" provision was never intended to prevent a panel trustee or a U.S. trustee from bringing evidence or information pertaining to "substantial abuse" to the attention of the court. These individuals, after all, are the most likely persons to be familiar with those types of facts in these cases. The "party in interest" phrase in section 707(b) was intended to mean creditors—not panel trustees or U.S. trustees.

Unfortunately, since 1984, many of the cases interpreting section 707(b) have concluded that a panel trustee (or a U.S. trustee) is also prevented from bringing questions of substantial abuse to the attention of the bankruptcy court. This result was simply not the goal of the conference committee or the Congress when that provision was formulated. Because of the confusion surrounding current law on this point, it must be clarified. That is why the conferees agreed to include language in section 707(b) making it clear that the U.S. trustee may move to dismiss based on substantial abuse.

Although the U.S. trustee brings the motion under this new provision, the conferees recognize that panel trustees are in a unique position to become aware of abuses in the course of performing statutory duties. Consequently, the conferees anticipate that frequently panel trustees will appear in support of motions filed by the U.S. trustees under section 707(b) as amended. It is also my hope that the Executive Office for U.S. trustees will issue uniform guidelines to U.S. trustees and panel trustees for identifying cases of substantial abuse and making section 707(b) motions—and for panel trustees to bring evidence of fraud or abuse to the attention of the U.S. trustees.

The conferees, addressing the third major subject of this legislation, resolved many differences in the details of farm bankruptcy provisions passed by the two bodies. The product of the conference committee is consistent with the objective of helping family farmers to keep their farms and satisfy creditors out of future earnings. A new chapter 12 for family farmers, patterned in a number of respects after existing chapter 13, is tailored specifically to the realities of a nationwide farm crisis. Conscious of the needs of farm lenders, the conferees attempted to include provisions that are fair to both creditors and debtors. The new chapter 12 will sunset after 7 years.

I wish to commend the gentleman from New Jersey [Mr. RODINO], the chairman of our Committee on the Judiciary, Senator THURMOND, the chairman of the Senate Committee on the

Judiciary, and the other conferees for their diligent efforts in drafting the final version of this legislation. Permit me specifically to acknowledge with appreciation the contributions of the other Republican conferees from this body, the gentleman from California [Mr. MOORHEAD], the gentleman from Illinois [Mr. HYDE], and the gentleman from Florida [Mr. SHAW]. The product of this effort, in my judgment, merits the support of our colleagues in both bodies.

Mr. Speaker, I reserve the balance of my time.

Mr. EDWARDS of California. Mr. Speaker, I yield 5 minutes to the gentleman from Oklahoma [Mr. SYNAR], who has been of immense help on this bill.

Mr. SYNAR. Mr. Speaker, first of all, let me join with all of those who have spoken before me, as well as those who are not with us this afternoon, to commend not only the gentleman from New Jersey [Mr. RODINO] for his leadership in this area, but most importantly, the gentleman from New York [Mr. FISH], for his leadership in consumer bankruptcy, as well as working with us through the farm bankruptcy legislation.

Let me also join in the accolades to Senator THURMOND, as well as Senator GRASSLEY, for their outstanding leadership, and particularly, CHARLES GRASSLEY, for his outstanding leadership in fashioning what I think is some innovative new bankruptcy law for our family farms.

Two particular features of this bill, I think, are going to be remembered from this session of Congress.

As we come to a close in this session, we will be remembered for a lot of things, including a tax bill, including, hopefully, some attack on the huge deficits which we have accumulated, and some pretty serious talk about trade.

□ 1655

I doubt there will be anything that we do that will have such an immediate impact in the grassroots of our country with respect to the situation that exists in most of the heartland, and that is in the agricultural sector, because with this new bankruptcy legislation we are going to do two things. First of all, with the creation of the bankruptcy judges, States like Oklahoma which are in desperate need of new bankruptcy judges in order to handle the explosive new load of bankruptcies that have occurred in Oklahoma City and Tulsa and throughout our State will have the opportunity hopefully to deal with the backlog. This is a major step in the right direction.

Second and more importantly, those family farmers who are facing that brink of disaster where they would have to be thrown off their farms can now look to this Congress and to this Government for new hope. That new hope is that we are going to give them the same standard that a small businessman or an individual has at this present time, which is the ability to reorganize.

Now, that means that not only are those farmers going to be winners by this legislation, but creditors who would see that they would only be able to get 10 cents on the dollar are going to be winners, and also those family farmers who surround those other farmers are going to be winners because we will not have that collapsing or domino effect from the equity of other farms going down when fellow farmers go bankrupt.

So this legislation is significant. It is important, because I think it is sending a message that we here in the U.S. Congress, we in this Government are sensitive to the family farmers who are facing this very terrible plight at this time.

You know, William Jennings Bryan in his famous speech, the Cross of Gold, almost 60 years ago, stated these words:

Destroy our cities and they will spring up again as if by magic; but destroy our farms, and the grass will grow in every city in our country.

This legislation will hopefully stem the tide that we have seen so recently in the massive bankruptcies in the family farm area.

This legislation will give us, hopefully, the new bankruptcy judges that will offer the sympathy, the sensitivity and the compassion to deal with this serious problem.

I join with my colleagues and, hopefully, this is the ray of hope that our family farmers have needed.

Mr. FISH. Mr. Speaker, I yield 2 minutes to a member of the committee, the gentleman from California [Mr. MOORHEAD].

Mr. MOORHEAD. Mr. Speaker, I am pleased that the conferees from the two bodies have reached agreement on legislation that authorizes 52 additional bankruptcy judgeships, provides for a nationwide U.S. Trustee Program, and modifies our bankruptcy law to include family farmer provisions.

We simply do not have enough bankruptcy judges today to keep up with the level of Bankruptcy Code filings. The bankruptcy adjudications problem is particularly acute in the central district of California. I am pleased that 7 of the 52 additional judgeships are designated for that district.

The U.S. Trustee Pilot Program has operated successfully for 7 years in a number of Federal judicial districts—including the central district of California—and merits extension nationwide. U.S. trustees are essential to the supervision of bankruptcy administration. A nationwide program offers the prospect of increased recoveries in bankruptcy cases and increased success in preventing fraud and abuse in the bankruptcy system.

This legislation recognizes the need for additional bankruptcy judgeships, the prospect for improved bankruptcy administration, and the potential for helping family farmers in financial distress to meet obligations out of future income. I urge the Members of this body to agree to the conference report.

Mr. FISH. Mr. Speaker, I yield such time as he may consume to the gentleman from Illinois [Mr. HYDE].

Mr. HYDE. Mr. Speaker, I am pleased to join with my colleagues in expressing support for the conference report on H.R. 5316, the bankruptcy judges, United States Trustees, and Family Farmer Bankruptcy Act of 1986. Additional bankruptcy judges are needed to respond to dramatically increased backlogs—and resulting court delays—in a number of Federal judicial districts. A nationwide U.S. Trustee Program is essential to improve oversight of bankruptcy cases, prevent abuses by the participants in the bankruptcy process, and increase the numbers of successful reorganizations. Special family farmer provisions of the Bankruptcy Code are necessary to address unique problems facing the agricultural sector of our economy.

I am particularly pleased that this legislation modifies section 523(a)(5) of the Bankruptcy Code—a provision that presently includes an exception to discharge for court-ordered support obligations. The change in this subsection will make support determinations nondischargeable regardless of whether they are made by courts.

Children are dependent on parental support regardless of whether support determinations result from court proceedings, administrative procedures, or expedited judicial processes. The Department of Health and Human Services has pointed out that "[a]llowing support debts established through administrative procedures to be discharged in bankruptcy provides a loophole to certain absent parents to eliminate their financial responsibility and may discourage states from implementing and using these more efficient and effective means of obtaining child support." It doesn't matter to the financially dependent child whether the support determination is made by a judge, hearing officer, or commissioner. The child's needs are the same regardless of whether the governmental entity involved in the determination is an agency, subagency, department, or court of a county, municipality, or State. The form of the determination—whether it is denominated a rule or an order, for example—also is unimportant from the child's standpoint. Paternity determinations in administrative proceedings are no less significant to the welfare of children than paternity determinations in judicial proceedings. The essential point is that our society must recognize the needs of children for support—and must not compromise that important principle for reasons extraneous to a child's welfare.

The modification to 11 U.S.C. 523(a)(5) is a Senate provision with only technical changes that in no way restrict the coverage of the original Senate language. The Senate provision originally took the form of legislation introduced by Senator DENTON for himself and Senator SIMON. They deserve credit for their successful efforts in the other body. I was pleased to have the opportunity to introduce a similar bill in this body, H.R. 4687.

Today I am gratified that the effort to provide additional protection for financially dependent children in our bankruptcy laws is reaching fruition. I urge my colleagues to support this legislation which includes a number of important provisions.

Mr. FISH. Mr. Speaker, I yield such time as he may consume to my colleague, the gentleman from Nebraska [Mr. DAUB].

Mr. DAUB. Mr. Speaker, because Nebraska has one of the highest backlogs of bankruptcy cases, we are the beneficiary in this legislation of an additional judge, for which we are very grateful and that is particularly important because of the farm and agricultural difficulties that we are experiencing. It is for that reason that I rise in support of this legislation.

Mr. FISH. Mr. Speaker, I yield 2 minutes to my friend and colleague, the gentleman from California [Mr. DANNEMEYER].

Mr. DANNEMEYER. Mr. Speaker, I rise in support of the conference report to accompany H.R. 5316, which authorizes additional bankruptcy judgeships nationwide. The need to authorize additional bankruptcy judgeships is undisputed as almost every judicial district has experienced an explosion in bankruptcy filings over the past 8 years.

California's Central Judicial District, of which my congressional district is a part, is one of the busiest in the country in terms of filings, cases pending, and terminations. Currently, the total number of filings per judge is 2,819. That contrasts with a national average of total filings per judge of 1,571. By making this bill a public law, seven additional bankruptcy judges will be added to California's Central District and the average filing per judge will be reduced from 2,819 to 1,780. Nationwide filings per judge will be reduced from 1,571 to 1,302. Clearly, this bill will assist the smooth operation of our bankruptcy system.

One item which was not to be addressed by this bill, was the allotment of the new judges within each judicial district. Orange County, which is a subdivision of California's Central District, has experienced a substantial caseload increase. As of May 1986, even though the two bankruptcy judges in Orange County have been working at a termination rate of 24 cases per day, or 1 every 20 minutes for an 8-hour day, there were still at least 4,278 cases pending per judge. No human can keep up that effort and it boggles the mind that they are able to perform at that level. When I offered the amendment in the Judiciary Subcommittee on Monopolies and Commercial to increase the number of new judgeships for California's Central District from 6 to 7, I wanted to specify that two of the new judgeships would be allotted to Orange County. Since subdistricts are not part of the statutory language and Congress does not choose to interfere with the internal organization of judical districts, I decided only to add one judge, with the understanding that the Judicial Conference or the central district judges themselves would be fair in apportioning the new judges. I am hopeful that the central district judges will agree with me that Orange County should receive 2 of the 7 new judges.

Finally, I want to thank the distinguished chairman of the Judiciary Committee, Mr. RODINO, and the distinguished ranking minority member, Mr. FISH, for their efforts to pass this bill. In addition, I would like to thank Mr. MOORHEAD, Mr. BERMAN, and Mr. EDWARDS of California, who are also members of the Judiciary Committee and greatly assisted my effort to add seven additional bankruptcy judges to California's Central District.

Mr. FISH. Mr. Speaker, I have no further requests for time, and I yield back the balance of my time.

Mr. EDWARDS of California. Mr. Speaker, I yield back the balance of my time, and I move the previous question on the conference report.

The previous question was ordered.

The conference report was agreed to.

A motion to reconsider was laid on the table.

———

(material omitted)

III. Excerpts from 132 Cong. Rec. 28592-28611 (Oct. 3, 1986)

BANKRUPTCY JUDGES, UNITED STATES TRUSTEES, AND FARMER BANKRUPTCY ACT—CONFERENCE REPORT

Mr. STEVENS. Mr. President, I submit a report of the committee of conference on H.R. 5316 and ask for its immediate consideration.

The PRESIDING OFFICER. The report will be stated.

The assistant legislative clerk read as follows:

The committee of conference on the disagreeing votes of the two Houses on the amendment of the Senate to the bill (H.R. 5316) to amend title 28 of the United States Code to provide for the appointment of additional bankruptcy judges, to provide for the appointment of U.S. trustees to serve in bankruptcy cases in judicial districts throughout the United States, to make certain changes with respect to the role of U.S. trustees in such cases, and for other purposes, having met, after full and free conference, have agreed to recommend and do recommend to their respective Houses this report, signed by all of the conferees.

The PRESIDING OFFICER. Without objection, the Senate will proceed to the consideration of the conference report.

(The conference report is printed in the House proceedings of the RECORD of October 2, 1986.)

Mr. THURMOND. Mr. President, I am pleased that the Senate is considering today the conference report on H.R. 5316, the "Bankruptcy Judges, United States Trustees, and Family Bankruptcy Act of 1986." A great deal of work has gone into this report by House and Senate conferees and I congratulate all who have played a part in moving this important legislation forward.

Mr. President, as my colleagues are aware, many Federal judicial district have been swamped by the significant increases in bankruptcy filings and have sought needed relief. The legislation before the Senate will provide that relief by establishing 52 new bankruptcy judgeships.

This legislation will also provide relief by making the U.S. trustee system a nationwide, permanent program. The U.S. trustee system was enacted as a pilot program in 1978. By most accounts, this pilot program has been a resounding success—contributing greatly to the orderly and efficient administration of the bankruptcy system in the districts where it has been established.

Mr. President, I am also pleased that the conference report on H.R. 5316 includes initiatives to address the increasing economic problems that have confronted family farmers. I especially want to commend my distinguished colleague from Iowa (Mr. GRASSLEY,) for his fine leadership in the development of the family farm provisions of this bill. Those provisions represent an innovative approach to a crisis which has reached serious proportions.

This legislation creates new and expanded protections for a majority of American farmers in the bankruptcy courts. It is important, however, that we remember that the family farm provisions of this bill are an extraordinary response to what is, hopefully, a temporary crisis.

This legislation modifies the provisions of adequate protection by eliminating lost opportunity cost and the "indubitable equivalent" language of 11 U.S.C. 361 (3). In essence, this is an experimental approach to address the concerns of some farmers who can not be financially restructured under current law. To address the experimental nature of this legislation the Senate insisted upon a sunset provision. The Senate preferred a 5-year authorization, however, the conferees agreed upon a 7-year period in which to use chapter 12. I am strongly supportive of the "sunset" provision in the family farm program and I strongly disagree with those who favor making the program permanent. In fact, I would have preferred a shorter "sunset" period than the 7-year period which was finally included in the report.

The legislation is meant to assist those farmers who have the true potential to reorganize and to allow them relief from heavy debt burden, and yet allow farmers to pay creditors what is reasonable under today's difficult economic situation. The conferees intended to maintain the balance in farm communities between suppliers, creditors, and farmers.

It is recognized that creditors should not shoulder all the burden of the current farm crisis and that creditors are at risk as well. When administering this chapter 12, the courts should strive to preserve this equity balance between creditors' and debtors' rights. They should appreciate the possibility of harsh consequences to secured and unsecured creditors in providing financial relief to farmers. Attempting to balance the conflicting objectives of farmer debtors and agricultural creditors has been a monumental task at best. We have insisted on a number of provisions which are supported by the creditors. We believe these improvements enhance the balance and equity of this legislation. I am informed that because of these improvements the Farm Home Administration and the American Bankers' Association no longer oppose this legislation.

I believe it will be necessary for Congress to monitor this program very carefully and to be prepared to act quickly to resolve any unintended consequences of its enactment. Perhaps the conditions which have led the Congress to enact the program will ease, making repeal of the program desirable before the 7-year sunset. We must recognize that a novel program such as this may be in need of further refinement. So I favor enactment of the family farm provisions, and urge careful and continuing analysis by the Congress to ensure the balance between the various parties involved in the agricultural sector.

Mr. President, I want to take this opportunity to commend my colleagues who have worked so hard on this legislation. I mentioned Senator GRASSLEY and his fine work on the family farm provisions, Senators HATCH, DECONCINI, and HEFLIN have also played major roles in the refinement of this bill.

I also want to commend the House members who contributed greatly to this report—especially House Judiciary Committee Chairman PETER RODINO and Congressman MIKE SYNAR.

Mr. President, I also want to commend the staff members who have worked long hours to prepare this conference report. Of my staff, Diana Waterman and Joe Buzhardt; on Senator HATCH's staff, Randy Rader and Bob Friedlander; on Senator GRASSLEY's staff, Sam Gerdano; on Senator DECONCINI's staff, Bob Feidler; and on Senator HEFLIN's staff, Karen Kremer.

Mr. President, these staff members have done a fine job in preparing this bill for passage, and I commend them for their efforts.

I ask unanimous consent to have a letter in connection with this matter printed in the RECORD.

There being no objection, the letter was ordered to be printed in the RECORD, as follows:

AMERICAN BANKERS ASSOCIATION,
Washington, DC, October 3, 1986.
Hon. STROM THURMOND,
Chairman, Senate Judiciary Committee,
U.S. Senate, Washington, DC.

DEAR CHAIRMAN THURMOND: On behalf of the American Bankers Association, I wish to express our appreciation to you, Mr. Chairman, to your entire group of Senate Conferees, and especially Senator DeConcini, and your staff for the excellent work you have done on H.R. 5316, the U.S. Trustees/Bankruptcy Judges bill.

As you know, earlier in this Congress, we testified in opposition to proposed farm bankruptcy legislation. Under your leadership, a number of key conference improvements were made to the legislation which we believe improves the balance between the concerns of agricultural creditors and farm debtors. Specifically, we strongly support the 52 additional bankruptcy judges, limitations to 90 days for debtors filing a plan, and the 7 year sunset of farm bankruptcy section.

Because of your assurances and that of Senator Grassley and Senator DeConcini to monitor closely the effects of this experimental legislation and assurances that you will address any major inequities in the next Congress, I wish to inform you that ABA does not oppose this legislation.

Again, we greatly appreciate the time and effort you and your excellent staff have devoted to the farm bankruptcy issue.

Sincerely,

EDWARD L. YINGLING.

FARM BANKRUPTCY SUBTITLE

Mr. GRASSLEY. Mr. President, I would like to briefly address myself to the farm bankruptcy subtitle of the conference report.

I am sure I need not remind the Members of this Chamber of the plight of our Nation's family farmers. The numbers of farms in financial trouble or on the brink of foreclosure is well known. But the measure of the crisis in agriculture isn't measured by cold numbers on a page. Instead, I measure it in terms of the human tragedy, the disruption of lives, and the despair of being a middle-aged farmer suddenly told to find another livelihood to support a family.

I hear it and I see it when I go back home every weekend. I know my colleagues have seen it too. We simply must stop the displacement. We must stop the bleeding on the farm.

Mr. President, I harbor no illusions about the ability of the Federal Bankruptcy Code to redress farmers' grievances. I know as well as anyone that the economic causes of the crisis in agriculture lie well beyond the realm of bankruptcy.

But hearings in the House and Senate led to the unmistakable conclusion that the Bankruptcy Code doesn't work for farmers.

The conference report subtitle on family farmer reorganization, approved by the conferees last Friday, is the culmination of more than 1½ years of effort by the House and Senate Judiciary Committees. The final product reconciles the unique attributes of farming into an existing bankruptcy framework, currently used by other small businesses and sole proprietors.

The subtitle creates an experimental, separate, chapter modeled after existing chapter 13, solely for use by family farmers with up to $1.5 million in debts.

Though the purpose is to give family farmers a fighting chance to reorganize their debts, the provisions ensure that only family farmers—not tax shelters or large corporate entities—will benefit.

Importantly, the new subtitle ensures that the bankruptcy system will not be abused. Earlier versions of this new chapter allowed a farm-debtor 240 days to file a plan. During this time, collateral could deteriorate without the promise of a confirmable reorganization plan. To address this problem, the exclusive period has been reduced to 90 days in the conference approved bill.

If time limits are not met, the case will be dismissed and cannot be refiled. This will be a powerful incentive to get these cases moving, rather than languishing in the courts. If fraud is found, the case will be dismissed or converted to chapter 7. This encourages good faith, and honest dealing by the debtor throughout the case.

The subtitle also contains a 7-year sunset, ensuring that Congress will reevaluate its effectiveness in allowing farmers to rehabilitate themselves. Let me add that I'd be the first to be willing to rethink provisions of this bill, if it proves to be unworkable. But I sincerely believe this will not be the case. It's a good, balanced product. It deserves a chance to work.

Mr. President, before leaving this bill, I would like to add my thanks and appreciation to those conferees who worked with me on this issue. First, I must thank the chairman of the Senate Judiciary Committee, Senator THURMOND, for his leadership and cooperation throughout this process. Diana Waterman, his general counsel, was of immeasurable assistance in the development of this final product. I would also like to thank Joe Buzhardt, counsel to the chairman, for his help. I would also thank Senator DeCONCINI, a cosponsor of my original chapter 12 bill, and his chief counsel, Bob Fiedler. I would also specifically thank Senator HEFLIN, who I know cares deeply about the application of our bankruptcy laws to farmers, and his chief counsel, Karen Kremer.

I cannot leave this list of "thank you's" without recognition of Bankruptcy Judges A. Thomas Small and Thomas Moore of the Eastern District of North Carolina. Their collective wisdom and experience have been critical to enactment of this legislation.

Finally Mr. President, I ask unanimous consent that a law review article by John C. Anderson, an attorney from Baton Rouge, LA, be printed in the RECORD at the conclusion of my statement. This article contains a detailed analysis of existing bankruptcy laws, and persuasively argues that these laws are inadequate for family farmers. I am confident that we have here taken a step to remedy this inadequacy.

There being no objection, the material was ordered to be printed in the RECORD, as follows:

AN ANALYSIS OF PENDING BILLS TO PROVIDE FAMILY FARM DEBTOR RELIEF UNDER THE BANKRUPTCY CODE

(By John C. Anderson*)

("The business of farming has always been subject to unpredictable financial problems, especially since the farmer's crops may be endangered by weather, insects, and natural disasters. Additionally, farmers face the normal problems of all business men, which may be increased by unusual changes in the economy. All businesses have suffered recently from increases in interest rates, fuel shortages, declines in prices offered for goods, inflation, and other general economic problems, and the farmer is no exception. In fact, the farmer's prospects have become even more bleak over the past two years, and his present and future financial problems are becoming a topic of national concern." [1])

I. INTRODUCTION

In 1982, this writer predicted that the financial problems and economies of the farming industry would rise to a level of national concern and that the exist-provisions of the Bankruptcy Code [2] were not adequate to deal with the problems of farmers and to reorganize them financially.[3] These predictions have come true, and the farming industry has virtually collapsed. The income derived by farmers from their crops has not been sufficient to keep up with the costs of operation, after taking into consideration the capital necessary to conduct the business and the natural disasters attendant with the business of farming.[4]

Because these dire predictions have become true, there is legislative movement in Congress to remedy the farmers' plight through amendments to the Bankruptcy Code which would give farmers financial relief.[5] This article will analyze the problems unique to farmers (creating their need for relief), pending family farm relief bills and legislation before Congress, and the provisions of the competing bills which should be adopted by Congress.

II. FINANCIAL PROBLEMS UNIQUE TO FARMERS AND NEED FOR RELIEF

All businesses are vulnerable to over-all economic problems, such as inflationary spirals, increases in interest rates, competition

---

Footnotes at end of article.

---

*Mr. Anderson received his J.D. from Louisiana State University Law School in 1972 and practices law in Louisiana with the firm of Due, Anderson & Adams. He is an associate member of the National Bankruptcy Conference and a member of its Committee on Farmer Insolvency. This article was prepared in conjunction with Mr. Anderson's work as a member of the Committee on Farmer Insolvency, and pursuant to a special request from counsel for the Committee on the Judiciary of the United States Senate to comment on the proposed family farmer bankruptcy bills. The National Bankruptcy Conference (the "Conference") is a voluntary organization composed of persons interested in the improvement of the Bankruptcy Code and its administration. It was formed in 1932 in connection with the 1938 revision of the Bankruptcy Act and has been active since that time on virtually all amendments to bankruptcy law. Members of the Conference include bankruptcy attorneys, law professors, and judges. On March 21, 1986, the Conference, composed of approximately sixty members and associates, met in Dallas, Texas for its mid-year meeting. The Conference's Committee on Farmer Insolvency reported to the Conference on the proposed bills pending before Congress pertaining to farmer insolvency and relief. This article is an analysis of that report and the Conference's proposed family farmer bill in comparison with the competing bills. This article represents only the position of Mr. Anderson, and it does not represent necessarily the position of the Conference or the Committee on Farmer Insolvency. All members of the Conference are free to take positions contrary to this article on any issue in representing a client, in court decisions, in legal publications, or otherwise. Mr. Anderson wishes to express his appreciation to the Committee on Farmer Insolvency for its help and particularly to Messrs. Herbert H. Anderson, Frank R. Kennedy, and Joe Lee for their comments and contributions to this article. The Committee on Farmer Insolvency of the National Bankruptcy Conference is composed of Messrs. Herbet H. Anderson (Chairman), Frank R. Kennedy, Lawrence P. King, Joe Lee, Morris W. Macey, Dennis Montali, Patrick A. Murphy, Gerald K. Smith, and John C. Anderson. Insight was also provided the author by Jeffrey W. Morris, Professor of Law, University of Dayton School of Law.

from the point of time in which the creditor could have foreclosed and sold the collateral (and continuing until the confirmation of a plan).

The Committee on Stays, Executory Contracts, and Property of the Estate for the National Bankruptcy Conference took issue initially with the *American Mariner* decision, arguing that the decision: (1) ignores the language of section 361 in general and section 361(3) in particular, which speaks of "adequate protection" of and the "indubitable equivalent" of the secured creditor's interest *in its collateral*; (2) misreads the House and Senate Reports, which make no reference (as admitted by the Court) to the "secured creditor's legal right to take possession of and sell the collateral" or its "equitable right to reinvest the proceeds of the sale," 734 F.2d at 430-1, which were written before the *indubitable equivalent* language was incorporated in section 361(3); (3) erroneously equates "indubitable equivalent" of the secured creditor's interest *in the collateral* in section 361(3) to "indubitable equivalent" of *the secured claim* in section 1129(b)(2)(A)(iii), where the latter phrase appears as an alternative to the discounted present value "as of the effective date of the plan" of deferred cash payments under the plan; (4) ignores the statutory scheme, which is that adequate protection under section 361 [with the back-up of super priority under section 507(b)] was designed to preserve only the value of the secured creditor's interest *in the collateral* in order to fix the amount of the secured claim, which must then be fully compensated by present value under the plan, whether the plan is confirmed under section 1129(a)(7) or under section 1129(b)(2)(A); (5) allows an undersecured creditor to obtain, early in the proceeding, the full value of its claim on the encumbered collateral, although the value of the unsecured creditors' claims on unencumbered collateral remains at risk throughout the case; and, at the same time, gives the undersecured creditor postpetition interest on the secured part of its claim by way of adequate protection, although section 506(b) does not allow any postpetition interest as part of the secured portion of the undersecured claim; (6) will jeopardize many reorganizations by enabling secured creditors to obtain, early in the Chapter 11 case, the full value of their claims, whereas the statutory scheme requires that they receive that value only on confirmation of a plan. This committee's recommendations are subject to further analysis before the National Bankruptcy Conference takes an official position for or against the committee's recommendations and arguments. However, this writer believes that the arguments of the committee are correct and highlight the errors in the rationale of the *American Mariner* decision. Further, the Court of Appeals for the Eighth Circuit has rejected the holding of *American Mariner*. *In re* Briggs Transp. Co., 780 F.2d 1339 (8th Cir. 1985); *but cf.* Grundy Nat. Bank v. Tandem Mining Corp., 754 F.2d 1436 (4th Cir. 1985) (wherein the Fourth Circuit adopted *American Mariner*).

It is highly doubtful that secured creditors "bargain for" any rights other than the liquidation value of their collateral, and so long as this primary right is reasonably maintained under any family farmer reorganization bill, there will be maintained an appropriate balance of policies (*i.e.*, a balancing which will arguably be more favorable to secured creditors than the Frazier-Lemke Act).

[187] *See supra* notes 71-88, 118-25 and accompanying text.

[188] *See supra* notes 90-117 and accompanying text.

[189] *See supra* notes 71-88 and accompanying text.

[190] 4 Bankr. Ct. Dec. (CRR) 462 (Bankr., S.D.N.Y. 1978). The holding of *KRO* was conditioned upon the debtor's amending its plan to provide some covenant or guaranty evincing a willingness to fulfill the repayment proposal contained on the debtor's plan. *See supra* note 143 and accompanying text.

[191] *See also* the authorities cited *supra* at notes 71-88 regarding cases under § 75 of the old Act. The result should be the same, if a farm was involved, rather than an office building.

[192] *See* Klee, *supra* notes 126 & 133, and accompanying text; *see also* the cases cited at note 136, *supra*.

[193] *See* the authorities cited *supra* note 126.

[194] 11 U.S.C. §§ 361(3), 506(a) (1986). When read together, §§ 506 and 361 operate to reinforce the existing *long-standing "rule to the effect the valueless junior secured positions or unsecured deficiency claims will not be entitled to adequate protection.* 2 W. Collier, *Collier on Bankruptcy ¶¶ 361-01 to -13 (15th ed. 1986); the reader should note that this treatise is the fifteenth edition and discusses bankruptcy law under the new Code; a discussion of the old Act is contained in the fourteenth edition, which is cited supra* note 9. *See* also the authorities cited *supra* note 105.

"The evidence before the District Court is not presented by the record. And as the Court of Appeals, if the appeal had been allowed, could have revised the ruling of the court below only in matter of law, it necessarily follows—and was conceded at the bar—that petitioners are bound by the findings of fact. Petitioners insist that their consent to the plan of reorganization was necessary or that their claims should have been accorded 'adequate protection.' But the adequate protection to which the statute refers is 'for the realization of the value of the interests, claims or liens' affected. Here the controlling finding is not only that there was no equity in the property above the first mortgage but that petitioners' claims were appraised by the court as having 'no value.' There was no value to be protected. This finding embraces whatever interests petitions may have as junior lienors under the Illinois law and, in the same aspect, the constitutional argument is unavailing as petitioners have not shown injury."

In re 620 Church St. Bldg. Corp., 299 U.S. 24, 27 (1936).

[195] 11 U.S.C. §§ 1129(b)(2)(A) (1986). *In re* Southern Missouri Towing Service, Inc., 35 Bankr. 313 (Bankr. W.D. Mo. 1983

[196] This hypothetical example is extracted from Anderson, *supra* note 1, which advanced a proposition similar to the one in the text accompanying this footnote.

[197] 11 U.S.C. § 1129(b)(2)(B) (1986). In the cases of the *In re* Pine Lake Village Apartment Co., 19 Bankr. 819 (Bankr., S.D.N.Y. 1982) and *In re* Marston Enters., Inc., 13 Bankr. 514 (Bankr., E.D.N.Y. 1981), debtors' plans were denied confirmation which attempted to allow the debtors to retain their real property and only pay secured creditors the fair market value of the property.

[197a] *Id; see* the cases cited at note 136, *supra*.

[198] *See* the authorities cited at note 136, *supra*.

[199] *Id.*

[200] Reconstruction Finance Corp. v. Denver & R.G.W.R., 328 U.S. 498 (1946); Group of Inst. Investors v. Milwaukee R., 318 U.S. 523 (1943); Consolidated Rock Prods. Co. v. DuBois, 312 U.S. 510 (1941); Case v. Los Angeles Lumber Prods. Co., 308 U.S. 106 (1939); for an expanded discussion *see* Blum, *supra* note 7; and for a discussion of how the rule of absolute priority has been modified under the new Code, *see* Klee, *supra* note 126; Anderson, *supra* note 7, § 12.24.

[201] *Accord*, Klee, *supra* note 126, at 150-56; Anderson, *supra* note 7, § 12.08.

[202] *Id.*

[203] See the authorities cited at note 136, *supra*.

[204] *See* authorities cited *supra* notes 71-88 and accompanying text.

[205] 11 U.S.C. § 1129(a)(10); *In re* Pine Lake Village Apartment Co., 19 Bankr. 819 (Bankr., S.D.N.Y. 1982); *In re* Marston Enters., Inc., 13 Bankr. 514 (Bankr., E.D.N.Y. 1981).

[206] *See* the authorities cited at notes 29 & 126, *supra*.

[207] *See, e.g., In re* Russell, 44 Bankr. 452 (Bankr., E.D.N.C. 1984); *In re* Lloyd, 31 Bankr. 283 (Bankr., W.D. Ky. 1983).

[208] 11 U.S.C. § 1325 (1986).

[209] 727 F.2d. 1379 (5th Cir. 1984).

[210] 11 U.S.C. § 303(a) provides that an involuntary case cannot be commenced against a farmer.

[210a] 11 U.S.C. § 1112(c) (1986).

[211] 747 F.2d 483 (8th Cir. 1984).

[212] *See, also, In re* Cassidy Land and Cattle Co., Inc., 747 F.2d (8th Cir. 1984) (liquidation plan may be confirmed over farmer-debtor's objection); *In re* J. F. Toner & Son, Inc., 40 Bankr. 461 (Bankr., W.D. Va. 1984) (same holding); *In re* Tinsley, 36 Bankr. 807 (Bankr., W.D. Ky. 1984) (same holding).

[213] *Compare, In re* Lange, 39 Bankr. 483 (Bankr., D. Kan. 1984) (liquidation plan can only be confirmed with the consent of the farmer-debtor); and *In re* Blanton Smith Corp., 7 Bankr. 410 (Bankr., M.D. Tenn. 1980) (same holding), *with* the cases cited at notes 209, 211 and 212, *supra*.

[214] 11 U.S.C. § 1112(c) (1986).

[215] Act of March 3, 1933, ch. 204 § 75, 47 Stat. 1467, 1470-73. This writer believes that the present legislative proposals to amend the Bankruptcy Code are not far removed in many respects from the legislation created under Section 75 of the old Bankruptcy Act.

[216] 11 U.S.C. §§ 1301, *et seq.*

[217] This writer believes that the House Bill, like Section 75, the farm relief provision of the old Bankruptcy Act, was enacted without sufficient study and analysis and that its approach to the problem (incorporation of farmer relief provisions into Chapter 13 is ill-advised. The existing Act does not have sufficient flexibility to meet the needs of farmer relief. Moreover, the farmer relief provisions should contain a "sunset" provision, causing the legislation to expire by its own terms after the farmer emergency situation passes.

Section 75 was enacted in 1933 and was not repealed by the Chandler Act of 1938, ch. 575, 52 Stat. 840 (1980). Rather, Section 75 was maintained in force until March, 1949, and was not made a permanent part of the Bankruptcy Act. 10 H. Remington, *A Treatise on the Bankruptcy Law* § 4002 (1947). The report of the House Committee on the Judiciary No. 1127, February 15, 1944, provides a historical discussion and commentary on the subject of the temporary nature of Section 75. Similarly, this writer believes that the unique problems of farmers cause a need for bankruptcy provisions different than Chapters 11 and 13 of the Bankruptcy Code, and for this reason, a separate chapter is needed for farmers. Since the proposed family farmer legislation attempts to rectify what may be only a temporary emergency situation, there appears to be good reason to have the proposed bills expire at some point in the future after the present emegency ends, unless extended by Congress in the future.

Mr. DENTON. Mr. President, I am pleased that the conference report on H.R. 5316, the Bankruptcy Judges and United States Trustees Act of 1986, maintains a provision which I introduced (originally as S. 1889) which amends the Bankruptcy Code to prevent the discharge of administratively ordered support obligations. The provision would amend the bankruptcy amendments contained in Public Law 98-353, and would fill a gap that currently permits discharge of certain spouse and child support debts through a bankruptcy declaration.

Mr. President, we enacted the Bankruptcy Amendments and Federal Judgeship Act, Public Law 98-353, in 1984. Section 454(b) of the act clarifies section 523(a)(5) of title 11, United States Code, to eliminate loopholes that formerly had allowed the discharge of spousal or child support debts through a judgment of bankruptcy.

Before the enactment of Public Law 98-353, only support debts created in separations, divorce decrees, or property settlements were protected from discharge by bankruptcy. The bankruptcy amendment extended the protection to debts established in other orders of a court of record, thereby preventing discharge in cases where a marriage has never taken place, (e.g. support awarded as a result of a court paternity determination).

Through inadvertence, however, the bankruptcy amendment did not contain a provision to protect support obligations established in State administrative proceedings.

Administrative proceedings are used by approximately 16 States to determine paternity suits and establish and enforce support obligations. Administrative proceedings have proved to be an effective and efficient procedure for resolving those disputes. It would be unfortunate if we were to prevent the States from using these procedures by denying protection from discharge by bankruptcy for administrative support judgments.

The efficient adjudication of paternity and support suits, and the enforcement of legally established support judgments, are or crucial importance to the economic health of our Nation. This provision was drawn to protect State administrative support judgments from discharge by bankruptcy, and thereby to encourage the States to resolve those suits as quickly as possible through efficient administrative forums.

In reviewing the provision, the House and Senate Conferees agreed to certain technical changes that do not restrict coverage in any way but rather ensure that support determinations made in accordance with State or territorial law (by a governmental unit as defined in 11 U.S.C. 101 (24)) are fully encompassed within the statutory language.

Mr. President, this provision will expand the exception to discharge in 11 U.S.C. 523(a)(5) to embrace support determinations involving various types of processes or procedures (e.g. administrative, expedited judicial) and various forms of determinations (e.g. rules, orders). Such determinations may be made by hearing officers or commissioners of agencies, subagencies, departments or courts of counties, municipalities or States—to cite some examples only.

I thank the conferees for supporting this provision and I urge my remaining colleagues to adopt it.

Mr. DeCONCINI. Mr. President, I have been an interested and active participant in the development of much of the legislation that is contained in the conference report that is now being presented for final passage. I support the overall package, but I do have reservations about some parts of the package. For the record, I would like to state my position on some aspects of the bill.

Title I of the bill creates 52 new bankruptcy judgeships. I have always been a strong supporter of the needs of the judicial branch and I have had a long, respectful, and satisfactory relationship with the bankruptcy judges of the Nation. I have often felt they have not received the treatment that their position and magnitude of their jobs deserves. By the same token, I was not convinced during the committee process that the caseload and workload of the bankruptcy judges demonstrated a need for more than 50 new bankruptcy judges. I would have supported a number closer to 30. The report that accompanied the Judiciary Committee action on the bankruptcy judgeship bill spells out in greater detail my reasoning and that of the

committee. I hope that is the future the judicial conference will review the report and respond in an appropriate manner. With judgeships running more than a quarter of a million dollars a year to maintain, we cannot engage in the luxury of having surplus judges. I urge the judicial conference to limit their judgeship request to those that are essential and to also review existing judicial position to see if they need to be maintained.

Subtitle B of title I, and title II of the bill deal with the extension and expansion of the U.S. Trustee Program. I have been a strong supporter of the U.S. Trustees, and am pleased that the provisions of this bill as they apply to the Trustees came out as they did. I regret, however, that the concept of "opt-out" as contained in the bill as it passed the Senate was not continued in a greater form. The bill provides that 88 of the judicial districts of the country will permanently go into the Trustee Program and that six districts, all located in Alabama and North Carolina, will be in a separate program much as exists presently, for 6 years. I believe that the theories of bankruptcy administration would have been better served had there been an opportunity for more districts to "opt-out" of the Trustee system and to participate in a program where a Bankruptcy Administrator within the judicial branch would have been responsible for bankruptcy case administration. As the bill stands, I don't believe the concepts of bankruptcy estate administration as advanced by the judicial conference will have a full and fair opportunity to prove themselves.

At this point I certainly want to compliment all the personnel of the U.S. Trustee Program for the outstanding job they have done in all district. They have a record of success, but with the added powers and authority contained in this bill, the need will be even greater for the Attorney General to closely monitor the Trustee activities to ensure that abuses of that power do not occur. Finally, I want to compliment the fine staff of various components of the Department of Justice for all their dedication and work on this bill. Names of people who have been especially important in the process include the Attorney General; the Deputy, Mr. Burn; Tom Stanton, Vince Lobisco and Barbara O'Conner of the executive office of U.S. trustees; and Jean FitzSimon, John Bolton and Tom Boyd from other sections of the Department of Justice. They are tireless proponents of the program and able technicians whose assistance was most appreciated.

Finally, Mr. President, I want to comment for a moment on section 255 of the bill which creates a new chapter 12 of the bankruptcy code especially designed to accommodate the family

farmer. This chapter is in response to the tremendous hardship that has afflicted many segments of the farm community with the large resulting number of bankruptcies. It was concluded that the present structure of the bankruptcy code simply didn't fit the special economic circumstances that attend the family farmer. I was proud to support the original Grassley bill on this subject in the Senate and I do feel that there is some merit in attempting to address the needs of the farmer through a separate chapter to the bankruptcy code. However, I am troubled by some provisions of the new chapter 12 which I fear might inadvertently cause substantial economic dislocation and bring about an unfair result.

I am very worried that the extremely debtor oriented provisions of this chapter may force our farm lender to write off hundreds of millions of dollars of farm debt with no hope of recovering this debt when the farm crisis ends. Can our credit community afford this? Can our rural banks, teetering now, take another hit? Can the Farmer Credit System take yet another significant economic reversal? Is it fair to ask the creditor to absorb the huge losses that can reasonably be expected to result from this bill? Will there be credit available for farmers in the future, or will this bill result in shutdown of credit in the agricultural area?

These are serious and far reaching questions to which I do not have the answer, but I fear we have tilted the pendulum too far in the direction of the financially troubled farmer. The result may well be that domino effect will occur that in the long run will prove detrimental to the farm sector.

The provision of this bill that troubles me the most is the provision that will permit a family farmer to go into bankruptcy, write down the secured debt to the current value of the land, and then begin to pay the creditor based on what amounts to a new mortgage based on the value of the farm. The thought that a person cannot pay their debt and yet may retain their property and only continue payments based on the value of the property as the filing of the bankruptcy is entirely new—and dangerous. Why won't every farmer with a substantially undercollateralized loan against his farm declare bankruptcy?

Let me put the theory into numbers. Let us assume that in the State of Iowa in 1980, a farmer purchased a piece of land for $1.2 million and took out a $1 million mortgage on the property. In the past 6 years, on the average, there has been a 60-percent decrease in land values in Iowa. In rough terms then, the farm purchased for $1.2 million is now worth $500,000. Another way to look at it is that the secured creditor now has a secured loan for $500,000 and an undercollateralized, unsecured loan for $500,000. Now what will happen under this bill? If the farmer declares bankruptcy under the new chapter 12, the farmer will (1) wipe out for all intents and purposes the $500,000 unsecured portion of the loan; (2) the farmer will only have to make payments on the new, depressed value of the farm—$500,000; and (3) the farmer keeps the farm! Why won't any farmer who finds himself in a situation like the above, where the farmer has a large debt service on property that has substantially depreciated, go into bankruptcy? I fear that we have created a legal atmosphere that may well encourage farm bankruptcies and that farmers who can now manage to work things out with their creditors in some satisfactory manner to both will no longer have that incentive to reach mutual agreement.

Figures on the amount of undercollateralized debt are hard to come by but I will throw out just a few by way of example of the potential magnitude of the problem. My best estimate is that about 40 percent of all farm debt held by institutional investors is undercollateralized. In dollar amounts, the figure exceeds $20 billion. Ninety percent of all debt is held by farmers whose debt is less than $1.5 million, the ceiling under this bill for farmers to take advantage of this chapter. In other words, almost all farmers will be eligible for this chapter. The Farm Credit System lists $2.1 billion in substantially undercollateralized debt. Who knows how much debt that is undercollateralized is held by the Farmers Home Administration—clearly a figure in the billions.

Mr. President, I don't want to be a "pollyanna" crying "wolf" needlessly, but it is my most sincere fear that we may regret our actions tonight. The farm title has substantially revised long held doctrines of the bankruptcy code such as the absolute priority rule and the theories of adequate protection. This bill by not including the doctrines embraced by 1111(b) of the bankruptcy code has precluded a creditor from any hope of participating in an upswing in the value of its collateral. In many other ways, our actions tonight are based on the utmost in good intent—but with no real knowledge of the implications. I urge the proponents of this new farm chapter, Senator GRASSLEY and Congressman SYNAR, to monitor the ramifications of this chapter closely and to resolve to redress inequities that may result in a prompt fashion. I greatly admire both of these gentlemen, and I fervently hope that my judgment is misplaced and that their judgment is fully rewarded.

In closing, I want to thank again the distinguished chairman of the Judici-

ary Committee, Senator THURMOND, and Senator HEFLIN for all their efforts on behalf of this bill. I also congratulate and thank Chairman RODINO on the House side for his yeoman efforts on behalf of this bill. Also in line for great praise for the roles they have played as "think tanks" on behalf of bankruptcy are all the members of the American Bankruptcy Institute and the National Bankruptcy Conference. Time and again we call upon these volunteer organizations for assistance and they respond with donations of their time and talent. Particularly to be commended are individuals such as Harry Dixon, Ken Klee, Rich Levin, Lawrence King, Robert Zinman, and William Perlstein. Finally, I would like to thank Bob Feidler of my staff for his many efforts on this bill and in the bankruptcy area.

Mr. HATCH. Mr. President, I rise in support of the Bankruptcy Judges and United States Trustees Act of 1986 (H.R. 5316). Despite the pessimists and the naysayers, and despite those who predicted that a satisfactory Bankruptcy Act could never meet the different perspectives and perferences of the varying regions of the country, we have developed a sound and solid conference bill. It is good bill. It establishes 52 much needed judgeships. It establishes 21 Federal judicial districts for the bankruptcy courts. It has refined and extended the bankruptcy trusteeship program, setting out in some detail the duties of the U.S. trustees, but also allowing some flexibility to the Attorney General to enlarge upon those duties if the occasion should rise.

This bill also allows a bankruptcy court to take any action on its own, or to make any necessary determination to prevent an abuse of process and to help expedite a case in a proper and justified manner. If necessary, a U.S. trustee can be designated to serve in one other region than his own, and a U.S. trustee can, in an emergency situation, serve as a case trustee after certification by the U.S. trustee that a disinterested person could not be found to fill the position of case trustee. This, helps to expedite matters and serves the interests of justice.

I have already indicated my concern over the precise wording of section 707(b) of the Bankruptcy Code. Several courts, primarily in Ohio, have taken the position that the bankruptcy trustee is technically "a party in interest" and may not bring evidence of abuse to the attention of the court. This was not the result we intended to achieve in the 1984 Bankruptcy Act. As a result of this conference bill, the U.S. trustee will have the opportunity to inform the court of fraud or abuse. This explicit authority will go a long way toward improving the current confusion and clarifying the real intent of the 1984 legislation.

The new provisions for the family farmer will aid in the preservation of the family farm while maintain at the same time the integrity of the bankruptcy system and meeting the needs of bona fide farm creditors. It also enables a family farm in trouble to undergo a reorganization without going under financially. That is for the good of all of us. I commend my colleague Senator GRASSLEY for this efforts in this regard. He has helped to improve a difficult situation for farmers and nonfarmers alike. The electronic case management demonstration project is an interesting means of evaluating by a cost benefit analysis the enormous caseload problem and the effectiveness of electronic case management remedy.

This is a bill that improves the law. It is a bill that improves the system. It is a bill which will assist creditors and debtors alike. I strongly support its passage, and I urge my colleagues to do the same. This will serve the interests of all parties, and by so doing, will serve the interests of the country.

UTAH BANKRUPTCY JUDGE

Mr. President, I commend the chairman of the Judiciary Committee, Senator STROM THURMOND, for his leadership in setting the bankruptcy courts of the United States on a firm constitutional footing. The adoption of the Landmark Bankruptcy Act in 1984 inaugurated a period of renewed commitment to sound judicial administration of our article I insolvency courts. This sound judicial administration, however, is jeopardized in some districts by inadequate resources to meet the needs. Accordingly, I once again commend the chairman for undertaking the important task of reviewing the need for additional judgeships to keep our bankruptcy system working smoothly.

In this connection, I introduced in March 1985 S. 618, a bill to provide for the appointment of an additional bankruptcy judge for the district of Utah. The need for enactment of this measure has been recently confirmed by the Administrative Office of the U.S. Courts which also requested creation of a new Utah bankruptcy judgeship to prevent disruption of the administration of justice in that part of the tenth circuit.

In making that request, the Administrative Office presented some alarming statistics regarding the massive caseload of the bankruptcy court of the State of Utah. Among the most reliable statistics in assessing the caseload of bankruptcy courts is the number of chapter 11 filings. Chapter 11 cases generally require extensive contested court hearings and adversary proceedings, while chapter 7 and 13 proceedings are generally very administrative and handled out of court. In 1981, the first year that applicable statistics were available, the total number of chapter 11 bankruptcy filings per judgeship in the State of Utah were 139—a figure many times in excess of the national average of 35. By 1985, the number of chapter 11 filings per judge has risen astronomically to 213—a figure still far above the national average of 92 per judge.

When compared with the national average of filings per bankruptcy judgeship in other categories, Utah's Bankruptcy Court must still be considered blatantly overburdened. For instance, the average number of petitions filed per judgeship in the Nation during 1985 was 1,586, while in Utah, the number stood at 1,979.

A clear indication that Utah's two bankruptcy judges are overworked is that they terminate an average of 77 of the complicated chapter 11 cases yearly, while national average for bankruptcy judges is 30—less than half the Utah totals.

This rigorous caseload clearly disrupts the administration of justice in this vital area of law. Utah bankruptcy judges must spend very long hours on the bench. Utah must often rely on visiting judges. And most distressing, Utah citizens and businesses must occasionally endure costly delays in seeking resolution of their claims.

In article I, section 8 of the U.S. Constitution we find that Congress has been empowered to create uniform bankruptcy laws. The efficiency of uniform bankruptcy laws, however, is imperiled when article I bankruptcy courts are presented with enormous caseloads. In fact, when compared with other districts in the tenth circuit, Utah falls even further behind in the acquisition of necessary bankruptcy adjudicatory resources.

Judge Ralph R. Maybey, a former Utah bankruptcy court judge with a national reputation, has often mentioned Utah's troubled position in the tenth circuit. The Utah district, in 1984, was dealing with almost four times the number of chapter 11 filings, more than two times the number of chapter 13 filings, and just under three times the number of adversary filings per judgeship as compared with other districts in the tenth circuit. Mr. Maybey, referring to the previous statistics, said, "Utah's problem is by far the worst of any in the circuit—and I dare say as bad as anywhere."

The Honorable Aldon J. Anderson, former chief judge of the U.S. District Court, district of Utah, prior to his recent resignation, repeatedly requested a third bankruptcy judgeship position in Utah. His pleas became increasingly emphatic as he saw the "trial calendars * * * backlogged approximately 2 years." He affirmed that the delay of appointment has not only been an inconvenience to the two presently overburdened judges, but also,

the delay "has worked in justice on litigants."

This situation is certainly worthy of congressional attention. If our court systems are to maintain the respect they require to dispense impartial and efficient justice, they must not fall into the dilemma currently facing the Utah bankruptcy bench. Accordingly, I urge my colleagues to join me in correcting this Utah situation and the same problems that have arisen in other districts that warrant this corrective legislation.

Mr. THURMOND. Mr. President, I would like to comment on one important provision in this conference report. Last May, when the Senate acted on this bill, I voiced my strong support for a provision sponsored by my distinguished colleague from Utah, Senator HATCH, to clarify the ability of the bankruptcy trustee to bring to the attention of the court information relating to substantial abuse of chapter 7 procedures. I am pleased to inform my colleagues that a similar provision is contained in the conference report. This provision explicitly allows the U.S. trustee not only to bring such information to the court's attention, but also to allow the U.S. trustee to move to dismiss the case on the grounds of substantial abuse. Obviously, the panel trustee will also be involved in this process, since he has important access to information concerning fraud and abuse. In order to further facilitate our intent and our goal in this area—protecting the integrity of the process by ensuring that the court receives all relevant information from objective sources—we expect the panel trustee to advise the U.S. trustee of all such pertinent information. The panel trustee would appear on behalf of any motion filed in this regard.

Mr. HATCH. If I might comment on the excellent presentation of the distinguished chairman of the Judiciary Committee, Senator THURMOND, I would like to add that it is our expectation that the Executive Office for U.S. Trustees will take all appropriate steps to facilitate close cooperation between the U.S. trustees and the panel trustees in these matters. This cooperation will thereby ensure the ability of the U.S. trustee to carry out his statutory responsibilities under section 707(b). In other words, Mr. President, this provision will enable the panel trustee and the U.S. trustee to work closely when dealing with any information or evidence relating to fraud or abuse. The conferees anticipate that the Executive Office for U.S. Trustees will issue uniform guidelines to both the U.S. trustees and the panel trustees for identifying cases of substantial abuse. This will serve to ensure the integrity of the bankruptcy system.

Mr. THURMOND. Mr. President, this legislation authorizes creation of 52 new bankruptcy judgeships, a na-

tionwide U.S. Trustee Program and significant reform in the area of farm bankruptcy. After close scrutiny and careful searching we have come to the conclusion that there are simply no new funds available for the 52 judgeships. Accordingly, we are now only authorizing the positions. The appointment of the new judgeships will not be made until funds are made available.

It is my understanding that efforts will be made to fund all 52 positions in a fiscal year 1987 supplemental and in fiscal year 1988 appropriations.

I ask my distinguished colleagues from New Mexico and Florida to be sure to include the funds for this authorization.

Mr. DOMENICI. I fully expect that in preparing the fiscal year 1988 budget resolution for function 750 including the Judiciary, the Senate Budget Committee will include the annualized fiscal year 1987 level including the impact of this bankruptcy authorization.

Mr. CHILES. I join Chairman DOMENICI in doing what we can to ensure a realistic fiscal year 1988 budget providing for the amount necessitated by this authorization.

Mr. THURMOND. I thank my colleagues for their kind assistance in this matter.

The PRESIDING OFFICER. The question is on agreeing to the conference report.

The conference report was agreed to.

CORRECTION OF TECHNICAL ERRORS IN H. CON. RES. 401

Mr. STEVENS. Mr. President, I ask unanimous consent that the Senate proceed to the consideration of House Concurrent Resolution 401.

The PRESIDING OFFICER. The concurrent resolution will be stated by title.

The assistant legislative clerk read as follows:

A concurrent resolution (H. Con. Res. 401) to correct technical errors in the enrollment of the bill S. 2069.

The PRESIDING OFFICER. Is there objection to the present consideration of the concurrent resolution?

Mr. BYRD. Mr. President, there is no objection on this side to the immediate consideration of the concurrent resolution.

The Senate proceeded to consider the concurrent resolution.

The PRESIDING OFFICER. The question is on agreeing to the concurrent resolution.

The concurrent resolution was agreed to.

Mr. STEVENS. Mr. President, I move to reconsider the vote by which the concurrent resolution was agreed to.

THE 1934 INDIAN REORGANIZATION ACT, THE 1972 CIVIL RIGHTS AMENDMENTS, AND *MORTON V. MANCARI*

I. Overview and Questions

The Indian Reorganization Act of 1934 followed several months of hearings and extended discussion within the committees responsible for Indian Affairs in both House and Senate. The comprehensive statute, which President Roosevelt described as "a measure of justice that is long overdue," extended to Indians new rights of local self-government as well as new opportunities for education and economic assistance. Section 13 of the bill, providing for preferential hiring of qualified Indians in the service of the agency that manages their affairs, is discussed in the House committee report and on the House and Senate floor.

Excerpts from the floor debate accompanying Title VII of the 1964 Civil Rights Act discuss the addition of a special provision preserving these preferential hiring practices for enterprises operating on or near Indian reservations. Excerpts from the floor debate accompanying the 1972 amendments to Title VII reflect no attention to or awareness of Indian hiring preferences.

1. The majority in *Morton v. Mancari* observes that a federal policy according some hiring preferences to Indians in the Indian service dates back as far as 1834 (Casebook, p.1083). Based on your review of the 1934 statute's legislative history, what motivated Congress to enact such preferences? Would you describe Congress's policy commitment as casual? Consciously committed? Deeply determined?

2. Does the length of time of, or degree of congressional commitment to, a statutory policy matter when seeking to determine whether there has been a repeal by implication?

3. Congress added two contiguous sections to its final version of Title VII of the 1964 Civil Rights Act. One clarifies that the law does not require employers to engage in preferential hiring to promote racial balance in their workforce. The other permits preferential hiring practices toward Indians by enterprises on or near reservations. Does the juxtaposition of these two sections reflect anything about the self-consciousness or intensity of Congress's position toward preferential hiring for Indians?

4. The 1972 Amendments to Title VII expanded the enforcement powers of the EEOC and extended the Act's anti-discrimination principles to state, local, and federal government employers. The new law made no mention of an Indian hiring preference for private or government employers. Is there anything in the 1934 or 1964 legislative history that counsels *against* understanding the 1972 Act as an implied repeal of previously enacted Indian preferences?

II. H.R. Rep. No. 73-1804 at 1, 4-8 (May 28, 1934)

73D CONGRESS 2d Session	HOUSE OF REPRESENTATIVES	REPORT No. 1804

READJUSTMENT OF INDIAN AFFAIRS

MAY 28, 1934.—Committed to the Committee of the Whole House on the state of the Union and ordered to be printed

Mr. HOWARD, from the Committee on Indian Affairs, submitted the following

REPORT

[To accompany H.R. 7902]

[page 4:]

SEC. 13. The Secretary of the Interior is directed to establish standards of health, age, character, experience, knowledge, and ability for Indians who may be appointed, without regard to civil-service laws, to the various positions maintained, now or hereafter, by the Indian Office, in the administration of functions or services affecting any Indian tribe. Such qualified Indians shall hereafter have the preference to appointment to vacancies in any such positions.

[page 5:]

STATEMENT

This measure has been under consideration by the committee for nearly 3 months. Extensive hearings were held, the first five parts of which have been printed and given the widest circulation. Every person or organization so desiring was heard or given opportunity to present a written statement. Testimony concerning all phases of the measure were received from a wide variety of interested persons, especially from the Indians themselves, from the Department, from numerous associations concerned with Indian welfare, from Members of Congress, from scientists, attorneys, and many others. Few measures have had more thorough consideration and discussion by those to be affected thereby than this proposed legislation.

6 READJUSTMENT OF INDIAN AFFAIRS

The hearings left no doubt as to the imperative need of comprehensive legislation to remedy the existing conditions among the American Indians generally. There was quite general agreement upon the purposes sought to be achieved by the proposed measure. However, a wide difference of opinion developed as to the wisdom of some features of the bill.

After careful consideration the committee ordered the bill reported with an amendment, striking out all after the enacting clause and inserting the committee substitute.

[page 7:]

Section 11 authorizes the creation of a revolving Indian loan fund of $10,000,000. Since the protective restrictions against the sale or encumbrance of his property bar the ward Indian from the customary sources of credit, it is imperatively necessary to set up a modest credit system.

Section 12 authorizes an appropriation of $250,000 annually for the vocational and technical education of Indians.

Section 13 enables the Secretary to establish standards which will admit to the Indian Service qualified Indians now barred by the severe academic requirements of the general civil-service examinations.

Section 14 restricts the act to the continental United States and Alaska.

Section 15 protects certain treaty rights of the Sioux depending for their fulfillment on the continued allotment of Sioux tribal lands.

[page 8:]

THE WHITE HOUSE,
Washington, April 28, 1934.

Hon. EDGAR HOWARD,
House of Representatives.

MY DEAR MR. HOWARD: The Wheeler-Howard bill embodies the basic and broad principles of the administration for a new standard of dealing between the Federal Government and its Indian wards.

It is, in the main, a measure of justice that is long overdue.

We can and should, without further delay, extend to the Indian the fundamental rights of political liberty and local self-government and the opportunities of education and economic assistance that they require in order to attain a wholesome American life. This is but the obligation of honor of a powerful nation toward a people living among us and dependent upon our protection.

Certainly the continuance of autocratic rule, by a Federal department, over the lives of more than 200,000 citizens of this Nation is incompatible with American ideals of liberty. It also is destructive of the character and self-respect of a great race.

The continued application of the allotment laws, under which Indian wards have lost more than two-thirds of their reservation lands, while the costs of Federal administration of these lands have steadily mounted, must be terminated.

Indians throughout the country have been stirred to a new hope. They say they stand at the end of the old trail. Certainly, the figures of impoverishment and disease point to their impending extinction, as a race, unless basic changes in their conditions of life are effected.

I do not think such changes can be devised and carried out without the active cooperation of the Indians themselves.

The Wheeler-Howard bill offers the basis for such cooperation. It allows the Indian people to take an active and responsible part in the solution of their own problems.

I hope the principles enunciated by the Wheeler-Howard bill will be approved by the present session of the Congress.

Very sincerely yours,

FRANKLIN D. ROOSEVELT.

III. Excerpts from 78 Cong. Rec. 9269-9270 (May 22, 1934)

1934   CONGRESSIONAL RECORD—HOUSE   **9269**

(material omitted)

[Page 9270:]

* * * *

I have always favored the employment of Indians who are competent and honest in the Indian Service, regardless of civil-service rules and regulations. In the event lands are purchased for Indians and administered as subsistence homesteads, those employed to assist the Indians in the cultivation of their lands, the harvesting of their crops, and the caring for their livestock should be Indians who live among them and speak the language and who are in sympathy with them.

We should assist the Indian in every way to earn a living and to qualify him to assume the full responsibility of citizenship and encourage him to take part in his local and State governments. We should inspire confidence in every Indian in his Government, because in the end he is destined to take his place along the side of his white neighbor and to become a part of the Government and to rely upon the protection of its laws. Most, if not all, restricted Indians have unrestricted relatives against whom this legislation would create a prejudice.

* * * *

[Mr. HASTINGS:]

* * * *

It is urged that the employees of an Indian community should be largely Indian. I am in sympathy with that suggestion. This could be done by amending the civil-service laws. I have always insisted that more Indians who could speak the language of the respective tribes should be employed, men and women, who are in sympathy with the members of the tribes, and who live their lives, instead of employing those from the eligible list of graduates from eastern colleges, but who have no practical knowledge of Indian affairs and who of necessity are not in as deep and continued sympathy with the Indians whom they serve. This would not require the chartering of a community.

* * * *

IV. Excerpts from 78 Cong. Rec. 11726-731 (June 15, 1934)

(material omitted)

Mr. HOWARD. Mr. Speaker, I feel I ought to acquaint the membership of the House with the fact that our splendid Committee on Indian Affairs has held no less than 29 different sessions for the consideration of this bill. I feel I should further state that when the bill was finally reported every element of controversy had been eliminated. Manifestly, we cannot speak at length regarding the merits of this legislation, but I am quite sure that every one of the members of my own committee is qualified to answer such questions as those who desire information may submit.

Mr. Speaker, it seems best that in the consideration of this measure, and in order to have it better understood, we should view somewhat the background of the present Indian problem.

Interwoven in that problem is the position of our Government, as guardian, with respect to the Indian, as ward. Bear in mind, please, that the status of ward was not of the Indians' seeking. It was forced upon him by our Government. On its part that relationship should be one of sacred trust. The proper administration of that trust is a matter which is vital to the Indian. As it raises or lowers the Indian in the social and economic scale, and thereby tends to make him self-supporting or a public charge, it is of direct interest to the American taxpayer.

Viewing the results of that guardianship, it is difficult for me to speak dispassionately. I shall not ask my colleagues to examine in detail a certain page of history upon which no American may gaze with feeling of pride. Suffice it to say that it reveals an almost uninterrupted succession of broken treaties and promises, and a record of the ruthless spoliation of defenseless wards. With all the vigor at my command I protest against allowing that shameful and inhuman treatment to continue a day longer without doing all in my power to put an end to it.

A few comparisons may be helpful in understanding the conditions which this bill is designed to correct. In making those comparisons I shall not turn back a single page of history. I shall only return to a period within the memory of most of us here today, to the year 1887, when the last major Indian policy, the general allotment law, was enacted. Indian statistics are somewhat incomplete and may not always be entirely accurate, but I believe those I shall now present are approximately correct.

In 1887 our Indian wards numbered 243,000. They owned 137,000,000 acres of land, more than one-third good farming land and a considerable portion valuable timberlands. Today they number about 200,000. Their land holding has shrunk to a mere 47,000,000 acres. Of this remnant only 3,500,000 acres may be classed as farming lands, 8,000,000 acres as timberlands of any value, 16,000,000 acres as good grazing lands, and 19,000,000 acres, almost one-half the Indian land remaining, as desert or semiarid lands of limited use or value.

The average holding of farm land per Indian in 1887 was slightly more than 160 acres, as against an average holding of 17 acres today.

In 1887 there were less than 5,000 landless Indians. Today there are more than 100,000.

In 1887 Indian trust funds, which are administered by the Government, aggregated $29,000,000. Notwithstanding the subsequent addition of more than $500,000,000, derived largely from the sale of Indian lands and assets, these funds today amount to but $13,500,000. A factor in the dissipation of these funds has been their use to pay the salaries of employees, generally whites, in the Indian Service. Although greatly reduced in recent years, the amount so used is still in excess of $2,000,000 per annum.

In 1887 the average Indian was self-supporting. Today nearly one-half are virtual paupers. The number of such is steadily increasing. A recent survey among typical Indian families by the Indian Office shows the average per capita income to be but $48 per annum in money and in produce raised and consumed.

The annual death rate among the Indian population in 1887 is given as 18 per thousand. Today it is 26 per thousand, more than twice that of the general population.

These comparisons tell a tragic story. They reveal a lamentable lowering of the social and economic status of the Indian. They show a startling loss of assets and an income diminished to the point where the burden of Indian care is becoming a heavy one upon the local and Federal Governments.

It is not my purpose at this time to dwell upon the responsibility for this sad state of affairs. In all fairness, it may be said that it is due in part to well-intentioned but mistaken policies, and in part to improper administration.

The failure of their governmental guardian to conserve the Indians' lands and assets, and the consequent loss of income or earning power, has been the principal cause of the present plight of the average Indian. The loss of land is primarily due to the Allotment Act of 1887 and the manner in which it has been administered. Often against their wishes allotments were forced upon Indians who were not prepared to manage their property. They have since sold their land or had it sold at tax sale. A large acreage of inherited allotted land has also been lost to the Indians through partition sales. Much so-called "ceded" or "surplus" Indian land has been sold to whites. Immense sums derived from the sale of Indian lands, timber, oil, and minerals have been squandered by the guardians. Whether these funds were disbursed to the Indians in per capita payments or whether they were paid as salaries to Indian Bureau employees, the result is now the same.

The deplorable conditions I have outlined were clearly developed in extensive hearings before the committee over a period of 3 months. Every interested person and organization, and especially the Indians themselves, were given opportunity to express their views. The hearings have been published in nine parts and are now available.

As a result of these hearings, there was general agreement that the present state of Indian affairs is far from satisfactory and that comprehensive legislation dealing with the subject was necessary. However, considerable controversy arose over many features of the original measure. In its desire to do all possible without further delay the committee, without a dissenting vote, has reported this substitute which embodies the features most urgently required, and eliminates controversial features upon which agreement could not be reached. The title creating a special Federal court of Indian affairs has been eliminated, as have the provisions authorizing the creation of chartered Indian communities. All compulsory features of the original measure have been omitted. Numerous other changes and eliminations have been made to meet objections raised.

While it is not as comprehensive as I personally would wish, this substitute measure contains many provisions which are fundamentals of a plan to enable the Indians generally to become self-supporting and self-respecting American citizens. Those provisions may be summarized as follows: Conservation of Indian lands; creation of a credit system for the Indians; extension of the trust period on Indian lands; organization of tribal councils responsive to the Indians and with authority to speak for them; education, vocational and technical, of the Indians; and admission of qualified Indians to the Indian Service.

Before submitting a more detailed discussion of this bill I desire to call special attention to a few sections which constitute the backbone of the measure.

Section 1 prohibits further allotments. It stops the big hole through which 90,000,000 acres of land have passed from Indian ownership. Note well the fact that those tribes which escaped partition and individual allotment have not lost an acre of land. Among these fortunate tribes are the Menominees of Wisconsin, the Red Lake Chippewas of Minnesota, the Pueblos of New Mexico, the Navajos and the Apaches of Arizona. Would that the Indians of my own State had been as fortunate.

Section 2 endeavors to conserve allotted lands still in Indian ownership by extending the trust period on all restricted lands until Congress shall otherwise direct.

Section 3 returns to tribal possession the remnant of between two and three million acres of the so-called " ceded " or " surplus " Indian lands which have not yet been sold.

Section 4 stops a dangerous leak through which the restricted allotted lands still in Indian ownership pass therefrom. Upon the death of an allottee the number of heirs frequently makes partition of the land impractical, and it must be sold at partition sale, when it generally passes into the hands of whites. This section endeavors to restrict such sales to Indian buyers or to Indian tribes or organizations. It, however, permits the devise of restricted lands to the heirs, whether Indian or not.

Section 5: The sections mentioned are designed to prevent further loss of Indian land. But prevention is not enough. The Indians now landless must be provided for. This section undertakes to do this gradually through an annual appropriation for the purchase of land.

Section 11 provides credit, now denied to the Indian because of his status as ward, to enable him to utilize his land and become fully self-supporting.

Section 13 permits the employment of qualified Indians in their own service, partly paid for from their own funds. The effect of existing requirements which bar them from such employment is grossly unfair.

I have tried to picture the Indian situation and, in a general way, to outline the manner in which this bill proposes to meet that situation. I make my most earnest plea in behalf of this measure. I am sure that a sense of justice and fair dealing will win the approval of this body for the bill, as it has won the approval of our President.

Mr. Speaker, analyzing somewhat more in detail the provisions of this measure, as they constitute a new policy in Indian affairs, let us examine that new policy to see wherein it differs from the old, which has brought disaster to the Indian, and to see how it offers a real hope for a way out of the admittedly evil conditions which confront us.

Reduced to its simplest terms, the present bill would prevent any further loss of Indian lands, would permit the purchase of additional lands for landless Indians, would set up a modern system of Indian agricultural and industrial credit, would permit Indian tribes or groups to incorporate for business purposes, would give Indian tribes the right to organize tribal councils for the promotion of the common welfare, would establish a special Indian civil service and give to qualified Indians the preference right to appointment in the Indian Service, and would create a loan fund for the vocational and professional training of Indians in order to qualify them for the Indian Service and for other employment.

It would strike a body blow at the twin evils of economic and social disintegration of the Indians. It would stop the sinister liquidation of Indian property and the equally sinister destruction of the Indian character wrought by generations of bureaucratic absolutism. It would give to the Indian at least a modest measure of economic security and economic opportunity. It would take him off the dole, out of the national poorhouse, and set him on the road to earning his own living, on the land, in the sweat of his brow. It would give to him what the white man has fought and died for over the centuries: The right to personal liberty and to a voice in the conduct of his daily life.

These objectives, I am convinced, are in keeping with the spirit of this Congress and this administration. The conduct of Indian affairs by the Federal Government for the past century has been a scandal and a blot on our name in every part of the world. Predatory interests have systematically and continually robbed the Indian of his property; the Government, by law, has supinely permitted this robbery, cloaking it under a sterile and sinister legality that was a travesty of justice and national honor and under a Federal " guardianship " that, with incredible complacency, watched through generations the destruction of the Indian estate and the Indian character.

I propose to discuss in some detail the method and result of this legalized robbery and of the Federal policy that has reduced the Indians to virtual peonage.

(material omitted)

(material omitted)

The Indians have not only been thus deprived of civic rights and powers, but they have been largely deprived of the opportunity to enter the more important positions in the service of the very bureau which manages their affairs. Theoretically, the Indians have the right to qualify for the Federal civil service. In actual practice there has been no adequate program of training to qualify Indians to compete in these examinations, especially for technical and higher positions; and even if there were such training, the Indians would have to compete under existing law, on equal terms with multitudes of white applicants. Today there are about 2,100 Indians holding permanent civil-service appointments in the Bureau of Indian Affairs, with a total permanent personnel of approximately 6,500. The great majority of these positions held by Indians are in the lower salary grades, such as clerks, matrons, cooks, boys and girls' advisers, and so forth. Considering the higher and technical positions, there are, for example, only 8 Indian foresters in a total forest personnel of 102; 250 teachers in a total teaching force of 966; 21 nurses in a total force of 345 nurses; only 8 Indian superintendents out of a total number of 103. The various services on the Indian reservations are actually local rather than Federal services and are comparable to local municipal and county services, since they are dealing with purely local Indian problems. It should be possible for Indians with the requisite vocational and professional training to enter the service of their own people without the necessity of competing with white applicants for these positions. This bill permits them to do so.

(material omitted)

(material omitted)

The development of Indian capacity for home rule will be greatly speeded up by providing better opportunities for vocational, technical, and professional education for able Indians. Section 12 authorizes the appropriation of not to exceed $250,000 annually for education of Indians in trade and vocational schools, of which not more than $50,000 per year shall be available for high-school and college education. These funds would be granted as reimbursable loans.

I have already spoken of the difficulty which Indians experience in meeting the civil-service requirements for entering the Indian Service. It should be possible for Indians to enter the service of their own people without running the gauntlet of competition with whites for these positions. Indian progress and ambition will be enormously strengthened as soon as we adopt the principle that the Indian Service shall gradually become, in fact as well as in name, an Indian service predominantly in the hands of educated and competent Indians. This does not mean a radical transformation overnight or the ousting of present white employees. It does mean a preference right to qualified Indians for appointments to future vacancies in the local Indian field service and an opportunity to rise to the higher administrative and technical posts. Section 13 directs the Secretary of the Interior to establish the necessary standards of health, age, character, experience, knowledge, and ability for Indian eligibles and to appoint them without regard to civil-service laws; and it gives to such Indians a preference right to appointment to any future vacancy. This provision in nowise signifies a disregard of the true merit system, but it adapts the merit system to Indian temperament, training, and capacity. Provision for vocational and higher education will permit the building up of an entirely competent Indian personnel.

* * * *

V. 78 Cong. Rec. 11123 (June 12, 1934)

* * * *

The PRESIDING OFFICER (Mr. TYDINGS in the chair). Eighty-seven Senators having answered to their names, a quorum is present.

Mr. WHEELER. Mr. President, the purpose of this bill is stated briefly in the report submitted by the Committee on Indian Affairs. This bill has the approval of the Bureau of Indian Affairs, of the Interior Department, and also has the approval of the Bureau of the Budget. The President himself has sent a letter stating that he desires to have the bill passed.

The purposes of the bill are as follows:

First, to stop the alienation, through action by the Government or the Indian, of such lands, belonging to ward Indians, as are needed for the present and future support of the Indians.

With respect to that, I will say that heretofore there has been pursued a policy whereby the Indians would get patents and fees to the lands, which would then be disposed of, and the Indians would find themselves without land and pauperized.

The second purpose is to provide for the acquisition, through purchase, of land for Indians now landless who are anxious and fitted to make a living on such land. The Committee on Indian Affairs and the Bureau of Indian Affairs have found that there are many Indians who have no lands whatsoever, and are unable to make a living. Consequently, the Government is constantly compelled to furnish money to these Indians; and it is thought by the Government that it would be much cheaper in the long run and would make better citizens of them if we could put them on small tracts of land where they could make their own living.

The third purpose of the bill is to stabilize the tribal organization of Indian tribes by vesting such tribal organizations with real, though limited, authority, and by prescribing conditions which must be met by such tribal organizations.

This provision will apply only if a majority of the Indians on any Indian reservation desire this sort of organization. As a matter of fact, however, it does not change to any great extent the present tribal organization, except that when a majority of the Indians want to establish this tribal organization and extend the provisions of the bill to it, they may do so.

The bill also provides that Indian tribes may equip themselves with the devices of modern business organization through forming themselves into business corporations. On some of the reservations the Indians are conducting fishing businesses, and on others they are conducting timber businesses. On other reservations they are conducting some other businesses. The bill provides that when a majority of the Indians on a reservation desire to form a corporation for the transaction of their business, they may do so in the manner prescribed in the bill.

The next provision is for the purpose of establishing a system of financial credit for Indians; that is, a revolving fund whereby the Government may loan to individual Indians in certain cases, and to the tribal organizations or the Indian corporations, certain money in the event that the Secretary of the Interior thinks they are worthy of such loans.

Then there is a provision to supply Indians with means for collegiate and technical training in the best schools. On many of the Indian reservations there are exceedingly bright, capable Indians who, as wards of the Government, are unable to get a higher education at the present time. There is no provision in the Interior Department by which the Department can make loans or provide funds to the Indians for such education.

The bill also has a provision to open the way for qualified Indians to hold positions in the Federal Indian Service on the Indian reservations. At the present time, by reason of the civil-service rules and regulations, we find that competent Indians are absolutely unable to take or hold positions in the Indian Service. For instance, we find many instances where Indian girls have graduated from a nursing school, are graduate nurses, but are unable to be employed in the Indian Service because of the fact that they have not had sufficient training outside, and they are unable to get the training because of the fact that most white training institutions would not give the Indian girls an opportunity to act as nurses in those institutions.

* * * *

VI. 110 Cong. Rec. 12722-23 (June 4, 1964)

[Page 12722:]

TE   *June 4*

CIVIL RIGHTS ACT OF 1963

The Senate resumed the consideration of the bill (H.R. 7152) to enforce the constitutional right to vote, to confer jurisdiction upon the district courts of the United States to provide injunctive relief against discrimination in public accommodations, to authorize the Attorney General to institute suits to protect constitutional rights in public facilities and public education, to extend the Commission on Civil Rights, to prevent discrimination in federally assisted programs, to establish a Commission on Equal Employment Opportunity, and for other purposes.

Mr. HUMPHREY. Mr. President, I have been discussing the changes in title VII.

MISCELLANEOUS CHANGES

I have stated the most significant changes in title VII. I shall now run through the title describing briefly the other principal changes which have been made:

First. In section 701—formerly 702—the definition of "employer" has been clarified to provide needed certainty as to coverage of employers where the number of employees fluctuates above and below the figure requisite to application of the title. Coverage is limited to those employers who employ more than the required minimum number of employees for at least 20 weeks out of the year.

Second. In section 701(b) a statement had been added that it is the policy of the United States to insure equal employment opportunity for Federal employees. This hardly represents a change in the law, but it was thought desirable because the United States, like all governmental units, State and local, is generally excepted from the category of employers covered by the title.

* * * *

Ninth. A new subsection 703(j) is added to deal with the problem of racial balance among employees. The proponents of this bill have carefully stated on numerous occasions that title VII does not require an employer to achieve any sort of racial balance in his work force by giving preferential treatment to any individual or group. Since doubts have persisted, subsection (j) is added to state this point expressly. This subsection does not represent any change in the substance of the title. It does state clearly and accurately what we have maintained all along about the bill's intent and meaning.

[Page 12723:]

1964   **CONGRESSIONAL RECORD — SEN**

(material omitted)

Tenth. A new subsection 703(i) has been added permitting enterprises on or near Indian reservations to follow preferential hiring practices toward Indians. This exemption is consistent with the Federal Government's policy of encouraging Indian employment and with the special legal position of Indians.

(material omitted)

VII. 110 Cong. Rec. 13702 (June 13, 1964)

Mr. MUNDT. Mr. President, I shall take only a few minutes of my time to explain my amendment. I have worked it out in cooperation with the representatives of the Bureau of Indian Affairs. The amendment involves the welfare of our oldest and most distressed American minority, the American Indians, the original landlords of America.

I have also discussed this amendment with the leadership on civil rights on both sides of the aisle. They have informed me that they will accept it. Therefore, unless there is other opposition we can approve it by a voice vote.

My amendment merely adds at the bottom of page 35 after "the United States, a corporation wholly owned by the Government of the United States," the words "an Indian tribe." The reason why it is necessary to add these words is that Indian tribes, in many parts of the country, are virtually political subdivisions of the Government. To a large extent many tribes control and operate their own affairs, even to the extent of having their own elected officials, courts, and police forces. This amendment would provide to American Indian tribes in their capacity as a political entity, the same privileges accorded to the U.S. Government and its political subdivisions, to conduct their own affairs and economic activities without consideration of the provisions of the bill.

Let me emphasize that Indian tribes in an effort to decrease unemployment and in order to integrate their people into the affairs of the national community, operate many economic enterprises, which are more or less supervised by the Indian tribes, the employees serving as apprentices in many instances, and as supervisors and regularly employed and paid employees in others.

My amendment has the support, among others, of the National Congress of American Indians. I ask unanimous consent to insert in the RECORD at this point a letter from the congress, and also some telegrams, as supporting evidence.

There being no objection, the material was ordered to be printed in the RECORD, as follows:

NATIONAL CONGRESS OF
AMERICAN INDIANS FUND, INC.,
Washington, D.C., June 9, 1964.
Hon. KARL MUNDT,
Senate Office Building,
Washington, D.C.

DEAR SENATOR: The National Congress of American Indians is in full support of those amendments which have been agreed to by the Senate leadership.

We urge that title VII, section 701(b) be amended to include Indian tribes as proposed. We also urge that title VII, section 703(i) be included in the Civil Rights Act of 1964 as proposed.

We favor these amendments because of the legislative history that surrounds the Indian tribes. As you know, our Indian tribes are suffering from a national unemployment rate of 50 percent and everyone is doing all that is possible to overcome this terrible unemployment rate. These amendments will greatly protect our business and enterprises on the reservations, and it will greatly increase the possibility of the tribes themselves progressing to overcome this unemployment figure.

We wish to thank all of you who are concerned about the American Indian people and we sincerely hope that these amendments will be enacted into law. With these amendments, we would fully endorse the principle of the Civil Rights Act of 1964.

Most sincerely,
ROBERT BURNETTE,
Executive Director.

———

ROSEBUD, S. DAK.,
June 4, 1964.
Senator KARL MUNDT,
U.S. Senate,
Washington, D.C.:

The Rosebud Sioux Tribe endorses proposed Civil Rights Act of 1964. We especially support section 703(I) which entitles Indian Reservations a preferential treatment because of past legislative and historical treatment. We urge that you support the Civil Rights Act of 1963.

CATO W. VALANDRA,
President, Rosebud Sioux Tribe.

———

CHADRON, NEBR.,
June 3, 1964.
Senator KARL MUNDT,
Senate Office Building,
Washington, D.C.:

The Oglala Sioux Tribe of Pine Ridge, S. Dak., fully endorse the proposed Civil Rights Act of 1964. We especially support section 703, subsection I, which entitles our Indian reservation to preferential treatment because of past legislative and historic treatment. We urge that you support Civil Rights Act of 1963.

ENOS POORBEAR,
President, Oglala Sioux Tribal Council, Pine Ridge, S. Dak.

———

ROLLA, N. DAK.,
June 8, 1964.
Senator KARL MUNDT,
Washington, D.C.:

Turtle Mountain Band of Chippewa Indians endorses the Civil Rights Act of 1963 provided that the Indian amendment title 7, section 701, subsection (B), and section 703, subsection (I), are made part of this act.

TURTLE MOUNTAIN TRIBAL COUNCIL.

———

DEVILS LAKE, N. DAK.,
June 8, 1964.
Senator KARL MUNDT,
Senate Building,
Washington, D.C.:

The Fort Totten Sioux endorses the Civil Rights Act of 1963, provided that the Indian amendment in title 7, section 701, subsection B, and section 703, subsection I are made a part of the act.

LEWIS GOODHOUSE,
Chairman, Devils Lake Sioux Tribe.

———

WASHINGTON, D.C.,
June 8, 1964.
Hon. KARL MUNDT,
U.S. Senate,
Washington, D.C.:

Cheyenne River Sioux Tribe favors amendment to section 701(B)(1) adding to line 24, page 35, after comma, "or Indian tribes," and adding to section 703 a new paragraph (I) as set forth in amendment No. 656 of May 26, 1964.

Thank you for looking after interests of American Indians.

FRANK DUCHENEAAX,
Chairman, Cheyenne River Sioux Tribal Council.

———

EL RENO, OKLA.,
June 9, 1964.
Senator KARL MUNDT,
Senate Office Building,
Washington, D.C.:

Cheyenne and Arapaho Tribes respectfully urge your continuing efforts to protect the Indians' rights in pending civil rights bill. Respectfully submitted.

WOODROW WILSON ACT,
Chairman, Cheyenne and Arapaho Tribes, Concho, Okla.

Mr. MUNDT. Mr. President, I do not believe there is any opposition to the amendment. I believe we all realize that equitable treatment for the American Indians is long overdue. This is an effort to take an important step in that direction. If there is no objection, there can be a voice vote on the amendment. That will be satisfactory to me.

In conclusion, Mr. President, I would like to say that if my present amendment is approved by the Senate, we shall have done an excellent job in this civil rights bill of protecting and promoting the welfare and opportunities of our American Indians—the one minority group in the United States which has suffered the longest and the most from the callous indifference and the poor judgment of Americans generally. An earlier amendment which I authored and offered to be of assistance to our Indians was, I am glad to say, approved and it is now part of the so-called package substitute which we all recognize will be the basic legislation which will be approved by the Senate next week after the current amendatory process has been completed.

My earlier amendment will be found on page 44 of the May 26 substitute package bill. It is identified as subsection (i) of section 703 of title 7—the so-called equal employment opportunity title of the bill. That amendment reads: "Nothing contained in this title shall apply to any business or enterprise on or near an Indian reservation with respect to any publicly announced employment practice of such business or enterprise under which a preferential treatment is given any individual because he is an Indian living on or near a reservation."

That amendment, Mr. President, together with the one I now have on the desk and which I trust will be approved will assure our American Indians of the continued right to protect and promote their own interests and to benefit from Indian preference programs now in operation or later to be instituted.

Mr. HUMPHREY. Mr. President, will the Senator yield?

Mr. MUNDT. I yield.

Mr. HUMPHREY. I have discussed this matter with the Senator from South Dakota. Any economic activity on the part of the Indian tribes must have the approval of the Secretary of the Interior. I see no reason to object to the amendment. We accept it.

* * * *

VIII. 118 Cong. Rec. 589-91 (Jan. 20, 1972)

TE   **589**

(material omitted)

Mr. HUMPHREY. Mr. President, I support the Equal Employment Opportunities Act, S. 2515, as reported by the Committee on Labor and Public Welfare.

The time has now come when we must firmly establish and guarantee the protections provided for under title VII of the Civil Rights Act of 1964. No longer can we permit millions of American citizens—women, blacks, Indian Americans, the Spanish speaking, and other minority groups—to continue suffering the indignities and injustices of discrimination in employment. No longer can we be content with a conciliatory approach to the resolution of complaints of civil rights violations committed against any American

590   **CO**‌**TE**

who wants a job or who seeks advancement to a position for which he or she is fully qualified. Nor, in the protection of these civil rights, can we now be satisfied with any enforcement procedure wherein the delay of justice means the denial of justice.

The experience of the past 7 years has shown us that by failing to provide the Equal Employment Opportunity Commission with effective enforcement powers, we established an agency under the 1964 Civil Rights Act which has been very successful in ferreting out the existence of discrimination, and pointing out to us how widespread and entrenched this discrimination is, but which has not been able to provide effective relief to eliminate this discrimination.

Our original view that employment discrimination consists of a series of isolated incidents has been shattered by evidence which shows that employment discrimination is, in most instances, the result of deeply ingrained practices and policies which frequently do not even herald their discriminatory effects on the surface. The EEOC has stressed many times that much of what we previously accepted as sound employment policy does, in effect, promote and perpetuate discriminatory patterns which can be traced back to the Civil War and earlier.

(material omitted)

January 20, 1972

[Page 590 continues:]

* * *

Coverage of State and local employees is another area where the existence of employment discrimination has been noted but no adequate remedy has been available. The presence of discrimination in State and local governments has been well documented by the U.S. Commission on Civil Rights in two extensive studies done during the past 2 years. And yet the protection of title VII available to the other segments of society have been denied State and local employees.

This situation is in clear conflict with our concept of government. Democracy is government by the people and for the people—all the people. That fundamental principle must be seen in government itself if it is to be believed. I feel that local governments, which most affect the daily lives of every citizen in the particular community, should be fully committed to maintaining equal employment opportunity. Any failure to promote this goal at the level of the State and local government can do nothing but breed discontent, mistrust, and harsh cynicism toward the entire process of government.

It is in this respect that S. 2515 extends the protections of title VII to all State and local employees. However, the bill does recognize the sovereign characteristics possessed by States, and accordingly does not extend the administrative process of the EEOC to them. Rather, if a charge against a State or local governmental agency is received by the EEOC, it will investigate that charge and attempt to conciliate. If it should fail, it will then submit the complaint to the U.S. Department of Justice where further legal action may be instituted by that Department. If the Justice Department decides not to act on a complaint, the individual would still have the opportunity to pursue his claim in court.

However, we cannot expect the advancement of equal employment opportunity in State and local governments to occur without establishing a firm example of Federal leadership at the forefront of this effort. The report of the Senate Committee on Labor and Public Welfare states this case with exceptional clarity:

The federal government, with 2.6 million employees, is the single largest employer in the nation. It also comprises the central policy-making and administrative network for the nation. Consequently, its policies, actions, and programs strongly influence the activities of all other enterprises, organizations and groups. In no area is government action more important than in the area of civil rights.

That is why I regard as of great importance the provisions in the bill giving expanded authority to the Civil Service Commission to eliminate discrimination in Federal employment, and expressly granting to Federal employees a right of private action to obtain relief from such discrimination.

We cannot be satisfied with reports of progress when minorities, representing almost one-fifth of Federal employment, are concentrated in the lower civil service grade levels, and when over three-fourths of the 665,000 women working for the Federal Government have positions below the level of GS-7.

The corrective remedies authorized in S. 2515 go beyond existing Executive order policy pronouncements to get at the real problems of discriminatory practices and effects that are institutional and regional in nature, more than they are the result of private, intentional wrongs.

Serious inadequacies are clearly present in existing Federal employee discrimination complaint procedures, in the credentials associated with civil service selection and promotion techniques and requirements, in procedures to assure bona fide plans and efforts by Federal agencies to accomplish actual results in the promotion of equal employment opportunity, and in the prohibition of employment discrimination at regional and local Federal installations as well as at national offices in Washington, D.C.

There can be no further delay in opening the higher civil service grades to women and minority groups. We must make absolutely clear the obligation of the Federal Government to make all personnel actions free from discrimination based on race, color, sex, religion, or national origin.

* * * *

(material omitted)

IX. 118 Cong. Rec. 1411-12 (Jan. 26, 1972)

(material omitted)

NATIONAL COMMITMENT TO ELIMINATE JOB DISCRIMINATION

Mr. BYRD of West Virginia. Mr. President, on September 14, 1971, I introduced S. 2515 for the distinguished junior Senator from New Jersey (Mr. WILLIAMS) and for 32 other Senators. Although I was not a cosponsor of that bill, I support the bill which is now before the Senate, and I shall vote for it on final passage.

There are some features of the bill

---

with which I am not in complete accord. Nonetheless, I hope that the bill can be improved when in conference with the other body.

(material omitted)

* * * *

The bill before the Senate would broaden the jurisdictional coverage of the Equal Employment Opportunities Commission, and would delete the existing exemptions for State and local government employees.

The U.S.-Attorney General would be given the authority to bring civil actions involving unlawful employment practices committed by State and local governmental agencies.

Employees of State and local governments are entitled to the same benefits and protections in regard to equal employment as are the employees in the private sector of the economy.

There are presently approximately 10.1 million persons employed by State and local governmental units. This figure represents an increase of over 2 million since 1964, and all indications are that the number of State and local employees will continue to increase more rapidly during the next few years. Few of these employees, however, are afforded the protection of an effective Federal forum for assuring equal employment opportunity. It is an injustice to provide employees in the private sector with the assistance of an agency of the Federal Government in redressing their grievances while at the same time denying assistance similarly to State and local government employees. The bill before the Senate would provide such assistance.

The Federal Government, with 2.6 million employees, is the single largest employer in the Nation. The prohibition against discrimination by the Federal Government, based on the due process clause of the fifth amendment, was judicially recognized in *Bolling v. Sharpe,* 347 U.S. 497 (1954) and cases cited therein.

Minorities represent 19.4 percent of the total employment in the Federal Government—15 percent are Negroes, 2.9 percent are Spanish-surnamed, 0.7 percent are American Indians, and 0.8 percent are Oriental. Their concentration in the lower grade levels indicates that their ability to advance to the higher levels has, in many instances, been restricted.

In many areas, the pattern at regional levels is worse than the national pattern. For example, a particularly low percentage of Federal jobs are held by Spanish-surnamed persons in areas of high residential concentration of such persons, particularly in California and the Southwestern States.

The position of women in the Federal Government has not fared any better. While women constitute 34 percent, or approximately 665,000 of the total number of Federal employees, 77 percent of the women are employed in jobs which are rated GS–1 through GS–6. Twenty-two percent are in grades GS–7 through GS–12, and only 1 percent are in grades GS–13 and above. The inordinate concentration of women in the lower grade levels, and their conspicuous absence from the higher grades is again evident.

The bill before the Senate should make possible the rectification of such situations wherein discrimination based on race, nationality, or sex is involved.

Recognizing the importance that the concept of due process places on the American ideal of justice, the bill insures fairness to the employer. Charges must be in writing. The allegations will not be made public by the Commission while it is investigating such, and the Commission will undertake to resolve each matter by informal means before issuing a complaint. Commission hearings must be on the record and will be covered by the provisions of the Administrative Procedure Act so as to provide maximum protection to all parties to the proceedings. The respondent would have the right to seek judicial review of a Commission decision which rules against him.

I believe that the Senate bill will provide the instrument for fulfillment of our national commitment to eliminate job discrimination based on race, nationality, religion, and sex. I, therefore, will vote for the bill.

———————

* * * *

THE 1967 AGE DISCRIMINATION IN EMPLOYMENT ACT AND THE MEANING OF "SUBTERFUGE"

I. Overview and Questions

The final Unit in this Supplement consists of an extended case study in which Congress and the Supreme Court address the meaning of the term "subterfuge" under the Age Discrimination in Employment Act (ADEA). This extraordinary prolonged dialogue between the two Branches is intriguing in its own right, and also may serve as a review exercise for students examining the uses and possible misuses of text and legislative history.

It is not uncommon for Congress to override the Court's interpretation of a particular word in statutory text. It is quite unusual, however, for Congress to do so twice with respect to the same word. Depending on one's separation of powers perspective, the interplay set forth below between Congress and the Supreme Court may be seen as vindicating the Court's "tough love" approach in the face of congressional insensitivity to explicit judicial reasoning, or as demonstrating the Court's arrogance in the face of a clearly expressed congressional purpose, or perhaps as reflecting both positions to a certain extent.

We present below excerpts from the 1967 ADEA text containing the term "subterfuge" and accompanying legislative history; the Court's 1977 decision in *McMann* construing that term and its legislative history; Congress's 1978 text and legislative history overriding the *McMann* decision; the Court's 1989 decision in *Betts* reaffirming its interpretive position from *McMann* on the meaning of "subterfuge"; and Congress's 1990 text and legislative history overriding the *Betts* decision. We also include excerpts from Congress's text and accompanying legislative history that explain the term "subterfuge" as part of the 1990 Americans With Disabilities Act (ADA).

As you review these materials, consider the following questions:

1. What was the primary legislative focus of the ADEA when enacted by Congress in 1967? How can you tell? Was the primary legislative focus the same in the 1978 amendments? What about in the 1990 legislation?

2. What is the basis for the Supreme Court's conclusion, in *United Airlines v. McMann*, that a pre-1967 plan cannot be a "subterfuge"? Are you persuaded by the Court's reasoning?

3. Can you challenge the *McMann* analysis regarding subterfuge, based on your reading of the 1967 legislative history? Based on any other factors?

4. On what grounds does the Court in *Betts* reaffirm its earlier conclusion that employee benefit plans adopted prior to enactment of the ADEA cannot be a subterfuge? Is the Court's treatment of legislative history persuasive? Does the 1978 Conference Report support the Court's position?

5. Review the House floor debate supporting the 1978 Conference Report. Do Representatives Hawkins, Weiss, and Waxman all have the same understanding of what the Report means?

6. Does the addition of a new section 4(k) in the 1990 legislation vindicate the Court's approach in *McMann* and *Betts*? Why or why not?

7. If you are Justice Scalia, confronted with a case raising the meaning of the term "subterfuge" in § 501(c) of the ADA, how do you interpret that term? What if you are Justice Stevens faced with the same problem? How would you interpret the term?

II. *An Act to Prohibit Age Discrimination in Employment, 81 Stat. 602 (1967)*

602   PUBLIC LAW 90-202–DEC. 15, 1967   [81 STAT.

Public Law 90-202

December 15, 1967
[S. 830]

AN ACT

To prohibit age discrimination in employment.

Be it enacted by the Senate and House of Representatives of the United States of America in Congress assembled, That this Act may be cited as the "Age Discrimination in Employment Act of 1967".

Age Discrimination in Employment Act of 1967.

STATEMENT OF FINDINGS AND PURPOSE

SEC. 2. (a) The Congress hereby finds and declares that—

(1) in the face of rising productivity and affluence, older workers find themselves disadvantaged in their efforts to retain employment, and especially to regain employment when displaced from jobs;

(2) the setting of arbitrary age limits regardless of potential for job performance has become a common practice, and certain otherwise desirable practices may work to the disadvantage of older persons;

(3) the incidence of unemployment, especially long-term unemployment with resultant deterioration of skill, morale, and employer acceptability is, relative to the younger ages, high among older workers; their numbers are great and growing; and their employment problems grave;

(4) the existence in industries affecting commerce, of arbitrary discrimination in employment because of age, burdens commerce and the free flow of goods in commerce.

(b) It is therefore the purpose of this Act to promote employment of older persons based on their ability rather than age; to prohibit arbitrary age discrimination in employment; to help employers and workers find ways of meeting problems arising from the impact of age on employment.

[page 603:]

PROHIBITION OF AGE DISCRIMINATION

SEC. 4. (a) It shall be unlawful for an employer—

(1) to fail or refuse to hire or to discharge any individual or otherwise discriminate against any individual with respect to his compensation, terms, conditions, or privileges of employment, because of such individual's age;

(2) to limit, segregate, or classify his employees in any way which would deprive or tend to deprive any individual of employment opportunities or otherwise adversely affect his status as an employee, because of such individual's age; or

(3) to reduce the wage rate of any employee in order to comply with this Act.

* * * *

(f) It shall not be unlawful for an employer, employment agency, or labor organization—

(1) to take any action otherwise prohibited under subsections (a), (b), (c), or (e) of this section where age is a bona fide occupational qualification reasonably necessary to the normal operation of the particular business, or where the differentiation is based on reasonable factors other than age;

(2) to observe the terms of a bona fide seniority system or any bona fide employee benefit plan such as a retirement, pension, or insurance plan, which is not a subterfuge to evade the purposes of this Act, except that no such employee benefit plan shall excuse the failure to hire any individual; or

[page 604:]

(3) to discharge or otherwise discipline an individual for good cause.

301

III. Age Discrimination in Employment, Hearing on S. 830 and S. 788 Before the Subcomm. on Labor of the S. Comm. on Labor and Public Welfare, 76th Cong. (1967)

AGE DISCRIMINATION IN EMPLOYMENT

HEARINGS

BEFORE THE

SUBCOMMITTEE ON LABOR

OF THE

COMMITTEE ON
LABOR AND PUBLIC WELFARE
UNITED STATES SENATE

NINETIETH CONGRESS

FIRST SESSION

ON

S. 830

TO PROHIBIT AGE DISCRIMINATION IN EMPLOYMENT

S. 788

TO PROHIBIT ARBITRARY DISCRIMINATION IN EMPLOYMENT
ON ACCOUNT OF AGE, AND FOR OTHER PURPOSES

MARCH 15, 16, AND 17, 1967

Printed for the use of the
Committee on Labor and Public Welfare

U.S. GOVERNMENT PRINTING OFFICE
WASHINGTON : 1967

76-941 O

COMMITTEE ON LABOR AND PUBLIC WELFARE

LISTER HILL, Alabama, *Chairman*

WAYNE MORSE, Oregon
RALPH YARBOROUGH, Texas
JOSEPH S. CLARK, Pennsylvania
JENNINGS RANDOLPH, West Virginia
HARRISON A. WILLIAMS, Jr., New Jersey
CLAIBORNE PELL, Rhode Island
EDWARD M. KENNEDY, Massachusetts
GAYLORD NELSON, Wisconsin
ROBERT F. KENNEDY, New York

JACOB K. JAVITS, New York
WINSTON L. PROUTY, Vermont
PETER H. DOMINICK, Colorado
GEORGE MURPHY, California
PAUL J. FANNIN, Arizona
ROBERT P. GRIFFIN, Michigan

STEWART E. McCLURE, *Chief Clerk*
JOHN S. FORSYTHE, *General Counsel*
EUGENE MITTELMAN, *Minority Counsel*

SUBCOMMITTEE ON LABOR

RALPH YARBOROUGH, Texas, *Chairman*

WAYNE MORSE, Oregon
JENNINGS RANDOLPH, West Virginia
CLAIBORNE PELL, Rhode Island
GAYLORD NELSON, Wisconsin
ROBERT F. KENNEDY, New York
HARRISON A. WILLIAMS, Jr., New Jersey

JACOB K. JAVITS, New York
WINSTON L. PROUTY, Vermont
PAUL J. FANNIN, Arizona
ROBERT P. GRIFFIN, Michigan

ROBERT O. HARRIS, *Counsel*
PETER C. BENEDICT, *Minority Labor Counsel*

II

* * * *

Senator JAVITS. My interest in preventing age discrimination in employment goes back to when I was attorney general of New York, serving with then Gov. Averell Harriman, now the President's roving Ambassador, and I am very gratified that following my efforts and those of then Governor Harriman, we did enact one of the very early bills against job discrimination because of age in New York.

Now, I think the time has come to act in the Federal Establishment. I am deeply gratified that the President has signalized this in his state of the Union message. The purpose of my testimony is to reconcile S. 788 with S. 830, the administration bill. Obviously, Mr. Chairman, it will be the efforts of the majority and I understand it perfectly well, to put S. 830 in shape.

Now, we have, in the Congress, begun to respond in many ways to the problems of older Americans. We have passed special legislation on housing, medicare, antipoverty, research, the Older Americans Act of 1965, and other programs. But, considering the enormous incidence of older people in the population attributable to marvelous advances in health, there is a great deal more we are going to have to do.

* * * *

Now, another problem is the operation of established pension plans, some of which provide benefits based to a certain extent on the age of the employee when first hired.

The administration bill, which permits involuntary separation under bona fide retirement plans meets only part of the problem. It does not provide any flexibility in the amount of pension benefits payable to older workers depending on their age when hired, and thus may actually encourage employers, faced with the necessity of paying greatly increased premiums, to look for excuses not to hire older workers when they might have hired them under a law granting them a degree of flexibility with respect to such matters.

That flexibility is what we recommend.

We also recommend that the age discrimination law should not be used as the place to fight the pension battle but that we ought to subordinate the importance of adequate pension benefits for older workers in favor of the employment of such older workers and not make the equal treatment under pension plans a condition of that employment.

Another problem which is not specifically dealt with in the administration bill is that of seniority. The seniority system, as it has developed in this country, operates to insure the job security of older workers, and thus constitutes a built-in protection against premature discharge, based on age alone. We must be sure that any age discrimination law which is adopted does not hamper the operation of bona fide seniority systems.

If we fail to take that precaution we will run into the strong opposition of both management and unions, and footdragging on the part both of employers and of trade unions in complying with the law.

So, Mr. Chairman, in order to meet these needs, I will introduce the following amendments to S. 830.

First, that administration and enforcement be placed in the hands of the Wage and Hour Division.

Second, that the criminal penalty in cases of willful violation be eliminated and a double damage liability substituted. This is an adequate deterent in a bill of this character, and there is no use giving people the argument that it has criminal sanctions as a reason for refusing to cooperate or testify in investigations or proceedings.

28   AGE DISCRIMINATION IN EMPLOYMENT

Third, that a fairly broad exemption be provided for bona fide retirement and seniority systems which will facilitate hiring rather than deter it and make it possible for older workers to be employed without the necessity of disrupting those systems.

Fourth, a provision guarding against preemption of the jurisdiction of a State agency performing a like function, but giving the Secretary of Labor a limited power to adopt uniform standards to which State agencies would have to defer.

Fifth, giving the Secretary of Labor power to adopt rules and regulations including the power to declare exemptions and to vary age limits but making that power subject to the requirement of the Administrative Procedure Act.

In my judgment, Mr. Chairman, and I have been devoted to this subject for years, this will materially improve the administration program as submitted.

In conclusion, I think we all agree on the ultimate objective of this hearing; that is, to report a meaningful bill to protect the opportunities of older workers to find employment. The differences are solely in the means to this objective. I am confident these means can be resolved, and I think that by resolving them we are better able to protect the older worker than if we did not resolve them and adopted some doctrinaire or stiff-necked attitude which, though it might look good on paper, would not result in the maximum hiring of older people.

We must break down the wholly irratioanl barriers to employment based on age alone which have been permitted to hinder the older worker in a search for employment opportunity.

(material omitted)

IV. *113 Cong. Rec. 7076-7077 (March 16, 1967)*

7076 CONGRESSIONAL RECORD — SENATE *March 16, 1967*

AGE DISCRIMINATION IN EMPLOY-MENT—PROPOSED AMENDMENTS TO S. 830 ADMINISTRATION'S BILL

AMENDMENTS NOS. 123 THROUGH 129

Mr. JAVITS. Mr. President, yesterday I testified before the Subcommittee on Labor of the Committee on Labor and Public Welfare, on the problem of age discrimination in employment. In my testimony I referred to certain amendments to the administration bill, S. 830, which I stated I was going to introduce, and explained the purpose of the amendments. I introduce, for appropriate reference, the amendments to which I referred—they are numbered 1 through 7—and I ask unanimous consent that my testimony before the Subcommittee on Labor explaining them be printed in the RECORD, together with the text of the amendments.

The ACTING PRESIDENT pro tempore. The amendments will be received, printed, and appropriately referred; and, without objection, the testimony of Mr. JAVITS will be printed in the RECORD, together with the amendments.

The testimony submitted by Mr. JAVITS is as follows:

ADMINISTRATION AGE DISCRIMINATION BILL MUST BE AMENDED

(Testimony of Senator Jacob K. Javits at hearings on Age Discrimination in Employment before the Labor Subcommittee of the Senate Labor and Public Welfare Committee, 10:00 a.m., March 15th, Room 4230, New Senate Office Building.)

(material omitted)

We must also be sure that the law which is passed does not in practice encourage rather than discourage discrimination against older workers. One of the problems which must be faced in this connection concerns the operation of established pension plans, some of which provide benefits based to a certain extent on the age of the employee when first hired.

The Administration bill, which permits involuntary separation under bona fide retirement plans meets only part of the problem. It does not provide any flexibility in the amount of pension benefits payable to older workers depending on their age when hired, and thus may actually encourage employers, faced with the necessity of paying greatly increased premiums, to look for excuses not to hire older workers when they might have done so under a law granting them a degree of flexibility with respect to such matters.

I do not mean to in any way minimize the importance of adequate pension benefits for older workers. Indeed, I have recently introduced a comprehensive bill to deal with this problem. I merely suggest that the age discrimination law is not the proper place to fight this particular battle.

Another problem which is not specifically dealt with in the Administration bill is that of seniority. The seniority system, as it has developed in this country, operates to ensure the job security of older workers, and thus constitutes a built-in protection against premature discharge, based on age alone. We must be sure that any age discrimination law which is adopted does not hamper the operation of bona fide seniority systems.

I have prepared and will introduce today, a series of amendments to the Administration's bill, which I believe will meet these various problems, while retaining the most desirable features of the Administration's bill, and of S. 788. Let me briefly describe them.

* * *

Third, a fairly broad exemption has been provided for bona fide retirement and seniority systems. As I previously noted, S. 830 contains only a limited exemption for retirement systems and no exemption for seniority systems.

(material omitted)

[page 7077:]

* * * *

I believe that adoption of these amendments will result in a law which is more efficient, at the same time fairer to all parties than the Administration's bill in its present form.

In conclusion, let me add that I think we all agree on the ultimate objectives of these hearings—that is to report meaningful legislation to protect the opportunities of our older workers to find employment.

Our differences concern the means to be utilized in achieving this objective. I am confident that these differences will be resolved and that this important legislation can finally be enacted. Without it we would be forced to fight the battle to protect our older citizens with one hand tied behind our backs. For all the counseling and retraining programs we may enact will be of only limited value if we cannot at the same time break down the wholly irrational barriers to employment, based on age alone, which have been permitted to spring up to hinder the older worker in his search for employment opportunities. This legislation is not the complete answer to all the problems of older workers, but it is certainly an extremely important weapon which our arsenal has for too long been without.

The amendments Nos. 123 through 129 were referred to the Committee on Labor and Public Welfare, as follows:

AMENDMENT No. 123

On page 6, beginning with line 7, strike out down through line 10 and insert in lieu thereof: "(2) to observe a seniority system or any retirement, pension, employee benefit, or insurance plan, which is not merely a subterfuge to evade the purposes of this Act, except that no such retirement, pension, employee benefit, or insurance plan shall excuse the failure to hire any individual; or".

* * * *

V. S. Rep. No. 90-723 (Nov. 4, 1967)

Calendar No. 707

90TH CONGRESS 1st Session	SENATE	REPORT No. 723

AGE DISCRIMINATION IN EMPLOYMENT ACT OF 1967

NOVEMBER 4, 1967.—Ordered to be printed
Filed under authority of the order of the Senate of November 2, 1967

Mr. YARBOROUGH, from the Committee on Labor and Public Welfare,
submitted the following

REPORT

together with

INDIVIDUAL VIEWS

[To accompany S. 830]

The Committee on Labor and Public Welfare, to which was referred the bill (S. 830) to prohibit age discrimination in employment, having considered the same, reports favorably thereon with an amendment in the nature of a substitute and recommends that the bill as amended do pass.

PURPOSE OF THE LEGISLATION

It is the purpose of S. 830 to promote the employment of older workers based on their ability. This would be done through an education and information program to assist employers and employees in meeting employment problems which are real and dispelling those which are illusory, and through the utilization of informal and formal remedial procedures where the education program has failed in its objective—the ending of employment discrimination based upon age. The prohibitions in the bill apply to employers, employment agencies, and labor organizations.

BACKGROUND

During recent years bills have been introduced in both the Senate and House to bar discrimination in employment on account of age. Also, during the last several years, significant legislation to bar discrimination in employment on the basis of race, religion, color, and sex have been enacted.

Section 715 of Public Law 88–352 (Civil Rights Act of 1964) directed the Secretary of Labor to make a study of the problem of age discrim-

★85–010—67

307

2 AGE DISCRIMINATION IN EMPLOYMENT ACT OF 1967

ination in employment. The product of that study was a report—"The Older American Worker—Age Discrimination in Employment"—issued June 1965. In his report, the Secretary recommended action to eliminate arbitrary age discrimination in employment and said:

> The possibility of new nonstatutory means of dealing with such arbitrary discrimination has been explored. That area is barren * * * A clear-cut and implemented Federal policy * * * would provide a foundation for a much-needed vigorous, nationwide campaign to promote hiring without discrimination on the basis of age.

Section 606 of Public Law 89–601 (Fair Labor Standards Amendments of 1966) directed the Secretary to submit "his specific legislative recommendations for implementing the conclusions and recommendations contained in his report on age discrimination in employment made pursuant to section 715 of Public Law 88–352." The President, in his Older American message of January 23, 1967, recommended the Age Discrimination in Employment Act of 1967, which was transmitted to the Congress by the Secretary in February.

The President's message, in the section on job opportunities, stated:

> Hundreds of thousands, not yet old, not yet voluntarily retired, find themselves jobless because of arbitrary age discrimination. Despite our present low rate of unemployment, there has been a persistent average of 850,000 people age 45 and over who are unemployed. Today more than three-quarters of the billion dollars in unemployment insurance is paid each year to workers who are 45 and over. They comprise 27 percent of all the unemployed, and 40 percent of the long-term unemployed.

(material omitted)

* * * *

SUMMARY OF MAJOR PROVISIONS

* * * *

Prohibition of age discrimination

Section 4 of the bill provides that:

A. It shall be unlawful for an employer of 50 or more persons (25 or more after June 30, 1968):

1. To fail or refuse to hire, or to discharge or discriminate against any individual as to compensation, terms, conditions, or privileges of employment, because of age;

---

4   AGE DISCRIMINATION IN EMPLOYMENT ACT OF 1967

2. To limit, segregate, or classify employees so as to deprive them of employment opportunities or adversely affect their status; or

3. To reduce the wage rate of any employee in order to comply with this act.

B. It shall be unlawful for an employment agency, including the U.S. Employment Service, to fail or refuse to refer any individual for employment, or to classify any individual for employment on the basis of age.

C. It shall be unlawful for a labor organization with 50 or more members (25 or more after June 30, 1968):

1. To discriminate against any individual because of age by excluding or expelling him from membership, or by limiting, segregating, or classifying its membership by age;

2. To fail to refer for employment any individual because of age, which failure may result in a deprivation of employment opportunities; or

3. To cause or attempt to cause an employer to discriminate against an individual because of age.

D. It shall be unlawful for an employer, employment agency, or labor organization:

1. To discriminate against a person for opposing a practice made unlawful by this act, or for participating in any proceeding hereunder; or

2. To use printed or published notices or advertisements indicating a preference, specification, or discrimination, based on age.

E. Exceptions to the forementioned unlawful practices:

1. Where age is a bona fide occupational qualification reasonably necessary to the particular business.

2. Where differentiation is based on reasonable factors other than age.

3. To comply with the terms of any bona fide seniority system or employee benefit plan which is not a subterfuge to evade the purposes of this act, except that no employee benefit plan shall excuse the failure to hire an individual.

4. To discharge or discipline an individual for good cause.

It is important to note that exception (3) applies to new and existing employee benefit plans, and to both the establishment and maintenance of such plans. This exception serves to emphasize the primary purpose of the bill—hiring of older workers—by permitting employment without necessarily including such workers in employee benefit plans. The specific exception was an amendment to the original bill and was favorably received by witnesses at the hearings.

(material omitted)

VI. *113 Cong. Rec. 31254-31255 (Nov. 6, 1967)*

31254

CONGRESSIONAL RECORD — SENATE

November 6, 1967

(material omitted)

We in America pride ourselves on our free enterprise system; particularly on the market as the only really objective test for the acceptance or rejection of the worth of goods or services. America was and still is the great land of opportunity, and the reason is clear: It is a land where a premium is put on ability—not rank, not privilege, and, if the system worked to perfection, not nationality, not religion, not sex, not race, and not age. But, Mr. President, we are confronted with the fact that as well as the system does work, there are still some shortcomings. We recognized this when, in the Civil Rights Act of 1964, we specifically prohibited discrimination on the ground of race, sex, religion, or national origin. At the time, we all recognized that the act left untouched another major problem: age discrimination. Although many of us, including myself, felt that the problem was severe enough and obvious enough to justify Federal legislation, the lack of any concrete information and statistics to show the full magnitude of the problem led us as a compromise in conference to direct the Secretary of Labor to make a report to Congress on age discrimination in employment.

In 1965, the Secretary filed his report and with it all doubt as to the need for this legislation vanished. The report found that a substantial amount of age discrimination in employment did exist and, furthermore, that almost all of it was completely arbitrary. As the report stated:

An unmeasured but significant proportion of the age limitations presently in effect are arbitrary in the sense that they have been established without any determination of their actual relevance to job requirements; and are defended apparently on grounds different from their actual explanation.

During this period the States were also manifesting their awareness of the age discrimination problem. At this date, some 24 States and Puerto Rico have enacted laws prohibiting age discrimination in employment. Half of those laws were passed since 1960, and all but three since 1955. The experience under the State laws has been varied. Unfortunately, most States have not made available sufficient funds or manpower to really make a dent in the problem. However, where forceful attempts have been made, especially in some demonstration projects, great success has been achieved.

What we have learned, essentially, is that a great deal of the problem stems from pure ignorance: there is simply a widespread irrational belief that once men and women are past a certain age they are no longer capable of performing even some of the most routine jobs. The answer to this kind of popular misconception is obviously a broad based program of information and education, and that is exactly what S. 830 provides for. At the same time, the experience of the States has shown that information and education alone are not enough; they must be coupled with the availability of formal remedial procedures to compel compliance with the law. S. 830 also provides these formal procedures through suits, either by the Secretary of Labor or the aggrieved individual, in the Federal or State courts.

The enforcement techniques provided by S. 830 are directly analogous to those available under the Fair Labor Standards Act; in fact, S. 830 incorporates by reference, to the greatest extent possible, the provisions of the Fair Labor Standards Act. This was accomplished through an amendment sponsored by Senator YARBOROUGH and myself which was adopted by the Subcommittee on Labor. The original version of S. 830 called for agency type enforcement, with hearings before the Secretary of Labor and then an appeal to the U.S. courts of appeals.

That was a departure from the approach which the Senate had actually adopted, at the urging of myself and Senators MURPHY, PROUTY, FANNIN, GRIFFIN, and SMATHERS when it incorporated a ban on age discrimination into the Fair Labor Standards Act amendments which passed the Senate last year. Although the age discrimination provisions were stricken in conference, the Secretary of Labor was directed to make specific legislative recommendations concerning age discrimination in employment to Congress this year. Those recommendations were embodied in S. 830, as originally introduced.

Although, as I have stated in my individual views, S. 830 was in most respects an excellent bill, the fact that it eschewed FLSA type of enforcement procedures in favor of an agency type process, which would have required the establishment within the Department of Labor of a wholly new bureaucracy complete with regional directors and attorneys, as well as hearing examiners, was most unfortunate. Happily, this defect has been corrected in the committee process. S. 830, as it has been reported out of committee, actually incorporates the best features of that bill, as originally introduced and S. 788, the bill which I, together with Senators ALLOTT, KUCHEL, MURPHY, and PROUTY introduced earlier this year based on the FLSA type of approach adopted by the Senate last year.

We now have the enforcement plan which I think is best adapted to carry out this age-discrimination-in-employment ban with the least overanxiety or difficulty on the part of American business, and with complete fairness to the workers. I think that is one of the most important aspects of the bill.

I can assure my colleagues that this bill was given the most careful possible attention by the Subcommittee on Labor and the full Committee on Labor and Public Welfare. Besides the change in enforcement technique to which I have already referred, many other amendments were adopted, some of which I had the honor of cosponsoring: among those amendments were the elimination of the criminal penalty in favor of a provision for double damage in cases of willful violation; an exemption for the observance of bona fide seniority systems or retirement, pension, insurance or similar plans and a provision specifically requiring the Secretary of Labor to promulgate rules and regulations under this act in accordance with the Administrative Procedure Act.

The amendment relating to seniority systems and employee benefit plans is particularly significant: because of it an

Mr. YARBOROUGH. Mr. President, will the Senator yield?

Mr. JAVITS. I yield.

Mr. YARBOROUGH. Mr. President, I commend and congratulate the distinguished senior Senator from New York for his long and diligent work and leadership in this field. He comes from a State that has a law against age discrimination. He served as attorney general of that State and his experience there has been invaluable in this committee.

Both the Senator from New York and I have had this experience of which he spoke of introducing bills year after year, and finally the consensus arrives.

As the Senator knows, this bill of mine, although I am the principal sponsor, is based on many provisions of his bill and the Department of Labor recommendations. In that sense it is an administration bill, so we might call it a consensus bill. It has had the overwhelming support of a majority of Senators on both sides. I do not know of any opposition to this bill which has been carefully worked out. I hope that it is passed by both Houses in this session of Congress. It was not easy to reach the consensus necessary to pass this bill because certain segments of our economy and society were opposed to this. It has taken years for them to see the necessity of it. The Senator from New York has been in the forefront of the fight.

Mr. JAVITS. Mr. President, I am grateful to the Senator for his generosity.

Mr. President, it is a sad day indeed when a man realizes that the world has begun to pass him by; that happens to all of us sooner or later. But it is surely a much greater tragedy for a man to be told, arbitrarily, that the world has passed him by, merely because he was born in a certain year or earlier, when he still has the mental and physical capacity to participate in it as energetically and vigorously as anyone else.

employer will not be compelled to afford older workers exactly the same pension, retirement, or insurance benefits as younger workers and thus employers will not, because of the often extremely high cost of providing certain types of benefits to older workers, actually be discouraged from hiring older workers. At the same time, it should be clear that this amendment only relates to the observance of bona fide plans. No such plan will help an employer if it is adopted merely as a subterfuge for discriminating against older workers.

One of the problems which arose before the committee, and which, happily, has been resolved in the bill, as reported, is the airline stewardess problem. I refer to the practice of a few airlines in requiring stewardesses to retire at the age of 32 or 35. At the present time, this practice exists only on a few airlines; most airlines have either never adopted the practice or, if they have, have now changed it voluntarily or as a result of collective bargaining. In their testimony before the Subcommittee on Labor, the stewardesses presented a very forceful case, and at one time the committee was seriously considering lowering the age limits in the bill to 32, or lower.

However, the Subcommittee on Labor and the full Committee on Labor and Public Welfare came to realize that while the stewardesses might have a good case, it was actually not within the province of this bill, directed as it is against the problem of discrimination against older workers. Thus, the committee, in my judgment, wisely decided to lower the age limit only to 40, since that is the age where, according to information currently available, age discrimination generally seems to start. We did however direct the Secretary of Labor to make a study of the feasibility of lowering the minimum age limits or raising the maximum age limits and report back his recommendations to us within 6 months. We anticipate that he will thoroughly study the stewardess problem as part of his overall study.

There are one or two other matters dealt with in the bill that I would like to call attention to. The full committee report is now before us, including not only my individual views, but those of the Senator from Colorado [Mr. DOMINICK], which I think are most important. Especially because of Senator DOMINICK'S individual views, I wish to ask a couple of questions of the manager of the bill, which I think will help very much to clarify some of the very intelligent points which Senator DOMINICK raises. I emphasize that he voted to report out the bill and he is permitting it to go through here. We are deeply indebted to him for his fine understanding and cooperation. I think he is entitled to have answers to certain of the very important questions he raises.

The first question, Mr. President, which also was raised with me by our minority leader, the Senator from Illinois [Mr. DIRKSEN] relates to that section 4(f)(2) of the bill, found at page 20, lines 20 to 25. As the Senator from Texas described it, that subsection provides an exemption from the prohibitions of the bill in the case of observance of bona fide

seniority systems or employee benefit plans such as a pension, retirement, or insurance plan.

The meaning of this provision is as follows: An employer will not be compelled under this section to afford to older workers exactly the same pension, retirement, or insurance benefits as he affords to younger workers. If the older worker chooses to waive all of those provisions, then the older worker can obtain the benefits of this act, but the older worker cannot compel an employer through the use of this act to undertake some special relationship, course, or other condition with respect to a retirement, pension, or insurance plan which is not merely a subterfuge to evade the purposes of the act—and we understand that—in order to give that older employee employment on the same terms as others.

I would like to ask the manager of the bill whether he agrees with that interpretation, because I think it is very necessary to make its meaning clear to both employers and employees. I ask whether he agrees with that interpretation of subsection (2) of section 4(f) of the bill, found on page 20, lines 20 to 25, inclusive.

Mr. YARBOROUGH. I wish to say to the Senator that that is basically my understanding of the provision in line 22, page 20 of the bill, clause 2, subsection (f) of section 4, when it refers to retirement, pension, or insurance plan, it means that a man who would not have been employed except for this law does not have to receive the benefits of the plan. Say an applicant for employment is 55, comes in and seeks employment, and the company has bargained for a plan with its labor union that provides that certain moneys will be put up for a pension plan for anyone who worked for the employer for 20 years so that a 55-year-old employee would not be employed past 10 years. This means he cannot be denied employment because he is 55, but he will not be able to participate in that pension plan because unlike a man hired at 44, he has no chance to earn 20 years retirement. In other words, this will not disrupt the bargained-for pension plan. This will not deny an individual employment or prospective employment but will limit his rights to obtain full consideration in the pension, retirement, or insurance plan.

Mr. JAVITS. I thank my colleague. That is important to business people.

As it now stands, the bill is limited to protecting people between the ages of 40 and 65. The Senator from Colorado, in his individual views, has raised the possibility that the bill might not forbid discrimination between two persons each of whom would be between the ages of 40 and 65. As I understand it, that is not the intent of the legislation. I do not think any such reading is justified by the terms of the bill. I think we should nail this down.

Section 4 of the bill specifically prohibits discrimination against any "individual" because of his age. It does not say that the discrimination must be in favor of someone younger than age 40. In other words, if two individuals ages 52 and 42 apply for the same job, and

the employer selected the man aged 42 solely—and I emphasize that word "solely"—because he is younger than the man 52, then he will have violated the act. The whole test is somewhat like the test in an accident case—did the person use reasonable care. A jury will answer yes or no. The question here is: Was the individual discriminated against solely because of his age? The alleged discrimination must be proved and the burden of proof is upon the one who would assert that that was actually the case. Would the Senator from Texas be kind enough to advise the Senate whether he agrees with that interpretation of the bill?

Mr. YARBOROUGH. I am glad that the Senator from New York has brought this question up for clarification. This matter was discussed in committee, but it was discussed in executive session. I think we should clarify this in the CONGRESSIONAL RECORD. It was not the intent of the sponsors of this legislation, including the distinguished Senator from New York, with all of his contributions, to permit discrimination in employment on account of age, whether discrimination might be attempted between a man 38 and one 52 years of age, or between one 42 and one 52 years of ago. If two men applied for employment under the terms of this law, and one was 42 and one was 52, naturally, the personnel officer or employer would have a choice to make. But if they were of equal capability, or one was higher than the other, he could not turn either one down on the basis of the age factor, he would have to go into the capabilities, experience, of the two men, or he might have to give them a test, either manual or mental, or whatever test that particular personnel officer would require, to see if they could do the work. The law prohibits age being a factor in the decision to hire, as to one age over the other, whichever way his decision went.

Mr. JAVITS. The last question raised by the Senator from Colorado [Mr. DOMINICK], and which I also think we should take account of, is the question of any conflict which might develop in the administration of the law as related also to the Civil Rights Act of 1964, which has some provisions in it with respect to discrimination in employment, or employment opportunity on grounds of race or color.

I do not think this presents any particular problem. The Civil Rights Act of 1964 does not cover age discrimination, and S. 830 does not cover racial or religious discrimination. The laws will operate completely independently of each other, as will the enforcement procedures.

I would ask my colleague again whether he would agree with that comment upon the particular concern expressed by the Senator from Colorado [Mr. DOMINICK].

Mr. YARBOROUGH. I agree with the answer to that comment in the remarks of the distinguished Senator from New York. I agree with his interpretation.

(material omitted)

VII. *United Airlines v. McMann, 434 U.S. 192 (1977)*

Supreme Court of the United States
UNITED AIR LINES, INC., Petitioner,
v.
Harris S. McMANN.
No. 76-906.

Argued Oct. 4, 1977.
Decided Dec. 12, 1977.

Mr. Chief Justice BURGER, delivered the opinion of the Court.

The question presented in this case is whether, under the Age Discrimination in Employment Act of 1967, retirement of an employee over his objection and prior to reaching age 65 is permissible under the provisions of a bona fide retirement plan established by the employer in 1941 and joined by the employee in 1964. We granted certiorari to resolve a conflict between the holdings of the Fifth Circuit in *Brennan v. Taft Broadcasting Co., 500 F.2d 212 (1974)*, and the Fourth Circuit now before us. See *Zinger v. Blanchette, 549 F.2d 901 (CA3 1977)*, cert. pending, No. 76-1375.

I

The operative facts were stipulated by the parties in the District Court and are not controverted here. McMann joined United Air Lines, Inc., in 1944, and continued as an employee until his retirement at age 60 in 1973. Over the years he held various positions with United and at retirement held that of technical specialist-aircraft systems. At the time McMann was first employed, United maintained a formal retirement income plan it had inaugurated in 1941, in which McMann was eligible to participate, but was not compelled to join. He voluntarily joined the plan in January 1964. The application form McMann signed showed the normal retirement age for participants in his category as 60 years.

McMann reached his 60th birthday on January 23, 1973, and was retired on February 1, 1973, over his objection. He then filed a notice of intent to sue United for violation of the Act pursuant to 29 U.S.C. § 626(d). Although he received an opinion from the Department of Labor that United's plan was bona fide and did not appear to be a subterfuge to evade the

purposes of the Act, he brought this suit.

McMann's suit in the District Court seeking injunctive relief, reinstatement, and backpay alleged his forced retirement was solely because of his age and was unlawful under the Act. United's response was that McMann was retired in compliance with the provisions of a bona fide retirement plan which he had voluntarily joined. On facts as stipulated, the District Court granted United's motion for summary judgment.

[1] In the Court of Appeals it was conceded the plan was bona fide "in the sense that it exists and pays benefits." But McMann, supported by a brief *amicus curiae* filed in that court by the Secretary of Labor, contended that the enforcement of the age-60 retirement provision, even under a bona fide plan instituted in good faith in 1941, was a subterfuge to evade the Act.

The Court of Appeals agreed, holding that a pre-age-65 retirement falls within the meaning of "subterfuge" unless the employer can show that the "early retirement provision . . . ha[s] some economic or business purpose other than arbitrary age discrimination." *542 F.2d 217, 221 (CA4, 1976)*. The Court of Appeals remanded the case to the District Court to allow United an opportunity to show an economic or business purpose and United sought review here.

We reverse.

II

Section 2(b) of the Age Discrimination in Employment Act of 1967, 81 Stat. 602, recites that its purpose is

"to promote employment of older persons based on their ability rather than age; to prohibit arbitrary age discrimination in employment; to help employers and workers find ways of meeting problems arising from the impact of age on employment." 29 U.S.C. § 621(b).

Section 4(a)(1) of the Act, 81 Stat. 603, makes it unlawful for an employer

"to discharge any individual or otherwise discriminate against any individual with respect to his compensation, terms, conditions, or privileges of employment, because of such individual's age . . . ." 29 U.S.C. § 623(a)(1).

The Act covers individuals between ages 40 and 65, 29 U.S.C. § 631, but does not prohibit all forced retirements prior to age 65; some are permitted under § 4(f)(2), 81 Stat. 603, which provides:

> "It shall not be unlawful for an employer . . . or labor organization--to observe the terms of a bona fide seniority system or any bona fide employee benefit plan such as a retirement, pension, or insurance plan, which is not a subterfuge to evade the purposes of this [Act], except that no such employee benefit plan shall excuse the failure to hire any individual . . . ." 29 U.S.C. § 623(f)(2).

See *infra*, at 448-450.

. . . .

[3] McMann argues that § 4(f)(2) was not intended to authorize involuntary retirement before age 65, but was only intended to make it economically feasible for employers to hire older employees by permitting the employers to give such older employees lesser retirement and other benefits than provided for younger employees. We are persuaded that the language of § 4(f)(2) was not intended to have such a limited effect.

In *Zinger v. Blanchette*, 549 F.2d 901 (1977), the Third Circuit had before it both the *Taft* and *McMann* decisions. It accepted *McMann*'s distinction between the Act and its purposes, which, in this setting, we do not, but nevertheless concluded:

> "The primary purpose of the Act is to prevent age discrimination in *hiring* and *discharging* workers. There is, however, a clear, measurable difference between outright discharge and retirement, a distinction that cannot be overlooked in analyzing the Act. While discharge without compensation is obviously undesirable, retirement on an adequate pension is generally regarded with favor. A careful examination of the legislative history demonstrates that, while cognizant of the disruptive effect retirement may have on individuals, Congress continued to regard retirement plans favorably and chose therefore to legislate only with respect to discharge." 549 F.2d, at 905. (Emphasis

supplied; footnote omitted.)

The dissent relies heavily upon the legislative history, which by traditional canons of interpretation is irrelevant to an unambiguous statute. However, in view of the recourse to the legislative history we turn to that aspect to demonstrate the absence of any indication of congressional intent to undermine the countless bona fide retirement plans existing in 1967 when the Act was passed. Such a pervasive impact on bona fide existing plans should not be read into the Act without a clear, unambiguous expression in the statute.

When the Senate Subcommittee was considering the bill, the then Secretary of Labor, Willard Wirtz, was asked what effect the Act would have on existing pension plans. His response was:

> "It would be my judgment . . . that the effect of the provision in 4(f)(2) [of the original bill] . . . is to protect the application of almost all plans which I know anything about. . . . It is intended to protect retirement plans." Hearings on S. 830 before the Subcommittee on Labor of the Senate Committee on Labor and Public Welfare, 90th Cong., 1st Sess., 53 (1967) (hereafter Senate Hearings). [FN6]

> > FN6. Section 4(f)(2) of the original administration bill provided: "It shall not be unlawful for an employer . . . to separate involuntarily an employee under a retirement policy or system where such policy or system is not merely a subterfuge to evade the purposes of this Act . . . ."

When the present language of § 4(f)(2) was later proposed by amendments, Mr. Wirtz again commented that established pension plans would be protected. Hearings on H.R. 4221 et al. before the General Subcommittee on Labor of the House Committee on Education and Labor, 90th Cong., 1st Sess., 40 (1967).

Senator Javits' concern with the administration version of § 4(f)(2), expressed in 1967 when the legislation was being debated, was that it did not appear to give employers flexibility to hire older employees without incurring extraordinary expenses because of their inclusion in existing retirement plans. His concern was not, as inferred by the dissent, that involuntary retirement programs would still be allowed. He said,

"The administration bill, which permits involuntary separation under bona fide retirement plans meets only part of the problem. It does not provide any flexibility in the amount of pension benefits payable to older workers depending on their age when hired, and thus may actually encourage employers, faced with the necessity of paying greatly increased premiums, to look for excuses not to hire older workers when they might have hired them under a law granting them a degree of flexibility with respect to such matters.

"That flexibility is what we recommend.

"We also recommend that the age discrimination law should not be used as the place to fight the pension battle but that we ought to subordinate the importance of adequate pension benefits for older workers in favor of the employment of such older workers and not make the equal treatment under pension plans a condition of that employment." Senate Hearings 27.

In keeping with this objective Senator Javits proposed the amendment, which was incorporated into the 1967 Act, calling for "a fairly broad exemption . . . for bona fide retirement and seniority systems which will facilitate hiring rather than deter it and make it possible for older workers to be employed without the necessity of disrupting those systems." Id., at 28.

The true intent behind § 4(f)(2) was not lost on the representatives of organized labor; they viewed it as protecting an employer's right to require pre-65 retirement pursuant to a bona fide retirement plan and objected to it on that basis. The legislative director for the AFL-CIO testified:

"We likewise do not see any reason why the legislation should, as is provided in section 4(f)(2) of the Administration bill, permit involuntary retirement of employees under 65. . . . Involuntary retirement could be forced, regardless of the age of the employee, subject only to the limitation that the retirement policy or system in effect may not be merely a subterfuge to evade the Act." Senate Hearings 96.

In order to protect workers against involuntary retirement, the AFL-CIO suggested an "Amendment to Eliminate Provision Permitting Involuntary Retirement From the Age Discrimination in Employment Act, and to Substitute Therefor Provision Safeguarding Bona Fide Seniority or Merit Systems," which would have deleted any reference to retirement plans in the exception. Id., at 100. This amendment was rejected.

But, as noted in Zinger, 549 F.2d, at 907, the exemption of benefit plans remained in the bill as enacted notwithstanding labor's objection, and the labor proposed exemption for seniority systems was added. There is no basis to view the final version of § 4(f)(2) as an acceptance of labor's request that the benefit-plan provision be deleted; the plain language of the statute shows it is still there, albeit in different terms.

Also added to the section when it emerged from the Senate Subcommittee is the language "except that no such employee benefit plan shall excuse the failure to hire any individual." Rather than reading this addendum as a redundancy, as does the dissent, post, at 454-455, and n. 5, it is clear this is the result of Senator Javits' concern that observance of existing retirement plan terms might discourage hiring of older workers. Supra, at 449. Giving meaning to each of these provisions leads inescapably to the conclusion they were intended to permit observance of the mandatory retirement terms of bona fide retirement plans, but that the existence of such plans could not be used as an excuse not to hire any person because of age.

There is no reason to doubt that Secretary Wirtz fully appreciated the difference between the administration and Senate bills. He was aware of Senator Javits' concerns, and knew the Senator sought to amend the original bill to focus on the *hiring* of older persons notwithstanding the existence of pension plans which they might not economically be permitted to join. See Senate Hearings 40. Senator Javits' view was enacted into law making it possible to employ such older persons without compulsion to include them in pre-existing plans.

. . . .

III

[4][5] In this case, of course, our function is narrowly confined to discerning the meaning of the statutory language; we do not pass on the wisdom of fixed mandatory retirements at a particular age. So limited, we find nothing to indicate Congress intended wholesale invalidation of retirement plans instituted in good faith before its passage, or intended to require employers to bear the burden of showing a business or economic purpose to justify bona fide pre-existing plans as the Fourth Circuit concluded. In ordinary parlance, and in dictionary definitions as well, a subterfuge is a scheme, plan, stratagem, or artifice of evasion. In the context of this statute, "subterfuge" must be given its ordinary meaning and we must assume Congress intended it in that sense. So read, a plan established in 1941, if bona fide, as is conceded here, cannot be a subterfuge to evade an Act passed 26 years later. To spell out an intent in 1941 to evade a statutory requirement not enacted until 1967 attributes, at the very least, a remarkable prescience to the employer. We reject any such *per se* rule requiring an employer to show an economic or business purpose in order to satisfy the subterfuge language of the Act.

Accordingly, the judgment of the Court of Appeals is reversed and the case is remanded for further proceedings consistent with this opinion.

Reversed and remanded.

. . . .

Mr. Justice WHITE, concurring in the judgment.

I

While I agree with the Court and with Mr. Justice STEWART that McMann's forced retirement at age 60 pursuant to United's retirement income plan does not violate the Age Discrimination in Employment Act of 1967, 29 U.S.C. § 621 *et seq.*, I disagree with the proposition that this bona fide plan necessarily is made lawful under § 4(f)(2) of the Act, 29 U.S.C. § 623(f)(2), merely because it was adopted long before the Act's passage. Even conceding that the retirement plan could not have been a subterfuge to evade the purposes of the Act when it was adopted by United in 1941, I believe that the decision by United to continue the mandatory aspects of the plan after the Act became effective in 1968 must be separately examined to determine whether it is proscribed by the Act.

The legislative history indicates that the exception contained within § 4(f)(2) "applies to new and *existing* employee benefit plans, and to both the establishment and *maintenance* of such plans." H.R.Rep.No.805, 90th Cong., 1st Sess., 4 (1967) (emphasis supplied); S.Rep.No.723, 90th Cong., 1st Sess., 4 (1967) (emphasis supplied), U.S.Code Cong. & Admin.News 1967, p. 2217. This statement in both the House and Senate Reports demonstrates that there is no magic in the fact that United's retirement plan was adopted prior to the Act, for not only the plan's establishment but also its maintenance must be scrutinized. For that reason, unless United was legally bound to continue the mandatory retirement aspect of its plan, its decision to continue to require employees to retire at age 60 after the Act became effective must be viewed in the same light as a post-Act decision to adopt such a plan.

No one has suggested in this case that United did not have the legal option of altering its plan to allow employees who desired to continue working beyond age 60 to do so; at the most it has been concluded that United simply elected to apply its retirement policy uniformly. See *ante,* at 447. Because United chose to continue its mandatory retirement policy beyond the effective date of the Act, I would not terminate the inquiry with the observation that the plan was adopted long before Congress considered the age discrimination Act but rather would proceed to what I consider to be the crucial question: Does the Act prohibit the mandatory retirement pursuant to a bona fide retirement plan of an employee before he reaches age 65? My reading of the legislative history, set out in Part

II of the Court's opinion, convinces me that it does not.

II

As the opinion of the Court demonstrates, Congress in passing the Act did not intend to make involuntary retirements unlawful. In recommending the legislation to Congress, President Johnson specifically suggested an exception for those "special situations . . . where the employee is separated under a regular retirement system." 113 Cong.Rec. 1089-1090 (1967). Pursuant to this recommendation, the House and Senate bills that were referred to committee expressly excepted involuntary retirements from the Act's prohibition, an exception which, with only slight changes, remained in the final version enacted by Congress. As the Court correctly concludes, the changes that were made in § 4(f)(2) were intended, not to eliminate the protection for retirement plans, but rather to meet the additional concern expressed by Senator Javits concerning the applicability of retirement plans to older workers who are hired. While the discussion in Congress concerning the language change was not extensive, it indicated that the change was intended to broaden the exception for retirement plans. I thus find unacceptable the dissent's view that Congress acceded to labor's suggestion that the protection for involuntary retirement be eliminated.

III

In this case, the Fourth Circuit recognized the fact that United's retirement plan is "bona fide" in the sense that it provides McMann with substantial benefits. The court, however, viewed as separate and additional the requirement that the plan not be a subterfuge to evade the purposes of the Act. I find no support in the legislative history for the interpretation of that language as requiring "some economic or business purpose." 542 F.2d 217, 221 (CA4 1976). Rather, as I read the history, Congress intended to exempt from the Act's prohibition all retirement plans--even those whose only purpose is to terminate the services of older workers--as long as the benefits they pay are not so unreasonably small as to make the "retirements" nothing short of discharges.

What little discussion there was in Congress concerning the meaning of the § 4(f)(2) exception indicates that the no-subterfuge requirement was merely a restatement of the requirement that the plan be bona fide. See 113 Cong.Rec. 31255 (1967). It is significant that the subterfuge language was contained in the original administration bill, for that version was recognized as being "intended to protect retirement plans." See *ante*, at 448. Because all retirement plans necessarily make distinctions based on age, I fail to see how the subterfuge language, which was included in the original version of the bill and was carried all the way through, could have been intended to impose a requirement which almost no retirement plan could meet. For that reason I would interpret the § 4(f)(2) exception as protecting actions taken pursuant to a retirement plan which is designed to pay substantial benefits.

Because the Court relies exclusively upon the adoption date of United's retirement plan as a basis for concluding that McMann's forced retirement was not unlawful, I cannot join its opinion. Instead, I would adopt the approach taken by the Third Circuit in *Zinger v. Blanchette*, 549 F.2d 901 (1977), cert. pending, No. 76-1375, and would hold that his retirement was valid under the Act, not because the retirement plan was adopted by United prior to the Act's passage, but because the Act does not prohibit involuntary retirements pursuant to bona fide plans.

Mr. Justice MARSHALL, with whom Mr. Justice BRENNAN joins, dissenting.

. . . .

434 U.S. 192, 98 S.Ct. 444

VIII. H.R. Rep. No. 95-950 (March 14, 1978)

95TH CONGRESS 2d Session	HOUSE OF REPRESENTATIVES	REPORT No. 95-950

AGE DISCRIMINATION IN EMPLOYMENT ACT AMENDMENTS OF 1978

MARCH 14, 1978.—Ordered to be printed

Mr. PERKINS, from the committee of conference, submitted the following

CONFERENCE REPORT

[To accompany H.R. 5383]

The committee of conference on the disagreeing votes of the two Houses on the amendment of the Senate to the bill (H.R. 5383) to amend the Age Discrimination in Employment Act of 1967 to extend the age group of employees who are protected by the provisions of such Act, and for other purposes, having met, after full and free conference, have agreed to recommend and do recommend to their respective Houses as follows:

That the House recede from its disagreement to the amendment of the Senate and agree to the same with an amendment as follows:

In lieu of the matter proposed to be inserted by the Senate amendment insert the following:

SHORT TITLE

Section 1. This Act may be cited as the "Age Discrimination in Employment Act Amendments of 1978".

SENIORITY SYSTEMS AND EMPLOYEE BENEFIT PLANS

Sec. 2. (a) Section 4(f)(2) of the Age Discrimination in Employment Act of 1967 (29 U.S.C. 623(f)(2)) is amended by inserting after "individual" a comma and the following: "and no such seniority system or employee benefit plan shall require or permit the involuntary retirement of any individual specified by section 12(a) of this Act because of the age of such individual".

(b) The amendment made by subsection (a) of this section shall take effect on the date of enactment of this Act, except that, in the case of employees covered by a collective bargaining agreement which is in effect on September 1, 1977, which was entered into by a labor organization (as defined by section 6(d)(4) of the Fair Labor Standards Act of 1938), and which would otherwise be prohibited by the amendment made by section 3(a) of this Act, the amendment made by subsection (a) of this section shall take effect upon the termination of such agreement or on January 1, 1980, whichever occurs first.

JOINT EXPLANATORY STATEMENT OF THE COMMITTEE OF CONFERENCE

The managers on the part of the House and the Senate at the conference on the disagreeing votes of the two Houses on the amendment of the Senate to the bill (H.R. 5383) to amend the Age Discrimination in Employment Act of 1967 to extend the age group of employees who are protected by the provisions of such Act, and for other purposes, submit the following joint statement to the House and the Senate in explanation of the effect of the action agreed upon by the managers and recommended in the accompanying conference report:

* * * *

PROHIBITION AGAINST MANDATORY RETIREMENT

Senate amendment

The Senate clarifies section 4(f)(2) of the act to prohibit the mandatory retirement of an employee within the protected age group pursuant to a bona fide employee benefit plan or seniority system which requires or permits such treatment.

House bill

The House bill is substantially the same.

(7)

8

Conference agreement

House recedes to the Senate amendment.

The conferees agree that the purpose of the amendment to section 4(f)(2) is to make absolutely clear one of the original purposes of this provision, namely, that the exception does not authorize an employer to require or permit involuntary retirement of an employee within the protected age group on account of age.

In *McMann v. United Airlines*, 98 S. Ct. 244 (1977), the Supreme Court held to the contrary, reversing a decision reached by the Fourth Circuit Court of Appeals, 542 F.2d 217 (1976). The conferees specifically disagree with the Supreme Court's holding and reasoning in that case. Plan provisions in effect prior to the date of enactment are not exempt under section 4(f)(2) by virtue of the fact that they antedate the act or these amendments.

* * * *

IX. *124 Cong. Rec. 7880-7888 (March 21, 1978)*

(material omitted)

* * * *

The Clerk read the statement.

(For conference report and statement, see proceedings of the House of March 14, 1978.)

Mr. HAWKINS (during the reading). Mr. Speaker, I ask unanimous consent that further reading of the statement be dispensed with.

The SPEAKER. Is there objection to the request of the gentleman from California?

There was no objection.

The SPEAKER. The gentleman from California (Mr. HAWKINS) and the gentleman from Minnesota (Mr. QUIE) will be recognized for 30 minutes each.

The Chair recognizes the gentleman from California (Mr. HAWKINS).

Mr. HAWKINS. I yield myself such time as I may consume.

Mr. Speaker, on March 2, the House and Senate conferees reached a compromise agreement on this vital piece of legislation. Today, my colleagues in the House will have the opportunity to support the conference report agreed upon by the House and Senate conferees. While the bill is not a perfect piece of legislation, we believe that it represents the first step in our long struggle to abolish the practice of mandatory retirement based solely on age.

Let me point out that in striving to achieve this goal in no way implies that we are opposed to retirement. Instead, we want to reaffirm our intent to protect the employment opportunities of older Americans and afford them the opportunity to make their own choice between employment and retirement. The legislation that we are considering today will provide older working citizens with that choice which has been denied them thus far. As we in the Congress strive to eliminate all forms of discrimination, it is imperative that we act to end age discrimination in employment as well.

Mr. Speaker, I would like to briefly describe the action which the conferees took in approving this bill.

RAISING THE UPPER AGE LIMIT

First, both House and Senate bills raised the upper age limit for coverage under the Age Discrimination in Employment Act for non-Federal employees from the current level of 65 years of age to 70 years of age. The House provision delayed this action until 6 months after enactment while the Senate bill specified January 1, 1979, as the effective date for raising the upper age limit. The House receded from its position and agreed to extend the effective date of this provision as a means of providing employers with the maximum leadtime in order to bring their plans into compliance with the new law. Moreover, the administration had requested that the effective date be extended to January 1, 1979, in order to evaluate the potential impact of the new law and make appropriate recommendations to the Congress if necessary.

(material omitted)

CONFERENCE REPORT ON H.R. 5383, AGE DISCRIMINATION IN EMPLOYMENT ACT AMENDMENTS OF 1978

Mr. HAWKINS. Mr. Speaker, I call up the conference report on the bill (H.R. 5383) to amend the Age Discrimination in Employment Act of 1967 to extend the age group of employees who are protected by the provisions of such act, and for other purposes, and ask unanimous consent that the statement of the managers be read in lieu of the report.

The Clerk read the title of the bill.

The SPEAKER. Is there objection to the request of the gentleman from California?

Mr. BAUMAN. Reserving the right to object, I do so only to ask someone as to what the program might be for the balance of the afternoon. Are we to take up any other legislation after the age discrimination conference report? Can the Speaker give us any enlightenment?

The SPEAKER. The Chair will report to the gentleman that in the event this will take less than an hour, we will go to the postal legislation.

Mr. BAUMAN. I thank the Speaker and withdraw my reservation of objection.

The SPEAKER. Is there objection to the request of the gentleman from California?

There was no objection.

(material omitted)

REMOVING THE UPPER AGE LIMITATION FOR FEDERAL EMPLOYMENT

An additional important provision contained in the conference agreement is the House amendment which entirely uncaps the upper age limitation for most civilian Federal employees. This amendment does not affect certain Federal employees whose retirement is required or otherwise authorized by statute. The Senate legislation did not affect the upper age limit with respect to Federal employees. However, the Senate conferees receded on this provision with an amendment that the effective date be delayed until September 30, 1978. The inclusion of Federal employees is largely the result of Senator PEPPER's tireless efforts to allow the Federal Government to serve as the model for private industry by abolishing mandatory retirement solely on the basis of age.

CLARIFICATION OF SECTION 4(f)(2)

Another significant provision contained in both House and Senate bills is the clarification of section 4(f)(2) of the act which prohibits mandatory retirement of an employee within the protected age group pursuant to a bona fide employee benefit plan or seniority system which requires or permits such retirement. The conferees agree that the purpose of this amendment is to make absolutely clear that this exception does not authorize an employer to require or permit involuntary retirement of an employee within the protected age group on account of age. This provision takes effect upon enactment with one exception. The conference agreement contains a provision which defers the effective date prohibiting mandatory retirement policies of persons aged 65 through 69 if such retirement is required or permitted by an employee benefit plan contained in a collective bargaining agreement in effect prior to September 1, 1977. The effective date of the prohibitions in these situations is the termination date of the collective bargaining agreement or January 1, 1980, whichever comes first.

In *McMann* v. *United Airlines, Inc.*, 98 S. Ct. 244 (1977), the Supreme Court ruled on the mandatory early retirement provisions in section 4(f)(2) for the first time, reversing a decision reached by the fourth circuit court of appeals (542 F. 2d 217 (1976)). Specifically, the Supreme Court upheld a plan which was established before the ADEA was enacted and which required retirement of all participants at age 60. Participation in the plan was voluntary, not compulsory. By virtue of this amendment, such a plan no longer falls within the section 4(f)(2) exception. Contrary to the Supreme Court's rationale, this amendment makes clear that regardless of when an involuntary retirement provision in a plan became effective—before or after the enactment of the ADEA or of these amendments—it is unlawful if it is triggered by the fact that an employee reaches an age within the protected age group. The conferees specifically disagree with the Supreme Court's holding and reasoning in that case, particularly its conclusion that an employee benefit plan which discriminates on the basis of age is protected by section 4(f)(2) because it predates the enactment of the ADEA.

WELFARE BENEFITS

Concerns have been expressed that these amendments will increase the costs of employee welfare benefit plans, such as those that provide disability, health, life and other forms of insurance for employees.

Benefits would not have to be equal where there is a legitimate economic or business purpose other than age which justifies the differential in benefits. The purpose of section 4(f)(2) is to encourage the employment of older workers by permitting age-based variations in benefits where the cost of providing the benefits to older workers is substantially higher. Any age-based differences in benefits would have to be evaluated under the standard in section 4(f)(2).

In view of the widespread interest in this subject, we would expect the Department of Labor to issue guidelines in the near future.

Mr. Speaker, I would like to take this opportunity to express appreciation to my colleagues in the House who have worked so long and so hard to bring us to this rewarding moment. Representatives PEPPER and FINDLEY, who authored this legislation and who sincerely represent the interests of this Nation's elderly, are to be congratulated for their outstanding leadership on H.R. 5383. In addition, Mr. WEISS and Mr. WAXMAN should be justly proud of this moment for their tireless efforts to end age discrimination in employment. I am also grateful for the support of my colleagues on the Subcommittee on Employment Opportunities as well as those members of the Select Committee on Aging who contributed significantly to the development of this legislation. I want to also acknowledge the 169 Members who cosponsored legislation to terminate age discrimination in employment. Finally, I want to express my appreciation to the 358 of my colleagues who joined with me in voting to pass this legislation last September 23.

I would be remiss if I did not thank our Senate colleagues, especially Senators WILLIAMS and JAVITS, who contributed so much to this final bill. I am well aware that there are countless others who have worked selflessly to help us reach this moment. We are also grateful to each and every one of you for your support.

Mr. Speaker, in closing, I urge the immediate adoption of this conference report.

(material omitted)

CONGRESSIONAL RECORD—HOUSE *March 21, 1978*

(material omitted)

* * * *

Mr. HAWKINS. Mr. Speaker, I yield 2 minutes to the gentleman from New York (Mr. WEISS), the author of one of the bills which is consolidated as part of this report.

Mr. WEISS. Mr. Speaker, I want to pay my deepest compliments to the chairman of the Subcommittee on Economic Opportunities for his patience and perseverance and wisdom which allowed us to arrive at a conference report of which for the most part we can be proud.

Also I want to pay my deepest respects to our colleague, the gentleman from California (Mr. WAXMAN), who coauthored with me the provisions of this legislation which correct one of the most blatant distortions which crept into the law over the last 10 years with respect to section 4(f)(2).

Mr. Speaker, since 1967, the Age Discrimination in Employment Act (ADEA) has served to protect the employment rights of Americans age 40 to 65. The amendments to this act, to which we give final legislative approval today, both expand coverage under the ADEA as well as clarify a major loophole in the existing law. It is the second function of this legislation to which I would like to address my remarks.

The original ADEA provides for three exceptions for coverage under its provisions. Section 4(f)(1) of the ADEA exempts situations in which age is a "bona fide occupation exception reasonably necessary to the normal operation of the particular business"; this is generally meant to exclude so-called hazardous occupations from the provisions of the act.

Section 4(f)(3) states that older workers can be discharged for good cause. While there is universal acceptance of these two provisions, the third exception, section 4(f)(2), has been subject to a variety of interpretations including, most recently, that of the Supreme Court in the case of *McMann* v. *United Airlines*, (98 S. Ct. 244 (1977)). It is the purpose of this legislation to clarify any misinterpretation of section 4(f)(2).

Section 4(f)(2) in its original form states the following:

It shall not be unlawful for an employer, employment agency, or labor organization—

To observe the terms of a bona fide seniority system or any bona fide employee benefit plan such as retirement, pension, or insurance plan which is not a subterfuge to evade the purposes of this act, except that no such employee benefit plan shall excuse the failure to hire any individual.

The original purpose of this exception was to facilitate the hiring of older workers without necessarily having to incorporate them fully into seniority or pension benefit plans.

Unfortunately, some employees have interpreted section 4(f)(2) as permitting mandated early retirement as long as such a requirement is included in the terms of a seniority or pension plan; under this interpretation an employer could mandate forced early retirement prior to the permissible age of this act by simply including such a provision in the employee's benefit package.

To remedy this situation, during subcommittee consideration of H.R. 5383, I introduced an amendment—based on legislation which Representative HENRY WAXMAN and I introduced in April, 1977—which closes the loophole in the existing section 4(f)(2). The amendment clarifies this section by adding the following clause to it:

* * * and except that the involuntary retirement of any employee shall not be required or permitted by any such seniority system or any such employee benefit plan because of the age of such employee.

The net effect of this amendment is to prohibit mandated early retirement provisions prior to the age of coverage of the ADEA in the terms of retirement, pension, or insurance plans.

It should be noted that it is not the intention of this amendment to have older workers cut off from their health and benefit plans the day they reach age 65. While employers, under this section, may not be required to fully integrate older workers into their seniority and pension benefit plans, they should not interpret the 1977 amendments to the ADEA as a license to cease to provide reasonable benefits to their older employees.

A second amendment which I proposed and which is part of this legislation permits seniority systems and pension plans under existing collectively bargained contracts to retain a mandatory retirement provision for workers age 65 and older for the duration of the contract or 2 years which ever first occurs. It will not be permissible for labor and management, however, to enter into new con-

tracts which would force early retirement.

There has been increased attention focused on section 4(f)(2) in light of the Supreme Court ruling in the McMann case. Again, my amendment to section 4(f)(2) makes clear that the section does not allow an employer to require or permit the involuntary retirement of an employee within the protected age group. In reversing a decision reached by the fourth circuit court of appeals (542 f.2d 217 (1976)), the Supreme Court upheld a plan which was established before the enactment of the ADEA and which required the retirement of all participants at age 60; participation in that plan was voluntary, not compulsory.

As a result of the amendment to section 4(f)(2), the plan in the McMann case would no longer qualify as an exception to the ADEA. Under this amendment—contrary to the Supreme Court's rationale—a provision in a pension or seniority plan which would mandate early retirement would be unlawful regardless of whether the plan came into effect before or after the enactment of the ADEA or these amendments.

It is important to note that the plan in the McMann case did not leave the employer the option of deciding to force participants to retire; the employer was required to retire every plan participant at age 60, where the employer has an option, the plan is clearly unlawful even under the McMann decision rationale, since the decision to force an employee to retire would have to be made after the enactment of the ADEA.

The effect of these amendments will be both immediate and widespread, according to an analysis of forced retirement provision in pension plans made available by the Department of Labor, some 2 million Americans are currently subject to pension plans which give the employer the complete option to retire qualified workers prior to age 65. These workers will be protected upon enactment of this legislation. Workers over 65 will be protected by this clarification of section 4(f)(2) upon the effective date of this legislation, January 1, 1979.

I am pleased that my amendments are a major component of this legislation.

Although this legislation represents a significant advance in the way in which Americans will view older workers in the labor market, I must take exception to the two exemptions concerning tenured professors and highly compensated executives which were proposed in the Senate amendment to H.R. 5383 and which in a modified version were accepted by the conferees.

I am vigorously opposed to exemptions based on occupation and I voiced this opposition when the House conferees initially confronted this issue. In fact, the entire conference was stalled for a period of 5 months in an attempt to arrive at a compromise between the House position of no exemptions and the Senate position which called for permanent exemptions for tenured faculty members and for highly compensated

executives with pension incomes of $20,000 per year. While the compromise agreed upon by the majority of the conferees is somewhat less onerous—it calls for a phaseout of the tenured professors exemption on June 30, 1982, and for a permanent exemption for executives with pension incomes of $27,000—it is no more logical than the original Senate proposal; the legislation as amended by these exemptions advocates an advance in the way in which society views the contributions of all workers age 65 to 70 as long as they are not tenured faculty members or are entitled to receive pension benefits of $27,000 a year or greater.

While my opinion of the exemptions ultimately was not shared by a majority of my colleagues on the conference committee, I am hopeful that this legislation, H.R. 5383, will provide the impetus to the elimination of all mandatory retirement provisions in our laws and that in the future the Congress will not burden what is essentially progressive and needed legislation with exemptions which are based upon occupational status or any other consideration.

Mr. HAWKINS. Mr. Speaker, I yield 2 minutes to the gentleman from California (Mr. WAXMAN).

Mr. WAXMAN. Mr. Speaker, I rise in support of the Conference Report on the Age Discrimination in Employment Act amendments. Final passage of the conference report will strike a major blow against age discrimination and for the rights of older Americans.

The ADEA amendments abolish compulsory retirement for most Federal workers and raise the mandatory retirement age for non-Federal workers from 65 to 70. My only regret is that the legislation is not stronger. As a strong supporter of the House bill passed last September, I was disappointed at the Senate's insistence on exempting tenured college professors and certain high level executives from the bill's protections.

The conference agreement provides that persons between the ages of 65 and 70, who for 2 years prior to retirement are employed as executives or in high-level profession capacities, and who have an annual retirement income exceeding $27,000, will remain subject to compulsory retirement. Similarly, college professors between the age of 65 and 70 will remain subject to mandatory retirement requirements until July 1, 1982. Both concessions are unjustified and regretable but I am pleased House conferees were successful in narrowing the scope of the Senate's exceptions.

LEGISLATIVE INTENT OF 4(f)(2)

As an original cosponsor of H.R. 6798, I am particularly pleased to see section 4(f)(2) of the Age Discrimination in Employment Act clarified. The confusion surrounding the original intent of Congress has lead to the involuntary retirement of workers prior to age 65. H.R. 6798, provisions of which were incorporated in H.R. 5383, sought to correct the misuse of this exception.

The purpose of the Age Discrimination in Employment Act was to "promote employment of older persons based on their ability rather than age; to prohibit arbitrary age discrimination in employment; to help employers and workers find ways of meeting problems arising from the impact of age on employment."

A study of the legislative history surrounding the 4(f)(2) exception reflects the intention that it further and encourage the employment of older workers. Congress feared that requiring participation of older workers in benefit plans would discourage employment of newly hired older workers.

The conference report clarifies any doubt surrounding the intent of the exception and specifically disagrees with the finding of the Supreme Court in *McMann* v. *United States* (98 S. Ct. 244 1977). The agreement prohibits mandatory retirement for persons under age 70 enrolled in a bona fide retirement or pension plan. Plan provisions in effect prior to the date of enactment are not exempt under section 4(f)(2) by virtue of the fact that they antedate the act. One exception to this prohibition would be persons between 65 and 70 subject to a collective bargaining agreement in effect prior to September 1, 1977.

Such persons would be exempt from the bill's protections until the collective bargaining agreement expires or until January 1, 1980—whichever comes first. It has come to my attention that there is some concern that employers may seek to evade the restrictions of 4(f)(2) by reducing or eliminating welfare benefits to employees over 65. It is argued that this practice may be justified, as health insurance and other benefits are sufficiently more costly for workers between 65 and 70.

I am hopeful, however, that employers do not terminate capable and healthy older workers from benefit plans solely on the basis of age. In the absence of actuarial data which clearly demonstrates that the costs of this service are uniquely burdensome to the employer, such a policy constitutes discrimination and a conscious effort to evade the purposes of the act.

While the conference committee did not specifically address the status of health benefits to older workers protected under this act, it is the intent of this Congress to prevent both open and subtle forms of age discrimination. Exceptions should only be applied in the strictest sense and only with full justification and cause.

(material omitted)

* * * *   * * * *

X. Act Discrimination in Employment Act Amendments of 1978, 92 Stat. 189 (1978)

PUBLIC LAW 95–256—APR. 6, 1978   **92 STAT. 189**

Public Law 95–256
95th Congress

An Act

To amend the Age Discrimination in Employment Act of 1967 to extend the age group of employees who are protected by the provisions of such Act, and for other purposes.

    Apr. 6, 1978
    [H.R. 5383]

Be it enacted by the Senate and House of Representatives of the United States of America in Congress assembled,

SHORT TITLE

SECTION 1. This Act may be cited as the "Age Discrimination in Employment Act Amendments of 1978".

    Age Discrimination in Employment Act Amendments of 1978.
    29 USC 621 note.

SENIORITY SYSTEMS AND EMPLOYEE BENEFIT PLANS

SEC. 2. (a) Section 4(f)(2) of the Age Discrimination in Employment Act of 1967 (29 U.S.C. 623(f)(2)) is amended by inserting after "individual" a comma and the following: "and no such seniority system or employee benefit plan shall require or permit the involuntary retirement of any individual specified by section 12(a) of this Act because of the age of such individual".

    Infra.

(b) The amendment made by subsection (a) of this section shall take effect on the date of enactment of this Act, except that, in the case of employees covered by a collective bargaining agreement which is in effect on September 1, 1977, which was entered into by a labor organization (as defined by section 6(d)(4) of the Fair Labor Standards Act of 1938), and which would otherwise be prohibited by the amendment made by section 3(a) of this Act, the amendment made by subsection (a) of this section shall take effect upon the termination of such agreement or on January 1, 1980, whichever occurs first.

    Effective date.
    29 USC 623 note.

    29 USC 206.

(material omitted)

XI. Public Employees Retirement System of Ohio v. Betts, 492 U.S. 158 (1989)

Supreme Court of the United States
PUBLIC EMPLOYEES RETIREMENT
SYSTEM OF OHIO, Appellant
v.
June M. BETTS.
No. 88-389.

Argued March 28, 1989.
Decided June 23, 1989.

KENNEDY, J., delivered the opinion of the Court, in which REHNQUIST, C.J., and WHITE, BLACKMUN, STEVENS, O'CONNOR, and SCALIA, JJ., joined. MARSHALL, J., filed a dissenting opinion, in which BRENNAN, J., joined, *post*, p. 2869.

Justice KENNEDY delivered the opinion of the Court.

The Age Discrimination in Employment Act of 1967 (ADEA), 81 Stat. 602, as amended, 29 U.S.C. § 621 *et seq.* (1982 ed. and Supp. V), forbids arbitrary discrimination by public and private employers against employees on account of age. Under § 4(f)(2) of the Act, 29 U.S.C. § 623(f)(2), however, age-based employment decisions taken pursuant to the terms of "any bona fide employee benefit plan such as a retirement, pension, or insurance plan, which is not a subterfuge to evade the purposes of" the Act, are exempt from the prohibitions of the ADEA. In the case before us, we must consider the meaning and scope of the § 4(f)(2) exemption.

I
A

In 1933, the State of Ohio established the Public Employees Retirement System of Ohio (PERS) to provide retirement benefits for state and local government employees. Public employers and employees covered by PERS make contributions to a fund maintained by PERS to pay benefits to covered employees. Under the PERS statutory scheme, two forms of monthly retirement benefits are available to public employees upon termination of their public employment. Age-and-service retirement benefits are paid to those employees who at the time of their retirement

(1) have at least 5 years of service credit and are at least 60 years of age; (2) have 30 years of service credit; or (3) have 25 years of service credit and are at least 55 years of age. Ohio Rev.Code Ann. § § 145.33, 145.34 (1984 and Supp.1988). Disability retirement benefits are available to employees who suffer a permanent disability, have at least five years of total service credit, and are under the age of 60 at retirement. § 145.35. The requirement that disability retirees be under age 60 at the time of their retirement was included in the original PERS statute, and has remained unchanged since 1959.

Employees who take disability retirement are treated as if they are on leave of absence for the first five years of their retirement. Should their medical conditions improve during that time, they are entitled to be rehired. § 145.39. Employees receiving age-and-service retirement, on the other hand, are not placed on leave of absence, but they are permitted to apply for full-time employment with any public employer covered by PERS after 18 months of retirement. Ohio Rev.Code Ann. § 145.381(C) (1984). Once an individual retires on either age-and-service or disability retirement benefits, he or she continues to receive that type of benefit throughout retirement, regardless of age.

B

Appellee June M. Betts was hired by the Hamilton County Board of Mental Retardation and Developmental Disabilities as a speech pathologist in 1978. The board is a public agency, and its employees are covered by PERS. In 1984, because of medical problems, appellee became unable to perform her job adequately and was reassigned to a less demanding position. Appellee's medical condition continued to deteriorate, however, and by May 1985, when appellee was 61 years of age, her employer concluded that she was no longer able to perform adequately in any employment capacity. Appellee was given the choice of retiring or undergoing medical testing to determine whether she should be placed on unpaid medical leave. She chose to retire, an option which gave her eligibility for age-and-service retirement benefits from PERS. Because she was over 60 at the time of retirement, however, appellee was denied disability retirement benefits, despite her medical condition.

Before 1976, the fact that appellee's age disqualified her for disability benefits would have had little practical significance, because the formula for calculating disability benefits was almost the same as the formula used to determine age-and-service benefits. In 1976, however, the PERS statutory scheme was amended to provide that disability retirement payments would in no event constitute less than 30 percent of the disability retiree's final average salary. Ohio Rev.Code Ann. § 145.36 (1984). No such floor applies in the case of employees receiving age-and-service retirement payments. The difference was of much significance in appellee's case: her age-and-service retirement benefits amount to $158.50 per month, but she would have received nearly twice that, some $355 per month, had she been permitted to take disability retirement instead.

Appellee filed an age discrimination charge against PERS with the Equal Employment Opportunity Commission, EEOC), and filed suit in the United States District Court for the Southern District of Ohio, claiming that PERS' refusal to grant her application for disability retirement benefits violated the ADEA. The District Court found that PERS' retirement scheme was discriminatory on its face, in that it denied disability retirement benefits to certain employees on account of their age. Betts v. Hamilton County Bd. of Mental Retardation, 631 F.Supp. 1198, 1202-1203 (1986). The court rejected PERS' reliance on § 4(f)(2) of the ADEA, which exempts from the Act's prohibitions certain actions taken in observance of "the terms of ... any bona fide employee benefit plan such as a retirement, pension, or insurance plan, which is not a subterfuge to evade the purposes of [the Act]...." 29 U.S.C. § 623(f)(2). Relying on interpretive regulations promulgated by the EEOC, the District Court held that employee benefit plans qualify for the § 4(f)(2) exemption only if any age-related reductions in employee benefits are justified by the increased cost of providing those benefits to older employees. Because the PERS plan provided for a reduction in available benefits at

age 60, a reduction not shown to be justified by considerations of increased cost, the court concluded that PERS' plan was not entitled to claim the protection of the § 4(f)(2) exemption. 631 F.Supp., at 1203-1204. [FN1]

> FN1. The District Court also found that PERS' disability retirement plan was not covered by § 4(f)(2) because PERS' actions were not taken pursuant to the terms of the plan, and because the plan impermissibly permits or requires involuntary retirement on the basis of age. 631 F.Supp., at 1204-1205.

A divided panel of the Court of Appeals affirmed. Betts v. Hamilton County Bd. of Mental Retardation and Developmental Disabilities, 848 F.2d 692 (CA6 1988). The majority agreed with the District Court that the § 4(f)(2) exemption is available only to those retirement plans that can provide age-related cost justifications or "a substantial business purpose" for any age-based reduction in benefits. Id., at 694. The majority rejected PERS' reliance on United Air Lines, Inc. v. McMann, 434 U.S. 192, 98 S.Ct. 444, 54 L.Ed.2d 402 (1977), which held that retirement plans adopted prior to the enactment of the ADEA need not be justified by any business purpose, concluding that Congress had "expressly repudiated" this decision when it amended the ADEA in 1978. 848 F.2d, at 694. Because PERS had failed to provide any evidence that its discrimination against older workers was justified by age-related cost considerations, the majority concluded that summary judgment was appropriate.

Judge Wellford dissented. Noting that PERS' plan was adopted long before enactment of the ADEA, he argued that under United Air Lines, Inc. v. McMann, supra, it could not be a "subterfuge to evade the purposes" of the Act. Judge Wellford rejected the EEOC's regulations requiring cost justifications for all age-based reductions in benefits, finding that nothing in the statute's language imposed such a requirement. We noted probable jurisdiction, 488 U.S. 907, 109 S.Ct. 256, 102 L.Ed.2d 245 (1988), and now reverse.

II

Under § 4(a)(1) of the ADEA, it is unlawful for an employer

"to fail or refuse to hire or discharge any individual or otherwise discriminate against any individual with respect to his compensation, terms, conditions, or privileges of employment, because of such individual's age." 29 U.S.C. § 623(a)(1).

Notwithstanding this general prohibition, however, § 4(f)(2) of the ADEA provides that it is *not* unlawful for an employer

"to observe the terms of ... any bona fide employee benefit plan such as a retirement, pension, or insurance plan, which is not a subterfuge to evade the purposes of this chapter, except that no such employee benefit plan shall excuse the failure to hire any individual, and no such ... employee benefit plan shall require or permit the involuntary retirement of any individual ... because of the age of such individual." 29 U.S.C. § 623(f)(2).

On its face, the PERS statutory scheme renders covered employees ineligible for disability retirement once they have attained age 60. Ohio Rev.Code Ann. § 145.35 (1984). PERS' refusal to grant appellee's application for disability benefits therefore qualifies as an action "to observe the terms of" the plan. All parties apparently concede, moreover, that PERS' plan is "bona fide," in that it " 'exists and pays benefits.' " McMann, 434 U.S., at 194, 98 S.Ct., at 446; see id., at 206-207, 98 S.Ct., at 451-452 (WHITE, J., concurring in judgment). Finally, whatever the precise meaning of the phrase "any ... employee benefit plan such as a retirement, pension, or insurance plan," see infra, at 2870 fn. 4, it is apparent that a disability retirement plan falls squarely within that category. Cf. 29 CFR § 1625.10(f)(1)(ii) (1988). Accordingly, PERS is entitled to the protection of the § 4(f)(2) exemption unless its plan is "a subterfuge to evade the purposes of" the Act. [FN2]

> FN2. As a result of the 1978 amendments, § 4(f)(2) cannot be used to justify forced retirement on account

of age. Appellee contends, and the District Court found, that appellee was forced to retire under the terms of PERS' plan, and that as a result § 4(f)(2) is unavailable to PERS. The Court of Appeals did not address this question, and we express no opinion on it, leaving its resolution to that court on remand.

We first construed the meaning of "subterfuge" under § 4(f)(2) in *United Air Lines, Inc. v. McMann, supra*. In *McMann*, the employer's retirement plan required employees to retire at the age of 60. After being forced to retire by the terms of the plan, McMann sued under the ADEA, claiming that the forced retirement was a violation of the Act, and that the mandatory retirement provision was not protected by the § 4(f)(2) exemption because it was a subterfuge to evade the purposes of the Act.. We rejected both positions. With respect to mandatory retirement, we found that the statutory language and legislative history provided no support for the proposition that Congress intended to forbid age-based mandatory retirement.

> FN3. When *McMann* was decided, § 4(f)(2) did not contain the final clause excluding from its protection benefit plans that "require or permit the involuntary retirement of any individual ... because of the age of such individual."

Turning to the claim that the mandatory retirement provision was a "subterfuge to evade the purposes of" the Act, we rejected the conclusion of the court below that forced retirement on the basis of age must be deemed a subterfuge absent some business or economic purpose for the age-based distinction. Instead, we held that the term "subterfuge" must be given its ordinary meaning as "a scheme, plan, stratagem, or artifice of evasion." Id., at 203, 98 S.Ct., at 450. Viewed in this light, the retirement plan at issue could not possibly be characterized as a subterfuge to evade the purposes of the Act, since it had been established in 1941, long before the Act was enacted. As we observed, "[t]o spell out an intent in 1941 to evade a statutory requirement not enacted until 1967 attributes, at the very least, a remarkable prescience to the employer. We reject any such *per se* rule requiring an employer to show an economic or business purpose in order to satisfy the subterfuge language of the Act." *Ibid.*

As an initial matter, appellee asserts that *McMann* is no longer good law. She points out that in 1978, less than a year after *McMann* was decided, Congress amended § 4(f)(2) to overrule *McMann* 's validation of mandatory retirement based on age. See Pub.L. 95-256, § 2(a), 92 Stat. 189. The result of that amendment was the addition of what now is the final clause of § 4(f)(2).

The legislative history of the 1978 amendment contains various references to the definition of subterfuge, and according to appellee these reveal clear congressional intent to disapprove the reasoning of *McMann*. The Conference Committee Report on the 1978 amendment, for example, expressly discusses and rejects *McMann*, stating that "[p]lan provisions in effect prior to the date of enactment are not exempt under section 4(f)(2) by virtue of the fact that they antedate the act or these amendments." H.R.Conf.Rep. No. 95- 950, p. 8 (1978), U.S.Code Cong. & Admin.News 1978, pp. 504, 511. See also 124 Cong.Rec. 7881 (1978) (remarks of Rep. Hawkins) ("The conferees specifically disagree with the Supreme Court's holding and reasoning in *[McMann]*, particularly its conclusion that an employee benefit plan which discriminates on the basis of age is protected by section 4(f)(2) because it predates the enactment of the ADEA"); *id.,* at 8219 (remarks of Sen. Javits); *id.,* at 7888 (remarks of Rep. Waxman).

[1] PERS disputes appellee's interpretation of this legislative history, asserting that it refers only to benefit plans that permit involuntary retirement and not to the more general issue whether a pre-Act plan can be a subterfuge in other circumstances. We need not resolve this dispute, however. The 1978 amendment to the ADEA did not add a definition of the term "subterfuge" or modify the language of § 4(f)(2) in any way, other than by inserting the final clause forbidding mandatory retirement based on age. We have observed on more than one occasion that the interpretation given by one Congress (or a committee or Member thereof) to an earlier statute is of little assistance in discerning the meaning of that statute. See *Weinberger v. Rossi,* 456 U.S. 25, 35, 102 S.Ct. 1510, 1517, 71 L.Ed.2d 715 (1982); *Consumer Product Safety Comm'n v. GTE Sylvania, Inc.,* 447 U.S. 102, 118, and n. 13, 100 S.Ct. 2051, 2061, and n. 13, 64 L.Ed.2d 766 (1980); *United States v. Southwestern Cable Co.,* 392 U.S. 157, 170, 88 S.Ct. 1994, 2001, 20 L.Ed.2d 1001 (1968); *Rainwater v. United States,* 356 U.S. 590, 593, 78 S.Ct. 946, 949, 2 L.Ed.2d 996 (1958); see also *McMann, supra,* at 200, n. 7, 98 S.Ct., at 449, n. 7. Congress changed the specific result of *McMann* by adding a final clause to § 4(f)(2), but it did not change the controlling, general language of the statute. As Congress did not amend the relevant statutory language, we see no reason to depart from our holding in *McMann* that the term "subterfuge" is to be given its ordinary meaning, and that as a result an employee benefit plan adopted prior to enactment of the ADEA cannot be a subterfuge. See *EEOC v. Cargill, Inc.,* 855 F.2d 682, 686 (CA10 1988); *EEOC v. County of Orange,* 837 F.2d 420, 422 (CA9 1988).

. . . .

492 U.S. 158, 109 S.Ct. 2854

XII. *S. Rep. No. 101-263 (April 5, 1990)*

Calendar No. 504

101st Congress 2d Session	SENATE	Report 101-263

THE OLDER WORKERS BENEFIT PROTECTION ACT

April 5 (legislative day, January 23), 1990.—Ordered to be printed

Mr. Kennedy, from the Committee on Labor and Human Resources, submitted the following

REPORT

together with

MINORITY VIEWS

[To accompany S. 1511]

The Committee on Labor and Human Resources, to which was referred the bill (S. 1511) to amend the Age Discrimination in Employment Act of 1967 to clarify the protections given to older individuals in regard to employee benefit plans, and for other purposes, having considered the same, reports favorably thereon with an amendment in the nature of a substitute and recommends that the bill as amended do pass.

CONTENTS

The amendment is as follows:
Strike all after the enacting clause and insert the following:

39-010

[pages 28-29]

E. Application of ADEA to pre-act employee benefit plans

In *United Air Lines, Inc.* v. *McMann*, 434 U.S. 192 (1977), the Supreme Court held that an employee benefit plan that pre-dated the ADEA could not be a subterfuge to evade the Act or its purposes. As a practical consequence, the Court's holding in *McMann* immunized any discriminatory employee benefit practice (including involuntary retirement) that was instituted prior to the enactment of the ADEA in 1967 and remained unchanged thereafter.

Congress promptly overturned the *McMann* decision in 1978 by adding a clause to section 4(f)(2) banning any involuntary retirement pursuant to a bona fide employee benefit plan. In the Confer-

29

ence Report, Congress expressed its disagreement with the Court's analysis in *McMann*:

> The conferees specifically disagree with the Supreme Court's *holding and reasoning* in that case. Plan provisions in effect prior to the date of enactment *are not exempt* under Section 4(f)(2) by virtue of the fact they antedate the act or these amendments.

H.R. Conf. Rep. No. 950, 95th Cong. 2d Sess. 8 (emphasis added).

Despite this unequivocal expression of congressional intent, the courts of appeals subsequently disagreed as to whether discriminatory benefit provisions that pre-dated the ADEA were "exempt" under section 4(f)(2). *Compare Betts* v. *Hamilton Board of Mental Retardation*, 848 F.2d 692 (6th Cir. 1988) *with EEOC* v. *Cargill*, 855 F.2d 682 (10th Cir. 1988). The Supreme Court resolved this conflict in *Betts* by reaffirming its decision in *McMann*. The Court held that the Pre-Act distinction established in *McMann* remained valid because the language upon which it was premised—the term "subterfuge" in section 4(f)(2)—was not specifically defined or modified by Congress in 1978.

Once again, the Committee intends to overturn the erroneous interpretation of the Supreme Court in this regard. We do so by removing the term "subterfuge" from the statute, and by adding a new section 4(k) making explicit the applicability of the ADEA to *all* employee benefit plans. Twenty-three years after enactment of the ADEA, the law simply should not permit employers who have been discriminating the longest—those with employee benefit plans that pre-date the Act—to continue to discriminate.

The Committee regrets that the Supreme Court in *Betts* chose not to credit the language of the 1978 Conference Report, language that appeared in the Congressional Record and was overwhelmingly approved by both Houses of Congress. The Committee hopes that in the future, the Supreme Court will take more seriously such expressions of legislative intent, particularly when they are subject to the same review and ratification as the language of the statute.

(material omitted)

XIII. Older Workers Benefit Protection Act, 104 Stat. 978-979 (1990)

104 STAT. 978   PUBLIC LAW 101-433—OCT. 16, 1990

Public Law 101-433
101st Congress

An Act

Oct. 16, 1990
[S. 1511]

To amend the Age Discrimination in Employment Act of 1967 to clarify the protections given to older individuals in regard to employee benefit plans, and for other purposes.

Older Workers
Benefit
Protection Act.
Pensions.
Health care.
29 USC 621 note.

Be it enacted by the Senate and House of Representatives of the United States of America in Congress assembled,

SECTION 1. SHORT TITLE.

This Act may be cited as the "Older Workers Benefit Protection Act".

TITLE I—OLDER WORKERS BENEFIT PROTECTION

29 USC 621 note.   SEC. 101. FINDING.

The Congress finds that, as a result of the decision of the Supreme Court in Public Employees Retirement System of Ohio v. Betts, 109 S.Ct. 256 (1989), legislative action is necessary to restore the original congressional intent in passing and amending the Age Discrimination in Employment Act of 1967 (29 U.S.C. 621 et seq.), which was to prohibit discrimination against older workers in all employee benefits except when age-based reductions in employee benefit plans are justified by significant cost considerations.

SEC. 102. DEFINITION.

Section 11 of the Age Discrimination in Employment Act of 1967 (29 U.S.C. 630) is amended by adding at the end the following new subsection:

"(l) The term 'compensation, terms, conditions, or privileges of employment' encompasses all employee benefits, including such benefits provided pursuant to a bona fide employee benefit plan.".

Retirement.   SEC. 103. LAWFUL EMPLOYMENT PRACTICES.

Section 4 of the Age Discrimination in Employment Act of 1967 (29 U.S.C. 623) is amended—

(1) in subsection (f), by striking paragraph (2) and inserting the following new paragraph:

"(2) to take any action otherwise prohibited under subsection (a), (b), (c), or (e) of this section—

"(A) to observe the terms of a bona fide seniority system that is not intended to evade the purposes of this Act, except that no such seniority system shall require or permit the involuntary retirement of any individual specified by section 12(a) because of the age of such individual; or

"(B) to observe the terms of a bona fide employee benefit plan—

"(i) where, for each benefit or benefit package, the actual amount of payment made or cost incurred on behalf of an older worker is no less than that made or incurred on behalf of a younger worker, as permissible under section 1625.10, title 29, Code of Federal Regulations (as in effect on June 22, 1989); or

"(ii) that is a voluntary early retirement incentive plan consistent with the relevant purpose or purposes of this Act.

Notwithstanding clause (i) or (ii) of subparagraph (B), no such employee benefit plan or voluntary early retirement incentive plan shall excuse the failure to hire any individual, and no such employee benefit plan shall require or permit the involuntary retirement of any individual specified by section 12(a), because of the age of such individual. An employer, employment agency, or labor organization acting under subparagraph (A), or under clause (i) or (ii) of subparagraph (B), shall have the burden of proving that such actions are lawful in any civil enforcement proceeding brought under this Act; or";

(2) by redesignating the second subsection (i) as subsection (j); and

(3) by adding at the end the following new subsections:

"(k) A seniority system or employee benefit plan shall comply with this Act regardless of the date of adoption of such system or plan.

XIV. Americans with Disabilities Act of 1990, 104 Stat. 327 (1990)

PUBLIC LAW 101–336—JULY 26, 1990   104 STAT. 327

Public Law 101–336
101st Congress

An Act

To establish a clear and comprehensive prohibition of discrimination on the basis of disability.

Be it enacted by the Senate and House of Representatives of the United States of America in Congress assembled,

SECTION 1. SHORT TITLE; TABLE OF CONTENTS.

(a) SHORT TITLE.—This Act may be cited as the "Americans with Disabilities Act of 1990".

(b) TABLE OF CONTENTS.—The table of contents is as follows:

July 26, 1990
[S. 933]

Americans with
Disabilities Act
of 1990.

42 USC 12101
note.

(material omitted)

[pages 369-370]

TITLE V—MISCELLANEOUS PROVISIONS

SEC. 501. CONSTRUCTION.   42 USC 12201.

(a) IN GENERAL.—Except as otherwise provided in this Act, nothing in this Act shall be construed to apply a lesser standard than the standards applied under title V of the Rehabilitation Act of 1973 (29 U.S.C. 790 et seq.) or the regulations issued by Federal agencies pursuant to such title.

(b) RELATIONSHIP TO OTHER LAWS.—Nothing in this Act shall be construed to invalidate or limit the remedies, rights, and procedures of any Federal law or law of any State or political subdivision of any State or jurisdiction that provides greater or equal protection for the rights of individuals with disabilities than are afforded by this Act. Nothing in this Act shall be construed to preclude the prohibition of, or the imposition of restrictions on, smoking in places of employment covered by title I, in transportation covered by title II or III, or in places of public accommodation covered by title III.

(c) INSURANCE.—Titles I through IV of this Act shall not be construed to prohibit or restrict—

(1) an insurer, hospital or medical service company, health maintenance organization, or any agent, or entity that administers benefit plans, or similar organizations from underwriting risks, classifying risks, or administering such risks that are based on or not inconsistent with State law; or

(2) a person or organization covered by this Act from establishing, sponsoring, observing or administering the terms of a bona fide benefit plan that are based on underwriting risks, classifying risks, or administering such risks that are based on or not inconsistent with State law; or

(3) a person or organization covered by this Act from establishing, sponsoring, observing or administering the terms of a bona fide benefit plan that is not subject to State laws that regulate insurance.

Paragraphs (1), (2), and (3) shall not be used as a subterfuge to evade the purposes of title I and III.

(d) ACCOMMODATIONS AND SERVICES.—Nothing in this Act shall be construed to require an individual with a disability to accept an accommodation, aid, service, opportunity, or benefit which such individual chooses not to accept.

(material omitted)

XV. H.R. Rep. No. 101-485, pt. 2, at 1, 136 (May 15, 1990)

101ST CONGRESS *2d Session*	HOUSE OF REPRESENTATIVES	REPT. 101–485 Part 2

AMERICANS WITH DISABILITIES ACT OF 1990

MAY 15, 1990.—Ordered to be printed

Mr. HAWKINS, from the Committee on Education and Labor,
submitted the following

REPORT

together with

MINORITY VIEWS

[To accompany H.R. 2273 which on May 9, 1989, was referred jointly to the Committee on Education and Labor, the Committee on Energy and Commerce, the Committee on Public Works and Transportation, and the Committee on the Judiciary]

[Including cost estimate of the Congressional Budget Office]

The Committee on Education and Labor, to whom was referred the bill (H.R. 2273) to establish a clear and comprehensive prohibition of discrimination on the basis of disability, having considered the same, report favorably thereon with an amendment and recommend that the bill as amended do pass.

(material omitted)

136

(material omitted)

With respect to insurance, section 501(c) of the legislation specifies that titles I, II and III of this legislation shall not be construed to prohibit or restrict—

(1) an insurer, hospital or medical service company, health maintenance organization, or any agent, or entity that administers benefits plans, or similar organizations from underwriting risks, classifying risks, or administering such risks that are based on or not inconsistent with State law;

(2) any person or organization covered by this Act from establishing, sponsoring or observing the terms of a bona fide benefit plan which terms are based on underwriting risks, classifying risks, or administering such risks that are based on or not inconsistent with State law; or

(3) a person or organization covered by this Act from establishing, sponsoring, observing or administering the terms of a bona fide benefit plan that is not subject to State laws that regulate insurance

provided that points (1), (2), and (3) are not used as a subterfuge to evade the purposes of titles I, II and III of this legislation.

As indicated earlier in this report, the main purposes of this legislation include prohibiting discrimination in employment, public services, and places of public accommodation. The Committee does not intend that any provisions of this legislation should affect the way the insurance industry does business in accordance with the State laws and regulations under which it is regulated.

Virtually all States prohibit unfair discrimination among persons of the same class and equal expectation of life. The ADA adopts tis prohibition of discrimination. Under the ADA, a person with a disability cannot be denied insurance or be subject to different terms or conditions of insurance based on disability alone, if the disability does not pose increased risks.

Because there was some uncertainty over the possible interpretations of the language contained in titles I, II and III, as it applies to insurance, the Committee added section 501(c) to make it clear that this legislation will not disrupt the current nature of insurance underwriting or the current regulatory structure for self-insured employers or of the insurance industry in sales, underwriting, pricing, administrative and other services, claims, and similar insurance related activities based on classification of risks as regulated by the States.

However, the decision to include this section may not be used to evade the protections of title I pertaining to employment, title II pertaining to public services, and title III pertaining to public accommodations beyond the terms of points (1), (2) and (3), regardless of the date an insurance plan or employer benefit plan was adopted.

For example, an employer could not deny a qualified applicant a job because the employer's current insurance plan does not cover the person's disability or because of the increased costs of the insurance.

(material omitted)

XVI. H.R. Rep. No. 101-485, pt. 3, at 1, 71 (May 15, 1990)

101ST CONGRESS *2d Session*	HOUSE OF REPRESENTATIVES	REPT. 101-485 Part 3

AMERICANS WITH DISABILITIES ACT OF 1990

MAY 15, 1990.—Ordered to be printed

Mr. BROOKS, from the Committee on the Judiciary,
submitted the following

REPORT

together with

ADDITIONAL AND DISSENTING VIEWS

[To accompany H.R. 2273 which on May 9, 1989, was referred jointly to the Committee on Education and Labor, the Committee on Energy and Commerce, the Committee on Public Works and Transportation, and the Committee on the Judiciary]

[Including cost estimate of the Congressional Budget Office]

The Committee on the Judiciary, to whom was referred the bill (H.R. 2273) to establish a clear and comprehensive prohibition of discrimination on the basis of disability, having considered the same, report favorably thereon with an amendment and recommend that the bill as amended do pass.

(material omitted)

71

Section 501(c)(3) provides that persons or organizations covered by the Act may continue to establish, sponsor, observe, or administer the terms of a bona fide benefit plan that is not subject to state laws that regulate insurance.

Section 501(c)(3) is designed to clarify that self-insured plans, which are currently governed by the preemption provision of the Employment Retirement Income Security Act (ERISA), are still governed by that preemption provision and are not subject to state insurance laws. Concerns had been raised that Sections 501(c) (1) and (2) could be interpreted as affecting the preemption provision of ERISA. The Committee does not intend such an implication. Until the preemption provision of ERISA is modified, these self-insured plans are subject to state law only to the extent determined by the courts in their interpretatioun of ERISA's preemption provision. Of course, under the ADA, the provisions of these plans must conform with the requirements of ERISA, just as the provisions of other plans must be based on or not inconsistent with state law.

Section 501(c) may not, however, be used as a subterfuge to evade the requirements of this Act pertaining to employment, public services, and public accommodations regardless of the date an insurance or employer benefit plan was adopted.

For example, an employer could not deny a qualified applicant a job because the employer's current insurance plan does not cover the person's disability or because of an anticipated increase in the costs of the insurance. Moreover, while a plan which limits certain kinds of coverage based on classification of risk would be allowed under this section, the plan my not refuse to insure or refuse to continue to insure, or limit the amount, extent, or kind of coverage available to an individual, or charge a different rate for the same coverage solely because of a physical or mental impairment, except where the refusal, limitation, or rate differential is based on sound actuarial principles, or is related to actual or reasonably anticipated experience.

(material omitted)

XVII. *136 Cong. Rec. 17293 (July 12, 1990)*

(material omitted)

[MR. WAXMAN:]

* * *

Finally, the bill explicitly notes that the exception for insurance underwriting may not be used as a subterfuge to evade the purposes of the ADA. I have been informed by those Members who are closely involved in the legislation to overturn the decision of the Supreme Court in *Public Employee Retirement System of Ohio* v. *Betts*, 109 S.Ct. 256 (1989) that the term "subterfuge" in the ADA should not be read as the Supreme Court read that term in Betts. Thus, there is no requirement of an intent standard under the ADA or a blanket exception for insurance plans that were adopted prior to the enactment of the ADA.

(material omitted)

XVIII. *136 Cong. Rec. 17378 (July 13, 1990)*

[SEN. KENNEDY:]

* * *

The ADA specifically provides that the exception for insurance underwriting and classification of risks may not be used as a subterfuge to evade the purposes of titles I and III of the act. It is important to note that the term "subterfuge," as used in the ADA, should not be interpreted in the manner in which the Supreme Court interpreted the term in *Public Employee Retirement System of Ohio* v. *Betts*, 109 S. Ct. 256 (1989). The term "subterfuge" is used in the ADA to denote a means of evading the purposes of the ADA. Under its plan meaning, it does not connote that there must be some malicious or purposeful intent to evade the ADA on the part of the insurance company or other organization. It also does not mean that a plan is automatically shielded just because it was put into place before the ADA was passed. The provision regarding subterfuge in section 501(c) should not be undermined by a restrictive reading of the term "subterfuge," as the Supreme Court did in Betts. Indeed, our committee recently reported out a bill to overturn the Betts decision. It is not our intent that the restrictive reading of Betts, with which we do not agree, should be carried over to the ADA.

(material omitted)